PROCEEDINGS OF A WORKSHOP ON
DETERRING CYBERATTACKS

Informing Strategies and Developing Options for U.S. Policy

D1560985

Committee on Deterring Cyberattacks: Informing Strategies and Developing Options for U.S. Policy

Computer Science and Telecommunications Board
Division on Engineering and Physical Sciences

Policy and Global Affairs Division

NATIONAL RESEARCH COUNCIL
OF THE NATIONAL ACADEMIES

THE NATIONAL ACADEMIES PRESS
Washington, D.C.
www.nap.edu

THE NATIONAL ACADEMIES PRESS   500 Fifth Street, N.W.   Washington, DC 20001

NOTICE: The project that is the subject of this report was approved by the Governing Board of the National Research Council, whose members are drawn from the councils of the National Academy of Sciences, the National Academy of Engineering, and the Institute of Medicine. The members of the committee that oversaw this project were chosen for their special competences and with regard for appropriate balance.

Support for this project was provided by the Office of the Director of National Intelligence under award number HHM402-05-D0011, DO #12. Any opinions, findings, conclusions, or recommendations expressed in this publication are those of the authors and do not necessarily reflect the views of the organization that provided support for the project.

International Standard Book Number-13: 978-0-309-16035-3
International Standard Book Number-10: 0-309-16035-9

Additional copies of this report are available from:

The National Academies Press
500 Fifth Street, N.W., Lockbox 285
Washington, DC 20055
(800) 624-6242
(202) 334-3313 (in the Washington metropolitan area)
Internet: http://www.nap.edu

THE NATIONAL ACADEMIES
Advisers to the Nation on Science, Engineering, and Medicine

The **National Academy of Sciences** is a private, nonprofit, self-perpetuating society of distinguished scholars engaged in scientific and engineering research, dedicated to the furtherance of science and technology and to their use for the general welfare. Upon the authority of the charter granted to it by the Congress in 1863, the Academy has a mandate that requires it to advise the federal government on scientific and technical matters. Dr. Ralph J. Cicerone is president of the National Academy of Sciences.

The **National Academy of Engineering** was established in 1964, under the charter of the National Academy of Sciences, as a parallel organization of outstanding engineers. It is autonomous in its administration and in the selection of its members, sharing with the National Academy of Sciences the responsibility for advising the federal government. The National Academy of Engineering also sponsors engineering programs aimed at meeting national needs, encourages education and research, and recognizes the superior achievements of engineers. Dr. Charles M. Vest is president of the National Academy of Engineering.

The **Institute of Medicine** was established in 1970 by the National Academy of Sciences to secure the services of eminent members of appropriate professions in the examination of policy matters pertaining to the health of the public. The Institute acts under the responsibility given to the National Academy of Sciences by its congressional charter to be an adviser to the federal government and, upon its own initiative, to identify issues of medical care, research, and education. Dr. Harvey V. Fineberg is president of the Institute of Medicine.

The **National Research Council** was organized by the National Academy of Sciences in 1916 to associate the broad community of science and technology with the Academy's purposes of furthering knowledge and advising the federal government. Functioning in accordance with general policies determined by the Academy, the Council has become the principal operating agency of both the National Academy of Sciences and the National Academy of Engineering in providing services to the government, the public, and the scientific and engineering communities. The Council is administered jointly by both Academies and the Institute of Medicine. Dr. Ralph J. Cicerone and Dr. Charles M. Vest are chair and vice chair, respectively, of the National Research Council.

www.national-academies.org

Preface

In a world of increasing dependence on information technology, the prevention of cyberattacks on a nation's important computer and communications systems and networks is a problem that looms large. Given the demonstrated limitations of passive cybersecurity defense measures (that is, measures taken unilaterally by an organization to increase the resistance of an information technology system or network to attack), it is natural to consider the possibility that deterrence might play a useful role in preventing cyberattacks against the United States and its vital interests.

At the request of the Office of the Director of National Intelligence, the National Research Council (NRC) undertook a project entitled "Deterring Cyberattacks: Informing Strategies and Developing Options for U.S. Policy." The two-phase project aimed to foster a broad, multidisciplinary examination of strategies for deterring cyberattacks on the United States and of the possible utility of these strategies for the U.S. government (see Box P.1 for the statement of task).

In the first phase, the Committee on Deterring Cyberattacks: Informing Strategies and Developing Options for U.S. policy produced a letter report, released in March 2010 and reprinted in Appendix A of this volume, that provided basic information needed to understand the nature of the problem and to articulate important questions that can drive research regarding ways of more effectively preventing, discouraging, and inhibiting hostile activity against important U.S. information systems and networks. The second phase of this project entailed selecting appropriate experts to write papers on questions raised in the letter report. A number of experts, identified by the committee, were commissioned to write these papers under contract with the National Academy of Sciences. Commissioned papers were discussed at a public workshop held June 10-11, 2010, in Washington, D.C., and authors revised their papers after the workshop.

In addition to commissioning papers, the NRC sponsored a prize competition for papers that addressed one or more of the questions raised in the letter report. Two of these papers were singled out for recognition as noted on p. xii in the Contents and have been included in Group 7 of this volume.

Although the authors were selected and the papers reviewed and discussed by the committee, the individually authored papers do not reflect consensus views of the committee. Under NRC guidelines for conducting workshops, workshop activities do not seek consensus, and proceedings (such as the present volume) cannot be said to represent an NRC view on the subject at hand. Furthermore, individual members of the committee may agree or disagree with the findings, conclusions, or analysis of

Box P.1
Statement of Task

An ad hoc committee will oversee a two-phase activity to foster a broad, multidisciplinary examination of deterrence strategies and their possible utility to the U.S. government in its policies toward preventing cyberattacks. In the first phase, the committee will prepare a letter report identifying the key issues and questions that merit examination. In the second phase, the committee will engage experts to prepare papers that address key issues and questions, including those posed in the letter report. The papers will be compiled in a National Research Council publication and/or published by appropriate journals. This phase will include a committee meeting and a public workshop to discuss draft papers, with authors finalizing the papers following the workshop.

any given paper in this volume, and the reader should view these papers as offering points of departure that can stimulate further work on the topics discussed.

The papers presented in this volume are published essentially as received from the authors, with some proofreading corrections made as limited time allowed.

The meeting agenda and biosketches of the speakers are provided in Appendixes B and C, respectively. Appendix D provides biosketches of the committee and staff.

Acknowledgment of Reviewers

This report has been reviewed in draft form by individuals chosen for their diverse perspectives and technical expertise, in accordance with procedures approved by the National Research Council's Report Review Committee. The purpose of this independent review is to provide candid and critical comments that will assist the institution in making its published report as sound as possible and to ensure that the report meets institutional standards for objectivity, evidence, and responsiveness to the study charge. The review comments and draft manuscript remain confidential to protect the integrity of the deliberative process. We wish to thank the following individuals for their review of the papers contained in this volume:

Amitai Aviram, University of Illinois
Robert Axelrod, University of Michigan
William Banks, Syracuse University
David Elliott, Stanford University
Anita Jones, University of Virginia
Cheryl Koopman, Stanford University
Ronald Lee, Arnold & Porter, LLP
Joseph Nye, Harvard University
Francesco Parisi, University of Minnesota
Joel Reidenberg, Fordham University
Jerome Saltzer, Massachusetts Institute of Technology
John Savage, Brown University
Dan Schutzer, Financial Services Technology Consortium
Walter Slocombe, Caplin & Drysdale
Jack Snyder, Columbia University
Joel Trachtman, Tufts University
Jenell Trigg, Lerman Senter, PLLC

Although the reviewers listed above have provided many constructive comments and suggestions, they were not asked to endorse the views presented in any of these commissioned and contributed papers, nor did they see the final draft of any of these papers prior to publication. The review of this report was overseen by Liz Panos, DEPS Report Review Officer. She was responsible for making certain that an independent examination of this report was carried out in accordance with institutional procedures and that all review comments were carefully considered. Responsibility for the final content of the commissioned and contributed papers in this volume rests entirely with the individual author(s).

Contents

---

[1]This paper was awarded First Prize in the National Research Council's Prize Competition for Cyberdeterrence Research and Scholarship "for original first steps in addressing the problem of third-party contributors to cyberinsecurity."

[2]This paper was awarded Honorable Mention in the National Research Council's Prize Competition for Cyberdeterrence Research and Scholarship "for raising important issues regarding active defense in cyberspace."

Group 1—Attribution and Economics

Introducing the Economics of Cybersecurity: Principles and Policy Options

Tyler Moore

Harvard University

ABSTRACT

The economics of information security has recently become a thriving and fast-moving discipline. Systems often fail because the organizations that defend them do not bear the full costs of failure. For instance, companies operating critical infrastructures have integrated control systems with the Internet to reduce near-term, measurable costs while raising the risk of catastrophic failure, whose losses will be primarily borne by society. So long as anti-virus software is left to individuals to purchase and install, there may be a less than optimal level of protection when infected machines cause trouble for other machines rather than their owners. In order to solve the problems of growing vulnerability and increasing crime, policy and legislation must coherently allocate responsibilities and liabilities so that the parties in a position to fix problems have an incentive to do so. In this paper, we outline in greater detail the various challenges plaguing cybersecurity: misaligned incentives, information asymmetries and externalities. We then discuss the regulatory options that are available to overcome these economic barriers in the cybersecurity context: ex ante safety regulation, ex post liability, information disclosure, and indirect intermediary liability. Finally, we make several recommendations for policy changes to improve cybersecurity: mitigating malware infections via ISPs by subsidized cleanup, mandatory disclosure of fraud losses and security incidents, mandatory disclosure of control system incidents and intrusions, and aggregating reports of cyber espionage and reporting to the WTO.

1 INTRODUCTION

Cybersecurity has recently grabbed the attention of policymakers. There have been persistent reports of foreign agents penetrating critical infrastructures, computer compromise facilitating industrial espionage, and faceless hackers emptying thousands of bank accounts. Furthermore, information security is now increasingly viewed as a matter of national security. The U.S. military has even recently established Cyber Command to defend the domestic Internet infrastructure and organize military operations in cyberspace.

When considering the national security implications of cybersecurity, it is tempting to think in terms of worst-case scenarios, such as a cyber "Pearl Harbor" where our enemies shut down the power grid, wreak havoc on our financial system, and pose an existential threat. Imagining such worst-case scenarios

3

is useful for concentrating the minds of decision makers and spurring them into action. However, there are downsides to focusing on the most extravagantly conceived threats—it gives the false impression that the situation is so dire that only a radical intervention might help.

In fact, many of the problems plaguing cybersecurity are economic in nature, and modest interventions that align stakeholder incentives and correct market failures can significantly improve our nation's cybersecurity posture. Systems often fail because the organizations that defend them do not bear the full costs of failure. Policy and legislation must coherently allocate responsibilities and liabilities so that the parties in a position to fix problems have an incentive to do so.

In this paper, we outline the key insights offered by an economic perspective on information security, and detail actionable policy recommendations that can substantially improve the state of cybersecurity. In Section 2, we describe four crucial aspects of cybersecurity which we later propose policy solutions for. First is online identity theft, which is the primary way cyber-criminals steal money from consumers. Second is industrial espionage, where trade secrets are remotely and often undetectably stolen. Third is critical infrastructure protection. The control systems regulating power plants and chemical refineries are vulnerable to cyber attack, yet very little investment has been made to protect against these threats. Finally, we consider botnets, a popular method of attack impacting nearly all aspects of cybersecurity.

In Section 3, we describe the high-level economic challenges to cybersecurity: misaligned incentives, information asymmetries and externalities. In Section 4, we study how policy may be used to overcome these barriers. We review the different ways liability is assigned in the law, giving an extended discussion to how the law has tackled various Internet vices by exerting pressure on intermediaries, principally Internet service providers (ISPs) and the payment system. Finally, we make four concrete policy recommendations that can improve cybersecurity.

2 CYBERSECURITY APPLICATIONS

While the intent of this article is to provide generalized advice to help strengthen cybersecurity, it is useful to consider particular applications where cybersecurity is needed. We now describe four of the most prescient threats to cybersecurity: online identity theft, industrial cyber espionage, critical infrastructure protection, and botnets.

2.1 Online Identity Theft

One key way in which malicious parties capitalize on Internet insecurity is by committing online identity theft. Banks have made a strong push for customers to adopt online services due to the massive cost savings compared to performing transactions at physical branches. Yet the means of authentication have not kept up. Banks have primarily relied on passwords to identify customers, which miscreants can obtain by simple guessing or by installing "keystroke loggers" that record the password as it is entered on a computer. Another way to steal passwords takes advantage of the difficulties in authenticating a bank to a consumer. Using a "phishing" attack, miscreants masquerade as the customer's bank and ask for credentials. Phishing sites are typically advertised via spam email purporting to come from the bank. Keystroke loggers can be installed using a more general ruse—for instance, fraudsters sent targeted emails to the payroll departments of businesses and school districts with fake invoices attached that triggered installation of the malicious software.[1]

Once the banking credentials have been obtained, miscreants need a way to convert the stolen credentials to cash. One option is to sell them on the black market: someone who can collect bank card and PIN data or electronic banking passwords can sell them online to anonymous brokers at advertised

---

[1]http://www.bankinfosecurity.com/articles.php?art_id=1732.

rates of \$0.40–\$20.00 per card and \$10–\$100 per bank account.[2] Brokers in turn sell the credentials to specialist cashiers who steal and then launder the money.

Cashiers typically transfer money from the victim's account to an account controlled by a "money mule." The mules are typically duped into accepting stolen money and then forwarding it. The cashiers recruit them via job ads sent in spam e-mails (Moore and Clayton 2008a) or hosted on websites such as Craigslist or Monster,[3] which typically offer the opportunity to work from home as a "transaction processor" or "sales executive." Mules are told they will receive payments for goods sold or services rendered by their employer and that their job is to take a commission and forward the rest, using an irrevocable payment service such as Western Union. After the mule has sent the money, the fraud is discovered and the mule becomes personally liable for the funds already sent.

2.2 Industrial Cyber Espionage

The rise of the information economy has meant that the valuable property of firms is increasingly stored in digital form on corporate networks. This has made it easier for competitors to remotely gain unauthorized access to proprietary information. Such industrial espionage can be difficult to detect, since simply reading the information does not affect its continued use by the victim. Nonetheless, a few detailed cases of espionage have been uncovered. In 2005, 21 executives at several large Israeli companies were arrested for hiring private investigators to install spyware that stole corporate secrets from competitors.[4] In 2009, the hotel operator Starwood sued Hilton, claiming that a Hilton manager electronically copied 100,000 Starwood documents, including market research studies and a design for a new hotel brand.[5] Researchers at the Universities of Toronto and Cambridge uncovered a sophisticated spy ring targeting the Tibetan government in exile (Information War Monitor 2009, Nagaraja and Anderson 2009). Employees at embassies across the globe were sent emails purporting to be from Tibetan sympathizers. When the employees opened the email attachment, their computers were infected with malware that stole documents and communications.

Many within government and the defense industrial base argue that, rather than occurring in a few isolated incidents, industrial cyber espionage is rife. The UK security service MI-5 warned British businesses that Chinese spies were systematically targeting them.[6] The security company Mandiant has claimed that an "advanced persistent threat" originating in China is being used to systematically steal intellectual property from businesses by computers infected with malware.[7] An anonymous survey of 800 CIOs revealed that many believed they were targeted by espionage, with each firm reportedly losing \$4.6 million annually.[8] On the record, however, businesses have remained mum, refusing to acknowledge the problem as such a significant threat to their profits.

2.3 Critical Infrastructure Protection

It is widely known that the process control systems that control critical infrastructures such as chemical refineries and the power grid are insecure. Why? Protocols for communicating between devices do not include any authentication, which means that anyone that can communicate on these networks is treated as legitimate. Consequently, these systems can be disrupted by receiving a series of crafted

---

[2]http://eval.symantec.com/mktginfo/enterprise/white_papers/b-whitepaper_internet_security_threat_report_xiii_04-2008. en-us.pdf.

[3]http://www.washingtonpost.com/wp-dyn/content/story/2008/01/25/ST2008012501460.html.

[4]http://www.guardian.co.uk/world/2005/may/31/israel.

[5]http://www.guardian.co.uk/business/2009/apr/17/industrial-espionage-hotel-industry-lawsuit.

[6]http://www.timesonline.co.uk/tol/news/uk/crime/article7009749.ece.

[7]http://www.mandiant.com/news_events/article/mandiant_releases_first_annual_m-trends_report_at_US_department_of_d/.

[8]http://www.cerias.purdue.edu/assets/pdf/mfe_unsec_econ_pr_rpt_fnl_online_012109.pdf.

messages. The potential for harm was demonstrated by researchers at Idaho National Laboratory who remotely destroyed a large diesel power generator by simply issuing SCADA commands.[9]

In order to carry out an attack, the adversary needs to know quite a bit of specialist knowledge about the obscure protocols used to send the messages, as well as which combination of messages to select. She also needs access to the system. This latter requirement is becoming easier for an attacker to meet due to the trend over the past decade to indirectly connect these control systems to the Internet. The main motivation for doing so is to ease remote administration. A related type of convergence is that the networks themselves are becoming IP-based. That is, the lower level network and transport protocols used to send control messages are now the same as for the wider Internet. This trend also makes it easier for an attacker, once access has been gained, to start sending spurious messages. Only a few control system engineers understand the transport protocols used by SCADA systems, whereas huge numbers of IT technicians and computer scientists understand Internet protocols. This certainly lowers the technical bar for carrying out attacks.

While many agree that critical infrastructures are vulnerable to cyber attack, few attacks have been realized. Anonymous intelligence officials have reported that Chinese and Russian have regularly intruded into the U.S. electrical grid.[10] Note, however, that no official has gone on the record to describe the intrusions. Nonetheless, the vulnerability cannot be disputed, and the worst case possibility has been demonstrated.

2.4 Botnets

Malware is frequently used to steal passwords and compromise online banking, cloud and corporate services. It is also used to place infected computers into a "botnet": a network of thousands or even millions of computers under the control of an attacker that is used to carry out a wide range of services. The services include sending spam, committing online-advertising fraud, launching denial-of-service attacks, hosting phishing attacks, and anonymizing attack traffic. Botnets are different from the previous three categories because they represent an attack method rather than a target. Botnets can be employed in attacks targeting all three of the above categories. For instance, some phishing attacks carried out by the rock-phish gang use a botnet infrastructure (Moore and Clayton 2007). The GhostNet/Snooping Dragon espionage of Tibetan authorities utilized a specialized botnet. Finally, botnets are useful for providing anonymous cover for cyber attacks such as those that might harm critical infrastructures.

Botnets are typically crafted for a particular purpose, which vary based on the preferences of the miscreant controlling the botnet, called a "botnet herder." Many botnets are designed to simply send spam at the behest of the botnet herder. For example, the Reactor Mailer botnet ran from 2007-2009, at its peak sending more than 180 billion spam messages per day, 60% of the global total (Stern 2009). At least 220,000 infected computers participated in the Reactor Mailer botnet each day. The Zeus botnet, by contrast, includes key logger software to steal online credentials which are relayed back to the botnet herder, and is estimated to be as large as 3.6 million computers.[11] Botnets can also be used to carry out denial-of-service attacks. Here, the herder directs the bots to make connections to the same websites, overloading the targeted site. Botnets were employed to carry out the denial-of-service attacks in Estonia[12] and Georgia.[13]

While the size of botnets varies, the more important factor is what purpose they are being put toward. The Conficker botnet was huge, infecting millions of computers,[14] but has not been associated

[9]http://www.cnn.com/2007/US/09/27/power.at.risk/index.html.
[10]http://online.wsj.com/article/SB123914805204099085.html.
[11]http://www.computerworld.com/s/article/9177574_Big_botnets_and_how_to_stop_them.
[12]http://www.wired.com/politics/security/magazine/15-09/ff_estonia?currentPage=all.
[13]http://www.zdnet.com/blog/security/coordinated-russia-vs-georgia-cyber-attack-in-progress/1670.
[14]http://news.techworld.com/security/114307/experts-bicker-over-conficker-numbers/.

with any harmful attack. We can see, however, that the proliferation of botnets is a worrisome trend and an important threat to cybersecurity.

3 ECONOMIC BARRIERS TO IMPROVING CYBERSECURITY

Each of the cybersecurity threats discussed in Section 2 possesses distinct technical characteristics, stakeholders and legal constraints. However, some commonalities remain, notably in the economic barriers inhibiting optimal levels of security investment. We now discuss the crucial common traits first, and then in Section 4 we will go through the legal and policy options available for each application.

3.1 Misaligned Incentives

Information systems are prone to fail when the person or firm responsible for protecting the system is not the one who suffers when it fails. Unfortunately, in many circumstances online risks are allocated poorly. For example, medical records systems are bought by hospital directors and insurance companies, whose interests in account management, cost control, and research are not well aligned with the patients' interests in privacy. Electricity companies have realized substantial efficiency gains by upgrading their control systems to run on the same IP infrastructure as their IT networks.

Unfortunately, these changes in architecture leave systems more vulnerable to failures and attacks, and it is society that suffers most if an outage occurs. Banks encourage consumers and businesses to bank online because the bank experiences massive savings in branch operating costs, even if the interface isn't secure and is regularly exploited by attackers. As pointed out by Anderson and Moore (2006), misaligned incentives between those responsible for security and those who benefit from protection are rife in IT systems. Consequently, any analysis of cybersecurity should begin with an analysis of stakeholder incentives.

There is a natural tension between efficiency and resilience in the design of IT systems. This is best exemplified by the push over the past decade towards network "convergence." Many critical infrastructure systems used to be operated on distinct networks with incompatible protocols and equipment—SS7 protocols managed the phone system, SCADA protocols controlled electrical grids, and so on. It is far cheaper to train and employ engineers whose expertise is in TCP/IP, and run the many disparate applications over a common Internet infrastructure. The downside, however, is that the continued operation of the Internet has now become absolutely essential for each of these previously unconnected sectors, and failure in any one sector can have spillover effects in many sectors. Yet an individual company's decision to reduce its operating IT costs doesn't take into account such an increase in long-term vulnerability. Reconciling short-term incentives to reduce operating costs with long-term interest in reducing vulnerability is hard.

Perfect security is impossible, but even if it were, it would not be desirable. The trade-off between security and efficiency also implies that there exists an optimal level of insecurity, where the benefits of efficient operation outweigh any reductions in risk brought about by additional security measures. For instance, consumers benefit greatly from the efficiency of online banking. The risk of fraud could be reduced to nothing if consumers simply stopped banking online. However, society would actually be worse off because of the added cost of conducting all banking offline would outweigh the total losses to fraud. When misaligned incentives arise, however, the party making the security-efficiency trade-off is not the one who loses out when attacks occur. This naturally leads to suboptimal choices about where to make the trade-off. Unfortunately, such a misalignment is inevitable for many information security decisions.

3.2 Information Asymmetries

Many industries report a deluge of data. Some even complain of being overwhelmed. However, in the security space there is a dearth of relevant data needed to drive security investment.

Testifying before the U.S. Congress on March 20, 2009, AT&T's Chief Security Officer Edward Amoroso estimated that cyber-criminals' annual profit exceeds $1 trillion.[15] That's right, *$1 trillion*. $1 trillion is a lot of money; it's bigger than the entire IT industry, and approximately 7% of U.S. GDP. It is also likely an extreme overestimate, perhaps triggered by a need to attribute enormous sums to any threat when competing for Congress's attention during this time of trillion-dollar bail-outs.

Note, however, we said it is *likely* an overestimate. The fact is we don't know the true cost of cyber-crime because relevant information is kept secret. Sure, we may never gain access to the miscreants' bank accounts. But we do know that most of revenue-generating cyber-crime is financial in nature, and most banks aren't revealing how much they're losing to online fraud.[16]

Look across the board, and there is an incentive to under-report incidents. Banks don't want to reveal fraud losses, for fear of frightening away customers from online banking; businesses don't want to cooperate with the police on cyber-espionage incidents, since their reputation (and their stock price) may take a hit; the operators of critical infrastructures don't want to reveal information on outages caused by malicious attack, in case it would draw attention to systemic vulnerabilities. Such reticence to share is only countered by the over-enthusiasm of many in the IT security industry to hype up threats.

However, such a combination of secrecy and FUD (fear, uncertainty and doubt) is dangerous. To understand why, let me first explain how the used car market works. George Akerlof (1970) won a Nobel prize for describing how markets with *asymmetric information*, such as the market for used cars, can fail. Suppose a town has 50 good used cars (worth $2000 each) for sale, along with 50 "lemons" (worth $1000 each). The sellers know which type of car they have but the buyers do not. What will be the market-clearing price? One might initially expect $1500, but at that price no one with a good car will sell, and so the market price quickly ends up near $1000. Consequently, the market is flooded with lemons, since no one with a good car would agree to sell at that price. The key insight is that buyers are unwilling to pay a premium for quality they cannot measure, which leads to markets with low-quality products.

Ross Anderson pointed out in 2001 that the market for secure software is also a "market for lemons": security vendors may assert their software is secure, but buyers refuse to pay a premium for protection and so vendors become disinclined to invest in security measures. A similar effect is triggered by refusing to disclose data on losses due to security incidents. The lack of reliable data on the costs of information insecurity make it difficult to manage the risk.

Unreliable information takes many forms, from security vendors overstating losses due to cyber-crime to repeated warnings of digital Armageddon caused by the exploitation of process control system vulnerabilities while suppressing discussion of any realized or attempted attacks. The existence of an information asymmetry does not necessarily mean that society is not investing enough in security nor that too much money is being allocated. Rather, it simply means that we are likely not investing in the right defenses to the ideal proportion. Ill-informed consumers and businesses are prone to invest in snake-oil solutions if they do not possess an accurate understanding of threats and defenses. Meanwhile, security companies may not be pressured to bring new technologies to market that protect against the most substantial threats. If we don't address the lack of reliable information soon, we are liable to end up with decision makers in industry and government refusing to take necessary protections because data explaining the magnitude and nature of the most significant threats just isn't there.

---

[15]http://commerce.senate.gov/public/?a=Files.Serve&File_id=e8d018c6-bf5f-4ea6-9ecc-a990c4b954c4.

[16]UK banks do report aggregated fraud losses. In 2009, the total reported losses due to all forms of payment fraud were £440 million (approximately $641 million). Of that total, £59.7 million ($87 million) was attributed to online banking losses. Source: http://www.paymentsnews.com/2010/03/uk-card-and-banking-fraud-losses-down-28-in-2009-to-4403mm.html. David Nelson at FDIC has been trying to collect similar figures from U.S. banks on a voluntary basis. He estimates that $120 million was collectively lost by U.S. banks due to malware infections targeting online banking services. Source: http://www.computerworld.com/s/article/9167598/FDIC_Hackers_took_more_than_120M_in_three_months?source=rss_news. In sum, a more accurate estimate of the annual proceeds from online crime is in the neighborhood of the low billions of dollars.

3.3 Externalities

The IT industry is characterized by many different types of externalities, where individuals' actions have side effects on others. We discuss three types in turn: network externalities, externalities of insecurity, and interdependent security.

The software industry tends toward dominant firms, thanks in large part to the benefits of interoperability. Economists call this a network externality: a larger network, or a community of software users, is more valuable to each of its members. Selecting an operating system depends not only on its features and performance but also on the number of other people who have already made the same choice. This helps explain the rise and dominance of Windows in operating systems, but also the platform dominance of iTunes in online music sales and Facebook in online social networks. Furthermore, it helps explain the typical pattern of security flaws. As a platform vendor is building market dominance, it must appeal to vendors of complementary products as well as to its direct customers. A secure operating system is more difficult to develop applications for, so security is not emphasized until market dominance has been achieved. Likewise, the opportunities made possible by being first to market explain why insecure software is readily pushed to market, and why software today is issued in perpetual "beta," or test, mode.

Network externalities also help explain why many of the secure upgrades to Internet protocols, such as DNSSEC and S-BGP, have failed to receive widespread adoption. The security benefits of such protocols aren't realized until many other users have also upgraded, which has discouraged early adoption. SSH and IPSec, by contrast, have been much more successful because they provide adopting firms with internal benefits immediately.

Insecurity creates negative externalities. A compromised computer that has been recruited to a botnet can pollute the Internet, harming others more than the host. As described in Section 2.4, botnets send spam, host phishing scams, launch denial-of-service attacks, and provide anonymous cover for attackers. In each case, the target of the malicious activity is someone other than the host computer. The societal losses due to control systems failure, such as prolonged power outages, exceed the financial loss to an individual utility in terms of lost revenue. Because the private risks facing utilities are less than the social risks, we would expect an underinvestment in protections against the social risks. Finally, we must also consider the positive externalities of Internet use that go squandered when people are afraid to use the Internet due to its insecurity.

A final type of externalities relevant to cybersecurity is interdependent security. Kunreuther and Heal (2003) note that security investments can be strategic complements: An individual taking protective measures creates positive externalities for others that in turn may discourage their own investment. Free-riding may result. Varian (2004) pointed out that free-riding is likely whenever security depends on the weakest link in the chain: firms don't bother investing in security when they know that other players won't invest, leaving them vulnerable in any case.

4 PROSPECTIVE SOLUTIONS

The economic barriers just discussed—misaligned incentives, information asymmetries and externalities—suggest that regulatory intervention may be necessary to strengthen cybersecurity. We next review several different approaches, assessing their suitability to the cybersecurity problem, followed by a series of concrete proposals for regulating cybersecurity.

4.1 Overview of Regulatory Options

4.1.1 Ex Ante Safety Regulation vs. Ex Post Liability

Much of the IT industry has thus far avoided significant regulation. Hence, many of the examples of existing regulatory efforts involving information security concern financial institutions, which face considerably more regulatory scrutiny. *Ex ante* safety regulation is designed to prevent accidents by prescribing safeguards before accidents occur. The bulk of information security regulation (both industry and government led) is compliance-driven, a type of ex ante regulation. Firms adopt security policies and "best practices" and test their own compliance with these rules.

One example of ex ante regulation can be found in the Financial Services Modernization Act of 1999 (a.k.a. the Gramm-Leach-Bliley Act), which obliges banks to "protect the security and confidentiality" of customer information. Federal banking regulators implemented this requirement by specifying processes that banks must comply with, such as adopting a written information security program and establishing programs to assess and manage operational risks. Notably, such regulations avoid technical prescriptions in favor of forcing compliance with organizational requirements. A process-based approach has the advantage of being less dependent on rapidly changing technologies, as well as making the job of compliance verification easier for regulators. On the other hand, the effectiveness of compliance-driven security policies has been called into question.[17] Given the poor state of cybersecurity, compliance-driven security is at best a qualified failure.

The alternative to proactive ex ante regulation is to assign *ex post* liability for failures to the responsible party. Here, the hope is that the threat of monetary damages arising from legal actions will encourage actors to take the necessary precautions to make failures unlikely.

Section 5 of the Federal Trade Commission Act (15 USC § 45) grants the FTC authority to take action against unfair or deceptive acts and practices that affect commerce. Since 2005, the FTC has occasionally charged companies with acting unfairly caused by a failure to adopt reasonable information security practices. Most of their efforts to date have been aimed at non-financial companies that have suffered massive breaches of personal information, including BJs wholesale club, DSW and ChoicePoint. Notably, the FTC's awareness to these security failures stems from the proliferation of mandatory breach disclosure regulations adopted by many U.S. states (discussed in the next section).

Software companies have long avoided any ex post liability for vulnerabilities in their own products (Barnes 2004). Many have argued that making Microsoft liable for the consequences of exploits targeting Windows would give it a strong incentive to secure it. This is undoubtedly true, but the question is whether it is too blunt an instrument to incent good behavior. For instance, Microsoft has already made huge investments in improving the security of Windows, leading to significant delays in the deployment of Windows Vista. This happened without the threat of liability (though one can argue that it was easier for Microsoft to spend money on security after having established its dominant market position).

A blanket assignment of liability to software developers—say by voiding all contract terms that disclaim liability for defects—is no panacea. First, introducing software liability would create significant negative side effects. The principal negative effect would be a reduction in the pace of innovation. If each new line of code creates a new exposure to a lawsuit, it is inevitable that fewer lines of code will be written. A move toward software liability will also damage the now-flourishing free software community. Graduate students might hesitate to contribute code to a Linux project if they had to worry about being sued years later if a bug they introduced led to a critical vulnerability. Resistance to software liability is one of the few points of agreement between open- and closed-source advocates. Second, it is not obvious that introducing liability would make software secure overnight, or even in the long term. This is because software development is inherently buggy. Even responsible software companies that rigorously test for weaknesses don't find them all before a product ships. To expect all software to ship free of vulnerabilities is not realistic.

A better approach, then, is to encourage responsible software development by vendors. Software companies might be required to demonstrate that its software development lifecycle includes adequate testing. The best policy response is to accept that security failures are inevitable, and to instead emphasize robust responses to security incidents (as exemplified by Recommendation 1 in Section 4.2). Furthermore, given the long-standing success of the IT industry in disclaiming software liability, this report

---

[17]http://www.rsa.com/products/DLP/ar/10844_5415_The_Value_of_Corporate_Secrets.pdf.

focuses on alternative regulatory arrangements more likely to receive broad stakeholder support. Ex post liability may still be a viable strategy for other aspects of the cybersecurity, notably process control system security.

Legal scholars have studied the trade-offs between ex post liability and ex ante regulation regimes. Shavell (1984) and Kolstad, Ulen and Johnson (1990) find that the best outcome occurs when both are used simultaneously. However, they also find that ex ante regulation does not work well when the regulator either lacks information about harms or is uncertain what minimum standards should be. Unfortunately, both of these conditions hold in the context of cybersecurity: security incidents are swept under the rug by affected firms, and regulators have yet to find a compliance regime that has significantly improved cybersecurity. Meanwhile, ex post liability runs into trouble when firms are not always held liable for harms created or when firms cannot pay full damages. These conditions, too, often hold for cybersecurity. Facing such a grim reality, we next turn to an alternative approach: information disclosure.

4.1.2 Information Disclosure

Given that information asymmetries are a fundamental barrier to improving cybersecurity, adopting policies that improve information disclosure may be attractive. Information disclosure has two primary motivations. First is the view, articulated by Louis Brandeis, that "sunlight is the best disinfectant." Bringing unfortunate events to light can motivate firms to clean up their act. Second, disclosure can be motivated by a sense of the community's "right to know." The Emergency Planning and Community Right-to-Know Act of 1986 forced manufacturers to disclose to the EPA (and, consequently, the public) the amount and type of toxic chemicals released into the environment. The aggregated data, known as the Toxic Release Inventory (TRI), has been effective in reducing the amount of toxic chemicals discharged into the environment (Konar and Cohen 1997). The TRI is now available to the public online,[18] and citizens can search the database by ZIP code to learn about chemicals (and the companies which released them) by geographic region. Mandatory information disclosure initiatives such as the TRI are well positioned as a lightweight regulatory alternative to ex ante regulation or ex post liability.

Another example relevant to cybersecurity is the flurry of privacy breach notification laws adopted in 44 states, led by the state of California in 2002.[19] Both public and private entities must notify affected individuals when personal data under their control has been acquired by an unauthorized party. The law was intended to ensure that individuals are given the opportunity to protect their interests following data theft, such as when 45 million credit card numbers were stolen from T.J. Maxx's information technology systems.[20] Breach-disclosure laws are also designed to motivate companies to keep personal data secure. Unquestionably, firms are now more aware of the risks of losing personal information, and have directed more investment in preventative measures such as hard drive encryption (Mulligan and Bamberger 2007).

Researchers have also found evidence that the information disclosure requirement has both punished violators and reduced harm. Acquisti, Friedman, and Telang (2006) found a statistically significant negative impact on stock prices following a reported breach. Meanwhile, Romanosky, Telang, and Acquisti (2008) examined identity theft reports obtained from the FTC from 2002 to 2007. Using time differences in the adoption of state breach disclosure laws, they found a small but statistically significant reduction in fraud rates following each state's adoption.

A final benefit of breach-disclosure laws is that they contribute data on security incidents to the public domain. This has reduced an information asymmetry among firms about the prevalence and severity of leakages of personal information. Unfortunately, there is currently no central clearinghouse

---

[18]http://www.epa.gov/tri/.
[19]California Civil Code 1798.82.
[20]http://www.businesswire.com/portal/site/home/permalink/?ndmViewId=news_view&newsId=20071130005355.

for breach reports, similar to the Toxic Release Inventory. Instead, the volunteer website datalossdb.org aggregates reports identified from news reports and letters sent to victims. Despite these limitations, privacy breaches offer the most empirical evidence among all classes of cybersecurity incidents, directly as a result of information-disclosure legislation.

However, there are important differences between the circumstances facing toxic chemical and privacy breach disclosures and the types of cybersecurity topics identified in Section 2. One key motivation of existing information disclosure regimes is consumer empowerment. In other words, there is a strong sense of a "right to know"—notification is required whenever *personal* information is lost, empowering consumers to check credit reports for any resulting suspicious activity. While consumers may also expect to know about cybersecurity incidents, it is often firms that lack the requisite information on cyber incidents necessary to invest in countermeasures. If the remote login to a power station's controls is compromised and the utility keeps mum about what happened, then other power companies won't fully appreciate the likelihood of attack. When banks don't disclose that several business customers have quickly lost millions of dollars due to the compromise of the company's online banking credentials, the business customers that have not yet fallen victim remain ignorant to the need to take precautions. Thus, in cybersecurity, we face information asymmetries across firms, not only between consumers and firms.

So might information sharing and analysis centers (ISACs) be a viable solution to the asymmetry between firms? ISACs are closed industry groups where participants can voluntarily share security-related information. ISACs were set up by Presidential Decision Directive 63 in 1997[21] as a way for the federal government to coordinate the protection of critical infrastructures (telecommunications, transport, water, chemical plants, banks, etc.) primarily owned by private industry.

While ISACs have been useful, they are no substitute for a policy of transparency and information disclosure. Many are classified, so any incidents being discussed are kept hidden from those not participating in the meetings, as well as the public. The rationale is that companies are more likely to voluntarily participate and be forthright if the information is kept secret. While this is true, it does underscore the value of the mandatory nature of existing information-disclosure efforts described above.[22] A greater awareness to incidents, even those industries would rather keep hidden, is made possible by mandatory disclosure. Furthermore, in cybersecurity, competitive interests often preclude voluntary private sector cooperation. For instance, security companies that remove fraudulent phishing websites do not share their data feeds with each other, causing a much slower response (Moore and Clayton 2008b).

To wrap up, information disclosure can be a powerful tool in reducing information asymmetries and correcting for misaligned incentives. However, simply righting an information asymmetry won't necessarily fix a problem when externalities are present.

4.1.3 Cyber-Insurance

Insurance is another mechanism for managing the risks presented by network and information security.[23] A robust market for cyber-insurance would offer several key benefits to society. Foremost, insurance could offer a strong incentive to individuals and organizations to take appropriate precautions. Insurance companies could reward security investment by lowering premiums for less risky actors. Second, because insurance companies base their competitive advantage on risk-adjusted premium differentiation, they have an incentive to collect data on security incidents where claims are made. Consequently, cyber-insurance is often touted as a solution to the informational challenges outlined in

---

[21]http://www.justice.gov/criminal/cybercrime/white_pr.htm.

[22]Occasionally, particularly egregious incidents are publicized, due to government prodding. For instance, in August 2009 the Financial Services ISAC issued a joint report with the FBI about business-level online banking fraud, describing how criminals had made off with over $100 million, stealing hundreds of thousands of dollars from each victim. Public disclosures remain the exception, however.

[23]See Boehme and Schwarz (2010) for a complete account of cyber-insurance's prospects and limitations.

Section 3.2. Third, like all types of insurance, cyber-insurance can help firms smooth financial outcomes by accepting the small fixed present cost of an insurance premium in place of future uncertainty of large losses.

Despite these advantages, the market for cyber-insurance has remained small for many years, and has repeatedly fallen short of optimistic growth projections. For instance, a conservative forecast in 2002 predicted the global cyber-insurance market would rise to $2.5 billion by 2005. However, the actual size by 2008 only reached 20% of the forecast for 2005 (Bandyopadhyay, Mookerjee, and Rao, 2009). Furthermore, the biggest benefits ascribed to cyber-insurance have not been realized. Rather than differentiate premiums by observed security levels, insurance companies base premiums on non-technical criteria such as firm size. Additionally, insurance companies have not amassed a large claims history documenting incidents.

Why has the market for cyber-insurance been such a disappointment? Factors on both the demand and supply side offer explanation. On the demand side, insurers complain of a lack of awareness to cyber-risks by firms. In fact, they point to mandatory breach disclosure legislation (as described in the previous section) as a significant step in the right direction, arguing that it has increased awareness at the executive level of this one particular category of threat. Consequently, policies that increase disclosure of cyber risks and incidents would help stimulate further growth in the cyber-insurance market. However, not all demand-side challenges can be dealt with by increased awareness alone. Responsibility for dealing with cyber-incidents must be clearly assigned to the appropriate party, otherwise no claims will need to be made. For instance, there is no need for ISPs to take out insurance against PC infections when they are not on the hook for mitigation. Legislation that clarifies liability for cyber incidents would go a long way toward remedying the lack of demand for cyber-insurance.

Barriers to the provision of cyber-insurance extend to issues of supply. First, information asymmetries—in particular, the difficulty of assessing the security of an insured party—help explain why insurance companies still don't differentiate premiums based on technical criteria. Certification schemes might help, but designing security certifications that cannot be gamed is hard. Examples of failed certifications include Common Criteria-certified "tamper-proof" PIN entry devices broken by cleverly-placed paper clips (Drimer, Murdoch and Anderson 2008) and more malicious websites receiving the TrustE seal of approval than legitimate sites (Edelman 2009). The other big supply-side problem is that losses from many types of information security risks are globally correlated. Given Windows' dominant market share, a new exploit that compromises Windows PCs will affect companies everywhere simultaneously. Whenever such correlations exist, then premiums must be raised, and often the resulting rise in premiums would price many firms out of the market (Boehme and Kataria 2006). In practice, insurance companies have avoided such correlations in their claims by adding exclusions to coverage such as excluding damage incurred by untargeted attacks. Such exclusions make cyber-insurance as offered today a far less attractive solution to mitigating risk.

To conclude, cyber-insurance may eventually be part of a long-term solution to improve cybersecurity, but it needs the right mix of policy to help make it viable.

4.1.4 Indirect Intermediary Liability

Perhaps surprising to non-lawyers, liability does not have to be placed on the party directly responsible for harm. Under indirect liability regimes, third parties are held responsible for the wrongs of others. At least three actors are usually involved: the bad actor, the victim, and a third party. A classic example of indirect liability comes from employment law: employers can be held liable for the actions of its employees. Why would indirect liability ever be desirable? Following the logic of Lichtman and Posner (2004), a number of conditions can make indirect liability attractive. First, the bad actors could be beyond the reach of the law, either because they cannot be identified or because they couldn't pay up even if caught. Second, high transaction costs could make designing contracts that dish out responsibility infeasible. Once either of these conditions is met, two additional factors should be considered.

First, indirect liability is attractive when a third party is in a good position to detect or prevent bad acts. Second, indirect liability is useful when the third party can internalize negative externalities by reducing the incidences of bad acts.

Lichtman and Posner argue that these conditions hold for ISPs in the context of cybersecurity. We defer discussion of the suitability of assigning liability to ISPs for cybersecurity to the next section. For now, we note that while strict liability has been avoided in virtually all Internet contexts, there are some areas where Internet intermediaries have been either obligated or protected from taking actions.

Section 230 of the 1996 Communications Decency Act (CDA) exempted Internet providers from liability for defamatory content contributed by its users. Until the CDA was passed, service providers were reticent to moderate any posts from users out of fear that doing so would expose them to liability for all content contributed by users. Section 230 of the CDA offered immunity to service providers that chose to voluntarily delete contributions from users deemed inappropriate. Note, however, that the CDA made no *obligation* to remove defamatory or slanderous content, even if it is illegal.

The Digital Millenium Copyright Act (DMCA) of 1998 took a different tack with respect to how service providers respond to users that violate copyright online. The DMCA also exempts service providers from liability for copyright infringement carried out by its customers. However, this time there's a catch: ISPs must comply with "notice-and-takedown" requests from copyright holders by expeditiously removing the content in question in order to obtain the liability exemption.

ISPs are not the only intermediary enlisted by Congress to help rid the Internet of "bad" actors. Payment networks (i.e., credit card networks such as Visa and MasterCard) are often seen as another intermediary where pressure can be applied. For instance, while early legislation aimed at stopping Internet gambling focused on ISPs, in the Unlawful Internet Gambling Enforcement Act (UIGEA) of 2006 Congress ultimately settled on payment processors as the intermediary to assign indirect liability. Payment processors were obliged to put in place procedures to stop Internet gambling transactions. Because all Internet gambling operations needed credit card payments to make money, leaning on the payment processors was an effective way to shut down operations. Note that the payment system has been used as an intermediary in the fight against a range of other online ills, including child pornography, controlled substances and tobacco sales to minors. MacCarthy (2009) offers a thorough explanation for how the law was applied in each case.

Payment card fraud is one area of cybersecurity where indirect liability is already used. The bad actors who commit account fraud victimize cardholders. Under the Truth in Lending Act of 1968, implemented by the Federal Reserve as Regulation Z, credit card holders are protected from liability for unauthorized charges on their accounts. Similarly, the Electronic Funds Transfer Act, implemented through Regulation E, protects debit card holders from liability for fraudulent use. Instead, the obligation to repay falls on banks operating the payment system, since the criminals are often out of reach.

It is instructive to examine how liability for payment card fraud has been allocated among intermediaries (MacCarthy 2010). For frauds occurring at brick-and-mortar stores, banks traditionally foot the bill, not the merchants where the fraud occurred. For online transactions, however, the merchant has to pay. This is because online transactions are riskier, since the card is not present. Banks and merchants have continued to fight over who should ultimately pay out in different circumstances. The Payment Card System Data Security Standard (PCI DSS) is a series of compliance requirements designed to improve the security of the payment system, particularly at merchants. Merchants found to be non-compliant with PCI requirements are assigned liability for fraud under industry rules. Merchants complain of the high costs of compliance and argue that PCI DSS is nothing more than a thinly veiled, industry-led liability shift from banks to merchants. Banks in turn argue that the issue is fairness, and that merchants must take responsibility for securing payment information and systems. A key take-home point when considering what to do about cybersecurity more broadly is that legal ambiguity about which intermediary must pay for remedies is undesirable and can lead to nasty legal battles.

To sum up, Congress has acted to regulate the undesirable activities of online users by articulating what intermediaries can or must do. There's a range of intervention possible, from "Good Samaritan" provisions protecting voluntary countermeasures to obligations of action in order to gain exemptions from liability. Most legislative interventions have been hands-off and lightweight, but unafraid to enlist the support of Internet participants to counter undesirable activity.

4.2 Recommendation 1: Mitigating Malware Infections via ISPs by Subsidized Cleanup

As described in Section 2.4, botnets comprising computers infected with malware present a substantial threat to many aspects of cybersecurity. This is because botnets are a preferred tool for carrying out a variety of online attacks. Hence, in our first recommendation we describe a way to counter botnets by overcoming the economic barriers described in Section 3 using policies inspired by the regulatory options discussed in Section 4.1.

Recommendation 1: Devise a program of malware remediation with the following attributes:

- ISPs are obliged to act on notifications that its customers are infected with malware by helping to coordinate the cleanup of affected computers. In exchange for cooperation, ISPs receive exemption from liability for the harm caused by the infected machines. If ISPs do not cooperate, then ISPs become liable for the harm caused by infected machines.
- The costs of cleanup will be shared between ISPs, government, software companies and consumers.
- Reports of infections (including ISP, machine OS type, infection vector, time to remediation, remediation technique) must be reported to a database and made publicly available on the data. gov website.
- Software companies contribute financially to a cleanup fund according to the number of reported infections affecting its software. Software companies receive exemption from liability for the harm caused by the infected machines in exchange for contributing to the fund.
- Consumer contribution to cleanup is capped at a small fixed dollar amount. Consumers are guaranteed that they will not be disconnected by their ISP in exchange for cooperating with cleanup efforts.

A substantial portion of Internet-connected computers are infected with malware. Estimates range from a few percent to 25% or more. Malware is frequently used to steal passwords and compromise online banking, cloud and corporate services. It is also used to place infected computers into a "botnet": a network of thousands or even millions of computers under the control of an attacker that is used to carry out a wide range of services. The services include sending spam, committing online-advertising fraud, launching denial-of-service attacks, hosting phishing attacks, and anonymizing attack traffic.

How does malware get cleaned up today? Sometimes the user will notice. If the user has installed anti-virus software, then the software may detect the malware after receiving updated signatures. However, this often doesn't work because most malware tries to disable new updates to the anti-virus software. Another option for Windows users comes through Windows Update. While far from complete, Microsoft's Malicious Software Removal Tool (MSRT) does automatically detect and remove popular types of malware. If these precautions fail, then the user often remains completely ignorant of the malware's presence. However, most malware-infected computers leave a trail of malicious activity that can be identified by third-party security companies which monitor Internet traffic. These companies often notify the relevant ISP of the activity. Some ISPs also actively detect computers that participate in botnets.[24] They then pass along lists of suspected IP addresses to the relevant ISPs. This cooperation stems from ISPs' long-standing cooperation in fighting spam, which is now sent via botnets.

---

[24]http://www.maawg.org/sites/maawg/files/news/MAAWG_Bot_Mitigation_BP_2009-07.pdf.

Once notified of malware on their customers' computers, ISPs have several options for taking action. At a bare minimum they can pass along the notice to consumers. In October 2009, Comcast announced a trial program to notify customers that they are infected via a browser pop-up, with links to instructions for removal.[25] Such notification-only schemes rely on customers to take the necessary steps, which sometimes works for tech-savvy users and on types of malware detectable by tools such as Microsoft's MSRT. Inevitably, though, malware is often not removed by users after they have been notified. For these cases, Comcast has partnered with McAfee to offer a remediation service by a skilled technician for $89.95. Australian ISPs recently announced a notification-based effort for all its ISPs.[26]

Another ISP-based option is to place infected computers into "quarantine." Once in quarantine, users are required to download and install anti-virus software and malware removal tools. They are then only permitted to rejoin the wider Internet once the security software is installed and the computer passes a network-based scan for malware. Quarantine is considerably more expensive than notification-only-based interventions, because special hardware must be installed at the ISP and more customer-support calls are made. Some ISPs use quarantine systems, but even those that do only use them for a minority of affected customers. Recently Dutch ISPs announced a signed agreement to notify and quarantine affected customers.[27] Note that in both the Dutch and the Australian cases many ISPs have joined together in common action. In part, this collective action is designed to allay the fear that customers might switch to a different provider rather than fix the underlying problem.

However, despite the increased interest among some ISPs, by far the most common response to notification that customers are infected with malware is to take no action. Why? The incentive for ISPs to intervene is very weak (van Eeten and Bauer 2008). Malware harms many victims, from consumers whose credentials are stolen to the targets of DDoS attacks. However, ISPs are not affected very much, apart from the prospects of being chided by other ISPs if too many customer machines are sending out too much spam. By contrast, ISPs face significant tangible costs by intervening. Above all, the costs of customer support in dealing with the phone calls that come in after sending out notices or placing customers into quarantine are very high. For the ISP, it is far less costly to ignore the notifications.

Consequently, the status quo of malware remediation is unacceptable. Many ISPs choose not to act, and even those that do avoid cleaning up the hard cases. Notification-only approaches leave many computers infected, while quarantine-based schemes can unfairly shut off the Internet connections of consumers that have followed all the steps but still remain infected. So what should the solution look like?

The first step in a comprehensive solution is to determine who should be responsible for taking action, and how to assign the responsibility. The ISP is a natural candidate for assigning indirect intermediary liability for cleaning up malware. This is because the miscreants actually carrying out the infections are typically beyond the reach of the law. Furthermore, as discussed above, ISPs are in a good position to detect and clean up computers infected with malware. But how should the liability be assigned?

Lichtman and Posner (2004) argue for ISPs to take on strict liability for the actions of its customers' computers. In other words, they suggest simply making the ISPs take the blame for malware-infected customers, and let them choose how they remedy the situation given the threat of legal responsibility. Given the history of exemptions ISPs have secured from responsibility for the actions of its customers in other contexts, we find such an aggressive approach unlikely to succeed. Instead, we look to the past examples discussed in Section 4.1.4 for inspiration.

The most cautious approach would be to follow the lead of CDA §230 and make cleanup voluntary, explicitly stating that ISPs have no obligation to fix infected computers, but that they are given legal leeway in the event they choose to intervene. While some ISPs are already actively intervening voluntarily, clarifying the legal right to do so might embolden wary ISPs to act. However, there are distinct

---

[25]http://www.comcast.com/About/PressRelease/PressReleaseDetail.ashx?prid=926.
[26]http://iia.net.au/index.php/section-blog/90-esecurity-code-for-isps/757-esecurity-code-to-protect-australians-online.html.
[27]http://www.darkreading.com/blog/archives/2009/09/dutch_isps_sign.html.

disadvantages of this approach. Notably, it does nothing to compensate for the weak incentives ISPs face in taking action, leading to incomplete remediation. Furthermore, by enshrining a lack of duty, ISPs may choose to intervene even less often than they do in today's more ambiguous environment.

A more ambitious approach (and the one we recommend) is to assign responsibility as has been done in the DMCA. Under a DMCA-like arrangement, ISPs get safe harbor from liability if they clean up infected customer machines upon notification. Notification of infected computers can come from an ISP's own efforts, detection by other ISPs, or from third-party security researchers, as already happens today. Safe harbor is granted if ISPs begin the cleanup process upon notification. They can attempt automated notification first, and continue ratcheting up efforts if notification fails to fix the problem. Quarantine may be tried next, followed by perhaps sending a technician to remediate the machine. Any legislation wouldn't be prescriptive in laying out the steps that must be tried and their order; rather, the scheme should be flexible in allowing ISPs to try different approaches so long as they are documented and the ultimate solution is a verified, timely cleanup of the affected computer.

ISPs that do not comply with notifications assume liability for the actions of the compromised machines. The amount of liability could be determined by the damages caused. Alternatively, since determining harm caused by a particular machine is difficult, liability could be assigned as a fixed penalty per ignored infection. Fixed penalties are used in other regulatory contexts. For example, in Europe airlines are assigned fixed penalties for flight overbooking, cancellations and excessive delays. Fixed penalties are useful because they avoid the problem of quantifying losses following every infringement. The threat of penalties should alter behavior so that, in practice, penalties are rarely issued. Anderson et al. (2008) recommended that the European Commission introduce fixed penalties for ISPs that do not expeditiously comply with notifications of compromised machines present on their networks. Such an approach could be effective in our context as well.

Three additional caveats to the designed countermeasure are still needed: a fair distribution of who pays for cleanup, transparency achieved through mandatory disclosure of reported infections, and consumer protection that ensures Internet connectivity is not threatened by cleanup efforts. We discuss each in turn.

Assigning ISPs the responsibility of ensuring its infected customers are cleaned up will impose a costly obligation on the ISP. This is somewhat unfair, since it is not the ISP's fault that the user has been infected. Yet indirect liability regimes need not be fair to be effective. However, a fair allocation of responsibilities is helpful to ensure that the proposal has broad support. Surely, the software companies who designed the insecure systems should bear some responsibility for cleaning up the mess it created. To that end, we recommend that the costs of cleanup should be shared between ISPs, government, software companies and consumers. ISPs already pay by the increased overhead in managing the cleanup process. Governments and software companies should pay by contributing to a fund that will help subsidize the ISP cleanup process. There is already precedent for cost-sharing between third parties in the cybersecurity context. First, Luxembourg is exploring the possibility of subsidizing malware cleanup (Clayton 2010). Second, as mentioned in Section 4.1.4, banks have negotiated arrangements with merchants to help pay for fraudulent transactions whenever standard security practices have not been met. For instance, Visa negotiated a payment of $40.9 million from TJX to reimburse banks following its breach affecting 46 million cardholders,[28] while in January 2010 Heartland agreed to pay MasterCard $41 million following its breach of 100 million credit card numbers.[29] Rather than negotiating one-off settlements between intermediaries, we recommend establishing a fund to receive regular payment from software companies, given the persistent nature of malware infections.

The government should pay for cleanup because it values clean networks and the reduction in denial-of-service attacks, corporate espionage and identity theft made possible by malware. Software companies should pay because holes in their software make the compromises possible. To make par-

---

[28]http://www.businesswire.com/portal/site/home/permalink/?ndmViewId=news_view&newsId=20071130005355.
[29]http://www.pcworld.com/businesscenter/article/196711/heartland_mastercard_settle_over_data_breach.html.

ticipation more palatable, we recommend that by helping to pay for the cleanup software companies be granted safe harbor from any harm the compromised machines have caused prior to cleanup. How much should companies pay? Payment could be distributed according to what caused the infections. If infection reports included the method of exploitation, then it is easy to figure out whether the culprit is Windows XP (Microsoft pays) or Acrobat (Adobe pays). Once the scheme is up and running, contribution amounts for the next quarter can be based upon the share of cleanup costs for the previous quarter. In this way, companies are rewarded for selling software that is more secure. In some cases, it will be difficult to track down the party responsible for developing the software that has been exploited (e.g., if the software is open source). In this case, the government can pay the unclassified share.

An absolutely critical component of the scheme is that it be transparent. We recommend mandatory disclosure of malware infections and cleanup in the same spirit as the privacy breach notification laws. Rather than requiring companies to notify only consumers of infections, we recommend mandatory disclosure of all de-identified data regarding notification of compromise and the cleanup process. Reports of infections (including ISP, machine OS type, infection vector, time to remediation, remediation technique) must be reported to a database and made publicly available on the data.gov website. The format for the incident data could adhere to the IODEF standard,[30] for instance.

Mandatory collection and publication of data is an essential component of the scheme and part of the grand bargain between ISPs and software companies receiving liability exemptions in exchange for cooperation with the cleanup process. It's not there just to help researchers. Mandatory disclosure of infections will help fix the information asymmetry plaguing information security investment (described in Section 3.2). Disclosure will put valuable security incident data in the public domain, and it is likely that it will trigger a similar "sunshine effect" as has been observed in environmental pollution due to the Toxic Release Index and in protecting personal information due to breach-disclosure laws. Some of the worst offenders (both ISPs and software companies) will be uncovered, raising awareness to the problem and providing an incentive for investment in defense. Progress will become measurable, not only to insiders but also to outside perspectives on the comprehensiveness of cleanup efforts. Public disclosure will help companies gain trust in the level of financial contributions required for assisting cleanup. Finally, transparent disclosure helps give credibility to the claim that improving cybersecurity is taken seriously at a government level. If the U.S. can demonstrate its commitment to cleaning up its own networks, then the resulting improvements in security can be used to apply pressure on other countries to follow suit.

We have already staked out the roles for governments, ISPs and software companies. What of consumer responsibility? Even customers who adhere to all of the best practices may become infected. According to Panda Security, 3.94% of U.S. computers scanned were actively running high-risk malware at the time of the scan. 8.21% of computers without antivirus software were running high-risk malware, but so did 1.64% of computers *with* antivirus software. Furthermore, attackers may craft "zero-day" exploits—attacks that exploit vulnerabilities previously unknown to the software provider or antivirus company—that no software can defend against. Finally, contrary to popular belief, getting infected is not caused by "irresponsible" web browsing habits such as visiting disreputable websites and installing dubious programs willy-nilly. A very common method of compromise is the "drive-by-download," where miscreants compromise popular websites so that when unsuspecting users visit the website, the site secretly downloads and installs malware onto the computer. In one study, researchers at Google found 3 million drive-by-download URLs, and furthermore that 1.3% of Google's incoming search queries return at least one drive-by-download link in its results (Provos et al. 2008).

Taken together, the evidence points to a situation where users cannot easily be blamed when malware takes over their computer. But in an economic analysis of liability, fairness takes a back seat to identifying the party in the best position to efficiently fix the problem. Consumers are generally not in a good position to defend themselves. They don't write the buggy software, and so they can't plug the

---

[30]http://xml.coverpages.org/iodef.html.

holes; they don't have a network-level view of Internet traffic, so they can't determine whether they are infected (as ISPs can). At best, they can take some safety precautions such as patch their computers and install antivirus. There's little more we can expect from them, and even if we got all consumers to automatically install patches and run antivirus software, we'd still have a problem. Consequently, consumers are not in the best position to cheaply fix the problem.

In light of this reality, any resulting policy should focus on ensuring that consumers are protected in the course of any cleanup efforts. Consequently, we recommend that any financial responsibility placed on the user be limited. Again, we have a precedent from the financial industry in Regulations E and Z, where payment card holders are not liable for fraudulent activity beyond a small fixed amount. A small remediation fee, capped at around $20 or so, would make the cleanup process smoother for malware victims while at the same time minimizing any moral hazard among some users. Perhaps the fee could be slightly higher for users that do not have antivirus software installed. It is also essential that the burden on the ISP is to actually remedy the infection. Disconnecting users' Internet connections is not an acceptable remediation, given the increasing reliance on the Internet to provide basic services. The only exception allowing disconnection could be if consumers do not cooperate with the cleanup efforts of the ISP. Otherwise, ISPs should have a duty to cleanup, capping the out-of-pocket expenses for consumers. This is to address concern that ISPs will choose to kick off users rather than clean them up (in Lichtman and Posner's words, "concern that liable ISPs will be overly cautious and thus inefficiently exclude marginal subscribers").

4.3 Recommendation 2: Mandated Disclosure of Fraud Losses and Security Incidents

Our second recommendation is considerably simpler than the first.

Recommendation 2: Establish a program to regularly publish the following aggregated loss figures related to online banking and payment cards on data.gov:

- Incident figures: # of incidents, total $ stolen, total $ recovered for specified # of incidents
- Victim bank demographics: # banks affected, # customer accounts impacted per bank, $ lost per customer, bank type, precautions taken by bank (2-factor authentication, back-end controls used)
- Victim customer demographics: business v. consumer breakdown—#s and losses
- Attack vector (if known): keyloggers, phishing, card skimming, payment network compromise, etc.
- Business category: online banking, payment cards (transaction type: retail, card present, card not present), ATM fraud

At present, no objective measures exist to answer seemingly straightforward questions: Is online identity theft increasing or decreasing? How many people and businesses fall victim to fraud online, and how much money is lost? Is online banking and e-commerce less safe than transactions in the real world? Without a way to answer these questions, effective policy cannot be developed to improve cybersecurity.

Fortunately, a low-cost solution is readily available: ask financial institutions to report back on fraud losses and aggregate their responses. It is not as though such information has to be kept secret. Banks in Spain, Britain and Australia regularly disclose aggregate information on payment card fraud. In 2009, for example, UK banks lost £440 million (approximately $641 million) due to all forms of payment fraud, while £59.7 million ($87 million) was attributed to online banking in particular.[31] Richard Sullivan, economist at the Federal Reserve, has argued that fraud statistics should be published in order to get a

---

[31]http://www.paymentsnews.com/2010/03/uk-card-and-banking-fraud-losses-down-28-in-2009-to-4403mm.html.

better grip on fraud levels and inform whether investments to secure the payment card infrastructure are needed (Sullivan 2009).

Within the U.S., there are some existing efforts to collect data on online frauds. David Nelson at the FDIC has been trying to collect fraud figures from U.S. banks on a voluntary basis. He estimates that $120 million was collectively lost by U.S. banks due to malware infections targeting online banking services.[32] The FBI runs the Internet Crime Complaint Center (IC3), which invites members of the public to submit reports of a wide variety of Internet scams. A few aggregate figures from the IC3 report are regularly made available in annual reports,[33] but most access to the IC3 data is restricted to law enforcement. The Financial Crimes Reporting Center collects suspicious activity reports from banks, but these mainly focus on money laundering activity. The Financial Services ISAC shares confidential, high-level information on threats between banks.

These efforts exhibit a number of significant limitations, compared to the mandatory disclosure we recommend. First, the reports are voluntary in nature, making them incomplete, unrepresentative, and impossible to draw reliable trends from. Very few privacy breaches were disclosed until the California law was passed, and we might suspect that the reports of online fraud are also inaccurately represented. In the case of IC3, the trouble is that quantifying losses is difficult for many circumstances, as this too relies on self-reporting. Second, they are often secret in nature—IC3 reports are shared only within law enforcement, the FS-ISAC is closed, and so on. Finally, efforts such as the FDIC tally of fraud figures are one-off samples, which make inferring trends over time impossible.

The principal justification for *mandating* public disclosure of incidents and losses is that the financial industry does not internalize all the costs of insecurity. Consumers are protected by Regulations E and Z, but businesses are not, and merchants are expected to share responsibility for covering the costs of fraud. If banks instead choose to cover all losses, then publishing loss figures is less crucial. As it stands, banks do not internalize all costs, and so the public deserves a fair and transparent accounting of who pays what share. This is why it is recommended to disclose, in addition to aggregated loss figures, a breakdown of the number and average loss of incidents for both consumers and businesses. Additionally, we should learn the distribution of losses between banks and merchants. These types of information can help answer questions such as how many people's lives are being disrupted by online fraud, whether any groups pay a disproportionate share, and whether this changes over time.

A second motivation for mandated disclosure is that payment systems exhibit significant network externalities. Visa, MasterCard and American Express have cultivated a very successful credit card network with millions of participating merchants and cardholders. The value of this existing user base is enormous, and presents a significant barrier to would-be new entrants offering a more secure payment alternative. Having already invested heavily in a less secure payment technology and achieved market dominance, existing payment networks may be reticent to invest further in security mechanisms to reduce fraud that is borne in part by third parties. Payment networks might reasonably retort that they are investing in security, and point to efforts already undertaken in Europe to upgrade to PIN-based smartcard authentication.

A credible reporting of financial fraud losses can settle any dispute over whether enough is being done, and it can serve as useful motivation for funding improvements to the security of the financial infrastructure. For instance, banks and payment operators are weighing whether to upgrade the payment network infrastructure to a more secure smartcard-based system (MacCarthy 2010). Comprehensive fraud statistics would help answer to banks *and* merchants whether there has been a substantial enough increase in card-not-present fraud to justify further security investment. Similarly, the National Security for Secure Online Transactions[34] being pitched by the White House needs buy-in from the private sector

---

[32]http://www.computerworld.com/s/article/9167598/FDIC_Hackers_took_more_than_120M_in_three_months?source=rss_news.

[33]http://www.ic3.gov/media/annualreport/2009_IC3Report.pdf.

[34]http://pindebit.blogspot.com/2010/04/national-strategy-for-secure-online.html.

to be successful. To get that buy-in, firms need to believe that improved online authentication is needed. How can firms agree to spend on security when they do not have an accurate picture as to how much is being lost due to the less secure infrastructure we have today? Publishing regular statistics on losses now will motivate future investment if the problem is truly as big as has been claimed.

4.4 Recommendation 3: Mandated Disclosure of Control System Incidents and Intrusions

We have received stark warnings from anonymous intelligence officials that the Chinese and Russians have regularly intruded into the U.S. electrical grid.[35] Yet no documented case of a successful cyber attack on process control systems has been publicly presented. In fact, when researchers from the Tuck School of Business interviewed an oil and gas refiner as part of a field study (Dynes, Goetz and Freeman 2007), they were told by the VP for refining that he "had never heard of" a cyber-incident shutting down a plant in the industry. The VP went on to state that he would only consider investing in process control systems security after a similar-sized refinery was attacked first.

Such different perspectives are hard to rectify—that attacks are already pervasive yet operators on the ground have yet to observe a single incident. One possible explanation is that the reports of incidents are exaggerated. Many of those sounding the alarm do certainly stand to gain from increased security investment. Alternatively, the existing mechanisms for exchanging information, the sector-specific ISACs, have failed. ISACs have been in operation for around a decade, which is sufficient time to assess the effectiveness of the voluntary, closed-door information exchanges. Either ISACs have failed to effectively communicate the severity of threats to relevant parties in the industry, or there hasn't been much to report.

Fortunately, there is a reasonable way to get to the bottom of this conundrum: adopt mandatory disclosure of all cyber incidents and intrusions, with a substantial public reporting capacity. If the intrusions are in fact happening, those who detect them should have a duty to report these. In fact, the ISACs could serve as the organization to receive reports, provided that there is a clear duty to produce public reports that receive widespread dissemination.

Recommendation 3: Mandatory disclosure of control system incidents and intrusions to the relevant ISACs, who provide further public dissemination.

There has been some tentative movement in this direction within the electricity industry. The self-regulatory body NERC has required power companies to start reporting to regulators any time they observe a disturbance suspected to have been caused by sabotage (NERC standard CIP-001). The reports themselves are kept secret, and as far as we know, not shared with other firms in the industry. This is a useful start, as it demonstrates an interest in keeping track of malicious disruptions. However, it is limited in the sense that reporting is only required when an outage occurs. Detecting that Chinese spies have penetrated the administrative interface into the SCADA system need not be reported, unless it caused the power to go out. It also has no explicit requirement to share the reported information with other utilities, which doesn't solve the problem of the oil refiner who is waiting to invest until he hears about others being attacked.

It must be mentioned that mandatory disclosure is no panacea. Disclosure will help address the lack of information on incidents, but the long-tail nature of cyber attacks on process control systems means that the effort could yield few reports. Furthermore, the problem of externalities remains.

---

[35]http://online.wsj.com/article/SB123914805204099085.html.

4.5 Recommendation 4: Aggregate Reports of Cyber Espionage and Report to WTO

Industrial espionage is claimed to be a significant problem for U.S. companies. However, these companies are naturally reticent to publicly discuss their experiences of espionage out of fear that their stock price may take a hit. Perhaps, though, the thinking is starting to change. In January 2010, Google disclosed that they had been the victim of a cyber attack apparently originating in China whose purpose was industrial espionage.[36] Subsequently it was revealed that at least 34 companies were affected, including Yahoo, Symantec, Northrop Grunman and Dow Chemical.[37]

Unfortunately, since the trade secrets were believed to be stolen by someone internationally, the Uniform Trade Secrets Act and Economic Espionage Act cannot easily be enforced. This does, however, leave one option: the TRIPS agreement of the World Trade Organization. Deciding to bring cases to the WTO is always politically delicate. However, if the U.S. suspects that industrial espionage is rife, and largely coming from a single country (i.e., China), then it may be worth preparing a complaint to the WTO. It's true that such a complaint could potentially harm the stock prices of the firms named victims. If espionage is anywhere near as pervasive as what has been uncovered in the Google case, then it may be in the strategic interest of the U.S. to take action.

5 CONCLUSION

An economic perspective is essential for understanding the state of cybersecurity today, as well as how to improve it moving forward. In this paper, we have described several key economic challenges: misaligned incentives, information asymmetries and externalities. We have also reviewed the policy options available for overcoming these barriers, notably information disclosure and intermediary liability. Our principal recommendations focus on getting Internet service providers to take a more active role in cleaning up infected computers, and to collect and publish data on a range of security incidents. These recommendations are designed to raise awareness to cybersecurity issues and assign responsibility for action within the private sector so that the risks to society may be mitigated.

REFERENCES

Acquisti, A., A. Friedman, and R. Telang. 2006. Is There a Cost to Privacy Breaches? An Event Study. *Proceedings of the International Conference on Information Systems (ICIS)*, Milwaukee, WI.

Akerlof, G. A. 1970. The Market for 'Lemons': Quality Uncertainty and the Market Mechanism. *Quarterly Journal of Economics* 84(3):488-500.

Anderson, R. 2001. Why Information Security is Hard—An Economic Perspective. *Proceedings of the 17th Annual Computer Security Applications Conference*, pp. 358-65. IEEE Computer Society.

Anderson, R., and T. Moore. 2006. The Economics of Information Security. *Science* 314(5799):610-13.

Anderson, R., R. Boehme, R. Clayton, and T. Moore. 2008. Security Economics and the Internal Market. European Network and Information Security Agency. Available at http://www.enisa.europa.eu/act/sr/reports/econ-sec/economics-sec/at_down load/fullReport.

Bandyopadhyay, T., V. Mookerjee, and R. Rao. 2009. Why IT managers don't go for cyber-insurance products. *Communications of the ACM* 52(11):68-73.

Barnes, Douglas A. 2004. Deworming the Internet. *Texas Law Review* 83(1), available at http://ssrn.com/abstract=622364.

Boehme, R. and G. Kataria. 2006. Models and measures for correlation in cyber-insurance. *Proceedings of the Workshop on the Economics of Information Security*, University of Cambridge, UK.

Boehme, R. and G. Schwarz. 2010. Modeling Cyber-Insurance: Towards a Unifying Framework. *Proceedings of the 9th Workshop on the Economics of Information Security*, Cambridge, MA, June 7-8. Available at http://weis2010.econinfosec.org/papers/session5/weis2010_boehme.pdf.

Camp, L. J., and C. D. Wolfram. 2004. Pricing Security: A Market in Vulnerabilities. In Economics of Information Security, Vol. 12, *Advances in Information Security*, ed. L. J. Camp and S. Lewis, 17-34. Boston: Kluwer Academic Publishers.

---

[36]http://www.darkreading.com/vulnerability_management/security/attacks/showArticle.jhtml?articleID=222700786.

[37]http://www.washingtonpost.com/wp-dyn/content/article/2010/01/13/AR2010011300359.html.

Clayton, R. 2010. Might Governments Clean-up Malware? *Proceedings of the 9th Workshop on the Economics of Information Security*, Cambridge, MA, June 7-8. Available at http://weis2010.econinfosec.org/papers/session4/weis2010_clayton.pdf.

Drimer, S., S. Murdoch and R. Anderson. 2008. Thinking inside the box: system-level failures of tamper proofing. *Proceedings of the IEEE Symposium on Security and Privacy*, pp. 281-295. IEEE Computer Society.

Dynes, S., E. Goetz and M. Freeman. 2007. Cybersecurity: Are Economic Incentives Adequate? In *Critical Infrastructure Protection*, pp. 15-27. Springer.

Edelman, B. 2009. Adverse selection in online "trust" certifications. *Proceedings of the 11th International Conference on Electronic Commerce*, pp. 205-212. ACM Press.

Information War Monitor. 2009. Tracking GhostNet: Investigating a Cyber Espionage Network. Available at http://www.scribd.com/doc/13731776/Tracking-GhostNet-Investigating-a-Cyber-Espionage-Network.

Kolstad, C., Ulen, T. and Johnson, G. 1990. Ex Post Liability for Harm vs. Ex Ante Safety Regulation: Substitutes or Complements? *American Economic Review* 80(4):888-901.

Konar, S., and M. Cohen. 1997. Information As Regulation: The Effect of Community Right to Know Laws on Toxic Emissions. *Journal of Environmental Economics and Management* 32(1):109-124.

Lichtman, D.G. and E.A. Posner. 2004. Holding Internet Service Providers Accountable. In *The law and economics of cybersecurity*, ed. Mark F. Grady, F. Paris, pp. 221-258.

MacCarthy, M. 2009. What Internet Intermediaries Are Doing About Liability and Why It Matters. *ExpressO*. Available at http://works.bepress.com/mark_maccarthy/1.

MacCarthy, M. 2010. Information Security Policy in the U.S. Retail Payments Industry. 9th Workshop on the Economics of Information Security, Cambridge, MA, June 7-8. Available at http://weis2010.econinfosec.org/papers/panel/weis2010_maccarthy.pdf.

Moore, T., and R. Clayton. 2007. Examining the Impact of Website Take-down on Phishing. *Proceedings of the Anti-Phishing Working Group eCrime Researchers Summit*, pp. 1-13.

Moore, T., and R. Clayton. 2008a. The Impact of Incentives on Notice and Take-down. In *Managing Information Risk and the Economics of Security*, ed. M. Eric Johnson, 199-223. New York: Springer.

Moore, T., and R. Clayton. 2008b. The Consequence of Non-cooperation in the Fight against Phishing. *Proceedings of the Anti-Phishing Working Group eCrime Researchers Summit*, pp. 1-14.

Mulligan, D., and Bamberger, K. 2007. Security Breach Notification Laws: Views from Chief Security Officers. *Samuelson Law, Technology & Public Policy Clinic, University of California-Berkeley School of Law*. Available at http://www.law.berkeley.edu/files/cso_study.pdf.

Nagaraja, S., and R. Anderson. 2009. The snooping dragon: social-malware surveillance of the Tibetan movement. *University of Cambridge Computer Laboratory Technical Report UCAM-CL-TR-746*. Available at http://www.cl.cam.ac.uk/techreports/UCAM-CL-TR-746.pdf.

Provos, N., P. Mavrommatis, M. Rajab, and F. Monrose. 2008. All Your iFrames Point to Us. *Proceedings of the USENIX Security Symposium*, pp. 1-15.

Romanosky, S., R. Telang, and A. Acquisti. 2008. Do Data Breach Disclosure Laws Reduce Identity Theft? *7th Workshop on the Economics of Information Security*, Hanover, NH. Available at http://ssrn.com/paper=1268926.

Shavell, S. 1984. A Model of the Optimal Use of Liability and Safety Regulation. *RAND Journal of Economics* 15(2):271-280.

Stern, H. 2009. The Rise and Fall of Reactor Mailer. *Proceedings of the MIT Spam Conference*, Cambridge, MA, March. Available at http://projects.csail.mit.edu/spamconf/SC2009/Henry_Stern/.

Sullivan, R. 2009. The Benefits of Collecting and Reporting Payment Fraud Statistics in the United States. *Payment Systems Briefing, Federal Reserve Bank of Kansas City*.

van Eeten, M., and J. M. Bauer. 2008. The Economics of Malware: Security Decisions, Incentives and Externalities. *OECD Science, Technology and Industry Working Paper No. 2008/1*.

Untangling Attribution

David D. Clark[1]

Massachusetts Institute of Technology

Susan Landau

PrivacyInk.com

INTRODUCTION

In February 2010, former NSA Director Mike McConnell wrote that, "We need to develop an early-warning system to monitor cyberspace, identify intrusions and locate the source of attacks with a trail of evidence that can support diplomatic, military and legal options—and we must be able to do this in milliseconds. More specifically, we need to reengineer the Internet to make attribution, geolocation, intelligence analysis and impact assessment—who did it, from where, why and what was the result—more manageable."[2]

This statement is part of a recurring theme that a secure Internet must provide better *attribution* for actions occurring on the network. Although *attribution* generally means assigning a cause to an action, this meaning refers to identifying the agent responsible for the action (specifically, "determining the identity or location of an attacker or an attacker's intermediary"[3]). This links the word to the more general idea of *identity*, in its various meanings. Attribution is central to *deterrence*, the idea that one can dissuade attackers from acting through fear of some sort of retaliation. *Retaliation requires knowing with full certainty who the attackers are.*

The Internet was not designed with the goal of deterrence in mind, and perhaps a future Internet should be designed differently. In particular, there have been calls for a stronger form of personal identification that can be observed in the network. A non-technical version of this view was put forward as: "Why don't packets have license plates?" This is called the *attribution problem*. There are many types of attribution, and different types are useful in different contexts. We believe that what has been described as the attribution problem is actually a number of problems rolled together. Attribution is certainly not one size fits all.

Attribution on the Internet can mean the owner of the machine (e.g., the Enron Corporation), the physical location of the machine (e.g., Houston, Estonia, China), or the individual who is actually

[1]Clark's effort on this work was funded by the Office of Naval Research under award number N00014-08-1-0898. Any opinions, findings, and conclusions or recommendations expressed in this paper are those of the authors and do not necessarily reflect the views of the Office of Naval Research.

[2]Mike McConnell, "Mike McConnell on How to Win the Cyberwar We're Losing," Washington Post, February 28, 2010.

[3]David Wheeler and Gregory Larson, "Techniques for Cyber Attack Attribution," Institute for Defense Analyses, October 2003, p. ES-1.

responsible for the actions. The differences between these varied forms of attribution motivate this paper. Our goal in this paper is to tease apart the attribution problems in order to determine under which circumstances which types of attribution would actually be useful.

In summary, we draw the following conclusions:

• The most challenging and complex attacks to deter are those we call multi-stage attacks, where the attacker infiltrates one computer to use as a platform to attack a second, and so on. These attacks, especially if they cross jurisdictional boundaries, raise technical and methodological barriers to attribution.

• Network-level addresses (IP addresses) are more useful than is often thought as a starting point for attribution, in those cases where attribution is relevant.[4]

• Redesigning the Internet so that all actions can be robustly attributed to a person would not help to deter the sophisticated attacks we are seeing today, such as the multi-stage attacks mentioned above. At the same time, such a change would raise numerous issues with respect to privacy, freedom of expression, and freedom of action, a trait of the current Internet valued by many including intelligence agencies.

To illustrate the utility of different sorts of attribution, we will use several examples of attacks. First we consider a distributed denial of service (DDoS) attack. As we discuss below, one aspect of dealing with DDoS attacks involves stopping or mitigating them as they occur. (This aspect may or may not be categorized as "deterrence," or instead just as good preparation.) To stop a DDoS attack, we want to shut off communication from the attacking machines, which would most obviously call for attribution at the level of an IP address. On the other hand, to bring the attacker—the bot-master—to justice requires a different type of attribution—a person, not a machine. Unlike the information for halting the attack, this form of attribution is not needed in real time. Next we consider a phishing attack, which attempts to extract information back from the recipient, so the attempted exploitation must include an IP address to which information is returned. The attribution question then becomes whether that address can effectively be translated into a higher-level identity. Attribution in the cases of information theft can be easy (relatively speaking) if the information is used in criminal ways (e.g., to generate false identities and open fake accounts) but extremely hard if the stolen data, such as flight plans for U.S. military equipment, disappears into another nation-state's military planning apparatus.

We start by putting attribution in the context of Internet communications, and then move to examining different kinds of cyber exploitations and the role attribution plays in these. We follow by considering attribution from four vantage points, enabling us to better discern what the real needs are for attribution.

A BRIEF INTRODUCTION TO INTERNET COMMUNICATIONS

In common parlance, all parts of the Internet are often rolled together into a single phenomenon called "the Internet." Calls for better security are often framed in this simple way, but it is important to start with a more detailed model of the Internet's structure.

To the designers of the network, the term "Internet" is reserved for the general platform that transports data from source to destination, in contrast to the various applications (email, the Web, games, voice, etc.), which are described as operating "on" or "over" the Internet. The data transport service of the Internet is based on *packets*—small units of data prefixed with delivery instructions. The analogy often used to describe a packet is an envelope, with an address on the outside and data on the inside.

---

[4]The companion paper by Earl Boebert in this collection [cite] focuses on sophisticated attacks of the sort a state-sponsored agency might launch, and concludes that for those sorts of attacks, attribution in the network is not a useful tool. For simpler and less sophisticated events, where one computer engages another directly, attribution may be a useful tool and we discuss the utility of IP addresses as a starting point for attribution in these cases.

A better analogy might be a postcard, since unless the data is encrypted it too is visible as the packet is moved across the Internet.

The Internet is made up of a mesh of specialized computers called *routers*, and packets carry a destination address that is examined by each router in turn in order to select the next router to which to forward the packet. The format of the addresses found in packets is defined as part of the core Internet Protocol (IP), and they are usually referred to as IP addresses. Packets also carry a *source IP address*, which indicates where the packet came from. This address thus provides a form of attribution for the packet. Since the routers do not use the source address as they forward a packet, much has been made of the fact that the source address can be forged or falsified by the sender. For a variety of reasons, it is not always easy for a router to verify a source address, even if it tries.[5] However, since the source address in a packet is used by the recipient of the packet to send a reply, if the initial sender is attempting to do more than send a flood of one-way packets, then the source address of the packet has to be valid for the reply to arrive back. For this reason, the source address found in packets often provides a valid form of source attribution.

Above the packet service of the Internet we find the rich space of applications—applications that run "over" the packet service. At this level, some applications employ very robust means for each end to identify the other. When a customer connects to a bank, for example, the bank wants to be very sure that the customer has been correctly identified. The customer similarly wants to be sure that the bank is actually the bank, and not a falsified web site pretending to be the bank. Encrypted connections from browser to bank,[6] certificate hierarchies, passwords and the like are used to achieve a level of mutual identification that is as trustworthy as is practical.

There are two important points to note about these application-level identity mechanisms. First, the strength of the identification mechanism is up to the application. Some applications such as banking require robust mutual identity. Other sites need robust identity, but rely on third parties to do the vetting, e.g., credit card companies do so for online merchants. Some sites, such as those that offer information on illness and medical options, are at pains not to gather identifying information, because they believe that offering their users private and anonymous access will encourage them to make frank enquiries.

Second, these schemes do not involve the packets. An Internet engineer would say that these schemes do not involve the Internet at all, but only the services that run on top of it. Certainly, some of these identity schemes involve third parties, such as credit card companies or merchant certification services. But these, too, are "on top of" the Internet, and not "in" the Internet.

In contrast to these two forms of identity mechanisms—IP addresses and application-level exchange of identity credentials, the "license plates on packets" approach would imply some mandatory and robust form of personal level identifier associated with packets (independent of applications) that could be recorded and used by observers in the network. This packet-level personal identifier, which might be proposed in the future for the Internet, is one focus of our concern.

CLASSES OF ATTACKS

It has become standard to call anything from a piece of spam to a carefully designed intrusion and exfiltration of multiple files an "attack." However, lumping such a wide range of events together does not help us understand the issues that arise; it is valuable to clarify terminology. As a 2009 National Research Council report on cyberattack delineated, some attacks are really *exploitations*. *Cyberattacks* and *cyberexploitations* are similar in that they both rely on the existence of a vulnerability, access to exploit

---

[5]One recent experiment concluded that nearly a third of Internet customers could spoof their source IP address without detection. Beverly, R., Berger, A., Hyun, Y., and Claffy, K. 2009. Understanding the efficacy of deployed Internet source address validation filtering. In *Proceedings of the 9th ACM SIGCOMM Conference on internet Measurement Conference* (Chicago, Illinois, USA, November 04-06, 2009). IMC '09. ACM, New York, NY, 356-369. DOI= http://doi.acm.org/10.1145/1644893.1644936.

[6]The relevant protocols go by the acronyms of SSL and TLS.

it, and software to accomplish the task,[7] but cyberattacks are directed to disrupting or destroying the host (or some attached cyber or physical system), while cyberexploitations are directed toward gaining information. Indeed a cyberexploitation may cause no explicit disruption or destruction at all. We will use that distinction. Attacks and exploitations run the gamut from the very public to the very hidden, and we will examine cyberattacks/cyberexploitations along that axis.

Bot-net Based Attacks

Distributed-denial-of-service (DDoS) attacks, in which a large number of machines from all over the network attack a site or a small set of sites, have the goal of disrupting service by overloading a server or a link. They have a unique character: visible and intrusive. DDoS attacks are designed to be detected. The attack is done by first penetrating and subverting a large stock of attack machines, forming them into what is called a "bot-net." A DDoS attack is thus a multi-step activity, first building the bot-net, then instructing the subverted machines to launch some sort of simultaneous attack on the target system. This step of the attack may be the sending of floods of packets, or just overloading the server with apparently legitimate requests.

Before the attack, it may be possible to take active steps to reduce the potency of an attack. There are at least two approaches to degrading the attack's strength—making it harder to penetrate and keep control of a machine, and identifying machines that are apparently infected, so they can be isolated if they participate in an attack. Machines that are seen as likely ultimate targets for DDoS attack can also prepare themselves by replicating their content on distributed servers, so that an attack must diffuse itself across multiple machines.[8]

During an attack, the relevant mitigation techniques involve turning off traffic from attacking hosts, or dropping it in the network before it reaches the point of overload. This response requires knowing the identity of the attacking machines to identify the traffic. Note that it is not necessary to know all of the machines, just enough to reduce the attack to manageable proportions. And depending on what steps are taken to block traffic from the attacking machines, there may be minimal harm from the occasional mis-identification of an attacker.[9]

After the fact, DDoS attacks represent a challenge for the objective of retribution. The attacker (the so-called bot-master or the client who has rented the bot-net from the bot-master) has usually taken care to be several degrees removed from the machines doing the actual attack. Tracing back through the attacking machines to find the responsible attacker may involve crossing jurisdiction boundaries, which adds complexity and delay. If the actual attack involved falsified source addresses, such traceback may be very difficult or even impossible. However, the range of attacks that can be executed without a two-way exchange of packets is very limited, and for many attacks today, the source address is not forged.[10] Because of these factors, there is a question as to whether after the fact retribution is a useful part of dealing with bot-net-based DDoS attacks.

---

[7]William A. Owens, Kenneth W. Dam, and Herbert S. Lin, *Technology, Policy, Law, and Ethics Regarding U.S. Acquisition and Use of Cyberattack Capabilities* (Washington D.C.: National Academies Press, 2009), p. 81.

[8]For example, a content provider might choose to outsource the hosting of its content to a Content Delivery Network (CDN). A leading provider of CDN service, Akamai, specifically claims that its infrastructure is massive enough that DDoS attacks will be ineffective against it. See http://www.akamai.com/dl/whitepapers/Akamai_Security_Capabilities.pdf?campaign_id=AANA-65TPAC, visited 20 April, 2010.

[9]For example, if the mitigation technique involved blocking traffic coming from a source for a few minutes, then if an innocent machine were mis-identified as part of the attack, the consequence would be only that the user of that machine could not reach the web site for that short time. That sort of failure can occur for lots of reasons, and might well be the outcome that the user perceived in any case while the target machine was under attack.

[10]This statement does not imply that forged source addresses are never seen in current attacks. For example, some attacks are based on the use of the DNS as a vector, and those attacks are one-way, and involve falsified source addresses. By sending a query to a DNS server with the source address of the machine to be attacked, the server will reply with a packet sent to that machine. See for example http://isc.sans.org/diary.html?storyid=5713.

Bot-nets are also used to send bulk unsolicited email—spam. From an attribution perspective, this application is different from DDoS attacks. When botnets are used for sending spam, spam provides traceback. Because merchants have to identify themselves in order to be paid, some attribution is possible. Spammers' protection comes not from anonymity, but from jurisdictional distance or ambiguity in legality.

Identity Theft

The term "identity theft" has received much attention in the press recently, but it is worth separating the different activities that are sometimes lumped together under a single term. The Identity Theft and Assumption Deterrence Act of 1998[11] criminalized identity theft, which the Federal Trade Commission describes as "someone us[ing] your personally identifying information, like your name, Social Security number, or credit card number, without your permission, to commit fraud or other crimes."[12] Under this definition, up to 9 million Americans suffer identity theft annually.[13]

This broad definition encompasses everything from the theft of a single credit-card number or misuse of a single account to a full-scale impersonation of an identity (involving the establishment of new credit accounts or identity documents in a person's name). The former constitutes the majority of identity theft. In 2006, for example, according to an FTC report, 6.8 million Americans suffered theft of their credit or account information, while 1.8 million had their identity information used to establish fraudulent accounts,[14] a ratio of three-and-a-half to one. Thus the 9 million number somewhat overstates the number of people subjected to full impersonation. The serious case of identity theft, in which new documents are established in someone else's name, happens about 2 million times a year in the U.S.

Identity theft is an interesting crime for a number of reasons. It is a multi-step crime—the identity in question must be stolen, and then exploited. The theft can occur in many ways. It may involve infiltration of a computer and installation of spyware that captures identifiers and passwords used for application-level authentication or the penetration of a merchant server and the theft of billing records. Such information may then be used by the original thief or sold to other criminals. Next, the identity must be exploited. If the exploit is on the Internet, this generally involves the use of the stolen credentials to mislead some sort of application-level authentication scheme, e.g., logging in as the user to lay a false attribution trail. Perhaps as a final step, some sort of money-laundering scheme is required to convert the exploit into money that is useful to the criminal.

Early Internet-based identity theft used "phishing," an attack in which a user is tricked into going to a web site that imitates a legitimate one (e.g., a bank) and typing in his name and password. Phishing attacks surfaced in 1996,[15] and by 2005, there were reports of as many as 250,000 phishing attempts being made daily against just one financial institution.[16] More lucrative than attempts at obtaining records about single individuals are efforts that download identity information about many individuals at once and then use that information to commit crimes.

One such incident involved a group from Russia and Estonia who, with the help of an insider, broke into a server at RBSWorldPay, an Atlanta-based card-processing company. Taking information on customer accounts—the card numbers and associated PINs and decrypting the protected information, the thieves created counterfeit debit cards, raised withdrawal limits on these accounts, and hired

---

[11]Public Law 105-318.

[12]Federal Trade Commission, *About Identity Theft*, http://www.ftc.gov/bcp/edu/microsites/idtheft/consumers/about-identity-theft.html [last viewed April 13, 2010].

[13]Ibid.

[14]Synovate, Federal *Trade Commission—2006 Identity Theft Survey Report*, November 2007, p. 4.

[15]Gunter Ollmann, The Phishing Guide: Understanding and Preventing Phishing Attacks, Next Generation Security Software Ltd. (white paper), 2004.

[16]Christopher Abad, "The Economy of Phishing: A Survey of the Operations of the Phishing Market," *First Monday*, Vol. 10, No. 9-5 (September 2005).

people for the day who withdrew $9 million from 21,000 ATMs in 49 cities.[17] Another attack involved Heartland Payment Services, a major processor of credit-card and debit-card transactions. Heartland's systems were penetrated, and unencrypted data in transit between merchant point-of-sale devices and Heartland was sniffed. The data collected included account numbers, expiration dates, and sometimes the account holder's name;[18] allegedly over 130 million accounts were compromised.[19]

The fact that internal bank and credit-card account records can now be accessed over the network has made theft of such records much easier. The pattern such as was employed in the RBSWorldPay case, in which a single insider transferred sensitive personal data to accomplices overseas, appears to be increasing in frequency.[20]

Data Exfiltration and Espionage

Foreign military and industrial espionage have long been problems for the U.S. Prior to the ubiquitous use of the network in modern enterprises, such espionage required people in place to make contacts at target facilities, receive the stolen information, etc. Moles might need to be in place for years before they had access to desired information. Such an enterprise was an expensive and time-consuming proposition. For example, in order to acquire Western technical expertise, hundreds of Soviet case officers were involved in Soviet-US collaborative working groups in agriculture, civil aviation, nuclear energy, oceanography, computers and the environment.[21]

The Internet has greatly simplified this process. Information that was once clearly inside a large enterprise may now be relatively easily accessible to people on the outside. Instead of all the work devoted to developing people in place, competitors, whether corporate or foreign governments, have discovered that the theft of secrets can be done over the network. Developing contacts, planting moles, and touring U.S. factories and development sites are efforts much less needed than they once were.

The first public reports of massive network-based data exfiltration surfaced in 2005. *Time* magazine reported a 2004 exploit in which U.S. military computers at four sites—Fort Huachuca, Arizona, Arlington, Virginia, San Diego, California, and Huntsville, Alabama—were, in a matter of six-and-a-half hours, scanned, and large numbers of sensitive files were taken. These materials were then apparently shipped to Taiwan and Korea, and from there, to southern China.[22] Since then numerous reports have surfaced of similar cyberexploitations, with the attempted intrusion method growing increasingly sophisticated over time.[23] The highly publicized intrusion into Google in 2009-2010 apparently followed this pattern.

Attacks of this sort are stealthy and often of small scale. Frequently they are individually tailored. Their preparation may involve taking over insecure intermediate machines, but only in small quantity, and perhaps highly suited to the task. These machines are used to transit the stolen information and hide its ultimate destination. The first step in the theft is to carefully scope out the target, learning where the files of interest are, and then, once target material has been located, to quickly pack and exfiltrate them, often in a matter of hours.

---

[17]United States Department of Justice, Office of Public Affairs, *Alleged International Hacking Ring Caught in $9 Million Fraud (November 9, 2009)*, and United States District Court, Northeastern District of Georgia, Atlanta Division, United States v. Viktor Pleschuk, Sergei Tsurikov, Hacker 3, Oleg Covelin, Igor Grudijev, Ronald Tsoi, Evelin Tsoi, and Mikhail Jevgenov, Defendants, Criminal Indictment 1-09-CR-492 (November 10, 2009).

[18]Kevin Poulsen, "Card Processor Admits to Large Data Breach," *Wired* (January 20, 2009).

[19]United States Department of Justice, Office of Public Affairs, "Alleged International Hacker Indicted for Massive Attack on U.S. Retail and Banking Networks" (August 17, 2009).

[20]Dan Schutzer, "Research Challenges for Fighting Insider Threat in the Financial Sector," in Insider Attack and Cyber Security: Beyond the Hacker, eds. Salvatore J. Stolfo, Steven M. Bellovin, Shlomo Hershkop, Angelos D. Keromytis, Sara Sinclair, and Sean D. Smith (New York: Springer, 2008), p. 215.

[21]Interagency OPSEC, Intelligence Threat Handbook (2004), pp. 32-33.

[22]Nathan Thornborough, "Inside the Chinese Hack Attack," *Time* (August 25, 2005).

[23]Bryan Krekel, *Capability of the People's Republic of China to Conduct Cyber Warfare and Cyber Network Exploitation*, prepared for the US-China Economic and Security Review Commission (2009).

Investigation of such theft is very difficult. To trace back across the network to the perpetrator may involve several stages through multiple machines in different jurisdictions. However, the data being stolen must follow some path back to the perpetrator, which raises the possibility of tracking. Possession of the stolen information may or may not be useful as evidence, depending on the sort of retribution contemplated. From a national-security perspective, these type of cases are the most important to deter. They are also the ones least likely to be solved solely through technical means.

CASCADES OF ATTRIBUTION AND MULTI-STAGE ATTACKS

Many attacks and exploits are *multi-stage* in character: A penetrates computer B to use as a platform for penetrating C, which is then used to attack D (for example). Deterrence means focusing on computer A. It does not do much good to ask what person or actor owns machines B and C—they were just penetrated in passing. Following the chain of attribution backwards toward A, it is IP addresses that lead back from D to C to B to A. If that trail can be followed, then the investigator can attempt to learn what can be discovered about A.

It is important to note both the limits of mechanisms for attribution and the intentional complexity of the various attacks and exploits, which have been crafted precisely to confound attribution. Looking at our earlier examples, we see patterns that are both *multi-step* and *multi-stage*. For example, a DDoS attack has a first step in which the array of attack machines (the bot-net) is assembled. This step will be taken in a multi-stage way, with the machines, as they fall prey to the initial event that infiltrates them, reporting back to some intermediate control computer that itself may have been first infiltrated and corrupted. Then in the step where the machines launch the attack, the instructions describing the attack will have been preloaded, and perhaps launched using a timer or a signal send through some complex signaling channel (e.g. a message to a chat channel), so that the controller is far away by the time that the attack is evident.

Of course, the multi-stage pattern is not unique to attacks and malicious behavior. Linking services together on multiple machines, such that A asks B to carry out some action, and B invokes C as part of the task, is the general idea behind composable services such as Web 2.0. In situations like this, A and B might exchange identity credentials, B and C might also do so, but C would not know who A is.[24] B is providing a service to its clients (e.g. A), and uses C as part of this service. Under normal circumstances, B would take on the responsibility of ensuring that the clients (e.g. A) are not undertaking unsuitable objectives when they invoke the service. In case of a bad event (consider the analog of a multi-car rear-end collision), C complains to B, and B complains to A.

When the multi-stage activity is malicious, of course, the issue is that the intermediate machine has been infiltrated and corrupted, so the machine is not acting in a responsible way or in ways that reflect the wishes of its owner/operator. The human operator of B may be seen at the origin of the attack, but is just a victim of a security flaw in his machine.

One of the conclusions of this paper is that multi-stage attacks must be a focus of attention when considering attribution and deterrence. First, many attacks fit in this category, including sophisticated and crafty attacks designed to avoid attribution. Assigning blame to such attacks is very challenging and difficult. Second, when computers are penetrated by an attacker to use as a platform for a further attack, that penetration usually bypasses any sort of end-to-end exchange of application-level credentials. So the only kind of attribution that can possibly be applied here is at the level of IP addresses. Personal-level attribution will not be a useful tool in tracing attribution or assigning blame, and dealing with these sorts of attacks does not provide a justification for requiring network-based, personal-level identification.

---

[24]One legitimate example of this occurs in federated identity management systems: the Identity Provider knows that Service Provider A and Service Provider B (for example, a hotel and a car-rental agency) are both providing services for the same customer, but through the judicious use of pseudonyms, no one else, including the two service providers, can determine that fact.

While multi-stage attacks represent a serious challenge, we urge the research community to consider what might be done to improve the options for tracking back to an ultimate source. Any solution or improvement that might be found will certainly not be purely technical, but will be a mix of technical and policy tools. For example, one might imagine every user of the Internet being urged to keep a log of incoming and outgoing connections. To avoid concerns about privacy, this log could be maintained under the control of the user himself—given today's technology, the sort of device called a "home router" could keep such a log with minimal additional cost for storage. But such a log would only be useful in a context where there are regulations as to when data could be requested from this log, by whom, etc. And of course, the user might have failed to maintain such a log. In such a case, the "punishment" might be that the ISP serving that user is required to log the user's traffic—the cost for failing to self-protect is a loss of privacy.

This idea may not be suitable—we offer it only as an example to illustrate how technology and policy will have to be combined as part of any solution, and also to illustrate that jurisdictional issues (and variation of regulation across jurisdictions) will be central in dealing with these sorts of attacks.

FOUR DIFFERENT ASPECTS OF ATTRIBUTION

As the discussion above points out, different types of cyberattacks and cyberexploitations raise different options for prevention and deterrence. We have found it useful to think about attribution from different vantage points:

- *Types:* if users are expected to be identified in some way, what is the source of that identity, and what can we conclude about the utility of different sorts of identity?
- *Timing:* what are the different roles of attribution before, during and after an event?
- *Investigators:* how might different parties exploit attribution as a part of deterrence?
- *Jurisdiction:* what are the variations that we can expect across different jurisdictions, and how might this influence our choices in mechanism design?

Types of Attribution

An IP address in a packet identifies an attachment point on the Internet. Roughly, by analogy to a street address, it indicates a location, but not who lives there. In many cases, of course, an address (both physical and Internet) can be linked to a person, or at least a family. Since residential Internet service is almost always provided by commercial Internet Service Providers (ISPs), they have billing information for all of their customers. If they choose to maintain a database that links billing information to the Internet addresses they give out to specific customers, they can trace back from address to personal identity. In the U.S. the organizations that work to deter copyright infringement have had laws passed allowing them to obtain a subpoena for such information from ISPs. But unless this connection has been made, Internet addresses have meaning only at the level of a network endpoint, which usually maps to one or a small cluster of machines.[25] Indeed, in many cases, an IP address cannot be identified with a particular machine because the machine has been on the network for a quite temporary period of time, such as in an airport lounge, hotel lobby, coffeehouse, etc.

In many application-level identity schemes such as the banking example above, identity has meaning at the level of an individual. The bank may keep track of Internet addresses as supplemental information to be used in case of abuse, but the design of their identity system is intended to tie directly to an

---

[25]Many homes have a device called a "home router, which allows a small number of computers in the home to share one network connection. As the Internet is currently used, all these machines share one Internet address, so starting with that address there is no way to distinguish among those different machines. At a larger scale, an ISP (or a country) might use this same sort of technology to map a large number of machines to one address, making this sort of attribution even less effective.

individual as the accountable agent, not a machine. The IP address is not used as part of establishing that identity.

A related kind of individual identity is the *pseudonym*. The idea of a pseudonym, as the term is usually used, is an identity that links to a specific individual, without revealing who that individual is. A pseudonym system should have two goals. First, the pseudonym should not be easily linked to an actual person—the goal is freedom from attribution. Second, the pseudonym should not be easily stolen and co-opted by another individual—the speaker, although anonymous, should have the exclusive use of that identity. Encryption schemes can be used in various ways to achieve this sort of functionality, which is a sort of "anti-attribution."

To fully protect pseudonymous speech and other types of anonymous activities, it is necessary to complement application-level "anti-attribution" mechanisms with tools to mask IP-level machine-based identity, since that can often be linked to human-level identity with some effort, as discussed above. Tools such as Tor[26] are used to give IP-level anonymity to communications; they are employed by activists and dissidents, journalists, the military and the intelligence community, and many others to mask with whom the communication is occurring. Law enforcement uses Tor to visit websites and chat rooms without leaving behind a tell-tale government IP address, while the military uses Tor to enable personnel "in place" to communicate with headquarters without revealing their true identity.

When Internet communications occur without the use of traffic analysis anonymizers such as Tor, the source and destination addresses in packets can be seen by every router that forwards the packet, and by any other sort of monitoring device that is in the path from the sender to the receiver. So these sorts of identity indicators are fairly public. In contrast, if two end points exchange identity credential between themselves over an encrypted connection, that exchange is private to those two end-points.[27] Even if a third party, such as a credit-card company, is involved in the identity verification, that third party has been invoked with the knowledge and concurrence of the initial end-points. The knowledge of the identity is restricted to those parties.

An analogy to monitoring IP addresses in the network might be security cameras. A camera on a public street captures our public behavior, and a likeness of our face. But it does not reveal who we are unless that face can be linked to some other aspect of identity. In contrast, in various circumstances we have to identify ourselves to some other entity (show a driver's license, passport, credit card, etc.) but this transaction is specific to the circumstances at hand, and is normally not visible to a third-party observer. A security camera in a store provides an analogy to the logging of IP addresses by an endpoint. The images might be more easily linked to a customer transaction, and thus to other aspects of identity. But the video captured by that camera is private to the store unless it chooses to reveal it (e.g., after a robbery) or it is demanded by an authorized third party (e.g., by a court order).

Using IP addresses as a starting point, one can try to derive forms of attribution other than at the level of the individual. IP addresses are usually allocated in blocks to Internet service providers (ISPs), corporations, universities, governments, and the like. Normally, the "owner" of a block of addresses is a public record, so one can look up an address to see who it belongs to. This can provide a starting point for investigation and subsequent fact-finding.

Another potential form of attribution is "where"—geo-locating the end-point associated with the IP address on the face of the physical landscape. IP addresses are not allocated in a way that makes geo-location automatic—they are given out to actors that may have large geographic scope. Nonetheless, for many IP addresses, one can make a very accurate guess about where the end-point is located, since many networks have a hierarchical design to their physical connectivity, and map the addresses to the levels of the hierarchy. Several commercial services now exist that provide the function of mapping an IP address to an approximate

---

[26]Tor is a tool developed by the U.S. Naval Research Lab to permit anonymous (at the IP level) use of the Internet. See www.torproject.org.

[27]The restriction of *encrypted* communication is critical here. If the observer is using technology called Deep Packet Inspection, or DPI, he can observe anything not encrypted, including identity credentials being exchanged end-to-end. Encryption does not hide everything; it is possible, for example, to determine the type of traffic (e.g., VoIP, video) even while the content itself is hidden.

location.[28] These services are designed to meet a number of customer needs, as their advertising suggests, including customization of Web content to different classes of customers and regulatory compliance. These services compete to provide accurate location information, and advertise their precision in their marketing information. Various firms claim that 99-99.9% of IP addresses can be accurately localized to within a country, and that 90-96% can be accurately localized to within a state, city or other similar region. These services are used today by commercial Web content providers to localize their content to the presumed location of the user (e.g., to pick the right language), or in some cases to block access to certain content based on the presumed locus (with respect to a jurisdiction), such as the blocking of Nazi memorabilia auctions to customers in France. They are designed to work in real-time (as part of processing a Web query) and can provide a rich, if approximate, mapping from IP address to other attributes.

The issue with many of these tools is that since the mapping is approximate, there is some degree of "plausible deniability" to assertions of responsibility. There have been proposals to "harden" the linkage between the IP address and other information. For example, the Chinese put forward a proposal to the ITU that as part of the conversion of the Internet from IPv4 to IPv6, addresses should be first allocated to states, which would then allocate them to the relevant private-sector actors. This would mean that the linkage from IP address to jurisdiction would be robust,[29] and that it would be possible for the Chinese government to be certain where downloaded material, whether software stolen from U.S. companies or human-rights information from U.S organizations, was going.

Of course, the transition from IPv4 to IPv6 is only one of the changes that may occur to the Internet over the coming years. A more dramatic change might be the introduction of a virtualized network infrastructure, which would permit multiple simultaneous networks to co-exist, each with its own approach to attribution. A future network that provides an information dissemination and retrieval service as part of its core function would imply some sort of binding between user and information that would be visible "in the network." We believe that our general conclusions will apply across a range of possible future network designs—the linkage between machine-level attribution and higher-level attribution (e.g. personal) will be a jurisdictional policy matter, not just a technical matter, and mechanisms for attribution must balance a range of policy objectives, not just focus on deterrence.

Timing

Before the Fact—Prevention or Degradation

Actions taken before the attack are the ones most commonly associated with "computer security"—they involve good defenses for computers (latest patches, good operating practices), good defenses for the network itself, and so on. None of these involve the need for attribution, but putting tools in place to implement good authentication and authorization are part of good security. For some classes of attacks, specifically DDoS events, it may be possible to degrade the viability of the bot-net or the potency of the attack by preventive actions that affect infected machines. In this respect, degradation of attacks can involve remote attribution (see below).

During the Fact: Mitigation

During an attack/event, the main objective is to stop or mitigate the event. Secondarily, one may want to gather evidence to be used after the fact. What one can do during an attack depends on the nature of the attack, and different approaches to mitigation place different requirements on attribution

[28]See, for example, http://www.maxmind.com/app/city, http://www.digitalelement.com/our_technology/our_technology.html, or http://www.quova.com/.

[29]There is some disagreement as to whether the original proposal was for *some* or *all* IPv6 addresses to be allocated to countries. For a 2004 statement that makes clear that the proposal was for only *some* addresses to be allocated in this way, see www.itu.int/ITU-T/tsb-director/itut-wsis/files/zhao-netgov02.doc.

for the attack. Different approaches will be needed to stop a DDoS attack and data exfiltration while it is happening.

After the Fact: Retribution

The traditional discussion of deterrence focuses on what would happen after the fact, when some sort of retribution would be exacted. For example, as discussed above, if the event is classed as a crime, this would trigger a police response. Primarily, police investigate crimes, identify the perpetrator, and gather the evidence for prosecution. Attribution is at the center of this role. Unless one can identify the perpetrator, retribution is hard to achieve. However, as we illustrated above in our examples of attacks, the actual situation is more complex in a computer-generated situation than this simple story might imply.

Ongoing: Attribution as a Part of Normal Activity

In fact, the "before the fact" phase above defines what should be the normal operating mode of the system. With good preparation, bad events might not occur. However, one should look at the role of identity and attribution in the ongoing operation of a system. The idea of authentication is well understood. Several sorts of ongoing activities are made more trustworthy not by trying to prevent misbehavior in real time, but by demanding strong accountability. For example, access to medical records in an emergency room may best be controlled by allowing the access but requiring that the doctor making the request be thoroughly identified so the request can be logged.

Investigators

There are various sorts of deterrence that might be imagined; these have different implications for the needed quality and precision of the attribution. Different actors—police, intelligence services, and the military—will benefit from different sorts of attribution. In the case of attacks that are described as crimes, the usual sort of deterrence is judicial—arrest and prosecution. This would seem to call for attribution at the level of the individual, and of *forensic* quality—sufficient to bring into court. However, this model of attribution may be over-simplified. First, the most important role of attribution may be during the course of the investigation, when evidence is being gathered. Having a clue about attribution that is sufficient to guide an ongoing investigation may be critical. One FBI agent put it this way, "I could do packet attribution and let's say it gets me to a physical location. Maybe I get a search warrant and I get back. How I get there is important."

After that point, forensic quality evidence matters. From the investigator's standpoint, "[What's] critically important is that you have evidence. Packet attribution is not beyond a reasonable doubt. The biggest thing in attribution is you're not looking for a computer; you're looking for a person." Prosecutors look for certain kinds of evidence to bring before a jury. Evidence of on-line identity, however robust technically, may be less compelling than evidence gathered from carrying out search warrants and following the money. Packet-level attribution may aid an investigation, but our world still demands that the real evidence come from the physical world.

Jurisdiction

Different parts of the Internet operate within different jurisdictions: different countries, different legal systems, and (within these jurisdictions) both as public and as private-sector activities. Any discussion of attribution must consider jurisdictional issues.

Variation in Enforcement

Some regions may be lax in their enforcement of laws and uninterested in making the investigation of cyberattack a high priority. This can be an issue in any attack, but becomes of particular importance in attacks that involve cascades of machines: machine A infiltrates machine B to attack machine C, and so on. If the jurisdiction within which B sits is not responsive, it becomes much harder to gather any evidence (which may be transient) that might link B to A. There is anecdotal evidence that attackers may "venue-shop" for regimes in which aggressive investigation is unlikely.

Evidence suggests that for single-stage events, so long as there are procedures in place within a jurisdiction, mapping from IP address to higher-level attribution is practical. For example, in the U.S. the RIAA, under the provisions of the Digital Millennium Copyright Act, regularly obtains information from ISPs about their customers hosting material covered by copyright for the purpose of bringing lawsuits. The conclusion reached from this example should be the importance of jurisdiction in such a network investigation. To determine traffic origin requires investigating the machines traversed by the communications. If a jurisdiction permits such an investigation, then attribution—and possible deterrence—is possible. But if it does not, because for example the jurisdiction does not view the activity as criminal, then tracing will not be possible.

This suggests that even if we were to push for a variant of the Internet that demanded very robust identity credentials to use the network, tracing would remain subject to barriers that would arise from variation in jurisdictions. Unless we imagine that all countries would agree to the election of a single, global identity authority, credentials would be issued by individual countries, where the quality of the process would be highly variable. In view of this, it is worth examining the issue of criminal versus national-security investigations more closely.

Criminal versus National-Security Investigations

"Follow the money" is surprisingly useful. That adage might seem odd in investigating crimes that are purely virtual, but the fact is that almost all criminal activity (including child pornography) involves money. Thus, for example, although their initial theft was of bits, if the RBSWorldPay criminals were to profit, in the end they needed to collect money from bank accounts. Even in child pornography cases, there are producers, organizers, users—and money.

Lack of laws against criminal activity on the Internet originally made prosecution of such activities difficult. Thus, for example, there were no charges brought against the Filipino developer of the 2000 ILOVEYOU virus; the Philippines only criminalized this activity three months after the release. A combination of the development of national laws and much greater international cooperation has greatly improved the ability to track and prosecute clearly criminal Internet activities (e.g., identity theft, child pornography, malware propagation, etc.). The key issue is what constitutes "clearly criminal." Economic espionage is not a crime in much of the world, and therefore other nations are unlikely to aid the United States in investigating or prosecuting such activities conducted against U.S. industry. That does not mean that investigation and consequences are not possible, only that they cannot follow the path of criminal prosecution the way, say, theft from RBS WorldPay has.

 If a nation-state is involved in the data exfiltration, then the problem is a national-security issue, not a law-enforcement case. The level of proof of the attribution need not stand up in court. Indeed, the level of proof used to determine the attribution may never be made public even if the accusations of spying are. Intelligence agencies deal with certain forms of espionage, such as cyberexploitations of national research labs, defense contractors, etc. Intelligence agencies do not usually try to bring spies into court—governments have their own ways of pushing back on attacks—forms of tit-for-tat that require a degree of attribution, but perhaps only at the level of the state actor responsible. Diplomats can enter into a "shall we confront or cooperate" negotiation with their counterparts, using evidence that might not stand up in court but which is sufficiently compelling to underpin the negotiation.

Finally, if a cyberattack occurs as part of what is seen as "armed conflict," there may be some form of military response. This form of response is not usually directed at a specific person, but at a state or non-state group. The level of attribution that is required is thus to some larger aggregate, not the individual. To the extent that the initial manifestation of attribution is at the level of the IP address, the question that arises is how, and with what precision, this can be associated with some collective actor. To the military, attribution at the level of an individual is not useful.

SUMMARIZING THE VALUE OF ATTRIBUTION

While there are probably many specific identity/attribution schemes, they seem to fall into general categories: the *machine*, the *person*, and the *aggregate identity*, such as a state actor. The term *principal* is often used to describe the person or other entity that is ultimately accountable for some action.

Machines may have their own credentials, and may store credential for principals, but machines act only on behalf of some agent, and that agent (individual or collective) is the entity that must be identified and held accountable if effective deterrence is to occur. Thus machine attribution plays an important role in attribution, but is not of great value by itself if the goal is holding that agent accountable.

Under many circumstances, it is possible, with some effort, to link an IP address to a higher-level form of identity, whether an individual, a family (for residential broadband access), a corporation, or a state. Making this connection may be very difficult if the alleged attacker is in another jurisdiction. More importantly, attacks that involve cascades of machines challenge us to make the linkage back to the computer that belongs to the attacker that should be held accountable.

During an attack, when the goal is mitigation, it is not generally useful to identify the responsible person; what is needed is to deal with the machines that are the source of the attack. This sort of attribution is usually associated with IP addresses.

Retribution is not typically directed at a machine; after all, one does not usually arrest a machine. However, one could imagine various forms of active defense, in which a system under attack reaches out and somehow disables the attacking machine. This could be seen as a form of tit-for-tat retribution. It is probably illegal under U.S. law, but would represent an example of punishing a machine rather than a person. The practical issue here is that if the machine is an intermediary belonging to an innocent user, the degree of punishment (if it is allowed at all) must be carefully crafted to fit the crime. Mitigating these sorts of attacks is important, and various proposals will have to be considered, such as asking the ISP hosting an attacking machine to disconnect it from the net for a few minutes. Any such scheme must be designed in such a way that it itself cannot be subverted into a tool for originating an attack. One might force a machine to reboot to see if this disabled the attack code, but this again looks like a direct attack.[30]

What Attribution Can Deliver

One can consider various different approaches: machine-level attribution, application-level attribution based on credentials exchanged between end-points, and redesigning systems so the costs of an attack lie partially on the attackers. We consider each of these briefly.

Machine-Level (IP address) Attribution

Much has been made of the fact that source IP addresses can be forged. However, the only sort of attack where a forged address is effective is a DDoS attack, where the goal is just to flood the destination with useless traffic. Any more sophisticated exchange, for example in support of espionage, will neces-

---

[30]Current recommended practice for ISPs is for the ISP hosting the infested machine to verify that the machine appears to be part of a bot-net, then use its billing records to translate from machine to person, and send the person a letter.

sitate a two-way exchange of information; this requires the use of valid source addresses. In a multi-step attack, the infiltration preparation of the intermediate machine requires meaningful communication; all but the last step will have valid source addresses.

Application-level Attribution

Especially if we were to redesign some protocols, the use of application level attribution based on credentials exchanged among end-points is the approach that has the best balance of implications. First, the applications, knowing what the task is, can pick the best tradeoff between strong accountability and the resulting protections and weaker (or no) accountability and its freedoms. A web site may want to allow access without demanding any identification, even though doing so weakens its access to retribution for attack. The site can compensate for this by limiting the consequences of attack—certainly there should be no confidential information on such a machine. DDoS may be the only real peril for such a machine, since defacement can usually be corrected quickly.

On the other hand, a machine storing highly confidential information should have no reason to permit any connection without strong identification of the other parties.

If a machine is attacked, we need a regime in which that machine can present evidence of attribution that it has gathered (both at the IP and application level), which it chooses to reveal because of the attack. Steps must be taken to prevent the end-point from falsifying this evidence; for example by means of some use of cryptography, or the use of trusted observers as witnesses. If this approach can be made to work, then the revelation of each party's identity is under the control of the other parties, but no others. This seems like a nice balance of features.

Approaching Attribution Orthogonally

One might conclude from the above discussion that the goal of improved deterrence based on better attribution is hopeless. This conclusion is over-pessimistic. The correct conclusion we draw is that change to the Internet to add some sort of public, person-level identity mechanism at the packet level is not useful and in fact counter-productive. But one might imagine various sort of clever "shifts in the playing field" that would make certain sorts of attribution easier to accomplish.

For example, would allocation of addresses to countries so that addresses could more easily and robustly be linked to a jurisdiction be a good idea? Such a change would have many implications, and careful thought would be required to consider whether such a change would be in the best interest of a majority of the actors on the Internet.

Would it make sense to hold owners of intermediate machines in a multi-stage attack responsible to some (perhaps minor) degree for the resulting harm of the attack? This approach might heighten attention to better security of computers attached to the Internet, and might lay the groundwork for a multi-stage trace-back system in which machines that allow themselves to be infiltrated become subject to third-party external surveillance as a consequence. To put this another way, the poor system maintenance would result in a loss of privacy.

Costs of Attribution

Few technical solutions have purely one-sided effects, and attribution is no exception to this general principle. Once a mechanism for attribution is put in place, we must expect that it will be used in differently in different jurisdictions, according to the laws and customs of each country. While in the U.S., we may talk about deterrence as a goal to stop the breaking of our laws; another country might use the same tools to repress dissidents. It would also be likely to use better attribution tools to detect our intelligence services at work. Making one task easier makes other tasks easier, unless we take specific actions to separate classes of activity in a technical way. This sort of separation would imply the use of different tools in different circumstances; a consequence of this is that attribution tools should not be built into the core fabric of the Internet.

CONCLUSIONS

Our fundamental conclusion is that "the attribution problem" is not actually a technical issue at all, but a policy concern with multiple solutions depending on the type of technical issue—e.g., DDoS attack, criminal activity, or data exfiltration—to be solved. Our conclusions are that, not surprisingly, solutions to the "attribution problem" lie outside the technical realm.

Conclusion 1

The occasions when attribution at the level of an individual person is useful are very limited. Criminal retribution requires identifying a specific person and assigning blame, but the evidence that is finally brought into court is unlikely to be "forensic quality" computer-based identity, but rather other sorts of physical evidence found during the investigation. Clues about identity may be more important during the course of an investigation.

Conclusion 2

There is an important distinction between what we call private attribution (private to the end-points) and public or third-party attribution.

In application-level attribution as we described it, each end-point may take steps to know who the other parties to the communication are, but that knowledge is private to the communicating parties. In public or third-party attribution, an "observer in the middle" is given enough information that they can independently identify the communicating parties. In the current Internet, the only form of observer attribution is based on IP addresses. Where public attribution is useful, it will be at the level of the machine, not the person. The most obvious case is "during the fact" DDoS mitigation, where nodes in the network need to take action based on source and destination addresses.

We believe that public attribution beyond what is available today (that is, not based on the IP address, but on finer levels that would identify a user) would seldom be of value in the Internet, and would, at the same time, be a major threat to privacy and the right of private action. Such a change would be inimical to many values intrinsic to the U.S., including rights protected by the First Amendment to read and write anonymously. As a corollary, we note that there are two kinds of observers, trusted (by one of the end points) and untrusted (or unaffiliated, perhaps). If and when observer-based attribution is useful, it will often be a specific case where one of the end-points invokes a trusted observer to monitor what is being sent, perhaps as a witness, or because the end-point machine is not itself trusted.

Conclusion 3

Multi-stage attacks, which require tracing a chain of attribution across several machines, are a major issue in attribution today.

This problem can be attacked in a number of ways, including making hosts more secure (a long-term effort) and making it harder for an infested machine to launch a subsequent attack. If this problem could be resolved, it would eliminate many uncertainties in attribution. Since it is not resolved, it imposes limits on the utility of attribution, no matter how it is structured. **Thus a prime problem for the research community is the issue of dealing with multi-stage attacks. This should be of central attention to network researchers, rather than (for example) the problem of designing highly robust top-down identity schemes.** Long term, we should look at what sorts of attribution would be of value if the multi-stage attack problem had been mitigated, as well as what is useful now.

Any attempts to deal with multi-stage attacks by tracing back the chain of machines involved will depend more on machine-level attribution at the intermediate steps, rather than personal-level attribution. Since the intermediate machines are normally being used without the permission (or knowledge) of their owners, knowing the identity of those owners is not very useful in trace-back. While one might imagine holding those owners accountable for some sort of secondary responsibility, the primary goal is to get back to the primary actor responsible for the attack, which involves following a chain of connections between machines.

Conclusion 4

We believe that pragmatically, the most important barrier to deterrence today is not poor technical tools for attribution but issues that arise due to cross-jurisdictional attacks, especially multi-stage attacks. In other words, deterrence must be achieved through the governmental tools of state, and not by engineering design.

Shifting the national-security problem of attribution to its proper domain, namely from the tools of technology to the tools of state, means several changes in thinking about how to tackle the problem. Rather than seeking solutions to the broad "attribution problem," networking researchers should move to considering the more narrowly focused problem of multi-stage attacks. Instead of seeking a purely technical fix, the U.S. government should move to diplomatic tools, including possibly treaties on cybercrime and cyberattack, to handle the multi-stage, multi-jurisdictional challenges of cyberexploitation and cyberattack. The efforts for top-down control of user identity and attribution, while appropriate and valid for critical-infrastructure domains such as the power grid, and financial and government services, have little role to play in the broader public network. Such efforts can be avoided, leading ultimately to better public safety, security, and privacy.

A Survey of Challenges in Attribution

W. Earl Boebert

Sandia National Laboratories (retired)

1 STATEMENT OF WORK

This paper was prepared under the following Statement of Work:

The consultant will research, draft, present, and finalize a commissioned paper on the problem of attributing cyber intrusions, both technical (can you determine which machine or machines are generating or controlling the intrusion?) and nontechnical (can you determine the party that should be held responsible for the intrusion?). Given that the "attribution problem" is seen as a major barrier to implementing any national policy to deter cyberattacks, this paper would lay out the technical and nontechnical barriers to attributing cyberintrusions, explore plausible aspirations for how these barriers may be overcome or be addressed in the future, and describe how and to what extent even perfect technical attribution would help to support national policy for deterring serious cyberattacks against the United States (that is, cyberattacks with a disabling or a crippling effect on critical societal functions on a national scale (e.g., military mission readiness, air traffic control, financial services, provision of electric power)).

2 INTERNET ATTACKS

2.1 Structure of the Internet

The Internet is a packet-switched network. In simplified form, such a network consists of interconnected nodes, each of which is given a number called an IP address. Units of data to be transmitted are cut up into pieces, or packets. Each packet is given a header which contains (in this simplified discussion) the source and destination IP address of the transmission and other control information. Packets are sent to routers which are provided with tables that give a "next reasonable router" for any given IP address. This relieves the routers from having to know all possible routes to all possible destinations. To use a geographic analogy, consider a router in Albuquerque that wishes to send a data element to New York. The element will be cut into packets whose source IP address will designate Albuquerque and destination IP address will designate New York.

To initiate transmission, the router in Albuquerque only needs to know the IP address of some intermediate router in the general direction, for example, Kansas City. That router, in turn, needs only to know that St. Louis is "on the way" and so forth, "hop" by "hop," until the destination is reached and the packet is joined with others to reconstitute the data element. The dynamic assignment of routes at each hop is what gives packet-switched networks their great resistance to failure.

Early in development of packet-switched networks it became obvious that numeric IP addresses were difficult for humans to cope with, and a second facility, called the Domain Name System or DNS, was developed to permit use of the symbolic domain names with which we are all familiar. The DNS is a distributed lookup system which, when queried, converts a symbolic name for a node, called a "hostname," to a numeric IP address.

2.2 The Nature of Attacks

The Internet shares the central vulnerability of all cyber systems: every action initiated by a human is performed indirectly by system functionality which cannot be directly observed. This vulnerability can be exploited by the insertion of malicious functionality in a node. Since the attacks take place on a packet-switched network, the malicious functionality that carries them out will, in general, be distributed over multiple nodes which must communicate over that network. Thus there are two basic elements to Internet attacks: malicious functionality and malicious packets. Malicious packets are those which are either used to communicate with a malicious functionality or used to shut down a target node by flooding it with traffic that it cannot handle.

If the malicious packets are part of a flooding attack, then the source IP address can be forged because no return communication is desired and attribution is not available from the packets themselves. If the hostile packets are control packets then technical attribution is at least theoretically possible, because they will contain a source IP address to permit return communication, as in an interactive session.

The well-publicized attacks on Estonia[1] and the nation of Georgia[2] were flooding attacks directed at the public interfaces of government services provided over the Internet. Such attacks are relatively easy to mount and very difficult to attribute, especially if they involve so-called "botnets" as described below. Major attacks against significant societal functions such as the military or power distribution require that the attacker gain access to internal network resources and not just direct streams of packets at public interfaces. Consider, for example, an electric power utility. If the utility were to be attacked the way Estonia and Georgia were, customers would not be able to pay their bills on line but power flow would not be affected. To disrupt power the attacker must penetrate the utility's security perimeter and be able to manipulate and destroy data and functionality on internal control networks. A similar situation exists with regard to the military, financial systems, and other major societal services in that their critical functions are not dependent upon the operation of public nodes such as World Wide Web sites.

It is unlikely that an adversary will initiate an attack on critical internal networks without first conducting both external and internal reconnaissance of the target network. Internal reconnaissance will generally be aimed at collecting "metadata," the internal information such as router tables, internal IP addresses and so forth which the network uses to manage itself. This data will be analyzed to determine network topography as well as what actions during the actual attack may produce the greatest degree of disruption to the service being provided by the target. The analogy here is with a sabotage team scouting a building to learn where to place their explosive charges for maximum effect.

The reconnaissance phase is the period where the attacker is most vulnerable to technical attribution. Since the attacker is, in effect, on a voyage of discovery through largely uncharted waters, it not only must exfiltrate large quantities of data but also typically must make repeated intrusions as its analysis raises questions that must be answered. A successful disruptive attack on a major network is a considerably more complex undertaking than flying an airplane into a building or setting off a truck

---

[1]Myers, Steven Lee. "Cyberattack on Estonia stirs fear of 'virtual war.'" *New York Times*, May 18, 2007. Available at http://www.nytimes.com/2007/05/18/world/europe/18iht-estonia.4.5774234.html. Accessed May 31, 2010.

[2]Anon. "War, redefined." *Los Angeles Times*, August 17, 2008. Available at http://articles.latimes.com/2008/aug/17/opinion/ed-cyberwar17. Accessed May 31, 2010.

full of explosives in a crowded street, and considerable planning is required to raise the probability of success to a point where a rational decision to proceed can be made.

2.3 The Attribution Problem

The general problem of attribution can be broken down into two subsidiary problems: technical attribution and human attribution. Technical attribution consists of analyzing malicious functionality and malicious packets, and using the results of the analysis to locate the node which initiated, or is controlling, the attack.

Human attribution consists of taking the results of technical attribution and combining it with other information to identify the person or organization responsible for the attack. There are significant barriers to both forms of attribution.

Both forms of attribution can be either positive or negative. Positive attribution yields positive information, such as where a node is or the identity or other characteristics possessed by an associated human. Negative attribution yields specific information, such as where the node is not located, or that the citizenship of an individual is not that of the U.S. or its allies. Negative attribution is useful in determining courses of action, such as whether suppressing a malicious node is a domestic law enforcement or a foreign covert action problem.

Both technical attribution and human attribution have degrees of uncertainty associated with them. One may know the country of registration of a machine, but not know the current physical location because the machine may be portable and accessing the Internet over long-distance telecommunication. Likewise, one may know the identity of attacker (e.g., through an informant or other "off net" information such as wiretap) but not know that person's affiliation or sponsorship, knowledge of which is important in determining what kind of retaliatory action is appropriate.

3 BARRIERS TO FORENSIC-BASED TECHNICAL ATTRIBUTION

3.1 Overview

The barriers described below represent impediments to conventional, forensic analysis, mostly of hostile packets retrieved from logs or captured by real-time monitoring on the Internet as it currently exists. This analysis, uncertain as it is, is only possible when administrators are alerted to a reconnaissance activity; in a large-scale disruptive attack, the first information to be destroyed by any competent attacker will be logs and other data which may facilitate attribution. There is, however, the possibility of post-attack analysis of logs saved in a protected fashion, such as off-site backups, with the aim of discovering the traces left by pre-attack reconnaissance.

Analysis of malicious functionality extracted from compromised machines is typically of greater value in determining the capabilities of the attacker and likely nature of the possible upcoming disruptive attack than it is in determining attribution. The amount of information on the Internet about malicious functionality is so large that a relatively low level of technical competence is required to exploit it. In the case of malicious software, it is not, as is the case with physical objects, to assert that a particular level of sophistication is an indication that a national laboratory produced the device. Brilliance in software development can be found anywhere, and the only physical resources required are a laptop and an Internet connection.

3.2 Botnets

A relatively new phenomenon is that of the botnet, which is a very large collection of nodes containing malicious functionality and operated under centralized control. Estimates of botnet sizes are highly uncertain and range from tens of thousands to millions of machines per net.[3] The principal use of botnets is the sending of spam email and flooding attacks called "DDoS" for "distributed denial of service."

Botnets are constructed by mechanisms which exploit vulnerabilities in operating systems or third party software to gain administrative privilege and install malicious functionality. These mechanisms can be self-propagating ("viruses" or "worms"), arrive by email ("phishing") or they exploit vulnerabilities in the DNS system. In these mechanisms a query for the IP address of some legitimate site actually returns the IP address of a malicious site that appears to be the legitimate one but really exists to insert malicious functionality in the visiting node.

There are two classes of victims of botnets. The first is the target of the coordinated attack; the second is the group of individuals whose machines have been captured by the botnet operator. In earlier virus and worm attacks, these two classes were identical, that is, the machine being infected by the virus or worm was also the target. This is not the case with botnets; the owner of the infected machine may not know nor care that some percentage of that machine's cycles and Internet bandwidth is being used to attack a third party. As a consequence, there is substantially less motivation for owners of infected machines to incur the expense and risk of removing the malicious software. In response, there have been calls to require the quarantining of machines that have shown signs of having been subverted.[4]

Botnets seriously complicate the technical attribution problem. Prior to their existence, attacks were generally mounted from single nodes. This meant that strings of malicious packets, such as those probing for misconfigured interfaces (so-called "port scans") could be readily correlated to form a picture of the actual attack, which in turn could be used for technical attribution or to guide a response such as discarding packets from that address.

In a botnet attack, the overall attack is distributed over tens to thousands of machines, all with different source IP addresses, thus seriously complicating the correlation problem. The resulting risk is most severe in the area of password guessing. Prior to botnets, password portals could be arranged so that some small number of incorrect password submissions from the same source IP address would cause the connection to be broken. Now one can encounter thousands of attempts at guessing a password, each from a different source IP address, and all coordinated by a single control node. If the attacker is patient and spaces the attempts out at intervals of minutes or even seconds, it may be days between the occurrence of the same source IP address in two different attempts. The attacker may thereby cycle through an arbitrarily large number of possible passwords with little chance of detection.

Botnets are also used for denial of service attacks aimed at shutting down a target node or set of nodes. The simplest method, as described above, is to flood the node with malicious packets. This technique is analogous to jamming in the radio frequency domain. It is most commonly used against World Wide Web sites by less technically capable attackers who object to the site's content or some behavior by the site's owner. More sophisticated botnet attacks involve port scanning or password guessing in order to gain administrator privilege, which in turn is used to corrupt or destroy data, or force shut down, of a critical node.

One technique for achieving technical attribution of a botnet control node is that of so-called "honeypots."[5] These are deliberately vulnerable machines that are placed on the Internet in the hope that they will have malicious botnet functionality installed in them. The malicious functionality, and the honeypot's communication with its control node, are then analyzed to determine the IP address of that control node. As noted below, botnet managers have options to make such analysis difficult.

[3]Daniel Woolls, "Spain: Mastermind of 'botnet' scam a mystery" *San Jose Mercury News*, March 3, 2010. Available at http://www.mercurynews.com/ci_14504717. Accessed 31 May 2010.

[4]Mason Rice, Jonathan Butts, Robert Miller, Sujeet Shenoi, An analysis of the legality of government-mandated computer inoculations, International Journal of Critical Infrastructure Protection, Volume 3, Issue 1, May 2010, Pages 5-15, ISSN 1874-5482, DOI: 10.1016/j.ijcip.2010.02.002. (http://www.sciencedirect.com/science/article/B8JGJ-4YC811B-2/2/790562795030f1a318fecc4c5bba0463). Accessed July 9, 2010.

[5]http://www.honeynet.org/. Accessed 31 May 2010.

3.3 Registration Privacy

In order for a symbolic hostname to be recognized by the DNS, it must first be registered by an organization authorized to do so, called a registrar. The registration must include a name, address, telephone number and email for an authorized point of contact for the host. In the early days of the Internet (and its predecessor, the Arpanet) this information was used for cooperation between administrators when network problems arose. The information was, historically, publicly available through a facility called "whois." A common forensic step, when confronted with a suspect packet, was to examine the source IP address, do a reverse DNS lookup to obtain the hostname, and then do a "whois" to obtain basic information such as country of origin. The usefulness of this step has been diluted in recent years with the rise of privacy protections on "whois" data. In some cases the protections are imposed by the registrars; in other cases, a proxy service is provided in which the hostname is registered by the service and the actual owner is not even known to the registrar. The steps needed to obtain the true "whois" information vary from service to service, and can range from simple telephone or letter requests to subpoena.

3.4 Proxies

Proxies are intermediate nodes that perform technical services during a transmission, such as caching packets to improve performance. Proxies, in general, complicate attribution because they change the source IP address of a packet from that of the actual sender to their own address in the course of performing their service. Two classes of proxies with particular impact on attribution are Network Address Translators and Anonymizing Proxy Servers.

3.4.1 Network Address Translation

The growing popularity of the Internet in the 1990s led to a shortage of IP addresses. One response to this was the development of a range of technologies called Network Address Translation or NAT. When IP addresses were first standardized, some numbers were reserved for private networks. An NAT "hides" a private network behind a public gateway. A variety of techniques are used to insure that two-way communication through the gateway is implemented without confusion. By this means large institutions with thousands or hundreds of thousands of machines connected to the Internet may display only a few hundred IP addresses to the public Internet. As a consequence, forensic examination of hostile packets may reveal a source IP address that indicates only the major institution from which the packet came. More detailed attribution requires cooperation of the institution, which may either be impossible (owing to absence of detailed logs) or not forthcoming. The latter is often the case when the packet in question has crossed national boundaries.

3.4.2 Anonymizing Proxy Servers

Other proxy servers are dedicated solely to anonymizing, and many of these are offered as a free public service. They are used by persons desiring privacy on the Internet, and also to bypass location-based content controls imposed by national regimes who seek to deny their citizens access to certain Internet sites. A site which tests and lists public proxy servers[6] documents, at the time of this writing, more that 200 servers in 14 countries.

It is a straightforward process to implement and operate a private anonymizing proxy server, either on one's own machine or one that has been compromised. Many public anonymizing services attempt to limit abuse by restricting their use to access of World Wide Web sites, and therefore would be useful only for external reconnaissance by potential attackers. There would be, of course, no technical limit on the

---

[6]http://www.publicproxyservers.com/. Accessed May 2010.

services that could be provided by a private anonymizing proxy server. One can easily visualize a botnet in which packets are passed through hundreds or more such servers in a given route, each of which is on a compromised machine with no overt connection to the individual controlling the botnet.

3.5 Dynamic Assignment of IP Addresses

Dynamic assignment is used principally by Internet service providers to minimize the number of IP addresses they need to support their customer base. The mechanism that performs this is called the Dynamic Host Control Protocol or DHCP. In this technique, when a customer machine contacts the provider through some facility such as DSL or television cable, an unused IP address is selected from a pool of addresses reserved for this purpose. This temporary IP address then becomes the source address of packets coming from the customer machine, but only for the duration of the connection, or less. This means that packets originating from a given customer machine may have different source IP addresses, and packets going to it have different destination IP addresses, as time passes.

The DNS service described above generally, but not exclusively, maintains a fixed relationship between symbolic hostname and numeric IP address. If the IP address of a particular machine is dynamically assigned by a protocol such as DHCP then the usual DNS can not be used to "advertise" its symbolic hostname to the Internet. There are, however, sites which provide what are called "dynamic DNS" services. These permit the owner of a hostname to rapidly change the IP address associated with that name, and do so in coordination with DHCP.

Dynamic DNS services can be used by botnet controllers to complicate forensics. If the malicious software in a single "bot" contained the IP address used to communicate with its controlling node, then that address could be used either to physically locate the node or to attack it over the net. Replacing an IP address in the "bot" software with a symbolic hostname provides no protection if that hostname refers to a fixed IP address, for then a forensic analyst could simply perform a DNS query and obtain that value. Instead, the dynamic DNS service is used to present the analyst with an ever-changing array of IP addresses with the intent of insuring that when and if a control node is identified it no longer is being used.

3.6 Onion Routing

Onion routing is an extensively documented technique for achieving anonymous communication within a packet-switched network. Implementations vary, but the basic principle is that of a virtual network of "onion routers" that runs on top of a conventional packet-switched network. Each "onion router" has a cryptographic subsystem based on a secret key known only to it and the initiator of the packet.

The initiator chooses a predetermined route through the "onion routers" to the intended destination. This contrasts with the dynamic routing described for the conventional network. Starting with the last "hop" the initiator puts source and destination addresses in the packet and then encrypts both it and the packet contents with the secret of the "onion router" that will initiate the last "hop." The initiator then makes that the contents of a packet, gives it the address of the "onion router" immediately before it, and encrypts it with that onion router's secret key. The initiator works backward in this fashion, router by router, adding a layer of encryption for each hop—hence the "onion" notion.

When the packet reaches a particular onion router, it decrypts it and obtains two things: the address of the next onion router to send it to, and contents that it cannot decipher. In this way compromise or observation of a given onion router yields only information about where the packet is to go next and does not show the source, destination, or contents.

Onion routing is publicly available on the Internet through a free service called "Tor,"[7] maintained by a U.S. registered nonprofit corporation. Volunteers worldwide host Tor routers, and the stated purpose of the service is to preserve privacy on the Internet.

---

[7]http://www.torproject.org/. Accessed May 2010.

Onion routing is a particularly attractive method for providing anonymous communication amongst elements of a botnet and sufficient documentation on the technique exists to permit implementation by technologists of a range of abilities.

3.7 Covert Communication

Covert communication is the transmission of information using system resources that were not intended for that purpose, i.e., "in a manner surprising to the authorities."[8] An example in the physical domain is the so-called "prison telegraph," where inmates communicate by rapping on the water pipes. In a sense, covert communication is the most powerful anonymizing tool in that it seeks to disguise the fact that communication is taking place at all.

Packet-switched networks in general, and the Internet in particular, provide ample opportunity for covert communication because of the large amount of control information carried in each packet. This information can be used to encode messages to malicious functionality, as can real-time phenomena such as packet sizes, timings, and sequences.

A well-publicized form of covert communication is steganography, in which messages are hidden in other messages or (more typically) pictures. This technique is less attractive as a way to communicate ith malicious functionality because of the overhead associated with extracting the information, but has been used for covert human to human communication.[9]

3.8 Future Indicators

The now almost universal use of digital media, with its ease of copying and transmission, has led to a rise in the unauthorized distribution of copyrighted works, most notably music and motion pictures. The copyright owners have responded to this in two broad areas. The first is the use of so-called "digital rights management," which seeks to impose technical controls on distribution. The second is to take legal action against those involved in unauthorized distribution, both providers and recipients.

In the past the copyright holders had initiated action against large numbers of recipients, such as students and other less powerful individuals in our society. After considerable adverse publicity, the music industry in particular dropped this approach[10] and focused on organizations that facilitate distribution.[11]

Recently, the owners of the copyright to a popular motion picture have resumed the practice of taking legal action against recipients.[12] In this action, as in previous suits by copyright holders against recipients, the plaintiffs have asserted repeatedly that IP addresses can be reliably associated with individuals. Setting aside the technical merits (or lack thereof) of such a claim, if it persists in the legal system then we can anticipate increased activity in the development of tools and techniques to prevent human attribution based on IP address.

In the area of covert communication, there has long been support by the U.S. Government for software that evades attempts by authoritarian regimes to censor the Internet.[13] Research in this area

---

[8]Morris, Robert, as reported in *Newsletter of the IEEE Technical Committee on Security and Privacy*, Winter 1991. Available at www.list.gmu.edu/misc_pubs/csfw/c91rep.pdf. Accessed May 31, 2010.

[9]Montgomery, David. "Arrests of alleged spies draws attention to long obscure field of steganography," *Washington Post*, June 30, 2010. Available at http://www.washingtonpost.com/wp-dyn/content/article/2010/06/30/AR2010063003108.html. Accessed July 9, 2010.

[10]McBride, Sarah and Smith, Ethan. "Music Industry to Abandon Mass Suits." *Wall St. Journal*, Dec 19, 2008. Available at http://online.wsj.com/article/SB122966038836021137.html. Accessed May 31, 2010.

[11]Plambeck, Joseph. "Court Rules that File Sharing Service Infringed Copyrights." *New York Times*, May 12, 2010. Available at http://www.nytimes.com/2010/05/13/technology/13lime.html?src=me. Accessed May 31, 2010.

[12]Smith, Ethan. "Thousands are Targeted over 'Hurt Locker' Downloads." *Wall St. Journal*, May 29, 2010. Available at http://online.wsj.com/article/SB10001424052748703957604575272843955251262.html. Accessed May 31, 2010.

[13]http://www.dit-inc.us/freegate. Accessed July 10, 2010.

continues,[14] and while the focus of the present tools is on passive observation of blocked Web pages, the basic technology can be applied to the covert communication requirements of attack tools. Whatever the motivation, it should be anticipated that technology that was once the exclusive domain of clandestine services will become more available to ordinary users, whether for good or ill.

4 ELIMINATING BARRIERS TO FORENSICS-BASED TECHNICAL ATTRIBUTION

None of the barriers described above will be particularly easy to eliminate. Proxies, NAT and dynamic assignment of IP addresses are now so deeply ingrained in the structure of the Internet that eliminating them would require significant cost and effort. DHCP and dynamic DNS are fundamental to a democratic Internet which has room for small and specialized servers. Covert communication, because it both exploits needed facilities and is extremely hard to detect, is virtually immune to elimination.

The three remaining cases are the overly privacy-preserving (and therefore attribution-preventing) services of Tor and Anonymizing Proxy Servers and Registration Privacy. Theoretically, all three could be eliminated by legislative action. However, owing to the transnational nature of the Internet, such action would have to be coordinated among multiple jurisdictions, or the service banned in one country would simply move to a "safe haven" where it was legal. Even if Tor as a service was eliminated, the underlying technology is so well known that the creation of a clandestine successor can be predicted with certainty; a similar argument can be made for the continuation of anonymizing proxy servers. If Registration Privacy were somehow to be outlawed, then malicious registrants would simply revert to the practices they used before it was available, and provide false identity, location and contact information on their registration documents.

A new low-level protocol for the Internet, called IPv6, is in the process of being deployed. The principal problem the protocol solves is the upcoming shortage of numeric IP addresses, which is rapidly becoming critical. IPv6 contains many new security features which, if they are properly implemented and administered, promise to reduce the difficulty of technical attribution. The concern amongst the technical community is that first, these features have not yet been subjected to serious attack, second, many of them are optional and may not be invoked by administrators who are under pressure to deliver network performance, and third, the protocol was designed over fifteen years ago and the art and science of attack has progressed significantly.[15]

5 ALTERNATIVES TO FORENSIC-BASED TECHNICAL ATTRIBUTION

5.1 Counterattack

The limitations of forensic-based attribution and the constant increase in the number and sophistication of attacks has led to more serious consideration of the option of counterattack or "hack back" in order to either obtain attribution or suppress attacks. This has reached the point where security researchers are publishing vulnerability information pertaining to the software used to convert an otherwise innocent machine into an element of a botnet.[16] Frustration with the current adverse trends in cyber security may well lead to an increase in "hack back" activity, with or without authorization, with concomitant risk to the overall stability of the Internet.

---

[14]Burnett, Sam et. al. "Chipping Away at Censorship Firewalls with User-Generated Content" to appear in the Usenix Security Symposium 2010. Available at http://www.gtnoise.net/papers/2010/burnett:usenixsec2010.pdf. Accessed July 11, 2010.

[15]Jackson, WIlliam. "Security will not come naturally with IPv6," *Government Computer News*, September 17, 2009. Available at http://gcn.com/Articles/2009/09/17/IPv6 security.aspx. Accessed May 31, 2010.

[16]Oudot, Laurent. "[Full-disclosure] TEHTRI-Security released 13 0days against web tools used by evil attackers." Available at http://archives.neohapsis.com/archives/fulldisclosure/2010-06/0423.html. Accessed July 1, 2010.

5.2 Preemptive Covert Operations

"Hack back," as the name implies, is a reactive strategy which is implemented upon detection of an attack; as with forensic-based methods, this may be too late. A further step in active defense is to mount preemptive covert operations against sites that are suspected to be planning or preparing attacks. These operations would focus on exploitation and intelligence-gathering, but could rapidly shift to suppression if an attack were detected. Awareness on the part of potential attackers that such "cyber patrolling" was being conducted would in and of itself act as a deterrent, since they would be faced with additional security tasks as well as the uncertainty as to the degree to which they may themselves have been penetrated and placed at risk.

5.3 Obstacles to Alternative Methods

There are no significant technical obstacles to the use of the techniques described above; they both are based on known and validated technology used by attackers themselves. Any obstacle that would potentially be raised would be of a legal and policy nature. One unresolved legal issue is the question of ownership of a subverted machine, such as an element of a botnet. One the one hand, it can be argued that the machine's Internet presence inherits the rights of the owner of the physical hardware. On the other hand, it can be argued that the machine's Internet presence is analogous to that of a vehicle which has been stolen and is being used in the commission of a crime, and which is then fair game for capture or suppression.

6 HUMAN ATTRIBUTION

The problem of converting technical attribution to human attribution is as old as crime and punishment. Barriers to it consist of all the known methods of evasion, deception, and denial. Consider, for example, a registered firearm which is linked by ballistics evidence to a crime. The person to whom the firearm is registered can, when confronted with this, simply claim that the gun was stolen. Similarly, a person who is associated with a machine known to be the source of malicious packets can simply claim that the packets were sent by malicious functionality that was installed without the person's knowledge. Given the power and deviousness of current techniques for doing so,[17] such claims are increasingly plausible.

Cyber forensics, as described above, are considerably less compelling than a ballistics test on a firearm. Whatever information is developed in the course of determining technical attribution must be combined with other information and analyzed in the context of the traditional investigatory triad of motive, means, and opportunity. The Internet adds further difficulties in that its transnational reach may, and in the criminal domain historically has, meant that investigations encounter severe jurisdictional constraints.

One technique that combines technical and human attribution, and that is limited in applicability but can yield valuable information, involves administrators establishing the means to capture and replay the real-time actions of an intruder who is conducting a reconnaissance exercise. Analysis of keystroke intervals, misspelling of command names, time of day and duration of intrusion and similar data can provide hints about the number, native language, and technical background of the group performing the intrusion. If multiple intrusions are detected, this form of analysis can also provide hints as to whether they represent a coordinated effort or are disjoint.

Whatever the technique, it is by no means certain that the benefits of effective human attribution would outweigh the adverse effects. Anonymity has been held to be an essential aspect of the effective

---

[17]Zetter, Kim. "Google Hack Attack Was Ultra Sophisticated, New Details Show." *Wired News*, Jan. 14, 2010. Available at http://www.wired.com/threatlevel/2010/01/operation-aurora/. Accessed May 31, 2010.

exercise of free speech.[18] A recent proposal by a member of the Obama administration for a voluntary system of Internet credentials has met with mixed response.[19] Besides the objections on the basis of personal privacy and freedom, there are serious questions of effectiveness and the degree to which any such system could resist techniques for identity theft. The latter concern is heightened by the phenomenon that any standardized and widespread security system becomes, by its ubiquitous nature, worth the expenditure of significant effort by hostile parties to defeat.

7 PERFECT TECHNICAL ATTRIBUTION AND DETERRENCE

7.1 Deterrence in General

The psychological theory of deterrence has been extensively studied, both for international relations and criminal justice.[20] The consensus is that individuals and organizations are deterred from aggressive action by two factors: first, that retribution is likely and will be unacceptably severe, and second, that risk of failure is too high. Before considering the role attribution may or may not play in deterrence, it is worthwhile to consider two factors which act to deter large-scale disruptive cyberattacks from any source.

The first of these is the risk of an unintended consequence that the initiator, or allies of the initiator, are harmed by the attack. For example, a crippling attack on the financial system of one nation by a transnational terrorist group carries the risk that the entire global economy may be adversely affected, which may in turn deplete the wealth of nations or individuals who are supporting that terrorist group.

The second factor is that a disruptive cyberattack is very unlikely to resemble a kinetic attack like a truck bomb, which achieves a near-instantaneous transition from normality to destruction. All but the most improbable scenarios for disruptive cyberattacks have them unfolding over time, time during which system administrators will be taking action to stop the attack and mitigate its effects. Thus the event will resemble a melee more than it will an explosion. The degree of uncertainty associated with such a widespread, dynamic, and interactive event and the associated difficulties of predicting success are an inherent obstacle to a decision to proceed with an attack.

7.2 The Deterrent Effect of Perfect Technical Attribution

The discussion to follow postulates an Internet in which there exists perfect technical attribution, that is, every action can be traced back to a specific human and every element of hardware and software can be identified as to source.

Whether perfect attribution would serve to deter an attack naturally depends on the nature of the actor considering a large-scale, society-disrupting attack. Given the scale of such attacks, and the magnitude of their possible consequences, these actors are not likely to be criminals or even large-scale criminal enterprises motivated by financial gain but rather state or non-state actors driven by geopolitical motives of power and influence.

There are four cases of where perfect technical attribution could be a factor: state-mounted attacks, state-sponsored attacks using non-state actors, state-tolerated attacks using non-state actors, and attacks by non-state actors with no state involvement.

State-mounted attacks are those conducted by the armed forces or covert action agencies of a nation state. The complex issues association with such attacks, as viewed from a U.S. perspective, are extensively treated in a previous National Research Council report.[21] Perfect technical attribution, in this case,

---

[18]Solove, Daniel J. *The Future of Reputation: Gossip, Rumour and Privacy on the Internet*, Yale University Press, 2007.

[19]Markoff, John. "Taking the Mystery Out of Web Anonymity," New York Times, July 2, 2010.

[20]McGill, William L. "Defensive Dissuasion in Security Risk Management," *Proc. 2009 IEEE International Conference on Systems, Man, and Cybernetics*, pp. 3516-3521.

[21]National Research Council, *Technology, Policy, Law, and Ethics Regarding U.S. Acquisition and Use of Cyberattack Capabilities*. National Academies Press, 2009.

adds little to deterrence. If a nation is preparing a cyberattack of a scale which is near or at the boundaries of an act of war, then that attack will most probably take place in an environment of international tension or imminent armed conflict. Attribution therefore becomes obvious, and the planners of the attack will have incorporated the chances and nature of retaliation in their calculus.

The involvement of non-state actors complicates the problem of assigning ultimate responsibility for the attack, and the existence of perfect technical attribution reduces that problem to one of determining a relationship between an identified non-state actor and some state. In the case of sponsorship, this determination can be made through traditional investigative and intelligence gathering techniques such as tracing financial transactions, interception of communications, and so forth. This process is complicated, and attribution obscured, by a common practice of clandestine services known as "false flag operations." In these, the service pretends to be that of some other state, in order to gain the sympathy and cooperation of a non-state actor. The elaborate steps, such as routing of financial transactions, location of meetings, etc., which are taken to convince the non-state actor of the false state affiliation can also mislead the target of the attack when it attempts to determine upon whom to retaliate. The principal deterrent effect of knowing "who did it" in this case, will be against the non-state actor. Since that individual or group is under state sponsorship, it is likely they will also be under state protection, and the deterrent effect will be minimal.

Further complications are introduced by state-tolerated attacks. These occur when the so-called "patriotic hackers" of a particular nation independently launch attacks whose nature and timing coincide with the interests of that nation. In this case there are no overt, detectable links between the national authorities and the attackers; rather, all the authorities need to do is refrain from taking action, possibly while protesting publicly that they are doing all they can to stop the assaults. There has been media speculation that the attacks from China on the United States,[22] attacks on Estonia,[23] and attacks on the nation of Georgia[24] were state-tolerated. Even a small scale-attack can escalate by having other hackers in other countries "pile on" as word of the attack spreads.[25] Later reports suggest that the Estonian attack was actually triggered by an Estonian citizen.[26]

Here the link between the actor and the state is even more tenuous than in the previous case, further reducing the chance that the state will suffer retaliation. Since retaliation against the actor or actors will, in general, require state cooperation, they also have little reason to be dissuaded from attacking, even if they are identified through the mechanism of perfect technical attribution.

Finally there is the case of a non-state actor that is not sponsored by, nor independently acting in the interests of, a particular state. This is the one instance where perfect technical attribution may act to deter: since an attack by such an actor readily fits into the criminal justice domain, the actor has no sponsor or protector, and in many jurisdictions punishment will be severe, perfect technical attribution and the associated fear of likely and unacceptable retribution will act as a deterrent.

8 SUMMARY

1. The Internet contains intrinsic features and extrinsic services which support anonymity and inhibit forensic attribution of cyberattacks.

---

[22]Delio, Michael. "Is This World Cyber War I?" *Wired News*, May 1, 2001.Available at http://www.wired.com/politics/law/news/2001/05/43443. Accessed May 31, 2010.

[23]Landler, Mark and Markoff, John. "Digital Fears Emerge After Data Siege in Estonia." *New York Times*, May 29, 2007. Available at http://www.nytimes.com/2007/05/29/technology/29estonia.html. Accessed May 31, 2010.

[24]Krebs, Bryan. "Russian Hacker Forums Fueled Georgia Cyber Attacks," *Washington Post*, Oct. 16, 2008. Available at http://voices.washingtonpost.com/securityfix/2008/10/report_russian_hacker_forums_f.html. Accessed May 31, 2010.

[25]Anon. "A cyber-riot" *The Economist*, May 10, 2007.

[26]Hruska, Joel. "Student behind DoS attack that rekindled bad Soviet memories." *ars technica*, January 24, 2008. Available at http://arstechnica.com/business/news/2008/01/student-behind-dos-attack-that-rekindled-bad-soviet-memories.ars. Accessed May 31, 2010.

2. Recent events in copyright enforcement may accelerate the technical evolution anonymizing services.

3. There are few if any plausible ways to overcome the barriers to forensic-based attribution imposed by these features and services.

4. It is too early to state with confidence that the move to IPv6 will have a significant effect on the ability to attribute cyberattacks.

5. In cases where forensic-based technical attribution is possible, it is most likely to be achieved in the reconnaissance phase of an attack.

6. Alternatives to forensic-based attribution include counterattack ("hack back") and sustained, aggressive covert intelligence gathering on potential attackers. The obstacles to these methods are primarily nontechnical.

7. Even if perfect technical attribution were achieved, it would have a significant deterrent effect in but a minority of cases where significant disruptive cyberattacks are contemplated by parties hostile to the United States.

8. Preemptive covert operations may have significant deterrent effect by raising uncertainty of success owing to the possibility that facilities controlling an attack may contain latent subversions.

Group 2—Strategy, Policy, and Doctrine

Applicability of Traditional Deterrence Concepts and Theory to the Cyber Realm

Patrick M. Morgan

University of California, Irvine

Deterrence is a common practice in the history of international politics and in many other social relationships, and was largely taken for granted until after World War II. Early in the Cold War analysts and policy makers began to seize on it as the ultimate recourse for preventing another great war, which led to developing the first extensive theoretical analysis of deterrence in international politics plus construction of a number of national deterrence strategies, postures, and policies. The topic here is what the U.S. might make use of or learn from Cold War deterrence, including what is not relevant and why, in seeking cybersecurity. The format is to select important highlights of, mainly American, deterrence thinking and practice and then indicate how they are relevant or not for the problem of cyberattacks.

BASIC ELEMENTS OF DETERRENCE

In international politics "deterrence" refers to efforts to avoid being deliberately attacked by using threats to inflict unacceptable harm on the attacker in response.[1] The threatened harm can be inflicted by a stout *defense*, frustrating the attack or making it too costly to continue, or by turning its success into a pyrrhic victory. Or it can be inflicted through *retaliation*. (And through a combination of the two.) The emphasis in international politics is on providing that defense or retaliation *militarily* but nonmilitary actions can also be used.

Normally, the most gratifying is a defense that discourages attacks by looking too tough and too costly to overcome. This is preferable to deterrence by retaliation because the defender largely determines the results if deterrence fails and an attack occurs. A potent defense is also simpler to understand and apply. But defending can be expensive and painful so getting effective *deterrence* from a defense is very welcome—security is achieved at less cost and no loss. In contrast, deterrence by retaliatory threats can be cheaper than deterrence by defense but offers slim comfort if it fails. A tough defense often had to compensate for failures in seeking deterrence by threats of retaliation. The distinctive reliance on deterrence by retaliatory threats in the second half of the 20th century resulted, beginning in the 1930s, from new weapons systems that could make known and prospective defenses much too porous. In

---

[1] Typically any attack is unacceptable, but an actor will have specific kinds of attacks it wants to prevent, in terms of the target(s), means used, size, and damage inflicted.

turn, the use of deterrence by threats of retaliation could readily exploit weaknesses in defenses. With nuclear weapons it became possible to deter by threatening terrible retaliation without maintaining any serious military defenses, but having to face devastating levels of harm, if deterrence failed, from a similarly armed opponent.

Modern states have had to decide how to try to deter. While relying at least somewhat on defense, using threats of retaliation is sometimes chosen even if a suitable defense is conceivable, for various reasons:

- A suitable defense is not yet ready;
- A suitable defense may not be achievable;
- The defense will be painful and/or expensive—it is better to avoid defending if possible;
- A suitable defense will not work for long—it will give way under sustained attacks or will soon be outmoded;
- Relative military capabilities shift rapidly and a suitable defense will eventually be outmoded.

Deterrence is a psychological relationship; the goal is to shape an opponent's perceptions, expectations, and ultimately its decisions about launching an attack. Thus deterrence requires an "opponent" who is thinking, or might readily think of attacking. Ideally deterrence short-circuits that thinking, convincing the opponent to reject undertaking even a seriously considered and prepared attack,[2] making it a deliberately contrived relationship with an *opponent*. (The U.S. is not deterring Canada). The Strategic Command's bombers and missiles are not deterrence, just capabilities useful for deterring. Deterrence requires threatening an opponent who has an attack in mind.

In mounting deterrence the policy maker works with three spectra. One consists of actions which can probably inflict what the opponent will consider unacceptable damage. Next is the set of actual actions available within the national defensive and retaliatory capabilities and their expected impact. Finally, there is a set of "acceptable" retaliatory responses—acceptable to oneself, one's allies, "world opinion" or the international community, future enemies, or whoever is deemed relevant. Conducting deterrence requires finding things to threaten to do that fall where the three spectra overlap. The boundaries of this area can readily change, not only over time but also during a confrontation, even just after an attack.[3]

It is important to note that deterrence is not only used to prevent attacks and war via threats of harm. It is often used *via* attacks and war, that is, deterrence by doing harm. China's ultimate effort to deter UN forces from completely occupying North Korea in 1950 was to launch several attacks on those forces to indicate it was prepared to fight if they approached the border. Often disputes are conducted by the repeated use of force, a kind of *serial deterrence*, in which the parties periodically punish each other to contain each other's behavior—as in Israeli interactions with the Palestinians during several periods. Cold War analysts talked about deterrence not only for preventing an East-West war but for using it to prevent escalation of one if it ever started. Of course, there is also the use of force against one

---

[2] In the usual usage an attack is a military action, but deterrence is used to discourage other unwanted acts as well.

[3] General works on deterrence in the Cold War era include: Freedman, L. 1981. *The Evolution of Nuclear Strategy*. New York: St. Martin's Press; Jervis, R. 1979. Deterrence Theory Reconsidered. *World Politics* 39: 289-324; Jervis, R. 1989. *The Meaning of the Nuclear Revolution: Statecraft and the Prospect of Armageddon*. Ithaca, NY: Cornell University Press; Morgan, P. M. 1983. *Deterrence: A Conceptual Analysis*. 2nd ed. Beverly Hills: SAGE; Powell, R. 1990. *Nuclear Deterrence Theory: The Search for Credibility*. Cambridge: Cambridge University Press; Wohlstetter, A. 1959. The Delicate Balance of Terror. *Foreign Affairs* 37: 211-234; Brodie, B. 1959. *Strategy in the Missile Age*. Princeton: Princeton University Press; Kahn, H. *On Thermonuclear War*. Princeton: Princeton University Press; Kahn, H. *On Escalation: Metaphors and Scenarios*. New York: Praeger; Schelling, T. C. 1960. *The Strategy of Conflict*. Cambridge, MA: Harvard University Press; Schelling, T. C. 1960. *Arms and Influence*. New Haven: Yale University Press; Mearsheimer, J. J. 1983. *Conventional Deterrence*. Ithaca: Cornell University Press; Jervis, R., R. N. Lebow and J. G. Stein, eds. 1985. *Psychology and Deterrence* Baltimore: Johns Hopkins University Press; Lebow, R. N. and J. G. Stein. Rational Deterrence Theory: I Think, Therefore I Deter. *World Politics* 41: 208-224; Lebow, R. N. and J. G. Stein. 1994. *We All Lost the Cold War*. Princeton: Princeton University Press; Snyder, G. 1961. *Deterrence and Defense: Toward a Theory of National Security*. Princeton: Princeton University Press.

opponent in order to deter other opponents in the future, a standard justification offered by the U.S. for its wars during the Cold War.

Relevance for Cyberattacks

The current explosion of concern about cyberattacks in the U.S. and elsewhere is the culmination of fears building for some time.[4] Many thousands of attacks on American cybersystems occur daily, with the damage often estimated in billions, even trillions.[5] It is said that important sectors, particularly in national defense, will be targeted in the future, resulting in very extensive damage, including paralysis of critical activities, if attacks are carried out.[6]

For a deterrence analyst this is puzzling. The threat is seemingly dire yet thus far the U.S. has done little to deter cyberattacks. Elaborate defensive arrangements exist or are being mounted, yet everyone agrees we are very vulnerable—the defenses are porous, and when they work they typically impose no serious cost on the attacker so the attacks continue to rise. No national strategy exists for deterring cyberattacks by retaliation either, with little indication available as to what sorts of retaliation are planned or under development. It is as if, having to choose deterrence by defense, retaliation or a combination of the two, the U.S. chose "none of the above." If the harm being done is severe and the prospective harm incalculable, including serious damage to national security, why isn't this a national crisis, with things being done intensively to deter attacks? This suggests that the harm is only now becoming enough to attract serious attention, and that scenarios depicting more devastating attacks are gaining in plausibility. Perhaps we have been grossly neglecting the threat, but given the highly developed threat-perception elements in our political system it is more likely that the cyberattack problem is still modest.[7]

This is reinforced by weak U.S. retaliation to date. Literature on deterrence of cyberattacks describes the many problems involved in retaliation, and there is little information about steps the U.S. is taking to retaliate.[8] Again, this strongly suggests the attacks are not terribly costly or bothersome—at least not yet. While retaliation may be practiced covertly, that seems unlikely—significant retaliation should be hard to hide unless the U.S. is using the difficulty of detecting sources of attacks to hide its actions. And deterrence normally benefits from retaliation and its effects being publicized.

---

[4]For an impressive, detailed analysis see Clark, R. A and R. Knake, 2010, *Cyber War: the Next Threat to National Security and What to do About It*, New York: HarperCollins.

[5]For examples of estimates see Blair, Dennis. February 2009. Annual Threat Assessment of the Intelligence Community for the Senate Select Committee on Intelligence. Washington, DC, 38-40, available at http://intelligence.senate.gov/090212/blair.pdf. Levett, C. February 15, 2010. U.S. Seeking Allies for Warfare in Cyberspace. Available at http://www.smh.com.au/technology/us-seeking-allies-for-warfare-in cyberspace-20100214-nzg2.html; Clark, W. K. and P. L. Levin. 2009. Securing the Information Highway: How to Enhance the United States' Electronic Defenses. *Foreign Affairs* 88, 6: 2-10; Moore, T. 2010. Introducing the Economics of Cybersecurity, this volume.

[6]Possible threats are explored in Kramer, F. D., S. H. Starr, and L. K. Wentz, eds. 2009. *Cyberpower and National Security*. Washington, DC: National Defense University Press.

[7]Kugler, R. L. 2009. Deterrence of Cyber Attacks. In F. D. Kramer, S. H. Starr, and L. K. Wentz, eds. *Cyberpower and National Security*. Washington, DC: National Defense University Press 309-340. The U.S. has a National Strategy to Secure Cyberspace dating back to 2003 which is vague. A description of the "cyber hawks" view of the threats to national security as quite serious, and a suggestion that the threat is not very serious for now, are offered in Libicki, M. C. 2009. *Cyberdeterrence and Cyberwar*. Santa Monica: RAND 35-37.

[8]The Obama Administration has adopted, and recently released information about, a Comprehensive National Cybersecurity Initiative which includes steps toward a deterrence posture. See Nakashima, E. 2010. White House Declassifies Outline of Cybersecurity Program. *Washington Post* March 3. This was a follow on to the Bush Administration's Comprehensive National Cybersecurity Initiative. The administration also has created a new high level coordinator on cyber affairs, and there is now a U.S. Cyber Command under the U.S. Strategic Command, while the Department of Homeland Security coordinates nonmilitary departments on cybersecurity matters. Theohary, C. A, and J. Rollins. 2009. Cybersecurity: Current Legislation, Executive Branch initiatives, and Options for Congress. Congressional Research Service Report for Congress, September 30. The new Cyber Command commander was confirmed in May 2010. The administration has also proposed development of a "voluntary trusted identity" system to restrict internet access to people with a special authenticated identification, which some analysts claim is too little too late. Markoff, J. 2010. Taking the Mystery Out of Web Anonymity. *New York Times*, July 4.

In fact, the United States is not practicing much deterrence at all. In place of grave warnings of the harm attackers will suffer are assertions we are getting serious about this and instituting new bureaucratic arrangements for doing so. Few cases are cited of attackers suffering significant consequences. How serious can the problem be? Even if the threat is still relatively limited, it is disturbing that the attackers are numerous and the vulnerable targets are so plentiful. Much that is at risk has little to do with national security but is still important—computers damaged by viruses, hackers stealing identities and funds, damaging traffic control systems, disrupting operations at locks and dams. And so on. And sometimes national security is involved. So why the relatively limited reactions to date? The answer, in part, is that the problem is serious but not yet in terms of *national security*, which is where deterrence is most salient. And in most cases the attacks are not from enemies or opponents in the classic sense, making deterrence of the usual sort in international politics difficult to apply.

Another straightforward reaction from a deterrence analyst would therefore be that in cyberattacks the nature of the opponents is certainly very different. Usually this is said about the many nonstate actors who launch attacks, but that isn't the heart of the problem. In the Cold War the enemies were "out there," beyond the nation's boundaries. However, rising interactions and interdependence among states and societies have shrunk the relevance of out there. Cyberspace is transnational. Thus the enemy is "in here," participating like the rest of us in, as a component of, the interactive and interdependent networks that constitute cyberspace. Unless and until we want to completely reorder, reorganize, and redesign cyberspace, to participate in it is to be vulnerable to attack. Attack capabilities are variants of the basic resources required for operating, and operating in, cyberspace.

The motivations of the attackers are different too. Many attacks apparently reflect a desire to defy authority, or assert oneself and one's daring and thereby gain prestige among peers, or make life more exciting. None of these fit the usual model of a deterrable actor. Many other attacks are criminal, mounted by deliberately risk-taking individuals/groups behaving with a selected subculture's norms and rejecting more generally accepted ones, making them poor targets for deterrence of the usual sort. As for the espionage attacks, even in regular international politics spying by *states* is not considered a crime—punishment is reserved for the individuals involved (and often skipped even then)—and thus rarely evokes severe retaliation, just stiffer defenses or spying efforts in return.

This means deterrence efforts must, for now, involve steps, disconnected from specifically designated enemies, that cannot readily be "tailored" to a single target within an established national strategy, or a few variants of it, for a few high priority opponents who clearly threaten national security. At least not now. Without clearly defined enemies, ranked in priority and capabilities to do harm, the general dimensions of the threats to be faced cannot be known and their nature cannot be reasonably specified. During the Cold War the ultimate threats could be depicted in terms of things like when and how well known enemies, familiar conflicts with them, and their clear capabilities for doing harm could suddenly coalesce into brutal violence. With cyberattacks, the fundamental *nature of the threat* to national security remains largely hypothetical. This is strange territory for the designing and application of deterrence.

We want deterrence for containing serious enemies who would use cyberattacks to do significant damage. This includes states that could readily be or are already enemies, nonstate actors our enemies support and assist, and people willing to facilitate such harm on their own or on behalf of those states and nonstate actors. Lesser kinds of attacks, up to and even including cyber espionage, call for versions of deterrence of far less relevance in international politics. Without specified real enemies with capacities to do major harm via cyberattacks, including harm roughly equivalent to that from *military* attacks or inflicted via aiding and abetting military attacks, it is much harder to draw on Cold War deterrence thinking and experience.

As for the U.S. having to choose how to deter, for cyberattacks it will have to rely on both defense and retaliation. Defense will be especially necessary because of the flood of attacks the U.S. already experiences; some capacity to block or mitigate them is vital and hopefully it will eventually be good enough to discourage them. Retaliation and retaliatory threats will not work well enough—they are not appropriate for the great majority of attacks, and the necessary preconditions for using them are unevenly present. Reversing the U.S. situation during the Cold War, for cyberattacks the deterrence supplied by defense must now compensate for the limits of deterrence based on retaliation.

Deterrence by defense, if much improved, will be very important as well for curbing the attribution problem which complicates deterrence by threat of retaliation. The more effective the U.S. defenses, the easier it will be to detail the nature of the severest, most threatening attacks. They will be the ones requiring the most resources, the most sophistication, the most elaborate planning, and the most penetrating advance intelligence work to pull off. That combination of capabilities will sharply limit the problem of figuring out "who done it" and provide a clearer focus for retaliation.

Finally, cyberattacks are very likely to turn out to be manageable primarily through applications of serial deterrence, repeated harmful responses over an extended period, to induce either temporary or eventually permanent suspensions of the most bothersome attacks or of attacks by the most obnoxious opponents. The attacks are already so common and come from so many sources that expecting to one day install a vigorous deterrence posture and virtually bring them to a halt is unrealistic. Successfully deterring one attacker will not discourage all the others.

DETERRENCE AND THE COLD WAR

The Cold War provided Americans with clear enemies, and the expectation that they were poised to strike at the U.S., its friends, allies and others important to American interests. In response the U.S. either had to defend those interests wherever they were attacked or, hopefully, avoid the attacks through deterrence. Interest in deterrence had begun to rise before World War II when vulnerability to being attacked, plus the harm that attacks might inflict, began to increase sharply for even the most powerful states. The more destructive a future war could be, even if one was victorious, the less attractive even "winning" became. When the 1930s international political situation, particularly great-power relations, made other ways of avoiding war unpromising, states' interest in deterrence climbed, but it did not prevent World War II nor do much to contain it. Not long after the war, nuclear weapons and the Cold War made *preventing* attacks vital, and interest in deterrence soon became intense.

The American armed forces' initial planning for another major war integrated nuclear weapons into standard strategic conceptions. Almost immediately some observers and analysts saw this as a mistake and grasped the central importance of deterrence and eventually led efforts to bring deterrence to the fore. But the initial American approach to deterrence in the 1950s, which envisioned winning a future major war by initial massive attacks and deterring by the threat of such attacks, was soon outmoded by events and the refining of deterrence theory. By the time new approaches were developed, it was difficult to add them to, or have them displace, what had already been set up.

The resulting nature, tone, and extent of Cold War deterrence strongly reflected the historical context from which it sprang, including the American experience of World War II and the behavior of its totalitarian opponents. The Cold War was seen as a conflict paralleling what World War II had been about, but with the nuclear age generating new conflict, and deterrence, capacities. The U.S. was again a status quo state facing a fierce aggressive challenge that must be deterred to prevent World War III. It took a while to appreciate:

- what was unique about the nuclear age in warfare, and strategy;
- what could and could not be done with nuclear deterrence;
- what could and could not be done with deterrence based on conventional forces; and
- whether and when nuclear weapons could be used.

It turned out that deterrence and related coercive efforts, with or without nuclear threats, worked unevenly. Nasty confrontations and serious crises occurred for years in the Cold War, alongside wars and other unhappy developments the U.S. had hoped to prevent. It also proved difficult to determine just when deterrence (nuclear and nonnuclear) worked and how well, or when it had failed and why.

Relevance for Cybersecurity

The U.S. has been slow to construct a substantial cyberdeterrence posture but that may turn out to be a good thing. It makes it possible to avoid going overboard on this. We are in the early stages of the cyber era and the cyberattack problem. On deterrence for cyberattacks we can presume that the context is in transition, with exciting improvements or nasty shocks to come in the technologies, international political situation, and our strategic thinking. We don't know enough about the future nature and sources of cyberthreats, all the things that could be done about them, plus the roles deterrence can play.

A similar situation existed early in the Cold War. Nevertheless, U.S. deterrence efforts rushed ahead with weapons, delivery vehicles, theory, strategy, policies—in a frenzied atmosphere. Deterrence seemed the crucial recourse for national security and the result was a quickly developed strategy, theory, and deterrence posture. It is not surprising that the posture soon fit badly with the theory and the strategy did not fit either of them. The deterrence capabilities and posture helped exacerbate the Cold War and make Soviet threats more fearsome,[9] while deterrence efforts tended to crowd out alternative approaches to dealing with the Cold War. Once the deterrence posture was firmly established it proved difficult to change—the basic elements were still in place when the Cold War ended and are still around today.

There is no frantic necessity today to risk making similar mistakes by claiming to know how deterrence will relate to cyberattacks and cybersecurity and making elaborate preparations accordingly. There is no intense political conflict among the major states to generate overwhelming fears of major cyberattacks, and virtually no U.S. conflicts with lesser states where a major cyberattack is likely. We do not see ourselves perched on the brink of a devastating attack. Thus there is no central security concern driving grand and military strategies, dictating priorities, shaping responses and forces, etc. when it comes to deterrence. While we worry about attacks on our friends, they seem mostly able to take care of themselves and, on the whole, act like being cyberattacked is not a grave concern.

There is an important political divide in the international system generating significant frictions but it differs greatly from the Cold War. The divide is between the developed, liberal, and democratic states and a number that are not like them. The former dominate the international system and are often seen by the others as expansionist and aggressive—they often depict themselves as having to deter "the West." Cyberspace, particularly the Internet, is a vehicle for Western "attacks" in their view, but less for inflicting crippling physical blows than as a purveyor of unacceptable ideas, norms, practices, and behavior. While we worry about and want to deter the misuse of cyberspace, an invaluable global resource, others worry that the basic nature of cyberspace as designed in the West is the real threat. This makes characterizing the relationship between deterrence and cybersecurity much more complicated than developing deterrence theory and strategy was in the Cold War.

It is, for instance, not clear what highly security-focused cyberattacks and a cyberwar would be about. They could be new ways of harassing or competing (such as in cyber-espionage) that substitute for warfare. They could improve the weapons in standard international conflicts and wars—a particular American concern since U.S. forces are exceedingly dependent on cyberspace for operations, and cyberattacks disrupting those operations could have impressive military effects. They could therefore someday constitute the essence of national strength and national standing in the world, making a cyberwar the ultimate expression of international conflict. Or they could be key instruments in struggles over the nature of cyberspace and who will dominate it. Each version would call for a different emphasis and policy orientation. Should we envision the emergence of MAD-like[10] cyberwar postures if international enmity deepens again? Extensive cyberwar–fighting capabilities for a new version of flexible response?

---

[9]Examples of this: megatonnage far beyond anything useful, highly vulnerable weapons, conventional forces on an unsustainable scale, many developments treated as affecting deterrence effectiveness far more than they turned out to do; repeated overestimates of opponent capabilities. (All of this eventually turned up in the Soviet Union too.)

[10]MAD—Mutual Assured Destruction—referred to the situation in which the U.S. and Soviet Union could readily completely destroy each other either by attacking or in retaliation for being attacked.

An extended conflict confined to cyberspace itself? Or would such plans be the latest examples of pre-paring to fight (or deter) the last war?

Will cyberwar be so technologically advanced that little physical harm and destruction results? Or put the survival of modern society at risk? Threats of the former would make retaliation less attractive than defense, necessitating a war-fighting, defense-dominant security posture. The latter would incite fears of defense inadequacy, putting the emphasis on deterrence by retaliation and making Cold War perspectives more relevant.

We cannot answer such questions, so we need to seize the opportunity to avoid the types of mistakes that characterized the early U.S. Cold War deterrence effort and the harmful long term consequences that resulted. Until we accumulate more evidence about the threats, problems, conflicts, and possibilities so our responses can rest on a sturdier foundation, we should treasure the chance to proceed cautiously in measured yet flexible "initial" responses.

The context is different from the Cold War in other ways as well. One example is how the U.S. is experiencing myriads of cyberattacks without wars or grave conflicts and few designated enemies. The world's most powerful nation suffers the most attacks! Many are crime-related, some resemble adoles-cent male joy-riding, others seem like probes or practicing—possibly by other states. Some are espionage. Obviously *deterrence cannot be asked to prevent all this*. But, as happened during the Cold War, it will continue to be difficult to determine when deterrence has failed, has worked, or is working, and why. Like in struggling to ward off disease, we will have so-so confidence in what we are doing, uncertainty about knowing when we are successful or not, and why. Like dealing with crime, the attacks will vary greatly and remain ubiquitous despite efforts to deter them; it will be difficult to know how deterrence is doing, whether and when it is successful. As with the drop in major crime in the past two decades, we will not be certain why a "success" has occurred or whether deterrence had much to do with it.[11]

An additional and important facet of cyberattacks is that the weapons are integral to the version of cyberspace in which we are immersed. The effects of attacks at one point can spread unpredictably, far beyond the target and even back to the attacker, given *the highly interdependent nature of cyberspace*. A cyberattack launched in retaliation might damage cyberspace in ways that harm the defender, not unlike earlier fears about the uncertain consequences of using ABC (atomic, biological, and chemical) weapons. But in contrast to those weapons, the point of developing cyberspace has been to promote rising interac-tions and interdependence through information availability and exchange. Its essence is what leads to vulnerability to attacks; to participate in it effectively is to also acquire capacities to damage cyberspace and harm others, deliberately or—just by leaving a computer inadequately protected—inadvertently.

This is responsible for still another difference from the Cold War. At that time national security con-cerns led to efforts to contain the spread of harmful weapons. Nothing like this applies to cybersecurity because, as noted, the relevant capabilities are integral to cybersystems.

BASIC CAPABILITIES NECESSARY FOR DETERRING

According to deterrence theory, in the abstract (and sometimes in reality) all that is necessary to deter is that the opponent *believe* you can and will harm him unacceptably if he attacks, whether or not this is true. Deterrence takes effect in the mind of the opponent—he ultimately determines whether he is deterred. What matters is his concluding that the harm will be "unacceptable." In theory, that is why he does not attack. Deterrence is therefore best pursued by having capabilities to impose such harm. Early in the Cold War analysts worked out what those capabilities should look like:

- Means (defensive and/or retaliatory) capable of inflicting unacceptable harm—typically mili-tary—on an attacker and able to sufficiently reach him (effective delivery systems);

---

[11]In terms of our major explanations for crime, the recession should have stimulated a resurgence in it but it hasn't.

- Effective capabilities for ordering and directing the necessary harmful steps—durable C2 (command and control); and
- The means and C2 being sufficiently survivable and effective to do that unacceptable harm after the opponent has launched his best attack and then puts up his best defense.

During the Cold War vast attention was paid to these things in designing and conducting deterrence.

Relevance for Cyberattacks

Applying this perspective, the first thing to note is the absence of substantial evidence about actors' attack capabilities in cyberspace. We are too early in the cyber age to know with any precision how much damage states or other actors can do or how much in the future they might reasonably be expected to do by cyberattacks, on their own or linked to other, probably military, attacks. We don't know how good attackers' abilities to ward off retaliation are either. For practicing deterrence we lack relevant information about how much damage an attacker would consider unacceptable, i.e. how much would be enough.

As noted above, rushing ahead almost blindly early in the Cold War was a mistake. While important conceptual and analytical progress was made when little was known about what nuclear war would be like, what military capabilities the opponent(s) possessed—how destructive, how reliable under stress, how survivable, how accurate—and how best to manage confrontations, much American thinking about these things did not survive serious encounters with reality. For instance, debates raged about whether a new age had emerged, outmoding much of the past, or much that seemed new was actually not and various lessons and thinking from the past still applied. Analysts and policy makers often got this wrong; determining what was really new was difficult.[12]

There is considerable secrecy now about American cyberattack capabilities and their survivability for purposes of retaliation. The U.S. is widely believed to have the best capabilities in the world, but little is available about how robust they would be after a major attack. There is more uneasiness than hard evidence about how damaging attacks by opponents or prospective opponents could be. Like early in the Cold War, discussion about how a conflict would go and what it will take to deter it is largely hypothetical.

It seems more important today, than it did early in the Cold War, to focus on the vulnerability of command and control of cyberattack defense and retaliatory capabilities. One Cold War concern was about how crippling attacks on national command centers and communications could affect negative control over unauthorized actions, particularly with nuclear weapons. Another was how antagonists' fears of attack could lead to nearly automatic retaliation upon receiving any serious warning signal of a possible attack. There seems to be little discussion about negative control over cyberwar and cyberattacks—concern about escalation seems mainly focused on how damage from initial attacks could generate a deliberately escalating conflict spiral rather than on a loss of control over national cyber capabilities that has them wreaking havoc on their own. This despite how negative control is now flimsy or nonexistent over so-called "patriotic" hackers in various countries.

Even more important is how C2 for many noncyber military capabilities is so heavily reliant on cyberspace. A failure of deterrence could be triggered by the temptation to seek a crippling first-strike capability not against defenses or retaliatory capabilities but the command and communication links for operating them. What kinds of responses to this problem might be employed?

During the Cold War, U.S. efforts to offset the effects of being attacked started with elaborately redundant attack capabilities, and eventually included redundant C2 arrangements as well: multiple

---

[12]Jervis, R. 1984. *The Illogic of American Nuclear Strategy*. Ithaca: Cornell University Press. Soviet thinking also remained deeply rooted in World War II, displaying an important conceptual lag. A recent illustration of this phenomenon is how the Gulf War came as a great shock to Chinese security perceptions.

and varied communications channels, information storage capabilities, repair resources, sites for storage of replacement equipment, command centers, and a strategic nuclear triad for retaliation. Much less effort now seems to be going into redundant cyberspace capabilities, particularly in the private sector. Since the public and private sectors are intertwined, the latter's deficiencies may be very harmful but cannot readily be corrected unless the government is willing to pay. Forcing the private sector to bear the costs seems unlikely since failure to comply cannot readily be detected. Meanwhile, redundancy in the public sector is always a convenient target, apt to be eventually regarded by some as waste and marked for elimination.

An alternative is simple and durable, or easily and cheaply repaired, components. This is a common preparation for military attacks in various countries. The emphasis is on systems with the ability to take hits and keep on going. The U.S., on the other hand, has normally gone for complex, hard to repair, advanced systems—much more potent but not necessarily very durable. Today, with respect to cyberspace the U.S. has the novel additional concern, steadily rising, about extreme dependence on foreign supplies of, and necessary backups for, many critical components of cyberspace and military systems.

Another alternative, seriously considered during the Cold War, was bolstering deterrence threats by arranging that decisions on responding to attacks, particularly with nuclear weapons, were decentralized in advance to regional and local military commanders—the response to an attack would be virtually instantaneous. However, this kind of arrangement soon looked too difficult to keep safe (worry about negative control) and too likely to generate escalation. Instead, control over American conventional forces and particularly American nuclear weapons was eventually extremely centralized. It is hard to know where we are on this with cyberattacks. On defenses, the initial responses have to be virtually automatic, with little central control. While immediate steps to counterattack are possible there seems to be uneasiness about making this automatic and also about officials ordering it through channels, particularly since the attacks might well have been routed through many locations and computers surreptitiously and thus the counterattacks would harm innocent parties. But punitive responses could be far more common, and essentially uncontrolled, from the private sector, and would be uncoordinated and possibly counterproductive, particularly for limiting escalation. The uneven cooperation now between the government and the private sector will make dealing with this problem serious and sensitive.

Decisions to more thoroughly retaliate can be centrally made but it is unclear how much central control there would be of the implementation. The crucial question is whether American cyberattack capabilities can inflict unacceptable harm. It is unclear how good others' defenses are and also how durable American resources will be under a sustained onslaught. One U.S. advantage is being the world's foremost bull's eye for cyberattacks: it has more experience spotting and coping with attacks than anyone, has been able to test more defenses, and presumably has more people used to dealing with attacks. However, the experience is apparently almost exclusively with *defenses*, and cyberspace defenses inflict little harm on attackers—at best they produce frustration and the costs of unsuccessful effort, not the extensive damage defenses often inflict in military combat. There is plenty of evidence about what cyberattacks can and cannot do against the cybersystems Americans are familiar with, but little about how effective American preemptive or retaliatory attacks might be. Lack of a potent American image and record of imposing unacceptable harm on attackers, by either defense or retaliation, makes effective deterrence next to impossible.

There are several possible reasons for this situation. The U.S., at least for now, may be unwilling to retaliate in noncyber ways. Perhaps it has potent defensive or retaliatory cyber capabilities in reserve but is unwilling to use them for fear of degrading their future effectiveness—to use them might be to lose them. Thus the U.S. prefers to rely on its (very uneven) reputation rather than to show what it can do. Another possibility is that using them would be too informative to others about profitable lines of research and development, or heighten foreign efforts to reproduce what the U.S. has.[13]

---

[13]The same applies to using noncyber responses to attacks—there could be reluctance because that might help opponents strengthen their defenses or better imitate U.S. capabilities.

If these are actually important considerations in the government, it is better for now to stress deterrence by *defense*, because those restraints on attacking others add significantly to its appeal. But defense is clearly far more expensive for the U.S. than attacking it is. This can be a serious problem and is often cited as a major deficiency of BMD—it costs more to build than ways around it do. There must be significant costs for an attacker in being thwarted by defenses—without compensating benefits—to get an effective rather than just annoying deterrence effect, and this is rarely the case for U.S. defenses now.

ADDITIONAL COMPONENTS OF EFFECTIVE DETERRENCE

In addition to the *image* of being able to seriously harm an attacker, it is important to effectively convey the *threat* to do so. Deterrence theorists quickly noted the difference between the two. Threats are not necessarily inherent in a military posture. A threat must reach the opponent and be understood, and may not work if it is garbled, is in the wrong "language," is aimed at the wrong party, or conveys an incorrect message by being, say, ambiguous, misleading, insincere, or too indeterminate.

While harmful capabilities sometimes convey a potent intrinsic threat and achieve a deterrence effect from this alone, this is rarely reliable enough. It is important that the deterrer specifically project the threat it feels is needed. But this can be hampered by vague diplomatic and other communications: alliances have escape clauses, threats are phrased so as to leave some avenues for retreat, they are interwoven with inducements and concessions, etc. There are various concerns as a result. The opponent may ignore or underestimate the threat; preoccupied with his own plans, he may neglect to carefully ascertain the other side's intent. Or he may be determined to attack no matter what. Or he may misinterpret the threat, seeing it as a sign he is about to be attacked (and must hurry to attack first) or dismissing it as empty posturing. Or he can treat threats as attempts to bully or humiliate, strengthening his desire to attack (leading to suggestions as to when and how threats are better conveyed privately). With such possibilities in mind, deterrence analysts stress the importance of offering not just threats of harm but reassurances that compliance will cancel that harm, but without indicating how to convincingly do this. Studies show that combining threats with incentives increases chances of success, but the opponent may instead treat the incentives as evidence the deterrer's commitment is weak.

Relevance for Cyberdeterrence

From a deterrence perspective it is therefore important to detect an emerging threat of attack well in advance, gaining time to assess it, design and implement appropriate deterrence threats, see how they are working, and make adjustments if needed, etc. Cold War era deterrence analysts often worked with an image of deterrence even in a crisis as conducted in the following fashion: rising conflict intensity and military preparations that threaten a possible attack lead to deterrence steps, which stimulate serious efforts by each side to ascertain the other's goals, intentions, plans, and determination—a learning process.

However, cyberattack preparations are likely to offer much less (maybe no) palpable evidence of an impending attack, and thus provide little inducement to mount a specifically targeted deterrence. And the necessary preparations to either defend vigorously or retaliate will also be much less visible. Evidence may have to come primarily from shifts in the intensity of the political conflict along with detectable increases in probing by each actor. Thus far, however, cyberattacks do not amount to such costly and deadly steps that they are *necessarily* preceded by a marked deterioration in relations. They are planned and prepared with virtually no signs, unlike most military attacks. Strategic nuclear attacks during the Cold War could eventually be launched on a few moments notice but there were some signs of going to a high level alert a deterrer might detect. Probes or shifts in behavior prior to military attacks were normally more costly to undertake and thus less likely to be exercises or a bluff. In contrast, there is a steady rain of cyberattacks today so even an opponent's probing may not necessarily or decisively stand out. Intelligence analysts fear that extensive but irrelevant information will drown out vital information; in the world of cyberattacks, such static is huge.

Thus deterrence of cyberattacks must rest on the necessary threat being *prominently displayed* virtually all the time. Not that it must always be carried out, but that readily detectable expressions of it are at least regularly displayed and periodically implemented. Much is made in the deterrence literature about harm from threats not being carried out, but this is because threats involving major military steps are reserved for a very serious crisis which rivets the attention of policy makers and onlookers. Under these circumstances backing down (in effect) from the threat can readily damage one's credibility. This is less true of general (noncrisis) deterrence, where threats are broader; not carrying them out might damage one's credibility but typically they offer more loopholes for the deterrer and are harder to interpret as backing down.

Cyberattacks on the U.S. occur constantly, and are not (yet) linked to deep political conflicts with other states, so they do not pose a crisis and a failure to fully defend or retaliate need not demean U.S. deterrence. The problem is to strongly establish the *principle* of a strong U.S. interest in deterring and in making preparations to punish attackers when, in fact, only a few attacks will evoke a truly harmful response. Deterrence has to be achieved not by making a response highly likely but via the *possibility* of one. This is hardly unique; international political threats often operate in this fashion, as statements not of certainties but about the risks of suitably harmful possibilities.[14] In deterrence such threats can be effective not in preventing all attacks but in reducing the highly provocative ones.

This is getting some virtue out of a necessity; ideally, a harmful response would be very common. Studies indicate that deterrence works best, with criminals for example, when coupled with a high probability of some harm being inflicted for attacks even if only on a low level, something which is not evident and not possible now for cyberattacks. Intermittent implementation of deterrence threats invites potential attackers to misinterpret them or misestimate the risks they would be taking.

THE SPECIAL CONCERN ABOUT CREDIBILITY—THE CREDIBILITY PROBLEM

Of the possible reasons deterrence might fail, what received most American attention during the Cold War was the credibility problem, primarily because it is inherent in the nuclear age for nuclear-armed states, plus the impact of the Munich analogy (from the late 1930s) and the steps leading up to the Korean War.[15]

Concern started with the fact that since deterrence seeks to persuade an opponent who has a significant incentive to attack, the deterrence threat must be believed (the opponent expects it to be carried out) and must be persuasive (the opponent sees the consequences as too harmful). In addition to factors mentioned earlier, analysts focused on "will." A deterrer's capabilities mean little if the deterrer can't convey a strong will to use them. If it is hard to do that, deterrence is in trouble. However, if rational decision making is assumed the deterrer, like the attacker, does a cost-benefit calculation and will not retaliate or defend if it feels it would suffer unacceptable harm as a result, and under *mutual*, particularly nuclear, deterrence how could retaliation be rational when the defender would risk suffering great additional harm from a severe counterretaliation?[16] By extension, this particularly applied to a low level attack when escalation might turn it into a nuclear war: why would the deterrer rationally choose to risk that by retaliating? In particular, why would it take such costs and risks on behalf of an ally or some other third party?[17]

---

[14]North Korea, for example, is constantly threatening to treat various actions by others as creating a "state of war" to which it will appropriately respond, when the likelihood of such a response is quite low.

[15]The Munich settlement was seen as having destroyed British and French credibility for Hitler, leading him to continue his expansion policies right on into starting World War II. The Korean War was held to be due to the U.S. having done almost nothing to generate a credible commitment to South Korea's survival. See Khong, Y. F. 1992. *Analogies at War*. Princeton: Princeton University Press; and Stueck, W. 1995. *The Korean War: An International History*. Princeton: Princeton University Press.

[16]This also applies to stoutly defending. Fear that defending will make the attacker do a great deal more damage in order to win can undermine the will to fight, as Czechoslovakia demonstrated twice in the 20th century, in the 1938 attack and in 1968.

[17]The worry was not only that an opponent would figure this out and decide to attack, but also that U.S. allies would see this and lose confidence in U.S. promises to fight for them.

The problem disappears if the deterrent threat will be carried out automatically if an attack occurs and the opponent knows this—that cancels the defender's opportunity to rationally decide not to retaliate. But there were obvious problems with this suggestion so it was never implemented. A highly sensitive warning system might falsely trigger the automatic retaliation, or it could set off retaliation after a relatively small attack that was not worth it—turning an "incident" into a war. Or it might erroneously detect an attack, mechanically or due to human error. And so on.

Alternatives ranged from making the response to an attack "semi-automatic," to upholding almost any minor commitment so as to build a reputation for doing so (the most influential solution in the US), to trying to convey a degree of irrationality in confrontations. The ultimate recourse was to count on the fact that since no government could guarantee to be highly rational after being attacked and might resort to a vicious response, resulting in disaster for the attacker, there was an existential deterrence associated with nuclear weapons and other powerful forces that provided considerable credibility.[18]

None of these were fully satisfactory. There was no definitive answer to the credibility problem, and deterrence had to be pursued without one. More broadly, the credibility problem arises because of the need to make a *very difficult decision* and a decision maker might not make it effectively for any number of reasons, rational or irrational.[19]

It is important to emphasize that in the Cold War much of the emphasis was on crude threats that had little to do with things like precise attribution and carefully tailoring the response to the specific nature of the attack. Massive retaliation was the ultimate posture here, initiated by the U.S. and eventually imitated by all other nuclear powers as at least part of their deterrence postures. When the U.S. sought to limit military responses to an attack to the lowest level needed to defeat it, European members insisted on a NATO posture prepared to initially fight hard and then readily escalate to the nuclear level, steadily and perhaps massively—increasing the indiscriminate destruction. They felt that the threat of indiscriminate destruction was the most effective deterrent.

Ultimately the U.S. and Soviet Union developed huge nuclear weapon stockpiles capable of many kinds of attacks, not just huge and indiscriminate ones—many of their weapons were, in fact, aimed at each other. But even very limited, and/or very precise attacks to limit damage could have set off escalation to larger and more destructive nuclear warfare; many analysts and observers, and also policy makers, believed this was very likely. And even small or precise nuclear attacks could readily have inflicted substantial collateral damage. Nuclear deterrence continued to seem very crude and imprecise in the harm being threatened.

Actually, deterrence operated during the Cold War despite real doubts about its credibility under many circumstances. Not only was it difficult to make a nuclear threat credible vis-à-vis another nuclear power, but it also became very difficult to make one credible vis-à-vis a nonnuclear state because of the so-called "nuclear taboo";[20] nuclear threats sometime had little effect on opponents' behavior. Conversely, a *nonnuclear* retaliatory threat could be hard to make credible against even a weak nuclear power for fear of escalation. Deterrence by nonnuclear threats against nonnuclear weapons states had always been complicated and problematic, not reliably successful, and this was true of nuclear deterrence in the Cold War era. After World War II U.S. officials expecting to have leverage on the Soviets and others from the U.S. nuclear weapons monopoly were regularly dismayed by the results. Later there

---

[18]This was typically phrased in terms of a defender irrationally provoking a *nuclear* war but it could readily apply to other cases. For instance, the Chinese decision to intervene in the Korean War confronted the U.S. with the risk of a much wider war, nuclear or conventional, if it retaliated directly in China.

[19]Nonrational reasons could include being frozen in panic or fear; no consensus on fighting; no certainty a decision to fight would be carried out; being tossed out of office before making or communicating a decision to fight; relevant orders lost or not believed by underlings, garbled in transmission, or misinterpreted. Examples of rational reasons for a decision to fight not being made: seeing that a counterretaliation will add too much to the damage already done; the planned response looks excessive or escalatory; the attack looks like a probe—retaliating could give the opponent valuable information about the deterrer's capabilities and plans.

[20]This is a great reluctance to abandon the history of nuclear nonuse since 1945 lest that encourage future uses of nuclear weapons and arouse international condemnation for breeching such an important threshold.

were instances of nuclear powers being attacked by nonnuclear states, even losing the wars or suffering other outcomes short of victory.

Cold War era deterrence had an uncertain (hard to ascertain) impact even on preventing wars among the great powers. While most analysts believe it was an important factor in preventing World War III, many now hold that often the Cold War opponents were not particularly interested in attacking each other, making for times when deterrence was not particularly responsible for upholding peace and security. Part of the deterrence contribution was the *possibility* of a very harmful outcome; it was the risk of *possible disaster* that (unevenly) deterred. U.S. deterrence benefitted from the American ability to mount a nasty conventional response, not just a nuclear one, but even at that level deterrence was a crude recourse with an uneven record—the Vietnam War, for example, being a long history of deterrence failures (on both sides).

Relevance of the Credibility Problem for Deterrence of Cyberattacks

This leaves no intrinsic reason empirically for concluding that deterrence should now work well against cyberattacks. The available evidence on the credibility problem suggests, in part, that it cannot work well. The credibility problem:

1. increases as the scale of harm to be inflicted from an attack or anticipated attack declines—at low levels of conflict threats to do very serious harm are often not credible;
2. increases with the possibility of a catastrophic counterretaliation;
3. increases to the degree the deterrer's primary or vital interests are not threatened;
4. usually increases for deterrence by collective actors (like the UN Security Council);
5. increases when the attacker is difficult to detect, identify, single out;
6. is somewhat independent of the deterrer's past behavior; credibility is not guaranteed by having upheld past commitments;
7. increases when the deterrer's upholding of commitments is irregular and infrequent;
8. increases in extended deterrence; and
9. increases when deterrers are seen by opponents as cautious, risk-averse.

The first of these applies directly to cyberattacks. Thus far the harm they inflict is below the threshold for triggering very harmful U.S. reactions—U.S. deterrence credibility here is quite low. The third point also applies—the U.S. is only now getting close to behaving as if cyberattacks threaten *vital* American interests.

The fifth point on attackers being difficult to detect is the most cited in analyses of deterrence of cyberattacks. They come from myriads of sources, often virtually anonymously. They can come from people associating themselves with a government which has not authorized and does not approve of their actions. And so on. With no way to link retaliation to the actual attacker, the credibility of threats to do so is diminished.[21] This is a serious complication. It appears in various forms in deterrence thinking. A standard concern in alliances is the danger an ally will connive to induce a conflict that drags its allies in—inciting the "attack" they respond to. A concern early in the nuclear age was that with nuclear proliferation a third party could provoke a war between the superpowers via an attack that looked like it came from one of them, or by reacting to an attack in ways that generated rapid escalation to its allies. (The basic rationale for British and French nuclear weapons was the implied threat that they could escalate to the nuclear level after a conventional Soviet attack and draw the superpowers into direct nuclear exchanges.) One of President Kennedy's concerns during the Cuban Missile Crisis was that NATO forces put on high alert in Europe would automatically break out their nuclear weapons, possibly alarming the Warsaw Pact states. Another was that in operating the

[21]For various views on the attribution problem see Libicki, M. 2009 *Cyberdeterrence and Cyberwar*. Santa Monica: RAND.

blockade during the crisis the Navy worked to force a Soviet sub to surface—an action not ordered by the president but how was Moscow to know that? In short, Cold War deterrence was not about only acting when responsibility for an attack was obvious.

This is equally true in conventional and subconventional military clashes where nuclear escalation is not a consideration. The Tonkin Gulf incident involved retaliation ordered when the exact nature of the incident was unclear. Various countries in the Cold War downed civilian airliners, yet the question of attribution remained open as to who specifically was responsible. A standard justification for inserting peacekeeping forces in conflict situations then and now is that incidents readily occur even when whether an attack really occurred, who did it, and who ordered it are in doubt.

On the other points, it is hard to say much about the credibility of threats that promise very great harm in response to cyberattacks: we have no examples yet. We can speculate that familiar things will result—the threats will be difficult to make credible and thus will often not be issued or not be effective. But they will be possible to implement and thus will have at least some credibility, particularly after the U.S. suffers serious attacks and is intensely irate.

There is no example to date of a collective actor attempting to deter cyberattacks. Collective actor deterrence has a difficult credibility problem for numerous reasons.[22] However, such a threat can more readily represent—if well organized and mounted—a daunting level of opposition to the attacker, a factor that gives threats credibility. Perhaps in the future primarily collective actors will be used to defend, or particularly to order retaliation, to make deterrence more credible and spread responsibility for carrying out the threats.

Does the credibility problem pose insuperable difficulties? No, deterrence can have some impact if there is a reasonable possibility that the U.S. will periodically do unacceptable damage, and occasional demonstrations of this occur. Such an effort should, of course, especially be made when the U.S. has major interests threatened or harmed. Failing to respond when the stakes are low does not undermine the credibility of all one's commitments; opponents normally take the threat more seriously when the stakes are high. If they attack anyway, failing to respond in that situation is a mistake.

This is likely to be particularly true for cyberattacks. With so many attacks occurring, the best deterrence posture will be to respond strongly when something important is threatened or harmed and mount occasional responses to lesser attacks. This would maximize credibility over a wide range of attacks, not precluding them but somewhat containing their incidence.

Next, there is no inherent reason the threatened response has to be "in kind" to be credible. Nothing in deterrence theory or past experience requires this. Many deterrence threats and their implementation ignore it. Examples include the use of sanctions to prevent or end a state's misuse of force, or the use of threats and force to curb gross domestic violations in human rights. In some cases it may even be unacceptable or unwise to respond in kind.[23] Thus analysts who suggest that deterrence of cyberattacks may well draw on a wide variety of painful responses—economic, military, political/diplomatic, cyber—are correct.[24]

Responses in kind are attractive for reasons that go beyond deterrence, such as conforming to a sense of what is the "right" thing to do, or to better highlight the attacker's offense and indicate a willingness to avoid damaging other relationships between the parties. Reasons for in kind reactions a deterrence perspective can endorse include, first, to have the response—by its limited nature—indicate types of restraint the opponent should adhere to in order to limit escalation, and second, to avoid breeching thresholds of damage that might invite future enemies to do the same.

As for the problem of attribution, in deterrence theory and past practice it has not been considered

---

[22]Morgan, P. M. 2003. *Deterrence Now.* Cambridge: Cambridge University Press 172-202.

[23]Thus expecting that a nuclear attack *must* bring a nuclear response, something U.S. allies sometimes promote, is not correct. The U.S. may want to respond in a devastating nonnuclear fashion. In the Gulf War the U.S. decided before the war to respond with conventional means even to an Iraqi use of weapons of mass destruction.

[24]For example, Kugler, R. 2009. Deterrence of Cyber Attacks. In Krasner, F. D., S. H. Starr, and L. K. Wentz, eds., *Cyberpower and National Security.* Washington, DC: National Defense University Press 309-340.

necessary to retaliate specifically against those who ordered or carried out the attack. Deterrence has typically been crude in this respect, one reason being that it is often not possible to identify the actual culprits. It is common to hold a state responsible for harmful actions coming from its territory, especially when it has been repeatedly given evidence of this and told it will suffer if the attacks continue. A government with weak control (it claims) over hackers can be threatened and punished for not developing effective control, just like one can be harassed for being a haven for drug traffickers or terrorists. The U.S. can use sanctions on China for tolerating piracy of American entertainment items, and it could do the same for China's allowing and even encouraging hackers to flourish and attack the US. Unwillingness to retaliate in this fashion is a choice made on the basis of what is deemed ethically or politically attractive, or practical; it is not endorsed by deterrence theory or past practice.

In principle, therefore, it is possible to establish a deterrence policy for cyberattacks based on threats of serious harm by defense and retaliation and which would be upheld periodically, directing the harm at a state actor or leaders of a nonstate actor whether they are specifically responsible or not, and even harming people not parties to the attacks. None of this behavior is without precedent. None would be absolutely unacceptable now, *if the scale of the attack and the damage caused that evokes the response is great enough.*

Reluctance to behave this way based on ethical or political considerations is understandable, and reflects concerns to be taken seriously. Today, normative constraints on using force are given far greater consideration and this is certainly welcome. Deterrence is always conducted within a *normative context*, which contributes to shaping what are considered appropriate or legitimate reactions to attacks, and thus the appropriate and legitimate kinds of deterrence threats to deliver. Norms pertain to such things as the scale of harm (as with the concept of proportionality—punishment fitting the offense), the *type* of harm, the threshold that, when crossed, justifies seriously harming an attacker, etc. Deterrence theory basically does not deal with this. Perhaps that is good since norms can change readily, are far from universal, and are often ignored under extreme provocation.

It is also not necessarily required to be highly sensitive to collateral damage in both the threats mounted and the harm inflicted if necessary. Deterrence was initially pursued in the Cold War with exactly the opposite approach: the harm threatened often included maximizing collateral damage. The earliest American nuclear deterrence strategy called for preparations to rapidly escalate a war with the communist world via a massive nuclear attack, with plans to inflict many millions of casualties. There was no concern for collateral damage to people, cultural objects, hospitals, churches, or anything else.

How was that possible? One factor was that the strategy emerged in the wake of an intense war without limits in which the U.S., like other participants, often inflicted indiscriminate destruction. Another was that the enemies were characterized in virtually the same terms as the ones in World War II—monstrous totalitarian regimes. Conducting the Cold War with this enemy in mind gave it considerable potential for sliding into another total war. U.S. deterrence ultimately rested on promising exactly that. The threat had significant credibility because similar consequences had been delivered in recent memory.

We reject thinking in those terms now because we have no conflict so intense, or enemies deemed so despicable.[25] Cyberattacks involve nothing like that. The normative context is therefore much more confining. This could quickly change if international conflicts greatly deepen and intensify and cyberattacks are part of why this happens (such as by becoming much more destructive). It is therefore impossible to specify the future of deterrence in cyberspace conflict. Deterrence is not nice—it is nasty behavior and meant to be so, threatening enough harm to get the opponent to desist. If, as is often the case, this would mean behaving in normally unacceptable ways and doing so is rejected when the time comes, that occurs because of self- or community-imposed constraints. Choosing to accept the constraints is a political decision, not inherent in deterrence.

---

[25]We come closest to thinking that way with Islamic terrorists in Al Qaeda and the Taliban and our behavior toward them reflects as much when it includes, for example, assassination efforts that include harm to family members or other noncombatants.

THE SPECIAL CONCERN FOR DETERRENCE STABILITY—THE STABILITY PROBLEM

In developing deterrence theory, "stability" received much attention, first in the context of mutual nuclear deterrence and then with respect to the entire Cold War. Stability referred, in the first instance, to deterrence preventing a war, particularly a nuclear war, then to preventing unacceptable escalation in a war—keep major states' wars small and prevent others' wars from drawing the great powers in so they became major wars. Deterrence was also to sustain stability by preventing the use of increasingly destructive weapons and actions in a war. Deterrence was believed less likely to fail, and escalation more likely to be avoided, by preventing proliferation of highly destructive weapons, grievous environmental damage from weapons and warfare, ruinous arms competitions, intense crises, and other dangerous conditions. These and other situations could lead to deterrence failures—destabilizing deterrence. Preventing all this eventually came to be put under the heading of arms control. Arms control covers many other things but its modern version in the Cold War was driven primarily by concerns about deterrence stability.

While a lack of credibility could contribute to deterrence failure, having credibility might not be enough. Deterrence stability is partially linked to the *strength of the opponent's motivation to attack*. Deterrence is supposed to adjust that motivation so an attack does not occur, but it can readily override credible deterrence threats. Often the more intense the opponent's motivation appears, the greater the reliance on deterrence to keep safe—deterrence becomes the ultimate recourse; but the stronger that motivation the less likely deterrence is to work. Deterrence is not at its best when it is needed most.

In terms of stability, therefore, the best time for deterrence threats is relatively early in a conflict, hopefully inhibiting the opponent's desire to attack before it has hardened, attack planning is far along, preparations well underway, etc. Deterrence stability is on better ground in noncrisis than crisis situations. An earlier, broader (general) deterrence is needed to help convince the opponent to abandon thinking about and preparing to attack. When a war occurs, the failure of deterrence began with a breakdown in general deterrence.[26]

Attacker motivation is also related to deterrence stability via concerns about irrationality. It is commonly said that deterrence is undermined if the opponent is irrational. Often what is meant is a fear that the opponent's desire to attack, due to his being irrational, will override deterrence threats.[27] The problem lies not in irrationality, but in *anything* producing an excessive motivation to attack. Sometimes irrationality is the problem, sometimes it is other things, but Cold War governments worried about possible irrationality in their opponents. An important concern in deterrence must be that using threats might enrage an opponent—that deterrence can sometimes provoke an irrational reaction.

Other facets of the stability problem were seen as structural. One was how nuclear weapons reinforced a strong desire in modern war for capabilities to win quickly and relatively cheaply. Nuclear weapons seemed ideal for this, allowing a preemptive attack so devastating the war would be over without a response. In a serious crisis if one side had such a capability it would have an enormous incentive to attack first, to win quickly and cheaply; deterrence would readily fail. In a serious crisis involving two states with such capabilities, each would be desperate to make the initial attack, would race to do so, and deterrence would collapse. The structure of the deterrence postures would be responsible for the disintegration of deterrence! This was referred to as the "crisis stability" problem.

Another structural concern pertained to alliances and related arrangements to enhance deterrence against attacks on the members. Deterrence would presumably depend in part on how cohesive the alliances were and Cold War alliances sometimes had problems on this score. The most powerful members worried that concerns about sustaining their deterrence credibility with the allies, or the need to back up an ally that was behaving provocatively, might draw them into wars they could otherwise avoid. The allies worried that their powerful patrons might, should the occasion arise, choose not to defend them and the deterrence they counted on would dissipate. The alliances imposed conflicting interests

---

[26]See Morgan, P. M. 2003 *Deterrence Now*. Cambridge: Cambridge University Press 80-86.

[27]The target's irrationality, per se, is not harmful to the success of deterrence threats—it is the nature of the irrationality that is important. Many forms of irrationality can enhance, not undermine, deterrence.

that might cause a failure of deterrence. This was a stability problem within the cluster of difficulties involved in extended deterrence (providing deterrence for another actor, typically an ally).

A third structural concern was the incentive for proliferation. Depending on an ally has always been risky, and Cold War allies had the further risk of involvement in a deadly war not of their making. Thus having their own weapons of mass destruction (WMD) could be seen as a better deterrent. Similar concerns promoted interest in proliferation among nonaligned states. Some analysts and governments argued that this would make the international system safer, more stable.[28] Most thought multiplying nuclear powers would increase deterrence failures via more accidents or more conflicts that escalated, or more irrational leaders inciting crises or displaying extreme behavior.

The ultimate impact of the stability problem was the sense that Cold War antagonists' security had become highly interdependent. Intellectual exploration of how to stabilize and supplement deterrence came to highlight cooperative efforts to make it more stable and maintain a political context in which stable deterrence would more readily endure. The resulting efforts were sometimes unilateral: making one's nuclear weapons more secure, less vulnerable to unauthorized use, safer from theft or a fire. Many involved opponents cooperating to make deterrence more robust. Others involved multilateral agreements and related implementation.

All this prodded analysts to go beyond primitive conceptions of how to use cooperation toward viewing Cold War conflict relationships as something like communities needing a degree of management. Cooperative management might include forgoing defenses to keep opponents vulnerable to each other's forces; or unprecedented information-sharing among antagonists about their weapons; or agreeing to forego certain weapons as destabilizing; or cooperating against WMD proliferation.

Relevance for Cybersecurity

In cyberspace security, American deterrence has little credibility to bolster its stability.[29] The U.S. is obviously an attractive target, and the lack of any apparent decline in the strength of motivations to attack it is a bad sign. At lower levels there is no deterrence stability at all. The only comfort is that no major failure, no attack, has generated a serious national security crisis. Not yet.

The most recognizable version of the stability problem at work in cyberspace is how technological change constantly outruns defenses and the global hacking community readily surprises defenders. The attackers may well be doing better than is publically indicated.[30] This readily invites pessimism about the prospects for successful defenses. In the nuclear age pessimism about defenses led to preoccupation with deterrence by threats of retaliation, but it is not yet clear that defenses against cyberattacks will be that ineffective. Highly capable defenses would markedly diminish the problem of cyberattacks. In the meantime, improving detection of and resistance to attacks is vital, as is developing restrictions on connections to systems with so many vulnerabilities. Improving defenses is doubly important because, unlike in the Cold War era, the alternative—deterrence by threats of retaliation—is in even worse shape. If the U.S. is to change this it will have to link threats of retaliation to actions that are more likely and more harmful than appears to be the case now.

A classic recourse for a weak deterrence posture is redundant capabilities for replacing what attacks damage or destroy or to provide sufficient operating capacity while recovery is undertaken. This is especially appealing for nations with large resources. If U.S. defenses remain porous, and retaliatory threats irrelevant, it will be imperative to have more redundant cyber resources and the things dependent on them, capabilities that are constantly changed to match developments. This will be particularly necessary for attack and retaliatory cyber capabilities and their command systems, and should be accompanied by efforts at cleverly hiding or protecting them.

---

[28]See Kenneth Waltz on this in Sagan, S. D. and K. Waltz. 1995. *The Spread of Nuclear Weapons: A Debate.* New York: W. W. Norton.
[29]As far as I know, no one else's deterrence on cyberattacks has real credibility either.
[30]See Bowden, M. 2010. The Enemy Within. *The Atlantic,* June, 72-83.

The most important version of the stability problem in cyber security would be cyberattacks able to inflict a rapid, cheap defeat of an American military effort abroad or as a direct attack on the U.S. itself. There is no certainty that cyberwar capabilities will ever be this potent, but it is vital to consider the possibility. The losses need not be directly military but could exploit the rising dependence of the U.S. and its friends on cyberspace in many areas, inflicting grave damage not readily corrected. The motivation to have this kind of attack capability will only be enhanced if it turns out to be attainable by even small actors; cyberattacks will become a great leveler and very attractive for that reason.

If this capability comes into existence, it will probably emerge unevenly and unpredictably, in sharp contrast with the Cold War when the initial states to take up nuclear weapons were obvious, they did so gradually and visibly, and only two possibly achieved universally applicable first strike capabilities. The cyberattack equivalent would more likely resemble how the U.S. acquired an enormous advantage in conventional warfare almost unnoticed, which came as a major shock to others in 1991. It could be even more startling. Deterrence postures could be rapidly outmoded, perhaps repeatedly, by the appearance of dangerous new versions of cyberattack capabilities. Deterrence postures would need to be very nimble indeed.

The most glaring stability concern in the Cold War era was the problem of reciprocal fear of surprise attack. One aspect was that, if badly designed, a visible military buildup taken to deter could incite fear that led to an opponent attacking instead. Fortunately, the initially destabilizing effects of developing similar cyber capabilities seem much more avoidable. There is no sign that preparations alone to defend against or retaliate for a cyberattack are necessarily so *vulnerable to being attacked first*—and so evident—that they will incite an attack.[31] The preparations would be difficult to detect.

On the other hand, since they will likely not be readily visible, the emergence of capabilities for disarming or otherwise very crippling preemptive cyberattacks will be a real nightmare, and just the possibility of this is therefore very disturbing. Indications that this might be happening will cause alarm not just for the actors involved but also for broader stability in international politics. Both a potential attacker and the target would have to prepare for the worst. This could lead governments basing defensive and retaliatory preparations on the opponent's *hypothetical* attack capabilities, with each side operating from what it infers, on the basis of its own research, cybersystems, and espionage efforts, about what the opponent has.[32] With cyberattacks more feasible and more readily mounted (given the right secret preparations) with little transparency, this could sharply escalate the hair trigger nature of serious confrontations via the reciprocal fear of surprise attack. Mutual cyber first-strike capabilities would set up the severe structural instability once again (the crisis stability problem) of states racing to use them first before they could be lost in an enemy attack, the instability exacerbated if each opponent was uncertain how advanced the other side's capabilities were and turned to a worst-case analysis.

As for alliances and the complications they pose for deterrence stability, the incentives to develop potent cyberattack capabilities will apply much more broadly. Compared with nuclear weapons, the costs seem likely to be modest. Many states and other actors may soon have considerable ability to do serious harm—*proliferation of relevant capacities is already widespread*. This will pose quite a different problem from the nuclear proliferation threat which has taken years to involve only a limited number of actors.

During the Cold War the superpower alliances somewhat inhibited proliferation via extended deterrence. The U.S. is already seeking cooperative relationships with allies for dealing with cyberthreats,[33]

---

[31]Apparently some analysts fear that those kinds of preparations may turn out to be vulnerable enough to invite attacks.

[32]This would be a throwback to aspects of Cold War deterrence. There were frequent instances then in which deterrence strategy and practice were heavily influenced by hypothetical threats, some described in very dramatic terms, leading to considerable arms racing, a good deal of which later proved unfounded.

[33]See for example: C. Levitt. February 10, 2010. U.S. Seeking Allies for Warfare in Cyberspace. Available at http://www.smh.com.au/technology/us-seeking-allies-for-warfare-in-cyberspace-20100214-nzg2.html; and Kyodo News. May 4, 2010. Japan-US to Cooperate in Combatting Cyber Attacks. *NAPSNet Daily Report* May 5, 2010. Available at www.nautilus.org/mailinglists/napsnet under Mailing lists—Daily Report.

and this will presumably expand, especially since the U.S. and its allies are integrating many cyber-systems for military cooperation purposes. However, the cyberattack cooperation involves exchanging expertise plus some relevant technology, and getting help from allies once a major attack occurs mainly in the form of visiting experts. It is not a matter of the U.S. specifically defending an ally, other than in the sense that when shared systems are under attack everyone will need to work together to beat it off. Pushing integration to where the U.S. would defend its allies systems would face strong objections that (a) this would expand American vulnerabilities via the integration of cybersystems, (b) an attack on an ally would automatically draw the U.S. into resisting it with no time to assess U.S. interests in doing so, and (c) many of the costs and burdens are much more affordable for the allies now than in the past.

It is difficult to assess the prospective stability problems associated with conflict escalation in cyber-attacks. If U.S. alliances are adjusted to include *retaliating* for cyberattacks on allies, which seems quite possible, then escalation can take place through U.S. retaliation and the responses it provokes. A more interesting route is that damage by cyberattacks into systems can spread out of control. This is not a form of escalation deterrence can handle. Whether the attack was launched deliberately or inadvertently, deterrence cannot be expected to prevent its consequences from expanding thereafter.

Finally, we come to how arms control was the ultimate Cold War response to various versions of the stability problem. The starting point was that even serious opponents had strong incentives to cooperate to manage their security relationship and the security environment because they have overlapping national interests. That also led to broader multilateral efforts at security management on conflicts and arms, reflecting how security interdependence affected everyone's welfare. Eventually, the cooperation extended across a wide range of activities. How does this experience apply to the cyberattack problem?

Interdependence in cyberspace has yet to become an equivalent threat, so that particular incentive to cooperate is not yet fully in play. But in the everyday conduct of very important activities, societies' interdependence in the cyber age is profound, is much broader and deeper, is much more apparent, and will continue to rapidly expand. The cybersecurity problem is already virtually universal in character; abuse of cyberspace can affect almost anyone. As long as cyberattacks are more annoying than deadly, they are a cost of interdependence that is more than offset by the benefits. But if they begin to pose grave threats to national security, or it becomes vital to prevent that, the arms control perspective will be increasingly relevant.

However, arms control was aimed at making deterrence stable, i.e. very effective, with deterrence considered the key to managing national and international security. Arms control was not an alternative to deterrence; it was making reliance on deterrence more successful and less burdensome. This is directly relevant to cybersecurity because the capacity to do harm to and via cyberspace cannot be eliminated (for the foreseeable future). It is necessary to make living with that fact less burdensome. Cooperation can reduce vulnerabilities to being harmed, strengthen the effectiveness of deterrence by defense, and improve the possibilities for deterrence by significant retaliation in response to attacks. This is cooperation to make cyberspace itself more safely manageable, resembling what Cold War arms control sought to achieve.

However, the prior effort was containing *destabilizing* aspects of security relations between intense opponents, including destabilizing effects their armaments provoked, but not by seeking to eliminate those arms and resolving or diminishing the intense conflicts. The arms were considered an important component of the arms control effort in that they provided much of the stability it was vital to preserve. Thus arms control adjustments of the international status quo were needed, but little had to be fundamentally changed. After all, stability via deterrence rested on living with an enormous ever-present threat.

In cyberspace the means for inflicting harm and resulting attacks are not essential; they threaten key qualities of cyberspace and disrupt its proper operations. Unlike national and international security during the Cold War, cyberspace is not meant to be a threat-based system or a threat-managed system. Thus the intended function of deterrence and its arms control component must be much different.

Cyberspace security requires reducing attacks or their effects as much as possible, so eliminating the capabilities for attacks or reducing the effects achieved by attackers as much as possible is quite appropriate. Arms control is needed not to facilitate and sustain the utility of deterrence, but to reduce the necessity of deterrence and curb the capacities to override it while other important things are done to improve cyberspace security.

Needed is a much differently designed and regulated cyberspace, including improved cooperation and more transparency among governments, societies, and private actors on cyberspace matters. All of this will be needed on a much broader scale than now and certainly more than Cold War arms control arrangements required. It will include more intrusive regulation and verification arrangements. Elaborate cooperation on threat perceptions, attack detection, and identification/apprehension of those responsible for attacks will be needed. New international organization arrangements for these efforts will be necessary. Deterrence is needed to help promote cooperative activities that sharply diminish the importance of deterrence. And arms control is needed not to stabilize deterrence but to funnel overlapping societal interests in the interactions in cyberspace into management that reduces its security threats, including the actors' capacities to do harm. Thus even though the threat of attacks will not be eliminated, by not making threat capacities the key to sustaining security the arms control needed is somewhat closer to disarmament than the arms control devised and practiced during the Cold War.

Next, while Cold War arms control sometimes involved numerous actors, fundamentally it was the work of a small number—especially in the major negotiations. Those who had to cooperate extensively were relatively limited, and some important steps could be taken unilaterally. Sustaining and stabilizing security in cyberspace will likely involve a great many more actors. Widespread cooperation will be needed to make significant adjustments, such as shrinking flaws, in cyberspace systems that generate such extensive vulnerabilities and therefore such strong inducements for attackers to do their thing.[34] Fortunately, and in contrast to the Cold War, such arrangements can be undertaken before a full blown version of the threat that cyberattacks may someday pose emerges. This valuable opportunity should be exploited.

The result will be a sharp departure from the Cold War model of uneven cooperation to secure limited constraints on states so as to enhance security management. Needed for this new kind of security problem is development of collaborative operation of cyberspace as a collective resource, involving states and a variety of other actors. It will be the difference between keeping specific grievous Cold War threats and conflicts in check via independent deterrence posture and collectively lowering threats and conflicts in cyberspace matters to a much more tolerable level.

Pessimism that all this can be done is certainly understandable. Cold War arms control, limited as it was, required strenuous efforts to get a much more modest level of cooperation. The conflictual, political, and bureaucratic obstacles were daunting and many observers felt that the achievements fell well short of what Cold War national and international security required, right up to when the Cold War began to dissolve.

However, pessimism should be tempered today by the extensive experience at such things, when clearly necessary, already accumulated in the international effort to contain and curb the terrorism problem or the threats from potential new epidemics, and the initial steps toward management of Earth's climate, or the threats of global economic collapse. Perhaps the most distinctive element of today's international system is its burgeoning interdependence across many fields via endlessly proliferating interactions. The problems stemming from this, facilitated or actively stimulated by rising interactions, are multiplying rapidly, and they already involve participation much broader and deeper, transparency much greater, and transnational operations much more penetrating and fine-grained than the international security cooperation projects we were used to in the past. The progress made to date is rather

---

[34]Some very appealing features of the web may be sacrificed: autonomy, anonymity, decentralization, considerable tolerance for misbehavior. For example, the Obama administration has proposed new arrangements that would curb the anonymity of internet users. See Markoff, J. July 4, 2010. Taking the Mystery Out of Web Autonomy. *New York Times*.

astonishing in historical perspective, as major cooperative international endeavors go, in such a short time. The problems with cyberspace are just an extension of the same underlying conditions. We are embarked on expanding the management of the international system in almost every direction; we need to embed cooperative management of cyberspace more deeply in this broader effort.

Finally, Cold War arms control got under way only after the United States had already constructed an enormous nuclear and conventional deterrence posture and the Soviet Union was busy catching up. The benefits of it came only slowly thereafter, swimming against a strong-running tide. We are still early in the emergence of major cyberattack capabilities, and have a chance to short-circuit their growth and spread and perhaps even reverse it. Cooperative efforts to deal with the problem of cyberattacks should be sharply escalated as soon as possible.

The main difficulty will be that the incentives for much greater cooperation are less potent now than the initial incentives were for Cold War arms control. The costs of major weapons, the intensity of the political conflicts they reflected, the environmental consequences of just having those major weapons, and the opportunity costs of the huge emphasis on military forces were all much higher then. Cyberattack capabilities, on all these measures, are more like biological weapons than nuclear and huge conventional weapons and forces in this regard.

CONCLUSION: WHAT SHOULD A GOOD CYBERDETERRENCE POSTURE LOOK LIKE?

Deterrence during the Cold War was developed for helping regulate a type of international politics that has been set aside and which we have every reason to want to never see again. Many of the most salient characteristics of that deterrence therefore have little relevance today. At present the cyberattack problem is quite different in scale and character. Some of the most applicable lessons of Cold War deterrence are essentially negative—on why it does not apply or should be avoided. A few can be be helpful in devising a less dominant, less imposing use of deterrence. However, the most important lesson from that period is that cooperative security management should be taken to heart and applied even more elaborately today because the scale and interpenetration of the interdependence embodied in cyberspace are so much greater. Cyberattacks represent not the threat of everyday order being overwhelmed in a vastly destructive conflict, but a manifestation of a dark side to some central features of everyday order now—a much less esoteric, more intimate threat.

To deal with it will require a cyberdeterrence posture that eventually consists of:

- **Defenses for immediately responding to attacks.** With cyberattacks, even a short delay in detecting and responding to an attack can be catastrophic. Defenses are needed that immediately provide protection, to mitigate the damage done, and that capability requires detection first. This is vital because there are so many attacks, often not all that important and springing from motivations deterrence cannot normally daunt. What is disturbing is that attackers are so often better at detecting weaknesses in systems vulnerable to exploitation than the defenses are.

- **Backup defenses that are much more impressive.** These are needed to handle the real concern: more serious, more deeply penetrating, and more elaborately crafted attacks. Such defenses are, beyond offering crucial protection, vital for a serious deterrence by defense. Much of the problem now is that attackers can keep on probing not only because this may not be costly but also because there is often no major backup when a defense is breached. This concern is familiar in shaping defenses of borders, with backup capabilities being the real heart of the defense. And some of the capabilities should be retaliatory, such as equipment that reaches out quickly to strike at, even destroy, machines used in attacks—equipment that should be used only when the harm from attacks is of very great concern.

- **Capacities for suitable retaliation when necessary in a more measured fashion.** These should encompass various forms of harm, cyber and otherwise, including military, economic, and political efforts and also steps to publicly provide evidence as to the identities of the attackers—seeking to embarrass the sources or generate greater pressure on them, in a fashion similar to the way this is done on human rights violations. The retaliation should inflict more harm than the U.S. currently practices, and threats to use it must be given more credibility than is now the case.

• **Significantly greater redundancy in cyberspace resources.** Deterrence is a sometime thing—attacks cannot be completely avoided. With regard to attacks, things are changing so fast that the backup resources will need constant updating based on sensitivity to technical and environmental changes. And the necessity to better defend, via redundant capabilities, the valuable private sector resources is critical.

• **Active promotion of collective arms control and related management in cyberspace.** This will require long, hard work. The universality of the problem and its growing scale must be stressed. Success will require considerable reordering of cyberspace, with much more regulation, plus new organizations and networks to oversee required norms and practices. In a familiar pattern, enhancing security will require more controls, less freedom of action, and less tolerance for a cyberspace wide open for reckless individualism.

Categorizing and Understanding Offensive Cyber Capabilities and Their Use

Gregory Rattray

Internet Corporation for Assigned Names and Numbers

Jason Healey

Delta Risk

OVERVIEW

This paper provides a framework for categorizing the offensive cyber capabilities across a range of potential scenarios to help further the dialogue on cyber deterrence and conflict management. Though not an in-depth analysis of the subject, this paper does include suggestions where further analysis might prove useful. Beginning with key features of the aspects of cyberspace that are most applicable for the offense, the paper outlines several key ways to categorize offensive operations. Attacks, for example, could be in support of existing kinetic operations and used in conjunction with other capabilities; however offensive capabilities could also be used as part of standalone engagements, operations and entire cyber campaigns.

Though many have posited notions on what a "real" cyber war would be like, we lack understanding of how such conflicts will be conducted and evolve. Accordingly, the third main section dives into an analysis of cyber war analogies, from the well-known "cyber Pearl Harbor" and "cyber 9/11" to less discussed analogies like a "cyber Vietnam." As cyber warfare is often compared to combat in the air, both in speed and range of operations and the loudly touted strategic effects, the paper also includes an extended case study on a cyber Battle of Britain fought force-on-force in cyberspace with little relation to fielded military forces.

For the purposes of this paper, offensive operations are those analogous to Computer Network Attacks (CNA), as defined by the Department of Defense,[1] and do not include acts of cyber espionage, or Computer Network Exploitation.[2] Though both types of operations may use similar technical techniques to access an adversary's networks, cyber exploitation is generally more akin to espionage than offensive operations. This paper's focus is therefore on Computer Network Attacks, whether operations between political actors operating across state boundaries or by non-state actors for political purposes.

---

[1]Joint Publication 1-02 (JP 1-02): Dictionary of Military and Associated Terms. Department of Defense. Washington, D.C., October 2009, available online at: http://www.dtic.mil/doctrine/new_pubs/jp1_02.pdf, accessed on March 1, 2010.

[2]Department of Defense Dictionary of Military and Associated Terms. Joint Publication 1-02, (JP 1-02), Department of Defense. Washington, D.C., October 2009, available online at: http://www.dtic.mil/doctrine/new_pubs/jp1_02.pdf, accessed on March 1, 2010.

CYBERSPACE AS A WARFIGHTING DOMAIN

From the birth of powered aviation in 1903, it was only fifteen years to the World War One battle of St. Mihiel, which involved the first mass operation of airpower during wartime. We are now rapidly approaching the 30th anniversary of the Internet and yet we have not yet had large-scale, coordinated military operations conducted to control cyberspace. As noted by the United States Air Force in the mid-1990s:

> Before the Wright brothers, air, while it obviously existed, was not a realm suitable for practical, widespread, military operations. Similarly, information existed before the Information Age, but the Information Age changed the information realm's characteristics so that widespread operations became practical.[3]

Just as aerodynamics drive military operations in the air, so do the physical and logical laws of cyberspace define military operations in that domain. Recognizing that understanding of cyberspace has changed, the *National Military Strategy for Cyber Operations* has put forth a military strategic framework that orients and focuses the actions of the Department of Defense in areas of intelligence, military and business operations in and through cyberspace. It defines cyberspace as "a domain characterized by the use of electronics and the use of the electromagnetic spectrum to store, modify and exchange data via networked systems and associated physical infrastructures."[4] Though cyberspace is fairly well understood as a warfighting domain there are a few key aspects that help us to better examine the role of offensive operations. Cyberspace is

1. Logical but physical;
2. Usually used, owned, and controlled predominantly by the private sector;
3. Tactically fast but operationally slow;
4. A domain in which the offense generally dominates the defense; and
5. Fraught with uncertainty.

Logical but physical. Though a warfighting domain, cyberspace has some striking differences from the other domains. "Unlike the land, sea, air and space where the laws of physics do not change, cyberspace is a man-made creation that continually changes and evolves."[5] However, it is not infinitely mutable. Cyberspace is physical because the information that transits through it is grounded in the physical infrastructure that creates and stores it and the physical infrastructure that gave rise to the domain is generally housed within states' borders. Cyberspace is also logical, as the information that transits through it, goes through on agreed-upon routing protocols. Certain logical aspects of cyberspace such as the functioning of open source code have no clear ownership, geographic basis or locus of responsibility. As described by Lawrence Lessig, cyberspace is governed by "laws of code" which are man-made and designed to achieve a wide variety of purposes.[6] This emergent synthesis of physical and logical attributes means that offensive operations can cross borders at great speed but with affects that are more likely to be reversible than other kinds of military attacks, as they often don't have actual physical impacts, such as destroying equipment or causing casualties.

This logical-physical disconnect is one of the reasons why cyber attacks thus far have tended to have effects that are either (1) widespread but limited in duration or (2) persistent but narrowly focused. Few attacks, if any, have so far been *both* widespread and persistent. We do note that the possibility of cyber attacks which cause physical destruction of equipment and cause events in physical space that

[3]Department of the Air Force. Cornerstones of Information Warfare, Department of Defense. Washington DC, 1995, available at http://www.iwar.org.uk/iwar/resources/usaf/iw/corner.html, accessed on March 1, 2010.

[4]Chairman of the Joint Chiefs of Staff. National Military Strategy for Cyber Operations. Department of Defense, December 2006, available at http://www.dod.gov/pubs/foi/ojcs/07-F-2105doc1.pdf, accessed on March 2, 2010.

[5]"Defending IT: Words from the New Military Cyber Commander." Gov Info Security, June 24, 2009, available at http://www.govinfosecurity.com/articles.php?art_id=1575, accessed April 10, 2010.

[6]Lessig, Lawrence. 1999. Code and Other Laws of Cyberspace. New York, NY: Basic Books.

result in deaths and possibly mass casualties does exist. So far, the known occurrences of such attacks have been highly limited.

Because of the current state of the logical and physical laws which govern cyberspace, attribution of particular attacks may be difficult, though it needn't rule out determining a particular nation responsible regardless of the technical attribution. Additionally, as the laws of code, technology and obligations of operators of cyberspace evolve, progress may well occur improving the attribution of attacks occurring within or from cyberspace.

Usually used, owned, and controlled predominantly by the private sector. Future conflicts in cyberspace are very likely to be won or lost in the private sector, which runs, owns, and depends on the underlying networks and information, at least in the most advanced economies. America does not primarily depend on cyberspace to support the U.S. military—it is one of the underlying engines of our economic advantages and productivity as well as a key way to export our culture of freedoms. Offensive operations undertaken by the U.S. military must consider that we could have much more to lose than to gain.

Similarly, when military planners consider conflicts in cyberspace, they often use metaphors from their own military service which may serve them poorly in the privately owned cyberspace. Consider aerial warfare: there is a lot of sky out there and very few aircraft, especially in a warzone. Pilots can "slip the surly bonds of earth,"[7] confident they will have little interaction with civilians and, if they do, the Air Forces will be in control. Nothing could be more different in offensive cyber operations. As soon as a military mission is "wheels up" from the base, it is likely to be transiting in some measure through a system owned, controlled, and used, by the private sector including in transit across global commons between international borders in undersea cables or through satellites. The targets of our offensive operations could include private sector targets and the attacks of our adversaries are even more likely to do so, hoping for asymmetric attacks against poorly defended targets.

Tactically fast but operationally slow. Cyberspace, where the computer is the battlefield, is widely considered to be an operational environment through which an attacker can strike with minimal investment while yielding potentially large-scale effects with great speed. While it is true that individual attacks can happen quickly—"approaching the speed of light" we are often assured[8]—the planning cycle for each attack to achieve a specific military effect is likely to be far longer than that. Cyberattack planning may take more time and effort than use of conventional forces due to the complexity of the environment and the targeted systems. Moreover, even well planned military attacks can have very transient effects. In past conflicts, to have a persistent strategic impact, an adversary needed to apply continuous pressure, to re-attack as the defenders repair damage, substitute for the disrupted goods or services, and re-establish themselves. There is little reason in this regard to believe that conflict in cyberspace will be different. The implication is that cyber wars, rather than consisting of a single, sharp attack, may instead be a long serious of tactical engagements, as part of larger operations, or as part of a larger campaign.

Fraught with uncertainty. Cyberspace is an extremely complex environment, characterized by rapid change and adaption, whose direction is difficult to predict. Though present in conventional warfare, uncertainty of effects is especially prevalent, and is often the dominant state, in conflict in cyberspace. This uncertainty stems from a variety of sources, as has been discussed in detail in the National Research Council report *Technology, Policy, Law, and Ethics Regarding the U.S. Acquisition and Use of Cyberattack Capabilities.*[9] In short, not only is there great uncertainty due to the normal fog and friction of military operations, but cyberspace also has particular challenges: rapid changes in the domain,

[7]Gillespie, Magee Jr. High Flight. Great Aviation Quotes, available at http://www.skygod.com/quotes/highflight.html, accessed on July 27, 2010.

[8]As is expressed on page 3 of: Chairman of the Joint Chiefs of Staff. National Military Strategy for Cyber Operations. Department of Defense, December 2006, available at: http://www.dod.gov/pubs/foi/ojcs/07-F-2105doc1.pdf, accessed on March 2, 2010.

[9]National Research Council. 2009. Technology, Policy, Law, and Ethics Regarding the U.S. Acquisition and Use of Cyberattack Capabilities. Owens, William A., Kenneth W. Dam, and Herbert S. Lin, eds. Washington, D.C.: National Academies Press.

insufficient knowledge of targets and dynamics, and uncertainty of cascading effects. This uncertainty imposes great demands on a military commander looking to use offensive cyber operations in a strictly controlled manner, as with any other application of force. The needs for intelligence support, target preparation, understanding of second and third order effects, and political and legal wavering make that commander's choice to rely on offensive cyber operations not as straightforward as it may seem at first. The challenges have been addressed in depth in *Strategic Warfare in Cyberspace*[10] as well as numerous studies conducted by the Department of Defense.

Ultimately, the inability to thoroughly plan and predict in cyberspace makes it difficult to achieve specific objectives through offensive cyber operations and seems to be one of the main brakes on more operational use of offensive operations.[11]

CATEGORIZING OFFENSIVE MISSIONS

Many previous attempts to categorize offensive cyber capabilities have focused understandably on what is new in the cyber domain. For example, cyber capabilities have often been categorized technically, such as the previous National Academy of Sciences paper[12] which looked at techniques for remote access (such as botnets, penetrations, worms and viruses, and protocol compromises) and close access (like compromising the supply chain or patch process). The United States Air Force was perhaps the first military organization to officially translate these technical categories into military operational terms.

In 1995, the Secretary and Chief of Staff of the Air Force signed out an official White Paper called *Cornerstones of Information Warfare*[13] which started the process of integrating cyber effects into defined military operations by listing "information attack" alongside physical attack and defining it as "directly corrupting information without visibly changing the physical entity within which it resides." This went several steps further in 1998 with new Air Force doctrine[14] which codified new missions of information warfare (that is, not just cyber) in parallel with those of more typical aerial warfare:

> Offensive counterinformation (OCI) includes actions taken to control the information environment. OCI operations are designed to limit, degrade, disrupt, or destroy adversary information capabilities . . .

> Defensive counterinformation (DCI) includes those actions that protect information, information systems, and information operations from any potential adversary.

This new Air Force doctrine made several key points on this new construct, including noting that "while the analogy is not perfect, there are strong parallels and airmen can apply many of the hard-won precepts of OCA-DCA to OCI-DCI." This statement helped tie what might be new in the cyber domain to the institutional lessons the Air Force had learned in its first fifty years.

Just as relevant to modern cyber operations, the Air Force was presciently highlighting that "the dividing line between [the offense and defensive missions of OCI and DCI] can be exceedingly thin and the transition nearly instantaneous." This rapid transition between defense and offense underlies the current direction of cyber conflict in the United States military with its increasing focus on "response actions" or "dynamic defense" to use more muscular methods to stop attacks.

---

[10]Rattray, Gregory J. 2001 Strategic Warfare in Cyberspace. Cambridge MA: MIT Press.

[11]For example, see Markoff, John, and Thom Shanker. Halted '03 Iraq Plan Illustrates U.S. Fear of Cyberwar Risk. *New York Times* online, available at http://www.nytimes.com/2009/08/02/us/politics/02cyber.html, accessed on 26 July 2010. Also see Nakashima, Ellen. Dismantling of Saudi-CIA Web Site Illustrates Need for Clearer Cyberwar Policies. *Washington Post* online, available at http://www.washingtonpost.com/wp-dyn/content/article/2010/03/18/AR2010031805464.html.

[12]National Research Council. 2009. Technology, Policy, Law, and Ethics Regarding the U.S. Acquisition and Use of Cyberattack Capabilities. Owens, William A., Kenneth W. Dam, and Herbert S. Lin, eds. Washington, D.C.: National Academies Press.

[13]Department of the Air Force. *Cornerstones of Information Warfare*, Department of Defense, Washington DC, 1995, available at http://www.iwar.org.uk/iwar/resources/usaf/iw/corner.html, accessed on March 1, 2010.

[14]Department of the Air Force. Air Force Doctrine Document 2-5: Information Operations (AFDD 2-5). Department of Defense, Washington, D.C., 1998, available at http://www.dtic.mil/doctrine/jel/service_pubs/afd2_5.pdf, accessed April 3, 2010.

These terms of OCI and DCI were not widely used (and have been since dropped[15]), soon displaced after by new terms approved in 1998[16] by the Chairman of the Joint Chiefs of Staff, and therefore applicable to all the military services. These terms remain in very common use and are still official joint doctrine[17]: Computer Network Attack (CNA), Exploitation (CNE) and Defense (CND).

Though these concepts brought needed doctrinal stability for over a decade, they did not have the same institutional parallels of offensive and defensive counterinformation. They categorized but they did not resonate, cutting off further deep thinking into how military operations in cyber conflict may differ or be similar to traditional missions and doctrines. The following is an illustrative list[18] of how such borrowed, customized doctrinal terms might help categorize military cyber missions (in each case, the definitions are from official Joint doctrine[19] with additions in italics):

- **Counter** *cyber*[20]: A mission that integrates offensive and defensive operations to attain and maintain a desired degree of *cyber* superiority.
- *Cyber* **interdiction:** An action to divert, disrupt, delay, or destroy the enemy's military cyber ~~surface~~ capability before it can be used effectively against friendly forces, or to otherwise achieve objectives.[21]
- **Close** *cyber* **support:** *Cyber* action against hostile targets' *information systems* that are in close proximity to friendly forces and that require detailed integration of each *cyber* mission with the fire and movement of those forces.
- *Cyber* **reconnaissance in force:** An offensive *cyber* operation *conducted by military (not intelligence) forces* designed to discover and/or test the enemy's strength or to obtain other information.
- **Suppression of enemy** *cyber* **defenses:** Activity that neutralizes, destroys, or temporarily degrades enemy *cyber* defenses by destructive and/or disruptive means.
- **Strategic** *cyber* **mission:** A mission directed against one or more of a selected series of enemy *cyber* targets with the purpose of progressive destruction and disintegration of the enemy's warmaking capacity and will to make war.

CATEGORIZING OFFENSIVE OPERATIONS

Offensive cyber operations (as distinct from their missions, above) can be categorized according to a number of factors. This list is neither mutually exclusive nor collectively exhaustive—indeed some even overlap or imply one another. Instead, these have been chosen as they seem to shed the most light in distinguishing between different kinds of offensive operations and ways that a cyber war might be fought, as analyzed in later sections of this paper. These key factors are summarized in the list below and briefly described after that:

---

[15]Department of the Air Force. Air Force Doctrine Document 2-5: Information Operations (AFDD 2-5). Department of Defense, Washington, D.C., 1998, available at http://www.dtic.mil/doctrine/jel/service_pubs/afd2_5.pdf, accessed April 3, 2010.

[16]Joint Publication 3-13, Joint Doctrine for Information Operations. Department of Defense, Washington, D.C., 1998, available at http://hqinet001.hqmc.usmc.mil/pp&o/PLN/Files/Op%20Planning%20Policies%20Procedures/Planning%20Process%20Dev/JP%203-13%20Joint%20Doctrine%20for%20Info%20Operations.pdf, accessed on March 7, 2010.

[17]Joint Publication 3-13, Joint Doctrine for Information Operations. Department of Defense. Washington, D.C., 2006, available at http://www.fas.org/irp/doddir/dod/jp3_13.pdf, accessed March 7, 2010.

[18]The authors are encouraged by the understanding that such an effort is currently underway within the Joint Staff, though any results will be published after this paper.

[19]Joint Publication 1-02 (JP 1-02): Dictionary of Military and Associated Terms. Department of Defense. Washington, D.C., October 2009, available online at: http://www.dtic.mil/doctrine/new_pubs/jp1_02.pdf, accessed on March 1, 2010.

[20]Please note, the crossed out text represents the word taken out and are not an editorial artifact.

[21]The Air Force, in *Cornerstones*, used this term back in 1995 explaining that "One approach to interdiction is wrecking bridge spans using laser-guided bombs. Alternatively, we might be able to alter the adversary's planners' information, falsely categorizing the bridges as destroyed, causing [them] to reroute forces and supplies."

Nature of Adversaries	Openness
Nature of Targets	Context
Target Physicality	Campaign Use
Integrated with Kinetic	Initiation Responsibility and Rationale
Scope of Effect	Initial Timing
Intended Duration	Initiation Attack

Nature of adversaries. Are the offensive operations being carried out by nation states on one side, both, or neither? If one or both adversaries are non-state groups, is there national encouragement or backing for one or both?[22] The nature of states' relationships with surrogate groups conducting offensive cyber operations has become one of the most significant and challenging aspects of understanding who is conducting offensive cyber operations. As a result, establishing effective deterrent and conflict management strategies in this environment remains challenging.

Nature of targets. Is the offensive operation against a military target, civilian target, or a dual-use target somewhere in between? This classification overlaps significantly with the nature of adversaries (above) when the offensive operation is a single attack—especially if it has tactical and short-term effects. For example, if an attack is looking to shut down power to a particular part of rail switching yard, then the target is civilian and the defender is the operator of that electrical system. However, if the offensive operations are part of a larger campaign (see below), especially if they are conducted over time, then it is likely that the adversaries are the nation states themselves. Even if particular targets may be operated by the private sector, nation-state governments may bear responsibilities for defending the targeted systems and enterprises.

Target physicality. Is the attack targeting the logical (e.g., disrupt a software service), the cognitive (convince or disrupt an adversary using false information), or the physical (breaking a generator)? Attacks with real physical effects are rare but they do exist[23] and they are likely to be far less reversible than other attacks with logical or cognitive effects. We can change our minds quickly, but new generators need to be ordered, built, delivered, and installed. We know little about the duration or impact of possible data corruption attacks but such attacks are certainly technically possible and hold significant disruptive potential.

Integrated with kinetic. Is the attack intended to be integrated or simply coincident with kinetic attacks? This could include either military attack legally conducted by a nation state or attacks by a terrorist, or other non-state, group seeking to combine cyber and physical attacks to cause more damage and panic or grab more media attention.

Scope of effect. Is the offensive operation meant for a narrow tactical or technical purposes (like disabling a botnet), achieving deep strategic gains (such as coercing a nation to stay out of an impending conflict), or something operational in between? Because of the nature of cyber space, offensive cyber operations have, like airpower, the theoretical ability to directly affect adversary centers of gravity far from his national borders and fielded military forces. On the other hand, cyber attacks can also have precise effects, which can make them appropriate for targeted operations with very limited impact.

Intended duration. Is the attack meant to have transient and short term effects (e.g., distract an adversary radar operator for a few minutes) or instead be persistent and long term (e.g., disrupt electrical transmission for the duration of a months-long conflict)? Though the duration of effects is likely to strongly correlate to the desired scope of effect (see above) this does not have to be the case. For example, a cyberattack might be intended to have a very short effect but right before a U.S. election, in an attempt to sway the results—a very limited duration attack but with strategic consequences.

---

[22]Healey, Jason. 2010. A Vocabulary for National Responsibility for Cyber Attacks. Cyber Conflict Studies Association. Available at http://www.cyberconflict.org/about-the-ccsa-board/-a-vocabulary-for-national-responsibility-for-cyber-attacks, accessed July 29, 2010.

[23]Meserve, Jean. 2007. Sources: Staged Cyber Attack Reveals Vulnerability in Power Grid. CNN. Online. Available at http://www.cnn.com/2007/US/09/26/power.at.risk/index.html, accessed 26 July 2010.

Openness. Where does the offensive operation fall between being overt and covert? Though as a rule adversaries conducting espionage do not want to be identified, often the participants in offensive operations do not take as much time to cover their tracks. For example, the "patriotic hackers" who attacked the U.S. from China in 2001 or Estonia from Russia in 2007 spent less effort trying to be covert than the group behind the GhostNet intrusions attempting to track the activities of the Dali Lama and his followers.[24]

Context. Is the offensive operation being conducted as part of a wider increase in tensions—even war—between adversaries, or is the attack truly an "out of the blue" pre-emptive or surprise attack? In the kinetic world, offensive operations from a nation against another rarely, if ever, take place at times of low geopolitical tensions. Even "surprise" attacks, like the 1941 strike on Pearl Harbor (US) or 1904 attack on Port Arthur (Russia), both by the Imperial Japanese military, followed a long period of perceived encroachments and tensions.

Campaign use. Is the offensive operation meant to be a standalone tactical attack or part of a larger cyber operation and campaign? In the public mind, cyberattacks are hackers conducting one-off events of maliciousness, such as defacing a web page and it may even be tempting for cyber defenders to treat every attack as a discrete technical event. As noted in some of the other categorizations in this section, there are strong reasons for stand-alone attacks. However, in other domains, offensive operations are typically characterized by a campaign, composed of operations, each of which is a string of tactical engagements. See Attachment 2 for a discussion of this perspective of cyber warfare.

Initiation responsibility and rationale. Is the United States the first actor to use cyber weapons or has another adversary initiated the cyber conflict? The U.S. military might be most likely to initiate offensive cyber operations alongside kinetic operations while other adversaries might initiate cyber attacks early to try to gain an asymmetric advantage.

Initial timing. Is the use of offensive operations a surprise, a pre-emption to an expected incoming attack, or a counter-attack to a previous cyber or kinetic attack? A surprise attack is not just a first strike, but one strategically "out of the blue" while a pre-emption would be a first strike conducted in expectation of imminently receiving such an offensive attack. Counterattacks could be a response to a traditional kinetic offensive ("You bombed us so we'll disrupt your information.") or an earlier cyberattack ("Hack *us*? Hack *this*. . .").

Initiation attack. If part of a campaign, are the offensive operations characterized by a massive initial set of strikes with many separate attacks? Or do the offensive operations build over time? Some theorists and movie script writers imagine a wave of attacks that debilitate the targeted adversary, whether a nation, company, or group. This is not the only tempo for an offensive cyber campaign, however, as graduated attacks could engage more targets with more profound effects over a course of weeks or months, similar to the aerial bombing of Yugoslavia as part of Operation Allied Force in 1999.

HOW MIGHT CYBER WARS BE FOUGHT?

One working definition for a "cyber war" is when between nations or groups there is an extended set of offensive operations that are each equivalent in effect to armed attacks conducted by militaries. If it is not an extended set of attacks, then given the transient nature of most certain cyber effects—the engagement is likely to be over fairly quickly, perhaps more akin to a natural disaster than a conflict. Similarly, any attacks with less than "effects equivalent to armed attacks" would not be similar enough to what militaries think of as warfare—even irregular warfare. If nations are at war, they get to stab the enemy, legally, and even civilian deaths can be acceptable if within the laws of armed conflict.

---

[24]Chinese Hack Into Indian Embassies, Steal Dalai Lama's Documents. 2009. Economic Times. Online. Available at http://economictimes.indiatimes.com/News/PoliticsNation/Chinese-hack-into-Indian-embassies-steal-Dalai-Lamas-documents/articleshow/4329579.cms, accessed 20 June 2010.

If this is an adequate description of cyber war, then the world has apparently not yet had one. So to think about how cyber wars might be fought, we have to use alternate methods of analysis. In the section above, this paper laid out ten characteristics of offensive operations, which can be combined to define characteristics of differing ways that cyber wars might be fought. For the next section, this paper will extend these ten characteristics to some well known, and less well known, analogies for cyber war.

This paper will start by tackling the two most often used analogies to think about cyber warfare. Newspapers splash headlines with "cyber Pearl Harbor" and "cyber 9/11," often using them interchangeably. However, both are handles that represent extremely different ways to employ force, which this paper will examine. The section after that will introduce several new analogies that capture additional possible ways cyber wars may be initiated and fought.

"Cyber Pearl Harbor" (or Surprise Attack by Military versus Military)

The Japanese attack on the U.S. military at Pearl Harbor on December 7, 1941 was a surprise attack during a period of high tensions that hoped to either dissuade the United States from engaging in protracted conflict in the Pacific theater or make that engagement at timing and terms greatly in the Japanese favor.[25]

A cyber Pearl Harbor, or "PearlHarbor.com" (see Table 1) might then be an initial, massive, integrated cyber offensive against the U.S. military in the hopes of quick strategic success, for example perhaps to coerce the United States or limit its ability to fight an upcoming conventional fight. This attack might be a tactical surprise but would be part of a larger geopolitical context of increasing tension and expectations of possible future combat.

One overlooked factor in discussions of a "cyber Pearl Harbor" is that it was just the opening strike of a larger campaign by the Japanese across the Pacific (including the Philippine Islands, Guam and Wake in the "eastern plan," and Hong Kong, Singapore, and other attacks as part of a "southern plan"). Moreover, these initial attacks were just the opening campaign of World War Two in the Pacific theater, a four-plus-year-long conflict that directly resulted from the sunken ships at Battleship Row. Likewise, any "cyber Pearl Harbor" could be reasonably expected to have the United States not succumb to coercion and angrily respond with all elements of national power.

So "cyber Pearl Harbors" can reasonably be expected to be followed by a major war, perhaps a traditional and kinetic war, possibly also though by a mix of major kinetic and cyber attacks (see "Cyber St. Mihiel" below) or an all-cyber fight (see "Cyber Battle of Britain" below). Of course, in that larger fight, the United States may not be again as talented and lucky as during the early 1940s, when Navy cryptographers could read the adversary's codes. However, any state adversary conducting such a massive surprise attack on the U.S. military must know that retaliation could come with devastating kinetic firepower even without 100% confidence of where the attack originated from. Non-state actors present a more challenging proposition in terms of retaliation. The 2003 U.S. *National Strategy to Secure Cyberspace* explicitly takes this approach in stating that "when a nation, terrorist group, or other adversary attacks the United States through cyberspace, the U.S. response need not be limited to criminal prosecution. The United States reserves the right to respond in an appropriate manner. The United States will be prepared for such contingencies."[26]

If there were a cyber Pearl Harbor against the United States, then obviously this kind of deterrence measure was clearly not enough to prevent the attack. The adversary may have judged its attack would be so successful the United States would be unable to withstand it, and would capitulate. However, deterrence might be able to limit the escalation, such as limiting the scope or lethality of follow-on attacks.

---

[25]Summary Report. U.S. Strategic Bombing Survey. Washington D.C., 1946, available at http://www.anesi.com/ussbs01.htm, accessed April 20, 2010.

[26]National Strategy to Secure Cyberspace. The White House. Washington, D.C., 2003, available at http://www.us-cert.gov/reading_room/cyberspace_strategy.pdf, accessed March 3, 2010.

Table 1: Analogy: "Cyber Pearl Harbor"

Nature of adversaries	Military versus military
Nature of targets	Military
Target physicality	Any
Integrated with kinetic	Any
Scope of effect	Strategic
Intended duration	Long-term
Openness	Fully overt
Context	Surprise during tensions
Campaign use	Larger campaign
Initiation responsibility	U.S. defending
Initiation timing	Surprise
Initiation attack	Massive

Table 2: Analogy: "Cyber 9/11"

Nature of adversaries	Non-state versus State
Nature of targets	Civilian
Target physicality	Any
Integrated with kinetic	Any
Scope of effect	Operational
Intended duration	Medium-term
Openness	Partially covert
Context	Surprise
Campaign use	Stand alone
Initiation responsibility	U.S. defending
Initiation timing	Surprise
Initiation attack	Massive

"Cyber 9/11" (or Surprise Attack by Non-State Versus Civilian Targets)

Though a "cyber Pearl Harbor" and "cyber 9/11" (see Table 2) seem to be used interchangeably, they would not be similar. The attacks on Pearl Harbor targeted the U.S. military and were conducted by a foreign military in a time of rising international tensions whereas the attacks on September 11, 2001 were conducted by non-state actor—the terrorist group Al Qaeda—and targeted civilians and civilian infrastructure. The U.S. response to both these attacks also led to a protracted military campaign fought both conventionally and unconventionally, this time against Afghanistan, which, nine years later, is still ongoing.

A "cyber 9/11" then would be an attack by a non-state actor attempting to destroy or disrupt key civilian infrastructure to result in catastrophe, perhaps across several sectors and simultaneously in several locations. However, as occurred after the real 9/11 when international public and legal opinion swung overnight,[27] America might be able to hold a nation responsible for a non-national group acting from its national soil possibly leading to longer-term conventional and unconventional military campaigns.

The damage from the real 9/11 was tragic, but the economic impact, although significant, was less than expected, ranging from GDP losses of $35 billion to $109 billion or between 0.5 percent and 1 percent of the GDP[28]) and limited, even in the short-term, as the New York Stock Exchange was closed for only four days.[29] This is likely also to be the case after a cyber 9/11, as typically disruptions from cyberattacks are either widespread or catastrophic but not both. So large-scale cyber disruptions might have severe impacts for a week, or even two, after which the economy may return to normal as indeed happened after 9/11 and other catastrophes like the volcanic air disruptions of 2010, Asia-wide earthquake-induced undersea cable outages in 2006, and the Northeast blackout of 2003.

In a classic cyber 9/11, the adversary would be a non-state actor, such as a terrorist group, attackers who may be difficult to deter from attacking by threatening punishing cyberattacks in return. It would be very difficult to attribute a large non-state attack with enough precision to undertake a counterblow. Even if it could be done, the terrorists would have no assets they value that would be susceptible to significant disruption. Though deterrence with offensive cyber capabilities may not be credible, deterrence with physical force (as happened to Al Qaeda and the Taliban) may be more so if the actor's center of gravity such as operating bases and sanctuaries can be located. Attacking computer systems to make

---

[27]Public Opinion Six Months Later. 2002 The PEW Research Center for the People & the Press. Available at http://people-press.org/commentary/?analysisid=44, accessed July 27, 2010.

[28]From a January 2010 report by the University of Southern California and referenced at "Study: Economic Impact of 9/11 Was Short Lived." 2010. NBC Los Angeles. Available at http://www.nbclosangeles.com/news/business/Study-bin-Ladens-Strategy-Was-Short-Lived.html, accessed April 2010.

[29]History of the New York Stock Exchange. NYSE Euronext. Available at http://www.nyse.com/about/history/timeline_2000_Today_index.html, accessed May 2010.

money or for kicks may be popular amongst hackers, but few would either want to cause significant damage and fewer still would be willing to face violent death or being a prisoner at Guantanamo Bay.

Though these two analogies, of Pearl Harbor and 9/11 are the most popular, there are a number of other ways that offensive operations could unfold. According, this section examines these and, where appropriate, draws a historical analogy. These additional five scenarios are not, of course, the only possibilities and perhaps are not even the likeliest, of how offensive operations fit into national military strategy and tactics. However, they are particularly illustrative of the possibilities and spotlight an additional framework for positing future cyber conflicts.

Covert Cyber Operations

Because of the difficulty of attribution, cyberattacks seem to lend themselves strongly to covert operations, whether by the United States or other states or adversaries, as a third option between "doing nothing (the first option) in a situation in which vital interests may be threatened and sending in military force (the second option)."[30] (See Table 3.) Even if the attack is detected and attributed to the nation of origin, the low barrier of entry for cyber attack capability always gives some level of plausible deniability.

Accordingly, it may be that the future of cyber conflict is not equivalent to larger, theater-level warfare but only to select covert attacks which could range across a wide set of goals and targets. It is plausible that every step of the "covert action ladder"[31] could be undertaken through offensive cyber operations: propaganda (least violent and most plausibly deniable) through political activity, economic activity, coups and paramilitary operations (most violent and least deniable). As these have been well-covered already in previous work by the National Academies,[32] they will not be repeated here.

Deterring covert operations would only be credible if attribution could pierce the veil of "plausible deniability." This may be difficult in many situations, especially if the standard of proof needs to be particularly high, such as to counterstrike. For many responses, though, less than perfect attribution may be "good enough." The attacked nation might privately threaten retribution to the suspected party or release sufficient details and suspicions to publicly smear them in the international press. This should be considered plausible as it parallels the responses to the GhostNet and Google cyber espionage cases, where non-state defenders went public with their details. This may not have achieved a completely successful deterrence effect against the presumed Chinese spies, but may be found in the future to have had some partial deterring effect on means, methods, targets, or frequency of attacks.

Direct Support for Special Operations

Unlike their use in a 9/11 or Pearl Harbor attack, offensive cyber operations could (even more easily) be used for very targeted, covert or clandestine attacks in support of special operations (see Table 4). For example, offensive operations could disable alarms or even create enough false alarms that operators learn to disregard the information on their screens. Likewise, voice-over-IP networks would be open to short term disruption to keep defenders from raising alarms or coordinating their defenses.

Gaining access is a critical first step for offensive cyber operations, so an attack in support of special operations may be characterized by unique access methods, not just over the Internet but also those enabled by corrupting a supply chain, the help of an insider, or having the special operators themselves use their physical access to the target to gain access to the target systems.

---

[30]Lowenthal, Mark M. 2008. Intelligence: From Secrets to Policy. Washington, D.C.: CQ Press. P 165.

[31]Lowenthal, Mark M. 2008. Intelligence: From Secrets to Policy. Washington, D.C.: CQ Press. P 170.

[32] See section 4.2 of the NAS study: Owens, William A., Kenneth W. Dam, and Herbert S. Lin. 2009. Technology, Policy and Law Regarding the U.S. Acquisition and Use of Cyber Capabilities. Washington, D.C.: National Academies Press.

Table 3: Covert Cyber Operations

Nature of adversaries	Intel versus any
Nature of targets	Any
Target physicality	Any
Integrated with kinetic	Any
Scope of effect	Any
Intended duration	Any
Openness	Covert
Context	Tension
Campaign use	Any
Initiation responsibility	U.S. initiating or defending
Initiation timing	Surprise or pre-emptions
Initiation attack	Limited

Table 4: Special Operations Support

Nature of adversaries	Military versus any
Nature of targets	Any
Target physicality	Any
Integrated with kinetic	Fully integrated
Scope of effect	Tactical
Intended duration	Short-term
Openness	Covert
Context	Surprise
Campaign use	Stand alone
Initiation responsibility	U.S. initiating or defending
Initiation timing	Any
Initiation attack	Massive

Furthermore, as more control systems and voice systems move to IP networks—making them more accessible in a wider range of conditions—the possibility for such surgical cyber support for teams working quietly in foreign countries seems strong. Obviously, because of the nature of these operations, the general public may never hear about these operations if conducted by the U.S. military. If an adversary conducted such a covert or clandestine attack, even the U.S. military or the targets of the attack itself may not know an attack has happened.

These cyberattacks would be difficult or impossible to deter by punishment, as the main effort of the attacker is the kinetic action of the commandos, which the cyber effect only enables.

"Cyber St. Mihiel" (or Operational Support for Traditional, Kinetic Military Operations)

St. Mihiel was the first mass operation of airpower during wartime, when in 1918 then-Colonel Billy Mitchell organized nearly 1500 aircraft in a synchronized campaign[33] to support one of the first solo U.S. offensives of World War One.

Though there have been Information Operations cells as part of military commands since the mid-1990s,[34] cyberattacks in support of military operations known cases of such operations are limited in number and not part of large-scale operations. However, in the future it could be that cyber conflict has an equivalent of St. Mihiel where cyber forces engage heavily, on both offense and defense, in support of more traditional military operations (see Table 5).

In such a scenario, computer network defenses fight off attacks to maintain U.S. communications, abetted by counterforce computer network attacks to suppress adversary offenses. Other computer network attacks could be used to disrupt critical infrastructure, such as the adversary's telecommunications centers, which would enable the offense to disrupt and delay the transit of information of the opposing military, and potentially disrupt or even destroy the command and control networks. Computer network exploitation missions might ensure access to key information like troop movements, learning the adversary commander's decisions and intent, combat assessment for kinetic and cyber strikes, and helping to direct new kinetic and cyber attacks to the enemy's weakest points.

In some cases, the adversary may have cyber capabilities to shoot back, but at other times, it may be that one side has superiority of the cyber domain. Either way, cyber deterrence not only has failed, but also is likely to remain of second importance to controlling the kinetic fight. It may still have a role though, especially if patriot hackers and copycat attacks confuse each side's national leaders, potentially derailing conflict resolution.

---

[33]Lt Col George M. Lauderbaugh. The Air Battle of St. Mihiel: Air Campaign Planning Process Background Paper. Airpower Research Institute. Online. Available at http://www.au.af.mil/au/awc/awcgate/ww1/stmihiel/stmihiel.htm, accessed May 2010.

[34]Maj Gen Gary Pounder, USAF. 2000. "Opportunity Lost." Aerospace Power Journal. Available at http://www.airpower.maxwell.af.mil/airchronicles/apj/apj00/sum00/pounder.htm, accessed July 26, 2010.

Table 5: Analogy: "Cyber St. Mihiel"

Nature of adversaries	Military versus military
Nature of targets	Any
Target physicality	Any
Integrated with kinetic	Fully integrated
Scope of effect	Operational
Intended duration	Medium-term
Openness	Overt
Context	Existing state of war
Campaign use	Campaign
Initiation responsibility	U.S. attacking and defending
Initiation timing	Attack or counter-attack
Initiation attack	Any

Table 6: Analogy: "Cyber Battle of Britain"

Nature of adversaries	State versus state
Nature of targets	Any
Target physicality	Any
Integrated with kinetic	None
Scope of effect	Strategic
Intended duration	Long-term
Openness	Overt
Context	Hostilities
Campaign use	Campaign
Initiation responsibility	U.S. attacking and defending
Initiation timing	All
Initiation attack	Any

"Cyber Battle of Britain" (or Overt Force-on-Force Cyber Conflict with Near-Peer Nation)

The Battle of Britain was the series of aerial campaigns fought between the Axis (predominantly Germany) and the British in 1940. The first large-scale contest between air forces, the German goal was originally to enable an invasion of the British Isles through attacks on ports and convoys. This targeting shifted over time to focus on the Royal Air Force before moving to direct attacks against key cities through terror bombing. In the end, these attacks meant to inflict strategic damage, either through a collapse of national morale and unity or through direct economic damage from destroyed infrastructure. The British goals were primarily defensive, to stop the German attacks, through a mix of defensive engagements combined with their own offensive strikes. This air war was fought largely independently from the fight in other domains and theaters.

The analogous conflict in cyberspace would be a standalone, overt cyber battle or war between nations, fought entirely within the domain of cyberspace and fully engaging each side's cyber attackers and defenders (probably both in government and the private sector) (see Table 6). Though tactical engagements might take place "at the speed of light" these would be mere dogfights in the context of the larger fight, with complete operations as part of offensive and defensive campaigns. A cyber Battle of Britain may develop slowly, through various phases (as did the original, 70 years ago) moving up from smaller, less-organized attacks before blossoming into a full force-on-force unleashing of violence. Each side may be deterred from making larger cyber attacks (as the Germans originally forfeited attacking cities) but continue to one-up the other nation in a progression of violence.

Though deterrence will have failed to prevent the initiation of cyber hostilities and escalation, a cyber Battle of Britain could still provide successful escalation control. Each adversary in this conflict might choose to limit themselves to only non-kinetic operations for a number of reasons, but perhaps the most compelling would be that neither adversary would be willing to escalate from cyber force to kinetic. Even if the effects of the offensive cyber campaigns were equivalent to those from a kinetic armed attack (death or significant property destruction), escalation to kinetic operations could entail possibly unacceptable risks to both sides—from international opprobrium for going kinetic first or uncertainty of how the other side might further escalate.

For a more extended case study on the strategic air war over Europe and implications for offensive cyber operations, see Attachment 1.

Large, Covert Cyber Conflict with Near-Peer Nation

A cyber conflict need not be overt to be destructive. It is possible that two national adversaries may choose to engage in a long series of offensive operations that neither is willing to admit to publicly (though they may be more frank with each other) (see Table 7).

Table 7: Large, Covert Cyber Conflict

Nature of adversaries	Intel versus Intel
Nature of targets	Any
Target physicality	Any
Integrated with kinetic	No
Scope of effect	Any
Intended duration	Medium-term
Openness	Covert
Context	Tension
Campaign use	Campaign
Initiation responsibility	U.S. attacking and defending
Initiation timing	Attack or counter-attack
Initiation attack	Any

Table 8: Below-Legal Threshold Campaign

Nature of adversaries	State versus state
Nature of targets	Any
Target physicality	Logical
Integrated with kinetic	No
Scope of effect	Strategic
Intended duration	Long-term
Openness	Overt
Context	Tension
Campaign use	Campaign
Initiation responsibility	Any
Initiation timing	Any
Initiation attack	Gradual

For example, here is one plausible (though certainly not probable) chain of events. The nation of Zendia has been conducting long-term and massive computer espionage against Ruritania, which is unable to stem the loss of information. The Ruritanian leadership, though unwilling to openly conduct counterattacks, authorizes covert offensive operations to dissuade the Zendians. After the first disruptions of manufacturing and electrical power, the Ruritanian leadership informs the Zendians that they were behind the attacks and provide credible proof, while continuing to deny it publicly. Instead of backing down, however, the Zendians conduct covert attacks of their own, disrupting logistics networks and financial transactions. Each side feels they were unfairly escalated against and continue retaliatory strikes, which are increasingly harsh while trying to retain plausible deniability.

A similar analogy may be the hot intelligence competition during the Cold War. The actions of spies and associated covert actions illustrate how two nations can fight in the shadows, maintain plausible deniability to the world (though the other side may know full well who was responsible), but still maintain tacit norms and boundaries. In the Cold War, an American agent might kill a Bulgarian or East German in the line of duty without significant retribution. But if a Russian were killed instead, the Americans would have been seen to have crossed a red line and would expect their own casualties in response.[35] In the cyber domain as much as the physical, tit-for-tat attacks had to be carefully measured, lest either side miscalculate and have a response be seen as an unwarranted escalation.

Understanding the correct retaliation is an exceptionally fine line, especially in cyber conflict, where the second- and third-order effects cannot be fully understood beforehand. A counterattack, even if precisely measured for a specific intent by an attacker, may be misunderstood by a defender and may have effects far worse than the attacker's intent.

Below-Legal Threshold Campaign

In the physical domains, there are many actions nations may take against each other that, while aggressive, fall beneath what the international community normally considers an "armed attack," the threshold set out by Article 51 of the United Nations Charter. These actions can take a range of forms including boycotts, broadcasts, stationing warships in international waters off the coast, increasing border patrols and improving defenses, missile tests, and large-scale exercises practicing an invasion.

It is possible that a nation would overtly use offensive cyber operations, kept similarly below the nebulous threshold of "armed attack," to coerce another nation (see Table 8). This may seem alluring to a nation's leadership, frustrated at the behavior of a rival; however any offensive operations kept deliberately below the threshold of armed attack may be more likely to be just a nuisance rather than a real challenge to coerce the adversary's leadership. This could mean a Below-Legal Threshold Campaign would be paired with a covert campaign. Of course, the nation on the receiving end of the sub-

[35]Discussion between author and Mark Lowenthal, 11 August 2010.

threshold overt attacks and over-threshold covert attacks would certainly suspect with a high degree of confidence which nation was behind both—and also attribute almost every other cyberattack from whatever source to their tormentor.

If the campaign were conducted over a long period of time or caused a certain amount of cumulative disruption it is possible the international community could decide it had become a de facto armed attack. This determination may not be a formal decision, such as the decision by the International Courts of Justice, but could be the consensus of international leaders and elite. Separately, democratic nations may have particular difficulties attempting to conduct a campaign of this type, as attacks would have to be crafted to not disrupt freedom of speech and diminish the moral authority of the attacking country.

"Cyber Vietnam" (or Long-term Irregular Warfare)

The Vietnam War was an extended irregular conflict, the first part of which was dominated by a guerilla war. The lightly armed Viet Cong insurgents fought asymmetrically—backed by the North Vietnamese regime—against the South Vietnamese and their American sponsors. Though the U.S. response was with traditional military forces, some units, such as the Special Forces, would attempt to engage the Viet Cong using guerilla-style tactics, albeit aided by more firepower and technology.[36]

An analogous irregular cyber conflict might involve few large-scale incidents with large-scale effects, but a continuing string of attrition attacks seeking to erode an adversary's power, influence, and will (see Table 9).[37] For example, an adversary (such as a group of Islamic radicals or extremist environmental or animal rights groups) could undertake only a handful of attacks in a year and whose effects may be very transient, disrupting operations of Wall Street for a day, or causing local blackouts of a few hours. However, these attacks could be significant enough to gain concessions from the U.S. government or get media attention for their political aims.

The targets of such offensive operations from a non-state adversary, like those of traditional guerillas, might target fielded military forces; headquarters or logistics; military and civilian institutions relied on by those forces (like payment systems); or prohibited targets like hospitals or schools; or civilians individually or en masse. Similarly, a nation state looking to fight an online guerilla war will be constrained from attacking these same targets sets.

A typical tactic of guerillas is to cause an overreaction from the other, more powerful, adversary as this can help push more people to supporting the guerillas' cause. Another is to ensure civilians are impacted directly or indirectly to force them to pressure their government to cease hostilities or influence the way the war is fought. In cyber conflict, these tactics could take the place of goading "hack-backs" of computers in neutral countries or against prohibited targets or attacks to coerce U.S. industries or individuals.

In a true "cyber Vietnam" the attacking group would also have the backing of a national sponsor, aiding and encouraging its campaigns, though possibly unwilling to commit their own cyber or traditional military forces. In this situation, nation states may attempt to re-establish some state-to-state responsibility especially for covert attacks.

A cyber guerilla campaign should not be mistaken for the acts of patriot hackers, conducting denial of service or defacements attacks for national reasons. These attacks hint at what a determined adversary might accomplish but fall far short of actual warfare.

Cyber Threat Removal

An offensive cyber operation might also be a small- or large- scale operation conducted to counter computers engaged in mass attacks (see Table 10). Such activities could be roughly analogous to naval

[36]Department of the Army. Appendix F: After Action Report: Operation Blackjack 33. U.S. Army Center of Military History. Available at http://www.history.army.mil/books/vietnam/90-23/90-23af.htm, accessed July 27, 2010.

[37]Department of Defense. 2007. Irregular Warfare Joint Operating Concept. Available at http://www.fas.org/irp/doddir/dod/iw-joc.pdf, accessed April 5, 2010.

Table 9: Analogy: "Cyber Vietnam"

Nature of adversaries	Non-state versus military
Nature of targets	Any
Target physicality	Any
Integrated with kinetic	Possible
Scope of effect	Any
Intended duration	Long-term
Openness	Overt
Context	Hostilities
Campaign use	Campaign
Initiation responsibility	U.S. attacking and defending
Initiation timing	Attack or counter-attack
Initiation attack	Any

Table 10: Cyber Threat Removal

Nature of adversaries	State versus any
Nature of targets	Any
Target physicality	Logical
Integrated with kinetic	No
Scope of effect	Technical
Intended duration	Short-term
Openness	Overt or covert
Context	Hostilities
Campaign use	Any
Initiation responsibility	Either
Initiation timing	Attack or counter-attack
Initiation attack	Any

operations against pirates that were common up until the 18th century and are becoming increasingly so in the 21st. In this scenario, a nation state would identify botnet zombies or controllers and use offensive operations to keep these offline. These attacks could be limited to "technical" counterattacks intended to counter specific adversaries, whether states, groups, or individuals. Instead they are focused on the means of the attack, the computers themselves.

Such an operation could be considered a counterattack if the nation were attacking botnets that were themselves targeting (or had targeted that nation); a pre-emptive move if there were intelligence that the nation would soon be a target; an initiating attack if none of those were true; or even a surprise attack if the nation did not announce the intention to carry out these kinds of attacks.

These attacks may be overt or covert and may or may not be part of an overall campaign. Some nations could in future decide to choose such operations as part of a persistent, constant presence to remove threats from cyberspace. It is highly unlikely that operations for cyber threat removal, whether a standalone engagement or part of a larger campaign, would be integrated with kinetic military operations. There may theoretically be a network so dangerous that offensive cyber operations would be teamed with Special Forces or kinetic covert action, but it is more likely, of course, that these cleanups would be integrated with law enforcement.

Deterrence would likely be very effective to dissuade threat-removal operations. If a nation clearly stated that it would see clean-ups of systems residing in its national borders as illegal or even acts of war, there likely would be far fewer such operations conducted than if such operations were conducted within the boundaries of more supportive nations (who might be convinced to see the cleaning up of the cyber commons as a public good).

CNE Campaign

A CNE Campaign would be a large-scale intelligence gathering campaign, probably by one nation (or the proxies of that nation) against the government or companies of another (see Table 11). Though this is a very likely kind of cyber conflict (and indeed may describe the current state of cyberspace), it is neither cyber warfare nor a use of offensive cyber operations, and so will not be given significant analysis in this paper and is included here only for completeness in describing possible future cyber conflicts. However, an effective CNE campaign is likely a critical enabler of many of the types of offensive operations described in this paper. Many of the key challenges regarding targeting, access and likely effects on targeted systems will be most directly addressed through the conduct of CNE.

FOR FURTHER RESEARCH AND CONCLUSION

This paper set out with the intention to outline important categories of offensive cyber operations and outline some ways cyber warfare might employ these capabilities. The framework here can be

Table 11: CNE Campaign

Nature of adversaries	State versus any
Nature of targets	Any
Target physicality	Logical
Integrated with kinetic	No
Scope of effect	Strategic
Intended duration	Not applicable
Openness	Covert
Context	Peacetime
Campaign use	Campaign
Initiation responsibility	U.S. spying or defending
Initiation timing	Not applicable
Initiation attack	Any

expanded with additional categories and trimming out of categories that lack power to analyze offensive operations as we have more empirical evidence about how these operations are conducted. Moreover, these analogies to how cyber wars might be fought are just a summary of a small subset of the possibilities. Further research can deepen the analysis of each of these analogies as well as add new analogies. Another potentially lucrative research path is utilizing the existing literature on coercive use of force to analyze how the frameworks, concepts and findings apply to cyber conflict, particularly as related to factors identified as underpinning the success or failure of cyber warfare.

Conflict in cyberspace—and offensive operations there—are new and novel, but as this paper has hopefully shown, traditional national security thinking can help illuminate the emerging issues. The ways to categorize offensive operations include adjectives typical also of modern kinetic military operations, such as whether the attack was a surprise, part of a larger campaign, or was covert or overt. Similarly, though "cyber 9/11" and "cyber Pearl Harbor" can have a deeper meaning than their popular associations, these handles can point how to apply military history and novel thinking to this new field.

ATTACHMENT 1: CYBER BATTLE OF BRITAIN

A complete, fully referenced exploration comparing the Battle of Britain to a future cyber conflict would require a separate full-length paper, so this attachment will cover only the most relevant points.

The Battle of Britain was the series of aerial campaigns fought between the Axis (predominantly Germany) and the British in 1940. This air war was the first large-scale contest between air forces and was fought largely independently from the war in other domains and theaters. The German goal was originally to enable an invasion of the British Isles through attacks on ports and convoys.[38] This targeting shifted over time to focus on the Royal Air Force before moving to direct attacks against key cities through terror bombing. In the end, these attacks meant to inflict strategic damage, either through a collapse of national morale and unity or through direct economic damage from destroyed infrastructure. The British goals were primarily defensive, to stop the German Air Force (Luftwaffe) attacks, through a mix of defensive engagements combined with their own offensive strikes both to stop the invasion (by destroying barges) but also deep strikes against Berlin, intended to target war-making capability. However, in response to the British attack against Berlin, the Germans countered with reprisal attacks against British cities.[39]

---

[38]Royal Air Force. The Battle of Britain. Available at http://www.raf.mod.uk/bob1940/phase1.html, accessed July 11, 2010.
[39]World War Two: Timeline 1939-1945, Fact File: the Baedeker Raids. BBC. Available at http://www.bbc.co.uk/ww2 peopleswar/timeline/factfiles/nonflash/a1132921.shtml?sectionId=4&articleId=1132921, accessed July 27, 2010.

Phases of Conflict

The original Battle of Britain was conducted nearly a year into formal hostilities by the combatants and the battles up to that point had been relatively conventional, in that there were not large-scale independent operations in the aerial domain. A cyber Battle of Britain need not follow either of those patterns, possibly being the opening battle without any earlier kinetic attacks. However, to follow the analogy more directly, the goals of the offense in such a battle would begin with a purely military operational focus, such as to enable or stop an invasion or coerce an adversary. The targets would be tied to the direct military objective. During the original Battle of Britain, the German objective was to invade so their original targets were ports and convoys.

However, if facing more difficult defenses than expected, the offensive cyber forces might shift targets, as the Luftwaffe did in mid-August (after a month of fruitless battles in the English Channel) to take the Royal Air Force on directly.[40] This phase of a cyber Battle of Britain would be a battle of attrition between offensive and defensive forces. In such a fight, either side might miscalculate its attacks and accidently prompt an escalation that neither side particularly wanted. After an attack on Berlin caused civilian casualties (mistakenly thought to be intentional), the Germans shifted to reprisal and terror attacks against civilian targets to defeat civilian morale. Unexpectedly, during this "Blitz" the populace of Britain became more cohesive, not less, and the shift gave relief to the RAF from the contest focused on the attrition of forces, which had been sorely pressed by attacks on their home airfields.[41]

Forces and Institutional Capability

As in an extended aerial campaign, in a cyber Battle of Britain success would favor the side with the most flexible employment of tactical and operational forces, especially if that side had a doctrine that most closely matched the conditions of the future battle.

Both the RAF and Luftwaffe entered the Battle of Britain with equipment and ideas based on pre-war doctrines that did not meet the needs of this new kind of warfare.[42] The British did not anticipate having to fight enemy fighters over their country, only bombers. Their resulting tactics were inflexible, locked into tight v-formations with only the leader free to scout for enemies. RAF commanders recognized this weakness but did not feel able to switch to more successful tactics in the middle of a key battle, meaning they were not as successful as they could have been had they correctly anticipated the nature of the coming air war. Similarly, German commanders, though with more appropriate fighter tactics, had not planned on long-term strategic bombing in favor of tactical bombing and close-air support to ground troops. Having underestimated the problems of strategic bombing campaigns, they assessed the entire aerial campaign would be over in weeks.[43] For both sides, weapons that made doctrinal sense did not perform as expected in actual warfare, such as for limited attack capability in force-on-force engagements (the RAF's Boulton Paul Defiance with no forward-facing guns) or unexpected vulnerability during unanticipated mission types (the Luftwaffe's Stukas).[44]

There will almost certainly be similar cascading doctrinal errors made by offensive and defensive cyber forces. For example, defenders may have expected deterrence to forestall any attacks or not planned properly to operate through disruptive attacks. Attackers might have a "cult of the offense," thinking that initial attacks would paralyze the defenders, making them incapable of successful defense,

[40]Royal Air Force. The Battle of Britain. Available at http://www.raf.mod.uk/bob1940/phase1.html, accessed July 11, 2010.

[41]The Blitz and World War Two. The History Learning Site. Available at http://www.historylearningsite.co.uk/blitz_and_world_war_two.htm, accessed July 28, 2010.

[42]Dye, Peter J. Logistics and the Battle of Britain. 2000. Air Force Journal of Logistics. Accessible at http://findarticles.com/p/articles/mi_m0IBO/is_4_24/ai_74582443/, accessed July 15, 2010.

[43]The Royal Air Force. The Battle of Britain: Background. Available at http://www.raf.mod.uk/bob1940/background.html, accessed 28 July 2010.

[44]Junkers-Ju 87. Academic Dictionaries and Encyclopedias. Available at http://en.academic.ru/dic.nsf/enwiki/10000, accessed July 27, 2010.

much less being able to counter with attacks of their own. Defenders may have underestimated the vulnerability of critical infrastructure targets protected by the private sector—or even overlooked their importance entirely. For a more detailed analysis of this dynamic between the lessons of aerial and cyber warfare, see *Strategic Warfare in Cyberspace* by Greg Rattray.

While attrition in aerial warfare is relatively easy to conceptualize (and measure) the concept also holds for cyber conflict. Each side would only have a certain number of trained "pilots" to handle offense and defense—these could easily be saturated. The attackers and defenders would also have a limited number of "airfields," "aircraft," and "bullets." These could be equivalent respectively to network capability, non-attributable attack hosts or botnets, and new exploits. Each of these resources can be replenished, in varying timeframes. Even more so than in aerial warfare, cyber operations favor the attacker. Defenders can be swamped with only one attack against a critical target, and so have a steeper exhaustion curve. A sophisticated adversary should be able to exhaust the defenders over time with comparatively less effort of their own.

Though the exhaustion curve of the offense may be less steep, the resources of attackers are not limitless and can be exhausted over time. Offensive forces may deplete their supply of new exploits to continue to inflict pain on the other side. Once an exploit is used, a skilled adversary would cover that defensive hole to make future, similar attacks difficult or impossible. In addition, there are fewer offensive operators, planners, and intelligence professionals than there are skilled defenders. The attacker's forces must balance these rare subject matter experts across their operational tempo, between combat assessment for yesterday's missions, conducting today's missions, and planning tomorrow's. Few nations would have the ability to surge a reserve to bring additional attacking forces to bear.

Key Enablers

The offense and defense in the Battle of Britain were enabled by a number of key factors, several of which might also have a cyber equivalent. Some of these factors are summarized in the list below:

- Ability to train weapon system operators and produce weapon systems. One factor to cessation of hostilities in 1940 was when the attacking Luftwaffe realized they could not destroy enough aircraft and factories to prevail.[45]
- Intelligence mismatch between offense and defense. The Germans had little targeting intelligence[46] to guide their next attacks and limited resources for battle damage assessment. Accordingly the offense could not adequately assess its past attacks or plan future missions whereas the defense had excellent situational awareness to detect and track incoming attacks.
- Strong defensive coordination that made the most of early warning and enabled operational flexibility to effectively counter attacks. A centralized command and control system with decentralized execution used advanced knowledge to counter attacks long before they reached their targets.
- Support crews to keep weapon systems operational with short turnaround times after each mission.

Defensive Coordination

The British held a decisive advantage with their "Dowding System"[47] to detect incoming attack formations and respond quickly and effectively. To detect attacks the British developed and employed both high-tech (radar) and low-tech (searchlights and observer corps) systems. Some elements, like the

---

[45]The Royal Air Force. The Battle of Britain: Background. Available at http://www.raf.mod.uk/bob1940/phase4.html, accessed July 27, 2010.

[46]"Battle of Britain." U.S. Centennial of Flight Commission. Available at http://www.centennialofflight.gov/essay/Air_Power/Battle_of_Britain/AP22.htm, accessed July 25, 2010.

[47]The Battle of Britain: The Dowding System. *Spiritus Temporis*. Available at http://www.spiritus-temporis.com/battle-of-britain/the-dowding-system.html, accessed July 21, 2010.

Chain Home radar stations, had to be set up well before the battle actually began while others developed over the course of the fight. For example, nearly a month into the battle a liaison unit was set up at Fighter Command to pass signals intelligence to fighter commanders.

The heart of this system was a central information center to gain comprehensive situational awareness based on all the incoming feeds, make quick assessments about the incoming attacks, and make defensive decisions, to be passed to operational commanders who would conduct their own interceptions.[48]

A defender in a cyber Battle of Britain, would have directly analogous needs, from equivalents radar (technology like deep-packet inspection at Tier 1 telecommunication providers to sense incoming attack) to observer corps (concerned users or companies reporting incidents to the government or information sharing centers). This information would have to pass to a command center empowered to see all the data and with sufficient authority to issue orders.

A cyber command center, for a cyber Battle of Britain, would present several tremendous disadvantages compared to the RAF's Fighter Command Headquarters. In a cyber conflict, attacks may target the private sector which may be outside of the military commander's authority. Accordingly there would have to be some way to pass situational awareness and coordinate defenses with key companies, including Tier 1 telecommunications providers, financial institutions, power companies and other likely targets. If the commanders don't hear about attacks because of a lack of sensors or the incident isn't reported (or even noticed), then there cannot be any Dowding-like coordination system or central defense. And while the RAF's operational commanders were able to issue orders to subordinate commands (under centralized control, decentralized execution), most Western nations lack any ability to issue orders to companies in the critical infrastructure sectors that would be the likely targets of attack. Few nations are likely to even have clear lines of authority to control their cyber defenses.

Moreover, the Germans did not know of the existence or the importance of most elements of the Dowding System so they were not countered, with the exception of some furtive strikes on radar stations, quickly abandoned as they were deemed not productive.[49] The command and control system may have been more fragile to dedicated attacks than airfields, if the Luftwaffe had had sufficiently good intelligence on its elements and locations. Cyber defenders in a cyber Battle of Britain may not be able to expect the same level of forbearance from their attackers. In many countries the major networks are well mapped and the major players known and basic emergency response plans published. All of these defensive elements are likely to be targeted early and often by a determined adversary.

Cessation of Hostilities

A cyber Battle of Britain may end the same way as the first one: the attacker realized it would not prevail and shifted its military attention to another adversary and theater, with no announcement, capitulation, or negotiation. If there were no other hostilities between the attacker and defender, this drift in a cyber conflict might mean each was willing to return to status quo ante especially if the attacks on either side were not catastrophic. The conflict could become a fight in the shadows, fought by intelligence forces stealing each other's secrets with periodic covert actions. Also, the two sides might just as easily decide on a more traditional agreement of armistice, though this may be hard to verify if there were copycat attacks or strikes by patriotic hacker.

Of course, the cyber force-on-force fight could expand into conventional, kinetic attacks. In this case, the offensive operations may take on a role more similar to a "cyber St. Mihiel," as airpower did after the Battle of Britain, taking on roles of intelligence, reconnaissance, or tactical and strategic strikes until there was a clear victor in the contest.

---

[48]The Battle of Britain: The Dowding System. *Spiritus Temporis*. Available at http://www.spiritus-temporis.com/battle-of-britain/the-dowding-system.html, accessed July 21, 2010.

[49]The Battle of Britain: The Dowding System. *Spiritus Temporis*. Available at http://www.spiritus-temporis.com/battle-of-britain/the-dowding-system.html, accessed July 21, 2010.

ATTACHMENT 2: TWO PERSPECTIVES OF CYBER WARFARE

There are two overlapping (but in some sense competing) perspectives of how cyber warfare will look. Both are valid and enlightening and both are needed to understand the likely course of future warfare in cyberspace. To help illustrate these perspectives, this section first charts the *military technical view of cyber warfare.*

(1) Attacks against the United States (in red [in the PDF of this volume]) are directed through unwitting hosts by a shadowy but sophisticated adversary (Figure 1).

(2) Subsequently, the United States—with the military Cyber Command in the lead—undertakes defensive counterstrikes to stop the pain while still defending against new strikes, as in Figure 2.

(3) Through skill and hard work (and luck), the United States is able to track back to the elusive adversary. Having established its identity sufficiently to convince the national leadership, Cyber Command begins the counterstrike to punish the foe and compel them to peace, as in Figure 3.

This military technical perspective is certainly valid, but also misses an important lesson of history. Typically traditional, kinetic wars—violent, large-scale conflicts between nations or armed non-state groups—take place as a series of unfolding tactical engagements over time.

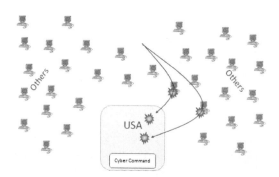

FIGURE 1 The Attack Begins: Military Technical View of Cyber Warfare

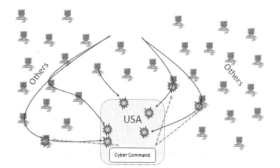

FIGURE 2 The Battle Is Joined: Military Technical View of Cyber Warfare

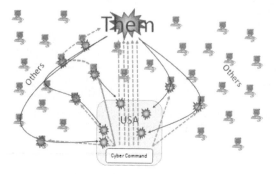

FIGURE 3 The Battle Reaches Crescendo: Military Technical View of Cyber Warfare

In the *traditional view of warfare*, it is entirely possible, even probable, that large-scale warfare in cyber space would follow the same model—a series of connected high-speed "dogfights" strung together into operations which are in turn, part of larger campaigns (see Figure 4). All happen in serial or parallel depending on the opposing forces and terrain, as part of a theater of war.

Of course, there may be combat operations in several theaters of war, either simultaneously or over the duration of a multi-year conflict, as in Figure 5.

An even more overlooked aspect of cyber warfare is that the interplay of the offensive and defensive cyber forces is likely to only be one field where the combatants compete with each other. They are likely to contend also with economic actions, like blockades or sanctions; rallying allies or international organizations; and with their intelligence forces, even through hostilities had ceased (Figure 6).

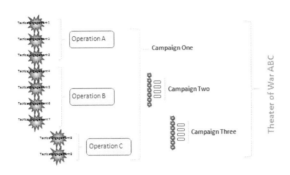

FIGURE 4 Traditional View of Warfare

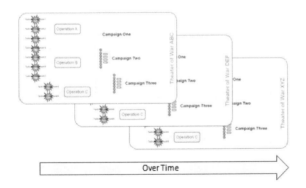

FIGURE 5 Traditional View of Warfare

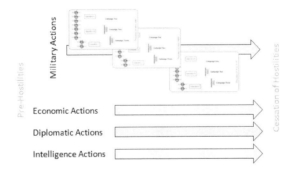

FIGURE 6 Traditional View of Warfare

A Framework for Thinking About Cyber Conflict and Cyber Deterrence with Possible Declaratory Policies for These Domains

Stephen J. Lukasik
Georgia Institute of Technology

A. DETERRING CYBER ATTACKS

The Role of Deterrence in Defense Against Cyber Attacks

Defending against attacks includes actions during three periods. The pre-attack period is the most important, for it is here that deterrence can possibly be effective. The trans-attack period is one where actions can be taken to limit damage, assuming one has real-time systems for sensing events and undertaking responses. The post-attack period is one of reconstitution and learning from the attack to improve the protection process to forestall or blunt future attacks. Schematically:

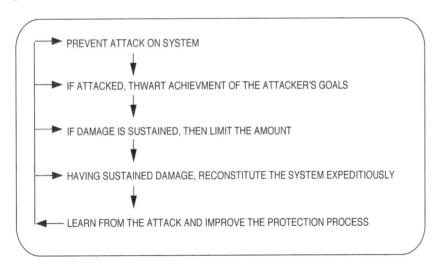

The first line describes the pre-attack period; the next two describe the trans-attack period; and the last two describe the post-attack period. All must be addressed when considering declaratory policy, although post-attack period actions are, by their nature, a result of failures during the two earlier periods. The most attractive actions are those that dissuade an adversary from attacking. In practice this includes deterring by detecting and defeating preparations for the attack, or preempting attackers before they can launch an attack.

Defeating attack preparations renders the attack ineffective. Hardening can serve either to deter, when hardening is seen by the attacker to be highly effective, or to reduce the effectiveness of the attack to the point where it judged to be an inefficient way for the attacker to expend resources. Distributing facilities, thus increasing the number of aim-points, creating virtual facilities behind which real facilities are hidden, adding redundancy, and deception can also serve to defeat attack preparations.

When these fail to deter, one seeks to limit the amount of damage in real-time. This is also a time for the cyber equivalent of civil defense, making users aware of an attack so they can take individual protective actions beyond the direct control of central authorities. Disconnection, either to disconnect the defender from an on-going attack or to disconnect the attacker, can be useful, though difficult to implement on a national scale currently.

Post-attack the defender reconstitutes what was destroyed and undertakes analyses to understand how the attack succeeded, what warning signs were present that were disregarded, and how the defense can be strengthened to reduce the likelihood or effectiveness of a future attack.[1]

Defense is a combination of all these, selected according to the technical capability of the defender, the value of assets to be protected, the costs to defend them, and the anticipated threat. All are part of the total picture. Deterrence, while attractive if one can pull it off, is not the only option open to a defender. The policy declarations proposed later address the full range of cyber defenses.

Defending What Against Whom

Defenders must deal with three kinds of attackers. *Nuclear states*, because they are cyber-capable as well, have global agendas, and may see the U.S. either as an obstacle or a military or economic threat to their agendas. *Non-nuclear states* are likely to see cyber weapons as an attractive counterbalance to U.S. conventional and nuclear capabilities. Cyber weapons are inexpensive, widely available, and relatively easy to master, and a cyberattack can be cost-free if attackers can remain anonymous. The attacker tier below states are *sub-state groups*. They can consist of terrorists and other criminal and extremist groups. The lowest level of attackers are *individuals*, the cyber equivalent of the Unibomber, but also including a wide range of "ankle-biters." The latter appear frequently in discussions of cyber defense although the threats they pose are not of a worrisome magnitude. Some individuals will, however, turn professional and thus can be viewed as potential recruits or as apprentice attackers.

Cyber technology has resulted in an active cyber underground and a commercial industry to write and distribute malware. Virus production has been automated and there is a malware market for goods and services to support spamming, phishing, and other potentially dangerous activities. A recent report notes:

> Half (52 percent) of new malware strains only stick around for 24 hours or less. The prevalence of short lived variants reflects a tactic by miscreants aimed at overloading security firms so that more damaging strains of malware remain undetected for longer, according to a study by Panda Security. The security firm, based in Bilbao, Spain, detects an average of 37,000 new viruses, worms, Trojans and other security threats per day. Around an average of 19,240 spread and try to infect users for just 24 hours, after which they become inactive as they are replaced by other, new variants. Virus writers—increasingly motivated by profit—try to ensure their creations go unnoticed by users and stay under the radar of firms. It has now become common practice for VXers to review detection rates and modify viral code after 24 hours. The practice goes towards explaining the growing malware production rate. The amount of catalogued malware by Panda was 18 million in the 20 years from the firm's foundation until the end of 2008. This figure increased 60 percent in just seven months to reach 30 million by 31 July 2009.[2]

---

[1]Stephen J. Lukasik, Seymour Goodman, and David Longhurst, *Protecting Critical Infrastructures Against Cyber-Attack*, Adelphi Paper 359, International Institute for Strategic Studies, London (2003).
[2]See <http://www.theregister.co.uk/2009/08/13/malware_arms_race/>.

Table 1

State-oriented cyber attacks	
Small attacks repeated frequently	1. Damage or bankrupt an economy
	2. Defraud or extort parts of an economy
Large attacks repeated less frequently	3. Damage or destroy a single infrastructure
	4. Exploit interdependencies among infrastructures
People-oriented cyberattacks	
Attacks on a large number of people	5. Destroy trust within a population
	6. Wear down resistance to policy change
Attacks on individuals or small groups	7. Attack reputations of leaders
	8. Destroy confidence in elites

State actors pose the greatest existential threat. They have resources and discipline, and can recruit and train numbers of personnel and manage large planned attacks. They have sovereign power to provide potential target intelligence and the means to acquire vulnerability information. They can have clear reasons for attacking other states. But against these advantages, they must have a realistic strategy for the use of force to achieve their larger objectives and to understand the role cyber force can play.

Sub-state groups pose a very different threat. They have more limited agendas than do states and must operate under everyone's radar. The fluid nature of their organizations, leadership, numbers, goals, and rapid changes in technology complicates assessing the threats posed by such groups. They may, in fact, represent the larger cyber threat to the U.S. because of their flexibility, the absence of a state organization to put at risk, and the attractiveness of cyber force because of its low cost and likelihood of success.

Cyber attacks are usually defined as software attacks, seen as arising from "outside" and to use the Internet or other network facilities to deliver attacker cyber force to the target. The attacker is seen as anonymous. The attack consists of transmitting software or data to the target such as to cause a computer to malfunction, or to enable the attacker to insert, destroy, copy, or modify data files contained therein. The modification can consist of encrypting the files so the attacker can hold them hostage for ransom. A network attacker can be part of the production and distribution supply chain for software and hardware as well, where the attack software is delivered "shrink-wrapped."

One can interrupt computer-enabled operations by attacking circuit board power supply logic, causing soft and hard failures. The target computer or system can be attacked by disabling the support systems on which operators depend: building security, fire protection, system power, and the like. One can induce soft or hard failures through electromagnetic pulse technology. Attacks on computer systems using physical force are attractive because, even in distributed systems, efficiency encourages concentrations of hardware: system control centers, server farms, and specialized facilities for manufacturing, maintaining, and distributing subsystems and components.

There are two kinds of targets to defend: the state and its people, either groups or individuals (Table 1). Attacks can be large or small, and repeated frequently or infrequently. The people-directed attacks have results that are similar to those of psychological operations, producing soft damage that is less easy to measure but is as central to warfare as physical damage.

Military doctrine calls for controlling strategic territory. Despite the distributed nature of public networks that seems to deny such a possibility, there are cyber analogs. The essence of a network is its connectivity. Controlling network connectivity thus amounts to control of strategic territory. International gateways will be important targets of such attacks.

Deterring Cyber Attacks by States

Cyber conflict between states is very different from conflict involving conventional and nuclear force. Concepts of deterrence formalized in the Cold War are of limited utility. Dissuading the Soviet

Union from launching an attack on the U.S. through fear of a certain and unacceptable response was the only plan that seemed to offer security early in the Cold War. Implicit was that both sides have comparable forces whose capabilities are known, that decapitating attacks can be made infeasible, that the survival of a retaliatory capability on each side is assured, and that firebreaks are fashioned so that escalation of the level of force in any conflict can be controlled. Deterrence had a psychological as well as a physical dimension.

Deterring cyber conflict requires expanding the concept of deterrence well beyond the framework of nuclear deterrence. When a conflict involves computers against computers, the psychological aspect of the threat is missing. National leaders may not even have a clear idea of the extent of the vulnerabilities of their computer networks.

Cyber attacks can have results similar to those of psychological operations. Sun Tsu said, "Those skilled in war subdue the enemy's army without battle." Commenting on Sun Tsu's strategy, Griffith explains, "Never to be undertaken thoughtlessly or recklessly, war was to be preceded by measures designed to make it easy to win. The master conqueror frustrated his enemy's plans and broke up his alliances. He created cleavages between sovereign and ministers, superiors and inferiors, commanders and subordinates. His spies and agents were active everywhere, gathering information, sowing dissention, and nurturing subversion. The enemy was isolated and demoralized; his will to resist broken. Thus without battle his army was conquered, his cities taken and his state overthrown. Only when the enemy could not be overcome by these means was there recourse to armed force."[3] Were there computers in 400 B.C. Sun Tsu would have enthusiastically adopted their capabilities.[4]

Beyond dissuading through fear of retaliation, dictionaries offer other synonyms for "deter." It can mean to discourage an attacker through effective defense or thwarting actions that make attacker success too uncertain. It can mean preventing by preemption. These broader meanings of deterrence suggest defense will play a larger role in cyber deterrence than in the nuclear case, where defenses were seen as destabilizing to the nuclear balance.

Warning systems, both strategic and tactical, are central to cyber deterrence. Without them, and the near-real time response they potentially enable, cyber attacks are certain to succeed eventually as attackers learn and defenders are mired down by the vastness of their systems. In this regard, cost-imposing strategies are important if they can make the probe-and-prepare-in-advance character of cyber attacks more difficult.

Strategic and tactical warning in cyber conflict can provide elements of deterrence through the ability to influence adversary perceptions. Cyber war-fighting, more akin to crisis management than conventional conflict, is possible at a low level of physical violence. An important cyber response capability is near-real time control of network connectivity.

While the details of deterrence will be different, there are three aspects of deterrence that remain invariant. A defender's response must be seen as technically *feasible*. In the nuclear case, very visible weapon tests and well publicized images of nuclear detonations and measured global radioactive fallout provided convincing demonstrations of feasibility. Second, the defender must be seen as *credible*, willing as well as able to respond. U.S. nuclear weapon use in WW II established that, and equivalent Soviet nuclear capabilities left little doubt what its response to a nuclear attack would be. Finally, defense through deterrence requires being *able* to respond, with in-being offensive capability. While response to a cyber attack need not be a cyber counter-attack, international principles of armed conflict speak to proportionality of response and escalation control favors responding in kind. Thus cyber offense is a component of cyber deterrence.

---

[3] *"Sun Tsu and the Art of War,"* translated and with an introduction by Samuel B. Griffith, Oxford University Press paperback, London (1973) pg. 39.

[4] The period Sun Tsu describes is uncertain; the date is for general orientation.

Deterring Cyber Attacks by Sub-State Groups

Deterring sub-state groups from cyber attacks differs from deterring sovereign states. With fewer fixed assets, sub-state groups have greater flexibility, and their independence from sovereign commitments insulates them from many types of sanctions or punishment approaches to deterrence. Their strength is in their followers and their commitment to an idea. Cyber weapons would seem to be attractive to them despite representing a departure from the simpler forms of violence and intimidation sub-state groups have employed to date. Nevertheless, the degree to which potential cyber capabilities are congruent with sub-state groups' operational code is relevant to U.S. planning.

To this end, it is illuminating to examine how one vocal sub-state group see the potential utility of cyber attacks. Jihadists, whose track record and declared antipathy to western values, provide one such example. Al-Qaeda, its affiliated terrorist groups, and its Jihadist supporters, like everyone else, use the Internet. There are currently at least 5,000 Jihadist websites.[5] The most important, large forums that serve as hubs for the virtual Jihadist community and clearinghouses for terrorist propaganda and tactical materials, have tens of thousands of registered members.

In spite of the enthusiasm with which these individuals—active terrorists as well as sympathizers—have embraced the use of cyberspace, currently the bulk of their online activities are unrelated to "cyber terrorism" in the traditional sense of launching destructive attacks over the Internet. Instead, they use the Internet for coordinating various functions related to terrorism, including funding, recruitment, propaganda, training in tradecraft, and intelligence collection.[6]

In recent years, however, a growing interest in using hacking methods to achieve various Jihad objectives has emerged. "Jihad" in both its technical meaning of "struggle" and its use by militant Muslims refers to a range of activities associated with combating the enemies of Islam and defending the pan-Islamic nation. This includes not only militant-style attacks, but also proselytizing, recruitment, fundraising, psychological influence, economic warfare, and a number of other activities.[7] Pursuant to the conception of Jihad as a holistic political struggle, the community's activities are broader than conventional cyber terrorism. Most fall into types of Jihad that is political but not immediately violent.

An illustrative example occurred during the online backlash to an incursion by Israel Defense Forces (IDF) into the Gaza Strip in December 2008. Hackers from the Muslim world self-mobilized to attack tens of thousands of Israeli websites. Most of these hackers executed simplistic attacks—defacing websites and leaving threatening messages, or they launched denial-of-service attacks to take the websites offline. Government, hospital, banking, and media sites were successfully attacked, in addition to the websites of thousands of large and small companies and organizations.[8] The stated motivations for the attacks

---

[5]MSNBC. "Pentagon Surfing 5,000 Jihadist Websites," May 4, 2006. See <http://www.msnbc.msn.com/id/12634238/>; Burleigh, Michael. "Some European Perspectives on Terrorism," Foreign Policy Research Institute, May 2008. See <http://www.fpri.org/enotes/200805.burleigh.europeanperspectivesterrorism.html>.

[6]Kohlmann, Evan F. "The Real Online Terrorist Threat," Foreign Affairs, Sept/Oct 2006; Timothy L. Thomas, "Al-Qaida and the Internet: The Danger of Cyperplanning," Parameters, Spring 2003.

[7]See, for example, the popular pamphlet "39 Ways to Serve and Participate in the Jihad." Variations on this document have been widely circulated on Jihadist websites since 2003. The pro-Jihadist translation service "Tibyan Publications" has published an English translation available at: http://www.archive.org/details/39WaysToServeAndParticipate. Indeed, the document supplies two definitions for "electronic Jihad:" one refers to organizing and distributing information on the Internet, the other refers to hacking. The hacking activities recommended involve taking offline American and other websites, and do not refer directly to any cyberterrorist scenarios.

[8]Project Grey Goose Phase II Report; available http://greylogic. US/?page_id=85. U.S. and NATO military websites were also attacked. A group of Turkish hackers defaced one of three subdomains of mdw.army.mil, the URL of the U.S. Army Military District of Washington, as well as the website of the Joint Force Headquarters of the National Capital Region. The same group left a threatening message on the NATO parliament site www.nato-pa.int. The message read: "Stop attacks u israel and usa! you cursed nations! one day muslims will clean the world from you!" See: McMillan, Robert. "Hackers Deface NATO, U.S. Army Web Sites," Computer World, January 9, 2009. The NATO defacement is available at: http://www.zone-h.org/content/view/15003/30/.

fell under the rubric of supporting Jihad, but were not immediately violent. The four most commonly articulated motivations for the anti-Israel hacks were:

- *Inflicting financial damage to Israeli businesses, government, and individuals*: A message on the Arabic hackers' site Soqor.net exhorted hackers to "disrupt and destroy Zionist government and banking sites to cost the enemy not thousands but millions of dollars. . . ."
- *Delivering threats of physical violence to an Israeli audience*: One Moroccan hackers' team posted symbols associated with violent Jihadist movements and an image of explosion, along with a threatening message for Israelis.
- *Using cyber attacks as leverage to stop Operation Cast Lead*: Many of the defacements contained messages indicating attacks on Israeli sites and servers would stop only when Israel ceased its violence in Gaza.
- *Fulfilling the religious obligation of Jihad*: Some hackers couched their activities in religious terms, insisting that cyber attacks were tantamount to fighting Jihad against Islam's enemies. One hacker wrote, "Use [the hacking skills] God has given you as bullets in the face of the Jewish Zionists. We cannot fight them with our bodies, but we can fight them with our minds and hands . . . By God, this is Jihad."[9]

This sort of Jihadist "hacktivism" has become a popular way for sympathizers to target perceived enemies of the faith. The Netherlands and Denmark have also been targeted by similar grass-roots campaigns in response to their newspapers' decisions to publish cartoons depicting the Prophet Mohammed in 2006.[10] U.S. websites have been targeted.[11] A smaller-scale effort targeted Chinese websites during Uighur-Han Chinese violence in 2009.[12] Such attacks may be popular because they are approved by the mainstream of the Muslim world. The Islamic university al-Azhar in Cairo, the single most influential religious institution in the Sunni Muslim world, issued a fatwa in October 2008 approving cyber attacks against American and Israeli websites. "This is considered a type of lawful Jihad that helps Islam by paralyzing the information systems used by our enemies for their evil aims," read the fatwa.[13] The fatwa explicitly endorsed attacks on websites, but it was not clear whether it could be extended to justify true cyber terrorist attacks.

While many of the Jihadist-hackers online have embraced a menacing form of hacktivism, there are intimations that others seek to harness these skills for cyber terrorism purposes. The prominent al-Qaeda strategist Abu Ubaid al-Qureishi has discussed the potential of cyber-terrorism. Al-Qureishi was a bilingual analyst who exploited English-language western sources, including writings by U.S. military, in the strategic documents he wrote in Arabic for the al-Qaeda core group in Afghanistan.[14]

In his essay titled "The Nightmares of America," al-Qureishi describes the five terrorism scenarios he asserts frighten the U.S. most. He explains that the purpose of his exercise was to exploit Western security analysis to uncover the greatest vulnerabilities in U.S. security. Al-Qureishi believed al-Qaeda should let these analysts, who publish prolifically in the open source domain, lead the way:

> In order to become acquainted with the enemy's hidden weak points, one must examine the studies that Western strategic analysts have written about the real or imagined security gaps and dangers threatening the security and safety of American society. Their fears must be studied carefully, because they usually point to weak points in American national security.[15]

---

[9]Motivations are excerpted from Project Grey Goose Phase II Report; available at http://greylogic. US/?page_id=85.

[10]Project on Jihadist Websites First Quarter 2008, International Centre for Political Violence and Terrorism Research, May, 2008, p. 24.

[11]The Israeli portals of American companies were among those aggressively targeted in the response to Operation Cast Lead.

[12]There was a mild campaign against Chinese websites during this time on Jihadist hacking forums.

[13]AKI. "Sunni Scholars Sanction Electronic Jihad," October 16, 2008.

[14]Sources vary as to whether al-Qureishi is still alive.

[15]Al-Qureishi, Abu Ubaid. "The Nightmares of America," February 13, 2002. Originally obtained from the Jihadist website *al-Qal'ah* (now defunct) on June 6, 2005.

Cyber terrorism is one of the five methods of attack outlined in the essay. Al-Qureishi describes four advantages of attacking over the Internet: cyber terrorist attacks can be conducted anonymously from a distance; the technology required is inexpensive; cyber attacks do not require exceptional skill; and few people are needed. His target list is from U.S. reporting on the subject: "As for the targets that the Jihad movements might choose, they range, in the view of American experts, from huge electrical grids to nuclear power plants, financial institutions, and the 9-1-1 emergency telephone network."[16]

He describes previous successes by hackers and concludes that, based on the rapid dissemination of hacker knowledge over recent years and the transformation of the U.S. economy into "a basically informational economy . . . [there is] a possibility [of launching] repeated, focused attacks with a very considerable effect."[17]

It is rare to find a document like al-Qureishi's essay that includes both the method of attack and possible targets. In discussing possibilities for violent attacks, Jihadists in terrorist forums rarely provide targeting information. Instead, their discussions focus on the techniques and tactics available to carry out an attack against an unspecified target. Jihadists write prolifically on surveillance, recruiting, kidnapping, executions, bomb-making, and other methods of violence, but have few discussions of specific terrorist plots against expressly identified targets. Targeting selection is assisted by higher-level strategic and theological documents, which provide religious justifications and strategic guidance for striking large classes of targets—such as oil targets in the Arabian Peninsula, or American tourists in the Middle East—without specifying particular locations. The objective is to distribute the tactical knowledge necessary for an entrepreneurial terrorist group to plan and execute its own attack, while minimizing the risk that the plot will be anticipated and disrupted.

The same is largely true of the Jihadist-hacker forums. The forums provide advice, manuals, and information on hacking tools and skills, usually without directing individuals to specific targets. Attacks are usually advertised after they have been successful.[18] A hacker will state his intention to use a certain hacking technique or tool against a general category of targets, such as "Zionist computers" or "Crusader websites."

The skills and knowledge observable in the forums must be considered in the context of intention. The forums are defined by explicit, overwhelming political motivations. While other hacking movements may be dominated by those professing criminal or ego-driven motivations, the Arabic-language hacking forums monitored consistently exhibit Jihadist-motivations.[19] While some may be content to fulfill their obligation to wage Jihad by defacing the homepages of Dutch newspapers, others are likely to have more dangerous ambitions against the U.S.

As evidence of this, one can examine other materials available to Jihadist-hackers on one of the hacker forums examined. This hacker forum is one section of a larger extremist website called the Electronic Mujahideen Network. A member of the hacker forum is also granted access to the other sections, which contain items encouraging terrorist operations, including bomb-making manuals and theological treatises justifying mass casualty attacks against infidels. The membership of the Electronic Mujahideen Network is likely to be more extremist and violent by nature than members of the Soqor.Net network, which is devoted entirely to hacking and IT-related topics. Moreover, by placing a hacking forum side-by-side with other forums devoted to more traditional terrorist methods, the administrators of the website are implicitly suggesting the use of cyber means towards violent ends. Other violent Jihadist websites have also included hacker sections.

---

[16]Ibid.

[17]Ibid.

[18]This is not always true, certainly there are posts in which one hacker will urge others to help him attack a certain site, but it is the case most of the time.

[19]Zone-H poll shows that roughly 1/10th of defacements worldwide are politically motivated, with another 1/10th motivated by "patriotism." Presentation by Kenneth Geers and Peter Feaver. "Cyber Jihad and the Globalization of Warfare." Available at: http://www.chiefofstation.com/pdf/Cyber_Jihad.pdf.

The skills and tools available in the hacking forums can be used to support conventional attacks. For example, Indonesian Jemaah Islamiya terrorist leader Imam Samudra organized the 2005 Bali bombings from his prison cell using a laptop provided to him by a prison guard. Samudra used the net to organize personnel and raise funds via online financial crime.[20] Samudra also authored a book in 2004 that contained a chapter advocating hacking for the sake of Jihad.[21]

Younis Tsouli, an aspiring terrorist living in the U.K., used his knowledge of cyber security to cover his tracks online while helping to coordinate the planning of potentially disastrous bombings in Canada, the U.S., Bosnia, and the U.K.[22] He functioned as the linchpin of an international network of aspiring terrorists who used Jihadist websites to communicate and obtain tactical information. His colleague, Tariq ad-Dour, was in charge of terrorist financing. He used Trojan horses and phishing scams to obtain 37,000 credit card numbers, to which he charged $3.5 million, including over 250 plane tickets. Ad-Dour laundered the money using online gambling websites.[23]

Tsouli, Ad-Dour, and a third accomplice aspired to be the Osama Bin Laden and Ayman al-Zawahiri of the new generation of terrorists, operating as terrorist "venture capitalists" who facilitate and finance plot ideas proposed to them by different entrepreneurial terrorist cells—as Bin Laden and Zawahiri have been reported to do. When the three were arrested in late 2005, they were associated with terrorist plots against targets in Sarajevo, Washington D.C., southern Ontario, and undisclosed cities in the U.K. They were also involved in plots against military bases in Georgia and Florida.[24]

Tsouli and his accomplices could have successfully combined their hacking skills A hacking primer he authored, "The Encyclopedia of Hacking the Zionist and Crusader Websites," is a popular download on the Electronic Mujahideen Network and other Jihadist websites.[25]

An attack that combines conventional and cyberattack is an electromagnetic pulse weapon (EMP) attack. EMP has garnered increased interest on Jihadist forums, especially the Electronic Mujahideen Network, where four articles on the subject have been recently published. The articles contain descriptive information on the construction and impact of EMP weapons. They are not so detailed as to suggest engineering experience or experimentation with building a prototype; rather, they reflect open source research performed in English and translated into Arabic.[26]

Another combination attack scenario is one in which terrorists exploit the timing of a natural disaster or economic downturn to amplify the impact of a cyber attack. During the severe downturn of late 2008, several Jihadist forum members urged their counterparts in the U.S. to take advantage of the country's vulnerable position to launch a terrorist attack.[27] Although this did not occur, it reflects an awareness of the power to amplify the impact of an attack—either cyber or conventional—by timing it correctly. Some believe hackers can make a significant impact on the economy without carrying out a large-scale attack if done during an economic downturn.

Deterring sub-state groups from cyber conflict differs from deterring states. Sub-state groups provide few targets and have no country to hold at risk. Instead one must seek to make possible attacks less desirable by imposing costs. Sub-state groups have many ways to achieve their long-term goals.

---

[20]AsiaNews.It. "Bali Terrorist Organised Attacks from Behind Bars," Indonesia Matters. Aug. 24, 2006.

[21]Sipress, Alan. "An Indonesian's Prison Memoir Takes Holy War Into Cyberspace," The Washington Post, December 14, 2004.

[22]NEFA Foundation, "Irhaby 007's American Connections," July 2007. Available at http://www.nefafoundation.org/miscellaneous/Irhaby007_AmericanConnections.pdf.

[23]Krebs, Brian. "Terrorism's Hook Into Your Inbox," The Washington Post, July 5, 2007. Available at http://www.washingtonpost.com/wp-dyn/content/article/2007/07/05/AR2007070501153.html.

[24]Katz, Rita and Josh Devon. "Web of Terror," Forbes, July 5, 2007.

[25]A translation of this manual is available from the CIA Open Source Center.

[26]One of the articles was a paraphrased translation of this paper by Australian researcher Carlo Kopp, available from global security.org. http://www.globalsecurity.org/military/library/report/1996/apjemp.htm.

[27]Project on Jihadist Websites Third Quarter 2008. International Centre for Political Violence and Terrorism Research, October 2008, p. 5.

Their current program of kinetic attacks is cost-effective. Such attacks require little technical skill when directed against soft targets, they provide results immediately visible too supporters and adversaries, and they fit into the long Muslim pattern of using what is immediately at hand for jihad.

Imposing costs is a matter of careful choice. There are two steps involved. The first is to establish models of sub-state cyber attackers and from these compile a set of possible interventions that if implemented and successful would result in substantial setbacks for attackers. Since initial lists of possible interventions will be a mixed bag, one has to subject them to a second step where one looks for favorable cost-exchange ratios, sorting ideas into what hurts the attacker most for least cost to the defender.

Determining cost-exchange ratios requires one, for each possible intervention, to estimate the cost to a defender to implement what is needed to be effective against the threat envisaged; and one must then estimate the regret of the attacker should that intervention be successful. To do this with the precision needed for approval of any new idea runs the risk of paralysis through analysis. But if one simply wants to filter lists of ideas to separate potentially useful interventions, warranting more study, from those that *a priori* look like losers, one can adopt a less rigorous approach.

For this, defender costs and attacker regret estimates are quantized into three levels. A "3" is used to denote an intervention that could be undertaken within current defender budgets and technical capabilities, but it is one that results, if successful, in minimal regret to the attacker. A "2" is used to denote an intervention that would require new defender expenditures beyond current budgets, for such matters as equipment development and testing, training personnel, and operational test and evaluation. When used as an estimate of attacker regret, it is something that hurts to the degree that the attacker suffers a major setback. A "1" is used for an intervention that would require much larger defender expenditures, e.g. for R&D because one may not know how to do what is proposed. The cost reflects the time required, the uncertainty of success, and implementation costs. But a "1" for the attacker means a major regret such as being exposed and punished, being put out of business, or subject to a major defender counteraction such as discussed in the following proposed declarations.

A test use of this methodology to prioritize potential defensive programs and to reflect various levels of attacker capabilities was undertaken. Two attacker models were constructed. One was for state-sanctioned attack groups, giving to them the advantages a state can provide for recruitment, training, target information, and secure operating facilities. A second model was for non-official attack groups: individuals, criminal groups, Jihadists, and the like. Defensive strategies were outlined against each for each phase of a cyber campaign from decision to focus on a target set; acquisition of personnel; acquiring target information; setting up facilities for training, exercises, probes, and attack operations; formulating a campaign plan; deploying operational attackers to staging areas; and executing the campaign plan over a period of time.

The first six of these phases are pre-attack. This is the most desirable time to defeat an attacker. Interventions in the last phase, trans-attack actions, are less desirable since they leave too much to last-minute chance. Each possible intervention received, for each phase of an attack where it is relevant, a defender cost "n" and an attacker regret "m."

The most attractive interventions are 3:1, cheap for the defender and killers for the attacker. Of the 27 identified interventions, there were 57 opportunities where one of them was applicable in one or more phases of an attack. There were 3 of the 3:1 type. The next most attractive defender interventions are 3:2: cheap for the defender and having a substantial impact on the attacker. There were 21 of these for the interventions identified. The last class of interventions having an attractive cost-exchange is the 2:1: killer impact on attackers but more expensive for the defender in terms of money and time. There were 17 of this type.

Thirteen of the 27 identified interventions were applicable to and had a satisfactory cost-exchange ratio in the pre-attack period. There were 18 of the identified interventions that were applicable to and had a satisfactory cost-exchange ratio in the trans-attack period.

In this illustration of the prioritizing methodology, the 27 possible interventions examined are by no means exhaustive. Other defenders will identify more and different possible interventions depending on the specifics of their concerns. But such a method can assist in guiding both R&D and in the implementation of defensive interventions.

Cyber Deterrence in Practice

While many countries can look to their own resources and their own defense, the U.S. position has, since WW II, been that collective defense is important for strong and weak alike. Coalition actions, some under the UN, some under NATO, and some ad hoc arrangements represent current examples. Extended deterrence, to be viable, requires demonstrations of capability so that allies and adversaries can adjust their expectations.

Demonstration of cyber power is thus a part of extended deterrence. There are, however, difficulties in demonstrating cyber offense and defense capabilities. Demonstrations of cyber power could be counter-productive if they are sufficiently impressive. It is difficult to conceive of potentially nation-harming cyber demonstrations that are safe. The U.S. policy has been to keep secure the extent of our cyber attack and defense capabilities. This has been successful, to the point that attackers may not be adequately aware of U.S. offensive and defensive capabilities. While good defense, it weakens deterrence.[28]

The current U.S. focus on protecting military computers, thus adhering to clear DoD areas of responsibility, is a politically sound course domestically, and it is fully justified as a force protection mission. But DoD "rides on" the economy and its interconnected infrastructures. Hence simply protecting itself is only the start of a wider set of necessary U.S. defensive actions.

Creating a cyber deterrent will depend on having something specific beyond the level of policy and doctrinal statements. One needs cyber plans of action. Talk depends on earned credibility, but executable plans of action are real. Plans of action can also serve to establish the level of "forces" required, the feasibility of specific attacks, targeting doctrine, intelligence requirements, consequences of execution, training and exercises needed, "cyber force" deployments, global situation awareness, and a host of practical matters. We need to know what the exercise cyber power means beyond the level of Power-Point charts.

Cyber power can effect both hard and soft results. Deterring the use of cyber force will depend on both forms of cyber power. Diplomatic and economic power are measured in ways quite different from the metrics of hard military power. Informational, i.e. cyber, power with aspects of both is not simply a subset of hard power. The integration of these three elements of power is not simple. The extension of military concepts and technologies devised for industrial war to counterinsurgency, counter-terrorism, and peace-keeping, all mixed hard and soft enterprises, reveal the difficulties in strategic integration.[29] DoD "Deterrence Operations Joint Operating Concept," issued December 2006, recognizes this:

> Deterrence requires a national strategy that integrates diplomatic, informational, military, and economic powers. The Department of Defense must develop strategies, plans, and operations that are tailored to the perceptions, values, and interests of specific adversaries.

Power is measured in known strengths, but uncertainty has value also. Deterrence depends not only on firm measures of strength, but also on uncertainty in the use of that power. A potential aggressor is deterred because he is not certain whether the post-attack period will be better or worse for him than the present. Thus the creation of uncertainty is as important for deterrence as projecting certainty.

---

[28]A recent NRC report, *Technology, Policy, Law, and Ethics Regarding U.S. Acquisition and use of Cyberattack Capabilities*, National Academies Press, Washington, D.C., April 29, 2009, makes substantially the same points. In Chapter 3, "Military Perspectives on Cyberattack," it notes, "At the date of this writing, an unclassified and authoritative statement of current joint doctrine for the use of computer network attack is unavailable, and it is fair to say that current doctrine on the matter is still evolving." In Chapter 9, "Speculations on the Dynamics of Cyberconflict," under Section 9.1, "Deterrence and Cyber Conflict," it notes, "It remains an open question as to whether the concepts of deterrence are relevant when applied to the domain of cyberconflict per se (that is, cyberconflict without reference to conflict in physical domains.")

[29]Rupert Smith, *The Utility of Force: The Art of War in the Modern World*, Random House/Vintage Books, New York (2007).

A Framework for Thinking About Cyber Conflict

Unless one has an understanding of cyber conflict, construction of policy declarations cannot lead anywhere. Cyber conflict is the delivery of "cyber force." Cyber force is the application and control of the inherent power of information and its transmission through public networks to achieve national goals. It takes place not in kinetic space but in the space of a myriad of electrical and logical connections. In practice, a "cyber attack" consists of transmitting software or data from one computer to another. The strategy and operational doctrines attending the exercise of cyber force have much in common with the corresponding concepts of kinetic conflict.

Control can be of physical systems, or of people. In the latter case cyber force produces effects previously the province of "psychological operations." This can include trust attacks, social alienation attacks, and exhaustion attacks. They have much in common with swarming attacks.[30]

Control of the cyber "battlespace" requires control of the network connectivity that makes such attacks possible. Connectivity maps are the cyber equivalent of topographic maps for ground combat. At a minimum controlling the battlespace means an attacker can disconnect what he threatens and the defender can, in response, disconnect the attacker. But matters are unlikely to come to that point. In this both real and abstract battlespace, a more delicate minuet takes place continually: a cat-and-mouse game, the thrust and feint of chess, fencing, or boxing. It has a parallel to the war between spam and spam filters we all fight, and traditional electronic warfare of measure, CM, CCM, . . . C^nM. Intelligence operations, particularly Sigint, cryptography, and deception are the essence. One might reasonably borrow the title of R.V. Jones' account of British scientific intelligence in 1939-1945, *The Wizard War*, to describe cyber conflict.

In this framework, preemption takes on a very different meaning from preemption in kinetic conflict. Preemption need not be to pass a point of no return. It can simply be to take the next step in the wizard war, the $C^{n+1}M$ to the C^nM adversary measures.[31]

The Relations Between Cyber, Conventional, and Nuclear Conflict

What we call "conventional," or more recently, "kinetic" conflict is conflict as conducted at least since Neolithic times. Nuclear conflict became a reality in WW II but nuclear states quickly mastered its conduct, or more importantly, how to avoid it. That understanding was based on an ordering of force, with conventional conflict seen as the normal, and preceding, form of conflict with escalation from the lesser to the greater inhibited by "firebreaks." Nuclear conflict has entered a new stage with the appearance of regional nuclear powers with small numbers of nuclear weapons and limited delivery range. Sub-state groups add to nuclear conflict possibilities through presumed capabilities to acquire nuclear weapons or fissile material from state inventories.

---

[30]A comprehensive study of swarming in kinetic conflict is the Pardee RAND Graduate School dissertation of Sean A. Edwards, "Swarming and the Future of Warfare," 2005. In contrast to linear warfare, swarming tactics are a characteristic of modern conflicts where forces undertake non-linear dispersed operations. He notes that swarming tactics are of two types: cloud swarms where the forces arrive at the target as a single mass and vapor swarms where attackers are initially dispersed and converge on the target. There are cyber equivalents to these: distributed denial of service in the case of the former and slow build-up of attacks over time that enable an overwhelming blow on a target in the latter. Swarming attacks can be defeated by, among other means, superior situation awareness, undermining attack enablers, and using "bait" tactics. Examples of these can be found in the declarations suggested in the following discussion.

[31]Michael Schrage argues, in "A Softer Way to Preempt Hostile Attacks," in the Washington Post, Aug 21, 2005 that "soft" preemption, consisting of disrupting information flows or other non-disruptive technical interference could arguably save lives if taken in lieu of conventional resorts to force. See <www.washingtonpost.com/wp-dyn/content/article/2005/08/20/AR2005082000108.html>.

The question then arises how cyber conflict "fits" into the current strategic and doctrinal structures that guide the management of force among state and sub-state actors. While the general question is examined elsewhere, a few conclusions are relevant.[32]

The analysis of the interactions of the three forms of force and conflict based on their employment can be examined combinatorially. They can be treated as employed singly, two at a time, or the three together. The case of cyber (Cy) force used singly has been the subject of the preceding discussion. Conventional (Co) and nuclear (N) used singly are outside the scope of this discussion.

The combinations of two forms of force, where one is Cy, are Cy + Co and Cy + N, used in order, i.e. (CyCo or CoCy.) The Cy and Co combinations are to be expected. Cy can be viewed as a defense suppression technique for an intended conventional conflict, a business-as-usual expectation, or they can be employed simultaneously. The CoCy order does not appear to be quite as plausible as the reverse but this is immaterial to the argument. Cy can be an adjunct to Co in a variety of ways. States with an adequate conventional force balance can be expected to continue to wage war as they have been trained and equipped to do, although one can quite possibly expect Cy to replace some Co force as its lesser cost, potentially greater effectiveness, covert nature, its "softness," and other characteristics come to be understood and appreciated. In this view, cyber force, and cyber conflict may be seen as preferable to conventional conflict by both attackers and targets. If this is the case, managing the CyCo firebreak may in the future take on the importance managing the CoN firebreak does currently. The low cost, combined with global reach, of cyber force may then make it the preferred choice of sub-state groups in the longer term also.

Granting the logic of these speculations, one can suggest the emergence of cyber force as a threat to the security of nations provides a certain counter-balance to nuclear threats. The direction the "balance" might move remains to be seen. The emergence of cyber force may simply add another terrible threat. Or it could result in reducing the attractiveness of nuclear weapons through the emergence of something "better" to an attacker.

B. DECLARATORY POLICY CONTRIBUTIONS TO CYBER DEFENSE

Perspectives on Declaratory Policy

Declaratory policies begin as words on paper. They can be ignored, overtaken by events, or become irrelevant under technological change. To be of value, there must be a plausible chain of events that could result in their implementation.

An example is the Universal Declaration of Human Rights adopted as UN General Assembly Resolution 217 A (III) in 1948. It asserts a number of human rights declared to be universal. Translated into 375 languages, it has spawned follow-on treaties dealing with elimination of racial discrimination (1969), elimination of discrimination against women (1981), a convention against torture (1984), and a convention on the rights of the child (1989). While many of these goals are still not universally recognized, the treaty structure has resulted in countless human rights watch groups, progress reports, political demonstrations, and international pressure to meet its ideals. It synthesizes widely felt concerns and stimulates action. To use a current expression, it is a declaration with "legs."

The fact a declaration is unilateral is not a limitation to its broader adoption. A declaration can be seen as a warning; as laying down an invitation for others to embrace its goals; or as proposing normative standards of behavior to be furthered through the declaration's logic and the appeal of its goals. When a few major states, supported by industry groups as well, undertake to implement its intent, the words begin to turn into actionable pressures and implementation decisions.

Apart from their possible adoption internationally, policy declarations serve internal purposes as well, to express needs so that divided parts of public and private bureaucracies can better see where

---

[32]Stephen J. Lukasik and Rebecca Givner-Forbes, "Deterring The Use of Cyber Force," December 14, 2009. See <www.cistp.gatech.edu/publications/files/cyber_deterrencev2.pdf>.

cooperation is needed on the national level. The ideas expressed can serve as a point of departure for refinement through further policy analysis and debate. They can guide R&D and allocation of resources. This is the sense in which the following declarations are offered. They should not be judged by whether a U.S. President would or would not be well-advised to adopt them at this point. They are to be seen as input to a policy process, not as output.

Recognizing that declarations could be a starting point on a path to formal international agreements, it is well to keep such a possibility in mind in considering them. There are four characteristics that would be important for more general international action:

(a) *Verifiable*—if declaratory policy is to effect change in something, actions taken or actions not taken, these should be observable. Being observable, parties to an international agreement can then decide if what is observed is consistent with the intent of the agreement. If it is not, the parties behaving in incompatible ways can be asked to clarify the events called into question, or the agreement itself can be amended to reflect changed circumstances.

(b) *Reciprocal*—all parties should be held to the same standards. A signatory wishing not to be a target of a prohibited action should be prepared to eschew that action itself.

(c) *Robust under change*—negotiating agreements is sufficiently complicated they should have more than a transitory period of applicability. A common driver of obsolescence is technology. In the cyber world, technology changes so rapidly that agreements must be capable of dealing with future capabilities very different from those existing when it was formulated.

(d) *Consistent with prior agreements*—prior agreements should be accommodated and their precedents recognized and used where possible. Consistency with prior agreements eases the acceptance of new proposals. Inconsistencies complicate reaching new agreement. On the other hand, if a new problem requires new frameworks and new solutions, states should be prepared to entertain that possibility.

Circumstances Addressable by Cyber-Related Declarations

The starting point for examining the domain of declaratory cyber policies is to define what concerns they could seek to address. Professional literature and the public media are rich in enumerations of concerns introduced by the convergence of digital technology, ubiquitous devices for manipulating digital representations, and the relative ease with which ideas can be communicated and widely accessed: the Internet, portable wireless devices, social networks, increasing bandwidth, and the educational, business, government, political, and social innovations that can be built on these capabilities.

The concern here is attacks of "national significance." The Department of Defense uses as the definition of an "incident of national significance":

> An actual or potential high-impact event that requires a coordinated and effective response by and appropriate combination of Federal, state, local, tribal, nongovernmental, and/or private-sector entities in order to save lives and minimize damage, and provide the basis for long-term community recovery and mitigation activities.

In 2005 the Department of Homeland Security offered fifteen National Planning Scenarios for "plausible terrorist attacks and natural disasters that challenge the Nation's prevention and response capabilities." Four provide some calibration for what might be addressed by declaratory policies: detonation of a 10 kT nuclear device; a major earthquake; a major hurricane; and a cyberattack. A commonly expressed concern in the cyber community is a "cyber Pearl Harbor." The 1997 report of the President's Commission on the Critical Infrastructure Protection referred to "cascading events" in what are believed to be unstable systems of systems.[33]

---

[33]*Critical Foundations: Protecting America's Infrastructures,* Report of the President's Commission on Critical Infrastructure Protection, The White House, October 1997.

Equating "significant" cyber attacks to 10 kT nuclear detonations, major earthquakes, and hurricanes conveys some sense of what is under discussion, but a link between damage, death, and computers is needed. For computer-inflicted damage to be crippling in the sense of a national economy, it must be long-lasting. Interrupting the operation of computers, however inconvenient, does not rise to the level of crippling. Computers, power systems, and communication systems fail regularly and states do not collapse. If such failures were to be widespread and coordinated, a nation would sustain larger economic losses. But engineers design, build, and operate systems to be robust under stress through backups, hot standbys, redundancies, rapid repair plans, other approaches to damage limitation and service restoration. What is needed to create long-lasting social and economic impacts from cyber attacks is to cause physical damage to large, expensive equipment for which spares are not available and for which manufacturing replacements is lengthy. This will be the case with damage to electrical generators, high voltage transformers, pumping stations, communication switches, routers, and server farms supporting information utilities such as cloud computing.

There are several examples of technical and regulatory issues relating to what we now call cyber war. Following the invention of the telegraph in the 1840s, states realized that technical standards were needed if the full potential of the new technology were to be realized. The history of telegraphy, and its parallels to our current circumstances, is elaborated on by Standage.[34]

The nineteenth century struggles for the regulation of international communications were renewed with the invention of radio and the introduction of wireless telegraphy in the early twentieth century. The history of this cyber war period is recounted by Rutkowski.[35] The parallels to today in both cases are striking and the measures adopted provide useful context for addressing present concerns. Rutkowski notes:

> The first U.S. interagency committee dealing with wireless cyberwar was convened in 1904 and primarily led by the Navy Department.
>
> As the years progressed during the 1900's, however, chaos emerged. Almost everyone was incented to get on the wireless internet. Commercial business, government, ordinary people, even the equivalent of "script kiddies" and hackers of today—the first radio amateurs—all got "on the net." Enterprises constantly pushed the state-of-the-art; new digital protocols were developed; nations were competing; network architectures and applications were continuously evolving; wireless cyberwar was becoming real . . .
>
> For years, the Washington political scene engaged in incessant wrangling as the wireless infrastructure and cyber security became progressively worse. Private enterprises claimed that technology and innovation would be impeded if the Berlin provisions [of 1906] were implemented, and argued that the infrastructure was overwhelmingly privately owned. Washington lobbyists warned against the dangers of Federal government involvement. There was a general antipathy against foreign nations and intergovernmental organizations. The military community wanted its own freedom of action to keep ahead of the rest of the world. And lastly, there was no consensus on what agency in Washington should act.
>
> On 22 April 1912, President Taft ratified the first multilateral agreement to which the U.S. became a party—the 1906 Berlin Convention—ending more than a decade of cyber conflict that was implicated as a causal factor in the sinking of the Titanic eight days earlier on 14 April 1912. The sinking and the subsequent investigations so inflamed public opinion that the 1906 Berlin treaty was quickly signed and an additional set of domestic and international actions undertaken by the U.S. government, together with other nations, in London in 1912, to mitigate further cyber conflict.
>
> It was the first acceptance of an international telecommunication treaty by the US—after refusing for nearly 50 years to become a party to any related agreements or instituting any regulation of the early wireless cyber environment.
>
> Any bright entrepreneur with a modicum of knowledge and inventiveness could become part of the emerging global infrastructure. Fortunes were made overnight. However, the problem was that any wireless transmitter could wreak havoc on a network somewhere else in the world . . .

---

[34]Tom Standage, *The Victorian Internet*, Walker and Company, New York (1998).
[35]A. M. Rutkowski, "Lessons from the First Great Cyberwar Era." Info, 12 Feb 2010.

The cybersecurity course proved cyclic over the years as each new cyber technology emerged, or administrations and appointees changed, or the U.S. global ambitions advanced or diminished. In general, however, the cycle remained the same. Excitement, euphoria, and innovation by geeks are followed by unfettered industry assimilation and exploitation, which gives rise to pervasive public implementations and then conflict among nations to maintain perceived advantages.

The lesson to take from this is that cyber security problems are not unique to our time. What are seen today as nearly insoluble problems, deriving from new technologies and complexities, have as good a chance of solution as did comparable earlier problems. The human mind can resolve problems the human mind creates.

Possible Policy Declarations

The following declarations are offered as a starting point for policy discussion, not an end point. They suggest one possible way that may reduce the problems that result from the interaction of computers existing under widely different state jurisdictions.

One type of declarations are those that establish a line past which we warn others not to venture. Drawing lines in the sand is treacherous, however, because they imply that anything not over the line is acceptable. Further, such a declaration must imply or define a threatened response, one intended to be serious enough to dissuade an attacker from the behavior defined. That carries with it the issue of credibility. How have individual states responded to similar situations in the past? It also binds a state to do something, or it loses credibility.

Another define normative behavior, goals we believe should serve as universal standards for all. Such declarations define ideal states that perhaps only a few states meet. There should be some reason to believe the proposed goals are realistic, as illustrated by the existence of at least some examples. As noted earlier, there should be some feasible path through which wider adoption can be facilitated. Because they call for changes in behavior, they must be viewed as long-term matters, but are important enough that any progress in these directions will be beneficial.

A third type of declarations serves to note ambiguous or unclear situations where further discussion and study is needed. These may be situations that identify matters requiring both domestic and international efforts. Or they can take the form of a statement such as "The state supports X under condition Y."

The following 11 possible declarations are suggested to encourage discussion of how declaratory policy might be employed in deterring cyber conflict. They are presented in an order from the possibly least controversial to those that are likely to engender the greatest barriers to adoption.

The set can be viewed as a logical package. All, individually and as a group, would aid in protecting users of the cyber commons, making it a safer place for the conduct personal and national business. But they are not inextricably linked. In this sense the set is a menu from which to select based on domestic and international priorities and opportunities.

---

1. Research and development of information technology should remain unfettered so that the greatest benefits can be secured for the well-being of all. To this end, potentially dangerous aspects of information technology should be openly discussed and international efforts undertaken to avert possible harm to all states and peoples.

Despite its flaws, it is clear that information technology has made major beneficial changes for people and for facilitating their interaction to exchange knowledge and to undertake economically important activities. This declaration simply says do not kill the goose that is laying the golden eggs. It is intended to head off the control or limitation of research and development in information technology. It does say, however, that the dark side of the technology, the misuse of the technology and the abuse of the cyber commons, is a problem and it calls on all states to openly discuss the issues and to discuss and cooperate on solutions.

Openly discussing the problem will be more difficult than one might expect. Cyber flaws are concealed to the extent possible. Matters of fault, liability, and loss of trust are part of the problem. Avoidance of national blame is another. Much is concealed under the rubric of national security, some quite justified, as when it would reveal vulnerabilities that could be more widely exploited, and some covered up to minimize unrelated political problems.

So this is a two-sided declaration, one to not fetter the technology, but also a call to openly discuss the problems, both technical and procedural that impact security.

The next declaration related to the facilities and operators of global public communications network.

---

2. Computer and information system resources connected by public international telecommunications facilities are critical for global discourse that is a human right and provide a common good from which all benefit. To this end, the availability of these open information resources to legitimate users should not be impeded.

This is consistent with the vision of the International Telecommunication Union, to which the U.S. is a signatory, that states, "By connecting the world and fulfilling everyone's fundamental right to communicate, we strive to make the world a better and safer place." It is a direct repetition of a principle regulating international communication going back to the earliest days of wire and radio telegraphy. There is a good body of internationally accepted behavior: non-interference with legitimate users; prior rights of incumbency; state control of what comes into its jurisdictions through the licensing of operators; and an obligation to help users in distress, either to provide back-up facilities or to identify sources of interference.

A recent NRC report notes "Users of information technology . . . should be able to use the computational resources to which they are entitled and [the] systems that depend on these resources."[36]

The declaration goes further, however, in that it declares open and unrestricted use of the public telecommunications facilities is a human right. This applies only to the public communication system, defined as the set of state-licensed carriers operating under the aegis of international communication agreements. There is flexibility in the declaration, in the word "legitimate." States are free to define "legitimate users" however they choose, but they should not interfere with the legitimate users of other states. Thus states maintain control of what their citizens do, but not what users over whom they have no jurisdiction can do.

The next two declarations begin to cut closer to the matter of identifying sources of abuse of the public network, particularly where the traffic is between computers.

---

3. Users of public international telecommunication facilities should, for the protection of all users, have a unique identifier supported by a verifiable mechanism available to them so that parties sustaining harm through misuse of those facilities can seek redress.

Attribution is impeded by the almost complete anonymity possible on the Internet and related TCP/IP networks. On the other hand, in many states this proposal would meet strong objections on grounds of privacy. In view of greatly varying needs for both privacy and security and the sensitivity of content of communications, it will be helpful to shift the security–privacy tradeoff to the user. The point of the declaration is to provide means for redress in the event of harm. Users willing to accept communications from unidentified users would do so at risk of denying themselves redress for consequent harm. The

---

[36]Seymour E. Goodman and Herbert S. Lin, Ed., *Toward a Safer and More Secure Cyberspace*, The National Academies Press, Washington, D.C. 2007, p. 53 item I in a Cybersecurity Bill of Right, Chap. 3.

unique identifier may be made available only by user request in the case of alleged harm suffered and be provided subject to the laws of the jurisdiction within which the harm occurs.

Unspecified here is the definition of "harm." Harm is culturally and politically dependent and it is unlikely that there will soon be global agreement on what is allowed and what is harmful and should be prohibited. By leaving harm undefined, the default definition is the way it is defined in the jurisdiction in which the harm is seen to have occurred. As in all cases where adjudication of claims is necessary, harm will in the end be defined by precedent and developing case law.

---

4. States shall establish a system of technical standards openly arrived at for all equipment attached to the public infrastructure, and the adequacy of those standards monitored though proof of performance publicly available.

This is in analogy to what is mandated in all systems, public or private. The integrity of the network requires that there be technical standards relating to what can and cannot be connected to the network. Whether one is talking about data formats, voltages, or pipe pressures, there must be limits set by the design conditions used as a basis for constructing the system. Engineers can design for wide ranges of operating conditions; they can provide alternatives to take care of special situations; and older devices are replaced over time by newer and more fault-tolerant versions. But "anything-goes" is not technically feasible.

This can be accomplished in various ways. In the case of regulated infrastructure systems, there can be central certification laboratories. In the U.S. telecommunications systems much of this has been made a responsibility of the manufacturer with provision for verification of the process as needed. Another powerful technique is provided by markets. Error-prone, unreliable, and inflexible devices disappear from the market. Each jurisdiction will have its own certification mechanisms. International standards bodies help a great deal. International inconsistencies can be dealt with through standing or new resolution procedures.

The point is to address faulty hardware, such as might be the result of building in vulnerabilities during the manufacturing process to provide attack channels, or it could be applied to address embedded or bundled software containing malware. There are precedents in some classes of equipment such as medical devices where faulty software can result in unsafe operation.

The next two declarations are a set intended to address current practices that render public telecommunication networks insecure.

---

5. The distribution of malicious software is incompatible with the free and beneficial use of public international telecommunications facilities. All nations shall undertake efforts to eliminate such activities within their jurisdictions that violate the rights of people everywhere, or they can be held complicit.

Malware is produced somewhere, in some state's jurisdiction. This does not say that malware production is prohibited, for there are many reasons why malware might be produced: for defensive R&D, as an intellectual puzzle, as a student exercise in computer security training, and as a form of free speech. What the declaration says is that its *distribution* is prohibited. The declaration then says it is the responsibility of each state to prevent the distribution of malware. Clearly this can only refer to international distribution. A state is free to allow its citizens to suffer from domestically produced malware if it chooses.

---

6. Seeking and/or obtaining unauthorized access to or control of computers outside the jurisdiction of a state shall be prohibited. States shall be expected to undertake actions to prevent such unauthorized access from within their jurisdiction, or they may be held complicit, and they shall be required to render assistance to states who have detected such unauthorized access.

This declaration addresses botnets. They are to be prohibited, and like the malware declaration, their detection and elimination is a matter for each state to accomplish within its own jurisdiction. But the prohibition is only when a computer in another jurisdiction is captured. A state is responsible for what it allows its citizens to do and that is mediated by its own laws. As with malware, a state that allows its citizens to capture a computer in another state and fails to prevent or eliminate the violation can be held complicit. What the declaration goes on to say is that regardless of the local *mores*, a state is required to render assistance when other states become aware of the intrusion into a computer in their jurisdiction.

The next four declarations address circumstances where cyber conflict through the facilities of the public telecommunication network is the issue.

---

7. In the event an attack, consisting of placing malicious software in the computers of another sovereign state, is detected by the target state, the attacker shall be required to remove the offending software under such terms of verification as mutually agreeable to the target and attacker states. States shall assist in determining the origin of such malicious software when called upon by the state detecting such software.

This declaration relates to a characteristic of cyber attacks that is quite different from attacks employing conventional or nuclear force. While all attacks require a great deal of planning and preparation, conventional and nuclear attacks announce themselves in a very obvious way, and with very direct means of attribution. The use of cyber force involves that the attacker violate the sovereignty of the target state long in advance. The attacker must probe the computer networks to be attacked to determine what vulnerabilities will be exploited. Malicious code will be inserted into the systems to be attacked. Viruses can be released that can wait for a signal to initiate the attack. Insiders may have been recruited and placed in critical locations. They may be active in providing current information or they may be sleepers.

The upside of advance software preparations is they can, in principle, be detected by the target nation. In such a case it may be in the interest of both parties to restore the pre-attack conditions as quietly as possible, in essence a no-harm-no-foul response. The declaration says a state can respond in such a case with cyber or other forms of force if it chooses, but an alternative resolution may be to require the offending state to withdraw its software, and to inform the injured state of the nature and locations of all such malicious software.

This leads to a cat-and-mouse game. What does the injured party know and can the attacker leave some of it software agents in place? If a state knows the attacker has not been fully compliant, does it call the attacker on it, revealing sources and methods, or does the state leave the software in place and monitor it, or even "double" it? Implicit is the ability to detect malicious but passive software. At a minimum what will be needed is that all software carry a digital signature and that all computers on the network be clean *ab initio*. In essence this reduces monitoring software environments to the equivalent of public health monitoring.

This recognizes that cyber conflict is not a matter of sudden violence but is much more like traditional intelligence operations, with move and counter move. Cyber conflict will consist of continual moves, not episodes of violence. To this end the current role of NSA in the newly created Cyber Command is well advised.

The next declaration returns to the matter of attribution. A previous declaration called for assistance in identifying the source, at least to the point of state origin and of the states through with attacks are mounted. The declaration is phrased in terms of the U.S. but it can easily be generalized.

---

8. In the event the U.S. suffers a cyber attack of national significance that threatens its economy and security, it will undertake to ascertain the circumstances that enabled it. All states are called upon to

assist in this determination. The U.S. will hold any states it believes to be complicit in the attack subject to such responses as are within its capability. An attribution of complicity can include all states whose communications facilities were wittingly employed in the attack or were employed through the negligence of a state to prevent such electronic communications from it.

This declaration says several things. First all states are called upon to assist in determining attack attribution. It says the U.S. can respond by any kind of force within its capability. But then it takes a draconian position, that any state whose telecommunication facilities were employed in the attack *can* be held complicit. "Can" allows the U.S. to let truly innocent states, innocent in its view of course, off the hook. But what it really means is that all states are responsible for seeing that attacks do not use their telecommunications facilities unimpeded. Some states will lack the resources to do adequate monitoring. The novelty of the attack may truly astound all. But it says that if states are to benefit from advances in information and communication technology, they have a corresponding responsibility to police their neighborhoods.

9. A state is entitled to seek information for the purpose of warning of a planned or impending electronic communication attack. It may do so in any way possible provided it does no harm to any states holding that information.

This declaration is, in essence, about what is euphemistically called cyber exploitation, known as intelligence collection. Given the continual nature of cyber conflict, and the need for an attacker to pre-place software, it says that a defender not only should look within his own computers for attack warning, but also should look for attack preparations in the computers of potential attackers. This is, in practice, no different from intelligence collection. But in the set of possible declarations it is best made explicit. The "do-no-harm" condition is what intelligence collectors do anyway, since one never wants a target to know what one has found out about him.

10. A strategic attack on the U.S. based on an electronic communications will be considered a use of force under the UN Charter. The U.S. will be entitled to undertake self-defense through "such action by air, sea, or land forces as may be necessary to restore international peace and security."

This is the only "line-in-the-sand" declaration in the group. In one sense it says the obvious, that an attack of national significance will be taken for what it is, an attack by a sovereign state which will trigger a justified self-defense response. What is a departure from current policy is that it puts cyber force in the category of force to which an armed response is justified. The quote is from the UN Charter.

11. Adjudication of disputes arising from the circumstances identified shall be undertaken through such international mechanisms as exist and are appropriate. States are expected to respect the rights and obligations cited for the mutual protection of their sovereignty and security.

The previous declarations have any state "plaintiff" able to charge "harm," and assign "complicity," This declaration says that these charges, while unilateral, are not final. Rather they must be submitted for adjudication to an international body. Several such exist and one can expect plaintiffs to forum-shop but the point is that the plaintiff is not prosecutor, judge, and enforcer. The international mechanism is unspecified, aside from being "appropriate." One can imagine special international bodies having particular competence in cyber commons violations. It goes without saying that time-critical emergencies requiring immediate self-defense will be dealt with and post-emergency claims of collateral damage addressed later. These are implementation matters that will evolve as situations arise and as new circumstances deriving from new technologies present themselves.

Assessing the Potential Utility of the Declarations

The 11 declarations are related to the cyber conflict issues raised in Part A (Table 2).

Stepping back to understand the relative importance of the 11 proposed declarations, the following structure emerges.

Declarations #2, 8, 10, and 11 are the central core. The keystone is Declaration #2, the assertion that the availability of the public telecommunication network is a right that should not be abridged. It recognizes that a state can define the terms of access for its citizens, but denies that any state can define the access available to citizens of other jurisdictions. Declaration #8 is the matching statement of the responsibility that must be discharged if a state is to avail itself of the right of access for its citizens in Declaration #2. Declaration #10 defines the conditions under which a state can justify self-defense in the case the right of access to the public telecommunications network is denied or harm is sustained though the malicious actions of another. The definition of "harm" is left to the state that sees itself as a victim, but in invoking such a right the merit of its complaint will ultimately be judged by its peers and the public. This last is the subject of Declaration #11.

The next set of Declarations, #5, 6, and 1, relate to the regulation of cyber "weapons." The first two suggest what should be prohibited through actions of each state exercising its responsibility for the cyber commons within its jurisdiction while Declaration #1 warns that cyber technology per se should not be limited, despite its downsides, because of its substantial upsides.

Table 2

1	Protection of cyber R&D	Technology aids defense as well as offense; proposes not to restrict it at this early stage in its development
2	Availability of public telecommunications resources	Proposed as a human right for personal and economic benefits
3	Identity management	Addresses the current anonymity on the public telecommunications network that defeats deterrence by impeding responses
4	Technical standards for network attachments	Addresses the need for assurance that devices, when first connected to the public telecommunications network are free of malware
5	Ban malware distribution	Malware is a cyber weapon that should be eliminated through actions by each of the states in the part of the Internet over which they have jurisdiction
6	Ban botnets	Botnets are the cyber weapon delivery system that should be eliminated through actions by each of the states of the part of the Internet over which they have jurisdiction
7	No-harm-no-foul conflict termination	Proposes a termination process that can be effective before the initiation of cyber conflict
8	Attribution of attacker	Establishes right of a state to seek information relating to attack attribution and to hold complicit states used as transit for the attack
9	Enables early warning activities	Provides a way to prevent damage pre-attack through preemption and trans-attack through damage limitation
10	Defines justification for self-defense against use of cyber force	Establishes the circumstance under which a state can avail itself of its right to self-defense
11	Adjudication mechanism	Requires a process for the investigation and settlement of claims

Declaration #7 proposes a conflict termination process that can be helpful in controlling escalation of cyber conflict.

Declaration #9 establishes the right of a nation to assure itself that other states are not preparing to launch a cyber attack. There are two aspects to this right. The first is that a nation should look inside its own computers, not those of others, because that is where the early warning evidence will be found. How this is done can constitute a privacy violation absent further definition of the process. One possibility is to extend personal identifiers to computers, with communications from those not "cleaned" so labeled in the same way unidentified users are apparent. The declaration implicitly recognizes that intelligence collection will be a part of a warning process as well. This is already a well-established "right" subject to the consequences a state risks if discovered.

The remaining two Declarations, #3 and 4, address implementation measures that will increase the difficulty with which cyber attacks can be carried out. In effect they raise the bar for successfully initiating cyber conflict and are, in effect, a mild form of cyber "arms limitation."

The eleven declarations can be assessed against the four characteristics proposed as measures of their potential for becoming part of multilateral agreements (Table 3).

Shown in Table 3 are some judgments regarding the degree to which the proposed declarations will meet the four conditions of being verifiable, whether all nations are likely to agree to the proposed limits on their activities, being robust under technical change, and being consistent with earlier international agreement that have been widely adopted in the past. "Y" indicates the characteristic can, in principle, be consistent with those metrics. "N" means it is not obvious that governments would accept such a limitation on their freedom of action.

The most promising are the declarations for protection of cyber R&D and the right of access to the global telecommunications systems. The other 9 declarations are problematic in varying degrees since they are likely to be seen as limiting future technical options for national security or commercial market positions. The easiest condition to satisfy is that of consistency with existing agreements, but this should not be surprising since the declarations proposed were formulated as logical extensions of existing international understandings.

The negatives in Table 3 should not be cause for discouragement. Declaratory policies are long-term enterprises. One chips away where one can and hopes that as time passes the need for the protections proposed will be more widely accepted. As a practical matter, the Internet is heavily influenced by the larger states so that even limited multilateral agreements can leverage a great deal of effective action. While not wishing ill, the frequent alarms over Pearl Harbor and 9/11 may have to occur before leaders and followers appreciate the seriousness of a wired global economy.

There remains the matter of plausible implementation processes. In much of the current discussion, there seems to be an acceptance that the problem of cybersecurity is too big for any but governments.

Table 3

	Declaration	Verifiable	Reciprocal	Robust	Consistent
1	Protection of cyber R&D	Y	Y	Y	Y
2	Availability of telecommunications resources	Y	Y	Y	Y
3	Identity management	Y	N	N	Y
4	Technical standards of network attachments	Y	Y	N	Y
5	Ban malware distribution	Y	N	Y	Y
6	Ban botnets	Y	N	Y	Y
7	No-harm-no-foul conflict termination	N	N	Y	Y
8	Attribution of attacker	Y	N	Y	Y
9	Enabling early warning activities	Y	N	N	Y
10	Self-defense against cyber force	Y	N	Y	Y
11	Dispute resolution	Y	Y	Y	Y

The enumeration of the difficulties then proceeds to point out that most of the world's cyber assets are privately owned, and that most owners see security as a cost rather than as a profit center. So the logic goes, not a great deal of substance will really happen.

This downward spiral into chaos need not be the way to read the situation. Governments are inevitably limited in what they can do: appropriations must compete with other needs; regulation is resisted; too strong a government hand is seen as big government and incursions on civil liberties and privacy. On the other hand, private owners of facilities and services can set their own rules, beholden only to market and shareholder expectations. This argues for purely private solutions. At each step those solutions will be limited but as the security situation worsens, more effective solutions will be demanded, and accepted, not because of government action but by market demands.

This oft-repeated call for "public–private" partnerships may be counter-productive, especially when each waits for the other to take action. Instead of private owners asking government what rules they must accept, faster progress may be possible if private owners tell governments what they need. It would seem to be worth a try. Meanwhile, the government can secure its own networks, fund the R&D it needs, and establish a market for strong security solutions. The declarations proposed can serve as directions for private actions. At the same time, developing voluntary technical standards, using the Internet and its social networks as a mechanism to encourage public and private exchange of solutions, and encouraging legally acceptable self-defense can be helpful.

THE BOTTOM LINE

Deterrence, on the Cold War retaliation model, is unlikely to be effective in dealing with cyber force. This model is a dead-end and continuing to pursue it simply distracts from doing something more useful. Deterrence itself is not impossible, but it must be based on broader concepts than retaliation and punishment.

Sub-state actors are not subject to deterrence based on threats of retaliation. They currently attack sovereign states, nuclear and non-nuclear, with impunity. Treating states and sub-state groups with a one-size-fits-all approach will result in addressing neither as well as they might. Sub-state groups are, for example, susceptible to cost-imposing measures.

Defense in cyber conflict is a critical part of cyber deterrence. It includes strategic and tactical warning, situation awareness, cyber order-of-battle, and the collection, retention, and analysis of cyber incident forensics.

Cyber force is quite unlike conventional and nuclear force. It can be "soft" in its effects, extended in time, and cumulative in its impact. Cyber attacks are not simply to be seen as the equivalent of strategic bombing without aircraft or missiles.

An important element of cyber defense will be real-time control of network connectivity. The cyber security problem arises from connectivity. Control of connectivity will be part of the solution.

Shared voluntary private efforts can contribute to cyber situation awareness and can provide a useful element of real-time cyber defense.

Declaratory policies are not ends in themselves. They are a beginning to a lengthy campaign to further a vision of a desired future. Declaratory policies are only useful to the extent that they leverage other forces and mechanisms to encourage beneficial use of the cyber commons. They are seeds, not trees.

ACKNOWLEDGMENTS

Part A of this work was supported by a grant from SAIC to the Georgia Institute of Technology Center for International Security, Technology, and Policy. The discussion of sub-state attackers in Part A is taken from the contributions of Rebecca Givner-Forbes to that work. Her assistance to this, as well as to other joint terrorism research projects, is gratefully acknowledged.[37] Part B was commissioned by the National Research Council. The discussion of cost-imposing strategies derives from research supported by the Office of the Secretary of Defense, Undersecretary for Policy.

The author also wishes to thank the colleagues who have provided helpful advice and guidance in developing this or earlier drafts: Dave Elliott, Sy Goodman, Tony Rutkowski, John Savage, Al Buckles, Michael Schrage, Greg Grove, and Tom Seivert.

---

[37]The full-text can be found in Stephen J. Lukasik and Rebecca Givner-Forbes, "Deterring the Use of Cyber Force," December 14, 2009. See <www.cistp.gatech.edu/publications/files/cyber_deterrencev2.pdf>.

Pulling Punches in Cyberspace

Martin Libicki
Rand Corporation

INTRODUCTION

Cyberwar can be considered a campaign that relies exclusively or mostly on operations in cyberspace. Examples might be the 2007 attacks on Estonia or the 2008 attacks on Georgia. States carry it out for strategic advantage. The advantage can be offensive—that is, to change the status quo. It can be defensive—to prevent others from changing the status quo (hence, deterrence et al.). States also carry out cyberwarfare—operations to support primarily physical combat: e.g., purported U.S. operations to disable Serbia's integrated air defense system during the Kosovo campaign.

Yet, a state may find that landing an all-out punch may not be its best strategy. It may, for instance, not convey the message that the state wishes to send. Certain acts of cyberwarfare, for instance, may violate understood norms about the legitimate use of force. Other acts may be escalatory or lead to violence.

Hence the question of this essay: under what circumstance *would* states pull their punches in cyberspace. The argument in this paper falls into five parts. It starts with short parts on the various types of cyberwarfare and a few features that distinguish cyberwarfare from physical warfare. The third part covers norms, specifically the application of existing laws of armed conflict to cyberwarfare and the case for norms more precisely tailored to the conflict in that domain. The fourth part is the paper's core: considerations that states may want to weigh in discussing how far to engage in cyberwar, either for deterrence or for more aggressive purposes. The fifth part addresses command-and-control to ensure that cyber-forces adhere to such limitations.

1 TYPES OF CYBERWARFARE

Cyberwarfare's motivations may be characterized thus:

- *Strategic:* to affect the will and capabilities of opposing states. A hypothetical example might be a Chinese strike on the U.S. infrastructure to warn the United States that the cost of intervening over Taiwan would be felt sharply at home. A strategic cyberattack might be carried out against the main military forces of a state to cripple its capabilities temporarily and allow other states leadtime to prepare for conflict.

- *Deterrence:* to affect the will of other states to carry out attacks, notably but not exclusively, cyber-attacks. Cyberattacks carried out in the name of deterrence may be demonstration attacks (although such attacks beg the question of what, in fact, is being demonstrated) and after-the-fact retaliation to convince the attacker to stop attacking, and deter it (as well as onlookers) from contemplating further mischief.
- *Operational:* to affect the conventional (physical) capabilities of opposing states engaged in current hostilities.
- *Special:* to achieve particular effects that are limited in time and place, largely outside the context of physical combat, and usually covertly. Examples may include attempts to hobble a state's nuclear weapons production, to target an individual, or to take down a hostile web site (or corrupt it with mal-ware that others might download). They are analogous to special operations.
- *Active defense:* a potpourri of techniques designed to limit the ability of others to carry out cyber-attacks or help characterize and attribute past cyberattacks. Some techniques may straddle the fuzzy line between defense, espionage, and offense.

Note that we specifically *exclude* computer-network exploitation (essentially, spying by stealing information from target systems) and techniques to facilitate computer-network exploitation (except insofar as they disable target systems).

2 WHERE CYBER IS DIFFERENT

The differences between cyberwar(fare) and its physical counterpart are so great that tenets about restraint in the use of physical force are imperfect guides to cyberspace. This part of the paper lays out critical differences between the two. Those interested in a fuller treatment are referred to the author's 2009 monograph, *Cyberdeterrence and Cyberwar* (MG-877-AF, Santa Monica [RAND], 2009).

Here is a summary:

Cyberattacks generally entail the use of information (bytes, messages etc.) to attack information systems, and, typically, by so doing, the information that such a system holds, and potentially affect the decisions made by humans and machines (e.g., power controls).

Cyberattacks are enabled by (1) the exposure[1] of target systems to the rest of the world, coupled with (2) flaws in such systems, which are then exploited. Empirically, systems vary greatly in their susceptibility to cyberattacks and susceptibility may vary over time (especially after systems recover from attack). System owners are typically unaware of all the flaws of their own systems (otherwise they would not be flaws very long).

The *direct* effects of cyberattacks are almost always temporary. Rarely is anything broken, and no one has yet died from a cyberattack (so far as anyone knows). The *indirect* effects can be more persistent: e.g., a target destroyed because a SAM was made to malfunction, a mid-winter power outage in which some people freeze to death.

Cyberattacks are self-depleting. Once a vulnerability has been exposed and deemed consequential, efforts usually follow to eliminate the vulnerability or reduce a system's susceptibility to further such attacks.[2]

The prerequisites of a cyberattack are clever hackers, cheap hardware, some network connection, intelligence on the workings and role of the target system, specific knowledge of the target's vulner-

---

[1] If one includes insider attacks, then one can talk in terms of the exposure of systems to insiders, although such a broad-brush application of "exposure" does not seem to add much since certain aspects of all systems are routinely exposed to authorized users.

[2] Depletion (of cyber-tricks) could mean that there are only so many tricks and they have been exhausted or the best tricks have been played and what remains (1) produces results that are less useful or easier to recover from before much has been damaged, or (2) works with less likelihood, (3) works under fewer circumstances which are less likely (e.g., the target machine is not in the required state very often). Alternatively the time required to find the next good trick grows steadily longer.

abilities, and tools to build exploits against such vulnerabilities. Cheap hardware possibly aside, none of these can be destroyed by a cyberattack (so, there is no basis for counterforce targeting in cyberwar). Furthermore, none are the exclusive province of states (although states have distinct advantages in acquiring these prerequisites).

Cyberattacks are very hard to attribute. Determining which box the originating attack came from is difficult enough, but even knowing the box does not prove that its owner was responsible, because there are many ways for a hacker to originate an attack from someone else's box. Even finding the specific hacker does not necessarily prove that a state was responsible for his or her actions.

The effects of cyberattacks are hard to measure. This applies even to those directed against well-scoped targets. Systems change constantly: processes that depend on affected systems (collateral damage) are not readily apparent and cannot necessarily be inferred from physical properties. The ultimate cost of, say, a disruption is often directly proportional to the time required to detect, characterize, and reverse its damage; all can vary greatly. Even after a cyberattack, it may not be clear what exactly happened; a data/process corruption attack, for instance, loses much of its force if the target knows exactly what was corrupted. Even disruption attacks, if aimed at processes that are rarely invoked or used as back-ups may not be obvious until well afterwards.

Cyberwar does not sit on top of the escalation ladder, or even very close to the top. Thus, it is not necessarily the last word between states.

3 NORMS

Which of the traditional Western laws of armed conflict apply to cyberwar? Without going through a legal exegesis, suffice it to say that the *technical* characteristics of cyberwar do not allow a particularly clean cross-walk between the laws of armed conflict as they apply in physical space and laws and their application in cyberspace. If norms would apply to offensive cyber operations, there must first be an understanding of the general principles and intentions behind such laws and then rethink their application to the unique circumstances of cyberspace. Some laws will carry over nicely; others will not.

Consider, therefore, the treatment of deception, proportionality, military necessity, and neutrality.

3.1 Deception

The laws of armed conflict frown on making military operators look like civilians, whether among shooters (hence the requirement for uniforms et al) or those being shot (no making command posts look like hospitals). But deception, in general, is the sine qua non of cyberwar. If a message sent to a target system announced "hey, I'm a cyberattack," the target system would doubtlessly keep it out. Cyber defenders take great pains to distinguish legitimate from illegitimate or harmful traffic—this is precisely the purpose of malware protection. Cyber offenders, in turn, take comparable pains to elude these detection mechanisms by masquerading as legitimate traffic. Another form of deception entails making an innocent system or network look interesting as a way of persuading offenders to waste their time rummaging through it, show their cyber techniques to the defender, befuddle them with erroneous information, and perhaps get them to leave the system (falsely) satisfied; such honeypots or honeynets are well-understood but not a common defense tactic.

Should norms frown on making military systems look like civilian systems (e.g., hospitals) in order to persuade offenders to roam elsewhere? The ability to hide looks different in the physical and the cyber world. In the physical world walls and roofs can mask what goes on inside a building—thus indications on the outside can belie what does on inside. In cyberspace, visibility can go all the way through or at least penetrate here and there (e.g., some files are open; others are encrypted). Conversely, in the real world, if walls and floors were invisible, it would be extraordinarily difficult to make the activities of a military command-and-control center look like the activities of a hospital. Absent deep inspection of content files, it may be difficult to tell what a given organization does simply by learning how it structures its information architecture.

3.2 Proportionality

Proportionality is tricky in both virtual and physical domains. If A hits B and B has grounds to believe that hitting back as hard would not deter subsequent attacks by A, B may conclude that it must hit back harder to convince A to knock it off. In cyberspace the problem of attribution makes overmatch ever more justified: if an attacker can expect to carry out *most* cyberattacks with impunity then the few times attribution is good enough for retaliation may justify striking back hard to make the *expectation of retaliation* an effective deterrent[3] That noted, proportionality is a norm not only because it is just but also because it is prudent if the attacker can counter-retaliate in an escalatory fashion.

Even if the *principle* of proportionality applies to cyberspace as it does physical space, the practical problems in modulating effects in cyberspace to preserve proportionality may be harder. As noted, battle damage may depend on details of the target system that the attacker does not know. Physical attacks at least have the "advantage" of physics and chemistry to work with. Because, say, the blast radius of a thousand-pound bomb is fairly well understood, one can predict what definitely lies outside the blast radius and what definitely lies inside. Error bands in cyberattack are much wider (although some effects can be tailored more precisely: one can corrupt files A and C without worrying about an intermediate file B). Broadly put, the likelihood that a physical attack that exceeds some operational minimum also exceeds some disproportionality point may well be higher in cyberspace than in real space.

The problem of the victim's responsibility about the ultimate damage is an issue in cyberspace, as it is in physical space but much more so. Iraq launched SCUDs against both Iran (in the 1980s) and Israel (in 1991). Far fewer people died per missile launch in Israel, partly because its building standards are better. Notwithstanding whether *any* such terror weapons can be justified, can Iraq be held responsible for the high level of casualties in Iran? Perhaps so because it knew or could have easily known the effects of a missile strike; Iran's building standards should not have come as a surprise. By contrast, matters are more opaque in cyberspace. In theory, well-written software should not fail in ways that break hardware, but poorly written software does exist (otherwise, cyberwar would be impossible). As such, an attack meant to disrupt electricity for a few days (not long enough to harm anyone) may create conditions under which hardware fails unexpectedly, disrupting electricity for months causing incidental deaths. Would it be the attacker's fault if those deaths lead others to judge some retaliation to be disproportionate?

3.3 Military Necessity and Collateral Damage

Can one avoid attacking civilians when seeking to strike the military? Often—especially when military networks are air-gapped, as prudent network management may suggest—but not always, particularly if the target actively seeks to immunize itself by daring the attacker to create collateral damage.

Attackers may have no way to know what services depend on the system being disrupted or corrupted. Some of this applies in the physical world. An attack on a power plant that cuts power to a military facility could also cut power to a civilian facility. One may not know exactly which buildings get their power from which power plants (especially if the target system is prone to cascading failures), but the visible artifacts of power distribution afford a halfway reasonable guess. In cyberspace, neither physics nor economics yield particularly good clues as to which servers satisfy which clients (although sufficient detailed penetration of the server may offer hints of the sort unavailable in the physical world). In an era of "cloud computing" a single server farm may serve any number of different customers, and many may be owned by neutral countries (China's primary airline-reservation systems are located in

---

[3]*Cf.* Lt. General Alexander's confirmation hearings testimony of April, 2010.

the United States). The problem is not just one of linking a service to its owner; the disruption of an obscure service for a wide variety of customers (e.g., one that reconciles different names into the same identity) can become a newly created bottleneck. The entanglement of services and hence the problem of collateral damage is only growing.

One issue of declining salience comes from replicating malware (e.g., worms and viruses). Although its use may help pry open a lot of doors, these days the preferred attack method is spear phishing—dangling a specific, albeit poisoned, document or link to a malware-infested web site before susceptible users in the hopes that they will bite, thereby introduce malware into their machines, thereby gaining a hacker initial access behind an organization's firewalls.

Avoiding gratuitous harm is a legitimate goal for cyberwar as with physical war, but both depend on some cooperation of the victim (as it does for physical combat). Thus, if the cyberattacker discovers that a particular system exists exclusively for civilian purposes, its disruption or corruption cannot be justified by military necessity (although it may be justified by the requirements of strategic deterrence). This goes double for attacks on systems that affect the personal health and civilian safety. Thus an attack on a dam's control systems that causes it to release too much water and therefore flood a city below it would be considered illegitimate; ditto, for attacking medical files that indicate which medicines go to which people. The target state, correspondingly, has an obligation not to co-mingle systems so that an attack on a legitimate target does damage to protected targets, or at least not co-mingle them more than business logic would otherwise dictate (thus, target states are not obligated to create separate DNS servers for life-critical, civilian, and national security systems).

So, how much knowledge of the attacked systems is required (a problem that applies to kinetic attacks as well)? If the knowledge is deficient and damage results, would opacity on the part of the adversary mitigate the attacker's responsibility? What constitutes a reasonable presumption of connectedness? What constitutes an unreasonable refusal by the attacker to exercise due diligence in examining such connections—does sufficient sophistication to carry out a certain level of cyberattack presupposes sufficient sophistication to determine collateral damage? The warriors-are-acting-in-the-heat-of-battle excuse does not pass the giggle test if warriors are hackers.

3.4 Neutrality

Generally, rules by which to judge neutrals are also more difficult in cyberspace. In the physical world, belligerents ought not cross neutral countries on the way to attack one another. Correspondingly, neutral countries that allow attacks to cross their countries assume a degree of complicity in that act.

But neutrals are not harmed by bad bytes traversing their networks. Can they even detect as much? If they could, then the target should be able to detect and filter them out as well—unless the neutral were (1) more sophisticated than the target, *and* (2) routinely scrubbed malware from traffic that traverses its borders.[4] If so, would it be obligated to report as much, particularly if it jealously guards the existence and capabilities of such a capability? In some cases—for instance, if a fiber optic line crosses a neutral's their territory without going through a local router or switch—it may be incapable of determining the fact of communications, much less their contents.

Regulating behavior *toward* neutrals is also different in cyberspace. In the physical world, country A is not enjoined from bombing a dual-use factory supplying military parts located in country B (with whom it is at war) even if the factory itself is owned by citizens of a neutral country C. Similarly, country A is not enjoined from taking down a server in country B even though it also provides critical services for country C (thus a Russian attack on U.S. servers that hold flight reservations data that could cripple China's air transport system). In practice, the world's information systems are collectively approaching spaghetti status in terms of their interconnections and dependencies. The advent of cloud computing,

---

[4]Akin to the still-controversial NSA-developed Einstein III programs that are being proposed to carry out deep packet inspection on packets flowing over federal government lines in order to filter out malware.

as noted, only adds complexity. If the threat of cyberwar proves serious, conforming states may have to regard some fraction of cyberspace (e.g., servers, systems, clouds) as off-limits to attack, but this leaves the question of how to assure that no target state uses sanctuary systems to host legitimate war targets (e.g., a logistics database).

If we restrict our consideration of cyberattacks to flooding (DDOS) attacks, some of these distinctions disappear and the laws of armed conflict that apply in the physical world apply somewhat better in the cyber world. Deception is not as important when it is the volume rather than the contents of the packets that creates the problem. The magnitude of the impact, at least the initial impact that can be gauged, and the targets are necessarily specific. But in all of today's fuss over DDOS attacks, they have very limited military utility. DDOS attacks are good at *temporarily* cutting off sites from the general public (and, as such, may affect information operations campaigns, except not necessarily in the desired direction) but militaries tend to be self-contained systems. Designing a communications architecture that mitigates DDOS attacks is not particularly complicated (Google, for one, would be glad to assist for a small fee).

3.5 New Norms for Cyberspace

Norms for cyberwar are better expressed in terms of their effects (what was done) rather than their method (how it was done)—that is, in terms of product rather than process. After all, the faster technology changes, the faster specific processes are retired. Thus a stricture against writing viruses ceases to have much meaning when viruses go out of fashion. Expressing norms in terms of effect are also easier to justify if such effects echo what earlier weapons could have produced; historic resonance helps legitimacy.

All these suggest that whatever norms in cyberspace are developed over the next decades might reflect the spirit of physical norms but they have to assume a different form altogether. So what might such norms look like?

3.5.1 Computer-Network Espionage

One place for norms might be the more acceptable practice of computer-network espionage. At the very least, states should disassociate themselves from criminal or freelance hackers. The practice is strategically deceptive as it permits states to get the benefit of criminal activity without necessarily having to face the international obloquy of whatever such hackers do. Such association also echoes the association between certain governments (notably Iran) and terrorist groups (notably Hamas and Hezbollah); all the major countries consider such associations reprehensible (at least when others do it) and properly so. Such an association is also bad policy: states may be thereby corrupted, may overlook non-hacking crimes carried out by its favored hackers, and may be subject to blackmail (a criminal group under pressure for non-hacker activities could threaten to reveal its links to state-sponsored crimes in cyberspace). It would be even better, of course, if such states took a more active role in prosecuting their own cyber-criminals, but norms against association are a start.

A similar norm might distinguish between national security espionage and all other espionage. The former at least has historical resonance. Spying may even contribute to international stability; U.S. spy satellites circa 1960 collected intelligence on Soviet capabilities thereby assuaging what might otherwise be unwarranted fears that could lead to overreaction. Commercial espionage is simply theft (if intellectual property or identifying information is stolen) or worse (if taking personal information creates the opportunity for blackmail). These norms may be more effectively and appropriately enforced in the commercial realm rather than the strategic realm (e.g., through retaliation or other hostile acts). Thus, by winking at the theft of intellectual property a state might affect its good standing within the international trade community (and violate at least the spirit of trade agreements). That noted, states that think they need CNE for economic development are unlikely to comply or willingly be party to negotiations that may end up depriving them of such capabilities. Even if they did, enforcement in trade courts (unused to who-done-its) is quite chancy.

A third CNE-related norm might dictate that implants to facilitate subsequent espionage should be distinguishable from implants that facilitate a later attack. Discovery of an implant meant to support subsequent attack may rightfully merit a more hostile reaction than a similar discovery meant to support subsequent espionage. Unfortunately, today's technology may not support the distinction: as a general rule, an implant allows *arbitrary* code to be sent to and run on someone else's system. One would have to engineer implants to forbid certain types of code to be run (including code that would disable the prohibition)—and it is by no means clear how to do that. Incidentally, none of this need mandate that implants in general be easy to find.

This suggests a fourth norm: if an attack on a system is off-limits, then espionage against such a system should be off-limits to the extent that the information acquired from such a system lacks a credible and legitimate purpose. For instance, it is hard to argue that a state must steal information from an organization which is willing to share such information. Although many targets of espionage have valuable intellectual property that they hope to employ overseas, many sensitive systems (e.g., for hospitals, electric power production) belong to organizations unlikely to be harmed if others overseas go about doing their business. Thus, if a state learns of such an implant originated by another state (admittedly, quite hard to determine), the burden of proof that such an implant was for (historically sanctioned) espionage rather than (much more hostile) sabotage should rest on the accused, not the accuser.

3.5.2 Reversibility

One norm appropriate for cyberspace (with little counterpart in physical world) is reversibility: every attack (not intended to break something) would have an antidote and the antidote should be made available to the target when hostilities cease. Thus, an attack which encrypts someone's data (assuming they lack a backup, which no one should, but some still do) should be followed by transfer of a decryption key when peace breaks out. Similarly, an attack that corrupts data should be followed by transfer of the true data (whether this replaced data would be trusted is another issue).

That noted, reversibility is not always necessary. CNE requires no antidote because nothing is broken.[5] Most attacks meant for disruption or even corruption can be reversed by the target's systems administrators in time. In many cases, the corrupted or encrypted data has a short half-life (e.g., the status of spare parts inventories on a particular point in the past) and, for practical purposes, its restoration may be more of a bother. However, this tenet imposes a requirement to refrain from attacks unless there *is* an antidote (this is akin to the rule that those who lay mines have to keep track of them). Thus, under such norms, a corruption attack would not be allowed to randomly alter information unless the true information were stored somewhere else. There may be circumstances where such a requirement is infeasible: storing the pre-corrupted data locally or sending offsite may cue defenders that something strange is going on and there may be no opportunity to ship the data anyhow (e.g., the malware that corrupts the data came from a removable device and the affected system is otherwise air-gapped). Such circumstances will have to be taken into account.

3.5.3 Against Hack-Back Defenses

Certain types of automatic defenses may also be put off-limits. A hack-back defense, for instance, may serve as a deterrent, but attackers who believe such defenses are used may make its attack seem to come from neutral or sensitive site (e.g., a newspaper, an NGO), automatic retaliation against which may create fresh problems. Such a capability is akin to an attractive nuisance (e.g., an uncovered swim-

---

[5]A separate question is whether the code that permitted or facilitated the CNE should be removed.

ming pool in a neighborhood with children). The automaticity of such an approach is redolent of the infamous Doomsday Machine from *Dr. Strangelove* (albeit with less drastic consequences).

3.6 Practical Matters

None of these tenets lends themselves to easy enforcement. Many of these distinctions are difficult to make technologically. Attackers can deny that they carried out attacks, or deny that the attacks they carried out were designed to have the proscribed effects that were credited to them. In many cases they can blame the targets, either with poor engineering (that inadvertently multiplied the effects of attacks) or, worse, with deliberately manufacturing evidence (e.g., discovered corruption without an antidote) and presenting it to credulous observers. As noted, some of these norms are premature pending the development of technology. The need for norms is vitiated by the upper limits of damage that cyberwar can cause compared to what old-fashioned violence can wreak. Nevertheless, if there are to be norms, these may not be bad places to start.

4 STRATEGIES

This section covers four overlapping issues associated with the management and control of offensive cyber operations: (1) retaliation, (2) *sub rosa* responses to cyberattack, (3) responses that promote de-escalation, and (4) offensive cyber operations in a wartime context. Retaliation will receive disproportionate attention insofar as it discusses matters that may be relevant to other sections.

The issues associated with the management and control of cyberwar parallel those of physical war because they are based on the same political-strategic challenges. However, the manifestation of these issues will look different in cyberspace, sometimes a lot different, and such differences will be explicitly noted.

4.1 Limits on Retaliation

The appropriate level and form of retaliation following a strategic cyberattack (that is, carried out against a nation's economy/society rather than only its military) is governed by several considerations. *First*, is it adequate—does it serve to convey discomfort to the attackers sufficient to make them rethink the logic of cyberwar? This usually sets a lower bound. *Second*, what does it convey about the posture and/or intentions of the retaliator? Such a consideration could ratchet up retaliation (for instance, if the retaliator has a declaratory policy and is worried about credibility), or tamp it down (if the attack appears part of a crisis that threatens to escalate out of control)? *Third*, is retaliation consistent with the recognized norms of conflict, at least as imperfectly translated into cyberspace? This tends to set an upper bound (at least if current Western norms are used). *Fourth*, would retaliation be considered escalatory—how likely is it to persuade attackers to respond with a quantitative or qualitative increase in effect or ferocity? This, too, tends to set an upper bound. *Fifth*, in the unlikely but not impossible event that retaliation is misdirected, what type of retaliation would be easiest to apologize for or even reverse? This consideration is more likely to shape the nature rather than the scope of retaliation.

4.1.1 Adequacy

Although the desire to assure adequacy tends to ratchet the response upwards, it need not do so. Deterrence, it should be remembered, arises from the ability to hit again, not the demonstrated ability to hit the first time—and in cyberspace the two may be quite different. The willingness to pull punches *in the interest of deterrence* is not as paradoxical as it might seem. One reason is that attacks reveal vulnerabilities in the target (and even software or hardware in common use) which are then more likely to be closed once revealed. The more attacks, the harder the target. Thus vulnerabilities disappear. A limited attack, particularly one that exploits known vulnerabilities unattended by the target's system administrators, reveals fewer new vulnerabilities and thus leaves more undiscovered vulnerabilities (aka zero-day attacks) to hold in reserve as the threat for the next time.

The other reason for restraint is to ensure that the response excites more fear than anger. Any attack may evoke both emotions: fear at an attack's recurrence, and anger at having been hit the first time. But only fear persuades others to do what you want; anger persuades them to do what you do not want.[6] Attacks with too little effect cannot induce enough fear and attacks with too much effect can persuade the target state to respond because it feels that the attacker cannot "get away" with what it did. Finding the sweet spot between fear and anger, if one exists (see Pearl Harbor), is particularly difficult in cyberspace. Not only are power disparities in that medium limited (there is no existential threat, and nations are talented in cyberspace in rough proportion to the extent they are dependent on cyberspace, itself), but the first attack tends to presage a *weaker* rather than *stronger* follow-up attack. Many tricks have been exhausted by being used, hence revealed,[7] and the target may reassess and reduce its current level of exposure to the outside world once it understands the adverse consequences of having been as exposed as it was. However, a relatively light attack that demonstrates capability and resolve (or at least aggression) may hint at the threat of wider and deeper effects without necessarily triggering a level of anger that overwhelms coercive effects.

4.1.2 Consistency with Narrative

Retaliation, particularly if its effects are obvious, makes a statement not only about the wages of sin, so to speak, but also the character of the executioner. This is true in the virtual and physical realm. There will be some nations that will seek to broadcast ferocity; others simply will not care—but the rest, the United States, one hopes, included, will want to make retaliation fit some master narrative about who they are and what kind of rules they would like the world to run by. At the very least, they will want the effects of attack and the means of retaliation to fit some morality play. Certain targets may be regarded as gratuitous and thus off-limits; conversely, if certain sectors of the population (e.g., opposing elites, leaders that hold obnoxious religious views) can be demonized a certain latitude, perhaps vigor, in retribution can be demonstrated. With rare exceptions (e.g., the 1986 raid on Libya) most punitive operations carried out by the United States have been means justified by specific ends: e.g., campaigns against dual-use facilities such as power plants or bridges in order to win wars, air strikes against SAM sites (the 1998 *Desert Fox* campaign against Iraq), or blockades to reduce supplies available to nations that misbehave (e.g., Israel's Gaza policy). Third party hurt was regarded as unfortunate but unavoidable.

What makes retaliation in cyberspace different is that it can rarely be justified by the need to disarm the other side for any length of time. The only justification is to change behaviors and thus harm to third parties such as civilians cannot be excused as instrumental to a tangible military goal. Thus, every reprisal must be judged by the narrative it supports. Such a narrative has to be robust enough to tolerate a wide range of unpredicted outcomes in both directions: fizzles and overkill—both are greater problems in the virtual rather than physical realm. The retaliator may have to pretend that the range of effects produced is a fairly good match for the range of effects sought lest it appear feckless (in promising what it cannot hit) or reckless (in creating more effects than it wanted to), or both at the same time. Precision in messaging is generally unavailable. Nevertheless a certain rough justice may be warranted. If the source of the attack, for instance, comes out of the universities but the state is clearly behind the move, then retaliation that targets financial elites may seem misdirected; conversely, if the attack appears to emerge from organized crime elements, then retaliation that targets the intellectual elite may seem

---

[6]Unless the point is to anger the target into over-reaction thereby mobilizing the population on behalf of the attacker; terrorism has long tried to exploit this logic.

[7]Although the attacker could have many types of attacks prepared, it presumably led with its best attack—in the sense of most damaging and/or most likely to succeed.

similarly misdirected. Overall, the more that the original attack comes as a surprise to the attacking state's population, the harder it is to justify retaliation that discomfits the same population (unless by doing so, one *intends* to alienate the population, persuade them to support the hackers, and justify the nature of the retaliation in retrospect).

Justification and legitimacy present big potential problems with the retaliation narratives. The attacking state may well deny everything and claim itself to be the victim of aggression (rather than retaliation) unless it chooses to boast of the attack to support a campaign of intimidation against the target state. The retaliator will have to determine how strong a case it can make in public to justify retaliation, but that hardly guarantees that those in the attacking state or friends of the attacking state will necessarily believe it. Very few people understand cyberspace well enough to evaluate the evidence of attribution in an objective manner, even if it were all laid out. Clearer cases in the physical world still beget confusion: after all, the evidence on who carried out the September 11th attacks is essentially accepted in the West, but half of those polled in the Islamic world believe otherwise. South Korea substantiated its claim that the March 2010 sinking of its naval vessel was an attack carried out by North Korea—but it remains to be seen how widely its evidence is believed.

The attacker's counter-narrative also has to be factored in; if it holds that the retaliator is an enemy of the local religion, then it will be reinforced by any cyberattack on religious institutions—hence the dilemma if the retaliator suspects that the original attack *did* come from religious institutions (e.g., that run universities that attackers attend). In the virtual realm, it is not so hard for the attacking state to then attack its own sensitive institution (e.g., a hospital run by religious authorities), demonstrate as much, and blame the supposed retaliator for having done so. Since cyberattacks rarely harm anyone, one moral bar for the attacking government is easy to surmount; after all, it is not causing its own to suffer greatly (indeed, with a little more work, it is possible that one can devise a counter-morality play in which valiant systems administrators stop matters just short of a disaster).[8] Without the kind of physical evidence that might prove exculpatory against such charges (e.g., we did not bomb a mosque because we know the tracks of every flight we sent out and none approached the mosque), the accused state (the retaliator, whether real or supposed) it cannot make its case. All the evidence of who done it is under the control of the attacking state, which can easily argue against giving it up on the grounds that releasing details would show others too much of the system and facilitate future attacks.

Other counter-narratives might take the attacking state off the hook. The state suffering retaliation can deflect the ire of its public against itself if retaliation targets institutions that are not controlled by the state (e.g., banks in some countries). It might do so by blaming the owners for having made themselves open to the schemes of hostile countries by exposing their systems to the outside world without sufficient security (again, this is an argument that almost everyone but the techno-cognoscenti will have to accept or reject on faith). Such a counter-narrative communicates the attacking state's refusal to be intimidated by retaliation, either directly (because it does not yield) or indirectly (because it need not accept the public's blame for the incident). To avoid such an argument, therefore the retaliator may have to find at least some targets that are the responsibility of the attacking state but damage to which is visible to the public (if the latter is the retaliator's intention).

4.1.3 *Prosecution Rather Than Retaliation*

Unless the attacking country is already at war with the target state (which tends to make retaliation secondary) or boasts of the attack—as it might if the effect was mean to coerce—target countries that profess to rule of law may be constrained to seek justice rather than retribution. Similar issues apply to terrorism, but rarely to conventional war. In the latter case, warfighters presume to act on the state's

---

[8]In cyberspace, however, accepting that kind of narrative is a matter of faith, with little evidence available to prove or disprove the story—and thus little opportunity for recognizably neutral umpires to call balls and strikes.

behalf, particularly if organized and armed by the state. In cyberspace where organization is a loose concept and being armed even looser, such a presumption may not necessarily apply.

The judicial route buys time. While prosecution is going on, the target state can allay popular ire while the source of the attack is ascertained. In contrast to military narratives that emphasize speed of reaction (re General Patton's aphorism: a good plan, violently executed . . . with vigor now is better than a perfect solution applied ten minutes later), legal processes are expected to be lengthy (the wheels of justice grind slow, but they grind exceeding fine).

Going to court hardly gets the attacking state off the hook. The target state can press the attacking state for access to individuals or information (e.g., let me look at these servers), and use the refusal to cooperate—which is hard to hide—as a justification for retaliation. NATO's invasion of Afghanistan was widely accepted as legitimate even though there is little evidence that the Taliban ordered or even knew about the September 11th attacks—it sufficed that the Taliban sheltered al Qaeda (following the East African embassy bombings) beforehand and refused to turn them over afterwards. UN sanctions were imposed on Libya following the latter's refusal to turn over two suspects in the Lockerbie bombing.

The disadvantages of the judicial route bear note. Many U.S. citizens are nervous about using civilian judicial methods against the leadership of an avowed enemy of the United States (al Qaeda) based, in part on the fear that the accused may escape punishment on a technicality. Arguably, until retaliation *does* ensue, there is no punishment and hence, by some measure, no deterrence. However, there is little to the argument that the failure to retaliate promptly leaves the offending government in place to carry out more mischief; retaliation in cyberspace cannot remove the government by force. Although a retaliation campaign may reduce popular toleration of the government, support for rogue governments tends to rise immediately after it gets into trouble. Governments that lose wars often fall after the war is over (e.g., the Galtieri government in Argentina following the Falklands, the Milosevic government in Yugoslavia following the Kosovo campaign), but this is hardly an argument for instant retaliation.

Conversely, delaying retaliation allows the attacker to bulwark its own cyber defenses so that delayed retaliation has much less of an effect for being postponed—but how much less? First, the attacker, with foreknowledge of possible retaliation, may have bulwarked its own defenses in advance of the attack; only non-governmental systems whose administrators did not get the memo about the upcoming attack would need to use the pause to get ready. Second, the cost and politics of the post-attack bulwarking cannot be ignored. Maintaining a high state of readiness for an extended period of time is costly. For the attacking state to call for systems owners to beef up their cyber defenses in advance of retaliation is to concede to many folks that some retaliation is coming even as it protests its innocence in the original attack. Third, if the two states are mutually hostile, the target may already have implanted malware into the attacking state's critical systems just in case. Implanting attacks do not guarantee that retaliation will work, but it does address much of the problem of gaining access before external barriers go up.

4.1.4 *Escalation*

Escalation in cyberspace—specifically, the relationship between retaliation and counter-retaliation it—can be a speculative topic. No tit-for-tat exchange in cyberspace has been seen. With no nation arguing that cyberwar is legitimate, few government officials have declared what might constitute thresholds of cyber escalation. The cyber equivalent of Herman Kahn's *On Escalation* is yet unwritten. Not only do we lack a discrete metric for cyberwar, but there is also no good way to measure the proportionality systematically and consistently (e.g., this act is more heinous than that act).

Consider a retaliator weighing between mild and hard retaliation in the physical world. A mild response may fail to convey sufficient displeasure or instill fear; indeed, it may embolden the attacker—who then believes that the retaliator is *unwilling* to strike back hard or *unable* to strike back hard, or both. This is a Munich world. Alternatively, an overly hard retaliation will induce anger in the attacker, shame in that it has lost face by revealing that others have no fear of retaliating against it in a serious way, or a sense of grievance that the punishment was disproportionate to the crime. This is the Guns of August world. History supports both points of view, but not for the same context. Thus, there is no universal agreement that a harder response is more escalatory than a milder response—let alone what the thresholds are.

Cyberwar adds further complexities. An attacker could be a state, state-sponsored, state-condoned, or just state-located. There is strategic logic in aiming retaliation at a state that did not attack but has the means of thwarting future attacks (e.g., by prosecuting hackers or at least by not harboring and supporting them) so as to persuade them to crack down. But it is unclear whether such retaliation would be considered *legitimate*—especially if the attacking state makes half-hearted attempts to look cooperative (e.g., we'd like to help, but we lack the resources, and letting you nose around in our systems looking for evidence would violate the privacy of our citizens, not to mention our sovereignty). Any non-trivial retaliation might be viewed as unfair, and hence an affront.

The attacking state may conclude it is best off denying everything. If so, non-trivial retaliation indicates that the retaliator thinks the accused attacker is not only a crook but a liar. For the attacking state not to take umbrage at that point is to concede it lied and lose face. It may matter little if the initial protestations of innocence were lies (not everyone will know that it is a lie); indeed, theories of cognitive dissonance suggest that the perceived insult felt by the attacker upon retaliation may be *greater* because the attacker has to work so hard to maintain that it *was* a lie—akin to protesting too much. All this, unfortunately, does not give the analyst much to work with in terms of determining thresholds since the relevant threshold (is retaliation non-trivial) may be quite low (retaliation was always going to be non-trivial). Thus the issue of whether retaliation is met by escalation may have little to do with how damaging the retaliation was; the attacking state will match or, alternatively, exceed the retaliation based on an altogether different set of strategic and political criteria.

Another complicating factor that is far more present in cyberwar than in other forms of response is the uncertainty in forecasting effects. Accidents have fostered escalation in the past (Germany's error that led it to bomb English cities opened the floodgates to city-busting in WWII). They could easily do so in cyberspace, especially if the mode of attack is not system/network disruption (whose effects are often instantaneous and obvious) but data/algorithm corruption (whose effects play out over time and may not be immediately evident to either side without extensive analysis and maybe not even then). If there *were* a recognized threshold in cyberwar, then the presence of great uncertainty in predicting effects argues for doing less rather than doing more as a way of minimizing the likelihood of unwanted escalation. However, the lack of such thresholds means one can be quite precise in predicting effects and quite imprecise in determining the other side's trigger point for escalation. Indeed, the other side may have no clue, or no activation threshold that it can maintain that is not highly context-dependent.

A third factor specific to cyberspace is the relatively narrow band between the least and the most damage one can do by retaliation. Violent war features very wide bands. If your country avoids war with a peer, the number of families that could be suddenly wiped out in any one day is quite low (e.g., from a car bomb or a bad accident). If your country goes to war with a nuclear-armed peer, it is possible that all families could be suddenly wiped out. There is a lot of scope for escalation within that band. Now consider cyberwar. In today's environment, cyberattacks are always taking place (even if acts of deliberate disruption or corruption are relatively rare). Given the number of sophisticated hackers around, one can assume that if a system with requisite vulnerabilities has something worth stealing, theft *will* take place and sooner rather than later. Because the general noise level is high in cyberspace, any retaliation that merits notice as such has to be loud. The top end may also be limited, as well. Who knows how much damage is possible through a no-holds-barred attack on a nation's critical infrastructure? No one has yet been killed in a cyberattack and there is scant indication that a full-blown attack could exceed the effects of a good-sized hurricane.[9] Similarly, there is little revealed information on fail-safe compo-

---

[9]The most commonly cited worst-case scenario concerns attacks on power companies that damage so much equipment that it would take months to restore power. Yet extracting from Idaho Lab's 2007 Aurora laboratory experiment to such a scenario is quite a stretch—most power equipment defaults to shutting down rather than going haywire.

nents of modern control systems (including for banking) or the extent to which timely and intelligent human intervention can mitigate the effects of cyberattacks. All we know about is what has happened so far, and, by standards of conventional warfare, the damage has not been terribly impressive. Thus the maximum damage may not be so great. All this suggests that the fact more than the level of retaliation will influence a state's counter-retaliation policy if it stays in cyberspace. Conversely, the level of retaliation may influence the original attacker to escalate out of the cyber realm to violence, whether via war or via state-sponsored terrorism.

A fourth complicating factor exists whenever the attacker *wants* retaliation. Terrorists often use attacks to goad the target into responding in an ugly and alienating manner. Fortunately, few states actually use goading as a strategy.[10] The danger is worse in cyberspace. States riven by competing bureaucratic factions may find that one or another faction has attacked the target state in cyberspace as a way of getting the rest of the country to rally behind its particular interests (e.g., a more belligerent stance) or rally against its particular *bête noire* (one bureaucracy may want to take on country A; the other to take on country B).[11] In the physical world, the faction that gets caught may blow its case; in cyberspace it is far easier for a faction to avoid getting caught. Even a state whose top leadership seeks no confrontation can be frustrated by difficulty of enforcing its writ on its own employees. As noted, clever hackers, sufficiently detailed intelligence on the target, and a modicum of hardware suffices to create a capability; thus a faction can, itself, have quite pernicious effects. At that point, the target's response is more likely to play into the hands of the faction that attacked it than into the alternative less-hostile faction—particularly if the suspect faction denies involvement and cites retaliation as proof of the target's/retaliator's malignant nature. Facing an attacker beset with such power struggles, the target state has to ask: would the positive deterrence effect from heavy retaliation trump the negative effect from aligning the state with the faction that identified the target state as the enemy? If the answer is no, the target state may prefer to keep retribution symbolic or even let the incident pass (if the attribution is less than certain, broadcasting doubts can be sufficient reason not to act), respond with judicial means as if the attackers were non-state entities that the state is morally obligated to look for, or try a subtle response (if one exists) which may disproportionately harm the attacking faction vis-à-vis the less hostile faction or the state and its public.

Fortunately, a response does not have to be disproportionate or even equivalent to the original attack to convince the attacker that its calculus of costs and benefits turned negative. Since cyberattacks cannot seize anything directly and only opens a narrow window to permit physical attacks, the tangible gains to the attacker may be modest, and may easily turn negative if the odds of attribution are respectable despite the retaliation being less than overwhelming. A response that is deliberately weaker than the attack may ward off escalation as long as the attacker does not make a case of how baseless *any* retaliation is.

Another approach to escalation asks: what sort of retaliation might put the attacker in a position where it may be forced to counter-retaliate. Clearly, there is a distinction between a cyberattack that kills someone and one that leaves no casualties. Almost as clearly, there is a distinction between a cyberattack with effects made for YouTube and more subtle versions (e.g., a blackout is more visible than a string of ATM failures, not to mention erroneous bank statements). If the attacking regime is nervous about its control over the population, then a cyber-retaliation that affects the performance of its domestic security forces may trigger a panicked and potential escalatory response—but it may also persuade the attacker to back off and argue that bigger stakes than information security are on the table. Systems that the attacker has put public prestige behind—perhaps because they allow it to fill an important promise, or because they have been (mistakenly) touted as secure—may also force the attacker to respond or even

---

[10]Bismark's Prussia, however, successfully goaded France into foolishly declaring war on it so that it could rally the south German states to its side, beat France, and thereby cement the creation of Germany—but with words, not war.

[11]Japan's army circa 1941 was more interested in combat with China and perhaps Russia; while Japan's navy had its eye on the West's colonies and thus was itching to go after the UK and the United States. The United States in the 1790s found itself divided between factions that favored France and those that favored Britain, each at war with the other.

escalate (without raising the stakes so high that it can be persuaded to call things off). But these are only guesses.

4.1.5 Taking It Back

The last consideration in limiting retaliation is the sneaking worry that one might be wrong. It can affect how one retaliates.

Historically, "oops" is not necessarily followed by "I'm sorry." Even after inspectors gave up looking for WMD, the United States never apologized for having invaded Iraq on false premises. Instead, administration officials argued that Saddam Hussein's failure to "come clean" (cooperate cheerfully with weapons inspectors) left him partially culpable for the West's mistake; it should have behaved as Libya did in renouncing nuclear weapons. False cyber-retaliation may be similarly justified if the supposed attacker failed to welcome the efforts of law enforcement officials with open arms, or did not abjure the capability for cyberattack or the closely related (albeit far better legitimized) capability for cyber espionage. Yet, putting the burden of proof on the supposed attacker to show that it *never* attacked may well be asking for the impossible. However, whereas in Iraq the regime changed (leaving no one to apologize to), such an outcome is far less likely for cyber-retaliation. Thus apologies may be needed to allay a now-hostile state.

Fortunately, it is easier to make amends in cyberwar than it is for physical war. Major destruction is unlikely; mass casualties even less likely. The likely effects of cyberwar are disruption and corruption. Both can be measured in economic terms—and thus if erroneously caused can be partially assuaged by cutting the victim a check. Cyberspace affords the retaliator an even better alternative. Attacks that scramble or corrupt data can often be repaired after the fact by releasing the (cryptographic) keys and thereby let the victim of retaliation unscramble the data or replace the corrupted data. This may not eliminate all the damage—scrambled data may be temporarily unavailable for use, and corrupted data may, conversely, have been used to ill effect—but it helps.

4.1.6 Conclusions to Limits on Retaliation

To reiterate, these five criteria—credibility, communications, norms, escalation control, and reversibility—suggest constraints on the means and extent of retaliation. The first says that retaliation must be noticed but cannot exhaust itself in the process; the next two suggest that it be carried out in a manner that compliments those carrying it out; the fourth suggests avoiding certain types of attacks even if it cannot ascertain a specific tripwire; the fifth suggests the wisdom of avoiding retaliation that is not reversible.

4.2 Sub Rosa Cyberattacks

A state's decision to engage only in *sub rosa* cyberattacks means that the attacks cannot awake the target's public and, by extension, everyone else's public. The only states that will know about the attack are the attacker, the target, and those that either side chooses to reveal the attack to. *Sub rosa* options are generally unavailable to attackers in the physical world. Such limitations are meant to ease the pressure on the target to respond by retaliation or escalation.

Table 1 locates *sub rosa* cyberattacks within the context of a broader attack-response matrix. The attacker can choose to carry out an overt attack—which is noticeable and boasted about (e.g., for the purposes of coercion). Alternatively, the attacks can be obvious—noticeable by the public but not owned up to. Finally, the attack can be covert; pains are taken not to make its effects public, and, no claim is made. (The fourth possibility—the attacker gives itself credit for an attack that it is at pains to hide—makes little sense). The retaliator has three choices: retaliate openly, retaliate in an obvious manner, or retaliate covertly.

Table 1

	Attack is Overt	Attack is Obvious	Attack is Covert
Response is Overt	Open cyber-war	Retaliator has to run the risk of explanation in the face of what may be the attacker's denials as well as the risk of possible error.	Retaliator has to reveal the attack (to mobilize its population, perhaps), and then run the risks of their denial.
Response is Obvious	Why bother? No one is fooled.	No one is fooled by the response, and error is possible. Yet, it lets both sides "deny" everything if they tacitly agree to settle.	Revealing the original attack would justify retaliation but point the finger at the retaliator; conversely if the retaliator is caught the *tu quoque* defense looks contrived.
Response is Covert	Puts the onus on the attacker to reveal what happened and explain why. Retaliator may have to answer to public about why no response.	Signals displeasure but also a desire not to let things get out of hand. May not deter third parties (except via rumor). Will also not protect against error.	*Sub rosa* cyberwar. Signals displeasure but also a desire not to let things get out of hand. Third parties know nothing. May protect against error.

Now consider the responder's options by type of attack (Table 1).

If the attack is overt, the responder is being dared to respond. It could take the dare openly. It could carry out an obvious cyberattack and not take credit, but it will be assigned credit anyhow because it has an obvious motive. Alternatively, it could respond covertly, leaving leave the original attacker to decide whether to reveal the retaliation—which, by the nature of a covert attack is likely to target state institutions that do not deal with the public—or keep quiet and boast that it attacked with impunity. The attacker's advantage lies in keeping quiet if interested in forging a tacit or covert agreement to stop. If the attacker does keep quiet, and particularly if it continues attacking, the responder will have to answer to its public (and others) why it did nothing. The responder's primary motive for keeping matters covert may be the hope that it can, in fact, persuade the attacker to stop without making it obvious to others *why* the attacker stopped.

If the attack is obvious but not overt, the primary consideration for the target is how certain it is of who attacked. Overt or obvious responses present similar considerations. Even with obvious responses, few who think about the matter will have serious doubts that the target was, in fact, the retaliator since only the target had an obvious motive.[12] The only reason to deny what is otherwise obvious is to permit both sides to save face ("What, hackers we?") while they come to a *modus vivendi*. Finally, a covert response to an obvious attack signals displeasure but also a desire not to let things get out of hand. It may lead to a tacit or at least covert settlement. The responder could concede that it had been attacked but claim it had insufficient facts to warrant a counterattack (and hope the target of its counterattack keeps quiet). A covert response will, however, not deter third parties, and it will not protect against error (see later in this section for why).

If the attack is covert, the responder has a deeper dilemma. It can respond overtly in order to make an example of the attacker—who is likely to deny its culpability and may even demand proof that such an attack took place. Such a strategy may be pursued to mobilize opinion against the attacker, particularly if the original covert cyberattack is a prelude to overt hostilities. An obvious response may be chosen because the target list with an obvious response is better. If the attacker reveals the attack, its doing so

---

[12] There are exceptions: (a) the attacker has struck multiple countries and so the retaliator can be one of several countries, (b) the attacker has multiple enemies even if they all have not been struck in cyberspace, or (c) the attack gives a third party who may dislike either the attacker or the target an opportunity to weigh in. In the last two cases, the real counter-attacker has to have something in wait ready to be sprung at just the right time. Nevertheless, the exceptions are exceptional.

will suggest to others who the true author of the response is. The risk is that if the responder is fingered and then claims it was attacked first, albeit covertly, such an argument will appear contrived.

The purest case is where both sides attack each other covertly. The attacker may wish to exert pressure on the target state's leadership without causing a public reaction that may constrain the ability of the leadership to act in the attacker's interest (or least not act against the attacker's interest). The retaliator may wish to dissuade further attacks without itself riling the attacker's public. In other words, both sides are likely to believe that each can come to an agreement and avoid escalation if each side's public is not, in effect, consulted on the matter. In the unlikely event that both side's leadership consist of hawks afraid that their publics are dovish, they can carry on at each other without undue interference (the less likely scenario inasmuch as having outsider observers tends to make concessions harder lest leaders lose face). And so the game goes on until someone concedes either explicitly or tacitly or until one or the other side's attacks are made public—either through one side's decision to reveal all or part of the exchange, or because what was supposed to be covert turns out to be overt. Alternatively, the exchange may continue indefinitely until the target systems have so hardened themselves that attacks are no longer worthwhile.

The retaliator may also wish to limit itself to covert responses because of attribution problems. If it is confident that it knows who the attacker is, but cannot or will not provide a convincing rationale to the rest of the world, then a covert response puts the onus on the target to explain why it is being attacked. But a covert response has a sneaky way of indemnifying the retaliator against the consequences of the retaliator's errors. If the retaliator is correct, the attacker will probably have a good idea who hit back because the attacker knows who it hit (unless the attacker was overly generous when selecting targets). If the retaliator is incorrect, however, the unfortunate victim of retaliation may be left hurt but confused: it does not know about the original attack and therefore has no reason to suspect the retaliator (to be sure, other evidence may reveal who the retaliator is, so a covert response is not entirely risk-free).

Sub rosa cyberwar can be quite tempting for the responder and even the attacker particular within the covert operations or covert intelligence community. No one has to produce evidence of attribution, and there is less pressure to reveal the particulars—methodologies and targets—of the attacks. Indeed, it is far easier, in most respects, to carry out rogue operations in cyberspace than it is to do so in the physical world: e.g., fewer prisoners to worry about. Unfortunately, what is most attractive to some becomes a weakness to others. The covert community lacks the public oversight that more overt parts of the national security community operate under. If it wishes to justify its actions, it has more control over what evidence is collected and presented; it has less to fear from contradictory material from neutral or hostile parties. Members of the covert community, despite their personal probity and honesty, tend to operate in a sealed world. Mistakes can go uncorrected for longer. When actions are criticized, there is a reflexive tendency to circle the wagons. Even those who argue that members of *our* covert community are like the rest of us, only in different professions, the same may not hold for members of *their* covert community where rule-of-law is noticeably weaker.

The second problem with *sub rosa* warfare is that each side's strategy is hostage to the exercise of discretion by the other side (not to mention the accidental revelation of covert attacks). Once revelations start everyone may end up looking bad: not only the attackers on both sides, but also the targets who could be called both feckless (for having been had) and sneaky (for covering it up). On the one hand, a primary rationale for keeping matters covert is to facilitate later settlement; on the other hand, those in the know—that is to say, the covert community—generally do not populate the sort of organizations whose primary motive is to reach accommodation with the other. Covert communities, by their nature, distrust all other covert communities. So, each side has to weigh whether it is better off pulling back the shades on these *sub rosa* exchanges or letting matters continue their subterranean course. The result may be a game of chicken. Each knows that revelation will make its side look bad not only to the public, but perhaps also to its own masters, but each may hope that the *threat* of revelation may make the other side look worse. Each side, may therefore be in a position to concede things to hide their common activities in ways that might be impossible were their "negotiations" subject to public scrutiny. The dangers seem obvious.

As noted, a covert cyberattack must abjure certain targets (i.e., a limit on offensive cyberwar options). Clearly, targets that affect the broad population are out; thus, attacks on critical infrastructures are incompatible with a *sub rosa* strategy. Perhaps, one can imagine an attack that could be and *would be* characterized as an accident but reported as deliberate (thereby achieving its dissuasive impact) by those who operate the infrastructure—but large conspiracies of this type are heir to leakage and hence failure. The same would hold for attacks on financial systems—unless bankers, too, want to play that game. That leaves as primary targets, parts of the government that do not interface with the general public (or whose interfaces can be controlled so that glitches in the interaction are made good or otherwise covered up). Still, those who run systems that were hacked have to be counted on to keep quiet about what they have seen. Ironically, this leads to two observations. First, that the best targets of *sub rosa* cyberattacks are systems associated with the covert community. The very best targets may be systems that the target state is reluctant to admit having.[13] That noted, intelligence systems tend to be air-gapped and thus essentially unavailable for attack. Second, as an open society, the United States is a poor target for a *sub rosa* attack because of the difficulty of keeping attacks secret. Closed societies offer good targets for *sub rosa* cyberattacks because they keep secrets better. This further implies, incidentally, that states at war offer more *sub rosa* targets than those at peace because wartime conditions tend to reduce the amount of information that traverse the boundary between a military and the rest of the world.

4.3 Promoting De-Escalation in a Crisis

How does a crisis begin?

War in the physical realm generally requires a concert of movements (e.g., tanks moving from garrison, leaves cancelled, civilians mobilized, supplies surging to the front) which must take place so many hours and days before conflict if forces are to be ready when war starts. No such physical or economic constraints spell the onset of conflict in cyberspace. Even attacks that have to be prepared, perhaps years in advance, cost only a little to maintain (e.g., to check if the intelligence is still good and if the implants are still functioning and accessible); they can be postponed for weeks and months often with little harm. Might a good indicator of an attack be an acceleration of bulwarking actions as the attacker braces against an expected retaliation? Perhaps, yet many such preparations can be made near-instantly if planned properly.

4.3.1 A Phony Crisis Can Start with Finding Implants

Indications of cyberwar are more likely to tell where than when (analogously, finding troops marching to your border says when, but finding them hidden in the hills says where). Current practice favors planting code into targeted systems well in advance of any crisis. An implant is designed to activate a subsequent strike; it allows the attacker to send arbitrary attack code to the target system confident that the target system will attempt to run the code at privilege levels which can cause serious damage to the system's functions or integrity.

Finding their attack code in your system may constitute a crisis—but what kind? As with an attack, attribution is more difficult if no attack has occurred. First, because an implant is not a time-specific preparation, there may be no real-world crisis going on at the time of discovery to suggest who may be planning a cyberattack. Those looking for what earlier crisis prompted the implant may be frustrated by the fact that intermediate servers that would allow one to trace the original infections may have long ago purged their memories. Even if the memories exist, one cannot know who did it if unable to trace back months' worth of packet traffic, a near-impossible task. Second, implants need not contain attack code,

---

[13]In the wake of the controversy over DARPA's Total Information Awareness program, funding was ended. If, as many believe, the program went underground into the intelligence community, those who run such systems may be quite reluctant to admit that they exist.

just enough code to permit attacks to be attached to operating system or common application. Without attack code to analyze whatever forensic clues exist in the code to trace it back to its putative writer are simply missing. The one advantage to finding an implant is that many attacks erase themselves after completion leaving nothing to analyze, but this is true only if they are completely successful and are not placed on machines that studiously archive everything to ineradicable media.

Last is the problem of distinguishing an implant prefatory to an attack from an implant prefatory to taking information. Most implants are in the latter category: they exist to keep the door open for the next attack or to facilitate the process of raising the privilege level of the rogue code to whatever is necessary to carry out its spying mission. Discovering an implant proves that the bad guys got in, but it does not prove that the attacked system can be harmed apart from having its files read.[14] It gives no clue to the likely success of the attack or its consequences.

So what does the target of an implant do? Presumably, the discovery prompts it to check its systems for similar implants in particular, or rescrub systems for implants in general (now that evidence of one suggests the possibility of others). If the state wishes its private and non-federal sector (or even its own less attentive bureaucrats) to scrub with alacrity, it may have to raise alarms about what it has managed to find. (Until these implants are vacuumed up, any emergency cyber-defense short of shutting off affected networks from the rest of the world may be meaningless; the enemy, so to speak, is already inside.)

Need the target state accuse specific others and thereby start an *external* crisis to allow it to meet an *internal* (clean-up) crisis?[15] In other words, need it make the case (tendentiously under the circumstances) that it has found a particular enemy's implant rather than simply an implant in general? Perhaps yes. It may want a crisis and this discovery furnishes as good a pretext as any. Similarly, it may wish to justify retaliation in another domain (e.g., to weaken the opponent). It may wish to embarrass an opponent, characterizing it as hostile (for having made the implant) and incompetent (for having let it be discovered) at the same time. In such circumstances, forbearance is secondary—the target state wants a crisis for its own purposes. Perhaps no. The target state may honestly be concerned that the supposed attacker should have been but was not been deterred from making an implantation. In today's world in which CNE is expected, the accusing state has to credibly argue that the implant could *only* have been meant for an attack. Not only is it unclear what would constitute evidence, but finding enough people who could and would evaluate such an argument on its merits may also be daunting—more daunting than, say, similar arguments about aluminum tubes made just prior to the 2003 invasion of Iraq.

In general whatever crisis follows finding an implant is one of choice not necessity.

4.3.2 A Real Crisis Needs an Attack

A nation that has been attacked, but has yet to respond and restore the *status quo ante bellum* can be said to be in a cyber-crisis. In common with most crises, a cyber-crisis has an internal component (managing domestic expectations) and an external component (managing international expectations and preserving one's "face" abroad).

In both cases the internal and external crises sharply change their character if and when there is a consensus on who attacked. Because people tend to blame others, notably specific others, for their problems, an internal consensus is likely to form first—indeed almost instantly (albeit not necessarily reliably) in some cases. States reluctant to escalate crises (which is most of them most of the time) may find themselves buffeted by internal popular pressures to respond and great uncertainty about whether that might start a completely unnecessary fight.

---

[14]The notion that any process that can read a file can also alter it is misleading—the process may not have sufficient write privileges, or the applications that read the data may ignore data that is not digitally signed, and the likelihood that a rogue process can replicate digitally signed data without access to the signing key is infinitesimal.

[15]At least one, "senior American military source said that if any country were found to be planting logic bombs on the grid, it would provoke the equivalent of the Cuban missile crisis." From *Economist*, July 3, 2010, "Briefing: Cyberwar," p. 28.

Until there is a *global* consensus on who attacked, the target can do nothing and not lose face *overseas*. Once such a consensus emerges—and it may emerge even if the technical analysis of the attack is quite incomplete—the target state will be viewed as having been challenged, as if slapped by a metaphorical glove in a duel. The challenge may be overt—attribution could be conceded and the attack justified as a response to a cyberattack, to the need to pre-empt a cyberattack (if it feels the target audience is unsophisticated and unaware that pre-emption is nearly impossible), a festering wound, to non-cyber forms aggression, or to mounting hostility from the target. The attacker may deny the attack directly but praise (and support) the attackers (e.g., the attitude of Iran towards Hezbollah). Or, the attacking state may deny everything with a wink and a sneer—as if it wanted to insulate itself from the automatic application of legal norms but wants the rest of the world to know that it has the capability to carry out such an attack and the target lacks the capability to ward it. Alternatively, the attacker may have been surprised to have been accused so soon, and turn sharply about-face and admit is culpability in order to wring whatever it can out of the target's humiliation (the 20th century is full of crises where the aggressor sought to humiliate others).

The target state, operating under the eyes of the world, can evaluate the attack in many ways: error (the attacker thought, erroneously, it was hit first), inadvertence (e.g., the attack was an accidental or unsanctioned act carried out by a rogue faction or at the behest of the attacking government), culminating (e.g., the act was undertaken to right a past wrong, or as a warning shot to defuse an existing crisis), or provocative (the act was a signal or prefatory to more hostile action). In the first three cases, the pressures on the target state emanate from its own citizens and from those in the rest of the world who may believe that the attack was provocative. The attacker, itself, may not view forebearance negatively but as deserved in the first case (error), a blessing in the second case (inadvertence), and a statement of maturity in the third case (culminating). Only in the last case (provocative) will it find a failure to respond to be an act of weakness that deserves further exploitation. The question for the attacker in the first three cases is whether it can provide enough political cover to the target to convince third parties that the failure to respond harshly cannot be considered a sign of the target's weakness but its strength in being able to see past recent pain to achieve more long-term goals. Or, the question may be moot: chances are the attacker (or supposed attacker) was accused because it was not on good terms with the target state in the first place.

In great contrast to physical war, the *direct security* implications of doing nothing are benign. A nation that does not respond to an invasion may cease to exist. One that does not respond to a raid, however, may continue. Cyberattacks are more like raids whose effects are temporary. Since retaliation cannot disarm the attacker, the failure to react has no bearing on the attacker's ability to do damage.

How a state's response appears to third parties has less to do with which category it comes in. The issue of whether the target should be embarrassed—and thus look vulnerable and perhaps pathetic—for having been fallen hard as a result of an attack remains, irrespective of the attacker's motive. This is not something that strike back will fix. Indeed, broadcasting a message of "how dare you expose my weakness" exposes it all the more by revealing the target's sensitivity to pain. As for deterrence, unless the attacker helps out (notably in the case of inadvertence or culmination)—apologizing or at least explaining the attack rather than boasting about it or denying it—motive may not matter terribly much either. This may put the target in an uncomfortable position if its interests vis-à-vis the attacker call for *not* retaliating (or not doing so in any but a nominal manner)—one reason to avoid declaring a deterrence olicy.

How should the target state distinguish the first three cases (where forbearance may be advisable) from the fourth case (where forbearance can be misinterpreted as weakness)? Forensics can help distinguish bad from good attribution, but its ability to distinguish inadvertence from deliberate attack is limited to its ability to distinguish one attacker from another within the same state, a weak clue about intention at best. One test of intentions may come from putting pressure on the attacking state to separate itself from the actual attacker; this is a test the attacker can pass (carrying out an open coercion campaign after conceding the rogue attacker seems illogical), but not necessarily fail—a lot depends on prior relationships (is the attacking state in thrall to the attacker's group?) or subsequent relation-ships (have the hackers been made heroes?). Finally distinguishing between a culminating attack and a prefatory attack depends almost entirely on political clues. Hints—but hardly proof—that the attack was culminating include statements to that effect, offers to reduce tensions, a visible turning to other matters, or a stand-down of forces (although how one can determine that cyber forces are standing down is a real puzzle).

4.3.3 Self-Restraints for the Attacking State

What should attackers, themselves, do to keep tensions in check?

Ironically, some of the question applies to falsely accused attackers. Unfairly or not, they may have some convincing to do. Simple denials may not communicate very much—indeed they are expected. Conclusive evidence that some named third party carried it out may be viewed with suspicion until verified. Offers of assistance with recovery may be viewed askance since it is difficult to help without get-ting privileged access to systems of the sort that the attacker would pay dearly to obtain. Unfortunately, the same fog of cyberwar that makes it difficult to prove who did it, also make it difficult to prove who did not do it. The least bad approach may be to give the target enough access to satisfy itself—unless the target is being driven by ulterior motives.

If escalation is to be avoided, a real attacker should make the case that it seeks no wider war; the attack in question was narrowly tailored in both scope and time, and not designed to permanently change relationships or power (it helps that the effects of cyberattack are usually temporary). If cyber-attacks are used as punishment and nothing more, there may be value in being explicit and even verifi-able (at least if facts matter to the target). *Thus, if an attacker would avoid escalation, it may help to put certain targets off limits so that its motives are not confused.*

One class of targets to avoid is systems whose malfunction can endanger others: e.g., health care, water supply, standalone safety systems (e.g., 911), system-specific safety systems (e.g., dam controls), and traffic management (unless declared explicitly in advance—e.g., do not fly after midnight). Such attacks are generally contrary to the laws of armed conflict, anyway.

Attacks that might threaten permanent changes in state power may contradict a narrative of limited effect. These include attacks that look prefatory to military action such as those on strategic warning systems, or more broadly, such as corruption attacks that may make the target worry about the quality of its command-and-control (including weapons C2). A related category may be morale-related attacks on armed forces on the basis that changes to morale are not restored when systems that support them are restored.

Similarly, crippling systems that hamper the ability of the target state to maintain its hold on power maybe misinterpreted as prefatory to a regime change campaign. To be avoided are disruptive but especially corrupting attacks on state-friendly media and internal security systems. Something like the Great Firewall of China would be off-limits as well, despite how richly apropos a target it may appear. A related set of attacks to avoid are those that undermine the basic trust that citizens have in their gov-ernment and comparable institutions: e.g., corruption attacks on the financial system.

So, what *would* be allowed—particularly if trying to impress a regime that only cares about the risk of permanent loss? Against such targets, the prospects for containing a crisis may be weak—but then the use of cyberattacks to get its attention may be pointless. Otherwise, if dealing with a state that pursues limited ends, and is willing to weigh the benefits of its counter-attacking you against the further costs you can impose on it, there are many ways to convey displeasure, and tilt its calculus without running afoul of your narrative. They include disruption attacks on infrastructures (even financial infrastruc-tures) as long as they are not aimed at causing much permanent damage or put lives at risk, disruption attacks on government agencies both civilian and military, and corruption attacks on both domestic and international intelligence activities (just enough to force the adversary to institute new more tedious procedures to ensure the quality of its information, but not enough to make it feel naked in its ignorance).

To reiterate a point made above, do not assume precision, or anything like it, in gauging the effectiveness of such attacks, or even the certainty with which attacks do or do not cross some line.

4.3.4 Forbearance in Wartime

The calculus of forbearance looks different in wartime. When blood flows, combating states will find that cyberattacks are the least of their reciprocal problems. Decisions elsewhere will overshadow their efforts at signaling one another in cyberspace. If, however, they are involved in testing one another (e.g., Egypt and Israel during their war of attrition), both sides may *want* to test their strength in cyberspace, believing full well that each can gauge the other side's capacity to give and take punishment without sparking the other to drive toward its capital (the tendency of each side to harden targets under conditions of cyberwar may echo similar but slower developments in other domains).

Those who limit their shooting to air, space, naval, or marine domains (offshore islands, remote possessions) because they fear uncontrolled escalation may similarly want to contain cyberwar. At the very least they would avoid targets whose disruption can only be justified by their effect on the national morale and the popular willingness to support further war. Military attacks directly associated with such a conflict (e.g., against air-defense radars) are presumably fair game and would not be seen as specifically escalatory. Even if cyberattacks precede violence, by the time both sides react physical force may already have been used (if the use of force is delayed too long the effect of the cyberattacks may have been reversed).

Can either side carry out cyberattacks against civilian targets to influence the fighting, *without* each touching the other's strategic nerves? Although similar issues arise over physical attacks (e.g., striking ports that support naval operations), they can often be dealt with through geographical limitations on combat (e.g., no bombs north of the Yalu River circa 1951). Boundaries in cyberspace are harder to define and confine. The reported U.S. strike on a jihadist web site[16] supposedly took out 300 servers around the world. Indeed, the information processing (e.g., C4ISR) support for combat operations generally need not be anywhere near the conflict (RF bandwidth permitting) and are more survivable if they are not (a subtle adversary may deliberately outsource such processing to cloud farms of third party countries within which one encrypted database is indistinguishable from another). Thus, the useful boundaries have to be logical rather than physical ones. Unfortunately, as Tom Schelling points out, for such boundaries to be effective in limiting the activities of both sides, they either have to be negotiated or so obvious as to suggest themselves (e.g., stopping at the river's edge). Otherwise they seem arbitrary and meaningless, or concocted to favor the side that advocates them. The nuclear threshold was one such boundary. The distinction between fatal and nonfatal cyberattacks may be another.

Asymmetries between opponents will complicate tacit agreements on what to leave intact in the cyber world, just as it does in the physical world. A local conflict between the United States and China over Taiwan will take place much closer to China: agreeing that homeland ports are off-limits favors them (they have no reasonable prospect of attacking debarking ports in California); the reverse favors the United States. One country may use coal to generate its electricity; the other, hydropower. A policy that has each side refrain, for safety reasons, from interfering with dam controls unfairly penalizes the coal-using state whose electrical generating capacity alone remains at risk. States that have built dedicated communications lines for defense are disadvantaged against states that must depend on dual-use infrastructures if both agree not to target dual-use nodes (routers and switches). Countries that feed intelligence to "patriotic" hackers to carry out cyberattacks are at an advantage over those who depend on their own employees if the onus against cyberattacks is levied on the basis of standard command-and-control dicta.

Attacking military facilities outside the field of war is often frustrated by the likelihood that they are air-gapped. Yet, many legitimate targets of cyberwar have dual uses—are they off-limits? Should one off-limits from a physical attack be off-limits from a cyberattack *that offers the potential of similar*

---

[16]Page A1 of the *Washington Post*, 19 March 2010.

collateral damage? Thus, if ports are off-limits for fear of harming civilian dockworkers, should cyberat-tackers refrain from corrupting its databases for fear of disturbing commercial operations overly much? In reality, attackers may now know what they damaged. They cannot count on help from information managers, reluctant to be seen as responsible for having poor cyber-defenses (leaving the ultimate victims, say shippers, wondering why schedules slipped)—but whose reticence to speak at least works against escalation.

Basing mutual forbearance on nuance and precision cannot be serious. Differences in judgments about who did it and what they did will persist. Third parties may also muddy the waters, particularly if they are interested in undercutting mutual forbearance. Apart from not wandering too closely to self-proclaimed limits, what can either side do to make its intent clear? Defenders can distinguish attacks by military opponents from others by reasoning that their foes have no interest in wasting their assets (knowledge of the opponents' vulnerabilities) on low-impact attacks—but only if they so choose. But little prevents the opponent from looking like (let alone making arrangements with) third parties for the same ends. The fog of war is an argument against forbearance.

This leaves a question as relevant in cyberspace as the physical world: if such gentlemen were so capable of negotiating such nuanced norms, why are they still resorting to fighting to settle their differences?

4.4 Proxy Wars

Another situation in which cyberwarriors may have to pull their punches is when going after the systems of a state which is helping an active combatant.

Local wars offer great powers the opportunity to contribute to the fight (and to upset their peers) by supplying information (e.g., about the battlefield or other information systems), information services, and cyberwar services to indigenous forces—and with seemingly little risk. Nevertheless, if proxy wars are not to escalate into general wars some boundaries on cyberattacks have to be set. In physical combat—using the Korean and Vietnam wars as examples—the bounds between allowable and pro-scribed targets were iffy but mostly observed. Chinese forces were fair game for U.S. forces below but not above the Yalu River. Russians avoided the Korean theater except for (rumors of) air combat. No one attacked U.S. forces out of theater. During the French-Indochina War, the United States was liberal in sending supplies, but not people. In the Vietnam War, similar rules applied: in theory Russian and Chinese "advisers" to North Vietnamese forces manning Russian or Chinese equipment (mostly SAMs) were not explicitly off-limits, but some U.S. policy makers worried about unintentionally killing them (while others were disappointed that they were rarely hurt).

The extent to which information systems of one great power will be considered off-limits to cyber-warriors of another great power (backing the other indigenous force) may depend on whether such help is considered akin to offering supplies (hence, largely protected) or offering forces (hence, less protected). The fact that information system assistance tends to involve activity on the part of (cyber) warfighters says forces, but the expected immunity of cyberwarriors from harm says supplies. The help offered by the great power by way of mapping opposing networks, revealing their vulnerabilities, and crafting exploit tools may be so complete, that the additional effort of sending commands to activate an attack would seem almost an afterthought—the fact that the great power does not pull the trigger may not reduce its culpability appreciably.

Even if both great powers agree to target only those systems in indigenous hands, the links between indigenous combatants and the systems of their great power friends may influence whether these great powers end up going after each other's systems. Can indigenous systems, in fact, be attacked without interfering with systems of their friends? Are the great powers' in-theater systems connected to its global systems? If one great power harms another great power's systems, would the target state want to make an issue of it? Can the attacker argue that such an attack was essential to helping its indigenous ally? Can the target retort that the attack was really meant to harm its systems and not indigenous systems?

Absent the right kind of firebreaks, one can imagine a continually escalating confrontation that requires either negotiations to establish mutual limits on the spot, or for one great power to back down unilaterally lest general war in cyberspace ensue.

So what norms should apply? One possibility is look for whatever opportunities exist to use physical boundaries as proxies for cyber boundaries. Thus, if the friend's systems are outside the war zone, perhaps they should be off-limits to a cyberattack even if they help the indigenous ally fight (as supplies destined for the war zone would be if they were sitting in the territory of the great power friend). This begs the question of how the attacker would know where any such systems sit. It also leaves the problem that cyberattacks against the indigenous combatant's systems may affect the great power's systems, something the attacker may have no way of knowing beforehand. A cross-infection may be *prima facie* indication that the two systems are not, in fact, virtually separated.

Asymmetries plague the application of such tenets in practice. For instance, the boundaries between systems of the great power and its indigenous friend may be well-defined and guarded on one side but not the other. Thus, the escalation risks from attacking the former would be low but the escalation risks from attacks on the latter would be high. Why should the more careless side get a free ride just because the attacks of the more careful side have the potential of riskier outcomes? Worse might ensue if attacks on the indigenous combatant's infrastructure end up bedeviling the lives of citizens of its great power friend (incidentally, such systems could easily sit in third countries).

Avoiding escalation in such scenarios might require proxy warriors to carefully separate their global systems from those sent to theater and require attackers to exercise great caution to ensure that their cyberattacks have precise effects. But it would not hurt for either external force to realize that accidents happen, especially in war zones.

5 IMPLEMENTATION

States that would pull punches in cyberspace must have appropriate command and control of their cyberwarriors. Instructions on what to avoid must be clear and the controls must be in place to ensure that such instructions are followed.

In the physical world, both command and control are getting better thanks to ever-more-ubiquitous surveillance and the proliferation of communications nets (e.g., cell phones). The effects of war can be meticulously documented and attributed. As more military equipment becomes digitized (and thus capable of hosting copious log files), the prospect of knowing exactly who did what when draws closer.

Not so in the cyberworld, where keystrokes can come from anywhere. Standard operating procedure (which is anyway rather thin for cyberwar) is a poor guide when one cannot state *a priori* exactly what the means of attack are (for instance, the route in often has to be determined in real time as the contours of the target's defenses are revealed) much less what the effects of attacks are. Any policy designed to attack up to some boundary but no farther is subject to two uncertainties: the difference between what was intended and what actually takes place, and the difference between what takes place and what is perceived to take place. If the odds and the cost of escalation are significant, the only possible lesson may be to stand as far away from the border as possible: in other words, do nothing in that domain. If one would act, clear and *thick* margins of some sort have to be established.

The burden of margin-setting will differ depending on whether one is worried about, alternatively, careful, careless, and rogue cyberwarriors.

Careful cyberwarriors are those that pay as much attention to constraints as they do to results. For them, clarity is the goal. The constraints on their behavior could include how to attack, and what results are unacceptable under which circumstances. They should be explicit, advertised, and somewhat stable (or at least not fluctuate arbitrarily). The rules that say what actions are permissible in what situations should be codified in advance of crisis because when the fighting starts, purposes are more fluid, and not necessarily broadcast to all (also true for physical combat). To make constraints work, it may be necessary to teach the basic principles of cyberwar as they apply to national security. Beyond such guidelines, the rules on how to attack or what constitutes non-excessive damage may be too context-specific to be specified too far in advance.

Careless cyberwarriors mean to follow the rules, but in the heat of combat, may convince themselves that carrying out a clear operational mission trumps conformance with often-ambiguous guidelines. All the rules for careful cyberwarriors apply to careless ones (who may be indistinguishable from careful warriors). The application may vary: the actions of careless warriors are apt to drift over the borders, and, being human, likely to blame their trespasses on unclear guidance, the ambiguities of cyberspace, and even the target's behavior (e.g., turning off the electric power substation to disable government bureaus was not supposed to put hospital patients at risk; where were the latter's backup generators?). If careless cyberwarriors are a problem, one approach would be to limit the amount of intelligence *all* cyberwarriors are provided with. To wit, if a particular target is likely to be off-limits, then probing such targets is neither resourced nor tolerated—but what if no target is not off-limits in some contexts? If so, there may be no target that cannot be probed for its susceptibility to cyberattack. Once such intelligence is gathered on such targets, they may be vulnerable to the efforts of careless cyberwarriors even if they are off-limits in that particular context. Postponing collection until war starts (and thus its context is clear) is problematic if collection becomes that much harder, afterwards. Such dilemmas have echoes in the physical world. Japanese F-15 fighters were designed not to have drop tanks, which thus limited their range, so as to demonstrate to the Soviet Union that Japan posed no *offensive* threat to Soviet territory.

The last category contains rogue warriors—so eager to strike the target that they take their work home with them, sometimes literally. Trained and filled with intelligence at work, they carry out attacks from platforms or intermediate conduits that are very difficult to trace and out of sight of their supervisors. Rogue warriors will not respond to constraints when freelancing (except as hints as to what to avoid appearing to do). Because they do not have to work in military formations or with unique military hardware, they are harder to detect and hence control than their equivalents in physical combat: e.g., the militias of developing nations. Not even keeping them (figuratively) chained to their desk in a crisis will eliminate mischief if they have found how to contact their own bots from their desktop—although such behavior may be suppressed if they have to account for every keystroke (unless the rogue operator creates malware that goes off unless specifically told not to). After all, even careful cyberwarriors are unlikely to carry out mischief from a ".mil" network lest the target of their attentions filter out their rogue packets simply by looking at their return address. Effective militaries have ways of filtering out most such rogue warriors and engineering social controls that keep potential rogue warriors in the force from straying. Having done what they can, states then have to determine whether the risks of violating self-imposed constraints merit reducing every cyberwarrior's access to the intelligence and tools necessary to mount the more sophisticated attacks.

6 CONCLUSIONS

Cyberwar is a messy, messy, messy, messy business. It is messy by the very nature of cyberspace where it is nearly impossible to know that the connections you cannot see do not, in fact exist. It is messy because the instruments of war are not necessarily monopolies of states, much less states in the immediate area of conflict. It is messy because knowledge of what happens to or what ensues from one's enemies is opaque and subject to manipulation. Finally, it is messy because one's own command-and-control is far less certain than for physical warfare. These, properly understood, create enough reasons to be skeptical about the instincts to declare that cyberwar unavoidable in one or another context.

In confrontations that are less than existential—and cyberwar, standing alone, clearly fits that description—an important role is played by the correct alignment of actions and narratives. The latter combines an interpretation of the relevant context of action in terms of a state's moral (and concomitant legal) structures. The adherence to norms, in turn, can be expression of the narrative, at least for states that take norms seriously rather than rhetorically.

The question of pulling punches gains another meaning in the context of war, but war may not necessarily be the best metaphor for the deliberate mischief that takes place in cyberspace. In many ways the metaphor of pollution is a better descriptor. In other contexts, cyberattacks may be said to be what happen if security engineering receives insufficient attention (just as accidents are what happen if safety engineering receives insufficient attention). A boat with a leak will take on water as fast in friendly waters as it does in hostile waters; the leak matters, the waters do not.

Group 3—Law and Regulation

Cyber Operations in International Law:
The Use of Force, Collective Security,
Self-Defense, and Armed Conflicts

Michael N. Schmitt

Durham University Law School, United Kingdom

INTRODUCTION

In April and May 2007, Estonia was victimized by massive computer network attacks.[1] The incident began with rioting incited by ethnic Russian cyber agitators in response to the government's decision to move a Soviet war memorial from the center of Tallinn to a military cemetery on the outskirts of the capital. Subsequent actions included direct cyber attacks against Estonian targets, including government and commercial Internet infrastructure and information systems such as the those of the President, Prime Minister, Parliament, State Audit Office, ministries, political parties, banks, news agencies, and Internet service providers. They involved denial of service (DoS), distributed denial of service (DDoS), defacement and destruction.

Because Estonia had invested heavily in networking following independence, the attacks proved devastating. By 2007, the country relied on information services for everything from banking and filing tax returns to paying for parking and public transportation. Internet services covered all of Estonia, with half the population enjoying access from their homes.

Most of the attacks emanated from outside the country, principally Russia. Their origin was also traced to at least 177 other countries.[2] Initially, they came from private IP addresses, although experts tracked a number to Russian government institutions. It remains uncertain whether the latter were launched with the government's knowledge. As the cyber attacks unfolded, they became increasingly sophisticated, evidencing considerable organization and command and control. While various pro-Russian activist groups apparently executed some of the second wave operations, there is no firm evidence that the Russian government either conducted or orchestrated them.

The impact of the cyber assault proved dramatic; government activities such as the provision of State benefits and the collection of taxes ground to a halt, private and public communications were disrupted and confidence in the economy plummeted. Was this "war"? After all, the scope and scale of the consequences far exceeded those that might have been caused by, for instance, a small-scale air

---

[1]For an excellent discussion of the attacks, see Eneken Tikk, Kadri Kaska, and Liis Vihul, *International Cyber Incidents: Legal Considerations* 14-33 (Tallinn: Cooperative Cyber Defence Centre of Excellence 2010).

[2]Charles Clover, "Kremlin-backed Group behind Estonia Cyber Blitz," *Financial Times*, March 11, 2009.

attack or a commando raid, both of which would signal the initiation of a "war" between Estonia and the State responsible for their execution.

Historically, the initiation of a war depended upon a formal act of State, generally a "declaration of war." It neither required hostilities, nor did hostilities alone amount to war. This traditional understanding of war has fallen into desuetude, replaced by a complex admixture of legal concepts. In the aftermath of the Second World War, the international community crafted a new normative scheme in the form of the United Nations Charter, which includes both a prohibition on the use of force in international relations and a system for enforcing the prescription. Today, the Charter, together with related customary international law norms,[3] governs how and when force may be employed by States. The carnage of the Second World War also prompted a reexamination of the rules applicable during warfare. During that process, the requirement for a declaration of war as the threshold for application of the "law of war" was abandoned.[4] Henceforth, this body of law (relabeled the "law of armed conflict" and usually referred to as "international humanitarian law" or IHL) would come into play whenever "armed conflict" occurred.

This article explores the contemporary international law governing cyber operations. In particular, it asks four questions, which together have supplanted the previous notion of "war":

(1) When does a cyber operation constitute a wrongful "use of force" in violation of Article 2(4) of the United Nations Charter and customary international law?;

(2) When does a cyber operation amount to a "threat to the peace, breach of the peace, or act of aggression," such that the Security Council may authorize a response thereto?;

(3) When does a cyber operation constitute an "armed attack," such that the victim-State may defend itself, even kinetically, pursuant to the right of self-defense set forth in Article 51 of the UN Charter and customary international law?; and

(4) When does a cyber operation rise to the level of an "armed conflict," such that IHL governs the actions of belligerents?

The attacks against Estonia, similar ones against Georgia during its armed conflict with Russia in 2008,[5] and the thousands of others directed against government, corporate and private systems worldwide on a daily basis aptly demonstrate the reality, immediacy and scale of the threat. It is one well-recognized by States. The May 2010 United States National Security Strategy cites cyber security threats as "one of the most serious national security, public safety, and economic challenges we face as a nation."[6] Similarly, the analysis and recommendations on NATO's new Strategic Concept prepared by a group of distinguished experts led by former U.S. Secretary of State Madeleine Albright singled out "cyber assaults of varying degrees of severity" as one of the three likeliest threats the NATO Allies will face in the next decade.[7]

Unfortunately, the existing legal norms do not offer a clear and comprehensive framework within which States can shape policy responses to the threat of hostile cyber operations. In particular, international law

---

[3]See fn 13 and accompanying text for a brief explanation of customary international law.

[4]Common Article 2 to the four 1949 Geneva Conventions provides that the treaties "shall apply to all cases of declared war or of any other armed conflict which may arise between two or more of the High Contracting Parties, even if a state of war is not recognized by one of them." Geneva Convention for the Amelioration of the Condition of the Wounded and Sick in Armed Forces in the Field, art. 2, Aug. 12, 1949, 6 UST. 3114, 75 U.N.T.S. 31; Geneva Convention for the Amelioration of the Condition of Wounded, Sick and Shipwrecked Members of Armed Forces at Sea, art. 2, Aug. 12, 1949, 6 UST. 3217, 75 U.N.T.S. 85; Geneva Convention Relative to the Treatment of Prisoners of War, art. 2, Aug. 12, 1949, 6 UST. 3316, 75 U.N.T.S. 135 ; Geneva Convention Relative to the Protection of Civilian Persons in Time of War, art. 2, Aug. 12, 1949, 6 UST. 3516, 75 U.N.T.S. 287 [hereinafter GC I–IV respectively].

[5]See Tikk, *supra* note 1, at 66-90.

[6]President Barack Obama, *National Security Strategy* 27 (May 2010).

[7]Group of Experts on a New Strategic Concept. *NATO 2020: Assured Security; Dynamic Engagement* (May 17, 2010) 17. The others are an attack by a ballistic missile and strikes by international terrorist groups.

as traditionally understood departs at times from what the international community would presumably demand in the cyber context. To some extent, this divergence can be accommodated through reasonable interpretation of the relevant norms. Where it cannot, the law would seem to require attention, either through treaty action or through the development of new understandings of the prevailing legal concepts.[8]

CYBER OPERATIONS AS A "USE OF FORCE"

The United Nations Charter, in Article 2(4), states that "[a]ll Members [of the United Nations] shall refrain in their international relations from the threat or use of force against the territorial integrity or political independence of any state, or in any other manner inconsistent with the Purposes of the United Nations." Despite the reference to territorial integrity and political independence, it is now widely understood that the prohibition applies to any use of force not otherwise permitted by the terms of the Charter, specifically uses of force authorized by the Security Council and defensive operations, each discussed separately below.[9]

Article 2(4) was revolutionary in its extension to threats. Of course, only those threats of a use of force that would otherwise be unlawful qualify.[10] For instance, threatening destructive defensive cyber attacks against another State's military infrastructure if that State unlawfully mounts unlawful cross-border operations would not breach the norm. However, threats of destructive cyber operations against another State's critical infrastructure unless that State cedes territory would do so.

The prohibition applies only to an explicit or implied communication of a threat; its essence is coercive effect. It does not reach actions which simply threaten the security of the target State, but which are not communicative in nature. Thus, the introduction into a State's cyber systems of vulnerabilities which are capable of destructive activation at some later date would not constitute a threat of the use of force unless their presence is known to the target State and the originating State exploits them for some coercive purpose.[11]

It is generally accepted that the prohibition on the threat or use of force represents customary international law.[12] Resultantly, it binds all States regardless of membership in the United Nations. Article 38 of the Statute of the International Court of Justice (ICJ) defines customary law as "general practice accepted as law."[13] It requires the coexistence of State practice and *opinio juris sive necessitatis*, a belief that the practice is engaged in, or refrained from, out of a sense of legal obligation (rather than practical or policy reasons).

Although simple in formulation, the norm is complex in substantive composition. It poses two key questions: "What is a use of force?" and "To whom does the prohibition apply?" Both bear heavily on the legality of cyber operations, which did not exist when the UN Charter was adopted by States in 1945. The difficulty of applying a legal provision which did not contemplate a particular type of operation is apparent.

---

[8]For book length treatment of these issues, see Thomas C. Wingfield. *The Law of Information Conflict* (Washington: Aegis Research Corporation 2000); Michael N. Schmitt and Brian O'Donnell, eds. *Computer Network Attack and International Law* (Newport: U.S. Naval War College International Law Studies, vol. 76, 1999); and the collected articles in 64 Air Force Law Review (2009).

[9]In its original form, the draft Charter contained no reference to territorial integrity or political independence, and their subsequent inclusion was controversial. The "other manner" language was inserted to make clear that their inclusion was not meant to limit the reach of the provision. See Doc. 1123, I/8, 6 U.N.C.I.O. Docs. 65 (1945); Doc. 784, I/1/27, 6 U.N.C.I.O. Docs. 336 (1945); Doc. 885, I/1/34, 6 U.N.C.I.O. Docs 387 (1945).

[10]This point was made by the International Court of Justice in Legality of the Threat or Use of Nuclear Weapons, Advisory Opinion, 1996 ICJ Rep. 226, ¶ 47 (July 8).

[11]Although a threat must be coercive in some sense, there is no requirement that a specific "demand" accompany the threat.

[12]See discussion of the issue by the International Court of Justice in Military and Paramilitary Activities in and Against Nicaragua (Nicar. v. US), 1986 ICJ Rep. 14, ¶¶ 187-191 (June 27) [hereinafter Nicaragua].

[13]Statute of the International Court of Justice, art. 38, June 26, 1945, 59 Stat. 1055, 33 U.N.T.S. 993. On customary law, see Yoram Dinstein, "The Interaction between Customary International Law and Treaties," *Collected Courses of the Hague Academy of International Law* 322 (Martinus Nijhoff, 2007).

Finally, it must be borne in mind that neither Article 2(4) nor its customary counterpart is remedial in nature. Rather, they merely set a threshold for breach of international law. The nature of the response to a wrongful use of force is instead determined by the law of State responsibility, the scope of authority of the Security Council and the law of self-defense. Each is addressed below.

Uses of Force

Do cyber operations constitute a "use of force" as that phrase is understood in relation to the prohibition? The interpretive dilemma is that the drafters of the Charter took a cognitive short cut by framing the treaty's prohibition in terms of the *instrument* of coercion employed—force. Thus, the norm did not outlaw economic and political coercion, but disallowed military force, at least absent an express Charter exception. Yet, it is seldom the instrument employed, but instead the *consequences* suffered, that matter to States. At the time the Charter was drafted an instrument based-approach made sense, for prior to the advent of cyber operations the consequences that Sates sought to avoid usually comported with instrument-based categories. Cyber operations do not fit neatly into this paradigm because although they are "non-forceful" (that is, non-kinetic), their consequences can range from mere annoyance to death. Resultantly, as the Commander of U.S. Cyber Command noted during his confirmation hearings, policy makers must understand that "[t]here is no international consensus on a precise definition of a use of force, in or out of cyberspace. Consequently, individual nations may assert different definitions, and may apply different thresholds for what constitutes a use of force."[14]

That the term "use of force" encompasses resort to armed force by a State, especially force levied by the military is self-evident. Armed force thus includes kinetic force—dropping bombs, firing artillery, and so forth. It would be no less absurd to suggest that cyber operations which generate consequences analogous to those caused by kinetic force lie beyond the prohibition's reach, than to exclude other destructive non-kinetic actions, such as biological or radiological warfare. Accordingly, cyber operations that directly result (or are likely to result) in physical harm to individuals or tangible objects equate to armed force, and are therefore "uses of force." For instance, those targeting an air traffic control system or a water treatment facility clearly endanger individuals and property. But cyber operations are usually mounted without causing such consequences, as illustrated by the case of Estonia. Are such operations nonetheless barred by the use of force prohibition?

The starting point for any interpretive endeavor in law is the treaty text in question.[15] In this regard, note that the adjective "armed" does not appear with reference to "force" in Article 2(4). By contrast, the Charter preamble cites the purpose of ensuring that "armed force shall not be used, save in the common interest." Similarly, the Charter excludes "armed force" from the non-forceful measures the Security Council may authorize under Article 41 and mentions planning for "armed force" with regard to forceful Article 42 measures.[16] And the Charter only allows forceful defensive actions in the face of an "armed attack."[17] This textual distinction suggests an interpretation of "force" that is broader in scope than the common understanding of the term.

When text is ambiguous, recourse may be had to "the preparatory work of [a] treaty and the circumstances of its conclusion."[18] The Charter's *travaux preparatoires*, indicate that during the drafting of the

---

[14]Unclassified Senate Testimony by Lieutenant General Keith Alexander, USA, Nominee for Commander, United States Cyber Command, April 15, 2010, www.senate.gov/~armed_services/statemnt/2010/04%20April/Alexander%2004-15-10.pdf.

[15]According to the Vienna Convention on the Law of Treaties, "[a] treaty shall be interpreted in good faith in accordance with the ordinary meaning to be given to these terms of the treaty in their context and in light of its object and purpose" which can be gleaned from the text, "including its *preamble* and annexes . . . ." May 23, 1969, art. 31(1)-(2), 1155 U.N.T.S. 331. The United States is not a party to the Vienna Convention, but treats most of its provisions as reflective of customary international law.

[16]The reference to planning is found in U.N. Charter, art. 46.

[17]U.N. Charter, art. 51.

[18]Vienna Convention, *supra* note 15, art. 32.

instrument a proposal to extend the reach of Article 2(4) to economic coercion was decisively defeated.[19] A quarter century later, the issue again arose during proceeding leading to the UN General Assembly's Declaration on Friendly Relations.[20] The question of whether "force" included "all forms of pressure, including those of a political or economic character, which have the effect of threatening the territorial integrity or political independence of any State" was answered in the negative.[21] Whatever force is, then, it is not economic or political pressure. Therefore, a cyber operation that involves such coercion is definitely not a prohibited use of force. Psychological cyber operations (assuming they are non-destructive) intended solely to undermine confidence in a government or economy illustrate such actions.

Suggestions to limit "force" to "armed force," or even the force required to amount to an "armed attack," were likewise rejected during the proceedings.[22] This seemed to indicate that "force" was not coterminous with "armed" force, thereby strengthening the significance of the absence of the term "armed" in Article 2(4). In the *Nicaragua* case, the ICJ expressly characterized certain actions which were non-kinetic in nature as uses of force.

> [W]hile arming and training of the contras can certainly be said to involve the threat or use of force against Nicaragua, that is not necessarily so in respect of all assistance given by the United States Government. In particular, the Court considers that the mere supply of funds to the contras, while undoubtedly an act of intervention in the internal affairs of Nicaragua . . . does not itself amount to a use of force.[23]

The determination that a use of force can embrace acts, like arming or training guerrillas, which fall short of armed force leaves open the possibility that non-physically destructive cyber operations may fall within the term's ambit. The threshold for a use of force must therefore lie somewhere along the continuum between economic and political coercion on the one hand and acts which cause physical harm on the other.

Unfortunately, unequivocal State practice in characterizing particular cyber attacks as (or not as) uses of force is lacking. In part this is because the Article 2(4) prohibition extends solely to acts of States, and very few States have definitively been identified as the initiator of a cyber operation which might amount to a use of force. Moreover, States may well hesitate to label a cyber operation as a use of force out of concern that doing so would escalate matters or otherwise destabilize the situation. Therefore, one can only speculate as to future State practice regarding the characterization of cyber operations.

Over a decade ago, this author identified a number of factors that would likely influence assessments by States as to whether particular cyber operations amounted to a use of force.[24] They are based on a recognition that while States generally want to preserve their freedom of action (a motivation to keep the threshold high), they equally want to avoid any harmful consequences caused by the actions of others (a motivation to keep the threshold low). States will seek to balance these conflicting objectives through consideration of factors such as those set forth below. The approach has generally withstood the test of time.

(1) *Severity:* Consequences involving physical harm to individuals or property will alone amount to a use of force. Those generating only minor inconvenience or irritation will never do so. Between the extremes, the more consequences impinge on critical national interests, the more they will contribute

---

[19]*See* Doc. 2, G/7(e)(4), 3 U.N.C.I.O. Docs. 251, 253-54 (1945). Economic coercion, which typically involves trade sanctions, must be distinguished from "blockade," which has the effect of cutting off trade, but employs military force to do so. It has historically been accepted that imposition of a blockade is an "act of war."

[20]Declaration on Principles of International Law Concerning Friendly Relations and Cooperation Among States in Accordance with the Charter of the United Nations, G.A. Res. 2625 (XXV), U.N. Doc. A/8082 (1970).

[21]U.N. GAOR Special Comm. on Friendly Relations, U.N. Doc. A/AC.125/SR.114 (1970); *See also* Report of the Special Committee on Friendly Relations, U.N. Doc. A/7619 (1969). The draft declaration contained text tracking that of Charter Article 2(4).

[22]Ibid.

[23]Nicaragua, *supra* note 12, ¶ 228.

[24]Michael N. Schmitt, "Computer Network Attack and Use of Force in International Law: Thoughts on a Normative Framework," 37 *Columbia Journal of Transnational Law* 885, 914-16 (1999).

to the depiction of a cyber operation as a use of force. In this regard, the scale, scope and duration of the consequences will have great bearing on the appraisal of their severity. Severity is self-evidently the most significant factor in the analysis.

(2) *Immediacy:* The sooner consequences manifest, the less opportunity States have to seek peaceful accommodation of a dispute or to otherwise forestall their harmful effects. Therefore, States harbor a greater concern about immediate consequences than those which are delayed or build slowly over time.

(3) *Directness:* The greater the attenuation between the initial act and the resulting consequences, the less likely States will be to deem the actor responsible for violating the prohibition on the use of force. Whereas the immediacy factor focused on the temporal aspect of the consequences in question, directness examines the chain of causation. For instance, the eventual consequences of economic coercion (economic downturn) are determined by market forces, access to markets, and so forth. The causal connection between the initial acts and their effects tends to be indirect. In armed actions, by contrast, cause and effect are closely related—an explosion, for example, directly harms people or objects.

(4) *Invasiveness:* The more secure a targeted system, the greater the concern as to its penetration. By way of illustration, economic coercion may involve no intrusion at all (trade with the target state is simply cut off), whereas in combat the forces of one State cross into another in violation of its sovereignty. The former is undeniably not a use of force, whereas the latter always qualifies as such (absent legal justification, such as evacuation of nationals abroad during times of unrest). In the cyber context, this factor must be cautiously applied. In particular, cyber exploitation is a pervasive tool of modern espionage. Although highly invasive, espionage does not constitute a use of force (or armed attack) under international law absent a nonconsensual physical penetration of the target-State's territory, as in the case of a warship or military aircraft which collects intelligence from within its territorial sea or airspace. Thus, actions such as disabling cyber security mechanisms to monitor keystrokes would, despite their invasiveness, be unlikely to be seen as a use of force.

(5) *Measurability:* The more quantifiable and identifiable a set of consequences, the more a State's interest will be deemed to have been affected. On the one hand, international law does not view economic coercion as a use of force even though it may cause significant suffering. On the other, a military attack which causes only a limited degree of destruction clearly qualifies. It is difficult to identify or quantify the harm caused by the former (e.g., economic opportunity costs), while doing so is straightforward in the latter (x deaths, y buildings destroyed, etc).

(6) *Presumptive legitimacy:* At the risk of oversimplification, international law is generally prohibitory in nature. In other words, acts which are not forbidden are permitted; absent an express prohibition, an act is presumptively legitimate.[25] For instance, it is well accepted that the international law governing the use of force does not prohibit propaganda, psychological warfare or espionage. To the extent such activities are conducted through cyber operations, they are presumptively legitimate.

(7) *Responsibility:* The law of State responsibility (discussed below) governs when a State will be responsible for cyber operations. But it must be understood that responsibility lies along a continuum from operations conducted by a State itself to those in which it is merely involved in some fashion. The closer the nexus between a State and the operations, the more likely other States will be to characterize them as uses of force, for the greater the risk posed to international stability.

The case of the Estonian cyber attacks can be used to illustrate application of the approach. Although they caused no deaths, injury or physical damage, the attacks fundamentally affected the operation of the entire Estonian society. Government functions and services were severely disrupted,

---

[25]In *The Case of the S.S. "Lotus,"* the Permanent Court of International Justice famously asserted that "[t]he rules of law binding upon States . . . emanate from their own free will as expressed in conventions or by usages generally accepted as expressing principles of law and established in order to regulate the relations between these co-existing independent communities or with a view to the achievement of common aims." S.S. "Lotus" (Fr. v. Turk.), 1927 P.C.I.J. (ser. A) No. 10, at 14 (Sept. 7).

the economy was thrown into turmoil, and daily life for the Estonian people was negatively affected. The consequences far exceeded mere inconvenience or irritation. The effects were immediate and, in the case of confidence in government and economic activity, wide-spread and long-term. They were also direct, as with the inability to access funds and interference with the distribution of government benefits. Since some of the targeted systems were designed to be secure, the operations were highly invasive. While the consequences were severe, they were difficult to quantify, since most involved denial of service, rather than destruction of data. Although political and economic actions are pre-sumptively legitimate in use of force terms, these operations constituted more than merely pressuring the target State. Instead, they involved intentionally frustrating governmental and economic functions. Taken together as a single "cyber operation," the incident arguably reached the use of force threshold. Had Russia been responsible for them under international law, it is likely that the international com-munity would (or should have) have treated them as a use of force in violation of the UN Charter and customary international law.

The criteria are admittedly imprecise, thereby permitting States significant latitude in characterizing a cyber operation as a use of force, or not. In light of the increasing frequency and severity of cyber operations, a tendency towards resolving grey areas in favor of finding a use of force can be expected to emerge. This State practice will over time clarify the norm and its attendant threshold.

Applicability of the Prohibition

By its own express terms, Article 2(4) applies solely to members of the United Nations. As discussed, the prohibition extends to non-Members by virtue of customary law. That is the limit of applicability. Non-State actors, including individuals, organized groups and terrorist organizations, cannot violate the norm absent a clear relationship with a State. Their actions may be unlawful under international and domestic law, but not as a violation of the prohibition on the use of force. Thus, in the Estonian case, and barring any evidence of Russian government involvement, none of those individuals or groups conducting the operations violated the Article 2(4) prohibition. But when can the conduct of individuals or groups be attributed to a State, such that the State is legally responsible for their actions? The law of State responsibility governs such situations.[26]

Obviously, States are legally responsible for the conduct of their governmental organs or entities.[27] This principle extends to unauthorized acts.[28] Accordingly, any cyber operation rising to the level of an unlawful use of force will entail responsibility on the part of the State when launched by its agents, even when they are acting *ultra vires*.

The fact that a State did not itself conduct the cyber operations at hand does not mean that it escapes responsibility altogether. States are also responsible for "the conduct of a person or group of persons . . . if the person or group of persons is in fact acting on the instructions of, or under the direction or control of, that State in carrying out the conduct."[29] The ICJ addressed the degree of control necessary for attribution in the *Nicaragua* case. There the Court considered attribution of the acts of the Nicaraguan Contras (a rebel group supported by the United States) to the United States, such that the United States would be responsible for breaches of IHL committed by the group. While finding the United States responsible for its own "planning, direction and support" of the Contras,[30] the Court limited responsibil-ity for the Contra actions to those in which the United States exercised "*effective control* of the military or

---

[26]This law is set forth, in non-binding form, in the International Law Commission's Draft Articles on Responsibility of States for Internationally Wrongful Acts, *in* Report of the International Law Commission on the Work of Its Fifty-third Session, UN Doc. A/56/10 (2001).

[27]Draft Articles on State Responsibility, *supra*, art. 4.

[28]Ibid., art. 7.

[29]Ibid., art. 8.

[30]Nicaragua, *supra* note 12, ¶ 86.

paramilitary operations in the course of which the alleged violations were committed."[31] Mere support for their activities did not suffice.

The Appeals Chamber of the International Criminal Tribunal for the Former Yugoslavia (ICTY) took a different tack in the *Tadic* case, where it held that the authority of the government of the Federal Republic of Yugoslavia over the Bosnia Serb armed groups "required by international law for considering the armed conflict to be international was *overall control* going beyond the mere financing and equipping of such forces and involving also participation in the planning and supervision of military operations."[32] It is essential to note that although the Tribunal expressly rejected the higher *Nicaragua* threshold of effective control, the technical legal issue was not State responsibility, but rather the nature of the armed conflict. Thus, while *Tadic* brings *Nicaragua* into question by proffering a lower threshold, it does not necessarily supplant the effective control test. It remains unclear whether effective control, overall control or some other test governs in international law, although the ICJ has twice reaffirmed its version.[33]

In the cyber context, then, States will be responsible for violating the prohibition on the use of force to the extent they either direct private individuals or groups to conduct the operations or are heavily involved in them. Determinations will be made on a case-by-case basis looking to the extent and nature of involvement by the State with the group and in the particular operations.

Even if conduct is not attributable to a State as under its control, it will nevertheless "be considered an act of that State . . . if and to the extent that the State acknowledges and adopts the conduct in question as its own."[34] The ICJ addressed this situation in the *Hostage* case, which involved seizure of the United States Embassy by Iranian militants in 1979. The Iranian government was uninvolved in the initial seizure, but later passed a decree which accepted and maintained the occupation of the embassy. According to the Court, "[t]he approval given to [the occupation of the Embassy] by the Ayatollah Khomeini and other organs of the Iranian State, and the decision to perpetuate them, translated continuing occupation of the Embassy and detention of the hostages into acts of that State."[35]

It should be cautioned that mere expressions of approval do not suffice for attribution; rather, the State must somehow subsequently embrace the actions as its own, for instance, by tangibly supporting their continuance, failing to take actions to suppress them, or otherwise adopting them. Adoption may either be express, as in the *Hostages* case, or implied, as when a State engages in conduct that undeniably constitutes adoption. In the Estonian case, had Russia publically encouraged further attacks, it would have borne responsibility not only for the subsequent attacks, but also those in the initial wave.

A State may also be held responsible for the effects of unlawful acts of private individuals or groups on its territory when it fails to take reasonably available measures to stop such acts in breach of its obligations to other States. In this situation, its violation is of the duty owed to other states, but its responsibility extends to the effects of the act itself. Applying this standard in the *Hostages* case, the ICJ found that the Iranian government failed to take required steps to prevent the seizure of the U.S. Embassy or regain control over it, in breach of its obligation to safeguard diplomatic premises.[36] The key to such responsibility lies in the existence of a separate legal duty to forestall the act in question, and an ability to comply with said duty. The ICJ articulated this principle in its very first case, *Corfu Channel*, where it held that every State has an "obligation to not allow knowingly its territory to be used for acts contrary to the rights of other States."[37] Of the many obligations States owe each other, ensuring their territory

---

[31]Ibid., ¶ 115. See also discussion in ¶ 109.

[32]Prosecutor v. Tadic, Case No. IT-94-1-A, Appeals Chamber Judgment, ¶ 145 (July 15, 1999).

[33]Armed Activities on the Territory of the Congo (Dem. Rep. Congo v. Uganda), 2005 ICJ General List No. 116, at 53 (Dec. 19); Application of the Convention on the Prevention and Punishment of the Crime of Genocide (Bosn. & Herz. v. Serb. & Mont.), at 391-392 (Judgment of Feb. 26, 2007).

[34]Draft Articles on State Responsibility, *supra* note 26, art. 11.

[35]United States Diplomatic and Consular Staff in Teheran, 1980 ICJ Rep. 3, ¶ 74 (May 24).

[36]Ibid., arts. 76-78.

[37]Corfu Channel Case (Merits), 1949 ICJ Rep. 4, 22.

is not a launching pad for the use of force or armed attacks (see discussion below) against other States certainly ranks among the most important. The fact that a use of force consists of cyber operations rather than traditional armed force would not diminish the responsibility of the State involved.

Finally, consider a situation in which the effects of a cyber operation extend to other than the targeted State. This is an especially relevant scenario in the cyber context, for networking and other forms of interconnectivity mean that a cyber use of force by State A against State B may have consequences in State C that would rise to the level of a use of force if directed against C. The causation of such effects would not amount to a violation of Article 2(4) vis-à-vis C. Article 2(4)'s requirement that Members "refrain in their international *relations*" from the use of force implies an element of purposely engaging in some action in respect of another specified State. Inadvertent effects caused in a State other than the target States do not constitute a form of "international relations."

However, even if the State did not intend such effects, it is clear that it bears responsibility for them. As noted in the Draft Articles of State Responsibility, "[t]here is an internationally wrongful act of a State when conduct consisting of an action or omission: (a) is attributable to the State under international law; and (2) constitutes a breach of an international obligation of the State."[38] In the envisaged case, since State A conducted the cyber operation, the action is directly attributable to it. Further, the wrongful use of force against B would constitute a breach of A's international obligation to refrain from the use of force. That the intended "victim" was B matters not. The criterion has been met once the breach of an international obligation has occurred. This is so even if the effects in C were unintended. As noted in the International Law Commission's Commentary to the relevant article:

> A related question is whether fault constitutes a necessary element of the internationally wrongful act of a State. This is certainly not the case if by "fault" one understands the existence, for example, of an intention to harm. In the absence of any specific requirement of a mental element in terms of the primary obligation, it is only the act of a State that matters, independently of any intention.[39]

Remedies for Violation

In the event of State responsibility for an unlawful act, the victim-State is entitled to reparation, which can take the form of restitution, compensation, or satisfaction.[40] With regard to cyber operations amounting to a use of force, compensation could be claimed for any reasonably foreseeable physical or financial losses. A State may also take any responsive actions that neither amount to a use of force nor breach an existing treaty or customary law obligation. As an example, a State may chose to block incoming cyber transmissions emanating from the State that has used force against it.

Additionally, the victim-State may take "countermeasures" in response to a use of force.[41] Countermeasures are "measures which would otherwise be contrary to the international obligations of the injured State *vis-à-vis* the responsible State if they were not taken by the former in response to an internationally wrongful act by the latter in order to procure cessation and reparation."[42] They are distinguished from retorsion, which is the taking of unfriendly but lawful actions, such as the expulsion of diplomats.

The wrong in question has to be ongoing at the time of the countermeasures, since their purpose is not to punish or provide retribution, but instead to compel the other Party to desist in its unlawful activi-

---

[38]Draft Articles of State Responsibility, *supra* note 26, art. 2.

[39]James Crawford, *The International Law Commission's Articles on State Responsibility: Introduction, Text and Commentaries* 84 (Cambridge UP 2002).

[40]Draft Articles on State Responsibility, *supra* note 26, arts. 34-37. Restitution is reestablishing "the situation which existed before the wrongful act was committed" (art. 35); compensation is covering any financially assessable damage not made good by restitution (art. 36); satisfaction is "an acknowledgement of the breach, an expression of regret, a formal apology or another appropriate modality" that responds to shortfalls in restitution and compensation when making good the injury caused (art. 37).

[41]Ibid., art. 49.1. See also Nicaragua, *supra* 12, ¶ 249; Gabcikovo-Nagymaros Project (Hung. V. Slovk.) 1997 ICJ 7, 55-56 (Sep. 25).

[42]Report of the International Law Commission, *supra* note 26, at 128.

ties.[43] Countermeasures must be proportionate to the injury suffered,[44] and the victim-State is required to have called on the State committing the wrong to refrain from the conduct (and make reparations if necessary), or, in the case of acts emanating from its territory, take measures to stop them.[45] Unlike collective self-defense (discussed below), countermeasures may only be taken by the State suffering the wrong.[46]

Countermeasures involving cyber operations would be particularly appropriate as a response to a cyber use of force, although the strict limitations placed on countermeasures weaken their viability in situations demanding an immediate reaction. On the other hand, it would be improper to respond with a cyber operation that rose to the level of a use of force, for "[c]ountermeasures shall not affect . . . the obligation to refrain from the threat or use of force as embodied in the Charter of the United Nations."[47] Responses amounting to a use of force are only permissible when falling within the two recognized exceptions to the prohibition on the use of force—action authorized by the Security Council and self-defense.

Although the limitation of countermeasures to non-forceful measures is widely accepted, in a separate opinion to the ICJ's *Oil Platforms* judgment, Judge Simma argued for what might be labeled "self-defense lite" in the face of an "unlawful use of force 'short of' an armed attack within the meaning of Article 51."[48] For Judge Simma, such "defensive military action 'short of' full scale self-defence" is of a "more limited range and quality of response" than that which is lawful in response to an armed attack in the self-defense context. The key difference with classic self-defense is that Judge Simma would exclude collective actions.[49] Reduced to basics, he is arguing for normative acceptance of forceful countermeasures.

The core problem with the approach is that it posits a tiered forceful response scheme. However, because the intensity of a defensive response is already governed, as will be discussed below, by the principle of proportionality, all that is really occurring is a relaxation of the threshold for engaging in forceful defensive actions. Such an approach is counter-textual, for the combined effect of Article 2(4) and 51 of the UN Charter is to rule out forcible responses by States against actions other than "armed attacks." Nevertheless, acceptance of such an approach by States would be significant in the cyber context because by it cyber operations which themselves would be a use of force under Article 2(4) may be launched in reaction to a cyber use of force that did not rise to the level of an armed attack under Article 51.

AUTHORIZATION BY THE SECURITY COUNCIL

Pursuant to Article 39 of the UN Charter, the Security Council is empowered to determine that a particular situation amounts to a "threat to the peace, breach of the peace or act of aggression." When it does, the Council "shall make recommendations, or decide what measures shall be taken in accordance with Articles 41 and 42, to maintain or restore international peace and security." Articles 41 and 42 set forth, respectively, non-forceful and forceful options for responding to such situations.

The scope of the phrase "threat to the peace, breach of the peace or act of aggression" has been the subject of much attention in international law. Breach of the peace would seemingly require the outbreak of violence; cyber operations harming individuals or property would reasonably qualify, but whether those falling short of this level would do so is uncertain. As to aggression, in 1974 the General Assembly adopted a resolution in which it characterized aggression as ranging from the "use of armed force"

---

[43]Draft Articles on State Responsibility, *supra* note 26, art. 52.3(a).

[44]Ibid., art. 51.

[45]Ibid., art. 52.1.

[46]Nicaragua, *supra* note 12, ¶¶ 211 & 252.

[47]Draft Articles on State Responsibility, *supra* note 26, art. 50.1(a).

[48]Oil Platforms (Iran v. US), 2003 ICJ Rep. 161, Separate Opinion of Judge Simma, ¶ 12.

[49]Ibid., ¶ 12-13.

and blockade to allowing one's territory to be used by another state to commit an act of aggression and sending armed bands against another State.[50] A cyber operation causing significant physical harm in another state would certainly rise to this level; whether others would is unclear.

This ambiguity is essentially irrelevant in light of the "threat to the peace" criterion. Little guidance exists on those acts which qualify, although they must be conceptually distinguished from activities constituting threats of the use of force in contravention of Article 2(4). In *Tadic* the ICTY opined that a threat to the peace should be assessed with regard to the Purposes of the United Nations delineated in Article 1 and the Principles set forth in Article 2.[51] This is a singularly unhelpful proposition, since said purposes and principles include such intangibles as developing friendly relations and solving social problems.

In fact, a finding that a situation is a "threat to the peace" is a political decision, not a legal one. It signals the Security Council's willingness to involve itself in a particular matter. There are no territorial limits on situations which may constitute threats to the peace, although they logically tend to be viewed as those which transcend borders, or risk doing so. Nor is there a limitation to acts conducted by or at the behest of States; for instance, the Council has repeatedly found transnational terrorism to be a threat to the peace.[52] No violence or other harmful act need have occurred before the Council may make a threat to the peace determination. Most importantly, since there is no mechanism for reviewing threat to the peace determinations, the Council's authority in this regard is unfettered. Simply put, a threat to the peace is whatever the Council deems it to be. This being so, the Council may label any cyber operation a threat to the peace (or breach of peace or act of aggression), no matter how insignificant.

Once it does, the Security Council may, under Article 41, authorize measures "not involving the use of armed force" necessary to maintain or restore international peace and security. Article 41 offers a number of examples, including "complete or partial interruption of economic relations and of rail, sea, air, postal, telegraphic, radio or other means of communication." Interruption of cyber communications would necessarily be included. An interruption could be broad in scope, as in blocking cyber traffic to or from a country, or surgical, as in denying a particular group access to the internet. Any other cyber operations judged necessary would likewise be permissible. Given the qualifier "armed force," operations resulting in physical harm to persons or objects could not be authorized pursuant to Article 41.

Should the Council determine that Article 41 measures are proving ineffective, or if before authorizing them it decides that such measures would be fruitless, it may, pursuant to Article 42, "take such action by air, sea, or land forces as may be necessary to maintain or restore international peace and security." The reference to operations by "air, sea, or land forces" plainly contemplates forceful military action, although a Security Council resolution authorizing the use of force will typically be framed in terms of taking "all necessary measures." To the extent that military force can be authorized, it is self-evident that cyber operations may be as well. It would be lawful to launch them alone or as an aspect of a broader traditional military operation. The sole limiting factors would be the requirement to comply with other norms of international law, such as the IHL prohibition on attacking the civilian population,[53] and the requirement to restrict operations to those within the scope of the particular authorization or mandate issued by the Council. Article 42 actions are not limited territorially or with regard to subject of the sanctions. For example, it would undoubtedly be within the power of the Council to authorize cyber attacks against transnational terrorist groups (e.g., in order to disrupt logistics or command and

---

[50]G.A. Res. 3314 (XXIX), annex, art. 3 (Dec. 14, 1974) ("Definition of Aggression").

[51]Prosecutor v. Tadic, Appeals Chamber Decision on the Defence Motion for Interlocutory Appeal on Jurisdiction, ¶ 29 (Oct. 2, 1995).

[52]See, e.g., S.C. Res. 1377 (Nov. 12, 2001); S.C. Res. 1438 (Oct. 14, 2002); S.C. Res. 1440 (Oct. 24, 2002); S.C. Res. 1450 (Dec. 13, 2002); S.C. Res. 1465 (Feb. 13, 2003); S.C. Res. 1516 (Nov. 20, 2003); S.C. Res. 1530 (Mar. 11, 2004); S.C. Res. 1611 (July 7, 2005); S.C. Res. 1618 (Aug. 4, 2005).

[53]Protocol Additional to the Geneva Conventions of 12 August 1949, and Relating to the Protection of Victims of International Armed Conflicts arts. 48, 51 & 52, June 8, 1977, 1125 U.N.T.S. 3 [hereinafter AP I].

control). It is important to emphasize that the measures only extend to restoring peace if breached, or maintaining it when threatened. No authority exists for taking punitive measures.

Pursuant to Article 25 of the Charter, UN members "agree to accept and carry out the decisions of the Security Council in accordance with the present Charter." This obligation applies even in the face of conflicting domestic or international legal obligations.[54] Consequently, if the Council ordered restrictions, for example, on cyber communications, individual States would be obligated to abide by them and ensure, to the extent feasible, their enforcement on their territory. How they do so is not the concern of the Council, so long as its decision is respected.

Since the United Nations does not itself control cyber networks or have the capability to mount cyber operations, it would have to rely on States to effectuate any cyber related resolutions. Originally, it was envisioned that the Security Council would have dedicated forces at its disposal to conduct Article 42 operations pursuant to "special arrangements" with contributing countries.[55] Such arrangements have never been executed. The Council has instead relied upon authorizations granted to individual States, ad hoc coalitions of States, security organizations such as NATO or UN forces consisting of troop contributions from its members. State practice has established that no obligation exists for States to provide military forces or finance specific operations that have been authorized. Therefore, if the Council were to endorse specific defensive or offensive cyber operations under Article 42, it would be wholly dependent on the willingness of States to provide the necessary cyber assets and forces to execute them.

Finally, it must be recalled that the entire UN collective security system depends on the readiness of the five Permanent Members of the Security Council (P5) to allow for action by refraining from exercise of their veto right.[56] In light of Russia and China's presence on the Council (cyber operations regularly emanate from their territory), this limitation may well prove the greatest obstacle to effective UN action in the face of those cyber operations which would in some fashion endanger international stability.

SELF-DEFENSE

The second recognized exception to the prohibition on the use of force is the right of States to take forceful actions to defend themselves. This customary international law right is codified in Article 51 of the UN Charter. In relevant part, it provides that "[n]othing in the present Charter shall impair the inherent right of individual or collective self-defence if an armed attack occurs against a Member of the United Nations, until the Security Council has taken measures necessary to maintain international peace and security." The article is the *conditio sine qua non* of the Charter, for although Articles 41 and 42 provide Member States some degree of protection from attack, their provisions rely upon implementation by the Security Council. Article 51 represents an essential safeguard in the event the collective security mechanism fails (or proves insufficiently timely), for it provides a means of defense requiring no Security Council approval. In practice, the right of self-defense has proven the principal means by which States ensure their security.

The right of self-defense bears solely on the remedies available to the victim of an armed attack, since all such attacks are "uses of force" in the context of Article 2(4) and customary law, with their legality determined by reference to those norms. By contrast, the issue in self-defense is the lawfulness of a forceful defensive response (including its nature, intensity, duration and scope) that would otherwise constitute an unlawful use of force by a State. This being so, it has no bearing on passive cyber defenses, which merely block attacks; all such defenses are lawful. It is only in the case of active defenses, whether kinetic or cyber in nature, that the law of self-defense comes into play by directly imposing physical costs on the group or State launching an attack.[57]

---

[54]U.N. Charter, art. 103.

[55]Ibid., art. 43.

[56]Ibid., art. 27.3.

[57]Note that one of the recommendations of the experts in NATO 2020 was that "NATO should plan to mount a fully adequate array of cyber defence capabilities, including passive and active elements." NATO 2020, *supra* note 7, at 45.

Further, States alone enjoy the right of self-defense. Private entities, such as a corporation that has been subjected to a hostile cyber attack, cannot respond pursuant to the law of self-defense regardless of its severity. Their responses would be governed by domestic and international criminal law norms. However, cyber attacks against a State's nationals may qualify as an armed attack on the State itself; there is no requirement in international law that State property or organizations be targeted. In such a case, the State may respond forcefully in self-defense should it choose to do so.

Armed Attack

The key text in Article 51, and the foundational concept of the customary law right of self-defense, is "armed attack." But for an armed attack, States enjoy no right to respond forcefully to a cyber operation directed against them, even if that operation amounts to an unlawful use of force. This dichotomy was intentional, for it comports with the general presumption permeating the Charter scheme against the use of force, especially unilateral action. In the *Nicaragua* case, the ICJ acknowledged the existence of this gap between the notions of use of force and armed attack when it recognized that there are "measures which do not constitute an armed attack but may nevertheless involve a use of force" and distinguished "the most grave forms of the use of force from other less grave forms."[58] Recall that the Court specifically excluded the supply of weapons and logistical support to rebels from the ambit of armed attack, but noted that such actions might constitute uses of force.[59] Simply put, all armed attacks are uses of force, but not all uses of force qualify as armed attacks.

As a result of the gap, the remedies for a use of force not meeting the threshold of armed attack are limited to lawful non-forceful actions, countermeasures or recourse to the Security Council. What this means in practical terms is that, absent Security Council authorization, a State subjected to a use of force may not respond in kind unless the use of force rises to the level of an armed attack. In light of the difficulties of identifying the source of a cyber operation, this cautious two-tiered system is especially appropriate in the cyber context. It is important to emphasize, however, that once it is established that an armed attack has occurred, no authorization from the Security Council is necessary before defensive actions, including those involving destructive cyber operations, may be mounted.

Consistent with the "use of force" prohibition, the Charter drafters elected an instrument-based approach to articulating the right of self-defense. And as with that norm, the intent was to preclude certain consequences (in this case, a premature forceful reaction by a State threatened with harm that would itself threaten community stability), while nevertheless allowing States to react forcefully when the consequences justified as much. But, again, the possibility of devastating consequences caused by a non-kinetic cyber attack was obviously not considered during the drafting process. Had it been, the drafters would surely have allowed for defense in the face of the severe consequences that can be caused by such attacks.

There is a problem in extending the notion of armed attack to address cyber attacks operations of this magnitude. The facts that the use of force language in Article 2(4) is not qualified by the term "armed" and that the phrase "use of force" has been authoritatively interpreted as not necessarily implying a kinetic action allow for interpretive leeway, and the resulting application of the seven factors set forth above. By contrast, the phrase "armed attack" tolerates little interpretive latitude.

Clearly, an armed attack includes kinetic military force. Applying the consequence-based approach, armed attack must also be understood in terms of the effects typically associated with the term "armed." The essence of an "armed" operation is the causation, or risk thereof, of death of or injury to persons or damage to or destruction of property and other tangible objects. Therefore, while an "armed attack" need not be carried out through the instrument of classic military force, its consequences (or likely consequences but for successful defensive action) must be analogous to those resulting from its employment.

---

[58]Nicaragua, *supra* note 12, ¶¶ 191 & 210. See also Oil Platforms, supra note 48, at ¶ 51.

[59]Nicaragua, *supra* note 12, ¶ 195.

A cyber operation that does not risk these results may qualify as an unlawful use of force, but will not comprise an armed attack permitting forceful defensive action.

In light of the grave consequences that cyber operations can cause without physically harming persons or objects, this interpretation may seem wholly unsatisfactory. Nevertheless, it is the extant law. It must be acknowledged that States victimized by massive cyber attacks, similar to or more aggravated than those suffered by Estonia, may choose to treat them as justifying a forceful response. If State practice along these lines became widespread and well-accepted, the Article 51 norm would shift accordingly through the natural process by which existing international law remains current. For the moment, that has not occurred.

Cyber operations that accompany military action otherwise constituting an armed attack have no bearing on the nature of the attack. For instance, cyber attacks would likely be conducted against enemy command and control or air defense systems as an element of a broader military operation. They can be responded to forcefully, regardless of whether they independently qualify as an armed attack, because they are a component of the overall military action. Similarly, cyber operations that are part of a lawful military response to an armed attack are obviously permissible so long as they comply with IHL, such as the prohibition on attacking civilians or civilian objects.[60] On the other hand, cyber operations need not accompany classic military operations. A cyber attack standing alone will comprise an armed attack when the consequence threshold is reached. Equally, States subjected to an armed attack may elect to respond solely with cyber operations.

In the *Nicaragua* case, the ICJ noted that not all attacks qualify as "armed attacks," citing the case of "a mere frontier incident."[61] According to the Court, an armed attack must exhibit certain "scale and effects." Unfortunately, the Court failed to prescribe criteria by which to resolve whether an attack meets the armed attack threshold. Not only has this proposition been fairly criticized, but in the *Oil Platforms* case the Court itself admitted that the mining of even a single ship could amount to an armed attack giving rise to the right of self-defense.[62] Consequently, by contemporary international law, qualitative indicators of attack (death, injury, damage or destruction) are more reliable in identifying those actions likely to be characterized as an armed attack than quantitative ones (number of deaths or extent of destruction). So long as a cyber operation is likely to result in the requisite consequences, it is an armed attack.

With regard to cyber operations, it must be cautioned that the mere destruction or damage (alteration) of data would not suffice. Were it to, the armed attack threshold would be so reduced that the vast majority of cyber operations would qualify as armed attacks. Rather, to comport with the accepted understanding of "armed attack," the destruction of or damage to the data would have to result in physical consequences, as in causing a generator to overheat and catch fire or rendering a train or subway uncontrollable such that it crashed. Destruction of data designed to be immediately convertible into tangible objects, like banking data, could also be reasonably encompassed within the scope of "armed attacks." But the destruction of or damage to data, standing alone, would not rise to the level of an armed attack.

It is sometimes argued that a cyber operation directed against a nation's military capability necessarily constitutes an armed attack. If the attack is physically destructive, there is no question that this is so. But the mere fact that cyber operations "compromise the ability of units of the DOD to perform DOD's mission" does not alone suffice.[63] Only when non-destructive cyber operations indicate that an attack is imminent ("preparing the battlefield") or represent the first step in an attack that is underway (as in bringing down an air defense radar network to facilitate penetration of enemy airspace) are force-

[60]AP I, *supra* note 53, arts. 48, 51 & 52.

[61]Nicaragua, *supra* note 12, ¶ 195.

[62]Oil Platforms, *supra* note 48, ¶ 72. See also, Yoram Dinstein, *War, Aggression and Self-Defence* 194-196 (Cambridge UP, 4th. ed. 2005); William Taft, "Self-defense and the Oil Platforms Decision," 29 *Yale Journal of International Law* 295, 300 (2004).

[63]National Research Council, *Technology, Policy, Law, and Ethics Regarding U.S. Acquisition and Use of Cyberattack Capabilities* 245 (William Owens, Kenneth Dam & Herbert Lin eds., National Academies Press, 2009).

ful actions in self-defense permissible. Obviously, it may be difficult to determine whether a particular cyber operation against military assets is either an indication or a component of attack; yet, that is a practical problem which does not affect the norm itself. As with the challenge of identifying an attacker or determining when attack is imminent (discussed below), the legal issue is whether the defender's conclusion is reasonable in the circumstances.

Finally, a cyber use of force by State A against State B may generate "bleed over" effects in State C. This situation does not, as noted earlier, constitute a use of force against C, although A would nevertheless be responsible for the consequences caused. However, if the effects in C rise to the level of those qualifying as an armed attack, C may respond in self-defense against A, even though C was not the intended target of the attack.[64]

The distinction arises from the fact that while the use of force prohibition solely pertains to the issue of whether there has been a particular violation of international law, the law of self-defense addresses whether a victim-State enjoys the right to employ force to protect itself. It would be incongruous to suggest that a State was barred from acting defensively when subjected to such effects. From its perspective (the correct vantage point in interpreting the law of self-defense), what matters is deterring or stopping the harmful actions; the intention of the actor is but a secondary consideration. Of course, the defensive actions must meet the criteria of self-defense set forth below, in particular the requirement that a forceful response be "necessary." Since C was not the intended target of the attack, it may suffice to simply notify A that it is suffering effects from the attack on B and demand that A takes steps to arrest them.

Anticipatory Self-Defense

Textually, Article 51 addresses only those situations where an armed attack is underway. Nevertheless, it is well-accepted that a State need not sit idly by as the enemy prepares to attack; instead, a State may defend itself once attack is "imminent."[65] The generally accepted standard of imminency was articulated in the 19th century by Secretary of State Daniel Webster following the famous *Caroline* incident. In correspondence with his British counterpart regarding an incursion into U.S. territory to attack Canadian rebels during the Mackenzie Rebellion, Webster opined that the right of self-defense applied only when "the necessity of that self-defense is instant, overwhelming, and leaving no moment for deliberation."[66] Although the incident actually had nothing to do with actions taken in anticipation of attack (the attacks in question were ongoing), Webster's formulation has survived as the classic expression of the temporal threshold for anticipatory defensive actions;[67] indeed, the Nuremberg Tribunal cited the *Caroline* case with approval.[68]

Following the events of September 11th, 2001, the United States suggested that a new self-defense paradigm was needed. As President Bush noted in his 2002 National Security Strategy,

---

[64]As the right of self-defense extends to armed attacks by non-State actors, an identical conclusion would apply to actions they undertake against one State having effects in another.

[65]Acceptance of the standard is not universal. For instance, Professor Yoram Dinstein argues against its existence, suggesting instead that such actions are better seen as "interceptive self-defense." He notes that "an interceptive strike counters an armed attack which is in progress, even if it is still incipient: the blow is 'imminent' and practically 'unavoidable.'" Dinstein, *supra* note 62, at 191. It might also be noted that whereas the notion of "*armed* attack" was interpreted with fidelity to the Charter text, this article accepts an interpretation of self-defense which runs contrary to the precise text of the UN Charter. The apparent inconsistency can be justified in a number of ways. Note that Article 51 refers to the "inherent" right of self-defense, which has been interpreted as either pre-existing (and thereby maintained in the Charter) or as inherent in the illogic of requiring States to suffer a potentially devastating strike before acting in self-defense. Additionally, Article 2 of the Definition of Aggression Resolution provides that the first use of force is merely *prima facie* evidence of an act of aggression. Definition of Aggression, *supra* note 50, art. 2. As such, it contemplates the possibility of a first use which does not qualify as an armed attack and which, therefore, can only be justified in terms of anticipatory self-defense.

[66]Letter from Daniel Webster to Lord Ashburton (Aug. 6, 1842), reprinted in 2 John Moore, Digest of International Law 411-12 (1906).

[67]See, e.g., Thomas M. Franck, *Recourse to Force: State Action against Threats and Armed Attacks* 97 (2002).

[68]International Military Tribunal (Nuremberg), Judgment and Sentences, 41 AJIL 172, 205 (1947).

For centuries, international law recognized that nations need not suffer an attack before they can lawfully take action to defend themselves against forces that present an imminent danger of attack. Legal scholars and international jurists often conditioned the legitimacy of pre-emption on the existence of an imminent threat-most often a visible mobilization of armies, navies, and air forces preparing to attack. We must adapt the concept of imminent threat to the capabilities and objectives of today's adversaries. Rogue states and terrorists do not seek to attack us using conventional means. They know such attacks would fail. Instead, they rely on acts of terror and, potentially, the use of weapons of mass destruction-weapons that can be easily concealed, delivered covertly, and used without warning . . .[69]

His conclusion was that the "greater the threat, the greater is the risk of inaction—and the more compelling the case for taking anticipatory action to defend ourselves, even if uncertainty remains as to the time and place of the enemy's attack."[70] The United States has maintained this approach to the present.[71]

Despite being characterized by some as revolutionary, even unlawful, the pre-emption doctrine represented a reasonable accommodation to the changed circumstances cited by the President. Indeed, it is arguable that the approach represented a *de minimus* departure from existing law. The underlying premise of anticipatory self-defense is that to effectively defend themselves, States must sometimes act before an aggressive blow falls. Traditionally, a standard requiring temporal proximity to the armed attack had been employed to assess the need. The underlying intent of the standard was to allow as much opportunity as possible for non-forceful measures to work in alleviating the crisis. Yet, as correctly noted in the National Security Strategy, the *modus operandi* of terrorists is to strike without warning, thereby denuding the opportunity the victim-State has to anticipatorily defend itself.

In such circumstances, the most reasonable accommodation of the law of self-defense to both the changed threat and to international law's rebuttable presumption against the legality of using force lies in restricting the victim-State from acting forcefully in self-defense until the point at which its window of opportunity to mount a effective defense is about to close. The imminency criterion should therefore not be measured by reference to the moment of armed attack, but rather with regard to the point at which a State must act defensively, lest it be too late.[72]

The "last feasible window of opportunity" standard must not be interpreted as permitting *preventive* strikes, that is, those against a prospective attacker who lacks either the means to carry out an attack or the intent to do so. The fact that an overtly hostile State is capable of launching cyber attacks—even devastating ones—does not alone entitle a potential victim to act defensively with force. Such hostility must mature into an actual decision to attack. The decision may be evidenced by, for example, preparatory cyber operations amounting to a demonstration of "hostile intent."[73] Moreover, the circumstances must be such that the pending attack has to be responded to immediately if the victim-State is to have any reasonable hope of fending it off. Consider a State's introduction of cyber vulnerabilities into another State's critical infrastructure. Such an action might amount to a use of force, but the victim-State may not react forcefully until it reasonably concludes that (1) its opponent has decided to actually exploit those vulnerabilities; (2) the strike is likely to generate consequences at the armed attack level; and (3) it must act immediately to defend itself. Until arriving at these conclusions, the victim-State's response would be limited to non-forceful measures, including countermeasures, and referral of the matter to the Security Council.

---

[69]The White House, *The National Security Strategy of the United States of America* 15 (Sept. 2002).

[70]Ibid.

[71]See, e.g., The White House, *The National Security Strategy of the United States of America* 18 (March 2006). The Obama National Security Strategy does not expressly adopt the doctrine of pre-emption, but nor is it rejected. It specifically reserves the right to act unilaterally. 2010 National Security Strategy, *supra* note 6, at 22.

[72]For a fuller discussion, see Michael N. Schmitt, *Responding to Transnational Terrorism under the Jus ad Bellum: A Normative Framework*, 56 NAVAL LAW REVIEW 1, 16-19 (2008).

[73]The U.S. Standing Rules of Engagement define hostile intent as "the threat of imminent use of force against the United States, U.S. forces, or other designated persons or property. It also includes the threat of force to preclude or impede the mission and/or duties of U.S. forces, including the recovery of U.S. personnel or vital USG property." CJCSI 3121.01B, June 13, 2005, at A-4.

Although, transnational terrorism represents the obvious justification for the approach, cyber operations present many of the same challenges to application of the traditional temporal criterion. Like terrorism, cyber operations are typically launched without any warning that attack is imminent. The time between launch of an operation and impact is measured in seconds at most, thereby often depriving the victim of an opportunity to foil the initial attack as it is unfolding; viable defenses could resultantly be limited to passive measures, such as firewalls and antivirus software. Moreover, although the immediate severity of a cyber armed attack may not reach the level of attacks with weapons of mass destruction, cyber operations have the potential, because of a networking, to affect many more individuals and activities. In light of these realities, an approach centering on a State's opportunity to defend itself is no less suitable in the context of cyber operations than in that of terrorism. Cyber or kinetic operations designed to foil an attack which has been approved, and which qualifies as an armed attack, would therefore be lawful when it reasonably appears that failure to act promptly will deprive the target State of any viable opportunity to defend itself.

Criteria for Engaging in Self-Defense

Actions in self-defense must meet two legal criteria—necessity and proportionality. The ICJ acknowledged both in the *Nicaragua* case, and later confirmed them in its *Oil Platforms* judgement.[74] Necessity requires that there be no reasonable option other than force to effectively deter an imminent attack or defeat one that is underway. This does not mean that force need represent the only available response; it merely requires that defense necessitate actions that are forceful in nature as a component of an overall response, which may well also include non-forceful measures such as diplomacy, economic sanctions or law enforcement measures.

Proportionality, by contrast, addresses the issue of how much force is permissible once it is deemed necessary. The criterion limits the scale, scope, duration and intensity of the defensive response to that which is required to neutralize a prospective attack or repel one that is underway. It does not restrict the amount of force used to that employed in the armed attack, since more force may be needed to successfully conduct a defense, or less may suffice. In addition, there is no requirement that the defensive force be of the same nature as that constituting the armed attack. Cyber operations may be responded to with kinetic operations and vice versa. The point of reference is the need to effectively defend oneself, not the character of the armed attack.

The key to the necessity analysis in the cyber context is the existence, or lack thereof, of alternative non-forceful courses of action. Should passive cyber defenses be adequate to thwart a cyber armed attack, forceful defensive measures would be disallowed. Similarly, if active cyber operations not rising to the level of force are adequate to deter armed attacks (prospective or ongoing), forceful alternatives, whether cyber or kinetic, would be barred. However, when non-forceful measures alone cannot reasonably be expected to defeat an armed attack and prevent subsequent ones, destructive cyber and kinetic operations are permissible under the law of self-defense.

Any forceful defensive cyber or kinetic operations must equally be proportionate. The victim of a cyber armed attack does not have a carte blanche to conduct its cyber or kinetic defense. Rather, the extent and nature of its response are limited to ensuring the victim-State is no longer subject to attack. The requirement should not be overstated. It may be that the source of the cyber armed attack is relatively invulnerable to cyber operations. This would not preclude kinetic or cyber defensive operations against other targets in an effort to compel the attacker to desist, although they must be scaled to that purpose.

Evidentiary Issues

Identification of an "attacker" poses particular problems in the cyber context. For instance, it is possible to "spoof" the origin of attack. Or the lone indication of where an attack originated from, or who

---

[74]Nicaragua, *supra* note 12, ¶ 194; Oil Platforms, *supra* note 48, ¶¶ 43, 73-74 & 76.

launched it, may be an IP address or other machine discernable data. And the speed by which cyber operations proceed dramatically compresses the time available to make such determinations. How certain must the target State be as to the identity of its attacker before responding in self-defense?

Although international law sets no specific evidentiary standard for drawing conclusions as to the originator of an armed attack, a potentially useful formula was contained in the U.S. notification to the Security Council that it was acting in self-defense when it launched its October 2001 attacks against the Taliban and Al Qaeda in Afghanistan. There, U.S. Ambassador Negroponte stated that "my Government has obtained clear and compelling information that the Al-Qaeda organization, which is supported by the Taliban regime in Afghanistan, had a central role in the attacks."[75] NATO Secretary-General Lord Robertson used the same language when announcing that the attacks of 9/11 fell within the ambit of the collective defense provisions of Article V of the North Atlantic Treaty.[76]

"Clear and compelling" is a threshold higher than the preponderance of the evidence (more likely than not) standard used in certain civil and administrative proceedings and lower than criminal law's "beyond a reasonable doubt." In essence, it obliges a State to act reasonably, that is, in a fashion consistent with the normal State practice in same or similar circumstances. Reasonable States neither respond precipitously on the basis of sketchy indications of who has attacked them nor sit back passively until they have gathered unassailable evidence. So long as the victim-State has taken reasonable steps to identify the perpetrator of an armed attack, cyber or kinetic, and has drawn reasonable conclusions based on the results of those efforts, it may respond forcefully in self-defense. That the State in fact drew the wrong conclusion is of no direct relevance to the question of whether it acted lawfully in self-defense.[77] Its responses are assessed as of the time it took action, not *ex post facto*.

Although the temporal aspect cannot be ignored, the time available to make the determination is merely one factor bearing on the reasonableness of any conclusion. In particular, automatic "hack-back" systems that might involve a response amounting to a use of force are neither necessarily lawful nor unlawful. Their use must be judged in light of many factors, such as the reliability of the determination of origin, the damage caused by the attack, and the range of available response options.

An analogous standard of reasonableness would apply in the case of anticipatory self-defense against an imminent cyber attack. International law does not require either certainty or absolute precision in anticipating another State's (or non-State actor's) future actions. Rather, it requires reasonableness in concluding that a potential attacker has decided to attack and wields the capability to carry out said attack, and that it must act defensively in anticipation of the attack lest it lose the opportunity to effectively defend itself. States could not possibly countenance a higher threshold, for such a standard would deprive them of a meaningful right of self-defense.

Admittedly, ascertaining a possible adversary's intentions in the cyber environment is likely to be demanding. Aside from the difficulties of accurately pinpointing identity discussed above, it will be challenging in the context of anticipatory self-defense to identify the purpose behind a particular cyber operation. For instance, is a cyber probe of a State's air defense designed merely to gather intelligence or instead to locate vulnerabilities in anticipation of an attack which is about to be launched? Obviously, such determinations must be made contextually, considering factors such as the importance of the matter in contention, degree of political tensions, statements by military and political leaders, military activities like deployments, exercises and mobilizations, failed efforts to resolve a contentious situation diplomatically, and so forth. The speed with which the defender may have to make such an assessment to effectively defend itself further complicates matters. Despite the factual and practical complexity,

---

[75]Letter dated 7 October 2001 from the Permanent Representative of the United States of America to the United Nations Addressed to the President of the Security Council, U.N. Doc. S/2001/946 (Oct. 7, 2001).

[76]Statement by NATO Secretary General Lord Robertson, NATO Headquarters (Oct. 2, 2001), http://www.nato.int/docu/speech/2001/s011002a.htm.

[77]Note by way of analogy to international criminal law, that pursuant to the Statute of the International Criminal Court, a mistake of fact is grounds for excluding criminal responsibility when the mistake negates the mental element required by the crime. Rome Statute of the International Criminal Court, art. 32.1, July 17, 1998, 2187 U.N.T.S. 90.

the legal standard is clear; a State acting anticipatorily in self-defense must do so reasonably. In other words, States in the same or similar circumstances would react defensively.

When a State asserts that it is acting in self-defense, it bears the burden of proof. In the *Oil Platforms* case, the ICJ noted that the United States had failed to present evidence sufficient to "justify its using force in self-defense."[78] Specifically, it could not demonstrate that Iran was responsible for a 1987 missile attack against an oil tanker sailing under U.S. flag or the 1988 mining of a U.S. warship during the Iran-Iraq "tanker war," to which the United States responded by attacking Iranian oil platforms. The Court rejected evidence offered by the United States which was merely "suggestive," looking instead for "direct evidence" or, reframed, "conclusive evidence."[79] "Clear and compelling" evidence would meet these requirements. Thus, States responding to a cyber armed attack must be prepared to present evidence of this quality as to the source and nature of an impending attack, while those acting in anticipation of an attack must do likewise with regard to the potential attacker's intent and capability.

Collective Responses

Unlike countermeasures, defensive actions may be collective. This possibility is explicitly provided for in Article 51's reference to "individual or collective self-defense." Collective self-defense may be mounted together by States which have all been attacked or individually by a State (or States) which has not, but comes to the defense of another. Although the basic norm is clear in theory, it is complex in application. As noted in the Experts Report on the new NATO Strategic Concept, "there may well be doubts about whether an unconventional danger—such as a cyber attack or evidence that terrorists are planning a strike—triggers the collective defence mechanisms of Article V (the North Atlantic Treaty implementation of Article 51)."[80]

The mere fact of an armed attack allows for collective defensive action; no authorization from the Security Council is necessary. But there are legal limits on exercise of the right. In the *Nicaragua* case, the ICJ suggested that only the victim-State is empowered to determine whether an armed attack has occurred, and it must request assistance before others act on its behalf.[81] Absent such a determination and request, collective actions would themselves amount to unlawful uses of force, and, depending on their nature, even armed attacks (paradoxically, against the State launching the initial armed attack). These requirements are designed to prevent States from claiming to act in collective self-defense as a subterfuge for aggression.

Given the practical difficulties of identifying a cyber operation's originator, this is a sensible limitation. It must be noted that some distinguished commentators challenge the strict application of these requirements. They argue that in cases where the collective defense actions occur outside the territory of the victim-State, other States may be entitled to act on the basis of their own right to ensure their security. The right arguably derives from breach of the duty to refrain from armed attack that the State initiating the armed attack bears.[82] This latter scenario is particularly germane in the cyber context since the effects of cyber armed attacks could easily spread through networks, thereby endangering States other than those which are the intended target. The prevailing view is nevertheless that there must be a request from the victim-State before the right of collective self-defense matures.

In many cases, a pre-existing treaty contemplates collective defense. Article 52(1) of the UN Charter provides that "nothing in the present Charter precludes the existence of regional arrangements or agencies for dealing with such matters relating to the maintenance of international peace and security

---

[78]Oil Platform, *supra* note 48, ¶ 57.

[79]Ibid., ¶¶ 59, 69.

[80]NATO 2020, *supra* note 7, at 20.

[81]Nicaragua, *supra* note 12, ¶ 199; The Court reiterated this position in the Oil Platforms case of 2003. Oil Platforms, *supra* note 48, ¶ 55.

[82]See discussion in Dinstein, *supra* note 62, at 270. This was the position adopted in Judge Jenning's dissent in Nicaragua. Nicaragua, Dissenting Opinion of Judge Sir Robert Jennings, *supra* note 12, at 544-46.

as are appropriate for regional action. . . ." Despite the reference to "regional" arrangements, the agreements need not be limited to States in a particular region or to actions occurring in a defined area. Such arrangements may take multiple forms, For instance, bilateral and multilateral mutual assistance treaties typically provide that the Parties will treat an armed attack against one of them as an armed attack against all.[83] As a practical matter, the effectiveness of collective defense provisions usually depends on the willingness of the treaty partners to come to each other's aid. A State that does not see collective defensive action as in its national interest may be expected to contest characterization of a cyber operation as an armed attack.

Military alliances based on the right to engage in collective defense also exist, the paradigmatic example being NATO. Pursuant to Article V of the treaty, Member States "agree that an armed attack against one or more of them in Europe or North America shall be considered an attack against them all and consequently they agree that, if such an armed attack occurs, each of them, in exercise of the right of individual or collective self-defence recognised by Article 51 of the Charter of the United Nations, will assist the Party or Parties so attacked by taking forthwith, individually and in concert with the other Parties, such action as it deems necessary, including the use of armed force, to restore and maintain the security of the North Atlantic area."[84]

The benefit of alliances is that they generally involve a degree of advanced planning for combined operations in the event of armed attack, and, as with NATO, military structures are often set up to coordinate and direct military operations. Preplanning and the existence of collective mechanisms for managing joint and combined action are especially valuable with regard to defending against cyber attacks. However, like mutual assistance treaties, alliance arrangements are subject to the reality that they are composed of States, which can be expected to act pursuant to their own national interests. In the case of NATO, for instance, decisions to act are taken by consensus in the North Atlantic Council; a single member State can therefore block NATO collective action. Indeed, had the cyber operations against Estonia risen to the level of an armed attack, it is not altogether certain that NATO would have come to its defense militarily, especially in light of Russia's place in the European security environment and the countervailing commitments of NATO allies elsewhere, especially Afghanistan and Iraq.

State Sponsorship of Attacks by Non-State Actors

The issue of State sponsorship of cyber operations was addressed earlier in the context of the responsibility of States for uses of force by non-State actors. There the question was when does a State violate the use of force prohibition by virtue of its relationship with others who conduct cyber operations? However, the issue of State sponsorship in the self-defense context is much more momentous. It asks when may forceful defensive actions, even kinetic ones, be taken against a State which has not engaged in cyber operations, but which has "sponsored" them? In other words, when is an armed attack attributable to a State such that the State may be treated as if it had itself launched the attack?

Until the transnational attacks of September 11, 2001, the generally accepted standard was set forth in the *Nicaragua* case. There the ICJ stated that "an armed attack must be understood as including not merely action by regular forces across an international border, but also 'the sending by or on behalf of a state of armed bands, groups, irregulars or mercenaries, which carry out acts of armed force against another state of such gravity as to amount to' (inter alia) an actual armed attack conducted by regular forces, 'or its substantial involvement therein.'"[85] The Court noted that the activities involved should

---

[83]For instance, the Japan-United States mutual defense treaty provides that "[e]ach Party recognizes that an armed attack against either Party in the territories under the administration of Japan would be dangerous to its own peace and safety and declares that it would act to meet the common danger in accordance with its constitutional provisions and processes." Treaty of Mutual Cooperation and Security Between Japan and the United States of America, Regarding Facilities and Areas and the Status of United States Armed Forces in Japan, art. V, Jan. 19, 1960, 373 U.N.T.S. 207.

[84]North Atlantic Treaty, art. V, Apr. 4, 1949, 34 U.N.T.S. 243.

[85]Nicaragua, *supra* note 12, ¶ 195.

be of a "scale and effects" that would equate to an armed attack if carried out by the State's military. Thus, "acts by armed bands where such attacks occur on a significant scale" would qualify, but "a mere frontier incident would not."[86]

By this standard, attribution requires (1) acts qualifying as an armed attack and (2) that the State dispatched the non-State actors or was substantially involved in the operations. As noted earlier, the ICTY took a more relaxed view of the degree of control necessary, accepting "overall control" as sufficient.[87] The events of 9/11 brought the issue of threshold to light in a dramatic way. Assistance provided by the Taliban to Al Qaeda met neither the *Nicaragua* nor *Tadic* standards, since the Taliban merely provided sanctuary to Al Qaeda. The cyber analogy would be doing nothing to put an end to the activities of cyber "terrorists" or other malicious hackers operating from a State's territory when it is within its capability, legal and practical, to do so.

Even though there was seemingly no legal basis for attribution to Afghanistan, when the Coalition responded with armed force against both Al Qaeda and the governing Taliban, no objection was raised. On the contrary, the Security Council condemned the Taliban "for allowing Afghanistan to be used as a base for the export of terrorism by the Al-Qaida network and other terrorist groups and for providing safe haven to Usama Bin laden, Al-Qaida and others associated with them."[88] It seems that the international community had lowered the normative bar of attribution measurably. While the underlying operations must still amount to an armed attack, it is arguable that today much less support is required for attribution than envisaged in either *Nicaragua* or *Tadic*. Far from being counter-legal, this process of reinterpretation is natural; understandings of international legal norms inevitably evolve in response to new threats to the global order. In that cyber operations resemble terrorism in many regards, States may equally be willing to countenance attribution of a cyber armed attack to a State which willingly provides sanctuary to non-State actors conducting them.

Armed Attacks by Non-State Actors

Although most cyber operations are launched by individuals such as the anti-Estonian "hacktivists," concern is mounting about the prospect that transnational terrorist organizations and other non-State groups will turn to cyber operations as a means of attacking States.[89] The concern is well-founded. Al Qaeda computers have been seized that contain hacker tools, the membership of such groups is increasingly computer-literate, and the technology to conduct cyber operations is readily available. In one case, a seized Al Qaeda computer contained models of dams, a lucrative cyber attack target, and the computer programs required to analyze them.[90]

International lawyers have traditionally, albeit not universally, characterized Article 51 and the customary law of self-defense as applicable solely to armed attacks mounted by one State against another. Violent actions by non-State actors fell within the criminal law paradigm. Nonetheless, the international community treated the 9/11 attacks by Al Qaeda as armed attacks under the law of self-defense. The Security Council adopted numerous resolutions recognizing the applicability of the right of self-defense.[91] International organizations such as NATO and many individual States took the same approach.[92] The United States claimed the right to act forcefully in self-

---

[86]Ibid.

[87]It must be emphasized that the legal issue involved in that case was not attribution of an armed attack, but rather the existence of an international armed conflict.

[88]S.C. Res. 1378, pmbl. (Nov. 14, 2001).

[89]This threat is cited in both the 2010 National Security Strategy (*supra* note 6, at 27) and NATO 2020 (*supra* note 7, at 17).

[90]Clay Wilson, Computer Attack and Cyber Terrorism: Vulnerabilities and Policy Issues for Congress, Congressional Research Service Report RL32114, Oct. 17, 2003, at 11-13.

[91]See, e.g., S.C. Res 1368 (Sept. 11, 2001); S.C. Res. 1373 (Sept. 28, 2001).

[92]See, e.g., Press Release, NATO, Statement by the North Atlantic Council (Sept. 12, 2001); Terrorist Threat to the Americas, Res. 1, Twenty-fourth Meeting of Consultation of Ministers of Foreign Affairs, Terrorist Threat to the Americas, OAS Doc. RC.24/RES.1/01 (Sept. 21, 2001); Brendan Pearson, *PM Commits to Mutual Defence*, Australian Financial Review, Sept. 15, 2001, at 9.

defense,[93] and no State objected to the assertion. Lest this approach be dismissed as simply an emotive reaction to the horrific attacks of 9/11, it must be noted that when Israel launched operations into Lebanon in response to Hezbollah's 2006 terrorism, the international community again seemed to accept a country's right to defend itself against armed attacks mounted by non-State actors.[94]

Despite acceptance by States of the premise that non-State actors may qualify as the originators of an armed attack, the ICJ seems to have taken a step backwards in two post-9/11 cases. In the *Wall* advisory opinion and the *Congo* case, the Court refrained from considering claims of self-defense against actions by non-State actors, noting that no assertion had been made that the relevant actions were imputable to a State.[95] Although the Court's reasoning was nuanced and fact-specific, it has nevertheless been widely criticized as inattentive to contemporary understandings of the relevant law. In particular, in the *Wall* case three judges expressly departed from the majority's approach on the bases that it ignored the fact that Article 51 makes no mention of the originator of an attack (while Article 2(4) specifically addresses uses of force by States) and that the Security Council had deliberately treated terrorist attacks as armed attacks in the aftermath of the 9/11.[96]

The Court's hesitancy to embrace the notion of armed attack by non-State actors is understandable in light of the risk of abuse. States might well apply it to engage in robust military operations against groups in situations in which law enforcement is the more normatively appropriate response. For instance, significant concerns have been raised regarding counterterrorist operations occurring outside an armed conflict mounted in States which do not consent to them. Such concerns are likely to be even more acute in relation to cyber operations, which are conducted not by armed members of groups resembling classic military forces, but rather by cyber experts equipped with computers. Nevertheless, as a matter of law, States seem comfortable with applying the concept of armed attacks to situations involving non-State actors. Should such groups launch cyber attacks meeting the threshold criteria for an armed attack, States would likely respond within the framework of the law of self-defense.

The point that the attacks must meet the threshold criteria cannot be overemphasized. There is no State practice supporting extension of the concept to the actions of isolated individuals, such as hacktivists or patriotic hackers. Further, the cyber operations must be severe enough to qualify as armed attacks, that is, they have to result in damage to or destruction of property or injury to or death of individuals. Finally, as the debate over minor border incursions demonstrates, it is uncertain whether attacks which meet the aforementioned threshold, but are not of significant scale, would qualify. As an example, a cyber attack that caused a single plant's generator to overheat, thereby temporarily interrupting service until it could be repaired, would presumably not, by the more restrictive standard, qualify as an armed attack. Rather, it would be the cyber equivalent of a border incursion.

Cross-Border Operations

When armed attacks by non-State actors emanate from outside a State, may that State take defensive actions against its perpetrators in the territory of the State where they are based? This question has been raised recently in the context of unmanned aerial vehicle strikes against terrorists in Pakistan

---

[93]"In response to these attacks, and in accordance with the inherent right of individual and collective self-defense, United States forces have initiated actions designed to prevent and deter further attacks on the United States. These actions include measures against Al-Qaeda terrorist training camps and military installations of the Taliban regime in Afghanistan. . . ." Letter from the Permanent Representative, *supra* note 75.

[94]See generally, Michael N. Schmitt, "'Change Direction' 2006: Israeli Operations in Lebanon and the International Law of Self-Defense," 29 *Michigan Journal of International Law* 127 (2008). Many commentators and States saw the actions as violating the proportionality criterion discussed above.

[95]Legal Consequences of the Construction of a Wall in the Occupied Palestinian Territory, Advisory Opinion, 2004 ICJ Rep. 136, ¶ 139 (July 9); Congo, *supra* note 33, at 53.

[96]Wall, supra *note* 95, Sep. Op. Judge Higgins, ¶ 33; Sep. Op. Judge Koojmans, ¶ 35; Decl. Judge Buergenthal, ¶ 6.

and elsewhere. It is no less pertinent to situations involving cyber armed attacks launched by non-State actors from abroad.

It is indisputable that one State may employ force in another with the consent of the territorial State. For instance, a State may grant others the right to enter its territory to conduct counterterrorist operations, as often occurs in Pakistan, or a State embroiled in an internal conflict with insurgents may request external assistance in restoring order, as with ISAF operations in Afghanistan or USF in Iraq. A State subjected to an armed attack, whether cyber or kinetic, could, with the acquiescence of the territorial State, equally launch cyber defensive operations into the State from which the attacks emanated.

The legal dilemma arises when operations are conducted without territorial State approval. By the principle of sovereignty (and the derivative notion of territorial integrity), a State enjoys near absolute control over access to its territory. In affirmation, the UN General Assembly has cited the use of force by a State on the territory of another as an act of aggression.[97] Yet, the right of States to use force in self-defense is no less foundational. When terrorists or insurgents seek sanctuary in a State other than that in which they are conducting operations, they bring the territorial State's right of sovereignty into conflict with the victim-State's right of self-defense.

Fortunately, international law does not require an either-or resolution when norms clash. Instead, it seeks to balance them by fashioning a compromise which best achieves their respective underlying purposes. In this case, such a balance would ensure that the territorial State need not suffer unconstrained violations of its sovereignty, but nor would the victim-State have to remain passive as non-State groups attack it with impunity from abroad. The resulting compromise is as follows. The victim-State must first demand the territorial State fulfill its legal duty to ensure actions on or from its territory do not harm other States and afford the territorial State an opportunity to comply.[98] If that State subsequently takes effective steps to remove the threat, then penetration of its territory by the victim-State, whether kinetically or by cyber means, is impermissible. But if the territorial State fails to take appropriate and timely action, either because it lacks the capability to conduct the operations or simply chooses not to do so (e.g., out of sympathy for the non-State actors or because its domestic laws preclude action), the victim-State may act in self-defense to put an end to the non-State actor's attacks. It matters not whether the actions are kinetic or cyber in nature, as long as they comply with the principles of proportionality and necessity.

ARMED CONFLICT

The *jus in bello* notion of "armed conflict" must be distinguished from the *jus ad bellum* concepts of use of force, threat to the peace, breach of the peace, act of aggression and armed attack. The *jus ad bellum* determines when a State has violated the international law governing the resort to force, and sets forth a normative flow plan for individually or collectively responding to such violations. By contrast, under the *jus in bello*, the applicability of IHL depends on the existence of an "armed conflict." This law is set forth in such treaties as the four 1949 Geneva Conventions and the two 1977 Protocols Additional (Protocol I for international and Protocol II for non-international armed conflict), and in customary international law.[99] In determining whether IHL rules like distinction (the requirement to distinguish combatants from civilians and military objectives from civilian objects), proportionality (the prohibition on attacks expected to cause harm to civilians and civilian object which is excessive relative to the military advantage anticipated to accrue from the attack), or direct participation (the loss by civilians of their protections when they take a direct part in hostilities) apply to cyber operations, the threshold question is whether an armed conflict is underway.[100]

---

[97]Definition of Aggression Resolution, *supra* note 50, art. 3(a).

[98]On the duty to police one's own territory, see Corfu Channel (U.K. v. Alb.), 1949 ICJ Rep. 4 (Apr. 9).

[99]GC I-IV, *supra* note 4; AP I, *supra* note 53; Protocol Additional to the Geneva Conventions of 12 August 1949, and Relating to the Protection of Victims of Non-International Armed Conflicts, June 8, 1977, 1125 U.N.T.S. 609 [hereinafter AP II].

[100]AP I, *supra* note 53, arts. 48, 51.5(b), 51.3.

There are two forms of armed conflict, international and non-international. The first refers to conflicts between States, whereas the second implies either conflicts between a State and a non-State organized armed group or those between such groups. Determining when a conflict is international or non-international is a highly complex matter, particularly in light of hostilties between States and non-State transnational actors, such as global terrorist groups. As an example of the uncertainty, consider that while the Israeli Supreme Court has characterized Israel's conflicts with terrorist groups such as Hamas and Hezbollah to be international, in part because they transcend Israeli territory, the U.S. Supreme Court has labeled the conflict with transnational terrorist groups like Al Qaeda as "not of an international character."[101] Although a full exploration of the characterization of conflict issue lies beyond the scope of this article, it is useful to examine the concepts in a general manner.

International Armed Conflict

Article 2 Common to the four Geneva Conventions states that they "apply to all cases of declared war or to any other armed conflict which may arise between two or more of the High Contracting parties."[102] This begs the question of the nature and scope of the referenced conflict. The International Committee of the Red Cross' official commentary to the provision provides that "any difference arising between two States and leading to the intervention of members of the armed forces is an armed conflict within the meaning of Article 2, even if one of the Parties denies the existence of a state of war. It makes no difference how long the conflict lasts, how much slaughter takes place, or how numerous are the participating forces."[103] Similarly, the ICTY has opined that "an armed conflict exists whenever there is resort to force between States."[104]

It is essential to distinguish states of "armed conflict" under the *jus in bello* from instances of *jus ad bellum* "armed attacks," for, as noted, some experts assert that minor incidents do not amount to the latter. Moreover, in the traditional treatment of the legal concept of "war," minor armed incidents did not necessarily signal the commencement of a war between States.[105] But so long as there is an armed exchange between the armed forces of two States, an "international armed conflict" exists. Actions by non-State actors operating under State control would also qualify, although actions by individuals or independent group would not. Hostilities need not even exist. By Article 2, the conventions apply in cases of "partial or total occupation . . ., even if said occupation meets with no armed resistance."[106] And it is equally accepted that there is an armed conflict if the forces of one State detain individuals protected by IHL, such as combatants.[107] It is irrelevant whether the parties to the armed conflict consider themselves to be "at war."

This leads to two alternative conclusions with regard to cyber operations standing alone. First, they must be the functional equivalent of a clash of arms between States. Applying the approach adopted in the context of the *jus ad bellum*, relevant actions must be likely to result in injury, death, damage or destruction to comprise an international armed conflict. Non-destructive computer network exploitation, espionage, denial of service attacks and other actions would not initiate an armed conflict, although they might, depending on the circumstances, qualify as a use of force. This is the mainstream approach among IHL experts, one focusing on the adjective "armed" in the phrase armed conflict.

However, the fact that an armed conflict can occur in the absence of combat arguably provides interpretive leeway. This is especially so in light of an ongoing debate among experts as to whether a cyber

---

[101]HCJ [High Court of Justice] 796/02, Public Committee against Torture in Israel et al. v. Government of Israel et al., ¶ 21(Dec. 13, 2006); Hamdan v. Rumsfeld, 126 S.Ct. 2749, 2795-96 (2006).

[102]Common art. 2 to GC I-IV, *supra* note 4.

[103]*Commentary to the Third Geneva Convention relative to the Treatment of Prisoners of War* 23 (ICRC, Jean Pictet ed., 1960).

[104]Tadic, Appeals Chamber Decision on the Defence Motion for Interlocutory Appeal on Jurisdiction, *supra* note 51, ¶ 70.

[105]Dinstein, *supra* note 62, at 11-13.

[106]Common art. 2(1) to GC I-IV, *supra* note 4.

[107]Pictet, *supra* note 103, at 23.

operation can amount to an "attack," as that term is used in IHL (e.g., the prohibition on "attacking" civilians and civilian objects).[108] The law defines attacks as "acts of violence,"[109] leading one school of thought to argue that only operations resulting in injury, death, damage or destruction are attacks to which the prohibitions apply.[110] Advocates would therefore likely accept the aforementioned limitation. A second school argues that the essence of such prohibitions is directing military operations against protected persons and places.[111] If this is so, then IHL would apply to certain non-destructive cyber operations against protected persons and objects, and, by extension, an international armed conflict would commence once a State or those under its control launched them.

The problem is that proponents of the second approach offer no criteria for distinguishing non-destructive "attacks" from non-destructive military operations that clearly do not qualify as attacks, such as lawful psychological operations. Presumably, consequence severity would be a key criterion, but how might that be determined (financial loss, disruption of essential State functions, etc.)? Indeterminacy may be acceptable in the context of identifying a use of force, for the issue there is merely whether a violation of law has occurred (and countermeasures cannot involve the use of force). By contrast, the consequences of finding an "armed conflict" are much more dramatic. Armed conflict renders violent actions by combatants lawful unless they breach a particular IHL norm, even when the initial resort to force by the belligerent State was unlawful. In other words, while IHL limits violence, it also legitimizes it. This interpretation is obviously problematic.

Non-International Armed Conflict

Determining when a non-international armed conflict exists is even more problematic. The relevant IHL is found primarily in customary international law, Common Article 3 to the Geneva Conventions and, for States party, Additional Protocol II (AP II). Although there is much controversy over the precise content of the customary law and the extent to which certain customary IHL norms apply in both international and non-international armed conflicts, it is undeniably a less detailed and less comprehensive body of law than that applicable in international armed conflict.

Common Article 3 to the Geneva Conventions defines non-international armed conflicts in the negative as those which are "not of an international character," a characterization reflective of customary international law.[112] There are two generally accepted criteria for such conflicts. First, Article 3 employs the phrase "each Party to the conflict." The term "Party" is commonly understood to refer to either States or to groups which have a certain degree of organization and command structure. Thus, cyber violence of any intensity engaged in by isolated individuals or by unorganized mobs, even if directed against the government, does not qualify. It would not amount to an armed conflict, and therefore would be governed by criminal law and human rights law, not IHL. The vast majority of the cyber operations conducted against Estonia would fall into this category.

The second criterion is intensity. It is generally agreed that a non-international armed conflict requires violence of a higher degree of intensity than international armed conflict. "Internal disturbances and tensions, such as riots, isolated and sporadic acts of violence and other acts of a similar nature"

---

[108]AP I, *supra* note 53, arts. 51 and 52.

[109]Ibid., art. 49.

[110]See, e.g., Michael N. Schmitt, "Warfare: Computer Network Attack and International Law," 84 (No. 846) *International Review of the Red Cross* 365 (June 2002).

[111]Knut Dörmann, Applicability of Additional Protocols to Computer Network Attack, Paper delivered at the International Expert Conference on Computer Network Attacks and the Applicability of International Humanitarian Law, Stockholm, November 17-19, 2004, http://www.icrc.org/web/eng/siteeng0.nsf/htmlall/68lg92?opendocument.

[112]Common art. 3 to GC I-IV, *supra* note 4 ("In the case of armed conflict not of an international character occurring in the territory of one of the High Contracting Parties, each Party to the conflict shall be bound to apply, as a minimum, the following provisions. . . .").

fall short of the threshold.[113] In non-normative terms, the criterion suggests that unrest which can be handled primarily by law enforcement entities, without resort to the armed forces, does not constitute non-international armed conflict even if carried out by armed groups. Along these lines, the ICTY has characterized non-international armed conflicts as involving "protracted armed violence between governmental authorities and organized armed groups or between such groups within a State,"[114] a formula adopted by the International Criminal Tribunal for Rwanda and in the Statute of the International Criminal Court.[115]

For parties to the instrument (the United States is not), AP II sets forth significant additional IHL norms. However, the threshold of applicability for this instrument is set at an even higher level than that of customary law and Common Article 3. In the case of AP II non-international armed conflicts, the non-State party to the conflict has to "exercise such control over a part of" a State's territory that it can "carry out sustained and concerted military operations."[116]

It would be exceptionally difficult for cyber operations standing alone to rise to the level of non-international armed conflict. First, operations launched by individuals and unorganized groups are not encompassed in the category, no matter how destructive. Second, the cyber operations would have to be protracted, that is, occur over a period of time. Sporadic attacks would not qualify, regardless of their destructiveness. Third, the requirement of intensity would augur against arguments that actions which are not destructive can sometimes meet the test, a weak argument even in the case of international armed conflict. Combined, the criteria mean that only significantly destructive attacks taking place over some period of time and conducted by a group that is well-organized initiate a non-international armed conflict.

Finally, as noted earlier, significant controversy surrounds the question of whether attacks by *transnational* non-State actors are international or non-international in character. The debate derives from the fact that non-international armed conflicts are typically seen as conflicts between a State and "rebels," in other words, civil wars. AP II seemingly makes this requirement explicit in its reference to conflicts taking place "in the territory of a State . . . between its armed forces and dissident armed forces or other organized armed groups."[117] Although Common Article 3 contains no such restriction, its reference to conflicts "occurring in the territory" of a Party to the 1949 Geneva Conventions has sometimes also been construed as excluding conflicts that transcend national borders. Thus, by one interpretation, such conflicts are international because they cross borders.[118] By an alternative interpretation, they are non-international because they do not involve States in opposition to each other, which has traditionally been the distinguisher for international armed conflict. Accordingly, they are conflicts which are "not of an international character."[119] It has also been argued that they are a new form of armed conflict to which only the general norms applicable to all armed conflicts, such as the principle of distinction, apply. This form of conflict has been labeled "transnational."[120] Finally, it might be argued that there is no armed conflict at all, but rather mere criminality. In fact, a strict reading of the law would suggest as much. However, this last approach begs the question of what law applies in the event of an armed attack (in the *ad bellum* context) to which a State responds forcefully, since absent an armed conflict, IHL is inapplicable. Whatever the correct characterization, it would apply equally to groups conducting cyber operations of the intensity required to constitute an armed conflict.

---

[113]AP II, *supra* note 99, art. 1.2, generally deemed to equally reflect the standard applicable to Common Article 3 and customary international law. See, e.g., Rome Statute, *supra* note 77, art. 8(2)(f).

[114]Tadic, Appeals Chamber Decision on the Defence Motion for Interlocutory Appeal on Jurisdiction, *supra* note 51, ¶ 70.

[115]Prosecutor v. Akeyesu, Case No. ICTR-96-4-T, Judgment, ¶ 619 (Sept. 2, 1998); Rome Statute, *supra* note 77, art. 8(2)(f).

[116]AP II, *supra* note 99, art. 1(1). It must also be able to implement the provisions of the Protocol.

[117]See text at fn 112.

[118]HCJ [High Court of Justice] 796/02, Public Committee against Torture in Israel et al. v. Government of Israel et al., ¶ 21(Dec. 13, 2006).

[119]Hamdan v. Rumsfeld, 126 S.Ct. 2749, 2795-96 (2006).

[120]See, e.g., Geoff Corn, "Hamdan, Lebanon, and the Regulation of Armed Conflict: The Need to Recognize a Hybrid Category of Armed Conflict," 40 *Vanderbilt Transnational Law Journal* 295 (2006).

FAULT LINES IN THE LAW

The legal analysis set forth above should strike most readers as unsatisfactory. Clear fault lines in the law governing the use of force have appeared because it is a body of law that predates the advent of cyber operations. The normative scheme made sense when close congruity existed between the coercive instruments of international relations, particularly military force, and their effects. To the extent one State disrupted order in the international community, it usually did so by using force to harm objects and persons. Resultantly, instrument-based normative shorthand (use of *force, armed* attack, and *armed* conflict) was employed as a means of precluding those effects (death, injury, destruction and damage) which were perceived as most disruptive of community stability, and as most threatening to State security. Debates such as whether actions short of military operations are uses of force or whether minor border incursions qualify as armed attacks demonstrate that the foundational concerns were actually consequence-based, for both reflect recognition that the instrument-based approach is not perfectly calibrated.

The advent of cyber operations threw the instrument-based approach into disarray by creating the possibility of dramatically destabilizing effects caused by other than kinetic actions. They weakened the natural congruency between the normative shorthand employed in the law governing resort to force and those consequences which the law sought to avoid as disruptive. Conceptually, the "qualitative" scheme, by which prohibitions were expressed in terms of types of activities (use of the military and other destructive instruments as distinguished from non-destructive ones) no longer sufficed to preclude those effects about which States had become most concerned. A non-kinetic, non-destructive means of generating effects which States cannot possibly countenance now existed; the qualitative shorthand no longer tracked the quantitative concerns of States.

The prohibition on the use of force has proven somewhat adaptable to this new reality because it has long been understood to extend beyond the application of kinetic force. Thus, it is reasonable to employ the criteria suggested in this article to identify situations in which non-kinetic actions will result in quantitatively unacceptable, and therefore prohibited, consequences. The UN Charter mechanism for Security Council-based responses to threats to the peace, breaches of the peace and acts of aggression is likewise adaptable because by it threats to the peace include, simply put, whatever the Council wishes.

However, the textual precision of the "armed attack" component of the individual and collective self-defense norm leaves little room for interpretive reshaping. By its own terms, "armed attack" does not reach many cyber-generated consequences to which States will wish to respond in self-defense. To a lesser extent, the same is true with regard to the notion of "armed conflict." It seems incongruent that a minor firefight would initiate an armed conflict, but a major non-physically destructive cyber attack against the cyber infrastructure of a State would not.

Evidence of disquiet abounds. In a recent report by the National Research Council, examples of armed attack included "cyberattacks on the controlling information technology for a nation's infrastructure (whether or not it caused immediate large-scale death or destruction of property)" and "a cyberattack against the stock exchanges that occurs repeatedly and continuously, so that trading is disrupted for an extended period of time (e.g., days or weeks)."[121] As a matter of law, they would likely qualify as uses of force, but not, by a strict interpretation of the self-defense norm, as armed attacks (or as initiating an armed conflict). The problem is that most States would surely treat them as such. In other words, the National Research Council report has misconstrued the law, but accurately identified probable State behavior.

When State expectations as to the "rules of the game" deviate from those that actually govern their actions, new norms can emerge. One method by which this can occur is through new treaty law. However, it is highly unlikely that any meaningful treaty will be negotiated to govern cyber operations in the foreseeable future. The greatest obstacle is that those States which are most vulnerable to cyber operations tend to be those which are also most capable of conducting them. Such tension will cause

---

[121]Technology, Policy, Law, and Ethics, *supra* note 63, at 254-55.

such States to hesitate before agreeing to prohibitions designed to protect them which may also definitively limit their freedom of action. This is especially so in light of the nascent nature of cyber warfare and the lack of experience of most States in these operations. In international relations, States are often comfortable with a degree of vagueness.

Much more likely is the emergence of new understandings of the existing treaty law which are responsive to the realities of cyber operations. While only subsequent treaty action can technically alter a treaty's terms, State practice can inform their interpretation over time. A well-known example involves veto action by Permanent Members of the Security Council. The UN Charter provides that a binding resolution of the Council requires the affirmative vote of all five Permanent Members.[122] However, State practice has been to treat the provision as blocking action only when a member of the "P5" vetoes a proposed resolution. This counter-textual interpretation is now accepted as the law.[123] The recent extension of the notion of armed attack to actions by non-State actors similarly illustrates normative evolution prompted by shifting State expectations.

In due course, similar evolution in the how the concept of armed attack is understood should be anticipated, as States increasingly accept the proposition that armed attacks must be judged qualitatively *and* quantitatively. Consequences will remain the focus of concern, but they will be assessed both in terms of nature and as to their impact on affected States. In this regard, the seven criteria proffered above in the use of force context can serve as useful indicators of whether States are likely to characterize particular cyber operations as armed attacks (or as initiating an armed conflict), and thus suggest the probable vector of the law. However, for the moment the existing law remains intact; it will be left to States to articulate the expectations and engage in practices that can serve to fuel the normative process necessary to transform *lex ferenda* into *lex lata*.[124]

---

[122]U.N. Charter, art. 27.3.

[123]See discussion in Bruno Simma, Stefan Brunner & Hans-Peter Kaul, *Article 27, in* I *The Charter of the United Nations: A Commentary* 476, 493-98 (Bruno Simma ed., 2d ed. 2002). The veto principle does not apply to votes on procedural matters.

[124]The law as it should be and the law that is, respectively.

Cyber Security and International Agreements

Abraham D. Sofaer

Hoover Institution

David Clark

Massachusetts Institute of Technology

Whitfield Diffie

Internet Corporation for Assigned Names and Numbers

Society has become dependent on cyber systems across the full range of human activities, including commerce, finance, health care, energy, entertainment, communications, and national defense. "The globally-interconnected digital information and communications infrastructure known as 'cyberspace' underpins almost every facet of modern society and provides critical support for the U.S. economy, civil infrastructure, public safety, and national security."[1] The U.S. is especially vulnerable to cyber insecurity because it depends on cyber systems more heavily than most other states. But cyber insecurity is a worldwide problem, potentially affecting all cyber systems and their dependent infrastructure.

Cyber insecurity can result from the vulnerabilities of cyber systems, including flaws or weaknesses in both hardware and software, and from the conduct of states, groups, and individuals with access to them. It takes the forms of cyber warfare, espionage, crime, attacks on cyber infrastructure, and exploitation of cyber systems.

Virtually all aspects of cyber insecurity have a transnational component, affecting users of cyber systems throughout the world. Nonetheless, current U.S. efforts to deter cyberattacks and exploitation—though formally advocating international cooperation—are based almost exclusively on unilateral measures.[2] Whether cyberdeterrence through these methods can provide an adequate level of cyber security for U.S. users is, in the view of the NRC Committee on Deterring Cyberattacks (hereinafter "Committee"), an open question. Proposals for the U.S. to consider additional, unilateral measures to deter cyberattacks through prevention and retaliation have been presented to the NRC Committee for

---

NOTE: This paper has benefited from valuable comments made by members of the NRC Committee on Deterring Cyberattacks, for which the authors are grateful. We also thank Seymour Goodman for his support, as well as Leisel Bogan, Courtney Matteson and Thomas Church for their invaluable research assistance.

[1] The White House, "Cyberspace Policy Review: Assuring a Trusted and Resilient Information and Communications Infrastructure," May 2009, p. iii.

[2] A recent example is the comprehensive and influential "Securing Cyberspace for the 44th Presidency," A Report of the CSIS Commission on Cybersecurity for the 44th Presidency (Washington, D.C. 2008), which contains numerous, sweeping recommendations to restructure government agencies and adopt national programs to secure various aspects of the U.S. cyber infrastructure, while proposing virtually no program of international engagement. This follows from the Report's premise that the activities of foreign states are the source of cyber insecurity in the U.S. (p. 11): "Foreign opponents, through a combination of skill, luck, and perseverance, have been able to penetrate poorly protected U.S. computer networks and collect immense quantities of valuable information."

its consideration. But, as the Committee has noted, measures associated with classical deterrence are difficult to employ against cyberattacks and exploitation.[3] States, groups, and even individuals can easily launch attacks upon or attempt to exploit cyber systems. The sources of attacks and exploitations are difficult to determine within time frames that enable victims to avoid damage, and any defensive measure is likely eventually to fail given the vulnerabilities of most cyber systems and the incapacities of users.

These considerations led the NRC Committee to conclude that, "whatever the useful scope for deterrence, there may also be a complementary and helpful role for international legal regimes and codes of behavior designed to reduce the likelihood of highly destructive cyberattacks and to minimize the realized consequences if cyberattacks do occur. That is, participation in international agreements may be an important aspect of U.S. policy."[4] Various forms of international cooperation do currently exist, and international agencies and private entities play or are attempting to secure significant roles in cyber security. For over a decade, however, the U.S. government—while complaining about cyberattacks, espionage, and exploitation by other states and non-state actors—has avoided international arrangements that go significantly beyond obligating a group of predominantly European states to criminalize and cooperate in prosecuting specified forms of conduct. This policy is, appropriately, changing. Both the Executive branch and Congress are now considering ways in which international cooperation and agreements could enhance cyber security.

The potential utility of international cybersecurity agreements deserves to be carefully examined. International agreements covering other transnational activities, including armed conflict, communications, air and sea transportation, health, agriculture, and commerce, among other areas, have been widely adopted by states to enhance safety and efficiency through processes that could well be useful in regulating cyber activities.

Transnational agreements that contribute to cybersecurity will only be possible, however, if they take into account the substantial differences that exist between activities regulated by established international regimes and cyber systems. Many states will be unprepared at this time to agree to limit their control of cyber activities they regard as essential to their national security interests. International agreements will also be impossible where irreconcilable differences in policies exist among states, particularly regarding political uses of the Internet, privacy, and human rights. But, while these factors limit the potential scope and utility of international cyber-security agreements, they do allow for international cooperation on many issues that could prove beneficial.

The potential for improving cyber security through international agreements can best be realized through a program that identifies: the activities likely to be subjects of such agreements and those that are not; the measures likely to be used by parties to improve cyber security in each area of activity appropriate for international cooperation; and the form which any international body that may be utilized or established for this purpose should assume, the authority such a body would be assigned, and the basis upon which its activities would be governed. International agreements negotiated on the basis of these practical premises could help to create a more secure cyber environment through measures that go beyond conventional forms of deterrence.

I. THREATS TO CYBER SECURITY

Retired Admiral Dennis Blair, former U.S. Director of National Intelligence, testified in early 2010 that increasingly sophisticated enemies "severely" threaten some U.S. information systems: "Sensitive

---

[3]See Chapter 9, National Research Council (NRC), *Technology, Policy, Law, and Ethics Regarding U.S. Acquisition and Use of Cyberattack Capabilities*, ed. William Owens, Kenneth Dam, and Herbert Lin (Washington D.C.: The National Academies Press, Washington, D.C., 2009). See also Section 2.2, (NRC) "Letter Report from the Committee on Deterring Cyberattacks: Informing Strategies and Developing Options for U.S. Policy" March 25, 2010, p. 6.

[4]Letter Report from the Committee on Deterring Cyberattacks: Informing Strategies and Developing Options for U.S. Policy, National Research Council, March 25, 2010, p. 19.

information is stolen daily from both government and private sector networks, undermining confidence in our information systems, and in the very information these systems were intended to convey. . . . Malicious cyber activity is occurring on an unprecedented scale with extraordinary sophistication."[5] Former Vice-Admiral Mike McConnell, Blair's predecessor and head of the National Security Agency ("NSA") from 1992 to 1996, wrote recently: "The United States is fighting a cyber-war today, and we are losing. It's that simple. As the most wired nation on Earth, we offer the most targets of significance, yet our cyber-defenses are woefully lacking."[6] Howard Schmidt, White House Cyber Security advisor, agrees that cyber threats exist, but denies we are in a "war"; others similarly criticize such statements as exaggeration.[7] It is widely agreed, however, that various vulnerabilities and forms of hostility have exposed cyber systems, including the Internet, to attack and infiltration, inflicting substantial costs in the form of financial losses and defensive measures and creating even more substantial, future dangers to the nation's critical infrastructures.[8] President Obama's 2009 Cyberspace Policy Review concludes: "a growing array of state and non-state actors such as terrorists and international criminal groups are targeting U.S. citizens, commerce, critical infrastructure, and government. These actors have the ability to compromise, steal, change, or completely destroy information."[9]

Cyber insecurity stems from the fact that cyber systems have been designed to facilitate access and utilization, rather than security. "The architecture of the nation's digital infrastructure, based largely upon the Internet, is not secure or resilient. Without major advances in the security of these systems to make them sufficiently secure or resilient, it is doubtful that the United States can protect itself from the growing threat of cybercrime and state-sponsored intrusions and operations."[10]

Threats to cyber security can be roughly divided into two general categories: actions aimed at and intended to damage or destroy cyber systems ("cyberattacks"), and actions that seek to exploit the cyber infrastructure for unlawful or harmful purposes without damaging or compromising that infrastructure ("cyber exploitation").[11] Cyberattacks may target government or private assets. They include efforts by states and non-state actors to damage and degrade computer software, hardware, and other aspects of computer operations, as well as to compromise cyber systems by infiltrating them without proper authority to obtain information or to control them in a variety of ways.[12] While some intrusions may not result in an immediate impact on the operation of a cyber system, as for example when a "Trojan Horse" infiltrates and establishes itself in a computer, such intrusions are considered cyberattacks when they can thereafter permit actions that destroy or degrade the computer's capacities.

---

[5]Admiral Dennis C. Blair, House Permanent Select Committee on Intelligence, *Annual Threat Assessment*, 111th Congress, 1st sess., 2009.

[6]Mike McConnell, "Mike McConnell on How to Win the Cyber-war We're Losing," *The Washington Post*, February 28, 2010, http://www.washingtonpost.com/wp-dyn/content/article/2010/02/25/AR2010022502493_pf.html (accessed on July 19 2010).

[7]See, for example, Evgeny Morozov, a Fellow at Georgetown University and a contributing editor to Foreign Policy, "Battling the Cyber Warmongers," Wall St. J., May 8-9, 2010, p. W3, col. 1, where he condemns "cyber-jingoism from former and current national security officials," including Richard Clarke and Mike McConnell, both of whom he notes are associated with security firms that have obtained or are seeking lucrative contracts with U.S. agencies and private firms. He refers to statements by Howard Schmidt that the notion of a "cyberwar" is "a terrible metaphor" and a "terrible concept." He acknowledges serious vulnerabilities but argues they stem largely from the incompetence of website managers and in any event do not require or justify the costly and privacy-restricting solutions being advanced by what he regards as alarmists.

[8]See generally the CSIS Commission Report on Cybersecurity, supra note 2; Richard Clarke and Robert K. Knave, *Cyber War: The Next Threat to National Security And What To Do About It* (New York: Harper Collins, 2010), 43-44.

[9]2009 Cyberspace Policy Review, 1. The Review quotes with approval the conclusion of the CSIS Commission Report, p. 11, that: "America's failure to protect cyberspace is one of the most urgent national security problems facing the new administration."

[10]2009 Cyberspace Policy Review, i.

[11]"Cyberattack refers to deliberate actions to alter, disrupt, deceive, degrade, or destroy computer systems or networks or the information and/or programs resident in or transiting these systems or networks." National Research Council, "Cyberattack Capabilities", National Academy Press, Washington, D.C., 2009, p. 1.

[12]Id., 360-67. A listing of the sources of threats is compiled in the very useful GAO Report, "Cyberspace: United States Faces Challenges in Addressing Global Cybersecurity and Governance," U.S. Government Accountability Office, Washington, D.C., 2010, p.4 (hereinafter "GAO July 2010 Report"): Bot-network operators; criminal groups; hackers; insiders; nations; phishers; spammers; spyware/malware authors; and terrorists. The Report also lists the "Types of Cyber Exploits" (p. 5).

Many forms of cyberattack have been identified, and new forms are continuously being devised. Among the cyberattacks of greatest concern are those conducted or supported by states and aimed at damaging or controlling cyber systems on which critical infrastructure depend, including power grids, air traffic control, and financial systems.[13] Many state and non-state actors seeking to attack or exploit U.S. cyber systems mask their identities by initiating their efforts from foreign countries, or by routing them through foreign computers and servers. Frequently, transnational attacks (some serious) are attributed to "patriotic" hackers, encouraged or tolerated by their governments.

Efforts to exploit cyber systems for the purpose of committing conventional crimes, or for other purposes regarded by states as harmful, are also common, and have caused significant losses and other costs. Cyber exploitation includes using the Internet and other cyber systems to commit fraud, to steal, to recruit and train terrorists, to violate copyright and other rules limiting distribution of information, to convey controversial messages (including political and "hate" speech), and to sell child pornography or other banned materials. Cyber systems contain vast amounts of data which criminals have been able to seize and utilize, such as Social Security numbers; and they enable criminals efficiently to approach millions of potential victims in attempted frauds and other schemes.

II. CURRENT CYBER-SECURITY MEASURES

The Internet currently is secured primarily through private regulatory activity, defensive strategies and products, national laws and enforcement, and some limited forms of international cooperation and regulation.

1. Private Measures

Non-governmental entities play major roles in the cyber security arena. Technical standards for the Internet (including current and next-generation versions of the Internet Protocol) are developed and proposed by the privately controlled Internet Engineering Task Force ("IETF"); the Web Consortium, housed at the Massachusetts Institute of Technology, defines technical standards for the Web. While the IETF was originally composed entirely of U.S. members, funded by and working for the U.S. government, it is today staffed entirely by volunteers, including network operators, academics, employees of private companies and government representatives. It establishes standards on a consensus basis. Membership and operations have become increasingly international, reflecting the growing interest of scholars, businesses, and governments throughout the world in the standard setting process.

Other privately controlled entities that play significant operational roles on aspects of cyber security include the major telecommunications carriers, Internet Service Providers ("ISPs"), and many other organizations, including:

- The Forum of Incident Response and Security Teams ("FIRST"), which attempts to coordinate the activities of both government and private Computer Emergency Response Teams ("CERTs") and is also working on cyber security standards;

---

[13]While state-sponsored attacks are often difficult to detect, for more than a decade states have used cyber warfare in retaliation to physical warfare or acts of aggression. In 1999, after a NATO jet bombed the Chinese Embassy in Belgrade, the Chinese Red Hacker Alliance launched a cyber assault on U.S. government websites. See Erbscholoe, Michael. Trojans, Worms and Spyware (NY: Butterworth-Heineman, 2005), 175. During the Second Chechen War, both sides engaged in cyber warfare with the Russian Federal Security Service responsible for knocking out key Chechen websites while Russian Troops engaged Chechen terrorists holding Russian civilians hostage. See Simons, Greg. Mass Media and Modern Warfare: Reporting on the Russian War on Terrorism (UK: Ashgate Publishing, 2010). During the Russia-Georgia war of 2008, the coinciding cyber assault was state-sponsored on both sides. There are suspicions that Iran and North Korea frequently promote state-sponsored cyberattacks though definitive evidence is often lacking. See Carr, Jeffrey and Shepherd, Lewis. Inside Cyber Warfare: Mapping the Cyber Underworld (Cambridge: O'Reilly Inc, 2009), 37. The GAO July 2010 Report (p.6) describes recent cyberattacks that illustrate potentially "debilitating impact on national security, " including a denial of service attack on Estonia (2007), an attack on DOD and other government computer networks (2008), attacks on California companies (2010), and attacks on Indian government computers (2009).

- The Institute of Electrical and Electronics Engineers ("IEEE"), which develops technical standards through its Standards Association and in conjunction with the U.S. National Institute of Standards and Technology ("NIST");
- The Internet Corporation for Assigned Names and Numbers ("ICANN"), which operates pursuant to a contract with the U.S. Department of Commerce (September 2009) transferring to ICAAN the technical management of the Domain Name System.[14]
- The International Electrotechnical Commission ("IEC") and the International Organization for Standardization ("ISO"), which together as non-governmental organizations, through their Joint Technical Committee, have developed information security standards for all types of organizations including one that addresses the development of information security management systems and the security controls that protect information assets (ISO/IEC 27001:2005);
- The European Telecommunications Standards Institute ("ETSI"), which is a non-profit, private entity with over 700 members from some 62 countries that produces through member-controlled committees globally applicable standards for Information Communications Technologies ("ICTs"), including for example the mobile Internet standards developed by its Third Generation Partnership Project ("3GPP");
- The Organization for the Advancement of Structured Information Standards ("OASIS"), another international, non-profit consortium that drives the development of e-business and web services standards through some 70 technical committees, and which did much of the work pursuant to UN request that led ultimately to an important, widely implemented standard, ISO 15000.

The standards promulgated by these bodies attempt to enhance security.[15] The standards are voluntary, however, in that the IETF and other, private standard-setting entities have no mechanism to mandate their use.

Protection from cyberattack and exploitation is primarily provided by private companies and individuals through passive, defensive measures: good software and equipment design, speedy and effective responses to weaknesses when identified, and the creation of various types of walls around systems or groups of users, including government agencies and public functions. ISPs and others responsible for infrastructure security invest in sound operational practices, redundant facilities, and other defensive measures that protect against most known forms of attack, but serious vulnerabilities exist (due among other things to inadequate maintenance and the failure of users to download patches), and new forms of attack are always being developed. Experts widely assume that attacks will be successful, and some believe that states, and perhaps other potential attackers, could, if they chose, inflict major damage on cyber systems and their dependent infrastructure.[16]

Security measures must be cost effective to get accepted. While the IETF has, for example, published standards that would, if adopted, increase the security of the Domain Name System ("DNS"), operators of the ".com domain" failed for a considerable period to turn on these protocols, claiming their implementation would double the infrastructure needed to handle the resulting increased message size.[17]

---

[14]ICANN is nominally a private, U.S., not-for-profit corporation, but is widely seen as U.S. controlled. It performs the functions of the Internet Assigned Names Authority, through which it establishes standards for the use and protection of names used in cyber communications. While it has some enforcement powers, it has thus far limited its exercise of powers to determining which entities are entitled to use which names, and has no useful authority to defend cyber systems from attack by individuals or groups prepared to disregard its rulings.

[15]We describe below specific examples of security-related IETF standards, such as secure BGP, IPSec, DNSSEC, RPKI, and encryption. More generally, all proposed IETF standards must include a security analysis as part of their specification.

[16]Clarke and Knave, 92. The authors anticipate that "logic bombs"—software that erases all programming, effectively negating further use of a device—will be used in attacks and may already be in place.

[17]DNS security flaws were identified in the early 1990s. Efforts to include security mechanisms led to the design of Domain Name System Security Extensions ("DNSSEC"), initially laid out in RFC 2535, an IETF paper. Despite being available for many years, DNSSEC is not more widely used because of backward compatibility issues, implementation costs, and perceived complexity of switching protocols. DNSSEC specifications (laid out in RFC 2535) have since been updated to make implementation more practical; See RFC 4033, 4034, and 4035 for updated DNSSEC-*bis* specifications.

Negligence by users also leads to costly breakdowns in defense. Victims, especially companies whose businesses depend on secure cyber activities, frequently fail to report flaws and successful attacks in order to avoid damaging their reputations. This in turn results in slower responses to attacks and greater damage. Inadequate sharing of information is a serious impediment to effective defense.

2. National Measures

Many national governments have adopted laws aimed at punishing and thereby deterring specific forms of cyberattacks or exploitation. The U.S., for example, has adopted laws making criminal various forms of conduct, including improper intrusion into and deliberate damage of computer systems.[18] These laws have little or no effect, however, on individuals, groups, or governments over whom the U.S. lacks or is unable to secure regulatory or criminal jurisdiction.

US national security experts almost exclusively emphasize the need for national measures for enhancing cyber security. They recommend national laws to protect the sharing of information about threats and attacks; methods for government bodies, such as the NSA, to cooperate with private entities in evaluating the source and nature of cyberattacks; and more effective defenses and responses to cyberattacks and exploitation developed through government-sponsored research and coordination pursuant to cyber security plans. Efforts of this sort are underway, and the U.S. government is examining what strategic defenses can be developed and utilized to protect critical infrastructure that depend upon vulnerable cyber systems.[19]

The GAO's July 2010 report details the specific roles being played by many U.S. agencies in efforts to enhance "global cybersecurity," but ultimately concludes that these efforts are not part of a coherent strategy likely to advance U.S. interests. It considers the National Security Council ("NSC") the "principal forum" for all national security matters requiring presidential involvement, and notes (p. 18) that the NSC's Information and Communications Infrastructure Policy Committee ("ICI-IPC"), created in March 2009, approved a subcommittee on "international cyberspace policy efforts (the International sub-IPC) composed of officials from the Departments of Commerce, Defense, Homeland Security, Justice, State, and Treasury, the Office of the U.S. Trade Representative, and the Federal Communications Commission. It describes the many functions performed by each of these agencies, including their participation in standard setting discussions, and in the work of international agencies such as the ITU and its study groups. (For each of the agencies the GAO provides a list of "efforts" in the form of tables to its report.) Many of the functions listed involve defensive preparations or investigation and prosecution for cyberattacks and exploitation. U.S. agencies engage in discussions in many international groups. But these activities have little significance, the GAO concludes, as they are not coordinated aspects of a plan but rather ad hoc "engagement" with other countries and groups. The GAO concludes (p. 32) that, as of the time its study was conducted, the U.S. lacks top-level leadership (the International sub-IPC does nothing more than ensure that all agencies are aware of each others' international activities), and that while multiple agencies are involved "in a variety of international efforts that impact cyberspace governance and security, the U.S. government has not documented a clear vision of how these efforts, taken together, support overarching national goals." It notes that officials from the Departments of State and Defense told the GAO that "an effort is currently under way to develop an international strategy for cyberspace," but concludes: "we have not seen any evidence of such activities . . . ." It also found that, even with regard "to information-sharing or incident response agreements with other countries, the federal government lacks a coherent approach toward participating in a broader international framework . . . ." This is due in part to national security concerns, and the Report notes (pp. 35-36) a comment by

---

[18]E.g., *Fraud and Related Activity in Connection with Computers*, U.S. Code 18, § 1030.

[19]The Wall Street Journal reported on an NSA program, through Raytheon, Corp., called "Perfect Citizen," to provide a "cyber shield" for critical infrastructure such as the electricity grid and nuclear power companies, that currently depend on insecure computer networks. The program is voluntary and part of the Comprehensive National Cyber-security Initiative, which is itself classified. July 8, 2010, p. A3.

a DOD official "that there is disagreement, particularly within the U.S. intelligence community, as to whether the benefits of showing cyber-threat information outweigh the risk of harm to U.S. security interests should sensitive data be leaked to an adversary of the United States."

3. International Measures

National governments often cooperate with each other informally by exchanging information, investigating attacks or crimes, preventing or stopping harmful conduct, providing evidence, and even arranging for the rendition of individuals to a requesting state. States have also made formal, international agreements that bear directly or indirectly on cyber security. Extradition treaties generally apply to a list of activities that constitute crimes in the states that agree to arrest and/or extradite individuals to each other. Mutual Legal Assistance Treaties ("MLATs") also generally apply to a list of agreed crimes; they require state parties to assist one another by providing information, evidence, and other forms of cooperation when requested to do so in such situations. These international agreements apply to the criminal activities specified, including situations in which the alleged criminals have used cyber systems in those activities.

International agreements that potentially bear upon cyber-security activities also include treaties (the UN Charter and Geneva Conventions) and universally accepted rules of conduct (customary law). Cyberattacks that have kinetic effects equivalent to a physical use of force, for example, are likely to be considered "armed attacks" under the UN Charter to the same extent as physical uses of force. The U.S. is reported to have proposed this concept as a governing principle in discussions with Russia and other states.[20] In addition, the right of states to exercise self-defense or to take countermeasures in response to such attacks would depend on their potential consequences. International law also provides rules related to the use of force during armed conflict that presumably apply to cyberattacks, including for example requirements that noncombatants and civilian institutions such as hospitals not be deliberately attacked, and that uses of force be restricted to measures that are necessary and proportionate. Considerable uncertainty exists, however, as to the application of rules written to regulate physical force to uses of cyberforce, and the issues are further complicated by the fact that the scope of use-of-force rules is far from universally agreed.

The most significant, multilateral arrangement that specifically addresses aspects of cyberattacks and exploitation is the Council of Europe Convention on Cybercrime ("CEC"). The CEC is a law-enforcement treaty designed to develop a common criminal-law policy aimed at defining, punishing, and thereby deterring cyber-related crimes. It requires all Member States (46 had signed and 30 had ratified as of June, 8th, 2010)[21] to adopt laws making criminal the following five types of actions against the integrity of cyber systems: illegal access; illegal interception; data interference; system interference; and misuse of devices. It also identifies types of conduct involving exploitation of cyber systems that Member States agree to make criminal, including fraud, forgery, child pornography, and violations of copyright laws. States are allowed to exempt from prosecution for some of these activities individuals who act without intent to harm. Member States are required to provide their domestic law enforcement agencies with the authority to investigate the covered conduct, and to cooperate with other Member States in their enforcement through extradition treaties and MLATs. States are entitled to make reservations that exempt themselves from prosecuting particular crimes, and to withhold cooperation in cases deemed inconsistent with their public policies or security.

The CEC's potential in providing cyber security is limited by the fact that its "law enforcement framework operates in many cases on a time scale that is too long to protect victims of cyberattack from

---

[20]John Markoff, "Step Taken to End Impasse Over Cybersecurity Talks," New York Times, July 17, 2010, A7, col. 1: "'The U.S. put forward a simple notion that we hadn't said before,' the diplomat said. 'The same laws that apply to the use of kinetic weapons should apply to state behavior in cyberspace.'"

[21]See Convention on Cybercrime CETS No. 185 at http://conventions.coe.int/Treaty/Commun/ChercheSig.asp?NT=185&CM=1&DF=&CL=ENG.

harm."[22] The CEC is no more effective in preventing cyberattacks than criminal law enforcement is in preventing conventional attacks. The treaty has no mechanism, moreover, for establishing or revising cyber-system practices or standards that could generally improve security. Furthermore, the CEC's potential in securing universal adherence is diluted by its inclusion of efforts to punish conduct based on content restrictions (such as fraud and child pornography) rather than focusing on efforts to punish cyberattacks that potentially damage the cyber infrastructure itself. Its limitations on "hate" speech seek to regulate an area in which states have strong differences, ranging from policies prohibiting all political speech to prohibiting only speech amounting to illegal conduct.

Another international agreement of significance is the Shanghai Cooperation Organization's ("SOC") set of principles or "action plan" related to Information Security adopted at the SOC's Seventh Council Meeting of Heads of State (China, Russia, Kazakhstan, the Kyrgyz Republic, Tajikistan and Uzbekistan) held on August 16, 2007 in Kyrgyz. The SOC principles are consistent with the law-enforcement approach of the CEC insofar as they relate to securing cyber systems from attack, but they differ markedly from the CEC by stressing the Members' intent to ensure national control over cyber systems and content. The agreement is signed by its six Member States, and like the CEC is open to approval by other states. The SOC principles confirm Member State control over the content of cyber communications, including any speech considered politically destabilizing.[23]

Many established international regimes have addressed or are considering cyber security issues. The CSIS Commission on Cybersecurity for the 44th Presidency noted the need to deal proactively with these efforts. The 2009 Cyberspace Policy Review notes that some of these efforts could result in regulations that overlap or conflict with each other, citing as an example the simultaneous development of forensics standards by both the International Telecommunications Union ("ITU") and the International Standards Organization ("ISO").[24] The GAO's July 2010 report strongly supports these conclusions, stating (pp. 36-37): "the sheer number of international entities engage in incident response can also impede international coordination." It provides several examples of the difficulties of working with states (even in Europe) and with CERTs, and concludes that coordinating bodies such as FIRST and the UN-created Global Response Center lack the demonstrated capacity "to provide a legitimate global information security service to benefit all participants . . . ."

These conclusions seem correct and significant, but they appear to understate the scope and intensity of current international activities that are taking place regardless of U.S. involvement, including in particular the ITU's plans.[25] Acting pursuant to annual calls by the UN General Assembly for greater international cooperation in dealing with cyber threats, and after numerous conferences and studies by a variety of private, national, regional and international groups, the ITU convened a World Summit on the Information Society ("WSIS") at which governments and world leaders called on the ITU to become the sole "Facilitator of Action" in what was designated Action Line 5: "Building confidence and security in the use of ICTs [Information and Communications Technologies]." After a series of meetings, declarations, programs, and considerable effort by experts and supporting governments, the ICT launched on May 17, 2007 and announced in 2008 its Global Cybersecurity Agenda ("GCA") "to provide a framework within which an international response to the growing challenges to cybersecurity can be coordinated and addressed." The GCA stresses the desirability of a concerted effort by all stakeholders "to build con-

[22]National Research Council, "Cyberattack Capabilities," 62.
[23]See ITU GCA, Global Strategic Report, 21.
[24]2009 Cyberspace Policy Review, 20-21.
[25]The ITU's Global Strategic Security Report (last update June 2008) summarizes the activities and "legislative" measures of regional organizations, including in addition to the CEC actions and declarations by the G8, the European Union, the Asian Pacific Economic Cooperation (which has an active Telecommunications and Information Working Group), the Organization of American States, the Commonwealth, the Association of South East Asian Nations, the Arab League, the African Union, and the Organization for Economic Cooperation and Development. See ITU Global Cybersecurity Agenda, "Global Strategic Report" (2009): 16-21. The Global Strategic Report is available at http://www.itu.int/osg/csd/cybersecurity/gca/global_strategic_report/index.html (accessed July 23, 2010).

fidence and security in the information society," but it sees the ITU as "uniquely placed" to be the lead agent in this effort. The ITU has 191 Member States and more than 700 Sector Members, and its sectors of operations (Radiocommunication, Standardization, and Telecommunication Development) are being rapidly expanded to include cyber-related issues. It is pursuing its perceived role through a broad range of activities in cyber security education and in the development and promulgation of a comprehensive array of plans and protocols intended to create a secure cyber infrastructure by dealing with cyber crime, technical standards, security requirements, capacity building, and even the promotion of child on-line safety.[26] The GCA calls for continued involvement of all existing stakeholders in the cybersecurity effort. At the same time, however, it clearly signals its determination to seek the implementation of standards issued by its own standards development body (ITU-D) and by the ISO, as well as its intention to play the leading if not the sole coordinating role in all aspects of cybersecurity.

Numerous other governmental entities play, or purport to play, significant roles on international cyber security issues. Various regional bodies have cybersecurity working groups, including the Asia-Pacific Economic Cooperation (APEC), the Association of Southeast Asian Nations (ASEAN), the European Union (EU), the Group of Eight (G8), the Organization of American States (OAS), and the Organization for Economic Cooperation (OECD). The North Atlantic Treaty Organization (NATO) has several defense-related cyber operations. INTERPOL, with 188 members, focuses on cyber crime and assists in investigations. Some of these entities go beyond merely discussing problems and seek to develop policies and standards to enhance security. The Meridian Conference and Process, founded in 2005, hosts government discussions regarding critical infrastructure protections. Any international negotiation will have to take into account the work of these and other governmental (and non-governmental) organizations that have become active in cyber-security issues, especially the claims and activities of such entities as the ISO and ITU.

III. POTENTIAL FOR INCREASED INTERNATIONAL COOPERATION AND REGULATION

The current, largely unilateral and defensive measures relied upon to provide cyber security in the U.S. (and elsewhere) are widely viewed as insufficient to ensure an adequate level of safety.[27] It may be possible, as CSIS and others have recommended, to provide adequate protection for certain, critical national security activities by isolating them from the Internet and other outside interventions. For most, current functions, however, some aspects of the principal security deficiencies identified can only be remedied or reduced through increased and more effective international cooperation.

The first recommendation for a multilateral treaty to deal with cybersecurity was published by Stanford University's Center for International Security and Cooperation in 2000. That draft proposed creating an international agency with regulatory authority similar to that of established specialized

---

[26]The measures listed in ITU reports include assistance to states in developing national cybersecurity strategies; the "ITU Toolkit for Cybercrime Legislation" and its study "Understanding Cybercrime"; several technology and security standards issued by ITU Study Group 17, which it calls "the lead study group on telecommunications security and identity management," a status the ITU notes was "confirmed by the ITU-T World Telecommunication Standardization Assemblies (WTSA) in 2000, 2004 and 2008, in close collaboration with ISO/IEC, as a tripartite joint action." In addition to numerous specific cyber-related standards that the ITU-T has issued (including for example its H.235.x series of recommendations for security infrastructure and service including authentication and privacy) is what it calls its ICT Security Standards Roadmap, which it states "promotes the development of security standards by highlighting existing standards, current work and future standards among key standards development organizations." See generally the ITU's GCA brochure and extensive materials available at http://www.itu.int/osg/csd/cyber security/gca/ (accessed July 23, 2010).

[27]The NRC "Cyberattack" report (39-40) notes that cyberattack capabilities are relatively inexpensive and increasingly available to both governments and non-state actors, and notes the inherent weaknesses of passive cyberdefense, "exploitable vulnerabilities will continue to be present in both civilian and military computer systems and networks of the United States. Thus, the U.S. information infrastructure is likely to remain vulnerable to cyberattack for the foreseeable future, . . . [C]yberconflict is quite unlike the land, air, and maritime domains in which U.S. armed forces operate, and enduring unilateral dominance with respect to cyberconflict is not realistically achievable by the United States."

agencies in other areas of transnational activity, but with heavy reliance on private expertise. It expressly excluded state action from its scope.[28] The U.S. has opposed such an approach, but support for multi-lateral understandings and activities has increased.[29]

General Assembly ("GA") resolutions commencing in 1998 (GA Res. 53/70) have been adopted annually, noting various aspects of the cyber security problem including crime, terrorism, critical infrastructure protection, spam, attacks on cyber infrastructure, and the need for capacity building.[30] In addition, conferences supported by the UN, individual governments, regional organizations, and others have been held on several occasions at various places in the world, resulting in calls for increased international cooperation to deal with threats to cyber security.[31] On January 6, 2006, the GA adopted Resolution 60/45, calling among other things for the appointment by the Secretary General of "a group of governmental experts, to be established in 2009 on the basis of equitable geographical distribution," to continue to study "existing and potential threats in the sphere of information security and possible cooperative measures to address them," and "to submit a report on the results of this study to the General Assembly at its sixty-fifth session." The Group of Governmental Experts representing 15 states, including China, India, Russia, and the U.S., met four times and on July 10, 2010 issued a report summarizing the threats currently faced by Information and Communication Technologies ("ICTs"), and recommending the following "further steps for the development of confidence-building and other measures to reduce the risk of misperception resulting from ICT disruptions":

1. Further dialogue among States to discuss norms pertaining to State use of ICTs, to reduce collective risk and protect critical national and international infrastructures;
2. Confidence-building, stability, and risk reduction measures to address the implications of State use of ICTs, including exchanges of national views on the use of ICTs in conflict;

---

[28]Abraham D. Sofaer and Seymour E. Goodman, "A Proposal for an International Convention on Cyber Crime and Terrorism," (CISAC, Aug. 2000) (with the assistance of several other scholars) (hereinafter "Stanford Draft"). Any current treaty should not be limited to "crime" and "terrorism" but rather should address cyber security in general.

[29]Dartmouth's Institute for Information Infrastructure and Protection issued a report in 2009, *National Cyber Security Research and Development Challenges,* addressing the international issues and calling for a multilateral international agreement:

> While there are U.S. laws and regulations that address physical border concerns, the issues become far less clear in the borderless reality of cyberspace. One participant observed, ". . . a world protocol is needed. We have a world economy, a world legal system . . . For information security, we need world conduct, ethics, monitoring, and response. The U.S. cannot do it alone." The object of the international doctrine should be to devise ways to eliminate threats, not just to identify ways to defend against them. Such a doctrine should specify clear roles and responsibilities regarding the security of IT components, from producers to customers. Moreover, the doctrine should codify normative behavior in cyberspace and should identify cyber attacks and abuse as crimes rather than national security issues.

Richard A. Clarke and Robert Knake call for a treaty modeled after the Strategic Arms Limitation Treaty (SALT) to address cyber war. They propose a "Cyber War Limitation Treaty, or CWLT" that would "establish a Cyber Risk Reduction Center. . . . coordinate with the United Nations . . . exchange information and provide nations with assistance . . . create international law concepts [for example] the obligation to assist and national accountability . . . ban first-use cyber attacks. . . . " They also call for banning cyberattacks on civilian infrastructure. In order to address the problem of non-state actors, they propose that the treaty "shift the burden of stopping them to the states party to the convention." Richard A. Clarke and Robert K. Knake, *Cyber War* (New York: Harper Collins 2010), 270.

[30]Among the most important of several General Assembly Resolutions on this subject is No. 55/63. It recommends: establishing a set of universally agreed principles for the use and protection of cyberspace; understandings by governments as to their responsibilities regarding their resort to cyberattacks or investigations; agreements by governments as to private activities that should be prohibited to enhance cyber security; commitments by governments to criminalize, prevent, investigate, prosecute and punish such activities; commitments by governments to provide forensic cooperation in cyber investigation and prosecutions by other governments, and to extradite or prosecute violators of agreed norms; agreements among states to allow within their territories certain types of investigation of cyberattacks by other governments; consideration and implementation through an agreed entity of protocols and standards designed to enhance cyber security; and the collective development and funding of an effective, multilateral program of support for cyber competence and capacity throughout the world to facilitate development and economic growth while instilling proper practices.

[31]In addition to the many ITU resolutions on the subject, the GCA report summarizes other, significant conferences held on related subjects at 22-23. The GAO July 2010 Report (pp. 8-17) also provides considerable, useful information on such transnational activities.

3. Information exchanges on national legislation, national ICT security strategies and technologies, policies and best practices;

4. Identification of measures to support capacity-building in less developed countries; and

5. Finding possibilities to elaborate common terms and definitions relevant to United National General Assembly resolution 64/25.[32]

This set of recommendations is far from a major step toward a cyber security treaty. Nonetheless, the report represents a breakthrough in the deadlock that had developed due to demands by some states for sweeping cyber security agreements, related especially to armed conflict, and U.S. opposition to international negotiations on cyber warfare and other aspects of cyber security. The willingness of the U.S. to begin discussions on state conduct, norms, defensive strategies, best practices, and capacity building represents a significant shift in national policy. It apparently results from the Obama Administration's willingness to consider international measures to enhance deterrence through international cooperation. Its 2009 Policy Review concluded that "International norms are critical to establishing a secure and thriving digital infrastructure," and that the U.S. should formulate its positions internally and attempt to implement them in all appropriate international forums.[33] While prior U.S. government policy pronouncements recognized a general need for international cooperation, the 2009 Policy Review specifically recommends that the U.S. government, working with the private sector, "should coordinate and expand international partnerships to address the full range of cybersecurity-related activities, policies, and opportunities associated with the information and communications infrastructure . . . ."[34]

Members of Congress, too, have signaled increased support for international cooperation to enhance cyber security. A 2009 GAO Report on national cybersecurity strategy called for an international agreement and a global cyber strategy.[35] In September 2009, Senator Dianne Feinstein called for an international agreement regulating cyber warfare much like regular warfare:

> In addition, the government must consider that effective cyber security inside the United States will require stronger diplomatic efforts and an international agreement on what will and will not be tolerated in cyberspace. An international framework on cyber warfare, much like international conventions on traditional warfare, is needed to govern this rapidly growing field.[36]

On July 10, 2009, Senator Kirsten Gillibrand introduced legislation that would encourage the Secretary of State to work with governments of other countries to coordinate cooperation on cybersecurity, and would require a report to Congress on the progress of those efforts.[37] On March 23, 2010, Senator

---

[32]Item 94 of the provisional list (A/65/100), "Developments in the field of information and telecommunications in the context of international security."

[33]2009 Cyberspace Policy Review, iv.

[34]2009 Cyberspace Policy Review, 20-21. The 2009 Cyberspace Policy Review, consistent with prior reports, places primary emphasis on domestic measures in its proposed plan to improve cyber security; it also refers, however, to the need for greater international cooperation and efforts, based on its conclusion that (17): "The global challenge of securing cyberspace requires an increased effort in multilateral forums . . .—in continued collaboration with the private sector—to improve the security of interoperable networks through the development of global standards, expand the legal system's capacity to combat cyber crime, continue to develop and promote best practices, and maintain stable and effective internet governance."

[35]U.S. Government Accountability Office, National Cybersecurity Strategy, testimony prepared for Subcommittee on Emerging Threats, Cybersecurity, and Science and Technology, 111th Cong., 1st sess., 2009, GAO-09-432T. The GAO has since then published two reports bearing directly on international cooperation and cyber security. Its March 2010 report—"Cybersecurity: Progress Made but Challenges Remain in Defining and Coordinating the Comprehensive National Initiative," GAO-10-338 (Washington, D.C.)—concluded that the U.S. lacks a formal strategy for coordinating outreach to international partners for standards setting, law enforcement, and information sharing. Its July 2010 Report, referred to at various points in this paper, reaffirms that conclusion on the basis of a comprehensive study of national and international activities.

[36]Senator Diane Feinstein of California, speaking for the Senate Resolution Supporting the Goals and Ideals of National Cybersecurity Awareness Month and Raising Awareness and Enhancing the State of Cybersecurity in the United States, on September 24, 2009, to the Senate, S. Res. 285, 111th Cong., 1st sess., Congressional Record 155 (September 24, 2009): S 9852-3.

[37]For the Senate bill, see International Cybercrime Reporting and Cooperation Act, S 3155, 111th Cong., 2nd sess., Congressional Record 156 (March 23, 2010): S 1873.

Gillibrand joined with Senator Orin Hatch to propose a more comprehensive bill coordinating global cybersecurity efforts. In a statement supporting the bill, Senator Hatch announced:

> Cybercrime is a tangible threat to the security of the global economy, which is why we need to coordinate our fight worldwide. Until countries begin to take the necessary steps to fight criminals within their borders, cybercrime havens will continue to flourish. We do not have the luxury to sit back and do nothing, and the International Cybercrime Reporting and Cooperation Act will not only function as a deterrent of cybercrime, but will prove to be an essential tool necessary to keep the Internet open for business. Countries that knowingly permit cybercriminals to attack within their borders will now know that the U.S. is watching, the global community is watching, and there will be consequences for not acting.[38]

The Senators announced that their bill had the support of such U.S. companies as Cisco, HP, Microsoft, Symantec, PayPal, eBay, McAfee, and major financial institutions.[39]

IV. FASHIONING EFFECTIVE INTERNATIONAL INITIATIVES

The potential advantages of securing agreements on international norms and standards related to cyber security stem from the view that states could by adopting and implementing such measures create a culture and practices more favorable to cyber security than currently exist. The important insight that the Internet and other cyber systems are (like other transnational activities) subject to state control,[40] implies that state support is necessary to achieve effective security norms and appropriate technology standards. Only states can limit their own destabilizing activities, and their cooperation is essential to curb so-called patriotic hackers and cyber crime. Harmonization of laws and practices cannot assure effective cooperation, particularly in enforcing rules or practices that fail accurately to reflect underlying differences in policy. But harmonization has not occurred and is essential to secure the benefits of criminal law enforcement through extradition treaties and MLATs, and to achieve interoperability of security systems. Harmonization, effectively applied, implies the existence of national plans and practices that enable the implementation of common international policies.

An enhanced capacity to implement norms, practices, and standards is another potential benefit of an international arrangement. Assuming—as we do—that the current, privately and professionally controlled process for reaching common technology positions on cyber activities is valuable and worth preserving, a mechanism whereby national governments could concur in such positions through an international structure could serve to achieve faster and more uniform acceptance, resulting in more secure and robust cyber networks. Finally, an international arrangement could serve to resolve some if not all the current political maneuvering over what agencies, states, or other entities should perform key transnational roles in ICT development and security. The current, de facto distribution of power appears to have ignited a competition for influence likely to disrupt rather than to enhance cyber security. An agreed redistribution of responsibilities that is acceptable to all stakeholders could ensure constructive cooperation in a highly complex undertaking.

But negotiating agreements that effectively exploit these potential advantages must satisfactorily address the difficulties and objections that thus far have led the U.S. (and others) to refrain from seeking international agreements beyond the CEC. Not all aspects of cyber insecurity are currently susceptible to international agreement. Some seem beyond the reach of acceptable resolution because the issues are novel or intractable. Others reflect major policy differences among potential member states concerning freedom of speech, privacy, or other social and political values. Others stem from the underlying premise that U.S. interests are inconsistent with international cooperation. Some states (including the U.S.) are

---

[38]Senator Orrin Hatch of Utah, speaking for the International Cybercrime Reporting and Cooperation Act, on March 23, 2010, to the Senate, S. 3155, 111th Cong., 2nd sess., *Congressional Record* 156 (March 23, 2010): S 1876.

[39]"Hatch, Gillibrand Introduce First of its Kind Measure to Bolster Cybersecurity," Orrin G. Hatch Newsroom, the Senator's Press Releases, March 23, 2010, http://hatch.senate.gov/public/index.cfm?FuseAction=PressReleases.Detail&PressRelease_id=8bcbfb97-1b78-be3e-e0e3-58aed09a749a&Month=3&Year=2010 (accessed July 21, 2010).

[40]Jack Goldsmith and Tim Wu, Who Controls the Internet: Illusions of a Borderless World (Oxford Press 2008).

as yet unwilling to be bound by limitations that their public complaints suggest they believe should bind others. Many U.S. officials and experts may in fact believe that U.S. security would be diminished through international cooperation rather than enhanced. Sharing information on cyber vulnerabilities, even with allies, could result in exposing those weaknesses to states prepared to exploit them. Sharing and improving the defensive capacities of all states would result in strengthening those whose networks the U.S. itself may seek to penetrate for intelligence or other purposes. Finally, even where agreement may be possible that an area of cyber activity is a likely subject of international agreement, the measures that are appropriate for that purpose will vary, and the form of the entity assigned the task of implementing those measures must also be agreed.

These difficulties and objections present real and challenging obstacles to international cooperation. They cannot be overcome by invoking sweeping generalities about the values of international cooperation. They do not, however, preclude international agreements on many aspects of cyber security. Rather, they reflect objections based on national security, political, and ethical concerns that are familiar from other areas of international engagement, and that can be effectively managed by adopting parameters for cyber agreements fashioned with due regard for such concerns. The U.S. pursues agreements in such areas, despite the risks, when they are expected to confer security and/or economic benefits. A useful example (based on incidents described in the GAO July 2010 Report, pp. 34-35) is the vigorous and successful effort by the U.S. Trade Representative to use international trade agreements as the basis for preventing China in 2007 from regulating (through testing and certification) the commercial sale of products such as routers, smart cards, secure databases and operating systems, and for convincing South Korea to drop a plan to mandate an indigenous encryption standard as part of a large-scale government adoption of voice-over-Internet Protocol systems. To the extent the U.S. adopts stringent cyber security standards for commercial sales of products, or otherwise erects cyber security-related trade barriers, it should expect that it will be unable to convince other states to open their markets to U.S. sales in similar circumstances. The optimal policy in such situations is to restrict those transactions that national security truly demands, while accepting and managing lesser risks where they are outweighed by countervailing advantages.

An appropriate approach would, taking into account such concerns, (1) limit at least initial efforts to **areas of activity** that are appropriate subjects for international cyber-security agreements; (2) determine and specify the **types of measures** that member states should undertake concerning each of the activities they include in such agreements; and (3) fashion the **administrative structure and functions** of any entity that should be utilized for this purpose in a manner that preserves what currently works well while improving what does not.

1. Determining the Activities to Include or Exclude from International Arrangements

International regulatory regimes regularly specify the areas of activity to which they apply or are considered inapplicable. The International Civil Aviation Organization ("ICAO"), for example, pursuant to the Chicago, Montreal, and other conventions, regulates civil aviation but has no authority over military aircraft and activities. Such limitations are common in international agreements, and are often necessary to attract the widespread support required for potentially meaningful cooperation.

The following areas of cyber activities are likely to be excluded from an international agreement at this time, or to be included only to a limited extent: (a) aspects of **cyber war**; (b) **cyber intelligence**; (c) politically related **content restrictions**; (d) proposals that unacceptably limit **privacy or human rights**; and (e) other concerns that states believe may prejudice their **national security** interests. This is not to say that these areas of activity should be ignored, but rather that they should be approached with an awareness of their likely sensitivity and correspondingly modest expectations.

(a). Cyber War

Cyber "war" is an area of great, public concern, and several proposals have been made to limit, or even to prohibit, cyber warfare. Russia proposed several years ago that all forms of cyber warfare be outlawed. China refused to accept so sweeping a restriction, viewing cyber warfare as an arena in which it could be successful in competing with the U.S. and other militarily powerful states. The U.S. for years indicated it was uninterested in even discussing limitations on cyber warfare. Military officials assigned leading roles in developing U.S. cyber capacities in fact announced their intent to "dominate" cyberspace.[41] The U.S. has created a Cyber Command, reflecting its view that cyber space is a new theater for national security activities analogous to the ground, sea, or air theaters of operations. Other states are responding to these developments by building their own capacities to engage in defensive, retaliatory, or anticipatory measures aimed at deterring or preventing cyberattacks.

The notion that the U.S. or any other state will be able to "dominate" cyber space seems unlikely ever to be correct. The use of such rhetoric—coupled with the announcement (uncoordinated with the Department of State) of the creation of a Cyber Command—has undoubtedly led other states to regard U.S. military policy as posing a threat to which they must respond. The critical response to this inflammatory posture may have led the U.S. recently to indicate for the first time an interest in pursuing agreements on cyber war issues. At his Senate confirmation hearing on April 15, 2010 to be Director of the NSA and Commander of the newly created U.S. Cyber Command, Lieutenant General Keith B. Alexander, said: "This command is not about efforts to militarize cyber space. Rather, it is about safeguarding the integrity of our military's critical information systems."[42] And in the UN sponsored Expert Group report, issued on July 17, 2010, the U.S. joined 14 other states, including China and Russia, in agreeing to consider "confidence-building, stability, and risk reduction measures to address the implications of State use of ICTs, including exchanges of national views on the use of ICTs in conflict."

Reaching agreement on cyber-war related issues will be difficult. The activities potentially covered by the concept of cyber warfare are numerous and important to the national security of potential member states. Furthermore, cyber capacities permeate modern warfare, and their use in armed conflict is already extensive and indispensable. The extent to which cyberattacks should or could realistically be treated as equivalent to conventional armed attacks is unclear. Individual computers could not reasonably be treated as analogous to conventional weapons. Verification of the performance of commitments would be difficult if not impossible. And violations would, absent some new forms of monitoring, remain difficult to trace and attribute to particular states.[43]

Despite these difficulties, agreements may be possible about specific aspects of cyber warfare. As the present NRC Committee's Letter Report notes, conventional arms control agreements may restrict the number, type, or use of weapons, may require advance notice of activities, and may establish rules limiting appropriate targets.[44] Agreements could be reached, for example, that apply certain established international-law principles to cyberattacks, as suggested recently by a U.S. diplomat familiar with the Expert Group negotiations. Governments would probably agree that a cyberattack by the armed forces

---

[41]Clarke and Knave, 41-44.

[42]Senate Committee on Armed Services, *Nomination of VAdm James A. Winnefled, Jr. USN, to be Admiral and Commander, U.S. Northern Commander, North American Aerpospace Defense Command; and Ltg. Keith B. Alexander, USA, to be General and Director, National Security Agency/Chief, Central Security Service/Commander, U.S. Cyber Command, 111th Cong. 2nd sess., April 15, 2010*, 9. Chairman Carl Levin described in his statement at the hearing the need for caution by the U.S. in resorting to cyberattacks (3): "Coupled with the fact that the United States economy and government are the most dependent in the world on the Internet and are therefore the most vulnerable to attacks, the Nation must not only invest in the effectiveness of its defense, but think carefully about the precedents that it sets, hopefully acting wisely in ways that we will accept if others act in the same or similar ways." He said the committee had been "assured that the Department of Defense leadership and the administration as a whole is committed to rapidly closing the cyber space policy gap. The committee has also been assured that the Defense Department is proceeding with appropriate caution and care regarding military operations in cyberspace."

[43]Comprehensive discussions of the application of existing international law to cyber warfare include the paper prepared for the current NRC study by Michael Schmitt, "Cyber Operations in International Law: The Use of Force, Collective Security, Self-Defense and Armed Conflicts" (NRC, 2010); and Scott J. Shackelford, "From Nuclear War to Net War: Analogizing Cyber Attacks in International Law," published in the *Berkeley Journal of International Law (BJIL)*, Vol. 25, No. 3.

[44]National Research Council Committee on Deterring Cyber Attacks, *Letter Report for the Committee on Deterring Cyber Attacks: Informing Strategies and Developing Options for U.S. Policy* (March 25, 2010), http://www.nap.edu/catalog/12886.html (accessed July 23, 2010).

of a state, with kinetic effects on the territory of another state equivalent to those of a conventional armed attack, should be treated in the same manner as a conventional attack, giving rise to the right of individual and collective self-defense, and allowing upon proper attribution resort to both cyber and kinetic responses. States could also confirm that targets normally immune during armed conflict from conventional attack, such as medical services and religious institutions, are also immune from cyberattacks. They could even agree that potentially appropriate targets during armed conflict, such as power grids, food supply, and financial infrastructure, should be immune from cyberattack under all circumstances.

One method for accomplishing limits on military activities (i.e., cyber war) without attempting directly to regulate national forces is exemplified by the protections established for civilian aircraft. The Chicago Convention (Art. 3) provides that it "shall be applicable to civil aircraft, and shall not be applicable to state aircraft"; and it also recognizes (Art. 1) "that every State has complete and exclusive sovereignty over the airspace above its territory." The Convention also, however, requires contracting states to issue regulations for their state aircraft "that they will have due regard for the safety of navigation of civil aircraft," an obligation that effectively limits the use of force other than in armed conflict (expressly excepted in Art. 89), and it grants certain qualified but significant rights of passage over the territories of all contracting states even to nonscheduled flights (Art. 5).[45] It may be possible, by analogy, to limit "cyber war" implicitly if not explicitly by granting protections to specified cyber activities or assets.

Identification protocols would likely be necessary to establish for protected entities or functions. Doing so in a manner that effectively limits abuse will pose problems, as states or groups having access to such protocols may use the information to target the entities and functions sought to be protected. The problem of accurate attribution of illegal cyberattack may tend to diminish the normal deterrent effect of potential uses of force in self-defense. Non-state actors may be particularly inclined to risk illegal attacks, since they lack corresponding institutions. A system for determining responsibility and imposing remedies, including monetary damages, against not only states but also ISPs and other responsible parties, could be a helpful supplement to responsive uses of force. But here, too, the difficulties will be substantial. International tribunals have lost their appeal. Furthermore, imposing damages on states for military activities is rarely acceptable other than on a voluntary (ex gratia) basis, and the threat of civil liability is likely to have no effect at all on non-state actors prepared deliberately to attack civilian infrastructure.

Considerable planning and negotiation will have to take place both within and among potential parties before progress can be expected on most cyber-war issues. While much public attention and official concern has been expressed about the dangers of cyber war, the U.S. will not be prepared to seek legal limits on such activities until it has determined that it is prepared to accept reciprocal obligations. No internal review has yet been made as to the cyber-war policies the U.S. should adopt or advocate in the international arena. Even after the U.S. has resolved internally its international cyber warfare policies, the appropriate, initial forum for implementing such policies may be with U.S. allies, in NATO for example, rather than through a multilateral arrangement with states that have different agendas and are less trusted. Given the difficulties in negotiating international agreements related to cyber war, that subject—though important and appropriate—should probably be handled separately from discussions on the ways in which states could cooperate in enhancing cyber security through the regulation of non-state conduct.

(b). Cyber Intelligence

Even less likely than cyber warfare to become a subject of international agreement is the use of cyber capacities by states for intelligence collection. Intelligence activities have long been and will continue

---

[45]Convention on International Civil Aviation, December 7, 1944.

to be conducted or sponsored by states subject only to national constraints. Informal understandings designed to avoid damaging cyber (or other) infrastructure may be possible between intelligence agencies of states, especially allies. But such understandings—or other agreements addressed to intelligence collection—are unlikely subjects of multilateral negotiations.

A different problem is posed by efforts of non-state actors to intrude upon and collect intelligence from government or private sources. Such intrusions seem an appropriate subject for international discussions. States may be able to fashion common norms and rules to restrict such conduct, at least in specified situations. Most if not all states have laws that prohibit private individuals from attacking other states without government approval. Such conduct appears in fact from the literature on cyber security to be common and troublesome. Efforts to penetrate private companies for commercial purposes may also be a subject that most if not all states will be willing to address, though where such efforts are officially sanctioned they are likely to be off the negotiating agenda.

(c). Content Restrictions

Virtually all proposals related to cyber security include support for some forms of content restrictions. The CEC includes agreements to prohibit messages that violate copyright laws, hate speech, and child pornography. The SOC acknowledges the right of Member States to prohibit messages that threaten political stability.

The parties to any multilateral negotiation should focus their efforts on securing agreement regarding its most important objectives. If the most important objective of a cyber security treaty is to protect the cyber infrastructure so it can perform its many essential functions, states should focus on protecting against cyberattacks and criminal exploitation that is damaging to ICTs. Negotiators should especially avoid efforts to pursue controversial restrictions of the content of cyber messages that jeopardize agreement on security-related issues. States whose participation in an international cyber regime would be indispensable have significant policy differences concerning the use of cyber networks for political and other forms of expression, and on the relationship of such efforts to national security. While the U.S. properly urges states to agree to allow unrestricted exchanges of ideas and political views,[46] convincing states such as China to alter their policies concerning freedom of communication seems unlikely for the foreseeable future. "A single answer to these . . . questions would leave the world divided and discontented. Decentralized answers to these questions help us get along."[47]

On the other hand, agreement to some content restrictions may be necessary to achieve agreement on cyber infrastructure protection. In such situations, it may be possible to separate such restrictions from infrastructure-protection provisions in order to allow parties to opt into or out of content requirements. At a minimum, the U.S. must insist on retaining the right to refuse to cooperate with political-speech restrictions. The Stanford Draft proposed no content restriction other than "narrow coverage of conduct described as the 'distribution of devices or programs intended for the purpose of committing' other conduct made criminal by the . . ." cyber treaty involved. This provision would permit "safe harbor" sites for discussions of computer vulnerability.[48]

(d). Privacy and Human Rights Limitations

Profound differences exist among potential member states to a cyber security agreement on the privacy and human rights to be accorded users. The U.S. and other democratic societies are justifiably concerned that cyber system regulation—and indeed some measures that strengthen cyber security—may

[46]Secretary of State Hillary Clinton, "Remarks on Internet Freedom" (speech, Newseum, Washington, D.C., January 21, 2010).
[47]"Who Controls the Internet? A Conversation with Jack Goldsmith," Defining Ideas, No. 1 (Stanford University: Hoover Institution, 2010), 100.
[48]Stanford Draft, 9.

also result in reducing the privacy and human rights of users. These concerns will surely compound the difficulties in reaching agreements to enhance security by limiting anonymity.

The ITU Constitution implicitly allows Member States to determine the scope of privacy and other human rights to the extent they are considered matters of domestic security.[49] Expressly recognizing such authority over cyber activities should be avoided, though with the realization that states will still have the power to regulate within their territories. Consensus should be possible, in fact, on including in any cyber-security agreement a reference to widely approved UN conventions bearing upon privacy and human rights, which may in the long run prove helpful in achieving progress on such issues. The Stanford Draft proposed making clear that member states would have no duty "to act in any manner that might infringe upon the privacy or other human rights of any individual or entity, as defined by the law of that State."[50] It proposed establishing within any international cyber-security entity created by agreement a committee of experts tasked with following and reporting on the protection of privacy and human rights, to serve as a forum for ongoing exposure and debate. It also proposed allowing any member state to refuse to cooperate with investigations and prosecutions it considered unfair or inconsistent with its national policies.

(e). National Security Exception

Transnational arrangements often raise issues regarded by states as potentially prejudicial to their national security. Treaties bearing on important national interests often exclude matters considered by any party to threaten its fundamental national security interests. Article XXI of the General Agreement on Trade and Tariffs ("GATT"), for example, states that nothing in the agreement "shall be construed to prevent any contracting party from taking any action which it considers necessary for the protection of its essential security interests," thereby exempting that activity from the regime's rules.[51] The WTO regime has operated effectively in a contentious area, despite its national-interests exception, perhaps because states have exercised that right with restraint, knowing that it is available equally to all parties and that its expansive exercise would deprive them all of the benefits of a regime that serves their interests.

Such situations are especially likely to arise in connection with the creation of cyber norms and standards. For example, sharing information is a fundamental characteristic and benefit of transnational regimes and would be an important aspect of any cyber-security agreement. A government may occasionally be faced, however, with a situation in which sharing information related to a cyber threat could prejudice its security by, for example, revealing vulnerabilities or defensive plans to a state or non-state actor suspected of supporting cyberattacks. States should be permitted, in their discretion, to invoke a national security exception in all such situations.

2. Measures Potentially Applicable to Covered Activities

After identifying those cyber activities (or aspects of such activities) that are likely subjects for international agreement, states considering such agreements must decide what measures to adopt to advance their agreed objectives. States have used or authorized a wide range of measures in international agreements, including: (a) **declarations** that establish common objectives and norms of conduct to achieve them; (b) **information sharing** to provide warnings of dangers and remedies to assist in dealing with them; (c) **prohibitions and punishment of conduct** which the parties agree to make criminal or impermissible under domestic law; (d) **law enforcement cooperation,** including mutual legal assistance and extradition; (e) **standards and practices** that establish mandatory requirements or recommendations

---

[49]Constitution of International Telecommunications Union, Chapter IV, Article 34: "Member States also reserve the right to cut off, in accordance with their national law, any other private telecommunications which may appear dangerous to the security of the State or contrary to its laws, to public order or to decency."

[50]Stanford Draft, 17.

[51]Article XXI(b), The General Agreement on Tariffs and Trade, 1947.

for equipment, training, and operational activities; (f) **enforcement measures**; and (g) **capacity building** for states requiring assistance.

(a). Declarations of Policy

International treaty regimes uniformly contain declarations of policy related to the subjects they cover. The Preamble of the Chicago Convention declares, for example, that it was adopted "in order that international civil aviation may be developed in a safe and orderly manner and that international air transport services may be established on the basis of equality of opportunity and operated soundly and economically." The Constitution of the ITU (Art. 1) includes among its purposes to "maintain and extend international cooperation between all Members of the Union for the improvement and rational use of telecommunications of all kinds," "to promote and to offer technical assistance to developing countries in the field of telecommunications," "to promote the development of technical facilities and their most efficient operation," and "to promote the use of telecommunication services with the objective of facilitating peaceful relations." In some areas of transnational activity, states issue such declarations without adopting significant, additional measures. Analogous declarations of policy could readily be crafted to express the purposes of an international cyber-security regime. A paper prepared for the NRC by Steve Lukasik describes some types of declarations that could be issued.[52]

Declarations of policy by a sufficiently widespread and influential group of states that confirm cyber security as a universal objective, and that describe appropriate norms of conduct to facilitate achieving that objective, could be useful in creating a more responsible, security-oriented environment than currently exists. Such declarations are commonly issued at the end of conferences, for example, with no expectation they will be treated as enforceable agreements. Alternatively, declarations could be issued that call for specific actions, or that establish specific arrangements or obligations; in the U.S., such agreements might have to be conveyed by the president to the Congress or ratified by the Senate.

(b). Information Sharing

A common feature of international agreements is a commitment to share information considered useful or essential by the parties. Usually, information sharing is only one aspect of a regulatory regime. For example, if a party to the Chicago Convention fails to implement a standard or practice issued with regard to civil aviation, it must under Article 38 "give immediate notification to" ICAO of the differences of its rules from those adopted by the agency. Some agreements are essentially limited to sharing information. In 1986, following the Chernobyl nuclear plant accident, the Convention on Early Notification of Nuclear Accidents required parties to notify each other and the International Atomic Energy Agency of nuclear accidents which have the potential for international transboundary release that could be of radiological safety significance for another state.[53] On December 16, 2000, the U.S. and Russia signed an MOU providing for pre- and post-launch notification of certain missile launches.[54]

Information sharing is certain to be a significant aspect of any international agreement that seeks to enhance cyber security. Parties could agree to share information about attacks or criminal activity; about software and hardware flaws they discover; about methods for increasing the security of computer operations or transactions; and of estimates of losses and damages caused by cyberattacks and exploitation. Efforts could be made on an international basis to overcome the reluctance of companies and individuals to reveal attacks, which typically delay the implementation of effective remedies.

---

[52]Steve Lukasik, "A Framework for Thinking About Cyber Conflict and Cyber Deterrence," this volume.

[53]"Convention on Early Notification of a Nuclear Accident," September 26, 1986, *Treaty Series: Treaties and International Agreements Registered or Filed or Recorded with the Secretariat of the United Nations* 1439, no. 24404.

[54]"Memorandum of Understanding on Notifications of Missile Launches," December 16, 2000.

(c). Prohibition and Punishment of Specified Conduct

Many international agreements identify types of conduct that parties agree to prohibit and punish. The Montreal Convention, for example, contains a commitment by all Member States to make criminal any form of aircraft hijacking, and to impose severe punishments on persons convicted of such acts.[55] The CEC is modeled on such agreements in that its parties commit to making criminal the forms of cyberattacks and exploitation specified. The ITU GCA identifies types of conduct that many states have agreed should be prohibited, especially attacks on cyber infrastructure, as well as forms of cyber exploitation, such as fraud and theft. States could agree to prohibit these and other activities, and add commitments to prohibit violations of copyright laws, "hate" speech, and other content restrictions. Limits on content have little if any relationship to enhancing cyber security, but their inclusion may be necessary to obtain consensus on security-related provisions.

(d). Law Enforcement Cooperation

Thousands of international agreements, bilateral and multilateral, provide for various forms of law enforcement cooperation. The CEC follows the traditional pattern, and it includes detailed provisions on the collection and preservation of evidence to be used in cyber-related prosecutions. Expanding the CEC regime to additional states and to additional forms of harmful conduct would enhance its effectiveness. This may only be possible, however, if CEC parties agree to join a regime formulated with the participation of non-European states whose support is critical to the successful prevention of cyberattacks and exploitation, and with their concerns in mind.[56] It may also be appropriate (and useful in securing consensus) to exclude from any agreement to prohibit certain types of conduct those interceptions and other activities that do no injury to cyber infrastructure and stem from the failure of users to exercise reasonable care.

As in most treaties calling for the extradition of alleged violators of specified laws of one party found in the territory of another party, member states of a cyber-security regime should be permitted to prosecute alleged violators rather than being required to extradite them. This authority enables a party to ensure that prohibited conduct is prosecuted without sending the individual involved to a state that might fail to provide a sufficiently high level of due process, that might impose unacceptably severe punishment, or for any other reason. In addition, each state could retain the right to treat alleged criminal behavior as immune from prosecution as political offenses or because non-prosecution is required by its national interests. For example, although virtually all states agreed to prohibit aircraft hijacking in treaties to protect civilian aviation, the U.S. and other parties have at times been unwilling to extradite or sometimes even to prosecute individuals for such a serious crime where, for example, the hijacking was done to escape unjust punishment by an oppressive regime. Some states will presumably be even less willing to cooperate in an international regime that strengthens the ability of undemocratic governments to prevent and punish political speech or otherwise restrict or deny fundamental human rights.

A particularly interesting law-enforcement issue is whether states should agree to permit other parties to engage in limited, unilateral actions within their territories to prevent or investigate cyberattacks or crimes in specified circumstances. The CEC's effectiveness has been undermined by its failure to extend this authority, since cyberattacks come suddenly and evidence required to prove who did them is soon lost. Without effective cooperation in preventing and prosecuting cyberattacks and crimes, states and non-state actors are likely to consider engaging in unauthorized and unilateral measures of self-defense, or conducting transnational investigations. The Stanford Draft considered such actions lawful only when based on "legally recognized authority," and acknowledged that "such efforts may affect

---

[55]Convention for the Unification of Certain Rules for International Carriage by Air," May 28, 1999, *Treaty Series: Treaties and International Agreements Registered or Filed with the Secretariat of the United Nations* 2242, no. 39917.

[56]The Stanford Draft (7), based on a review of then current statutory law, proposed including a commitment by parties to prosecute cyber-related violations of widely approved anti-terrorism treaties.

innocent third parties [even when they] may be reasonable."[57] (A separate paper on such "hackback" or investigative activities has been prepared for the NRC committee).[58]

It would be desirable for parties to a cyber-security agreement to allow limited, specified forms of intrusion of their "cyber space" for information collection and in self-defense, with prompt notification requirements. This authority could be exercised by international teams subject to oversight by all parties in order to avoid the danger that states might abuse such authority for the purpose of conducting an attack or intelligence operation. Standards to govern defensive measures could be developed by an international agency, if one is established, to implement cyber security initiatives. Officially sanctioned and regulated defensive actions would be preferable to unregulated efforts more likely to be overbroad, ineffective, and offensive to the state into whose territory such defensive or investigative actions are undertaken.

(e). Standards and Practices

International governmental organizations ("IGOs") established to protect and foster many types of transnational activities have been given authority (in a variety of forms) to establish rules. In ICAO, these are called (Art. 37) standards and recommended practices ("SARPs"), but are given other names at other IGOs, such as "codes" or simply "rules." These "rules" are often intended to enhance security, safety, and efficiency, objectives that states would seek in negotiating any cyber security agreement. ICAO's SARPs, for example, deal with such matters as airworthiness, registration and identification of aircraft, navigational aids, airports, licensing of pilots and engineers, collection and exchange of meteorological information, investigation of accidents, and other matters "concerned with the safety, regularity, and efficiency of air navigations as may from time to time appear appropriate."

The "rules" adopted by IGOs rarely constitute "law" in the sense of enforceable obligations. States sometimes give IGOs law-making powers, but usually for limited and essential purposes. Normally, states grant IGOs authority to establish what they consider appropriate standards and practices to deal with particular issues, but reserve to all parties the option of declining to implement the rules proposed. Since member states of such institutions participate in fashioning and thereafter approving the standards and practices developed, and because of the frequent need to abide by such rules in order to obtain the benefits of access to the territories and cooperation of other member states, it is rare that states actually decline to follow duly approved rules. While rules adopted by specialized agencies are therefore appropriately characterized as "soft law," they are rarely challenged (though sometimes ignored).[59]

Examples of "soft law" rule making by IGOs abound. In civil aviation, ICAO's thirty-five member Council is empowered to adopt SARPs as (non-compulsory) annexes to the Chicago Convention, and these generally become effective within a designated period unless a majority of Member States disapprove. Though not formally binding, these rules are authoritative, being important for the safety and efficiency of civil aviation. The World Meteorological Organization ("WMO") occasionally adopts technical resolutions through its Congress as "decisions" that it calls on all Member States to do their "utmost" to implement. When these decisions relate to the agency's important World Weather Watch program states able to comply with its requirements generally do so. The International Maritime Organization ("IMO") has established numerous requirements related to navigation, safety equipment, and pollution avoidance, generally approved by its Assembly. While the Assembly consists of representa-

---

[57]Stanford Draft, 8.

[58]Jay Kesan and Carol Mullins Hayes, "Thinking Through Active Defense in Cyberspace," this volume.

[59]Even legally binding rules can prove ineffective. The World Health Organization ("WHO") Health Assembly is, for example, given express authority by its Member States to adopt regulations binding on all parties except those that reject or make reservations to them by a designated time. The Assembly has rarely exercised this authority, and its most significant action—adoption of its Health Regulations intended to prevent the spread of diseases—was legally upheld but ineffective at securing compliance from the states that it unambiguously bound. Frederic L. Kirgis, Jr., "Specialized Law-Making Processes," in *United Nations Legal Order*, ed. Oscar Schachter and Christopher C. Joyner, Vol. 1, (ASIL, Cambridge Press 1995), 132.

tives of all Member States, it operates through Sub-Committees that deal with technical subjects. It has adopted many nonbinding codes, guidelines, or standards that "are prepared with great care by IMO committees," which are generally successful because "many of the individuals who shape them are also heavily involved in implementing them, either as government officials charged with responsibility for shipping or as representatives of shipping interests."[60]

The Internet (and other cyber systems) currently operate without any formal international institution to set standards or practices, the sort of "soft law" established by many international agencies. The Internet is indeed based on standards, but the term as used by network engineers means something quite different from a SARP. The IETF sets the standards that define the technology of the Internet, but these are "interoperability" standards, and are voluntary. No agency is required to mandate the use of these standards; any actor wanting to participate in the Internet must conform in order to be operating in a manner compatible with the standards being applied by other actors. Similarly, network operators meet as members of the North American Network Operators Group ("NANOG") (which operates internationally despite its name), to discuss operational issues and to set informal standards based on interoperability without being convened by an IGO. Other NGOs, such as ETSI and OASIS, discussed above, operate in the same manner.

Interoperability standards of this sort are common in other areas of transnational activity. In maritime operations, for example, the standards that define the shape and fitting on a shipping container are interoperability standards, and there is no need for an international institution to mandate their use; a non-conforming container would not be shippable. On the other hand, many standards in other areas of transnational activity go beyond being interoperability standards, and must be complied with even though they are not essential in order to function. The standard for the display of navigation lights on vessels of different sizes, for example, is a mandatory requirement, approved by an international institution and enforced by states as a standard or practice.

A significant aspect of the inadequate level of security in cyber operations may stem from the limits to what can be achieved using informal organizations with no power even to adopt "soft law" rules. For example, the Internet community has been discussing the migration from IPv4 to IPv6 for years, with only slow progress. The IETF has defined standards to secure the DNS (the Domain Name System Security Extensions or DNSSEC), which currently has inadequate security, but deployment has been slow due to concerns that should have been resolved in a more timely manner. Similarly, the IETF, working with major equipment vendors, has set standards for a more secure inter-region routing protocol (secure BGP), but these have not been deployed. It is possible that the effectiveness of organizations such as the IETF, ICANN, ISO, ETSI, OASIS, and NANOG could beneficially be complemented by some institution empowered to consider and establish a timetable for the implementation of the standards they propose with the greater authority commonly accorded "soft law" rules promulgated by IGOs.

Establishing cyber-security standards through an international governmental regime seems manageable in some areas, such as criminal law enforcement. Rules have been developed under the CEC that provide deadlines for responding to requests, procedures concerning the seizure of data, production orders, expedited presentation, and disclosure.[61] Similarly, standards or practices could be published concerning notification of attacks, including disclosure requirements, without unmanageable controversy. Another subject that might profitably be addressed in or through a cyber security agreement is how and when disclosure should be made of security flaws in programs, hardware, websites, and other

---

[60]Frederic L. Kirgis, Jr., "Shipping," in *United Nations Legal Order*, vol. 2, ed. Oscar Schachter and Christopher C. Joyner (ASIL, Cambridge Press 1995), 717. 727-28

[61]See "Convention on Cybercrime." For measures taken at the national level, see Chapter I (specifically Section 2 Article 18 for production order, Article 19 for search and seizure). For measures taken regarding international cooperation, see Chapter II (specifically section 1 Article 24 for extradition, Article 27 for provisions regarding mutual assistance requests). Full text is available at http://conventions.coe.int/Treaty/Commun/QueVoulezVous.asp?NT=185&CM=8&DF=&CL=ENG (accessed July 23, 2010).

CITs. Disclosures currently can create considerable controversy or even lead to criminal prosecution.[62] Established methods that guaranty safe harbors for such revelations, and perhaps appropriate rewards or recognition, could advance security.

Other problems that could be addressed through standards that go beyond interoperability include, for example, the continued use of software programs considered insecure by the public and even by government agencies performing sensitive tasks;[63] creating agreed bases for liability (by identifying best practices, minimum reliability requirements, and other consensus-based measures) for damages caused by inadequate products or performance by ISPs and other providers; proposals for identifying users being considered by private and government bodies; and the various uses of encryption to enhance reliability without revealing identity.

Presumably, any governmental agency established to consider and promulgate cyber-security standards and practices would build on the interoperability standards fashioned by the IETF or other standard creating bodies and already universally deployed. Such an agency could become a vehicle for considering and adopting existing and future IETF and other acceptable standards with a view toward giving them the authority generally associated with standards promulgated by IGOs. If states agreed to a system that authorized a cyber-security agency to set time periods within which an agency recommended standard should be fully debated, modified, and deployed, the current, informal and uncoordinated system could be strengthened.

(f). Enforcement Measures

International agreements often leave the power to enforce their requirements to the states that join the regimes they operate. IGOs are, however, sometimes assigned authority to collect evidence, hold hearings, make determinations, or impose and enforce remedies against offending states for violations of commitments. The very first, modern, multilateral arrangements, adopted to regularize the collection of tariffs, encourage commerce, and reduce pollution in the Rhine River authorized officials to determine whether violations of commitments were taking place, and ultimately to collect and distribute tariffs to the parties in accordance with an agreed formula.[64] A more recent example is ICAO's power to make and issue findings that an airport is insufficiently secure, where "the practical effect of such a declaration would be to close the airport to international use."[65]

A variety of enforcement powers could conceivably be given to entities assigned cyber-security tasks. Among the most common types of enforcement measures would be the usual powers to establish a budget, to allocate financial obligations to parties, and to suspend the voting rights (or right to participate) of parties that fail to pay their shares of the financial burden of the agency's operations. Authority could also be created for determining responsibility for cyberattacks or exploitation and imposing penalties on non-state actors, including monetary damages and the suspension of licenses.

---

[62]An example of a controversial disclosure is discussed in a Wall Street Journal article published on June 14, 2010, "Compute Experts Face Backlash," B6, col. 1, describes how a group collectively called Goatse Security disclosed a flaw in AT&T's website that made iPad owners' email addresses public. Other experts condemned the disclosure, and the FBI reportedly opened an investigation of the incident. Jeff Moss, founder of the Black Hat security conference said: "We've been having this conversation for 15 years," and still not everyone agrees what is "responsible" disclosure.

[63]Experts appear to regard Windows to be relatively insecure, for example, creating widespread vulnerability. Google, Inc., is reported to have recently instructed its personnel that they may not use Windows on the company's non-portable computers. David Gelles and Richard Waters, "Google ditches Windows on security concerns," *Financial Times*, May 31, 2010, http://www.ft.com/cms/s/2/d2f3f04e-6ccf-11df-91c8-00144feab49a.html.

[64]Thomas Bernauer and Peter Moser, "Reducing Pollution of the River Rhine: The Influence of International Cooperation," *The Journal of Environment Development* vol. 5 no. 4 (December 1996): 389-415. Bernauer and Moser find that such international efforts were modestly and indirectly helpful, and that informal solutions were more effective than formal arrangements.

[65]See Frederic L. Kirgis, Jr., "Aviation," in *United Nations Legal Order*, vol. 2, ed. Oscar Schachter and Christopher C. Joyner (ASIL, Cambridge Press 1995), 853. For more, see the Universal Security Audit Programme (USAP) of ICAO, <http://www2.icao.int/en/ssa/asa/usap/Pages/default.aspx>.

Alternatively, the IGO may be given authority to make determinations, while private actors, such as ISPs, would be relied upon to impose remedies; such private actors will be far more likely to enforce standards against uncooperative users if they are able to rely on approved, international standards or findings to justify enforcement actions.

(g). Capacity Building

Many international regimes include commitments by the parties to provide equipment and training to enable less developed states to acquire the capacities necessary to perform their obligations under the agreement at issue. As a consequence, these states may be able to apply the capacities they acquire to enhance their economic well being. ICAO, for example, together with the United Nations Development Program, engages in many programs each year, involving 80 or more personnel, to "provide training, technical advice, and help in purchasing necessary equipment" to states unable to perform commitments they are prepared to undertake by joining the treaty regime.[66] The ITU has established and is implementing a program to develop cyber security capacities in several states, consistent with its announced, global strategy.

Major programs to assist less developed states develop cyber capacities, including security know-how, are needed in many places. Current efforts along these lines by the U.S. and some other states are limited, and leave many governments incapable of assisting in any cyber investigation or preventive or remedial actions that may be required within their territories. The 2009 Cyberspace Policy Review recommends that the U.S. "should increase resources and attention dedicated to conducting outreach and building foreign capacity. For example, the United States should accelerate efforts to help other countries build legal frameworks and capacity to fight cybercrime and continue efforts to promote cybersecurity practices and standards."[67] Providing this assistance through an international organization would encourage less developed states to join the treaty regime, thereby advancing the objective of creating a uniform and effective set of agreed and binding commitments.

3. Administrative Structure and Powers

The third set of issues that must be addressed in fashioning international agreements regarding transnational activities, including cyber security, are the administrative arrangements and allocations of authority to perform the functions agreed. If the parties to an arrangement agree only on issuing declarations of policy, no administrative structure would be required. The more complex and substantive the functions to be performed on the international level, the more pivotal the process of establishing an effective administrative structure with appropriate allocations of authority. Crafting a suitable structure for an international institution would be critical to its success. To the extent the outcomes desired are rules that are to be adopted as regulations in member states, some sort of governmental approval process will be required. Parties may be prepared to have certain functions performed internationally with one set of administrative arrangements but not with another.

Most IGOs that consider and promulgate rules tend to be structured along established patterns. Several have two representative bodies: a plenary body in which all member states are represented and which usually grants ultimate approval of major decisions; and a smaller, governing body of restricted membership that decides what projects to undertake and manages the process. The technical work of IGOs is often performed by committees of experts that fashion proposals for the IGO's consideration. A Secretariat performs the administrative services required. Voting within the bodies of IGOs varies both as to the body involved, and sometimes as to the issues being determined.[68]

[66]Stanford Draft, 15.
[67]2009 Cyberspace Policy Review, 21.
[68]See generally, Paul Szasz, "General Law-Making Processes," in *United Nations Legal Order*, vol. 1, ed. Oscar Schachter and Christopher C. Joyner (ASIL, Cambridge Press 1995), 48-58.

In fashioning an IGO, or a new assignment for an existing IGO, the treaty-making states are free to specify arrangements that suit their objectives. Important differences exist among IGOs, by design, with regard to the allocation of power to make and approve proposals. A variety of voting arrangements exist, even within the same type of representative body, depending on whether the issue involved is a matter of internal IGO administration (such as its budget), or a matter of external concern.

The potential differences in allocations of responsibilities and authority are especially significant in considering the possibility of international regulation of cyber systems in at least the following respects: (a) whether the current system of **private, professional control over cyber security standards** could continue in its essential composition and methodology; (b) how to ensure **speed and flexibility** in responding to security problems; and (c) what **allocation of powers** to establish among member states regarding agency proposals and internal agency operations.

(a). Maintaining Private, Professional Control over Cyber Security Standards

Perhaps the most fundamental of all issues in considering whether to support international agreements that allocate significant functions related to cyber systems to an IGO is who would participate in developing and approving standards, and how the IGO would relate to existing organizations such as the IETF, ETSI, and ICANN. The current, dominant role of private individuals, entities, and companies in creating, managing, developing, and defending the cyber infrastructure is one of its defining features. The creation of an IGO need not—and in our view should not—entail a shift in the power to perform those functions from the private, volunteer and professional entities and forces that currently dominate cyber standard-setting, to international appointees who may lack the expertise and commitment that private groups have provided since the Internet was created. Such a shift would generate tremendous resistance, since it might place control of standard setting in persons with particular political allegiances inconsistent with universal access and technological progress. Great expertise has been developed regarding cyber threats and security, moreover, within existing private-sector entities, and the support and involvement of these experts would improve the prospect that policies and rules proposed internationally will reflect industry needs and professional opinion rather than political objectives and professionally inadequate conclusions.

Instead of a shift in power, the assignment to an IGO of authority over cyber-security issues could (and should) be fashioned so that it creates a complementary source of power to existing arrangements. An international treaty establishing a specialized agency to regulate cyber security can be fashioned in a manner that preserves private sector influence over the development of cyber system rules. Many multilateral treaty regimes convey substantial influence—amounting in some instances to effective control of key issues—to private sector representatives or entities. The established method for dealing with subject matter that requires "a great deal of technical knowledge" is to grant authority to committees of private-sector experts to fashion technical standards.[69] In ICAO, for example, the 33 member Council is empowered to adopt standards and practices, but these standards and practices must first be considered and recommended to the Council by the Air Navigation Commission (Chicago Convention, Art. 56), a body of fifteen persons with "suitable qualifications and experience in the science and practice of aeronautics" appointed by the Council from nominees of Member States. The ITU operates similarly "with heavy reliance on private-sector expertise and involvement,"[70] though its current internal structure provides no guaranty of professional control over the content of the standards the technical committees propose.

The current standard-setting processes for the cyber world could be incorporated with necessary modifications into an international legal regime assigned this responsibility. Entities such as the IETF, ETSI, OASIS, and ICANN could, for example, be made into or treated as technical committees whose approval of proposed standards is required as a prerequisite to their adoption. This change could not only preserve

---

[69]Szasz, 53.
[70]Stanford Draft, 14-15.

the current advantages of a private, professional standard-setting regime, it could also, as explained above, enhance its effectiveness. That current privately developed standards are voluntary serves important interests; but in cases related to security and the migration of the core infrastructure to new standards, such as IPv6, an international agency empowered to review, approve, and establish a process for deploying proposed standards could be a useful complement to existing, expert standard-crafting bodies.

Considerable competition has developed in recent years, however, over which agency or agencies will be designated or formed to perform the leading roles associated with a cyber-security regime. The ITU in particular, as noted above, regards itself as having been invested with the role of sole facilitator on cyber security, a role it interprets expansively to include every major function likely to be performed in such a process. The U.S. and other potential parties to an international cyber-security agreement would have to weigh the ITU's possible advantages (existing, experienced, expert, non-duplication of functions, representative) and disadvantages (bureaucratic, political, unwieldy, inefficient, one state-one vote system, lack of guaranteed professional control over standards) in considering its potential cyber-security roles. The ITU and its supporters have not, however, been waiting for the U.S. or any other particular state to make up its mind on how to structure an international cyber-security regime. It will be difficult at this point, therefore, to find a formula for protecting established, privately dominated processes that work well, within a new regime that is essentially governmental and in danger of being subject to politically driven influences.

One significant development over the last several years lends support to the possible preservation of authority for standard setting in private and professional hands. While the Internet Society, the IETF, and ICANN were quite naturally originally dominated by U.S. members and influence, they have become increasingly international entities. Further changes to advance this process without compromising high-quality outcomes could be negotiated, including conceivably the reallocation of "control" the U.S. government has claimed but does not exercise over the authoritative "root" server for domain names and numbering.[71] In addition, highly competent and effective, non-US international standard-setting bodies have become established and represent broad segments of the private sector while also including government participants. Treating these entities as the expert committees on which an agency such as the ITU would be committed to depend could provide a basis for preserving current advantages while expanding the role of other states to an extent consistent with analogous regimes. While the one-state, one-vote formula could be retained for existing functions of an organization such as the ITU, for example, other voting rules could be devised for the IGO's new functions, such as an alternative voting formula for the approval of "soft law" rules, with the usual opt-out option. The possible arrangements that could be developed can only be known through an actual negotiating effort, and further delay in undertaking one is likely to narrow remaining options.[72]

(b). Speed and Flexibility

States can, in fashioning an international agreement, take into account the special needs and characteristics of the activities to be affected. Most specialized agencies of the UN proceed with their work at a slow pace. In some areas, however, speed is essential, and deadlines must be met for the activity to achieve its

[71]Goldsmith and Wu treat the "root" server issue as fundamental. See discussion in Who Controls the Internet, pp. 170-72. The U.S. has responded to complaints on this issue from the EU by establishing the Internet Governance Forum in which states debate and recommend Internet policy issues; it should, if necessary, also consider arrangements that would enable it to share with other states its largely theoretical "ultimate" authority over the process in such a manner that enables it to prevent changes that are unacceptable, as is the case with regard to substantive matters considered by the Security Council.

[72]Opposition is intense to any negotiation that might result in the U.S. agreeing to an ITU role in cyber security. A recent article by Robert M. McDowell, a Commissioner of the Federal Communications Commission condemns the FCC proposal to regulate broadband Internet access services under laws written for "monopoly phone companies" as opening the door to ITU ambitions to regulate the Web. He states: "The best way to keep the Internet open, operating and growing is to maintain the current model." Yet, he also acknowledges that international support for ITU jurisdiction over at least parts of the Internet may be beyond the power of the U.S. to prevent, since "Unlike at the U.N. Security Council, the U.S. has no veto power at the ITU . . . ." Wall St. J., July 23, 2010, p. A17.

intended purpose. For example, information about the discovery of a dangerous infection in a particular area must be conveyed and utilized by health authorities there and throughout the world as quickly as possible, and WHO requirements call for the immediate transfer of such information.[73] A threat to an aircraft in international air space must be dealt with quickly enough to prevent it from being realized.

Care is also taken by some IGOs to ensure that international rules or other actions establish objectives rather than specify the means for achieving them. ICAO, for example, does not require that every party use the same type of equipment to track aircraft or perform some other agreed function; it requires only that each party adopt some method that enables it to perform its agreed function in a satisfactory manner. Similarly, the IMO requires vessels to be able to perform certain activities; it does not normally mandate the purchase of specified equipment or insist upon a particular technology for satisfying those purposes.[74]

Preserving the already limited ability of states to act swiftly and flexibly is particularly important in the cyber security area. The cyber sector is dynamic, with changes that often are faster than expected and impossible to predict. National planners should, if possible, use any international arrangements they negotiate to improve response times to attacks and other threats, perhaps by establishing separate units of politically unaffiliated experts assigned to deal with emergencies. Cyber threats, and their potential defenses, also evolve in ways that are impossible fully to anticipate, and measures adopted to deal with threats sometimes have adverse consequences requiring adjustments. To deal with this problem, international cyber security norms and standards established by declaration, by treaty, or through rules, should be expressed in terms of the results sought, rather than as mandating the use of specific technologies or procedures. The ITU is aware of this potential problem, and has indicated that its proposals will avoid rigid requirements likely soon to be outdated. Preserving the current, private sector control mechanisms for cyber security would help to ensure that these objectives are achieved.

(c). Allocation of Powers

The allocation of powers generally adopted for IGOs could be an appropriate starting point for negotiators in fashioning an entity to perform the functions contemplated in a cyber security agreement. If, for example, the parties agree to continue using the IETF and other private, professional entities as the source of technical cyber security proposals, effective protection would thereby exist against political or technically ill-advised initiatives. Approval of the products of such expert deliberations, by a body backed by governmental authority, on the other hand, is an entirely appropriate political prerequisite for such initiatives to obtain the degree of legal authority agreed upon by the parties. (Some protective mechanism may be required to prevent modifications by the representative entities that do not meet the approval of the technical committee that develops them.) Paul Szasz explained why this mix of power allocation may be optimal:

> The object here is to make certain that any instruments developed will be both technically correct and politically tolerable. This combination may be attained by assigning the task of formulation to a carefully composed expert organ, and having the latter's work vetoed [i.e., reviewed] by a strictly representative one, which may lack technical competence but can make sure that procedures followed at the expert level were satisfactory. These experts would also ensure that there are no major subjective obstacles for any significant state or group of states in the proposed norms.[75]

If it is impossible satisfactorily to integrate existing, private standard-setting bodies into a system within an IGO, it may be preferable to maintain their separate status, counting on their expertise and

---

[73]World Health Assembly, "Global health security: epidemic alert and response," Resolution WHA54.14, Fifty Fourth World Health Assembly, May 21, 2001.

[74]See Key Principles of IMO's Technical Co-Operation Programme in "IMO and Technical Co-Operation in the 2000s," *IMO Resolution A.901(21),* November 25, 1999.

[75]Szasz, 95.

influence with users to lead the agency to utilize and integrate the privately created standards into agency approved rules and options. In that event, however, the IGO with its separate, expert committees, bureaucratic ambitions, and likely political agenda, could resist privately developed proposals in favor of its own priorities, triggering competitive actions that become an obstacle to continued, technical progress.

V. DIFFICULTIES IN NEGOTIATING INTERNATIONAL AGREEMENTS

Any effort to secure a formal international agreement inevitably entails difficulties and costs, some predictable but others impossible to anticipate. Agreements that are declarations of policy and include no formal commitments pose few problems. But the more formal and inclusive the agreement sought, the greater the uncertainties. Informal declarations of policy may be useful in some situations. But formal and universal commitments are sometimes essential for an agreement to achieve its purposes. Formal commitments to prohibit and punish cyberattacks, to cooperate in prosecuting attackers and criminals, and to adopt agreed measures to enhance safety, would hold more promise of real results than mere verbal pronouncements.

Though more valuable than informal declarations, multilateral agreements providing universal coverage are difficult and time consuming to negotiate, and ultimately provide no assurance that all signatories will abide by their commitments. Conventions related to air and sea terrorism, genocide, and torture have obtained virtually universal agreement from states, but even these fundamental obligations are sometimes violated by parties and high ranking officials. Such agreements are nonetheless made, with full awareness of their imperfections, because of their expected benefits.

The process of securing international agreement on the many controversial issues associated with cyber security is certain to be complex, with uncertain outcomes on some possibly critical issues. Multilateral efforts that the U.S. originally supported concerning climate change, land mines, and an international criminal court resulted in treaties that the U.S. has refused to ratify. Other states have been unwilling to join agreements that the U.S. finds acceptable, notably the CEC. Efforts to extend the reach of a multilateral cyber security agreement to areas of activity where no true international consensus exists seem especially likely to do more harm than good.

The potential costs and uncertainties in securing international agreements, and particularly of utilizing UN mechanisms, can be limited through procedural measures and careful planning. Bilateral and informal arrangements could be used to build toward a broader set of understandings sufficient to justify attempting to create a more conventional, multilateral agreement. Preparatory work with key states should enable participants to identify areas of activity related to cyber security that should be excluded from the negotiating process for reasons identified in this paper, or put on a separate track. Methodical consideration should be given to each type of measure that could be helpful in the development of a more secure cyber infrastructure, keeping in mind that it is unrealistic to identify specific solutions to problems during the negotiating process and that such efforts must be left to the entities the parties agree should be entrusted to implement their policies. The willingness of states—and especially of the U.S.—to accept any significant degree of international, governmental control over cyber security standards and practices will depend on the administrative structures established to exercise the authority conferred.

VI. CONCLUSION

Increased interest in resorting to international cooperation and agreements to enhance cyber security presents a potentially useful opportunity if it is carefully considered and exploited. The areas of cyber activity over which international agreements are most likely to contribute to cyber security must be identified, and they are necessarily those subjects on which the U.S. and other states are prepared to adopt objectives and policies applicable to their own conduct. Cyber warfare (with important exceptions based on existing international law norms), cyber intelligence collection, and content regulation or standard setting that restrict political speech or limit privacy or human rights, are subjects on which states have conflicting interests, objectives, and policies. On the other hand, cyber infrastructure security seems an area in which all states have strong and consistent interests that they may be prepared to advance through international cooperation and agreements.

Competition over which groups should control the Internet and other cyber systems has long existed. A former battleground for influence was between private groups and the U.S. government, "where over time a form of technocratic self-governance has emerged under the ultimate guarantees provided by the U.S. government."[76] A new and more challenging competition has emerged, however, as states and IGOs seek to establish roles for themselves in a process that Goldsmith and Wu have called "the beginning of a technological version of the cold war, with each side pushing its own vision of the Internet's future."[77] The competition will be resolved either through negotiation or through various forms of conflict likely to be costly and with uncertain results.

In our view, the potential of cyber systems will be most effectively realized by continuing to enable— and indeed enhancing the authority of—an essentially international, diverse, specialized, private and professional set of entities over the technical aspects of the Internet and other, publicly utilized systems. This outcome may, in fact, be more likely through international negotiation and agreement than by continuing a policy of shunning such engagement and allowing the growing competition over power to continue. In the process, the U.S. and other states could enhance security in several areas of cyber activities by authorizing an IGO to perform the many, useful roles such institutions have performed in other areas of transnational activities, while providing governmental backing for rules proposed by the private, professional groups that have made this area of transnational activity so economically productive and socially transformative.

[76]Goldsmith & Wu, 182.
[77]Id. 184.

The Council of Europe Convention on Cybercrime

Michael A. Vatis

Steptoe & Johnson LLP

I. BACKGROUND

The Convention on Cybercrime is an international treaty that seeks to harmonize national laws on cybercrime,[1] improve national capabilities for investigating such crimes, and increase cooperation on investigations.[2] The Convention was drafted by the Council of Europe (COE) in Strasbourg, France.[3] In addition to COE Member states, Canada, Japan, South Africa, and the United States participated in the negotiation of the Convention as observers.[4] The U.S., despite its official "observer" status, played an especially influential role, in part because it had more experience than other countries in addressing cybercrime and entered the process with well-formulated positions.[5]

---

[1] By "cybercrime" I mean those computer-related offenses specifically prescribed by the Convention, as discussed below in Part II.A.

[2] The Convention is available on the website of the Council of Europe at http://conventions.coe.int/Treaty/en/Treaties/Html/185.htm; accessed July 30, 2010.

[3] The Council of Europe comprises 47 member States, including all 27 members of the European Union (Austria, Belgium, Bulgaria, Cyprus, Czech Republic, Denmark, Estonia, Finland, France, Germany, Greece, Hungary, Ireland, Italy, Latvia, Lithuania, Luxembourg, Malta, Netherlands, Poland, Portugal, Romania, Slovakia, Slovenia, Spain, Sweden, and the United Kingdom) plus Albania, Andorra, Armenia, Azerbaijan, Bosnia and Herzegovina, Croatia, Georgia, Iceland, Liechtenstein, Moldova, Monaco, Montenegro, Norway, Russia, San Marino, Serbia, Switzerland, The Former Yugoslav Republic of Macedonia, Turkey, and Ukraine. *See* Council of Europe website, available at http://www.coe.int/aboutCoe/index.asp?page=47pays1europe&l=en; accessed June 5, 2010. The COE was established in 1949 primarily as a forum to uphold and strengthen human rights, and to promote democracy and the rule of law in Europe. Over the years, the CoE has been the negotiating forum for a number of conventions on criminal matters in which the United States has participated. Non-European states may also participate in activities of the COE as observers.

[4] *See* Convention on Cybercrime, Explanatory Note ¶ 304, available at http://conventions.coe.int/Treaty/EN/Reports/Html/185.htm; accessed June 6, 2010. Other states that have been invited to accede to the Convention, but have not yet signed or ratified it, are Chile, Costa Rica, the Dominican Republic, Mexico, and the Philippines. *See* Council of Europe website, available at http://conventions.coe.int/Treaty/Commun/ChercheSig.asp?NT=185&CM=8&DF=02/06/2010&CL=ENG; accessed June 6, 2010.

[5] *See, e.g.,* Computer Crime and Intellectual Property Section, U.S. Department of Justice, *Council of Europe Convention on Cybercrime Frequently Asked Questions and Answers,* available at http://www.cybercrime.gov/COEFAQs.htm#QA2; accessed June 7, 2010 ("The United States, represented by the Departments of Justice, State and Commerce, in close consultation with other U.S. government agencies and interested private parties, actively participated in the negotiations in both the drafting and plenary sessions, working closely with both CoE and non-CoE member States. Because the provisions in the Convention were generally adopted by consensus both in the drafting and plenary groups, rather than by member State vote, the United States had a real

One critical, but often overlooked, aspect of the Convention is that many of its procedural provisions are not limited to cybercrimes. Rather, they extend to *any* crimes for which it is necessary to collect evidence "in electronic form."[6] Thus, the Convention obliges ratifying states to create laws allowing law enforcement to search and seize computers and "computer data," engage in wiretapping, and to obtain real-time and stored communications data, whether or not the crime under investigation is a cybercrime.[7] In many ways, then the "Convention on Cybercrime" is a misnomer—or is at least a misleadingly narrow description of the Convention's substance.

The origins of the Convention date back to November 1996, when the European Committee on Crime Problems (CDPC) recommended that the COE set up an experts committee on cybercrime.[8] From the beginning, the CDPC recognized that "[t]he trans-border character of [cyber-space] offences, e.g. when committed through the Internet, is in conflict with the territoriality of national law enforcement authorities."[9] Accordingly, the CDPC opined then, "a concerted international effort is needed to deal with such" crimes, and "only a binding international instrument can ensure the necessary efficiency in the fight against these new phenomena."[10]

Following the CDPC's advice, the COE Committee of Ministers, in February 1997, established the "the Committee of Experts on Crime in Cyber-space."[11] The Committee of Experts' charge was to examine the following subjects and to draft a "binding legal instrument" addressing them, "as far as possible"

- "cyber-space offences, in particular those committed through the use of telecommunication networks, e.g. the Internet, such as illegal money transactions, offering illegal services, violation of copyright, as well as those which violate human dignity and the protection of minors";
- "other substantive criminal law issues where a common approach may be necessary for the purposes of international co-operation such as definitions, sanctions and responsibility of the actors in cyber-space, including Internet service providers";

---

voice in the drafting process."); J. Martin, U.S. Department of Justice, *The United States Experience* 1 (November 19, 2001) (The U.S. participated in negotiations in part "because we believed that given our long history with cyber crime, and our role in the development of networked communications systems, we could make valuable contributions to the negotiations."); ibid. at 5 ("During the negotiations, the U.S. delegation met frequently with representatives from industry and privacy groups, as well as interested individuals, to listen to their concerns and encourage an open process.").

The U.S. strongly supported inclusion in the Convention of the provisions to "create expedited channels of communication between countries and to reduce the number of hurdles required to exchange information," including: the 24/7 points-of-contact network; the requirements to preserve evidence without requiring dual criminality; and the requirement of expedited cooperation "not only for crimes committed by and against computers, but also for any crime involving electronic evidence." Ibid. at 4. The U.S. also "opposed measures that would permit countries to place untenable conditions on the exchange of information between law enforcement agencies, . . . proposals that would have required industry to deploy new technologies to assist law enforcement, or to routinely collect and retain data for long periods of time[,] . . . definitions of offense that were too general, thereby inadvertently creating criminal liability for legitimate commercial activities[,] . . . and measures that require the private sector to destroy critical evidence." Ibid. at 4-5. In addition, the U.S. sought the inclusion of the "federal clause," whereby Parties "may reserve the right to assume obligations under Chapter II of this Convention consistent with its fundamental principles governing the relationship between its central government and constituent States or other similar territorial entities," thus making clear that such constituent States or territories are not each bound by the Convention. Art. 41. *See* J. Martin, *supra*, at 6.

[6]*See* Convention on Cybercrime, Art. 14(2)(c). *See also* Convention on Cybercrime, Explanatory Note ¶ 141 ("The Convention makes it explicit that Parties should incorporate into their laws the possibility that information contained in digital or other electronic form can be used as evidence before a court in criminal proceedings, irrespective of the nature of the criminal offence that is prosecuted.").

[7]*See* Convention on Cybercrime, Arts. 18-21.

[8]*See* Convention on Cybercrime, Explanatory Report, ¶ 7. The CDPC is a COE committee that advises the COE's Committee of Ministers on crime problems. The Committee of Ministers comprises the Foreign Ministers of all the COE's Member states, and acts as the COE's decision-making body. *See* Council of Europe website, available at http://www.coe.int/t/cm/aboutCM_en.asp#P25_338; accessed June 6, 2010.

[9]Convention on Cybercrime, Explanatory Report, ¶ 8.

[10]Ibid., ¶ 9.

[11]*See* ibid., ¶ 12.

- "the use, including the possibility of transborder use, and the applicability of coercive powers in a technological environment, e.g. interception of telecommunications and electronic surveillance of information networks, e.g. via the Internet, search and seizure in information-processing systems (including Internet sites), rendering illegal material inaccessible and requiring service providers to comply with special obligations, taking into account the problems caused by particular measures of information security, e.g. encryption";
- "the question of jurisdiction in relation to information technology offences, e.g. to determine the place where the offence was committed (*locus delicti*) and which law should accordingly apply, including the problem of *ne bis idem* in the case of multiple jurisdictions and the question how to solve positive jurisdiction conflicts and how to avoid negative jurisdiction conflicts"; and
- "questions of international co-operation in the investigation of cyber-space offences. . . ."[12]

The Committee of Experts negotiated and drafted the text of the Convention (and its Explanatory Report) over the next four years, culminating in the final draft that was approved by the CDPC in June 2001 and then adopted by the COE's Committee of Ministers on November 8, 2001. The Convention was then submitted for signature by Member states and observer states in Budapest, Hungary on November 23, 2001.[13]

The Convention, by its own terms, would not take force until five nations had ratified it, including three COE Member states.[14] That occurred on July 1, 2004, after Lithuania had ratified it.[15] (Albania, Croatia, Estonia, and Hungary had already ratified the Convention, in that order.)[16] As of June 5, 2010, 29 nations have ratified the Convention.[17] Seventeen other states have signed the Convention but not ratified it.[18] The United States signed the treaty on November 23, 2001, and ratified it on September 29, 2006.[19] The Convention entered into force in the U.S. on January 1, 2007.[20]

The Convention is open to signature and ratification by any COE member states and any non-Member states that "have participated in its elaboration."[21] Additional states may be invited by the

---

[12] Ibid., ¶ 11.

[13] *See* Council of Europe website, available at http://conventions.coe.int/Treaty/Commun/QueVoulezVous.asp?NT=185&CM=8&DF=02/06/2010&CL=ENG; accessed June 5, 2010.

[14] *See* Convention on Cybercrime, Art. 36.

[15] *See* COE, Convention on Cybercrime website, available at http://conventions.coe.int/Treaty/Commun/ChercheSig.asp?NT=185&CM=8&DF=02/06/2010&CL=ENG; accessed June 5, 2010.

[16] *See* ibid.

[17] The states that have ratified the Convention as of June 5, 2010, are: Member states Albania, Armenia, Azerbaijan, Bosnia and Herzegovina, Bulgaria, Croatia, Cyprus, Denmark, Estonia, Finland, France, Germany, Hungary, Iceland, Italy, Latvia, Lithuania, Moldova, Montenegro, Netherlands, Norway, Portugal, Romania, Serbia, Slovakia, Slovenia, The Former Yugoslav Republic of Macedonia, and Ukraine, and non-Member state the United States of America. *See* ibid.

[18] The states that have signed but not yet ratified the convention are: Member states Austria, Belgium, Czech Republic, Georgia, Greece, Ireland, Liechtenstein, Luxembourg, Malta, Poland, Spain, Sweden, and Switzerland, and United Kingdom, and participating non-Member states Canada, Japan, and South Africa. Ibid. Five Member states (Andorra, Monaco, Russia, San Marino, and Turkey) and five non-Member states (Chile, Costa Rica, Dominican Republic, Mexico, and Philippines) have not signed the Convention. *See* ibid.

[19] *See* ibid. The United States made a number of technical declarations and reservations in its instrument of ratification. The declarations and reservations of all the ratifying states, including the United States, can be found on the COE, Convention of Cybercrime website, available at http://conventions.coe.int/Treaty/Commun/ListeDeclarations.asp?NT=185&CM=8&DF=02/06/2010&CL=ENG&VL=1; accessed July 30, 2010.

[20] *See* COE, Convention on Cybercrime website, available at http://conventions.coe.int/Treaty/Commun/ChercheSig.asp?NT=185&CM=8&DF=02/06/2010&CL=ENG; accessed June 5, 2010. The U.S. Department of Justice and the U.S. Senate took the position that the Convention required no implementing legislation in the United States, since "[a]n existing body of federal laws will suffice to implement the obligations of the Convention, although some minor reservations and declarations are needed." U.S. Sen., Exec. Rpt. 109-6, *Council of Europe Convention on Cybercrime (Treaty Doc. 108-11)* at 6 (November 8, 2005). *See also* Statement of Attorney General Alberto R. Gonzales on the Passage of the Cybercrime Convention (August 4, 2006) ("The Convention is in full accord with all U.S. constitutional protections, such as free speech and other civil liberties, and will require no change to U.S. laws."), available at http://www.justice.gov/opa/pr/2006/August/06_ag_499.html; accessed June 7, 2010.

[21] *See* Convention on Cybercrime, Art. 36.

COE's Committee of Ministers to accede to the Convention, after the Committee consults with and obtains the unanimous consent of "the Contracting States to the Convention."[22]

On November 7, 2002, the Committee of Ministers adopted the Additional Protocol to the Convention on Cybercrime.[23] The Additional Protocol requires ratifying Member States to pass laws criminalizing "acts of racist or xenophobic nature committed through computer networks." This includes the dissemination of racist or xenophobic material, the making of racist or xenophobic threats or insults, and the denial of the Holocaust and other genocides. It also commits ratifying nations to extend to these crimes the investigative capabilities and procedures created pursuant to the main Convention.

The Additional Protocol opened for signature on January 28, 2003. It came into force on March 1, 2006, after 5 states had ratified it.[24] As of June 5, 2010, 17 states have ratified the Additional Protocol.[25] Another 17 nations have signed but not ratified it.[26] The United States participated in the drafting of the protocol but did not sign it because of concerns that it was inconsistent with guarantees of the United States Constitution.[27] Ratification of the main Convention does not oblige a ratifying state to take any action under the Additional Protocol.

II. THE CONVENTION'S PROVISIONS

The Convention states as its goal the "protection of society against cybercrime" by "providing for the criminalisation of such conduct . . . and the adoption of powers sufficient for effectively combating such criminal offences, by facilitating their detection, investigation and prosecution at both the domestic and international levels and by providing arrangements for fast and reliable international co-operation."[28] The Convention is divided into three principal parts. The first part addresses the substantive cybercrime offenses that each ratifying state is obliged to adopt in its national law. The second part concerns investigative procedures the states must implement. And the third part relates to mechanisms to enhance international cooperation.

A. Cybercrime Offenses

The Convention requires Parties (*i.e.*, ratifying states) to "adopt such legislative and other measures as may be necessary to establish as criminal offences under its domestic law, when committed intentionally"[29]:

---

[22]*See* ibid., Art. 37.

[23]The Additional Protocol is available at http://conventions.coe.int/Treaty/EN/Treaties/html/189.htm; accessed June 6, 2010. The Explanatory Report accompanying the Additional Protocol is available at http://conventions.coe.int/Treaty/EN/Reports/Html/189.htm; accessed June 6, 2010.

[24]*See* COE, Convention on Cybercrime website, available at http://conventions.coe.int/Treaty/Commun/ChercheSig.asp?NT=189&CM=8&DF=05/06/2010&CL=ENG; accessed June 5, 2010.

[25]The following Member states have ratified the Additional Protocol: Albania, Armenia, Bosnia and Herzegovina, Croatia, Cyprus, Denmark, France, Latvia, Lithuania, Montenegro, Norway, Portugal, Romania, Serbia, Slovenia, The Former Yugoslav Republic of Macedonia, and Ukraine. *See* ibid.

[26]The 17 nations that have signed but not ratified the Additional Protocol are: Member states Austria, Belgium, Estonia, Finland, Germany, Greece, Iceland, Liechtenstein, Luxembourg, Malta, Moldova, Netherlands, Poland, Sweden, and Switzerland, and participating non-Member states Canada and South Africa. Seventeen participating states have not signed the Additional Protocol: Member states Andorra, Azerbaijan, Bulgaria, Czech Republic, Georgia, Hungary, Ireland, Italy, Monaco, Russia, San Marino, Slovakia, Spain, Turkey, and United Kingdom, and participating non-Member states Japan and the United States of America. *See* ibid.

[27]*See* U.S. Department of Justice, Computer Crime and Intellectual Property Section, *Council of Europe Convention on Cybercrime, Frequently Asked Questions and Answers*, available at http://www.justice.gov/criminal/cybercrime/COEFAQs.htm; accessed June 5, 2010.

[28]Convention on Cybercrime, Preamble.

[29]The Convention also obligates Parties to criminalize intentional aiding and abetting of the offenses described in the text. *See* ibid., Art. 11. In addition, the Convention requires Parties to enact measures holding corporations criminally, civilly, or administratively liable for any listed offenses committed by an individual "who has a leading position" in the corporation and commits

- "the access to the whole or any part of a computer system without right"[30];
- "the interception without right, made by technical means, of non-public transmissions of computer data to, from or within a computer system, including electromagnetic emissions from a computer system carrying such computer data"[31];
- "the damaging, deletion, deterioration, alteration or suppression of computer data without right"[32];
- "the serious hindering without right of the functioning of a computer system by inputting, transmitting, damaging, deleting, deteriorating, altering or suppressing computer data"[33];
- "the production, sale, procurement for use, import, distribution or otherwise making available of," or the possession of: "a device, including a computer program, designed or adapted primarily for the purpose of committing any of the offences [described above]," or "a computer password, access code, or similar data by which the whole or any part of a computer system is capable of being accessed," where the action is taken "without right" and "with intent that it be used for the purpose of committing any of the offences [described above]"[34];
- "the input, alteration, deletion, or suppression of computer data, resulting in inauthentic data with the intent that it be considered or acted upon for legal purposes as if it were authentic," when done "without right"[35];
- "the causing of a loss of property to another person by . . . any input, alteration, deletion or suppression of computer data . . . [or] any interference with the functioning of a computer system, with fraudulent or dishonest intent of procuring, without right, an economic benefit for oneself or for another person," when done "without right"[36];
- the production for the purpose of distribution, the offering or making available; the distribution or transmission, the procurement, or the possession of child pornography on or through a computer system, when done "without right."[37]

---

the offense for the benefit of the corporation. *See* ibid., Art. 12(1). Parties must also provide for the liability of a corporation where "the lack of supervision or control" by a person with "a leading position" in the corporation allows another person under the authority of the corporation to commit one of the listed offenses. *See* ibid., Art. 12(2).

[30]Ibid., Art. 2. However, "[a] Party may require that the offence be committed by infringing security measures, with the intent of obtaining computer data or other dishonest intent, or in relation to a computer system that is connected to another computer system." Ibid.

The term "without right" is meant to "refer to conduct undertaken without authority (whether legislative, executive, administrative, judicial, contractual or consensual) or conduct that is otherwise not covered by established legal defences, excuses, justifications or relevant principles under domestic law." Convention on Cybercrime, Explanatory Report ¶ 38. In particular, the Convention "leaves unaffected conduct undertaken pursuant to lawful government authority (for example, where the Party's government acts to maintain public order, protect national security or investigate criminal offences). Furthermore, legitimate and common activities inherent in the design of networks, or legitimate and common operating or commercial practices should not be criminalised." Ibid.

[31]Ibid., Art. 3. However, "[a] Party may require that the offence be committed with dishonest intent, or in relation to a computer system that is connected to another computer system." Ibid.

[32]Ibid., Art. 4. However, "[a] Party may reserve the right to require that the conduct . . . result in serious harm." Ibid.

[33]Ibid., Art. 5.

[34]Ibid., Art. 6(1). However, "[a] Party may require by law that a number of such items be possessed before criminal liability attaches" on the basis of possession of one of the listed items. Ibid., Art. 6(1)(b). In addition, a Party may reserve the right not to enact into law any of the offenses described in this Article other than those concerning "the sale, distribution or otherwise making available of a computer password, access code, or similar data by which the whole or any part of a computer system is capable of being accessed." Ibid., Art. 6(3).

[35]Ibid., Art. 7.

[36]Ibid., Art. 8.

[37]Ibid., Art. 9. "Child pornography" is defined as including "pornographic material that visually depicts: a) a minor engaged in sexually explicit conduct; b) a person appearing to be a minor engaged in sexually explicit conduct; or 3) realistic images representing a minor engaged in sexually explicit conduct." Ibid., Art 9(2). However, each Party may reserve the right not to criminalize all offenses concerning the procurement or possession of child pornography. Ibid., Art. 9(4). In addition, a Party may reserve the right not to criminalize the listed activities if they involve a person appearing to be a minor engaging in sexually explicit conduct, or realistic images of a minor engaging in such conduct, if the material does not actually involve a minor. Ibid.

The Convention also requires Parties to criminalize the "willful" infringement of copyright and related rights when done "on a commercial scale and by means of a computer system."[38] In addition, Parties must ensure that all of the listed offenses "are punishable by effective, proportionate and dissuasive sanctions, which include deprivation of liberty."[39]

B. Investigative Procedures

The second principal part of the Convention requires Parties to enact certain procedural mechanisms and procedures to facilitate the investigation of cybercrimes or any crimes committed with a computer or for which evidence may be found in "electronic form."[40] The provisions in this part require states to "adopt such legislative and other measures as may be necessary to:

- "enable its competent authorities to order or similarly obtain the expeditious preservation of specified computer data, including traffic data, that has been stored by means of a computer system," in order to give authorities the opportunity to seek disclosure of the data[41];
- with respect to preserved traffic data about a communication, "ensure the expeditious disclosure to the Party's competent authority...of a sufficient amount of traffic data to enable the Party to identify the service providers and the path through which the communication was transmitted"[42];
- empower its authorities to order "a person in its territory" to produce "specified computer data in that person's possession or control,"[43] and to order "a service provider offering its services in the territory of the Party" to produce "subscriber information relating to such services"[44];

---

[38]Ibid., Art. 10. A Party may reserve the right, however, not to criminalize such acts "in limited circumstances," as long as "other effective remedies are available" and the reservation does not derogate from the Party's obligations under other international agreements. Ibid., Art. 10(3). Copyright infringement was included in the Convention because "copyright infringements are one of the most widespread forms of computer- or computer-related crime and its escalation is causing international concern." Convention on Cybercrime, Explanatory Report ¶ 35.

[39]Convention on Cybercrime, Art. 13(1). For corporations, such punishment must include "monetary sanctions." See ibid., Art. 13(2).

[40]Specifically, the Convention requires that these procedures be available to investigate the substantive offenses described in the Convention, "other criminal offences committed by means of a computer system," and "the collection of evidence in electronic form" of any type of criminal offense. Ibid., Art. 14(2).

The Convention also requires that these mechanisms and procedures include "conditions and safeguards" necessary "for the protection of human rights and liberties," including "judicial or other independent supervision, grounds justifying application, and limitation of the scope and the duration of such power or procedure." Ibid., Art. 15.

[41]Ibid. Art. 16. If a Party implements this requirement "by means of an order to a person to preserve specified stored computer data in the person's possession or control," such order shall require preservation of the data "as long as necessary, up to a maximum of ninety days," with the preservation period subject to renewal. Ibid., Art. 16. Parties must also ensure that the person directed to preserve the data keeps the undertaking confidential. See ibid., Art. 16.

[42]Ibid., Art. 17.

[43]Ibid., Art. 18. The drafters of the Convention intended that data within a person's "possession or control" not be limited to data that is stored in the territory of the state. "The term 'possession or control' refers to physical possession of the data concerned in the ordering Party's territory, and situations in which the data to be produced is outside of the person's physical possession but the person can nonetheless freely control production of the data from within the ordering Party's territory (for example, subject to applicable privileges, a person who is served with a production order for information stored in his or her account by means of a remote online storage service, must produce such information). At the same time, a mere technical ability to access remotely stored data (e.g. the ability of a user to access through a network link remotely stored data not within his or her legitimate control) does not necessarily constitute 'control' within the meaning of this provision." Convention on Cybercrime, Explanatory Note ¶ 173.

[44] Convention on Cybercrime, Art. 18. "Subscriber information" means "subscriber information" means any information held by a service provider "relating to subscribers of its services other than traffic or content data," and which relates to "the type of communication service used" and technical aspects of the service; the "period of service"; "the subscriber's identity," address, "telephone and other access number"; "billing and payment information"; and "any other information on the site of the installation of communication equipment, available on the basis of the service agreement or arrangement." Ibid., Art. 18(3).

- "empower its competent authorities to search or similarly access" and to seize "a computer system" or a "computer-data storage medium" in its territory, and to search and seize data stored therein[45];
- empower its authorities to "collect or record through the application of technical means" on its territory, "traffic data, in real-time, associated with specified communications in its territory[46] transmitted by means of a computer system," or to "compel a service provider, within its existing technical capability,"[47] to do the same or to cooperate and assist the authorities' own collection or recording"[48];
- empower its authorities, in the case of "serious offences," to "collect or record through the application of technical means" on its territory "content data, in real-time, of specified communications in its territory transmitted by means of a computer system," or to "compel a service provider, within its existing technical capability," to do the same or to cooperate with the authorities' own collection or recording[49];
- establish jurisdiction over any of the substantive offenses set forth in the Convention that are committed in the state's territory[50]; and

---

[45]Ibid., Art. 19(1). Parties must also ensure that if their authorities search a computer system and then have reason to believe that the data they are seeking is stored in another system in the state's territory and that "such data is lawfully accessible from or available to the initial system," the authorities "shall be able to expeditiously extend the search . . . to the other system." Ibid., Art. 19(2). In addition, Parties must empower their authorities "to order any person who has knowledge about the functioning of the computer system or measures applied to protect the computer data therein to provide, as is reasonable, the necessary information, to enable the" search or seizure of the relevant computer systems or data. Ibid., Art. 19(4).

[46]The reference to "communications in its territory" (in the provisions dealing with collection of both traffic data and communications content) is meant to be expansive, and includes situations where one of the parties to a communication is in the state's territory, or where a computer through which the communication passes is in the territory. *See* Convention on Cybercrime, Explanatory Note ¶ 222 ("For the purposes of this Convention, it is understood that a communication is in a Party's territory if one of the communicating parties (human beings or computers) is located in the territory or if the computer or telecommunication equipment through which the communication passes is located on the territory.").

[47]The reference to a service provider's "existing technical capability" (in the provisions concerning both collection of traffic data and communications content) is intended to make clear that providers are not legally obliged to build or acquire the technical capability necessary to effectuate a collection order. "The article does not obligate service providers to ensure that they have the technical capability to undertake collections, recordings, co-operation or assistance. It does not require them to acquire or develop new equipment, hire expert support or engage in costly re-configuration of their systems. However, if their systems and personnel have the existing technical capability to provide such collection, recording, co-operation or assistance, the article would require them to take the necessary measures to engage such capability." Convention on Cybercrime, Explanatory Note ¶ 221.

[48]Convention on Cybercrime, Art. 20(1). A Party must also enact such measures as are necessary "to oblige a service provider to keep confidential the execution" of such power "and any information relating to it." Ibid., Art. 20(3). Note, however, that a Party may reserve the right to apply this authority only to the same "serious offenses" for which it authorizes real-time collection of communication content under Article 21. *See* ibid., Art. 14(3). It may also reserve the right not to apply this authority to communications on computers transmitted within a computer system that "is being operated for the benefit of a closed group of users" and "does not employ public communications networks and is not connected with another computer system." *See* ibid., Art. 14(2), (3).

[49]Ibid., Art. 21(1). A Party must also enact such measures as are necessary "to oblige a service provider to keep confidential the execution" of such power "and any information relating to it." Ibid., Art. 21(3).

[50]Ibid., Art. 22(1)). The Convention also calls on Parties to establish jurisdiction over cybercrimes committed "on board a ship flying the flag of that Party," "on board an aircraft registered under the laws of that Party," or "by one of its nationals, if the offence is punishable under criminal law where it was committed or if the offence is committed outside the territorial jurisdiction of any State." Ibid. However, Parties may reserve the right not to assert jurisdiction in such cases, or only in specific cases or circumstances. *See* ibid., Art. 22(2).

The Convention does not define what "committed in the state's territory" means. In the Explanatory Note accompanying the Convention, the drafters remark, "Each Party is required to punish the commission of crimes established in this Convention that are committed in its territory. For example, a Party would assert territorial jurisdiction if both the person attacking a computer system and the victim system are located within its territory, and where the computer system attacked is within its territory, even if the attacker is not." Convention on Cybercrime, Explanatory Note ¶ 233. The drafters' examples do not include—nor do they exclude—a situation where the computer system attacked is outside the state's territory but the attacker is within it. From the perspective of international cooperation, it is perhaps most critical that states extend their jurisdiction to cybercrimes that emanate from their states even if the effects are felt elsewhere, since those states will have the greatest ability to investigate the origin of the attack and to arrest the perpetrator.

- establish jurisdiction over any of the substantive offenses set forth in the Convention "in cases where an alleged offender is present in its territory and it does not extradite him or her to another Party, solely on the basis of his or her nationality, after a request for extradition," and where the offense is punishable in both states by deprivation of liberty for a maximum period of at least one year.[51]

C. International Cooperation

The third principal part of the Convention sets out mechanisms by which Parties to the convention will assist each other in investigating cybercrimes and other crimes involving electronic evidence. The Convention provides that Parties "shall co-operate with each other . . . to the widest extent possible for the purposes of investigations or proceedings concerning criminal offences related to computer systems and data, or for the collection of evidence in electronic form of a criminal offence."[52] However, this cooperation shall occur "through the application of relevant international instruments on international co-operation in criminal matters, arrangements agreed on the basis of uniform or reciprocal legislation, and domestic laws."[53] This suggests that cooperation may be limited or delayed if required by law or other arrangements. The specific cooperation measures are described below.

First, Parties must regard the substantive offenses set forth in the Convention as extraditable offenses, as long as the offense is punishable in both states by deprivation of liberty for a maximum period of at least one year, "or by a more severe penalty.[54] However, "[e]xtradition shall be subject to the conditions provided for by the law of the requested Party or by applicable extradition treaties, including the grounds on which the requested Party may refuse extradition."[55] If a Party refuses to extradite a person solely on the basis of his nationality, "or because the requested Party deems that it has jurisdiction over the offence," the requested Party must refer the case (if requested by the Party seeking extradition) to its own competent authorities "for the purpose of prosecution."[56] Such authorities "shall take their decision and conduct their investigations and proceedings in the same manner as for any other offence of a comparable nature."[57] But there is no requirement that the person actually be prosecuted. Rather, the Requested party must simply "report the final outcome to the requesting Party in due course."[58]

Second, Parties must "afford one another mutual assistance to the widest extent possible for the purpose of investigations or proceedings concerning criminal offences related to computer systems and data, or for the collection of evidence in electronic form of a criminal offence."[59] Parties must "accept and respond to" requests made by "expedited means of communication, including fax or email, to the extent

---

The U.S. delegation to the CDPC interpreted this provision of the Convention as calling for states to assert jurisdiction over cybercrimes committed by persons within their territory against computers outside their territory. *See* K. Harris, U.S. Department of Justice, *Jurisdiction and international cooperation provisions in the Convention* 2 (Nov. 20, 2001) (paper submitted to nations considering signing the Convention) ("Since sophisticated locally based cybercriminals may also target victims in other countries, the exercise of territorial jurisdiction also plays an important role in reducing international cybercrime."). It is worth noting, too, that the U.S. Department of Justice for many years took the position that the principal American "cybercrime" law, the Computer Fraud and Abuse Act (CFAA), 18 USC. § 1030 et seq., applied to cases in which the attacker was inside the United States but the victims were not. But this position was not explicitly embodied in the CFAA until 2001, when the definition of "protected computer" in the CFAA was amended by the USA PATRIOT Act, Pub. L. 107-56, § 814(d)(1), so that it included a computer "which is used in or affecting interstate or foreign commerce or communication, including a computer located outside the United States that is used in a manner that affects interstate or foreign commerce or communication of the United States." 18 USC. § 1030 (e)(2)(B).

[51]Convention on Cybercrime, Art. 22(3).

[52]Ibid., Art. 23.

[53]Ibid.

[54]*See* ibid., Art. 24(1)-(4).

[55]Ibid., Art. 24(5).

[56]Ibid., Art. 24(6).

[57]Ibid.

[58]Ibid.

[59]Ibid., Art. 25(1).

that such means provide appropriate levels of security and authentication," but may require "formal confirmation to follow."[60] However, Parties may refuse cooperation on any ground provided for under its domestic law "or by applicable mutual assistance treaties," except that a Party shall not exercise its right to refuse assistance in the case of cybercrimes "solely on the ground that the request concerns an offence which it considers a fiscal offence."[61]

Third, Parties may, to the extent permitted by their domestic laws, spontaneously forward to another Party information that it has uncovered that it thinks might assist the receiving party in investigating a cyber crime.[62] Before providing such information, the "providing Party may request that it be kept confidential or only used subject to conditions. . . . If the receiving Party accepts the information subject to the conditions, it shall be bound by them."[63]

The fourth set of mutual assistance provisions applies when two Parties do not have an existing mutual legal assistance treaty or some other formal arrangement between them (or when the Parties agree to apply the Convention provision in lieu of their existing arrangement).[64] The Convention requires each Party to "designate a central authority" responsible for sending, answering, or executing requests for mutual assistance.[65] The COE Secretary General shall keep an updated register of these central authorities.[66] Parties agree to execute requests "in accordance with the procedures specified by the requesting Party, except where incompatible with the law of the requested Party."[67] The Convention provides, however, that Parties may refuse assistance not only for reasons specified in their domestic law or in existing MLATs, but also on the ground that "the request concerns an offence which the requested Party considers a political offence or an offence connected with a political offence" or that "execution of the request is likely to prejudice its sovereignty, security, *ordre public* or other essential interests."[68] In addition, a "requested Party may make the supply of information or material in response to a request dependent on the condition that it is: a) kept confidential . . ., or b) not used for investigations or proceedings other than those stated in the request."[69]

Fifth, Parties must "take all appropriate measures to preserve [computer data] expeditiously" at the request of another, where such data is located in the requested Party's territory and the requesting party intends to follow up with a request to search, seize, or disclose that data.[70] Such data must be preserved

---

[60]Ibid., Art. 25(3).

[61]Ibid., Art. 25(4). In the Explanatory Note to the Convention, however, the drafters suggest that a Party's right to refuse cooperation is more limited than the text of the Convention suggests on its face. The Explanatory Note explains that certain provisions of the Convention must be implemented regardless of existing domestic laws or treaties, such as the obligation "to provide for the forms of co-operation set forth in the remaining articles of the Chapter (such as preservation, real time collection of data, search and seizure, and maintenance of a 24/7 network)." Convention on Cybercrime, Explanatory Note ¶ 258. Though the meaning of this statement is far from pellucid, it appears that Parties must implement "the forms of cooperation" required by the Convention, but they may refuse to actually cooperate if doing so would violate the terms of their domestic laws or existing treaties (or if non-cooperation is expressly allowed by some specific provision of the Convention, such as Article 27's reference to refusing to assist if executing a request would prejudice the requested State's sovereignty or security).

[62]*See* Convention on Cybercrime, Art. 26(1).

[63]Ibid., Art. 26(2).

[64]*See* ibid., Art. 27(1).

[65]*See* ibid., Art. 27(2). "In the event of urgency," however, "requests for mutual assistance...may be sent directly by judicial authorities of the requesting Party to such authorities of the requested Party," with a copy sent simultaneously to the requested Party's central authority through the central authority of the requesting Party. Ibid., Art. 27(9).

[66]Ibid., Art. 27(2).

[67]Ibid., Art. 27(3). In addition, "[t]he requesting Party may request that the requested Party keep confidential the fact of any request. . . . If the requested Party cannot comply with the request for confidentiality, it shall promptly inform the requesting Party, which shall then determine whether the request should nevertheless be executed." Ibid., Art. 27(8).

[68]Ibid., Art. 27(4). The requested Party may also "postpone action on a request if such action would prejudice criminal investigations or proceedings conducted by its authorities." Ibid., Art. 27(5).

[69]Ibid., Art. 28(2).

[70]Ibid., Art. 29(1), (3).

for at least sixty days.[71] A party may not refuse a preservation request in a case involving a cybercrime (*i.e.*, one of the substantive offenses set forth in the Convention) on the basis of "dual criminality"—*i.e.*, that the offense at issue is not an offense in the requesting state.[72] However, a requested Party may refuse a preservation request if it concerns an offense that "the requested Party considers a political offence or an offence connected with a political offence" or "the requested Party considers that execution of the request is likely to prejudice its sovereignty, security, *ordre public* or other essential interests."[73]

Sixth, a Party must respond to requests to search, seize, or disclose computer data located within its territory.[74] Notably, however, the Convention states that the requested Party shall respond "through the application of relevant international instruments on international co-operation in criminal matters, arrangements agreed on the basis of uniform or reciprocal legislation, and domestic laws."[75] This suggests that a response to a request to search, seize, or disclose data may be delayed or rejected where so required by relevant laws or arrangements.

Seventh, the Convention permits a Party, "without the authorisation of another Party," to "access or receive, through a computer system in its territory, stored computer data located in another Party, if the Party obtains the lawful and voluntary consent of the person who has the lawful authority to disclose the data to the Party through that computer system."[76] This means, for instance, that a law enforcement agency in Country A may remotely access a computer in country B if it obtains the consent of the owner of that data. Less clear is whether this authority extends to a situation where an LEA in Country A obtains a court order *requiring* the data owner (who may have an office in Country A and thus is susceptible to Country A's jurisdiction) to disclose the data or to allow the LEA to access the computer in Country B.

The issue of "unilateral" access to data stored in another country was controversial during the negotiations of the convention.[77] Apparently some states were in favor of allowing greater authority for unilateral action across borders to access computers and data, while others were opposed. The drafters settled on the two sorts of unilateral actions all could agree on—access to data with the consent of the

[71]*See* ibid., Art. 29(7). In addition, if, in the course of executing a preservation request, a requested Party "discovers that a service provider in another State was involved in the transmission of the communication," it must "expeditiously disclose to the requesting Party a sufficient amount of traffic data to identify that service provider and the path through which the communication was transmitted." Ibid., Art. 30(1). A requested Party may withhold such data only if the preservation request "concerns an offence which the requested Party considers a political offence or an offence connected with a political offence" or "the requested Party considers that execution of the request is likely to prejudice its sovereignty, security, *ordre public* or other essential interests." Ibid., Art. 30(2).

[72]*See* ibid., Art. 29(3). However, dual criminality may be a reason to reject a preservation request in cases involving other types of crimes. *See* ibid., Art. 29(4).

[73]Ibid., Art. 29(5).

[74]*See* ibid., Art. 31(1), (2). A Party must respond "on an expedited basis" when "there are grounds to believe that relevant data is particularly vulnerable to loss or modification;" or when relevant laws or arrangements otherwise permit expedited cooperation. Ibid., Art. 31(3).

[75]Ibid., Art. 31(2), citing Art. 23.

[76]Ibid., Art. 32. In addition, a Party may, "without the authorisation of another Party . . . access publicly available (open source) stored computer data, regardless of where the data is located geographically." Ibid.

[77]As the Explanatory Note to the Convention says: "The issue of when a Party is permitted to unilaterally access computer data stored in another Party without seeking mutual assistance was a question that the drafters of the Convention discussed at length. There was detailed consideration of instances in which it may be acceptable for States to act unilaterally and those in which it may not. The drafters ultimately determined that it was not yet possible to prepare a comprehensive, legally binding regime regulating this area. In part, this was due to a lack of concrete experience with such situations to date; and, in part, this was due to an understanding that the proper solution often turned on the precise circumstances of the individual case, thereby making it difficult to formulate general rules. Ultimately, the drafters decided to only set forth in Article 32 of the Convention situations in which all agreed that unilateral action is permissible. They agreed not to regulate other situations until such time as further experience has been gathered and further discussions may be held in light thereof. " Convention on Cybercrime, Explanatory Note ¶ 293. *See also* K. Harris, *supra*, at 6 ("The establishment of rules to permit direct, unilateral access in other cases proved elusive, and it was decided to wait until further experience has been gained before attempting to fix further rules in this area.").

data owner, and access to open source information.[78] However, the Explanatory Note to the Convention also makes a point of stating that other types of unilateral access "are neither authorized, nor precluded" by the Convention.[79]

Eighth, the Convention provides that "Parties shall provide mutual assistance to each other in the real-time collection of traffic data associated with specified communications in their territory transmitted by means of a computer system."[80] This mandate is subject to the caveat that the "assistance shall be governed by the conditions and procedures provided for under domestic law."[81] However, Parties are obligated to provide the requested assistance "at least with respect to criminal offences for which real-time collection of traffic data would be available in a similar domestic case."[82] This provision is meant to allow Parties "to trace the source of an attack in real time, while a transmission is in progress."[83]

Ninth, "[t]he Parties shall provide mutual assistance to each other in the real-time collection or recording of content data of specified communications transmitted by means of a computer system to the extent permitted under their applicable treaties and domestic laws."[84] This means Parties must assist each other by engaging in wiretapping of computer communications, but only to the extent permitted under their domestic laws. This does not necessarily mean that if a requested state may wiretap when investigating the same type of offense, it must render the requested wiretapping assistance when another state is investigating an offense. The requested state may have jurisdictional requirements, among other things, that would preclude it from wiretapping in order to assist the Requesting State.

Finally, "[a] Party shall designate a point of contact available on a twenty-four hour, seven-day-a-week basis, in order to ensure the provision of immediate assistance for the purpose of investigations or proceedings concerning criminal offences related to computer systems and data, or for the collection of evidence in electronic form of a criminal offence."[85] These 24/7 points-of-contact are responsible for "facilitating" or "directly carrying out" the necessary assistance, including by providing technical advice, preserving data, collecting data, providing legal information, and locating suspects.[86] Each Party must ensure that the 24/7 points-of-contact are "trained and equipped" to fulfill these requirements and "facilitate the operation of the network."[87] The 24/7 network was modeled on a similar network created by the G8 group of nations in 1997 and subsequently expanded to include 20 nations by 2001.[88]

The Convention does not have any enforcement mechanism, *per se*, to ensure that Parties comply with their obligations under the Convention. Instead, the Convention provides that "[t]he European Committee on Crime Problems (CDPC) shall be kept informed regarding the interpretation and application of this Convention."[89] It also contains a dispute resolution provision, which states that Parties who disagree "as to the interpretation or application of th[e] Convention...shall seek a settlement of the dispute through negotiation or any other peaceful means of their choice, including submission of the dispute to the CDPC, to an arbitral tribunal whose decisions shall be binding upon the Parties, or to the International Court of Justice, as agreed upon by the Parties concerned."[90] Nevertheless, if one

---

[78]*See* Convention on Cybercrime, Explanatory Note ¶ 293. Although the Explanatory Note says that "all agreed" on these two types of unilateral cross-border action, Russia—which is a COE member—has reportedly maintained a continuing objection to this provision. *See* J. Markoff and A. Kramer, *In Shift, U.S. Talks to Russia on Internet Security*, N.Y. Times (December 12, 2009), available at http://www.nytimes.com/2009/12/13/science/13cyber.html; accessed June 7, 2010.

[79]Convention on Cybercrime, Explanatory Note ¶ 293.

[80]Convention on Cybercrime, Art. 33(1).

[81]Ibid.

[82]Ibid., art. 33(2).

[83]K. Harris, *supra*, at 6.

[84]Convention on Cybercrime, Art. 34.

[85]Ibid., Art. 35(1).

[86]Ibid.

[87]Ibid., Art. 35(3).

[88]K. Harris, *supra*, at 6.

[89]Convention on Cybercrime, Art. 45(1).

[90]Ibid., Art. 45(2).

party refuses to submit to such arbitration, the other Party has no real recourse under the Convention as to that dispute.

III. REACTION TO THE CONVENTION

When the Convention entered into force, it was opposed by many civil liberties groups, which feared that the new investigative authorities that would be created in many ratifying states, and the increased law enforcement cooperation, would erode privacy and other rights.[91] The view of private industry was mixed, with copyright owners strongly supporting the convention, but Internet service providers and other network operators concerned about the increased burdens the Convention might place on them in the form of additional requests for interception and stored traffic data and subscriber information.[92] In more recent years, however, the opposition has been more muted. It is not clear whether this has been because the fears of opponents have not been borne out, or because the Convention is now seen as a *fait accompli*, at least in many countries.

One notable and continuing source of criticism has been Russia. Although a member of the COE, Russia has not signed the Convention, let alone ratified it. As discussed below, Russia has, since the mid 1990s, proposed a cyber arms control treaty in the United Nations that would restrict what nation-states can do with cyber weapons. With regard to the Convention, Russia has reportedly been opposed to the section of the provision allowing unilateral trans-border access by law enforcement agencies to computers or data with the consent of the computer- or data-owner, seeing this as a violation of national sovereignty.[93] Some have suggested that Russia's real reason for not signing the convention is its desire to avoid taking on an obligation to assist other nations in cybercrime investigations given the numerous cyber attacks that emanate from Russia, including some that many people suspect are state-sponsored.

The United Nations Office on Drugs and Crime has recently recommended that "the development of a global convention against cybercrime should be given careful and favourable consideration."[94] It cited the slow progress in getting nations to sign onto the COE Convention, and the reluctance of non-COE states to accede to a treaty that they had no hand in developing.[95]

The International Telecommunication Union (ITU), a U.N. agency responsible for information and communication technology issues, has also questioned whether the Convention should be adopted as a global standard. ITU General Secretary Hamadoun Touré has cited the fact that the Convention was developed solely by COE members and four observer nations. He has also reportedly said that the Convention is now "a little dusty."[96] As an alternative, the ITU sponsored the creation of the "ITU Toolkit

---

[91] *See* J. Pryce, *Convention on Cybercrime*, Privacy & Security Law Report, Vol. 5, No.1, p. 1451 (BNA, Inc., October 16, 2006). Some of the comments and concerns expressed by civil liberties groups and others can be found on the websites of the Center for Democracy and Technology, available at http://optout.cdt.org/international/cybercrime/; accessed June 7, 2010; the American Civil Liberties Union, available at http://www.aclu.org/technology-and-liberty/international-cybercrime-treaty; accessed June 7, 2010; and the Electronic Privacy Information Center, available at http://www.aclu.org/technology-and-liberty/international-cybercrime-treaty; accessed June 7, 2010.

[92] J. Pryce, *supra*, at 1451. Many of the initial concerns that had been raised by industry during the drafting process had been addressed by the time the final Convention went into effect. For example, amendments were made to clarify that the Convention did not mandate data retention or the use of specific interception technologies, to make clear that states would not criminalize the development or use of network security testing tools, and to limit the vicarious liability of corporations. *See* ibid.

[93] *See* J. Markoff and A. Kramer, *In Shift, U.S. Talks to Russia on Internet Security*, N.Y. Times (December 12, 2009), available at http://www.nytimes.com/2009/12/13/science/13cyber.html; accessed June 7, 2010.

[94] Secretariat of the United Nations Office on Drugs and Crime (UNODC), *Recent developments in the use of science and technology by offenders and by competent authorities in fighting crime, including the case of cybercrime*, Working Paper submitted to the Twelfth United Nations Congress on Crime Prevention and Criminal Justice (Jan. 22, 2010) at 15, available at http://www.unodc.org/documents/crime-congress/12th-Crime-Congress/Documents/A_CONF.213_9/V1050382e.pdf; accessed June 7, 2010.

[95] *See* ibid. at 11-12.

[96] M. Emert, *ITU will IP-Adressen verwalten*, heise Netze (October 21, 2009), available at http://www.heise.de/netze/meldung/ITU-will-IP-Adressen-verwalten-835928.html; accessed June 7, 2010.

for Cybercrime Legislation."[97] Drafted through the American Bar Association's Privacy & Computer Crime Committee, Section of Science & Technology Law, "with global participation," the toolkit serves as model legislation for countries to adopt. The goal of the Toolkit is to harmonize national legislation without requiring nations to join an international treaty. Still, the Toolkit's substantive provisions were based in part on the Convention, and its sections on international cooperation that resemble those in the Convention. The ITU has also promoted its own cyber-warning organization, the "International Multilateral Partnership against Cyber-Threats" (IMPACT), which is ostensibly modeled after the Centers for Disease Control and Prevention and strives to serve as an international "early warning system" for cyber attacks, but has relatively few members.[98]

The COE, however, has pushed back against the criticism, and said that what is needed is to get more countries to accede to the Convention, not to "reinvent the wheel."[99] The COE Secretary General has asserted that the Convention "has received strong support by the Asia-Pacific Economic Cooperation, the European Union, Interpol, the Organisation of American States and other organisations and initiatives as well as the private sector."[100]

In addition, the COE's Committee of Experts on Terrorism has stated that, for now, at least, no separate Convention is necessary to deal with the use of the Internet for terrorist purposes, including terrorists' attacks on computer networks, since "large scale attacks on computer systems appeared to be already covered by the Cybercrime Convention."[101] It stressed that "at the present stage primary focus should be on ensuring the effective implementation of the Cybercrime Convention and the Convention on the Prevention of Terrorism, as new negotiations might jeopardize their increasing impact on the international fight against cybercrime and terrorism."[102] Instead, the Committee recommended that the COE urge more nations to accede to the Convention on Cybercrime.[103] The Committee also stated, though, that "further consideration could be given to the question of responsibility of Internet providers."[104]

IV. EVALUATION OF THE CONVENTION

The Convention represents the most substantive, and broadly subscribed, multilateral agreement on cybercrime in existence today. It offers a relatively comprehensive approach to harmonizing national legislation to address cybercrime both substantively and procedurally, and presents a framework for international cooperation that did not exist before except on a bilateral or ad hoc basis.

---

[97]The ITU Toolkit is available at http://www.itu.int/ITU-D/cyb/cybersecurity/projects/cyberlaw.html; accessed June 7, 2010.

[98]See M. Emert, *ITU calls for global cybersecurity measures*, The H Security (May 24, 2009), available at http://www.h-online. com/security/news/item/ITU-calls-for-global-cybersecurity-measures-741711.html; accessed June 7, 2010. Information about IMPACT's membership, mission, and services is available at http://www.impact-alliance.org/; accessed June 7, 2010.

[99]J. Kirk, *Council of Europe pushes for only one cybercrime treaty*, NetworkWorld (March 23, 2010), available at http://www.networkworld.com/news/2010/032310-council-of-europe-pushes-for.html; accessed June 7, 2010. At a COE cybercrime conference earlier this year, Maud de Boer-Buquicchio, the COE Deputy Secretary General, reportedly said, ""I think we will have the best chance to succeed if we unite around one international instrument that already exists." Ibid.

[100]Thorbjørn Jagland, Contribution of the Secretary General of the Council of Europe to the Twelfth United Nations Congress on Crime Prevention and Criminal Justice (February 16, 2010) at 18 (citations omitted), available at http://www.coe. int/t/dghl/cooperation/economiccrime/cybercrime/Documents/Reports-Presentations/SG%20Inf%20_2010_4%20-%20 UN%20Crime%20congress_ENGLISH.pdf; accessed June 7, 2010.

[101]Council of Europe Committee of Experts on Terrorism (CODEXTER), Opinion of the Committee of Experts on Terrorism (CODEXTER) for the Attention of the Committee of Ministers on Cyberterrorism and Use of Internet for Terrorist Purposes (2008) at 1, available at http://www.coe.int/t/e/legal_affairs/legal_co-operation/fight_against_terrorism/4_theme_files/Cyberterrorism%20opinion%20E.pdf; accessed June 7, 2010.

[102]Ibid. at 3.

[103]See ibid.

[104]Ibid.

A U.S. Department of Justice official involved in cybercrime issues rates the impact of the convention as "very positive."[105] Although there are no statistics by which to meaningfully compare pre- versus post-Convention rates of international cooperation, the DoJ official states that such cooperation has increased "radically" in recent years, and that at least some of this increase is attributable to the Convention.[106] The greatest observable increase has occurred in countries that have ratified the Convention.[107]

In serious investigations, in which time is of the essence, cooperation has improved "remarkably" in the last few years, according to the DoJ official.[108] This includes cases involving destructive cyber attacks (such as denial of service attacks, viruses, and worms).[109] A good deal of this improvement is based on the Convention, in particular the ability to require preservation of evidence until authorities can seek its disclosure; the authority to engage in "spontaneous" cooperation; the creation of the 24/7 points-of-contact network; and the ability to engage in remote searches (though this authority is probably not used often).

Still, the shortcomings of the Convention are obvious. While a good number of European countries (and the United States) have ratified the Convention, a notable number of major players have not. Most conspicuously absent are Russia and China, which have been the source of many of the most serious cyberattacks in recent years, some of which are suspected to be state-sponsored or, at least, state-tolerated. Beyond that, there is not a single nation from Asia, Africa, or South American that has ratified the treaty. When asked how the Convention might be improved, the DoJ official involved in cybercrime stated that more nations needed to become parties to the Convention.[110]

Substantively, the Convention is fairly comprehensive in addressing the most common categories of cybercrimes and the most common types of investigative tools used by law enforcement. And it clearly prescribes mechanisms and procedures for international cooperation, including expedited responses to requests for assistance. But the Convention also allows Parties to refuse to assist in many instances where assistance would conflict with domestic law or, notably, where a country claims that providing assistance would prejudice its sovereignty, *ordre public*, or "essential interests." Thus, where a Party is suspected of being responsible for an attack—or of tolerating it for its own purposes—that Party would likely be able to refuse to cooperate and still be in compliance at least with the letter of the Convention. And the Convention contains no enforcement mechanism by which countries that do not receive requested cooperation (and/or are the victims of cyber attacks emanating from or transiting through a Party) may seek redress.

Moreover, the Convention does not address the particular concerns that may be raised by cyber attacks that are not just criminal acts, but may also constitute espionage or the use of force under the laws of war. This may be because the negotiators of the Convention were primarily representatives of law enforcement, justice, and foreign affairs ministries and agencies, or it may be that nations simply refused to discuss military and intelligence matters in that setting. Whatever the reason, the Convention does not begin to deal with the issues that might arise when, for instance, a nation finds itself under a devastating cyber attack and cannot afford to wait to see if the countries that the attacks are coming from (or going through) will render the necessary cooperation.

Beyond having more nations ratify it, the Convention itself could be improved in several ways, so that it is a more useful tool for dealing with damaging cyberattacks. Some of the proposals that follow

---

[105]Telephonic interview of DoJ Official by author, July 29, 2010.

[106]Ibid.

[107]Ibid. The DoJ official notes, though, that "dozens" of countries that are not parties to the Convention have nevertheless enacted domestic legislation modeled on it. Ibid. The official also observes s that cooperation has increased not just in cybercrime investigations, but also in investigations into other crimes involving electronic evidence (including kidnapping cases and threats of violence communicated via email). Ibid.

[108]Ibid.

[109]Ibid.

[110]Ibid.

seem unlikely to be accepted by a majority of the parties to the Convention, out of concern over infringement of their sovereignty interests. Nevertheless, they at least offer a basis for discussion.

First, the grounds for rejecting a request for assistance under the Convention might be narrowed. Allowing nations to deny assistance based on "prejudice" to their "sovereignty, security, *ordre public* or other essential interests" allows them too much flexibility to reject assistance without offering specific and credible reasons. A nation that is itself responsible for the attack (or is purposely tolerating an attack carried out by private citizens within its borders) thus has an easy way to continue to hide its involvement. At the very least, the Convention could require that a requested nation that denies assistance provide *specific* reasons for doing so, in writing. This might at least have some deterrent effect against illegitimate denials of requests for assistance.

Second, a meaningful enforcement mechanism could be added to the Convention, by which a nation that is denied assistance can seek redress. One simple way to do this would be to amend the Convention's existing dispute resolution mechanism so that review by a neutral arbiter is mandatory whenever it is requested by a country whose request for assistance is denied, without requiring the agreement of the requested party before an arbiter can even hear the case. It seems unlikely that nations would agree to give a neutral arbiter the power to compel assistance. But the arbiter might at least be given the authority to declare whether the requested Party's denial of assistance was legitimate. This, too, would have some deterrent effect.

Third, a reporting requirement could be added to the Convention, so that denials of assistance requests—and the reasons for the denials—get reported to the CDPC (or some other entity). This information could then be published in some form, or at least shared with all ratifying states. Such a reporting requirement would also have some deterrent effect on illegitimate or baseless denials of assistance.

Fourth, and most radically, one could imagine an amendment that would authorize requesting Parties that are denied assistance, *without a legitimate, credible reason*, to engage in unilateral, cross-border investigative action, such as remotely searching computers in the requested nation. Such an amendment would go beyond the existing remote search authority in the Convention, which permits a Party to conduct a remote search only when it "obtains the lawful and voluntary consent of the person who has the lawful authority to disclose the data to the Party through that computer system." An amendment along these lines could—as a logical matter, at least—go even further and allow the requesting Party—in the event of a destructive cyberattack—to remotely destroy or disable the computer(s) from which the attack is emanating. But such amendments would need to be drafted very carefully (to say the least), so that the circumstances in which such remote searches or counterattacks are authorized are clearly defined.

Even if amendments along the lines of the preceding paragraph could be drafted sufficiently clearly and tightly, in a way that avoids allowing a requesting Party to rely on them as a pretext for its own espionage or cyberattack, it seems highly unlikely that the Parties to the Convention would agree to them. A more realistic alternative, then, might be for Parties to state unilaterally that they reserve the right to engage in such measures when they experience a highly damaging attack and the requested Party denies a request for assistance without a legitimate, credible reason.

V. ALTERNATIVES TO THE CONVENTION

The principal alternative to the Convention that has been put forward thus far is Russia's proposal for an international cyber arms control treaty. Beginning in 1998, Russia has urged United Nations action to limit cyber attacks, likening the destructive effect of cyber weapons to that of weapons of mass destruction.[111] It sponsored a U.N. resolution, adopted by the General Assembly in 2000, that called upon

---

[111] *See* I. Ivanov, Letter dated 23 September 1998 from the Permanent Representative of the Russian Federation to the United Nations addressed to the Secretary-General (September 30, 1998), available at http://www.un.org/ga/search/view_doc.asp?symbol=A/C.1/53/3&Lang=E; accessed June 7, 2010.

Member States to consider "existing and potential threats in the field of information security, as well as possible measures to limit the threats emerging in this field" and to examine "international concepts aimed at strengthening the security of global information and telecommunications systems."[112] Russia also proposed a set of principles which, among other things, would have required states to "refrain from . . . [t]he development, creation and use of means of influencing or damaging another State's information resources and systems; . . . [t]he deliberate use of information to influence another State's vital Structures; . . . [u]nauthorized interference in information and telecommunications systems and information resources, as well their unlawful use; . . . [or e]ncouraging the activities of international terrorist, extremist or criminal associations, organizations, groups or individual law breakers that pose a threat to the information resources and vital structures of States."[113] And in 2008, Vladislav Sherstyuk, a deputy secretary of the Russian Security Council, reportedly described a proposed treaty that would prohibit secretly embedding malicious code in another country's computers for later use in the event of hostilities.[114] Russia has also proposed prohibiting attacks on noncombatant systems and on using deception in cyberspace.[115]

The United States has been cool (at best) to the Russian proposal, at least until recently. Late last year, the Obama Administration reportedly began meeting with Russian officials to discuss cybersecurity issues, including possible restrictions on the military use of cyber weapons, and agreed to begin talks in the U.N. Disarmament & International Security Committee.[116] Talks have continued this year, including at a Russian-sponsored cybersecurity conference in Garmisch-Partenkirchen, Germany in April. And in June 2010, Gen. Keith Alexander, the Commander of the U.S. military's new Cyber Command and the Director of the National Security Agency, said that "we have to establish the rules [for cyberwarfare] and I think what Russia's put forward is, perhaps, the starting point for international debate."[117] He also stated that "it's going to take all countries" to establish the rules of the road for how governments operate in cyberspace, and emphasized that the key to any new agreement will be enforcement mechanisms.[118] But he also suggested that the United States should develop a counterproposal to Russia's proposed treaty.[119]

It remains to be seen whether Russia's proposal gains any traction, in particular from the United States, which seems unlikely to agree to a ban on the offensive use of cyber weapons anytime soon. But even if Russia's proposal—or any other proposed treaty to limit nations' use of cyberattacks or to set norms of behavior in "cyberspace"—were adopted, such a treaty would not really be an *alternative* to

---

[112]U.N. Resolution 55/28, Developments in the field of information and telecommunications in the context of international security (November 20, 2000), available at http://disarmament.un.org/vote.nsf/511260f3bf6ae9c005256705006e0a5b/d368c1f35 906aa318525697d00752cc6?OpenDocument&ExpandSection=3,5#_Section3; accessed June 7, 2010.

[113]Report of the U.N. Secretary General, Developments in the field of information and telecommunications in the context of international security (July 10, 2000) at 5, available at http://www.un.org/documents/ga/docs/55/a55140.pdf; accessed June 7, 2010.

[114]*See* J. Markoff and A. Kramer, *U.S. and Russia Differ on a Treaty for Cyberspace*, N.Y. Times (June 27, 2009), available at http://www.nytimes.com/2009/06/28/world/28cyber.html?_r=1&scp=3&sq=Vladislav%20Sherstyuk&st=cse; accessed June 7, 2010.

[115]*See* Ibid.

[116]*See* J. Markoff and A. Kramer, *In Shift, U.S. Talks to Russia on Internet Security*, N.Y. Times (December 12, 2009), available at http://www.nytimes.com/2009/12/13/science/13cyber.html; accessed June 7, 2010.

[117]Transcript of Remarks by Gen. K. Alexander at the Center for Strategic and International Studies, Washington, D.C. (June 3, 2010) at 11, available at http://www.nsa.gov/public_info/_files/speeches_testimonies/100603_alexander_transcript.pdf; accessed June 7, 2010.

[118]Ibid. at 14.

[119]*See* ibid. at 11-12. In July 2005, the United States, Russia, China and several other countries reportedly reached agreement on a set of recommendations directed at reducing the threat of attack on each others' networks. *See* E. Nakashima, Washington Post (July 17, 2010), available at http://www.washingtonpost.com/wp-dyn/content/article/2010/07/16/AR2010071605882. html; accessed July 30, 2010. The group reportedly "recommended that the U.N. create norms of accepted behavior in cyberspace, exchange information on national legislation and cybersecurity strategies, and strengthen the capacity of less-developed countries to protect their computer systems." Ibid. However, the author has been unable as of July 30, 2010 to find a copy of these recommendations.

the Convention, since it probably would not provide mechanisms for cooperation when a cyber attack does occur. Thus, for example, Russia might legally bind itself to a treaty banning nation-state attacks on civilian computer networks. But if an attack then occurs that appears to emanate from Russia, that treaty would probably not address how countries that have been attacked may respond, or whether Russia would have any obligation to assist in investigating the attack.

Therefore, a treaty on cyberattacks and the Convention on Cybercrime are not mutually exclusive. Indeed, the Convention could bolster a cyber attack treaty in some senses. For example, if a Party to the Convention rejects a request for assistance in investigating a cyber attack without a legitimate, credible reason, that rejection could be regarded as an indication (though not proof in and of itself) that the Party was directly or indirectly responsible for the attack, and thus in violation of the cyber attack treaty. Thus, even as the United States continues to explore the possibility of a multilateral agreement on cyberattacks, it should continue to urge other nations to ratify the Convention. It should also consider proposing ways of improving the Convention to deter illegitimate or inappropriate denials of assistance by requested Parties.

Group 4—Psychology

Decision Making Under Uncertainty

Rose McDermott
Brown University

Decision makers are often confronted with threats and risks they may not understand, but nonetheless need to address. Among these kinds of problems, cyberattacks may present novel technical and political challenges which leaders are not adequately prepared to properly resolve. Under such circumstances, policymakers strive to reduce uncertainty, often believing, rightly or wrongly, that the quality of decisions based on more information, and more certain intelligence, will prove superior. Decisions based on more, or more certain, information may not always emerge normatively better, but decision makers may feel more confident of the choices they make under such conditions. This proclivity to favor certainty in the face of conflict exists in the realm of cyberattacks. In fact, cyberattacks constitute an attack on certainty itself; indeed, creating uncertainty in the population about the security of particular systems, such as the electrical grid, may represent part of the goal of an attack. Importantly, the central problems confronting decision makers in the realm of cyberattack remain fundamentally and intrinsically psychological in nature because they so often involve high degrees of uncertainty about the source of the attack, and the motivations of the perpetrator. Yet these psychological problems, which often incorporate technical elements about which decision makers often remain either uneducated or unaware, nonetheless require decisive political remedies. In order to achieve this goal, decision makers must learn to accept and manage uncertainty even under conditions of stress and threat.

American leaders in particular tend to look for solutions to complex problems in terms of technological fixes, since such remedies appear straightforward and direct. But such responses can fail, as often occurs in intelligence when signals intelligence is privileged over human intelligence, often to the detriment of accuracy; such a difference may explain part of the reason the Israelis were less surprised than the Americans by the fall of the Shah in 1979. Similarly, problems may exist for which no technical solution yet exists.

Several specific classes of psychological biases tend to plague decision makers confronting uncertainty. In the case of cyberattack, the tendency for aggression to become heightened in anonymous circumstances raises the risk for unnecessary confrontation, and processes of social contagion intensify the time pressure under which leaders may have to operate. Ironically, awareness of such proclivities does not necessarily diminish their occurrence. Indeed, overconfidence can further exacerbate such effects.

The following discussion outlines potential ways to reduce uncertainty, concentrating on the biases which can infuse processes of decision making under such conditions. To begin at the end, cyberdefense and cyberoffence will remain inadequate to address the extent and scope of the impending challenge, accurate and confident attribution will prove enormously difficult if not impossible to achieve, and other technical solutions are likely to remain impossible for the foreseeable future. As a result, gaining an adequate appreciation of the ways in which systematic psychological biases surrounding attribution and confidence, in particular, can influence decision making under uncertainty in particular ways can help cut off the tendency to create the very problems we seek to ameliorate. In order to make appropriate decisions under conditions of unavoidable uncertainty, leaders should be made more aware not only of the technical nature of the challenges they face, but also of the psychological biases which may impede optimal choice when options remain limited, uncertain or truncated. Institutional strategies for reducing the influence of such biases, including efforts to increase transparency across response options, may help reduce the negative influence of these tendencies. In addition, improving expertise and calibration could reduce the prospects for disproportionate responses to cyberattack, which may lead to undesirable unintended consequences.

DECISION MAKING UNDER UNCERTAINTY

The central psychological problem in addressing uncertainty results from the fact that individuals tend to jump to conclusions prematurely in a desperate attempt to gain some sense of control, however artificial, over the situation at hand. When this happens, several consequences follow. First, leaders, like others, strive to fit a given situation into a pre-existing category they already have in mind for "what kind of conflict" this resembles, or "who is to blame" for a particular outcome. These desires, however normal, can lead to systematic biases because they encourage decision makers to fit a novel situation into a pre-existing theoretical category, which then serves to shape and structure incoming information in ways which conform to those pre-existing beliefs. For example, they readily accept information which conforms to those beliefs without sufficient interrogation, they reject intelligence which refutes those ideas without investigation and they interpret ambiguous information in ways which conforms to, and supports, those pre-existing ideas (Lord, Ross & Lepper, 1979). In other words, individuals tend to apply different criteria to incoming information based on the degree to which it aligns with their pre-existing theories of the world.

This process can be exacerbated up the chain of command when many decision makers share a particular world view, as occurs when individuals of a given generation share a powerful historical analogy, such as Munich, Vietnam, or 9/11 (Khong, 1992). These analogies then serve not only to organize information but also to provide appropriate ready-made responses, although oftentimes these alternatives do not derive from successful choices in the past, but rather emerge from what leaders thought might have solved the problem in hindsight. So, for example, those who opposed appeasement of Hitler at Munich might assume that standing firm against future potential tyrants will prevent the outbreak of war. This can work so long as the current challenge closely resembles the historical one in critically important ways; however, often the new threat contains novel elements which require greater ingenuity in generating a response. When this occurs, trying to fix a current problem with a past solution works about as well as trying to fit a computer into a typewriter case.

The second main consequence that follows from premature cognitive closure in the face of uncertainty is that the initial judgments then come to serve as anchors for future assessments of the situation (Webster & Kruglanski, 1997); under this circumstance, individuals tend to "seize" on early information and then "freeze" on those evaluations even as new contradictory information may emerge. These tendencies appear to vary across situations but represent pretty stable aspects of individual personality differences. The preference for "seizing" early seems to derive from an impetus for urgency, while the propensity toward "freezing" appears to result from a desire for permanence, or stability. When this occurs, decision makers prove much less likely to re-evaluate earlier decisions than they would if they were still making up their mind about the nature of an attack and their options for response. These initial evaluations, often based on very little information but tremendous urgency to achieve certainty, will be heavily influenced by prior beliefs and images regarding the nature and capabilities of given adversaries.

These tendencies will likely exert themselves strongly when confronting the prospect of cyberattack because the nature of the threat is reasonably new and many leaders may not be familiar with the technology or its level of complexity. Knowing how to prepare people to respond without necessarily having to teach them the technical aspects of the problem will prove challenging. Leaders may be unsure how much information they need in order to be confident regarding how best to response. They may have very clear suspicions about who constitutes an enemy, and what kinds of responses will deter which kinds of attacks, but they may not have enough information to go public with their claims.

ENSURING APPROPRIATE ANALOGIES TO GUIDE DECISION MAKING

The goal of preventing cyberattacks against the United States is important, but the presumptive analogy of deterrence upon which it rests seems misguided, if pervasive. Deterrence as a theory developed in the context of kinetic attacks which allowed some attribution, albeit often biased, regarding instigation and intent. But unlike most military attacks, cyberattacks defy easy assessments of perpetrator and purpose. Deterrence dominated as the strategy of choice during the Cold War between the United States and the Soviet Union. However, cyberattack looks much more like the current threats posed by non-state terrorists than like those posed by hegemonic state actors. As with terrorism, the very point of cyberattack, at least in part, is to increase uncertainty. Applying possibly anachronistic notions of deterrence to such a threat may lead decision makers away from the most creative approaches, and constructive responses, to these challenges.

One of the main problems with deterrence was noted by Robert Jervis (1979, 1982) in his work on nuclear deterrence; the fundamental logic of deterrence rests on assumptions of rationality which do not accurately depict human decision making processes. Deterrence depends on a credible threat to respond and deny the adversary any advantage from an attack, and yet such an ability requires decision makers to clearly give and receive clear signals of intent and capability. In the context of nuclear weapons, Jervis noted the many psychological obstacles that might prevent leaders from properly evaluating the opponent's values, credibility, or perceptions; all these calculations provide the basis upon which reliable deterrence depends. Recent evidence from psychology and neuroscience only serve to validate and clarify such reservations regarding human decision making.

The misuse of the deterrence analogy should prove instructive to those who remain skeptical that leaders fall prey to such inappropriate historical references. In the case of cyberattack, a more apt analogy might be drawn from the risks posed by pandemic disease and the principles of disease surveillance employed to try to contain such threats. Pathogens co-evolve in the human immune system, often operating as parasites, but also working to facilitate useful functions, such as digestion. From a public health perspective, many pathogens only constitute a threat when they become unusually virulent or prevalent. Similarly, most people can use their computers normally without it posing a risk to the broader community. However, when a particular computer gets taken over, especially without its owner's knowledge, the person who controls the machine can wreck public havoc, just as an individual can spread disease prior to actively experiencing symptoms himself. While epidemiologists need not broadcast their surveillance of disease prevalence, and such watchdogs rely on primary care physicians for providing first responder information, systematic monitoring remains crucial to any attempt to keep potential epidemics under control, or to limit their spread and destructiveness once they emerge. In the case of a pandemic disease such as the flu, public health officials try not to kill infected individuals, but rather seek to kill the dangerous pathogen. Efforts to monitor and control the emergence of botnets can serve a similar goal of providing firewall protection to the wider public by containing the dangerous computers, rather than going after those who control them remotely since these individuals are much more difficult to identify and locate.

The specter of cyberattack raises similar concerns regarding attitudes toward regulation and surveillance as well as the nature of underlying security relationships. The influence and effect of some cyberattacks, like some diseases, may only become fully evident over time. Some attacks may initially appear worse than they are, like Legionnaire's disease, while the lethality of others, such as AIDS, may simply prove incomprehensible upon first appearance. Like a lethal pathogen, the adversary in cyberattacks is often supremely adaptive and quick to respond to efforts to stop their grown and activity. Hardening defenses often only serves to redirect the energy of the assailant to more vulnerable areas. As with disease, in the case of cyberattack, it may prove less effective and efficient to go after the adversary than to simply target the infected machines, thus denying the adversary the means of delivery.

APPROACHES TO REDUCING UNCERTAINTY

When confronted with uncertainty, leaders will naturally seek to reduce that uncertainty by obtaining more information about the nature, source, intent and scope of the perceived threat or attack. There is nothing wrong with this inclination; problems arise when such intelligence is treated with a degree of confidence which the evidence cannot support. When subsequent actions are then based on these inferences, numerous negative consequences can arise, from increasing the risk of blowback by potentially harming innocent parties, to initiating actions that end up harming one's own systems, to escalating a conflict beyond expectation or desire. Awareness of the processes by which such decisions might become skewed can help to design institutional constraints and checks, as well as foster greater transparency and accountability.

When responding to a potential cyberattack, leaders confront a variety of questions, not least those relating to the source and intent of the attack. What is the purpose of the attack? Who instigated it? Can we stop it? Should we retaliate, and, if so, how? In striving to answer these questions, leaders have a variety of tools and strategies available to them; however, basing such decisions on an atavistic model of deterrence only serves to restrict creative responses to these challenges by enforcing an analogy based on assumptions of kinetic systems and psychological rationality which do not apply in the cyber realm.

There are many ways in which these assumptions can undermine optimal decision making, defined as maximizing democratic goals of peace, prosperity, freedom and openness in the context of working actively to suppress any given threat. There are at least three domains where leaders can, and should, strive to operate effectively to reduce the risk posed by those who would try to disrupt American cyber capabilities; each of these areas can remain plagued by uncertainty. The first relates to issues of offense and defense, the second to questions surrounding attribution, and the third revolves around additional technical solutions.

One way in which leaders try to reduce threat is through the use of offensive and defensive counter strategies, which can be active or passive in nature. In current discussions, defense tends to solicit most of the attention, with a lot of effort going into passive efforts, such as establishing anti-virus software, firewall protection, or improving password strength and encryption. However, these strategies can often create the very problems they are intended to prevent, as occurred with the recent McAfee security update error which precipitated a global crash of tens of thousands of PCs.[1] Active defense work, which in the case of cyberattack may involve some kind of offensive counter-attack, but could also include more typical police investigation strategies, is also available to leaders. Offensive strategies, including cyberattack and cyberexploitation, on the other hand, tend to be classified in nature.

Yet clearly attributing the identity of an attacker in a cyberattack scenario presents one of the most difficult and salient challenges facing defenders. This issue of identification and responsibility often lies at the crux of the uncertainty facing decision makers in determining the nature of the threat they confront, and the possible responses they might take in reaction. Note that such problems pose threats not only for the United States, but also for other countries which might react to attacks as well. Foreign

---

[1]http://www.wired.com/threatlevel/2010/04/mcafeebungle/.

leaders may also share similar constraints and uncertainties in their decision making as well, and U.S. leaders should be careful not to assume that adversaries or allies have a clearer understanding of attribution, or how best to respond to it, than we do. How such attacks affect others can also compound the effect on U.S. systems; there will be inevitable interconnections in how their responses affect our own systems, and U.S. defenders may need to stay attuned to such interaction effects.

The problem with attribution in cyberattack, of course, is that even if it is possible to locate the IP address of the attacking machine, it may be impossible to know who exactly is controlling that machine. Even if investigators find a particular location, they may never be able to locate the computer which launched an attack, as for example might occur if a Starbucks with open wireless networks served as the instigating location. Plausible deniability results from the very real possibility that a given computer was hacked and taken over by another with no knowledge on the part of the host about the nefarious activities his machine subserved. Because the knowledge required to learn how to become an expert hacker, unlike that required to make a nuclear bomb, for example, is relatively accessible and inexpensive, it may be impossible to determine the source of any given attack. Clever attackers can use many machines as stepping stones and hide their electronic tracks with still other machines, and victims may remain quite limited in what they can do to overcome it, undermine it, or learn about its original source (Stoll, 2005).

Efforts to improve and strengthen authentication can only take investigators so far because assertions of identity requires some kind of credentialing that may itself seem untrustworthy. If, for example, the Google attacks from China were launched from various students at two different universities, would the United States be more likely to believe they had nothing to do with the Chinese government if they had credentials from the Chinese government saying they were merely students and not government operatives? Just as forensic computer programmers may not trust any information they obtain from a machine they judge to have been compromised, and taken over by another, agents of the United States government may not trust any government-issued identification as either authentic or accurate. As a result, it is unclear how much effort is worth dedicating to processes of authentication. Such validation only works in a larger context of trust, whose very existence would vitiate the need for such credentialing in the first place. In order to understand this phenomenon intuitively, it may help to consider the mirror counter-factual experience. Imagine, for example, how the United States might expect other governments to respond to a claim that a hacker was working entirely independently out of an American city. Would the government expect Britain to believe such an argument more than, say, China?

Attributions of identity matter because they are used, at least in part, to infer intent. The United States may not like it if it finds the British or Israelis penetrating our defense IT network, but the sense of threat and fear will be much less than if similar acts were attributed to the Chinese or the Iranians. And yet an attack emanating from Iraq might appear to come from a computer in London just as easily as from one in Tehran. In one of the first coordinated cyberattacks discovered in early 1998, although apparently going on for a year or more prior, the so-called Moonlight Maze incident, an attack on the United States Department of Defense, NASA, and other government agencies appeared to emanate from Moscow, although it remained unclear whether that was the original source of the attack. The Soviets denied any involvement. But the identity of an attacker remains central to making inferences about intent, just as the apparent goal of an attack can provide information about its potential source. This inferential process highlights the importance of the influence of emotion on assessments of uncertainty and outcome; fear and anger affect predictions of probability in systematic ways which will be addressed in greater detail below. Suffice it to note here that fear leads to more pessimistic evaluations, while anger produces more optimistic assessments regarding future outcomes (Lerner & Keltner, 2000).

Another reason accurately identifying an attacker can prove critical is because any American president, or other leader, may remain reluctant to take a decisive action in retaliation for an attack if the source of such an attack remains unknown or uncertain. Yet accurate assessments take time, providing another reason to diminish the basis for effective models of deterrence to function. If the source of an attack cannot be identified with certainty, how can a counterattack, either a cyberattack or a kinetic one, be initiated without risking the possibility of unwanted collateral damage or potential blowback?

But sometimes leaders may feel more confident of their attributions of villainy than the objective evidence might support, particularly if they have jumped to conclusions based on judgments resulting from the salience of recent attack. In this way, leaders may emphasize the utility or destructive consequences of a potential attack over its probability. By highlighting potential damage in making risk assessments, and privileging value over probability in making decisions about how to respond, decision makers may adopt a worst case scenario approach to a cyberattack and jump to unwarranted conclusions out of an understandable desire to prevent future damage. If a leader gets this assessment wrong, his estimate of the possibility that a particular perpetrator instigated the attack will be higher than if his assessment was correct. The interaction between these biases can thus complicate accurate judgments concerning attribution.

However, technical analysis alone is unlikely to allow a decision maker to accurately speculate about the source of a cyberattack. Intelligence will most likely fail, and even sophisticated observers may never know if what they see represents the actual source, or whether someone else has engaged in deliberate deception to make it appear that a proxy machine constitutes the real source of an attack. Indeed, one of the sequelae of premature cognitive closure in the face of threat is that leaders will be more prone to assume threats will emerge from places where they have seen similar attacks emanate previously. If a secondary attack closely followed the one launched against Google, assumed to originate from China, it would be much easier for decision makers to assume that the subsequent attack similarly emerged from China. For this reason, catalytic conflict, or conflict between two countries initiated by a third party, remains a significant concern. Yet such attribution may or may not prove accurate. Uncertainty regarding source, and often intent as well, remains inherent in the domain of cyberspace itself, inextricably bound to the nature of the technology itself.

Moreover, lest observers appear naïve, it may remain in the best interests of the United States government to be able to hide behind attributional equivocation and uncertainty, not only in order to engage in unacknowledged retribution against attackers, but also to protect concealed sources whose skills may allow the United States to conduct powerful offensive cyberattacks as well. Such ambiguity might serve at least two important purposes. One, it allows the United States to engage in the kind of plausible deniability about initiating attacks which, while criticizing other governments for so doing, nonetheless allows the government to take aggressive action against potential threats while keeping the means of such attack secret. Second, a presumed veil of ignorance surrounding the source of attacks might allow the U.S. government to take back door advantage of presumed aggressors, or even try to take over particular machines, much like intelligence agents tried to turn spies into double agents during past wars.

Yet, as with the brief superiority which the United States had with regard to Multiple Independently Targetable Re-entry Vehicles (MIRV) technology in the days of the land based Intercontinental Ballistic Missile arms races with the Soviet Union, dominance may eventually give way to parity, as is likely already the case in this arena. Or, in the case of cyberattack, the most sophisticated technology could also reach into the hands of terrorists who may not be content to only try to steal money or information, but rather seek to wreak mayhem and destruction on the power grid, air traffic control, banking, and military command and control. As with the use of any other mercenary, states and other actors can gain rapid advances by paying skilled individuals to sell what they know to the highest bidder. Such prior experiences in the kinetic domain encourage caution and skepticism about the value of seeking to achieve or retain dominance in any rapidly changing and progressing technology.

PSYCHOLOGICAL ISSUES IN ADDRESSING UNCERTAINTY

The fundamental problems related to decision making under conditions of uncertainty, such as those which remain pervasive in the nature of cyberattack, involve psychological issues. And the appropriate remedies need to rest on primarily political, as opposed to technical, grounds because the inherent risks affect political values and calculations, and often remain immune to any quick technological fixes designed to assure attribution. There are several significant psychological insights which can be brought to bear in an analysis of this topic. The most relevant include biases surrounding judgment under uncertainty, attribution, contagion and social validation, and confidence. Each will be discussed in turn below.

Judgment Under Uncertainty

In the original psychological work on judgment under uncertainty, Slovic, Kahneman & Tversky (1982) described three biases which they found systematically affect the way people render assessments concerning future probabilities. To be clear, in combination with their work on decision making, most prominently explicated under the rubric of Prospect Theory (Kahneman & Tversky, 1979, 1984; Tversky & Kahneman, 1992), they made a distinction between judgment under uncertainty and decision making under conditions of risk. Judgment refers to those assessments about the likelihood that a certain event or person belongs in a particular category, or probability of a particular event occurring in the future, for example. These judgments primarily constitute assessments of an objective reality about the real external world. Decision making, on the other hand, refers to the primary internal calculations that individuals make, which can involve trade-offs between values, as the classic guns versus butter debate best exemplifies in the political realm. Decision making under risk occurs when the decision maker faces a threat to something of value; the actor must contemplate how much of something of value might be lost if different alternatives are chosen. The right choice may allow the person to move forward in a positive way, but the wrong choice may precipitate the loss of important values, including money, status, reputation, or some other significant thing of subjective worth or import. Judgmental biases relate to the part of a rational model that refers to probability; decision making biases mirror the aspects of a rational model that refers to assessments of utility. This distinction remains meaningful in analytic terms when describing the relevant judgmental heuristics which can bias judgment.

The original work on judgmental biases, which remains robust in its demonstration of these processes, identified three primary heuristics, or basic rules of thumb individuals typically utilize in rendering predictions about the likelihood or frequency of events. By and large, these biases work effectively and efficiently, particularly in the midst of the ecological context in which they evolved, but they can lead to systematic and predictable biases, particularly when abstracted to unfamiliar contexts (Gigerenzer, 1996).

The first, representativeness, showed how people rely on similarity to make judgments about whether a particular event or person fits into a specific category; profiling individuals to determine whether they are likely to be terrorists represents a systematic attempt which depends, at least in part, on this same kind of procedure. The second, availability, suggests that individuals rely on ease of accessibility and imagination to judge how likely a future event might be. Attempts to protect the airlines from a suicide terrorist represent an example of the ways in which salient experiences not only bias judgments of probability, but also restrict imagination of future events to overweight those which have occurred in the past. The last, anchoring and adjustment, refers to the way in which people tend to gravitate to a particular focus or target, even when they know that it is irrelevant to the judgment they are being asked to make. They then often fail to make proper accommodations for the ways which the event or individual they are being asked to judge differs from the original target. This proclivity provides a basis for the use, and misuse, of historical analogies to explain and analyze modern crises. Similarly, this dynamic explains, in part, why leaders often try to fight a current war using the strategies they believe would have succeeded in the last one.

Two specific so-called fallacies merit particular discussion in light of the issues raised by cyberattack. First, the conjunction fallacy has been shown to operate in many contexts, including political forecasting, estimates of criminal activity and decision making under risk (Tversky & Kahneman, 1983). In basic probability theory, no combination of factors can be more likely than either of its separate components. Yet both representativeness and availability can operate to make such a combination appear more likely than either of its parts. As a result, people may judge particular events or scenarios more likely than they are in reality either because they appear similar to something familiar (i.e., this is what happened in the Estonian attacks), or because they are salient for some reason (i.e, Google just sustained a similar attack). When this happens, observers can overestimate the probability of a particular event that seems more representative and available and simultaneously underestimate the probability of events which appear less representative and available. This phenomenon exerts its pull even when true probability is uncertain or even unknowable.

This dynamic becomes relevant not only in thinking about how leaders make judgments about whether a particular person or country, like China, belongs in a particular category, such as enemy or hacker, but also in rendering assessments regarding the likelihood that a particular kind of event, like a computer virus, results from either relatively benign or malicious intent. And even if malicious intent appears clear, the category of intrusion can matter in making decisions about how to respond: Is the intruder after money, information, or seeking to cause destruction? Each of these kinds of assessments requires placing individuals or actions within particular categories whose base rate probability remains unknown or unclear. Under such circumstances, similarity and salience can drastically affect assessments of probability in ways which do not accurately reflect actual likelihood, but can nonetheless profoundly influence political decisions about how to respond to a given threat or attack.

A related dynamic, called the disjunctive fallacy (Bar-Hillel & Neter, 1993), occurs when individual rank the probability of a category more likely than its superordinate categories. For example, when someone says they think it was more likely they saw a dog than an animal, or more likely someone is from Brazil than South America, they fall prey to his fallacy. These assessments, as with the conjunction fallacy, fly in the face of standard probability theory, but possess a strong psychological pull. In each instance, estimates of probability can be drastically affected in systematic ways by psychological processes which do not rest within the realm of acceptable normative models of rationality or probability. In such a way, a university source of attack may be judged less likely than a state sponsored attack, although the actual ability to distinguish between such sources remains more apparent than real.

In addition, these processes can interact with emotion in ways which exacerbate these biases under crisis situations involving fear or anger. For example, angry people tend to have more optimistic assessments of future probabilities (Lerner & Keltner, 2000); if the attacks on 9/11 made a person very angry, he would have been more likely to believe that responding with violent action would prove successful in stopping the terrorists than someone who was made sad by the same event. On the other hand, fearful people evince a more negative assessment of the future, as might be expected by those who worry about the worst coming to pass. Similarly, in considering potential responses, emotions can significantly affect a leader's decision regarding the nature of appropriate response (Sabini & Gault, 2000). Angry individuals appear much more likely to seek retributive justice, while fearful ones tend to support more rehabilitative types of outcomes. Thus, a leader, and a public, more scared about future attacks will likely support quite different choices than those who, in contrast, remain angry.

Attribution

One of the main problems with attribution concerns assessments of agency. Computers represent disembodied extensions of the actors who control them; these actors, in turn, can disavow any knowledge of any given interface, thus ensuring plausible deniability regarding both action and intention if victims manage to trace a given source.

While it may not seem entirely viable to work on developing various procedures which might allow for a higher probability of accurate attribution in such attacks, research on attribution can speak to the way in which technical and non-technical information can be combined to triangulate in on greater confidence surrounding the identity of an attacker. The analogy here is similar to that of epidemiology, using patterns of infection to trace a disease back to its source.

Attribution theory (Kelley, 1967) focused particularly on consensus, distinctiveness and consistency as the three key feature of appropriate causal inference in attribution. While this work did not specifically seek to discern identity, the lessons apply to such attributions as well as those regarding other causal inferences. Consensus emerges when many observers make the same judgment concerning causality. Distinctiveness occurs when an actor engages in a behavior that diverges from what other actors in that same situation do, thus making their actions unique or distinct in some way. Consistency refers to the notion that a given actor does something that appears in keeping with behavior she has undertaken in the past, or seems in line with basic tendencies that observers have witnessed from that person before, or in other situations. A combination of distinctiveness and consistency may look like what a poker player would consider a "tell" in an opponent, an idiosyncratic and reliable indicator of intent or, in this case, identity.

In trying to apply these theoretical notions to attributing identity in the case of cyberattack, observers might use these same characteristics to ascertain the identity of an attacker by employing a combination of these categories. It is important to keep in mind, for example, that actors can identify online in a variety of ways. They can visually self-identity (i.e, with a picture), they can verbally self identify (i.e. with a name) or they can discursively self-identity, as when they provide identifying information, or a verbal tell, which can uniquely be associated with a particular actor, or type of actor. Such revelations may be as simple as always mis-spelling a particular word in the same specific way. The first two might be faked, but the last may be unconscious, or, at the very least, put forward by someone who has close familiarity with the target actor.

In trying to triangulate on the identity of a particular perpetrator, using attribution theory for a guide, and perhaps focusing on more discursive forms of self-identification, observers might examine the extent to which an attack is consistent with prior attacks from known sources, the degree to which allies and other trusted sources with access to the same information converge on the same putative source, and the manner in which the attack appears distinctive to a particular actor, or embodies a specific Modus Operandi for a known actor. Such a process can help hone in on a particular locale, organization or actor. This is similar to using background information in an audio or video tape to try to identify the location of the speaker.

Other Social Psychological Processes:
Anonymity, Social Validation, and Contagion Effects

In their astute analysis of some of the social psychological effects which fed the First Internet War, which involved a distributed denial of service attack on Estonian government sources for several days in early 2007, Guadagno, Cialdini, and Evron (2010) pointed to several significant social psychological factors which, while not unique to cyberspace, certainly have effects which can be magnified within it. The endemic character of these forces retain prominence in circumstances of cyberattack to a greater degree than in kinetic warfare primarily because of the speed and vast potential dispersion of Internet effects. When something goes viral in cyberspace, millions of people can receive information almost instantaneously. This level of simultaneous and instantaneous exposure to mass experiences remains essentially unprecedented in prior human history. Furthermore, an attack which degrades communication may itself render an effective response to such an assault more difficult to achieve.

Anonymity provides a key to both the aggressiveness that can manifest in cyberthreats, as well as the difficulty of tracing attribution. Those who interact online have more anonymity than those who see each other face to face precisely because such visual cues are absent (Bargh & McKenna, 2004); indeed, many individuals experience a sense of depersonalization when interacting with people who are not there (Postmes et al., 2002), which can help explain why increasing time spent online can increase anxiety, diminish social capital, and heighten experiences of alienation. Yet, interestingly, Derks et al. (2008)

found *greater* frequency and explicitness in emotional displays in computer mediated communication than in face to face interactions. This may partly result from the need to convey emotions explicitly online which would be evident through non-verbal expressions and vocal intonation in personal interactions. While such emotional mediation may help explain why more than 3% of last year's marriages began with eharmony, it also reflects the fact that hostility, as well as attachment, is more frequently and easily expressed in anonymous and mediated contexts as well.

Social psychologists have suggested that anonymous forms of interaction, such as those that rule cyberspace, decrease individuals' attention to their normal standards of behavior, releasing inhibitions which might govern their behavior in face to face interactions (Joison, 2001; Matheson & Zanna, 1989; Sassenberg et al., 2005).

These models rest on earlier work on the effect of deindividuation on the propensity for violence. Deindividuation, such as occurs in large groups, or when anonymous engagement is possible, can increase the likelihood that individuals will disregard their own internal standards and espouse the established group social norm, even if that norm encourages aggressive actions. In the case discussed by Guadagno et al. (2010) in Estonia, they cite this process as one of the reasons inciting Russian sympathizers to join in a dedicated denial of service against Estonian government agencies. The medium may be different, but the process is identical to that employed by members of ACT-UP in the late 1990s with their strategy to phone-bank the FDA, denying access and egress, until the agency agreed to allow AIDS patients to try experimental drug therapies on a fast track approval basis (Carpenter, 2002).

The social identity of deindividuation model (SIDE) (Reicher et al., 1995) has been investigated in the context of computer mediated interaction to examine the effect of minority influence on majority opinion in such contexts (Moral-Toranzo et al., 2005). SIDE argues that under anonymous conditions, individuals become more attentive to the group than to themselves, and thus more likely to behave in ways which both manifest and represent group norms. This model suggests that anonymity will potentiate minority influence under conditions where group identity becomes salient, but these predictions were not sustained in the empirical work. This may be at least partly because the majority opinion represents the modal group norm to which members predominantly adhere.

Furthermore, the rapidity and broad reach of the Internet potentiates and speeds the influence of social validation and contagion effects. Social validation effects grow out of an adherence to the group norms which dominate and persevere in deindividuated environments such as those which rule the Internet. Along with liking, social proof provides one of the most powerful tools of persuasion available (Cialdini, 2001). Together, activities which make others like us for doing something everyone else is doing become particularly attractive. People are much more likely to do something once they see others engaging in the same behavior; this phenomena helps explain a lot about the cascades that precipitously occur in all sorts of social processes from economic markets to morale in combat (Rosen, 2005) where one person's behavior, or that of a small group, quickly grows into a contagion effect. As when videos of great interest go viral, so too can acts of mayhem and destruction, as long as careful instructions and sufficient motivation are provided by sophisticated organizers.

Social observers (MacKay, 1841) going back to Freud (1922) sought to understand the nature of mass hysteria, panics, and contagion effects, each of which represent a kind of social proof and validation. Interestingly, Heath & Heath (2007) demonstrate that some ideas are much more likely to prove contagious; those which contain an emotional element, such as disgust, appear to possess the ability to both spread more rapidly and endure longer in popular culture than other constructs. But clearly Internet technology potentiates the speed and rapidity with which any idea which hits the zeitgeist can spread.

The speed and breadth of these effects influence many social processes, but by far one of the most important relates to recruitment efforts. The social manipulation of identity becomes infinitely easier when those who orchestrate such identities do not necessarily have to conform to them in person in a physical way. Hitler was remarkable for his ability to perpetuate an Aryan dream when he himself was short and dark; few people have the charisma, courage or craziness to try to pull off such discrepancy between idea and image on a large scale. But such a maneuver is much easier to pull off when the discrepancy remains out of sight. A tactical leader can recruit potential suicide bombers using extreme religious rhetoric for strategic political reasons, and do so while sitting in a fancy house filled with materialist possessions, just as easily as an old, fat, overworked grandmother can change diapers while working at a job doing phone sex; in such a context, "oh, baby" takes on an entirely different meaning. Nature abhors a vacuum and fantasy can fill in anonymous spaces with the beliefs individuals want to attribute to one other. Sophisticated actors can generate social movements to engage in dedicated denial of service attacks by hitting upon emotional appeals that motivate myriad respondents to take action; contagion effects then operate to recruit enormous amounts of labor instantaneously.

One of the most important aspects of these social psychological phenomena and processes, including those related to attribution, is that targets and observers are unlikely to know about, become aware of, or understand these processes or how the work. This means, among other things, that both groups are much more likely to assume that large states or other main actors are responsible for large attacks than may be the case, simply by the natural tendency to associate a large effect with a big causal force or actor. This belief itself represents a form of representativeness, assuming, by the logic of similarity, that big effects must spring from equally big and powerful sources, when this may not necessarily be the case. Particularly in the realm of cyberspace, where large effects can be perpetuated by a lone individual at low cost, such assumptions can prove dangerous to veracity.

Confidence

Confidence can influence the response to attacks in two ways, either by underconfidence or overconfidence. The latter is by far the more prevalent phenomena, but both effects operate in distinct ways analytically. Underconfidence can afflict a leader who tries to attribute the source of an attack to a particular entity. As with the police who may know who committed a crime, but not be able to prove it, underconfidence can afflict a leader who believes he knows who is responsible for a cyberattack, but who does not have enough evidence to be able to publicly justify a hostile response should something go wrong.

Underconfidence can also precipitate the emergence of worst-case scenarios, as when an intrusion is uncovered the intent of which remains unclear. Underconfidence may encourage a leader to assume that he must treat the invasion as an attack, and not, for example, as an attempted exploitation, because the *political* effects of appearing to do nothing may be untenable. If that is the case, the tendency to react as though every intrusion represented a worst case scenario may lead to over-reaction in certain cases.

However, the experience of overconfidence appears much more endemic and destructive in nature. Overconfidence refers to the belief that you are better and more skilled than you actually are in reality. In work on aggression in simulated war games Johnson et al. (2006) found that overconfident people held much higher expectations about their likelihood of success in combat and thus proved more likely to attack, even without prior provocation.

Significantly, this study found tremendous overconfidence among male participants in particular, who remained remarkably resistant to appropriate recalibration in the face of failure. Subjects were asked to estimate how well they would do in the game prior to play. Most men claimed that they would do extremely well, while most women estimated that they would perform at about average level. Significantly, once participants had information about whether or not they won or lost their particular game, calibration based on feedback did not fall in line with normative expectations. Women who lost recalibrated strongly downward, but did not make sufficient adjustment upward in the wake of victory. Men, on the other hand, tended to recalibrate quickly to winning, and in fact tended to overestimate their newly demonstrated skill, while failing to downregulate adequately in the face of failure.

These findings remain largely consistent with the overall literature on overconfidence and conflict (Johnson, 2004). In their evolutionary model of overconfidence, Johnson & Fowler (2009) show how overconfident individuals will make more challenges in uncertain environment. They also illustrate how environments with lots of resources can thus prove more likely to create more conflict. They suggest that overconfidence makes evolutionary sense by maximizing fitness whenever the value of resources exceeds twice the cost of competition. Of course part of the challenge posed by uncertainty is that participants often do not know ahead of time the exact value of the resources at stake, or the cost it might extract in order to protect them. This challenge of such a calculus represents precisely why uncertainty can impose such a high psychological cost on decision makers seeking to protect central values at the lowest possible cost without incurring undue waste.

Ironically, overconfidence often tends to go hand in hand with incompetence (Ehrlinger et al., 2008). People tend to grossly overestimate their skills in all kinds of social and intellectual tasks. This appears to result from the fact that they lack the skills necessary to realize their own limitations. Failure to see the nature of their own mistakes leads incompetent people to have higher estimates of their own performance than is warranted by objective judgments. Thus, incompetence exacerbates overconfidence to the detriment of well-calibrated decision making.

Uncertainty of Outcomes

One of the real psychological challenges in trying to understand and appropriately respond to a cyberthreat derives from the kind of uncertainty related to potential outcomes. A National Research Council report (2009) outlines several types of uncertainties in this area: those that result from the use of any kind of weapon; those that derive from the use of a new weapon (what Slovic (1999) might refer to as "dread" risk, related to fear of the unknown); and those that emerge from unexpected interaction effects between military and civilian communication systems.

The first kind of uncertainty raises the specter of collateral damage, which in the cybersphere can be quite large. Businesses, hospitals, utilities and many other aspects of the commercial sector now largely depend on a functioning Internet in order to conduct their daily affairs; any action taken to deny access to an attacker could result in serious damage to interests the government seeks to protect. Also important in a democratic, free-market society is that potential technical responses that might provide greater potential protection in some circumstances, may also pose greater threats to both privacy and freedom. In addition, these processes might also affect the profitability of large sectors of the economy, such as the Starbucks mentioned above, which rely on open and inexpensive access to the Internet, not least for purposes of shopping.

The second kind of uncertainty poses the risk of blowback, whereby in an attempt to block or attack an intruder, unexpected consequences can emerge which come back to harm or destroy one's own machines, possibly even damaging the possibility for such machines to locate and desist future activities on the part of the invader. Much like the use of a biological weapon in war, which can risk damage to one's own troops depending on the way the wind is blowing, the opportunity to uncover the existence of many possibly unknown links between intermediary machines may outweigh the expected benefits of denying access, especially if such benefits cannot guarantee permanent destruction of the enemy.

The third type of uncertainty clearly overlaps with the first, but also raises additional concerns related to unpredictable system effects (Jervis, 1998), whereby unintended consequences can emerge from the attempt to separate intrinsically intertwined systems into components whose manipulation will not undermine a highly interdependent system.

CONCLUSIONS

Clearly, the risk of cyberattack, like other forms of terrorism, poses an important challenge for future decision makers. The traditional notion, built around kinetic weapons, of using deterrence to prevent an attack may not prove a viable strategic model because it rests on assumptions of rationality that do not reflect accurate notions of human decision making capability. For deterrence to work, actors must believe that they can credibly threaten retaliation that would deny the attacker the spoils of victory. Yet such a notion rests on the belief that leaders can both identify attackers and respond in kind. Neither of those assumptions credibly holds true in the world of cyberspace. A more appropriate analogy rests on a public health model of disease prevention, where defenders engage in active surveillance to discover and monitor infections early, thus reducing the risk for lethal catastrophe.

Technical solutions may improve the ability to attribute the source of an attack to a particular machine, but there is no technical way to credibly link any given machine to a particular actor who can then be held accountable for his actions. That plausible deniability remains inherent in the anonymous nature of the technological systems themselves. Further, defensive technologies fail as offensive strategies overcome them, just as has occurred over time with kinetic weapons. While the United States and other countries such as China clearly seek dominance in cyberattack capabilities, ultimately such dominance, and the ability to maintain it, appears ephemeral in nature since so many people can acquire the skills to hack into machines and use other machines as proxies, with resources they can secure on their own at relatively little expense. The cost and sophistication of a machine does not remain commensurate with the obstacles that confront those who seek plutonium for purposes of building a nuclear bomb. Such a reality also increases the difficulty of finding and thwarting the many actors operating in this realm for different purposes. Therefore, if offensive and defensive technologies will ultimately prove inadequate, and adequate means of attribution remain impossible, decision makers are left in the realm of having to respond to attacks which by their very nature impose, and are intended to incur, high degrees of uncertainty.

If such is the case, then the game that is being played between attacker and target is primarily psychological in nature, even if the solutions need to be political in response. Under conditions of uncertainty, several psychological processes exist which exacerbate the decisional challenges which confront leaders under even the best of certain conditions. First, judgmental biases work to make certain scenarios appear more plausible than probable because of their similarity to known or previous events, or because of their salience. Emotions such as fear or anger can exacerbate the desire to respond in a conciliatory or hostile manner, respectively. Second, attributional strategies related to assessments of consensus, distinctiveness and consistency can be used to try to get at least an internal sense of likely, if not definitive, attribution, based on discursive identity revelation. Third, many social psychological processes, including anonymity, deindividuation, social validation and contagion effects, work to enhance the prospects for terrorist entrepreneurs to recruit followers to engage in destructive processes, including dedicated denial of service attacks. Careful thought should go into the best way to mobilize similar public forces in service of the national interest; greater public awareness of the stakes in simple, emotional language (i.e. "How long could you live without email?") might serve to balance the forces on this front. Fourth, overconfidence poses a real threat to obtaining accurate estimates of the likelihood of success in counterattack, and increases the probability of undertaking hostile retaliatory action without adequate or accurate information. Such responses may precipitate the kind of collateral damage and blowback which may serve to damage the very elements of society that the government is supposed to protect.

Importantly, all these forces combine to produce an aggregated effect whereby leaders will tend to leap to premature conclusions when faced with the threat or reality of cyberattack. This will happen particularly under conditions of stress, or when leaders fall prey to either groupthink, or its opposite but equally destructive force, emotional isolation (Bar-Joseph & McDermott, 2007). They may quickly jump beyond the evidence available, often with a great deal of confidence in the accuracy of their judgments, to reach conclusions about who is responsible and what they are trying to accomplish. Such beliefs will then prove unusually resistant to modification in the face of later information or further analysis. Furthermore, such ideas will be heavily influenced by the beliefs and images such leaders hold about the potential strength and malignant intent of various enemies. In this way, context will provide critical information by establishing the category into which a particular threat or attack is placed. However, such assessments may also convey inaccurate indications regarding the nature of a current attack by highlighting the source of a recent similar threat, or stressing the influence of a particular actor. These judgments can thus skew the perception of leaders who strive to achieve certainty in order to know how best to respond. Appropriate responses may not require certainty to be effective, but leaders are likely to be reluctant to make decisions without such assurance, however false, inflated or self-created.

Given what we know about the psychological propensities to which individuals appear prone, what mistakes are leaders most susceptible to making in the area of cyberattack, as opposed to another realm? The two most significant relate to anonymity, and its tendency to increase aggression through processes of deindividuation, and social contagion, because of the speed and extent of spread which can occur on the Internet. Importantly, the effects of anonymity do not only confer to the aggressor, but also the target. If a leader has no personal knowledge of his opponent, it may be easier to order more extreme responses than if he was aware of mitigating or explanatory circumstances on the part of the assailant. Similarly, social contagion can exert effects far beyond the ability of any government to control, since the diffusion can take on a life of its own quickly through the neurocomputational mutations that can occur in cyberspace. It would be a mistake for governments to underestimate their speed or potency, or to overestimate their ability to predict or control these events.

How might such psychological tendencies be addressed to mitigate potentially harmful effects? Recall that, like with psychotherapy, awareness of a process does not necessary incur protection against its effect. Knowing that these biases exist does not prove sufficient to eliminate their effects. However, placing options side by side in ways which render transparent the effect of these biases at the time of decision can lead to more reliable choices. In addition, competence matters. Training leaders, especially those from cyber command who will be tasked with providing information to a decision maker in a time of crisis, with as much information as possible about both the technical and political aspects of attribution, may prove enormously helpful. In this regard, simulations where such leaders learn to more properly calibrate their judgments, and their confidence, with immediate feedback as to accuracy, can go a far distance toward increasing skill, decreasing overconfidence, and rendering more informed choice. Such procedures could be instigated as part of clear institutional promotion and training requirements for relevant jobs.

Prospects for cyberattack will not diminish. Developing appropriate response strategies in the face of various potential scenarios will prove challenging. But marshalling the forces of human psychology in support of such procedures constitutes a stronger edifice upon which to build defense than theories modeled on assumptions of rationality without empirical support.

REFERENCES

Bar-Joseph, Uri & McDermott, Rose. 2007. Personal Functioning Under Stress Accountability and Social Support of Israeli Leaders in the Yom Kippur War. *Journal of Conflict Resolution* 52(1): 144-170.

Bargh John & McKenna KYA. 2004. The Internet and social life. *Annual Review of Psychology* 55:573-90.

Bar-Hillel, Maya & Neter, Efrat. 1993. How alike is it versus how likely is it: A disjunction fallacy in probability judgments. *Journal of Personality and Social Psychology* 65(6): 1119-1131.

Carpenter, Daniel. 2002. Groups, the Media, Agency Waiting Costs, and FDA Drug Approval. *American Journal of Political Science* 46 (3): 490-505.

Cialdini, Robert. 2001. *Influence: science and practice, 4th ed.* New York: HarperCollins.

Derks, Daantje, Agneta H. Fischer, Bos, and E. R. Arjan. 2008. The role of emotion in computer-mediated communication: A review *Computers in Human Behavior* 24(3):766-785.

Ehrlinger, Joyce, Johnson, Kerry, Banner, Matthew, Dunning, David & Kruger, Justin. 2008. Why the Unskilled Are Unaware: Further Explorations of (Absent) Self-Insight Among the Incompetent. *Organ Behav Hum Decis Process* 105(1): 98-121.

Freud, Sigmund. 1922/1990. *Group Psychology and the Analysis of the Ego.* New York: W. W. Norton & Co.

Gault, Barbara & Sabini, John. 2000. The roles of empathy, anger, and gender in predicting attitudes toward punitive, reparative, and preventative public policies *Cognition & Emotion*, 14, (4):495-520.

Gigerenzer, Gerd. 1996. On narrow norms and vague heuristics: A reply to Kahneman and Tversky. *Psychological Review* 103(3): 592-596.

Guadagno, Rosanna, Cialdini, Robert, & Evron, Gadi. 2010. Storming the Servers: A Social Psychological Analysis of the First Internet War. *Cybertechnology, Behavior and Social Networking* 13: 1-8.

Heath, Chip & Heath, Dan. 2007. *Made to Stick: Why Some Ideas Survive and Others Die.* New York: Random House.

Jervis, Robert. 1979. Deterrence Theory Revisited. *World Politics* 31 (2): 289-324.

Jervis, Robert. 1982-1983. Deterrence and Perception. *International Security* 7 (3): 3-30.

Jervis, Robert. 1998. *Systems Effects: Complexity in Political and Social Life.* Princeton, NJ: Princeton University Press.

Johnson, Dominic. 2004. *Overconfidence and War*: The Havoc and Glory of Positive Illusions. Cambridge, MA: Harvard University Press.

Johnson, Dominic, McDermott, Rose, Barrett, Emily, Cowden, Jonathan, Wrangham, Richard, McIntyre, Matthew & Rosen, Stephen Peter. 2006. Overconfidence in wargames: experimental evidence on expectations, aggression, gender and testosterone. *Proc Biol Sci.* 273(1600): 2513-2520.

Johnson, Dominic & Fowler, James. 2009. The Evolution of Overconfidence. Unpublished ms.

Joinson AN. 2001. Self-disclosure in computer-mediated communication: the role of self-awareness and visual anonymity. *European Journal of Social Psychology* 31:177–92.

Kahneman, Daniel & Tversky, Amos. 1979. Prospect Theory: An Analysis of Decision under Risk. *Econometrica* 47 (2): 263-291.

Kahneman, Daniel & Tversky, Amos. 1984. Choices, Values and Frames. *American Psychologist.* 39(4): 341-350.

Kelley, Harold. 1967. Attribution Theory in Social Psychology. *Nebraska Symposium on Motivation* 15: 192-238.

Khong, Yuen Foong. 1992. *Analogies at War: Korea, Munich, Dien Bien Phu and the Vietnam Decisions of 1965.* Princeton, NJ: Princeton University Press.

Lerner, Jennifer & Keltner, Dacher. 2000. Beyond valence: Toward a model of emotion-specific influences on judgement and choice. *Cognition & Emotion* 14 (4): 473-493.

Lord, Charles, Ross, Lee & Lepper, Mark. 1979. Biased assimilation and attitude polarization: The effect of prior theories on subsequently considered evidence. *Journal of Personality and Social Psychology* 37 (11): 2098-2109.

MacKay C. 1841. *Extraordinary Popular Delusions and the Madness of Crowds.* New York: Farrar, Straus, & Giroux.

Matheson K & Zanna Mark. 1989. Persuasion as a function of selfawareness in computer-mediated communication. *Social Behaviour* 4:99–111.

Moral-Toranzo, Felix, Canto-Ortiz, Jesus, & Gomez-Jacinto, Luis. 2007. Anonymity effects in computer-mediated communication in the case of minority influence. *Computers in Human Behavior* 23 (3):1660-1674.

National Research Council. 2009. *Technology, Policy, Law, and Ethics Regarding U.S. Acquisition and Use of Cyberattack Capabiltities.* Washington, D.C.: National Academies Press.

Postmes T, Spears R, & Lea M. 2002. Intergroup differentiation in computer mediated communication: effects of depersonalization. *Group Dynamics* 6:3-15.

Reicher Stephen, Spears R, & Postmes T. 1995. A social identity model of deindividuation phenomena. In Stroebe W, Hewstone M, eds. *European review of social psychology, vol. 6.* Chichester: Wiley.

Rosen, Stephen Peter. 2005. *War and Human Nature.* Princeton, NJ: Princeton University Press.

Sassenberg K, Boos M, Rabung S. 2005. Attitude change in face-to face and computer-mediated communication: private selfawareness as mediator and moderator. *European Journal of Social Psychology* 35:361-74.

Slovic, Paul.1999. Trust, Emotion, Sex, Politics, and Science: Surveying the Risk-Assessment Battlefield. *Risk Analysis* 19(4):689-701.

Slovic, Paul, Kahneman, Daniel & Tversky, Amos. 1982. *Judgment Under Uncertaitny: Heuristics and Biases.* New York: Cambridge University Press.

Stoll, Clifford. 2005. *The Cuckoo's Egg; Tracking a Spy Through a Network of Computer Espionage.* New York: Pocket.

Tversky, Amos & Kahneman, Daniel. 1983. Extensional versus intuitive reasoning: The conjunction fallacy in probability judgment. *Psychological Review* 90(4): 293-315.

Tversky, Amos & Kahneman, Daniel. 1992. Advances in prospect theory: Cumulative representation of uncertainty. *Journal of Risk and Uncertainty* 5(4): 297-323.

Webster, Donna & Kruglanski, Arie. 1997. Cognitive and Social Consequences of the Need for Cognitive Closure. *European Review of Social Psychology* 8.

Zimbardo, Philip. 1970. The human choice: individuation, reasons, and order versus deindividuation, impulse, and chaos. In Arnold WJ, Levine D, eds. *Nebraska Symposium on Motivation* 17:237-307. Lincoln: University of Nebraska Press.

Group 5—Organization of Government

The Organization of the United States Government and Private Sector for Achieving Cyber Deterrence

Paul Rosenzweig*

Red Branch Consulting

INTRODUCTION

A few years ago, the Central Intelligence Agency (CIA) working cooperatively with Saudi Arabia set up a "honey pot" website[1] to attract jihadi sympathizers. By all reports the website served as a useful intelligence gathering tool, giving the unseen CIA and Saudi observers insights into the activities and interests of the terrorists who frequented the site. By 2008, however, it had become apparent that some were using the website to make operational plans to infiltrate jihadists into Iraq where they would join the insurgency, potentially threatening the lives of American troops. The National Security Council (NSC) convened a group of representatives from the Department of Defense (DoD), CIA, Department of Justice (DOJ), the Office of the Director of National Intelligence (ODNI), and the National Security Agency (NSA) to consider the matter. Eventually, over the CIA's objections, a DoD team from Joint Functional Component Command–Network Warfare (JFCC-NW) "took down" the website. Its actions caused collateral effects as far away as Germany, and disappointed our Saudi collaborators.[2]

The incident illuminates a host of definitional and policy issues and challenges in the cyber realm, many of which are considered in companion pieces for this study. But equally clear from this anecdote are the challenges we face from the lack of any effective, purpose-built, standing organizations or processes within the U.S. government for developing policy or making decisions about cyber attacks and cyber defense. Rather, as this particular event makes clear, critical decisions that may set precedent are frequently made in an ad hoc manner often without the benefit of either the time or inclination for a broader and comprehensive consideration of the policy implications of the decisions.

---

*Principal, Red Branch Consulting, PLLC, and Professorial Lecturer in Law, George Washington University School of Law. The author expresses his thanks to Nicholas Rueter, a J.D./M.A. candidate at Duke University, for his able research assistance. I am indebted to the participants in the NAS workshop, the anonymous reviewers of this paper, and particularly to the members of the panel, for their thoughtful review and comments which have improved this paper. The remaining errors are, of course, my own.

[1]A "honey pot" is a website that is designed with features intended to lure and entice potential visitors, much as honey attracts bees, or Winnie the Pooh.

[2]The details of this event were disclosed in Ellen Nakashima, Dismantling of Saudi-CIA Web site illustrates need for clearer cyberwar policies, Wash. Post at A01 (March 19, 2010) [available at http://www.washingtonpost.com/wp-dyn/content/article/2010/03/18/AR2010031805464.html].

The organizational deficit is two-fold: It is, first and foremost, a lack of structures for the *making* of a comprehensive policy and a lack of organizational cohesiveness in driving solutions forward in a way that includes all relevant stakeholders. It is, secondarily, a lack of adequate structures for *implementing* the policy decisions that have been made and for auditing our success (or failure) in doing so. This organizational deficit is not for a lack of effort. For more than 10 years, various Executive boards, agencies and working groups have struggled to create a cohesive framework for cyber decision-making.

Yet, today, most observers would agree that the U.S. has yet to develop a stable solution. As two well-regarded observers recently noted:

> [W]e also developed on an *ad hoc* basis over the last two decades various organizational structures in response to the cyber threat. Yet those infrastructure protection boards and cyber commissions typically lacked leadership, had no real authority, and were often made up of individuals who did not have combined expertise in national security, cyber security, policy, and law.
>
> Meanwhile, the private sector, owners of most of our critical cyber infrastructure, pursued an unstructured response to the threats, relying in the first instance on government systems for cyber security.[3]

A number of legitimate reasons explain why we have yet to develop these structures and processes. There are, first, several unique challenges inherent in deterring or preventing cyber attacks. These include the well-known attribution problem, the dependence of the civilian economy and military capability on information technology, and the difficulty in distinguishing between attack and exploitation. More prosaically, despite the proliferation of boards and commissions we simply have not paid enough sustained attention to the problem: organizational structures for the United States government to support our cyber deterrence activities have developed organically, over the past 20 years, through episodic and often reactive attention, rather than the product of a concerted policy-making process.

Then, too, by virtue of the nature of the cyber intrusions we have experienced, our organizational efforts have focused systematically on defensive measures rather than offensive ones. As a consequence, though our organizational structures for cyber defense are incomplete and lack coherence, with gaps and overlaps in responsibility and authority that have yet to be resolved, our structures for controlling attack/response mechanisms are even more immature and have yet to evolve to permit consideration of a "whole of government response" that would bring to bear all aspects of government power.

The lack of coherence is magnified because existing structures tend to conflate two distinct operational functions—those of policy decision-making and those of implementation. The function of setting deterrence policy and deciding a course of action will typically rest with governmental authorities. However, in the cyber domain (unlike, say, the nuclear domain), aspects of the implementation of those decisions will affect private sector actors who deploy their own defensive mechanisms and whose networks may be used to deliver a cyber response. The complex interaction between civilian, governmental, and military organizational structures for both offensive and defensive operations requires simplification.

This paper begins with a review of the history of existing American structures and processes within the Executive branch and examines the role of non-executive structures in the Legislative and Judicial branches of government. From this background the paper proceeds to a consideration of several particularly challenging questions relating to cyber deterrence policy and organization. This, in turn, allows for the development of recommendations for the improvement of the current structures.

I. A BRIEF INTERLUDE—A TAXONOMY OF DETERRENCE STRUCTURES

To some degree, a paper considering questions relating to the organization of the U.S. government's cyber deterrence response is premature. The organizational structures and procedures that the United States adopts to implement a policy of cyber deterrence should, optimally, be designed to implement the chosen underlying policy of deterrence itself. Form ought, ideally, to follow function, and in the absence of a clearly defined policy, defining a structure to implement a policy is hazardous, at best, and quite possibly counter-productive.

---

[3]William Banks & Elizabeth Rindskopf-Parker, Introduction, 4 J. Nat'l Sec. L. & Plcy. 1, 3 (2010).

Nonetheless, certain preliminary thoughts about organizational structures can be offered. But doing so requires the development of a taxonomy of deterrence, since in the cyber domain (as much, if not more so as in the physical world) our deterrence efforts will operate along several different tracks.

Broadly speaking traditional deterrence strategies are implemented through policies of denial and punishment.[4] In the context of the cyber domain, denial activities will involve a multifaceted approach that includes significant civilian participation. Punishment activities may well involve non-cyber responses that incorporate non-military (and possibly traditional kinetic military) actions. As a result, our cyber deterrence structures will need to be broad and wide ranging, and will likely vary depending upon which function the structures seek to support.

To that end, it is useful (or, at least, this author finds it useful) to identify certain subcategories of potential cyber deterrence activities for purposes of assessing the utility of current structures and processes. Within the area of denial, one can identify at least three distinct types of activity:

- *Cyber defense*—Classic activities of cybersecurity involving the detection and prevention of cyber intrusions or attacks.
- *Cyber resilience*—Activities relating to the strengthening of cyber networks so that even successful attacks have only limited effect because of redundancy and repair capacity built into the system.
- *Cyber systems assurance*—Activities relating to providing assurance that the cyber systems in use are not subject to foreign penetration or control.

Likewise, the area of punishment will, conceptually, involve at least two reasonably distinct activities that might require distinct structures:

- *Cyber attack*—Activities relating to a response to a cyber attack involving retaliatory (or preemptive) cyber action.
- *Non-cyber response*—Activities in response to a cyber attack not involving a cyber response (whether kinetic military acts or non-military acts).

And, finally, overarching all of these structures there exists a need for strategic-level structures that enable the *cyber coordination* of these various activities.

Not all of the structures that one can conceive of taxonomically have found a real-world analog within the federal government (or the private sector). To the contrary, while some (like cyber resilience structures) have a relatively long history (in cyber terms), others (like those relating to cyber assurance) are almost non-existent. In this section, we examine the existing federal organizational structures and processes and how they came to be.

A. Cyber Defense and Cyber Resilience to Protect Critical Infrastructure

Though conceptually distinct, the U.S. government has treated cyber defense and resilience functions as interrelated, and developed structures that seek to address both aspects of deterrence/denial through a single set of mechanisms.

Early Efforts

President Clinton made the first significant U.S. effort to address cyber defense and resilience issues with the issuance of Presidential Decision Directive (PDD)-63 in May 1998.[5] The directive noted the potential vulnerability of American infrastructure (ranging from transportation to water systems) and set forth a process for the development of an infrastructure assurance plan to protect critical assets. Nota-

---

[4]National Research Council, William Owens, Kenneth Dam & Herbert Lin, eds., Technology, Policy, Law, and Ethics Regarding U.S. Acquisition and Use of Cyberattack Capabilities, § 9.1 (National Academes Press 2009).

[5]PDD/NSC-63, Critical Infrastructure Protection (May 22, 1998) [available at http://www.fas.org/irp/offdocs/pdd/pdd-63.pdf].

bly, the directive treated cyberspace as a *mode* by which threats to infrastructure would be propagated and did not identify cyberspace, itself, as a critical infrastructure asset. Each sector of the economy was to identify its vulnerabilities and propose remedies for them. The directive called for development of response plans to minimize the damage of attacks on infrastructure and reconstitution plans for restoring capabilities rapidly.[6]

PDD-63 also devised a coordination structure that has, in effect, become the model for all succeeding cyber defense and resilience activities. Within the Federal government, each economic sector was associated with a "lead agency" that would have the principal responsibility for coordinating activities with the private sector and developing the Federal plans. As one might expect, these designations followed the regulatory functions of then-existing Federal agencies: Treasury was the lead for banking activities; HHS for public health; Energy for electric power and so on.[7] These agencies would appoint senior officials to serve as "Sector Liaisons" who would, in turn be coordinated by a "National Coordinator for Security, Infrastructure Protection and Counter Terrorism" who would, himself, be a subordinate of the National Security Advisor (that is, part of what today we would call the National Security Council). The work of this Federal organization would be supplemented by the appointment of a board of prominent non-Federal leaders (infrastructure providers and state and local officials) who would provide advice under the auspices of the National Infrastructure Assurance Council (NIAC), a board that continues to exist today.[8]

ISACs

As a direct result of PDD-63, the U.S. government fostered the creation of sector-specific Information Sharing and Analysis Centers (ISACs). The purpose of the ISACs, as the name suggests, is to enable the sharing of information, within each sector, about threats and vulnerabilities to that sector. Since 1998, ISACs have been created in many of the critical infrastructure sectors (e.g. Financial Services; Real Estate; and Electricity). Most notably, an Information Technology ISAC was one of the first created. The current reach of the ISACs to the various critical infrastructures is extensive. When considered collectively, the individual private/public sector ISACs possess an outreach and connectivity network to approximately 85% of the U.S. critical infrastructure.

The ISAC structure is intended to provide each sector with 24/7 information sharing/intelligence capabilities; allow the sector to collect and analyze threats based on its own subject matter analytical expertise; and coordinate with the government on sector-specific impacts. The efforts have been moderately successful in disseminating information, but complaints from industry continue to arise that the government is not effectively using private sector expertise to leverage its capabilities,[9] and does not (often for classification reasons) adequately share threat information in the cyber domain.[10]

---

[6]PDD/NSC-63 §8.

[7]PDD/NSC-63, Annex A.

[8]PDD/NSC-63 § VI.

[9]For example, initially few, if any, private sector participants were routinely invited to the large-scale TOPOFF exercises in which U.S. government officials examine their response to predicted future terrorist incidents. *See* ISAC Council White Paper, "The Integration of ISACs in to Government and Department of Defense Homeland Security and Homeland Defense Exercises, (January 2004) [available at http://www.isaccouncil.org/whitepapers/files/Integration_of_ISACs_Into_Exercises_013104.pdf]. Though this particular issue has been resolved in more recent exercises it is emblematic of the challenges faced in integrating a public and private sector response.

[10]There have been no significant recent studies of the effectiveness of ISACs by outside sources. A dated review, conducted by GAO in 2005, reports a number of breakdowns in information sharing. *See* Critical Infrastructure Protection: Department of Homeland Security Faces Challenges in Fulfilling Cybersecurity Responsibilities, at 32 (GAO-05-434 May 2005). A slightly more recent study from 2006 found that successful integration varied widely across the ISAC sectors. *See* Critical Infrastructure Protection: Progress Coordinating Government and Private Sector Efforts Varies by Sectors' Characteristics (GAO-07-39 Oct. 2006).

Recent Developments

President Bush sought to advance the Clinton initiative, and gave voice to the first "National Strategy to Secure Cyberspace."[11] For the first time, the strategy recognized that cyberspace was a separate infrastructure in its own right, worthy of protection because of its inherent value (rather than, as before, because it provided a means by which attacks on other infrastructure could occur). The principal noteworthiness of the strategy, for purposes of this inquiry, lay in its call for the development of a public-private architecture for responding to national cyber incidents.[12]

This recognition of the uniqueness of cyberspace as an independent infrastructure was confirmed in Homeland Security Presidential Directive (HSPD)-7, which defined critical infrastructure as "both physical and cyber-based" assets so vital to the United States that the incapacity or destruction of such systems and assets would have a debilitating impact on American interests.[13] HSPD-7 sought to define the coordinating role of the Department of Homeland Security (DHS) in protecting cyber assets, directing the DHS Secretary to "maintain an organization to serve as a focal point for the security of cyberspace. The organization will facilitate interactions and collaborations between and among Federal departments and agencies, State and local governments, the private sector, academia and international organizations. To the extent permitted by law, Federal departments and agencies with cyber expertise, including but not limited to the Departments of Justice, Commerce, the Treasury, Defense, Energy, and State, and the Central Intelligence Agency, will collaborate with and support the organization in accomplishing its mission."[14]

As the laundry list of involved agencies makes clear, the coordinative function on cybersecurity issues is a daunting task. The challenge is magnified when one considers the multivariate nature of the tasks that comprise a government-wide approach to cybersecurity. In January 2008, President Bush adopted a Comprehensive National Cybersecurity Initiative (CNCI), portions of which were declassified by President Obama in 2010. The CNCI identifies 12 broad cybersecurity initiatives, ranging from increased cyber education and cyber domain situational awareness to a call for the development of a comprehensive cyber deterrence strategy (of which this study is a small part). All but 3 of these initiatives are fairly characterized as requiring efforts of cyber defense and/or cyber resilience.[15]

The complexity of the coordination task was highlighted by the principal recommendation of President Obama's Cyber Space Policy Review, a comprehensive review of American cyber policy undertaken at the start of the President's Administration.[16] Recognizing the difficulty of coordinating so many initiatives in so many agencies, the Review called for the appointment of a White House-level policy coordinator (colloquially knows as a "Cyber Czar") who would "anchor" leadership on cyber issues within the White House.[17] Indeed, the need for leadership was so palpable that the Review's first chapter was entitled "Leading from the Top." Responding to this call, in December 2009, President Obama appointed Howard Schmidt as the first Special Assistant to the President and Cybersecurity Coordinator.

The Cybersecurity Coordinator's powers remain, however, consultative and coordinative rather than directive and mandatory. As the Review made clear, the coordinator does not (and was not intended to) have any operational authority or responsibility, nor the authority to make policy unilaterally. Rather

---

[11]The National Strategy to Secure Cyberspace (February 2003), [available at http://www.dhs.gov/xlibrary/assets/National_Cyberspace_Strategy.pdf].

[12]National Strategy to Secure Cyberspace at 20-24.

[13]Homeland Security Presidential Directive-7 (Dec. 17, 2003).

[14]HSPD-7 § 16.

[15]Comprehensive National Cybersecurity Initiative (declassified version) [available at http://www.whitehouse.gov/cyber security/comprehensive-national-cybersecurity-initiative]. Three of the initiatives (calling for a cyber counter-intelligence policy; development of a deterrence strategy; and adoption of a supply change risk management strategy) have aspects of cyber defense or resilience to them, but more appropriately are characterized as policies of cyber assurance, cyber attack or non-cyber response. As with any taxonomy, the categorization of policies is indefinite at the margins and of utility only insofar as it aids analysis.

[16]Cyber Space Policy Review: Assuring a Trusted and Resilient Information and Communications Infrastructure (May 2009).

[17]Cyber Space Policy Review at 7; *see also id.* at vi (recommendation #1, calls for appointment of NSC-level policy cyber coordinator).

the coordinator is intended to act through the normal interagency process to harmonize and coordinate policy across inter-agency boundaries.[18] Here too, as the CNCI's task-list makes clear, the predominant effort for the Coordinator has been in the realms of cyber defense and cyber resilience.

B. Cyber Systems Assurance

Other cyber threats arise, not from direct attack on the system, but from threats that originate from within the system itself. Some of those threats might arise from insider activity—as when an enemy agent successfully poses as an insider to gain access to the cyber system. Conceptually, however, this insider threat (whether to a U.S. government target or a private commercial target) poses no problems distinct from those posed by any other insider effort. Likewise, the systems we have developed and put in place to protect against more traditional insider threats of espionage—security clearances and background checks—are likely also appropriate to counter the cyber insider threat. Thus, there is little reason to suspect that any organizational or process issues exist that are unique to cyber insiders.

The same cannot be said of the inside threat posed to cyber systems by the workings of the hardware within the various routers, switches, operating systems and peripherals that comprise the real-world manifestations of cyberspace or the code in the software purchased from foreign sources.[19] History records several examples where a state actor has taken advantage of its position as a system supplier to surreptitiously introduce systems subject to its own control or influence.[20] It is thus a matter of significant concern that over the past decades the United States government has become increasingly reliant on commercial off the shelf technology (COTS) for much of its cyber supply needs. Indeed, counterterrorism experts have sometimes opined that American reliance on COTS computer technology, that is often manufactured and/or maintained overseas, poses a greater vulnerability to U.S. cyber systems than traditional cyber attacks.[21] Or, as the Defense Science Board opined in 2007: "The current systems designs, assurance methodologies, acquisition procedures, and knowledge of adversarial capabilities and intentions are inadequate to the magnitude of the threat."[22]

The situation has changed little in the past three years. For this reason, the CNCI identified "global supply chain risk management" as one of the initiatives critical to enhanced cybersecurity.[23] Yet, the U.S. has a very limited set of systems and processes in place to respond to this challenge. Indeed, as observers have noted, there is a disconnect between our counter-intelligence, which is often aware of risks to our cyber supply chain, and our procurement processes, which cannot have access to classified information regarding supply chain threats. Setting aside intelligence concerns, the prospect of creating a "black list" of unacceptable products for purchase is fraught with problematic issues regarding liability

---

[18]Cyber Space Policy Review at 8.

[19]The dependence of the Department of Defense on commercial, non-domestic software and hardware was identified as a significant vulnerability by the Defense Science Board. *See* Report on Mission Impact of Foreign Influence on DoD Software (Defense Science Board, Sept. 2007). The vulnerabilities identified are not, of course, limited to DoD, but pervade any IT system (whether governmental or private-sector operated) that uses foreign-sourced hardware or software.

[20]A recent RAND study, for example, noted two such instances—the British "gift" of Enigma machines to other countries and a Russian use of black market systems controllers to disrupt pipeline activity. *See* Martin Libicki, Cyberdeterrence and Cyberwar, at 21 & nn. 27, 28 (RAND 2009).

[21]Libicki, Cyberdeterrence and Cyberwar at 22; National Security Threats in Cyberspace at 24-25 (ABA/National Strategy Forum, 2009 [hereinafter "National Security Threats"].

[22]Defense Science Board, "Foreign Influence," at vi.

[23]CNCI, Initiative #11. It bears noting that supply chain security is not exclusively an issue of national security. Many of the same problems and challenges are posed by the possibility of fraud and the delivery of counterfeit products. The magnitude of the problem is daunting. A recent Department of Commerce report cited nearly 9,000 instances of counterfeit electronics encountered by original component manufacturers in 2008 alone. *See* Department of Commerce, Bureau of Industry and Security (OTE), "Defense Industrial Base Assessment: Counterfeit Electronics," (Jan. 2010) at 11. The Semiconductor Industry Association has reported the seizure of more than 1.7 million counterfeit chips since its Anticounterfeiting Task Force began in 2007. *See* Michael Aisenberg, "The Information Technology Supply Chain: Survey and Forecast of Emerging Obligations for Industrial Vendors," at 2 (ABA Info Sec. Quarterly, Spring 2010) [copy on file with author].

and fidelity.[24] And, even if we could devise a means of giving the procurement process access to sufficient information and if liability issues could be overcome, it might well be the case that no significant alternative sources of supply exist.

At present, there are only two notable structures in operation within the U.S. government that provide a means of addressing supply chain security issues—and neither is particularly adept or well suited to the task.

One is the Committee on Foreign Investment in the United States (CFIUS). CFIUS is an inter-agency committee authorized to review transactions that could result in control of a U.S. business by a foreign person (known as "covered transactions"), in order to determine the effect of such transactions on the national security of the United States.[25] If CFIUS determines that the proposed transaction poses a risk of some sort it may prohibit the transaction altogether or, far more frequently, it may enter into a mitigation agreement that puts in place mechanisms and requirements that it deems necessary to ameliorate the risk. Though CFIUS was initially created to focus on the sale of companies that would result in foreign control of defense-critical industries, in the post-9/11 world it has come, as well, to focus on sales that will effect critical infrastructure (such as the now-infamous sale of port facilities to Dubai Ports World). This focus has, on at least one publicly acknowledged occasion, involved the review of a purchase that implicated cybersecurity concerns.[26]

Likewise, an interagency working group known as "Team Telecom" reviews questions relating to the acquisition of an ownership interest in American telecommunications companies by foreign interests. The Federal Communications Commission has statutory authority to review transactions where a foreign entity seeks to purchase more than a 25 percent indirect ownership stake in U.S. common carriers licensed by the FCC. When such a transaction is proposed the FCC will, as a matter of policy, defer to the Executive branch and coordinate the application with the Executive branch for national security, law enforcement, foreign policy, or trade concerns. The applications are referred to Team Telecom, which is co-chaired by staff from the Department of Homeland Security and the Department of Justice, including the FBI, and which also includes representatives from the Departments of Commerce, Defense, State, and the Treasury, and the Office of the United States Trade Representative. Based on its review, Team Telecom may have no comment on an application or may request that the FCC condition grant of the application on compliance with assurances made by the applicant in either an exchange of letters or a formal security agreement. In this way, as well, the U.S. government will on occasion have a process in place for addressing cyber assurance concerns that result from the foreign purchase (note that both processes are limited to the acquisition of ownership interests) of an interest in a cyber-related industry.[27]

In recent years a number of ad hoc working groups have sprung up to consider the COTS challenge. Many of them operate in a classified environment. A recent survey by the Co-chair of the ABA Information Security Committee identified no fewer than five separate industry and Federal initiatives.[28] The

---

[24]National Security Threats at 24-25.

[25]CFIUS operates pursuant to section 721 of the Defense Production Act of 1950, as amended by the Foreign Investment and National Security Act of 2007 (section 721) and as implemented by Executive Order 11858, as amended, and regulations at 31 C.F.R. Part 800. The DNI is tasked with conducting an intelligence assessment of the risks posed by certain transactions and reporting to the committee on his findings. His representative sits, *ex officio*, on the committee and brings a counter-intelligence perspective to its deliberations where appropriate.

[26]*See* James Jackson, "The Committee on Foreign Investments in the United States (CFIUS)" at 9 (Congressional Research Service, Feb. 4, 2010) (reporting that the Israeli firm Check Point Software Technologies decided to call off its proposed $225 million acquisition of Sourcefire, a U.S. firm specializing in security appliances for protecting a corporation's internal computer networks, because of a CFIUS inquiry). The author is personally aware of several similar transactions, the details of which are protected by the confidentiality rules that apply to CFIUS activities.

[27]One other, rarely used, mechanism is section 232 of the Trade Expansion Act of 1962 (19 USC. § 1862). Section 232 authorizes the Department of Commerce, in consultation with DoD and other appropriate agencies, *see* 15 CFR Part 705, to block the importation of goods that would displace domestically produced materials essential to the defense industrial base. Given the infrequency of its application, section 232 is of little practical import.

[28]Aisenberg, "Information Technology Supply Chain," at 1 & n.3, 6-8. The author is indebted to Michael Aisenberg of MITRE, whose comments on the initial draft of this paper allowed the development of the analysis in this section.

most notable are two recent data-collection initiatives documenting the extent to which counterfeits infiltrate our supply chain: a recently completed study by the Department of Commerce, which documented the prevalence of counterfeit parts in the Navy's IT supply chain,[29] and ongoing pilots within the CNCI, Task 11, collecting detailed data on vendors, components, product integration and deployment of cyber products within DoD and DHS.[30]

C. Cyber Attack and Non-Cyber Response

The U.S. military has moved aggressively to establish doctrine and structures for the control of military operations in cyberspace. The Army, for example, has developed a concept of operations and a set of capabilities requirements for military action in cyberspace.[31] Likewise, the Navy has created a Fleet Cyber Command and reactivated the 10th Fleet for cyber warfare.[32] Similarly, the Air Force has designated its existing Space Command as the locus for its cyberspace mission and has begun inculcating its Airmen with the need to be "Cyber Wingmen."[33]

To coordinate these sometimes disparate efforts, on June 23, 2009, the Secretary of Defense issued a memorandum creating a new command, the U.S. Cyber Command (USCC), within the structure of our military forces. More particularly, the Secretary created Cyber Command as a sub-unified command subject to the authority of the commander of the U.S. Strategic Command.[34] As detailed in section 18.d(3) of the DOD Unified Command Plan, the USCC is tasked with securing American freedom of action in cyberspace and mitigating the risks to national security that come from dependence on cyberspace. It is, therefore, the home of both offensive and defensive military cyber missions of all sorts. A catalog of its missions includes:

- integrating cyberspace operations and synchronizing warfighting effects across the global environment;
- supporting civil authorities and international organizations in cyberspace activities;[35]
- directing global information grid operations and defense;
- executing full spectrum military cyberspace operations;
- de-conflicting offensive cyberspace operations;
- providing situational awareness of cyberspace operations, including indications and warnings; and
- providing military representation to U.S. and international agencies on cyberspace matters.

In short, USCC is anticipated to serve as a broad-based, comprehensive locus for U.S. military cyberspace operations, with significant impact on non-military civilian operations. And, consistent with

---

[29]The report is summarized in a useful briefing, available at www.combatcounterfeits.com/files/bis-counterfeit-briefing.ppt.

[30]Aisenberg, "Information Technology Supply Chain," at 10.

[31]TRADOC PAM 525-7-8, Cyberspace Operations Concept Capabilities Plan (Feb. 2010).

[32]Navy Stands Up Fleet Cyber Command, Reestablishes U.S. 10th Fleet (Jan. 29, 2010) [available at http://www.navy.mil/search/display.asp?story_id=50954].

[33]*See* Memorandum for All Airmen, Air Force Cyberspace Mission Alignment (Aug. 20, 2009).

[34]The new commander of USCC is dual-hatted and also serves as the Director of the NSA. A useful summary of the political considerations that led to this unusual result can be found in Richard A. Clarke & Robert K. Knake, Cyber War (Harper Collins 2010), pp. 32-44.

[35]Presumably this support to civil authorities will be provided consistent with existing military doctrine. DoD Directive 5111.13 (March 2009) defines Defense Support to Civil Authorities (DSCA) as: "Support provided by U.S. Federal military forces, National Guard forces performing duty in accordance with [Title 32, U.S. Code], DoD civilians, DoD contract personnel, and DoD component assets, in response to requests for assistance from civil authorities for special events, domestic emergencies, designated law enforcement support, and other domestic activities. Support provided by National Guard forces performing duty in accordance with [Title 32, U.S. Code] is considered DSCA, but is conducted as a State-directed action. Also known as civil support."

existing joint doctrine, the commander of USCC will, generally, have the freedom to select and approve specific courses of action to achieve the mission objectives set by his superiors.[36]

It is, of course, difficult to develop a concrete sense of what USCC actually will do. The command has not yet been fully activated and will not become so until October 2010. It was only recently, in May 2010, that its first nominated commander was confirmed by the Senate. Nor has the command developed a set of policies and doctrines that will guide its actions; its first comprehensive strategy is anticipated late in 2010.

Thus USCC is, ironically, a virtual command at this juncture and the most that can be said is that it appears to be quite flexible in its scope. The authorizing documentation provides DOD with ample ability to develop within USCC any number of cyber-related missions. With respect to cybersecurity matters (what this paper classifies as cyber defense and cyber attack) it is likely in the end that the limitations on the scope of activity in USCC will be more in the nature of resources and external competition with other U.S. government agencies, rather than inherent limitations in its authorities. In short, we have a new cyber command, but the policy and doctrine that will define its objectives remain to be better defined.

The military is not, of course, the only U.S. governmental institution that would be responsible for a cyber response. The dynamics of the domain will necessarily involve other governmental agencies in any cyberaction. To cite the most obvious example, as the Cyber Space Policy Review, the National Cybersecurity Strategy and the recent CSIS study on Securing Cyberspace all recognize, the internet is a uniquely borderless domain.[37] Thus any effective deterrent strategy will necessarily require a governmental organization and process that enables international engagement. While one could, in theory, imagine a situation in which all of our cyber responses were enabled by military-to-military interactions the prospects for such a scenario are dim. Rather, one can readily anticipate that international engagement will require engagement across the domain of diplomacy, law enforcement and infrastructure protection, with a necessarily wide variety of international interlocutors.

Likewise, our government's cyber capabilities are not only useful as a cyber response measure. They may well play a role when kinetic military strikes would be viewed as too drastic or disproportionate, or even as a response to diplomatic disagreements, both overtly and covertly. And, of course, these capabilities can and will be used as a tool to supplement more traditional military operations to disable an enemy's command and control structures. We have only begun our efforts to build the structures necessary to direct these multiple missions.[38]

---

[36]*See generally,* Unified Command Plan § 18.d(3); Advanced Questions for Lieutenant General Keith Alexander, USA Nominee for Commander, United States Cyber Command in Hearings Before the United States Senate Armed Services Committee (April 13, 2010) [available at http://www.washingtonpost.com/wp-srv/politics/documents/questions.pdf] [hereinafter "Alexander, Advanced Questions"].

[37]National Security Strategy at 49-53; Cyber Space Policy Review at 20-21; CSIS, Securing Cyberspace for the 44th Presidency at 20-23 (Dec. 2008).

[38]No description of the organizations and processes necessary for cyber deterrence would be complete without acknowledgment of the need for structures to ensure that activities intended to prevent a successful cyber attack by U.S. opponents or to enable a successful cyber attack by our own government are pursued in conformance with the laws and policies of the United States. As other papers in this collection make clear, a number of potential activities in support of a cyber deterrence policy have significant privacy and civil liberties implications.

This paper consciously leaves aside this very significant implementation question, though it is clearly one that *must* be addressed. Existing oversight structures range from agency level privacy officers and inspectors general to executive level institutions such as the Intelligence Oversight Board of the President's Intelligence Advisory Board (established by E.O. 13462), and the Privacy and Civil Liberties Oversight Board (created by Pub. L. 110-52, 9/11 Commission Act, § 801, though as of the writing of this paper inactive). These executive mechanisms are supplemented through congressional oversight and, where appropriate, judicial review of executive actions. As new deterrence policies are developed and implemented it is likely that new privacy protective systems will also be developed (indeed, this paper suggests one such system as part of its description of a new public/private model of cooperation). This paper does not, however, provide a complete description of existing structures. The failure to address the question, however, is by no means a diminishment of its importance.

II. CHALLENGING QUESTIONS—THINKING ABOUT ORGANIZATION AND PROCESS

Most are familiar with the unique aspects of cyberspace that make a deterrence policy challenging to develop. The difficulties of attributing an attack to a particular actor are well-documented. Likewise, the independence (or purported quasi-independence) of certain cyber actors from state sponsors further complicates the equation of attribution, and the surreptitious nature of some intrusions often makes attacks difficult to perceive (and thus respond to).

But the particular challenges for conceptions about the organization and processes of the U.S. cyber deterrence policy lie not in these difficulties, for they are more technological than organizational. They will likely not be resolved by a decision on how the government and private sector are organized. Put another way it is hard to imagine how an organizational change in the U.S. government would increase (or decrease) our ability to resolve the attribution question on a routine basis.

Rather, for purposes of this paper, it is useful to consider difficulties that particularly give rise to organizational challenges in our defense of cyberspace. Given the uncertainties surrounding the cyber realm and its rapidly mutating nature, no paper of any reasonable length can identify, much less address, all of the salient organizational challenges. Below, this paper offers thoughts on six issues—the failure of the market; the assumption of the need for a rapid response; the asymmetry of risk; the challenge of hardware reliance; the disablement of private self-help; and unseemly federal competition.

A. The Public/Private Dilemma

The fundamental question is: Who should be responsible for protecting the cyber domain? Why, after all, are cyber defense and resilience even a matter of governmental concern? Ought we not to anticipate that the private sector would address these matters on its own initiative? With over $1 trillion in losses from cyber theft annually,[39] a traditional theory of the efficient market would posit the development of a robust market for security solutions.

This has not been the case. Rather, the prevalence of security vulnerabilities in the system appears to reflect a systematic market failure.[40] Because the costs of inadequate security are often (though not always) borne by the customers of the cyber service provider (rather than the provider itself), the costs of security failures are, quite naturally not internalized by private sector actors in a way that incentivizes them to take adequate protective steps. Security for the broad system of the internet (both its private components and the government components) is a classic market externality whose pricing is not adequately captured in the costs experienced by individual users. The situation will only get worse: "there is widespread agreement that this long-term trend of grabbing the economic gains from information technology advances and ignoring their security costs has reached a crisis point."[41]

The difficulty in developing a private cybersecurity solution is exacerbated by systematic limitations on information sharing necessary to combat cyber threats. Private enterprises have little incentive to publicly identify their own vulnerabilities. This is especially true in the cyber domain, where the private sector actors are notoriously distrustful of government interference and regulation. And the converse is also true—government institutions like the NSA with (perhaps) superior knowledge of threat signatures and new developments in the arsenal of cyber attackers are deeply reluctant to share their hard won knowledge with the private sector at the risk of compromising their own sources and methods. At this

---

[39]Elinor Mills, Study: Cybercrime Costs Firms $1 Trillion Globally, CNet.com (Jan. 28, 2009) [available at http://news.cnet.com/8301-1009_3-10152246-83.html].

[40]National Security Threats at 11-14. An extended discussion of cyber space as a "commons" can be found in Rattray, Evans & Healey, "American Security in the Cyber Commons," *in* Denmark & Mulvenon, eds., "Contested Commons: The Future of American Power in a Multipolar World" (CNAS Jan. 2010).

[41]Jack Goldsmith and Melissa Hathaway, "The Cybersecurity Changes We Need," Washington Post (May 29, 2010) [available at http://www.washingtonpost.com/wp-dyn/content/article/2010/05/28/AR2010052803698.html].

point, the sad truth is that, despite efforts within the ISACs, we have yet to successfully develop the political will to create the culture where information sharing enables cybersecurity improvement.

This has led some to contemplate organizational changes that would enable the Federal government to take direct responsibility for securing the cyber domain. At present, Federal organizations exist for this purpose but the scope of their activities is limited: the Department of Homeland Security has begun deployment of an intrusion detection system (known as Einstein 2) to protect the .gov domain and has started the development of an intrusion prevention system, called Einstein 3.[42] The military has taken similar steps to protect nodes on the .mil domain. One can at least conceptually envision a Federal organization that would deploy the same sorts of protective technology on private sector portions of the internet to protect the civilian domains (.com, .net., and .edu). Indeed, given that government traffic is often dependent on the private sector network for transmission, some (including, most recently, the Deputy Secretary of Defense) have expressed the view that Federal protection of private sector networks is affirmatively desirable for governmental purposes, independent of any benefit to the private sector.[43] Such an organization, if created, would eliminate some of the information sharing problems but would bring with it a host of privacy-related concerns that might prove insurmountable, for it would place the Federal government in the position of monitoring and controlling private sector internet traffic.

Indeed, to summarize the problem, a *government operated* system will raise the specter of "Big Brother" and engender significant opposition from privacy advocates, while a *privately operated* system has proven impossible to develop naturally, lacks transparency, and has less ready access to NSA-generated threat signature information. If we do not solve the dilemma of enabling public-private cooperation we are unlikely to get cyber defense and cyber resilience right.[44]

B. The Assumption of Rapidity

One of the unique aspects of cyberspace that will particularly affect our organizational structures and processes is the *rapidity* with which cyber activities occur. When a cyber domain attack is perceived to occur at the pace of milliseconds, it may be that the deterrent or defensive response will need to occur with equal rapidity. As LTG Keith Alexander, the first Commander of U.S. Cyber Command, recently told the Senate, "[A] commander's right to general self-defense is clearly established in both U.S. and international law. Although this right has not been specifically established by legal precedent to apply to attacks in cyberspace, it is reasonable to assume that returning fire in cyberspace, as long as it complied with the law of war principles (e.g. proportionality), would be lawful."[45] We therefore face a situation where it is possible (indeed, likely) that some subordinate commanding officer may feel compelled (and authorized) to act without higher authorization if the commander perceives that a cyber attack has

---

[42]Privacy Impact Assessment for the Initiative Three Exercise, DHS Privacy Office (March 18, 2010) [available at http://www.dhs.gov/xlibrary/assets/privacy/privacy_pia_nppd_initiative3.pdf].

[43]*See e.g.* William J. Lynn, III, "Defending a New Domain: The Pentagon's Cyberstrategy," 97 at 104 (Foreign Affairs, Sept./Oct. 2010) (recommending that policy makers consider extending NSA intrusion detection and prevention capabilities "beyond the .gov domain" to, for example, domains "undergirding the commercial defense industry").

[44]One final complexity deserves mention at this juncture—nobody actually owns or operates the Internet itself. While private sector and government actors own pieces of the cyber domain (various routers and nodes, for example) the actual rules for how the cyber domain works are set by the Internet Engineering Task Force which is an "open international community of network designers, operators, vendors and researchers concerned with the evolution of the Internet architectures and the smooth operation of the Internet." "Overview of the IETF" [available at http://www.ietf.org/old/2009/overview.html]. This community operates by the promulgation of technical standards which, in the end, become *de facto* operating requirements for any activity in cyberspace. Thus, some questions about cyber defense and resilience may, necessarily, require engagement with an engineering community that is both internationalist and consensus-oriented, characteristics that may be inconsistent with effective U.S. government action.

[45]Alexander, Advanced Questions at 24; *see also* Lynn, "Defending a New Domain," at 103 (U.S. military must "respond to attacks as they happen or even before they arrive").

begun. And what is true for the military may also be true of private actors who are protecting their own networks—they may feel the need to act instantaneously without the benefit of reflection.

This perception of the need for rapidity reflects a sea-change in concept. The physics of the internet destroys time and space.[46] Even in the nuclear domain, the imminence of the threat was measured in minutes, allowing the development of processes (like the classic nuclear code "football") that permitted a considered, albeit hurried, human response. The cyber domain is often characterized as one in which a near-instantaneous response is necessary.

That characterization may not, however, be accurate and its prevalence may actually be pernicious. A counter-response may be essential immediately as a purely defensive measure, but it is likely that a deterrence-based cyber response can be delayed without significant cost. As Martin Libicki pointed out in a recent RAND study, a cyber response is unlikely to be able to disable a cyber attacker completely. As a consequence, for deterrence policy, "[m]ore important than [the] speed [of the response] is the ability to convince the attacker not to try again. Ironically, for a medium that supposedly conducts its business at warp speed, *the urgency of retaliation is governed by the capacity of the human mind to be convinced, not the need to disable the attacking computer before it strikes again.*"[47]

This is a central insight that ought to govern organizational structures for U.S. cyber deterrence policy. Our task is relatively simple to describe (though difficult, in practice, to achieve);

- Begin, by dividing potential decisions into:
  - o those that may require immediate action (e.g. rapid military cyber defense or attack); and
  - o those for which time may be taken (non-military responses, for example, or long-term cyber resilience initiatives)
- For those decisions requiring either long-term preparatory action, or less rapid response, put in place purpose-built organizations and institutions to achieve defined objectives and provide adequate leadership and resources to achieve those ends;
- For those decisions that will require immediate action, set up structures now to permit consideration of "pre-approved" responses to anticipated situations; and
- In the absence of pre-approved responses, determine in advance who will make the necessary immediate decisions.

In short, in the case of cyber deterrence policy, perhaps function should follow form. The purpose of our organization should be to slow the responsive system down, where feasible, to allow consideration of alternatives and, where not feasible, to allow the prior consideration of response scenarios in advance of the need to implement the response. The worst of all possible worlds would be a lack of structure that permitted mature and thoughtful consideration of reasonable alternatives.

C. Risk Asymmetry

It is a relatively uncontroversial assessment of the current state of affairs to say that, in the cyber domain, the risk to the U.S. is asymmetric. Our nation, with its highly technology-dependent systems,[48] is comparatively more vulnerable to cyber attack than are many of our nation-state peer adversaries. And our comparative vulnerability is significantly greater than that of many non-state actors.

---

[46]Remarks of Kim Taipale, Duke University Center on Law, Ethics and National Security (April 2010) [available at http://www. law.duke.edu/lens/conferences/2010/program].

[47]Libicki, Cyberdeterrence and Cyberwar at 62 (emphasis supplied).

[48]The military, alone, has over 15,000 networks and 7 million computing devices. Its systems are probed thousands of times and scanned millions of times each day. *See* Lynn, "Defending a New Domain" at 97-98. Multiply that by the vulnerabilities in other Federal departments (not to mention State, local, and private sector networks) and the scope of the problem becomes impossibly daunting.

We have yet, however, to internalize the implications of this asymmetry for deterrence organization and policy. Our conception of deterrence is effected by memories of the Cold War, where the threat and response were relatively symmetric. We assumed that a nuclear attack would merit a nuclear response.

But there is no reason to believe that a cyber attack of any form *necessarily* requires a directly proportionate cyber response. Indeed, given the reality of asymmetric cyber reliance by our adversaries, the implication is that our response to a cyber attack should not be confined to a cyber response. While it is likely (indeed, almost certain) that a cyber-based response will form a portion of any deterrent strategy, it is equally likely (indeed, also equally certain) that our actions will engage the full panoply of U.S. governmental authority—ranging from economic sanctions to diplomatic endeavors, to espionage, to criminal prosecution and even to non-cyber kinetic military responses as the circumstances may require.

In a recent speech on internet freedom, Secretary of State Clinton emphasized this point, suggesting the broad scope of potential United States responses to cyber threats: "States, terrorists, and those who would act as their proxies must know that the United States will protect our networks. Those who disrupt the free flow of information in our society or any other pose a threat to our economy, our government, and our civil society. Countries or individuals that engage in cyber attacks should face consequences and international condemnation. In an internet-connected world, an attack on one nation's networks can be an attack on all. And by reinforcing that message, we can create norms of behavior among states and encourage respect for the global networked commons."[49]

And yet, at this juncture, the structures for a coordinated whole-of-government response to cyber threats and for the delivery of a non-cyber response are immature. A recent GAO study made clear that the White House has retained fairly tight control of the development of any deterrence strategy, assigning responsibility for the task directly to the National Security Council (rather than, say, assigning it to a DoD/State working group for development).[50] But, as the vignette which opened this paper makes evident, the White House-coordinated structures have yet to develop a doctrine for the expression of cyber policies.

What is necessary is a structure and organization that will allow the entire panoply of governmental responses to be considered (below, the author suggests a response to the need for such a structure— creation of a "Cyber Defense Options Group"). These will range across the entire domain of Federal activity (often requiring international cooperation) and could include (and this is just a sampling of possibilities):[51]

- *Public exposure and shaming*—The United States might, for example, publicize data and information identifying cyber intrusions and countries whose weak or ineffective civil justice system permits or fosters illegal activity;
- *Diplomatic condemnation*—We could work to develop international norms of behavior, including cooperation in the suppression of cyber intrusions, and then use diplomatic processes to develop shaming techniques that might modify state-actor behavior;
- *Economic sanctions*—One can readily imagine a role for economic sanctions in response to cyber intrusions. For example, one might impose retributive tariffs on non-cooperative countries. More aggressively one might boycott or blacklist products from countries known to introduce malicious hardware into COTS technology, and seek to convince other nations to adopt similar sanctions;

---

[49]Speech of Secretary of State Hillary Clinton (Washington DC Jan 21, 2010) [available at http://www.state.gov/secretary/rm/2010/01/135519.htm].

[50]GAO, "Cybersecurity: Progress Made But Challenges Remain in Defining and Coordinating the Comprehensive National Initiative," at 13 (GAO-10-338) (March 2010) [hereinafter "GAO Cybersecurity"].

[51]Current conceptual thinking in conflict management broadly recognizes that "soft power" systems will often be effective supplements to the hard power of a kinetic response. *E.g.* Joseph Nye, Soft Power: The Means to Success in World Politics (Public Affairs 2004). Theorists characterize the panoply of soft power instruments through the mnemonic "MIDLIFE"—that is Military; Intelligence; Diplomacy; Law enforcement; Information; Financial; and Economic instruments of power. All, conceivably, could be of use in deterring cyber attacks and intrusions.

• *Cyber sanctions*—Sometimes cyber acts will beget cyber sanctions. If a country persists in misusing internet domain name directories, for example, international organizations might, in turn, limit or restrict the development of new domains within that country. More extreme sanctions (for example, bandwidth throttling) are also conceivable;

• *Financial punishments and criminal sanctions*—Administrative, civil and criminal sanctions may be available in situations where an actor (or an intermediary) may be readily identified. In traditional conceptions of deterrence theories, these sorts of sanctions are considered effective as a response to malfeasant individual conduct;

• *Expulsion from international organizations*—In conjunction with any of these sanctions one might, in significant cases, consider suspending or expelling a country from relevant international organizations as a sanction for its activities (or those within its borders);

• *Espionage and other covert responses*—Naturally, one response to covert cyber activities will be covert activities by America. Indeed, it may well be that covert cyber activities will be a critical enabler for the effective implementation of other whole-of-government responses, providing essential intelligence to enhance effective targeting of the response;

• *Cyber intrusions or attacks*—Of course the fact that other responses are possible does not mean that a cyber response is inappropriate. It may often be the case that a like-for-like cyber response will be deemed to have the maximum deterrent effect while achieving proportionality;

• *Kinetic military attacks*—And, finally, there is no reason to suppose that a cyber attack with kinetic or near-kinetic effects on American targets must, necessarily, be responded to with an equivalent cyber response. It is at least plausible to consider the possibility that a traditional kinetic response will be the more proportionate and responsible one.

Our organizational structures and processes must be designed to accommodate and foster the consideration of these various options. Contrast that with our nuclear deterrence structures which were principally intended to verify that an attack had been launched and allow the President the opportunity to respond if he deemed it necessary. Indeed, one of the lessons from our experience with nuclear deterrence is that often the lens through which response actions can be taken needs to be broadened (as it was, for example, in our response to the Cuban missile crisis). In the cyber domain, the need to institutionalize that broadening of response will likely be even greater. Our structures must provide for a less focused response and allow for the consideration of all feasible action options. Instead of narrowing the structure and focusing on a single decision the cyber response structure must be necessarily more diffuse, lest we run the risk of conceiving of the cyber domain in predominantly military terms and thus militarizing a fundamentally civilian environment.

There are, of course, likely to be costs to this broadening. Most notably, it risks frustrating decision-making altogether. But if the structures and processes are properly defined and well-led, that challenge can be overcome. And the virtues of a whole-of-government response likely outweigh the costs associated with a more complex decision-making process.

D. Hardware Failures

If you ask counter-intelligence experts which they fear more, American vulnerability to an external cyber attack or the potential compromise of the operation of the hardware innards of our computers and internet switches, they almost certainly will say that the hardware threat is more challenging. The globalization of production for both hardware and software makes it virtually impossible to provide either supply chain or product assurance.[52]

The vulnerability is made acute by the fact that the U.S. government (and the private sector) have come to rely on commercial off-the-shelf technology. These COTS technologies have many obvious

---

[52]National Security Threats at 2. The observation as to the prioritization of threats was made by a participant whose comments were subject to Chatham House rules—they were for the public record but not for direct attribution.

advantages—they are generally cheaper than custom-built proprietary solutions and, because they are produced in the private sector, they are modified and upgraded more rapidly in a manner that is far more consistent with the current technology life-cycle. Particularly in the cyber realm, where upgrades occur with increasing frequency, reliance on COTS allows government and the private sector to field the most modern equipment possible.

One example of the COTS phenomenon, as recounted by an International Telecommunications Union workshop, will serve as an example: "In the mid-1980's, the DoD mandated the use of the ADA programming language. ADA never gained popularity in the commercial sector, which evolved from programs such as Cobal and Fortran to C and C++ as common programming languages. While ADA was optimized for real time and rapid conversion of analog to digital information, much faster microprocessors and digital sensors circumvented most of these advantages."[53] As a consequence ADA fell into disuse and the DoD systems moved away from their specially designed, non-commercial programming language to a commonly available commercial one. But, in doing so, the U.S. adopted a structure where it was vulnerable to the same types of attacks and hacking as commercial systems. The vulnerabilities that come from running commercial operating systems on most government computers would not exist in the same way if our computers operated on a non-commercial system.[54]

This is equally true for our hardware purchases. Because COTS systems have an "open architecture" design few of them have integrated security architecture. Increasingly, knowledge of the design of the systems and their manufacture is outsourced to overseas production. We therefore live in a world where a significant fraction of the innards of our computers are manufactured overseas, often in plants located in peer-competitor nation states.[55] Likewise, much of the service of existing systems is conducted overseas.

A process for dealing with these vulnerabilities is by no means clear. It is unlikely that the United States government and private sector will return to a time when all of its systems were "made in the USA." Doing so would be prohibitively expensive and would forego a substantial fraction of the economic benefits to be derived from the globalization of the world's economy.

A "made in the USA" response would not eliminate the COTS problem, as even hardware constructed in the United States could be built with malicious intent. However, the origin of hardware components may create a significant difference in the nature of the problem. For U.S.-built components the threat is in the nature of an insider threat and we can have reasonable confidence that the quality control and security processes of the U.S.-domiciled manufacturer are intended to negate that threat, rather than foster it. For non-U.S. companies the same will often be true, at least for components manufactured in countries that take an equivalent approach to hardware assurance. But we may sometimes have less confidence in the efficacy of those processes in countries where quality control and security are less well-developed. Even more troubling, we may sometimes reasonably doubt whether the company's processes are truly designed to achieve those goals or whether the intent works at cross-purposes with America's interests. It is significantly more difficult for the inspection processes of the purchaser to provide for hardware or software assurance than it is for those of the manufacturer.[56]

---

[53]A Collective Security Approach to Protecting the Global Critical Infrastructure at 13 n.14 (ITU Workshop on Creating Trust in Critical Network Infrastructures, Document CNI/09, May 2002).

[54]It is true that all operating systems necessarily have vulnerabilities, and that would be true of government systems that run on ADA, or Windows, or Linux. The degree of comparative vulnerability of these operating systems is hotly debated. *See, e.g.,* Geer et al., Cyber*In*security: The Costs of Monopoly (available at http://cryptome.org/cyberinsecurity.htm) (arguing that monoculture of Microsoft Windows increases vulnerability). The point here is a much more limited one—when the operating system is constructed exclusively by the government, then the government has much greater control against the deliberate insertion of vulnerabilities and it will tend to minimize the extent to which it is subject to non-purposeful malware attacks.

[55]DoD has reported finding counterfeit hardware in systems that the Pentagon has purchased. *See* Ellen Nakashima, "Defense Official Discloses Cyberattack," Wash. Post (Aug. 24. 2010) (available at http://www.washingtonpost.com/wp-dyn/content/article/2010/08/24/AR2010082406154.html?hpid=topnews). The Army's concept of cyber operations for the future recognizes the need to address hardware vulnerabilities. *See* TRADOC PAM 515-7-8 at 12.

[56]Lynn, "Defending a New Domain" at 101 (hardware tampering is "almost impossible to detect and ever harder to eradicate").

And so, though the continued purchase of COTS from a globalized supply chain is inevitable, it would be inappropriate to disregard the threat posed by the foreign origin of much of our hardware. And, notably, the risk is not posed simply by the hardware purchases we make. Many of the service functions that our cyber domain requires are also procured from foreign providers. The commonplace chestnut is the complaint that all of the help lines are answered in India, but the far more significant fact is that many of the repair and maintenance services used for our cyber systems are also provided by foreign suppliers—and so the risk is not just that we purchase hardware from overseas sources but that we rely on those same sources for much of our operational repair and maintenance capacity.

The Comprehensive National Cybersecurity Initiative recognized this vulnerability with its initiative to "develop a multi-pronged approach for global supply chain risk management." But "multi-pronged approach" is often code for "this is a very big problem that we don't have a handle on." Thus, it is somewhat distressing (though utterly unsurprising) that the CNCI initiative to address this problem consists of little more than anodyne platitudes: "This initiative will enhance Federal Government skills, policies, and processes to provide departments and agencies with a robust toolset to better manage and mitigate supply chain risk at levels commensurate with the criticality of, and risks to, their systems and networks."[57] Far more concrete action is necessary, perhaps even action that is moderately intrusive on the free flow of globalized commerce.

E. The "Right" of Self-Defense

The failure to develop structures that effectively protect the private sector from cyber intrusion creates a challenge for private sector actors who are obliged to defend their own networks: Consider the cyber deterrence problem from the perspective of the private sector actor whose systems are subject to an attack. The vulnerability is particularly acute as we come to realize that our adversaries *may* be planning acts that are designed to target private infrastructure.[58] Private sector actors who are contemplating a response to such attacks may well find themselves on the horns of a dilemma—neither able to rely on the government to defend them nor legally authorized to respond themselves.

As with other actors in the cyber domain those defending private sector networks will frequently be unaware of the identity of their attackers, and they may often be equally unable to distinguish a true attack from a probe or an unlawful intrusion. In such an ill-defined situation, those who act in response to an attack may do so in violation of law. The Neutrality Act makes it illegal for an American to wage war against any country at peace with the United States.[59] It preserves, at least in theory, the power of the Congress to declare war and the monopoly power of the Executive to use force in the face of an external attack. Similarly, the Logan Act,[60] forbids American citizens from negotiating with foreign governments. It, too, is intended to preserve an zone of exclusive Federal policy control. Both Acts provide, in theory, for punishment as felonies.

---

[57]CNCI Initiative #11.

[58]Most notably, in recent months Congress has heard testimony about Chinese research that examines the possibility of creating a cascading failure in American electrical grids. *See* Wang & Rong, Cascade-based Attack Vulnerability on the U.S. Power Grid, 47 Safety Science 1332 (2009) [available at http://www.docstoc.com/docs/30535594/Cascade-Based-Attack-Vulnerability-on-the-US-Power-Grid%E2%80%9D].

[59]In its present form, the Act provides: "Whoever, within the United States, knowingly begins or sets on foot or provides or prepares a means for or furnishes the money for, or takes part in, any military or naval expedition or enterprise to be carried on from thence against the territory or dominion of any foreign prince or state, or of any colony, district, or people with whom the United States is at peace, shall be fined under this title or imprisoned not more than three years, or both." 18 USC. § 960.

[60]"Any citizen of the United States, wherever he may be, who, without authority of the United States, directly or indirectly commences or carries on any correspondence or intercourse with any foreign government or any officer or agent thereof, with intent to influence the measures or conduct of any foreign government or of any officer or agent thereof, in relation to any disputes or controversies with the United States, or to defeat the measures of the United States, shall be fined under this title or imprisoned not more than three years, or both." 18 USC. § 953.

But a private sector actor may well, either purposefully or perhaps even through inadvertence or mistake, trench upon these prohibitions.[61] Leaving aside whether a particular cyber response is a "military expedition" (i.e. a use of military force—which is, in fairness, a significant question), it is entirely plausible that a private sector response to an intrusion may involve taking action against a state actor or a quasi-affiliated state-sponsored entity. More commonly, it might involve communicating with the state actor in a way that could be construed as a "negotiation." Thus, a private sector actor might well be responsible for firing the first shot of a cyber war or conducting the first cyber negotiation. Put more prosaically, how should a private electric company react if its grid appears to be subject to infiltration from an unidentified Chinese source? Is it disabled from taking action by the potential that the foreign source might be operating at the direction of Chinese authorities?

Likewise, under the Computer Fraud and Abuse Act (CFAA), it is a crime to intentionally access any protected computer (that is one used in or effecting interstate or foreign commerce) without authorization, or in excess of authorized access, and thereby obtain information from the computer.[62] Since almost invariably, any protective action by a private sector actor will involve accessing a protected computer without authorization and obtaining information from it, virtually every aspect of private sector self-help is, at least theoretically, a violation of the CFAA and therefore a crime. The specter of criminal prosecution may disable or deter private sector self-help and may also have the effect of causing the private sector to outsource protective activities overseas.[63]

But the other side of the equation is equally troubling. Private sector actors will engage in self-defense when they have to, at least in part because they cannot (and currently do not) rely on the U.S. government as a protector. In the context of kinetic warfare it is quite reasonable to insist upon a governmental monopoly on the use of force. The Constitution, after all, charges the government with the obligation to "provide for the common defense" and, by and large, the Federal government has taken on that role in the kinetic sphere. Thus far, however, it has not done so in the cyber domain, and its failure to do so leaves private sector actors with no good option. If the government cannot provide for a defense (whether because it chooses not to or because it lacks the organization and structures to do so), it seems deeply problematic to prevent private sector actors from using whatever tools they have available to protect themselves.

F. Federal "Competition"

Given the many challenges faced by the Federal government, it is unsurprising that some see a continuing lack of adequate coordination at the Federal level in our cyber resilience and, particularly, defense activities. As the GAO reported earlier this year, though several coordinating groups exist at the White House, agencies continue to have "overlapping and uncoordinated responsibilities for cybersecurity activities."[64] To the extent the lack of coordination is discussed publicly, the perception is that there is an ongoing fight for control of the domestic cybersecurity effort pitting the National Security Agency against the Department of Homeland Security.

The perception of, at best, a lack of coordination and, at worst, continuing conflict over control of the cyber defense mission is only exacerbated by acts which at least facially suggest a continuing dissonance. A recent example was the announcement by NSA in October 2009 that it was breaking ground on a new facility in Utah to provide "intelligence and warnings related to cybersecurity threats,

---

[61]The analysis in this section was spurred by a question posed at a recent conference by Stephen Dycus, a member of the National Research Council committee that oversaw this project.

[62]18 USC. §1030(a)(2)(C).

[63]It is notable, for example, that the private sector efforts to track the Chinese intrusion into the Dali Lama's computer system (known as GhostNet) were conducted by a Canadian company. *See* Tracking GhostNet: Investigating a Cyber Espionage Network, Information Warfare Monitor (Mar. 29, 2009) (available at http://www.scribd.com/doc/13731776/Tracking-GhostNet-Investigating-a-Cyber-Espionage-Network).

[64]GAO, Cybersecurity at 2.

cybersecurity support to defense and civilian agency networks, and technical assistance" to DHS. In November 2009, DHS opened its own new facility, the National Cybersecurity and Communications Integration Center, in Arlington, Virginia. This facility will "house the National Cyber Security Center, which coordinates cybersecurity operations across government, the National Coordinating Center for Telecommunications, which operates the government's telecommunications network, and the United States Computer Emergency Readiness Team, which works with industry and government to protect networks and alert them of malicious activity."[65] The two new facilities are, at least facially, somewhat duplicative (both, for example, purport to have a warning and alert function and both also anticipate assisting civilian networks in protecting themselves against attack) and indicative of a continuing need for strategic level cyber coordination.

Duplicative effort and the waste it entails are not the only risks posed by uncoordinated Federal activity. There may well be instances where the division of responsibility impedes essential information sharing of threat signatures (as the discussion of the ISACs above suggests). There may also be occasions where the comparative lack of transparency at NSA precludes effective oversight and control of executive activity by the legislative branch and the public.[66] But perhaps most significantly, the lack of coordination reflects an inability to bridge a cultural gap between the operational environment of the private sector and that of the national security environment. To be sure, DHS as an institution does not fully reflect the robust, competitive private sector environment of Silicon Valley. But allowing NSA or CyberCommand to have the predominant role will, inevitably bring a more militarized or intelligence-focused perspective to the problem than would be the case if the civilian DHS agency had a primary role. Thus, it matters significantly which agency is assigned as the lead for protecting civilian networks. As Rod Beckstrom (former Director of the DHS National Cybersecurity Center) noted, which agency leads the cybersecurity effort makes a difference because an "intelligence culture is very different from network operations or security culture."[67]

To some degree the dissonance between DHS and NSA activities is a product of a significant disparity in their resources and expertise. As the DHS Inspector General recently reported, DHS/US-CERT lacks both the authority to compel other federal agencies to follow its recommendations and the staff to adequately conduct operations.[68] The NSA, by contrast, is well-funded and staffed and has, within the domain of its own operations, ample authority to act—authority that has only been enhanced by the creation of CyberCommand. Indeed, despite DHS's statutory authority and responsibility for protecting civilian infrastructure it appears that it is NSA (and not DHS) that has begun a program, called "Perfect Citizen," to detects cyber assaults on private infrastructure.[69] Though details of this new program are hazy[70] it appears possible that the program will conflict with or duplicate programs operated by DHS. It may also presage an effort by NSA and the Pentagon to exert more control over civilian networks generally.

At present, the White House cyber coordinator lacks the authority to de-conflict these competing structures. His role, avowedly, lacks any authority over operational decisions or budgetary priorities.

---

[65]J. Nicholas Hoover, "NSA to Build $1.5 Billion Cybersecurity Data Center," Information Week (Oct. 29, 2009) [available at http://www.informationweek.com/news/government/security/showArticle.jhtml?articleID=221100260].

[66]This brief paper is neither the time, nor the place, to debate recent controversies over NSA activities. Suffice it to say that the controversies are real, and the public confidence in NSA's rectitude comparatively diminished.

[67]See Letter from Rod Beckstrom to Janet Napolitano (March 5, 2009) [available at http://epic.org/linkedfiles/ncsc_directors_resignation1.pdf]. Beckstrom resigned his position as Director of the National Cybersecurity Center in part because of his perception that NSA was, inappropriately "control[ing] DHS cybersecurity efforts." Id.

[68]Statement of Richard L. Skinner, Inspector General, Department of Homeland Security, Before the Committee on Homeland Security, U.S. House of Representatives (June 16, 2010).

[69]The existence of the Perfect Citizen program was disclosed in Siobhan Gorman, "U.S. Plans Cyber Shield for Utilities, Companies," Wall St. J. (July 8, 2010).

[70]NSA has denied aspects of the initial report. See "NSA Launches Infrastructure Cybersecurity Program," Information Week (July 9, 2010) [available at http://www.informationweek.com/news/government/security/showArticle.jhtml?articleID=225702741&cid=RSSfeed_IWK_News].

The result, beyond the perception of conflict, is confusion among the public and likely the creation of gaps and overlaps in authorities and responsibilities.[71]

III. RECOMMENDATIONS

Rationalize the Federal Structure

The current Administration has, through the appointment of a cyber coordinator, made a real effort to address the lack of cross-government coordination. But, as the recent GAO audit makes clear, there continues to be a confusion and overlap of responsibilities. The dry language of the GAO masks a traditional Washington concern—a battle over turf and budgets—and makes clear that more effort is required.

The outcome of this battle matters, profoundly. Authority follows responsibility, and who the Federal government charges with principal responsibility for cyber defense and resilience will determine whether our cyber response is primarily influenced by concerns grounded in intelligence or in network security. Our present plan, which divides responsibility for different domains among different agencies does not reflect the reality of the connectedness of the internet. It is all well and good to say that NSA and Cyber Command will defend the .mil networks, that DHS will bear responsibility for the .gov networks, and that the private sector will address problems in the .com and .edu domains. But the reality is that cyber traffic crosses domains; except for a few narrowed "walled garden" networks (like the government's classified networks), .gov and .mil traffic all travels through non-governmental nodes. Dividing responsibility for protection does not reflect the actual geography of the domain, which is precisely why the Department of Defense is aggressively planning to provide assistance through military capabilities to protect civilian networks.[72]

But the reality of current capabilities is such that no organizational plan is likely to succeed if a single federal agency is given a comprehensive lead responsibility. One would expect that sensitivities are too great to ever permit, for example, the NSA or CyberCommand to be responsible for protecting all parts of the Internet (though the Perfect Citizen program may well be an effort to do just that). Conversely, though it has the requisite statutory authority, DHS lacks the experience and expertise necessary to achieve results. What is required is decisive leadership from the White House to resolve the current confusion and provide a focal point for private sector coordination.

This is easier said than done. Precisely the same arguments were made in support of the creation of an Office of the Director of National Intelligence and in the creation of a Department of Homeland Security. In both cases a central focal point was thought necessary to achieve effective coordination of executive action. Both efforts may fairly be characterized as "ongoing works in progress" whose ultimate efficacy has yet to be conclusively determined. And just as the subordinated agencies have resisted inclusion within ODNI or DHS, it is likely (indeed nearly certain) that DoD and DHS would resist the strengthening of any White House control of cyber issues. It is highly likely any cabinet secretary will resist any organizational rules that constrain his or her ability to direct and control the personnel and resources within the Department.

There are two answers to this problem. One, reflected in the next section, is to have a strongly coordinated planning and policy development process at the White House/NSC level, so that disputes over implementation plans are minimized. The second, more controversial one is to recognize that the

---

[71]Emblematic of the challenges faced by the cyber coordinator is the recent memorandum allocating responsibility between OMB and DHS for federal agency compliance with the requirement of the Federal Information Security Act of 2002 (FISMA). *See* "Clarifying Cybersecurity Responsibilities and Activities," M-10-28 (July 6, 2010) [available at http://www.whitehouse.gov/omb/assets/memoranda_2010/m10-28.pdf]. Irrespective of the merits of that allocation, the memorandum is notable for the fact that it was co-signed by the cyber coordinator and the Director of OMB and issued on OMB letterhead, reflecting the coordinator's lack of directive authority.

[72]Lynn, "Defending a New Domain," at 104.

cyber domain requires giving directive, rather than coordinative, authority to an NSC-level official (who likely will require Senate confirmation and be subject to Congressional oversight).

This sort of change in organizational structure will be opposed by existing Cabinet members. It will require a strong commitment from the White House and a significant increase in the power of the cyber coordinator, and, no doubt, will necessitate legislative changes from Congress. To achieve a fully integrated cyber response, it would be necessary to give the coordinator authority to:

• Create a unified cyber security budget account within the President's annual budget submission and work with OMB and the NSC to set budget priorities with that account;
• Lead and coordinate the development of cyber security policy (including through chairmanship of the policy planning group described below, if that is created);
• Direct agency action in conformance with the budgetary and policy priorities set;
• Have dotted line authority over and a role in the selection of sub-cabinet cyber leaders (e.g. the commander of Cyber Command and the head of US-CERT); and
• Develop an enhanced set of objectives derived from the CNCI that will contain a set of measurable performance goals and objectives for cyber defense and resilience.[73]

To achieve this level of coordination and secure the cooperation of other federal agencies, it is almost certain that the cyber coordinator will need to, effectively, have cabinet-rank and report directly to the President. Any lesser degree of empowerment will, with near certainty, foreclose any realistic possibility of success. In short, if it wishes to advance the coordinative function in a meaningful way the White House must take ownership of the cybersecurity issue and work with Congress to endow the cyber coordinator position with the authority necessary to achieve a set of clearly defined and articulated goals.

The cyber coordinator will also have the difficult task of incorporating private-sector perspectives into the development of any Federal policy and in its implementation. Typically, Federal policy is informed by private sector views through the offices of the constituent cabinet agencies who participate in the policy development. Somewhat less frequently, private sector views are formally solicited through advisory committees and other less formal means of interaction. In the cyber domain, uniquely, Federal policies will have an impact on private sector equities and implementation issues will require private sector coordination. A critical task for the cyber coordinator will be the development of an effective mechanism for incorporating those view points.

Finally, it is worth acknowledging that we should not be completely sanguine at the prospects for success in achieving this sort of restructuring. In addition to opposition from agencies whose roles and responsibilities will be modified, we should anticipate significant opposition from both Congress and the regulated community. Congressional inertia and interest in protecting jurisdictional prerogatives[74] is widespread, as is regulatory resistance to any activity that empowers governmentalcontrol. Coordinated budgeting will require the cooperation of the Appropriations Committees in both houses of Congress in consolidating their consideration of the President's budget request. To the extent that legislative enactments are required to achieve centralizing objectives, their passage will require a significant investment of Presidential political capital.

Plan, Don't React

Instances of threat and response have been and, for the foreseeable future are likely to remain, subject to decision on a one-off, ad hoc basis within the context of working groups that create policy in reaction

[73]By way of analogy, Homeland Security Presidential Directive-5 designates the Secretary of Homeland Security as the principal federal official responsible for domestic incident management. Whether by statute or by executive order, similar (indeed greater) authorities could be afforded the cybersecurity coordinator.

[74]Witness the current divergence between competing cybersecurity bills proposed by the Senate's Commerce and Homeland Security committees.

to particular events. Thus, for the non-cyber responses to cyber threats, current structures appear to contemplate the development of alternative courses of action in a case-specific decision making process and not through a purpose-built decision making mechanism guided by an overarching policy. In such a situation choices among the various options (which can run the gamut of governmental responses) is likely to reflect as much existing capabilities as it is defined policy.

That sort of organizational structure and planning process does not do justice to the panoply of cyber attack and non-cyber response options. For purposes of a comprehensive cyber deterrence policy apparatus, the President should charter an NSC-led committee (notionally called the "Cyber Defense Options Group") whose initial task would be to survey and compile the potential modes for a whole-of-government response to a cyber intrusion or a cyber attack. Here, too, the cyber coordinator will need to find a mechanism for incorporating private sector perspectives.

Once this catalog of potential U.S. government actions is compiled, the response options should be subject to a rigorous risk-based analysis of consequence through red-teaming and other war game activities. In this way, the Federal government can create a menu list of possible responses that reflect a comprehensive range of potential activity and tie those potential responses to particular types of intrusions or attacks. The end result would be a coherent cyber deterrence policy that, in so far as possible, provides guidance in the anticipation of need.[75]

Maintain Human Control

The problem for cyber response is, in some ways, the same organizational challenge faced in other domains. The issue is "how to sustain human control [that is, maintain a] man-in-the-loop. . . . For example, control structures can have human control to unlock weapons systems, or automatic system unlock with human intervention required to override. An example of the former is the control of nuclear weapons and of the later, the control of a nuclear power reactor. This may be high tech, but the big questions are political and organizational."[76] Indeed, the problems associated with automated responses were demonstrated, in a more prosaic fashion, just recently when automated trading rules caused a 1000 point decline in the Dow Jones Industrial Average in less than 10 minutes of trading on the New York Stock Exchange.[77]

Our organizational structures and processes have not yet matured sufficiently in the cyber domain to understand this distinction, much less enable the implementation of policies that maximize the sustainment of human control at senior policy levels. To the contrary it would appear today that the default in response to a cyber attack is to permit critical decisions to be made at an operational level, informed only by system assurance necessity.

Such a structure is problematic. As an urgent matter, as part of the same options analysis recommended above, the Federal government should include within the ambit of the inter-agency study a charge to determine the means of maintaining policy level control of any cyber attack response to the maximum extent practicable. The governing rule should be, wherever possible, to "go slow" and permit human control. We have already seen how easy it is for automated systems to create a "flash crash;" we want to make sure that they don't start a "flash war."

And in those situations where a rapid response is deemed essential, default policies that must be implemented without human intervention should be identified in advance for consideration and human review. We should anticipate limiting these automated rapid response to essential defensive measures and affirmatively limit the extent to which offensive, aggressive measures are pre-authorized. The study group's proposals should, optimally, also be informed by consultation with the legislative branch.

---

[75]An important corollary benefit of the Cyber Defense Options Group would be to allow policy options to be developed with the input of those who would implement them, but not with their exclusive control. In general, the development of policy is best served when it is informed by but not subservient to the necessities of implementation.
[76]Tom Blau, "War and Technology in the Age of the Electron," Defense Security Review 94, 100 (London 1993).
[77]Nelson Schwartz & Louise Story, "When Machines Take Control," New York Times at B1 (May 7, 2010).

Create a True Public-Private Partnership

Engagement with the private sector has been only partially successful thus far. Many argue, correctly, that private sector information sharing networks exist at the technical level and are effective. But the reality is that we have yet to find a structure that enables strategic information sharing between the private sector and the federal government in an appropriate way.[78] Frequent reliance on cooperative councils, like the ISACs, has produced little more than the repetitive refrain that government can't share intelligence with the private sector and the private sector sees little to gain by sharing with the government.

Perhaps the time has come to consider a different organizational structure for cyber defense, for which the author offers this novel idea:[79] We might think about whether or not we should formalize the public-private partnership necessary for cyber defense by creating a Congressionally-charted, non-profit corporation (akin to the American Red Cross and the Millennium Challenge Corporation). One might notionally call it the "Cybersecurity Assurance Corporation" or "CAC."[80]

This potential organizational adaption would address many of the concerns that have frustrated the purely private or public responses. It would eliminate the "first mover" economic problem by federalizing the response. And it would allow greater maintenance of the security of classified information within the ambit of a government corporation. As a corollary, the quasi-public nature of the CAC might (if appropriate legal structures were adopted) provide a forum in which defense-related private sector information could be shared without fear of compromise or competitive disadvantage. Thus the CAC would provide a secure platform that allowed the government and the private sector to fully utilize our information assurance capabilities and call on both public and private resources.[81]

Indeed, the premise is that with the proper incentives private sectors actors can self-organize to achieve tasks.[82] It is simply the case that the current economic structures of cyber security do not provide those incentives. One significant benefit of the CAC structure would be to change the incentive structure to provide a secure, non-competitive forum where collaboration could be fostered.

At the same time, the quasi-private nature of the organization would provide greater assurance that legitimate concerns for privacy and government overreaching were suitably addressed. The centralization of the effort would allow for a unified and continuous audit of privacy compliance. The maintenance of a private sector control structure would further insulate against misuse and abuse by governmental authorities. And the absence of return on investment concerns would allow the organization to focus on privacy protection and network integrity.

Thus, a suitable organization would have some form of the following characteristics:

- *Board of Directors*—It is likely that an independent board would have appointees from government and the private sector. It might also possibly have non-governmental representatives from the privacy community;
- *Executive structure*—Any new corporation will require the full panoply of C-level managerial functions. At a minimum these will include a chief executive officer, and chief operations, finance, legal, and management officers;

---

[78]National Security Threats at 14.

[79]I am indebted to my former colleague at DHS, Adam Isles, whose thoughts on the idea of public-private partnership in a different context sparked this idea.

[80]This paper serves only as an outline of certain aspects of the CAC. The author acknowledges that significant further consideration and development of the idea are necessary, but offers these preliminary thoughts for the purpose of generating discussion. *See* Rosenzweig, "The Cyber Assurance Corporation," (forthcoming).

[81]Appropriate legal structures might include mandatory reporting; anonymization of information given to the CAC; compartmentalization of information that cannot be anonymized; and the development of a penalty structure for the misappropriation of CAC-protected information.

[82]*E.g.* DARPA Network Challenge (a/k/a Red Balloon Challenge), as described at https://networkchallenge.darpa.mil/default.aspx].

• *Security structure*—Given that the proposed CAC will be a repository for both classified information derived from government sources and confidential business information derived from private sector sources it will likely, itself, be the subject of both traditional espionage and cyber intrusions. A robust internal security structure will be essential;

• *Audit/privacy protective structure*—The critical innovation of the CAC is the creation of a unique structure that fosters the sharing of information. The principal goal of this structure is to assure transparency of operations while insulating the operations of the organization from political interference. Thus the most significant requirement (at least from the perspective of public acceptance) will be organizational structures that provide for a robust set of oversight mechanisms, including some sort of inspector general (IG)-like official with the responsibility for auditing compliance matters.

By far the most important requirement will be the drafting of an institutional charter clearly delineating the authorities and responsibilities of the CAC. What, after all, will the CAC actually do and how will it do it? At a minimum, one expects that the CAC will serve as a centralized information sharing system for threat information, much as the ISAC does now, but with a greater capacity to marry that information to government-derived data and, potentially, with the capacity to anonymize and re-distribute threat information more successfully than ISACs currently do. Indeed, the expectation is that, because of its particular authorities, the CAC will be able to achieve greater sharing than under current structures. If we judge that it cannot then the entire enterprise is not worth the effort.

In addition, the CAC should also be authorized to conduct the following additional functions: incident review and reporting; threat assessment and analysis; and the operation of intrusion detection and prevention systems. Of course, the devil is in the details: current owners of networks will be unwilling to delegate the responsibility for intrusion protection to the CAC unless they see a significant benefit from the collectivization of a security response. Again, if the CAC cannot achieve that objective the enterprise is without benefit. But, as this paper has argued earlier, the current model of complete reliance on private incentives to create the optimal level of intrusion detection and prevention has, plainly, not worked. The potential inherent in a CAC structure provides a half-way house that, if successful, will eliminate the natural instinct of the Federal government to fully federalize a response.

The initial charter will then need to identify the means by which the CAC can achieve its objectives. Will it have, for example, authority to define security standards and best security practices? Will it have regulatory authority to create and mandate private sector compliance? Will participation in its intrusion and detection activities be voluntary or mandatory? Will it be authorized to collect fees or reimburse expenses incurred by its private sector partners? And given the privacy sensitivities, under what rules will the CAC be authorized to cooperate with U.S. government authorities?

Many additional practical questions would, of course, need to be answered regarding the development of the CAC. Most notably the specifics of the governance structure of the organization will be critical. There will be detailed issues, including, for example:

• What qualifications are required for the Board of Directors?
• What would be the appointment/selection process?
• What degree of control would the Board have over the day-to-day executive leadership of the institution?
• Would anyone outside the board have a role in the appointment of executive level leaders?
• Would, as seems likely, the corporation be wholly private?
• Who would appoint the IG? To whom would the IG report?
• What powers of compulsion (if any) would the IG have?

One should not, of course, think that the creation of such a structure will be easy. It would require Congressional authorization, after all. Of equal significance, the start up costs of the CAC will require a

Congressional appropriation and the long-term funding needs will have to be addressed through some sort of fee mechanism. These are not modest challenges to the development of the CAC structure.[83]

Address Service and Non-Ownership Vulnerabilities

Finally, we need to give more concerted attention to the problems posed by the insecurity of our supply chain. Our current system (which, in a very limited way, reviews threats to our supply chain in some situations where a foreign entity takes corporate control of a critical systems manufacturer) plainly does not serve (and was not intended to serve) so broad a purpose. It is safe to say that under the current CNCI initiatives the U.S. government is still in the "information gathering stage" as it seeks to assess the scope of the problem and devise a workable set of solutions.

Recent recommendations for addressing the COTS problem reflect the difficulties that face us in devising a comprehensive solution. As the Defense Science Board recognized (and, indeed, recommended) the U.S. government will continue to purchase commercial goods for use.[84] It simply is untenable to suppose that the United States will ever forgo the economic benefits of a globalized purchasing system. Yet such a system inherently carries with it the risks associated with the off-shore production of goods and services critical to an infrastructure.

But strategies to eliminate the risk are non-existent and those required to mitigate it seem to be mostly nibbling around the edges. The Defense Science Board, for example, recommends:

- Increased intelligence efforts to understand adversarial intentions;
- Allocation of assurance resources on a prioritized bases to mission's whose failure would have the greatest impact;
  - Better quality DoD software (to make malicious attacks more readily observable);
  - Development of better assurance tools and programs;
  - Better knowledge of suppliers processes and trustworthiness; and
  - A robust research agenda.[85]

Likewise, the Department of Commerce, Office of Technology Evaluation, recommends relatively modest steps:

- Creation of a centralized counterfeit reporting database;
- Clarification of the Federal Acquisition Regulations to allow a "best value" purchase of IT components;
- Federal guidance to industry on the scope of criminal and civil liability for dealing with counterfeits and responsibility for reporting to the federal government;
  - Broader law enforcement investigations of counterfeit activities;
  - Federal leadership in disseminating best practices to industry;
  - International agreements to limit the flow of counterfeit technology; and
  - Better lifecycle planning to reduce the need to rely on problematic and unreliable vendors.[86]

The reality, however, is that steps such as these will not eliminate the risk to cyber assurance posed by the use of commercial systems. The dispersed nature of the cyber domain only serves to exacerbate the international character of the problem and render it seemingly insoluble. To supplement the ongoing CNCI Task 11 initiatives, the government should charter a broad-based study program (perhaps through

---

[83]One final note: It may well be that to foster some quasi-competition we might wish to charter more than one CAC.

[84]Defense Science Board, "Foreign Influence," at 51.

[85]Defense Science Board, "Foreign Influence," at 51-68.

[86]Department of Commerce, "Defense Industrial Base," at 208-211.

the National Academies) focused exclusively on the problem of COTS and supply chain security. Developing a comprehensive risk mitigation plan is both essential and, likely the best that can be achieved.[87]

As the government's examination of the COTS issue moves forward, the author offers two suggestions for additional steps that do not, thus far, appear to have been actively considered:

- We should consider expanding governmental review authorities to include situations where foreign entities take control of service activities that affect the cyber domain, or where foreign influence is achieved without purchasing full control (as in, say, a lease arrangement). Neither of these situations falls within the current domain of CFIUS or Team Telecom—yet the threat is no different whether Cisco's router production system is purchased by a foreign entity or all service for the routers is provided by that same foreign entity;
- We should also consider actions that would diversify the types of hardware and software systems that are used within the cyber domain. Such a diversification would, in effect, create a "herd immunity" against attack by malicious actors through both software and hardware intrusions.[88] For federal actors (and other governmental actors) creating herd immunity might be as simple as changing the Federal Acquisition Regulations to require product purchasing diversity. For private sector actors the government might achieve the same result by more vigorously enforcing the antitrust laws.

The author recognizes that both these suggestions are moderately controversial. Yet it seems self-evident that in the absence of concerted action the potential vulnerability posed by the reliance on COTS will not be alleviated.

CONCLUSION

As noted at the outset, any effort to identify optimal governmental structures and processes for cyber deterrence ought, in the long run, to be informed by the underlying deterrence policies adopted. Form should, in the end, follow function, not lead it.

That having been said, it seems clear that at this juncture our governing structures are not yet well developed and do not facilitate the adoption of coherent policies, much less permit their successful implementation. To a very real degree our failure to adopt a rational structure is a reflection of the medium with which we are dealing. The cyber domain is a non-hierarchical interconnected web of systems; we should be little surprised that our efforts to impose a hierarchical system of order on a fundamentally disordered structure have, to date, met with less than complete success.

But that does not mean that we should not try. Indeed, despite the difficulty, we must. If we are to maintain the utility of the web as a tool of communication and control we necessarily must adopt some form of hierarchy to protect the cyber domain. Whatever the policy chosen, clearer lines of authority within the Federal government and a more coherent structure of public-private interaction are necessary to allow for effective action. In sum that structure must:

- Provide for greater and more effective control of the Federal effort;
- Assure political control of any cyber response;
- Provide a means that will effectively allow for a public-private collaboration; and
- Find some means of providing for supply chain security.

The task, though simply stated, is a daunting one.

---

[87]Department of Commerce, "Defense Industrial Base," at 211.

[88]The author pretends no expertise in the epidemiology of herd immunity. What little understanding he possesses comes from a few useful review articles. *E.g.* P. Fine, "Herd immunity: history, theory, practice" 15(2) *Epidemiol Rev* 265–302 (1993). Notably, adoption of this approach is consistent with recent conceptual thinking suggesting that cybersecurity issues are analytically akin to public health problems. *E.g.* IBM, Meeting the Cybersecurity Challenge: Empowering Stakeholders and Ensuring Coordination at 11-23 (Feb. 2010); K.A. Taipale, Cyberdeterrence (Jan. 2009) [available at http://papers.ssrn.com/sol3/papers.cfm?abstract_id=1336045].

Group 6—Privacy and Civil Liberties

Civil Liberties and Privacy Implications of Policies to Prevent Cyberattacks

Robert Gellman

Information and Privacy Consultant

I. INTRODUCTION

The purpose of this paper is to consider the civil liberties and privacy implications of potential policies and processes to prevent cyberattacks. Other than the general topic and a request to consider the possibility of licensing Internet users, little direction was offered. The topic raises a host of unbounded, complex, difficult, and contested legal and constitutional issues. Almost any one of the issues could be the subject of an entire paper, book, or even treatise.

What can be accomplished here is to consider some of the issues raised by possible proposals aimed at preventing cyberattacks and to suggest some of the major fault lines that demarcate the borders of what is possible from what is uncertain from what is prohibited. To characterize the analysis another way, how far can prevention policies and processes go before they hit possible legal, constitutional, or other barriers? This paper is an analysis of *selected* issues raised by this question.

The analysis of any proposal can differ significantly depending on who is performing an activity and where that activity is being performed. The federal government cannot do some things that private companies can do. Some activities would be less objectionable when done in a private, access-controlled network than when done on the Internet in general. Some activities can be more readily accomplished with the consent of data subjects than without consent. The laws of other nations may impose restrictions that are absent in U.S. law, or vice versa, which can complicate prevention of cyberattacks on a global scale.

The discussion here is organized under four main topics, search, speech, information privacy, and due process. Many potential cyberattack prevention policies and processes raise concerns under more than one of these topics, and the placement of issues under these topics is somewhat discretionary. For example, a requirement that Internet Service Providers (ISPs) retain data about a user's Internet activities raises concerns under the First Amendment, Fourth Amendment, privacy, and due process.[1] In this paper, data retention is considered in the search section.

---

[1] The text of the U.S. Constitution and its amendments can be found at http://topics.law.cornell.edu/constitution, accessed August 30, 2010.

273

II. ISSUES RELATING TO SEARCH

1. Surveillance

Cyberattack prevention activities will at times make use of the surveillance authority given to the government. It is not possible to summarize that authority in this document. There may be no more convoluted area of privacy law in the United States than surveillance law. One scholar describes the law of electronic surveillance as "famously complex."[2] The standards vary enormously, depending on numerous factors. Some of the factors that determine the nature of the surveillance that is permissible, the procedures that may be required as a prerequisite to surveillance, and the uses of the results of the surveillance include:

- who is undertaking the surveillance (the government or a private party)
- why the surveillance is being conducted (for law enforcement, national security, foreign intelligence, or private purposes)
- whether the target of the surveillance is a U.S. citizen (including a permanent resident), foreign national, or agent of a foreign power
- the form of a communication (e.g., telephone call, electronic mail)
- whether a communication is stored by a third party or is in transit
- whether a communication is transmitted by a wire
- whether the surveillance captures video or sound
- what is being intercepted (e.g., content of a communications or a telecommunications attribute, such as the telephone number dialed)
- what is under surveillance (e.g., a public place, home, workplace, locker room, toilet stall)
- where the surveillance is conducted from (e.g., a public place, a private place, an airplane, a place of employment)
- the extent to which a place under surveillance has been protected from observation
- whether the surveillance is subject to state law or to federal law
- whether the technology used to undertake the surveillance is in general public use.

The history, scope, and shortcomings of the Electronic Communications Privacy Act of 1986[3] (ECPA) are most relevant here. There are three titles to ECPA: the first amends the Wiretap Act; the second contains the Stored Communications Act; and the third addresses pen registers and trap and trace devices. The first two titles are most relevant here.

The Wiretap Act is a criminal statute that seeks (1) to protect the privacy of wire and oral communications, and (2) to set out the circumstances and conditions under which the interception of wire and oral communications may be authorized.[4] In 1986, ECPA amended the existing Wiretap Act to extend to electronic communications protections against unauthorized interceptions that existed previously only for oral and wire communications via common carrier transmissions.

The Stored Communications Act[5] seeks to protect electronic communications and voice mail from unauthorized access by defining unlawful access as a crime. The goal was to protect the confidentiality, integrity, and availability of such communications stored by providers of electronic communication service pending the messages' ultimate delivery to their intended recipients.

---

[2]Orin S. Kerr, *Lifting the "Fog" of Internet Surveillance: How a Suppression Remedy Would Change Computer Crime Law*, 54 Hastings Law Journal 805, 820 (2003). See also Gina Marie Stevens & Charles Doyle, *Privacy: An Overview of Federal Statutes Governing Wiretapping and Electronic Surveillance* (2009) (Congressional Research Service), available at http://assets.opencrs.com/rpts/98-326_20091203.pdf; accessed on March 23, 2010.

[3]Public Law 99-508, 100 Stat. 1848 (1986).

[4]18 U.S.C. § 2511.

[5]18 U.S.C. § 2701.

One of the law's exception permits access to electronic communications by service providers, and this provision allows employers who directly provide (as opposed to using a third party service provider) email service to employees the ability to monitor email.[6] That monitoring ability could support the cyberattack prevention activities. Public employers remain subject to Fourth Amendment requirements and may be more limited in their ability to review email.[7] Privacy policies and terms of service established by an ISP could also be relevant to a user's expectation of privacy and could authorize monitoring of email by the ISP.

It is widely recognized today that ECPA's assumptions about technology are outmoded and that the protections that ECPA sought to provide now operate inconsistently because of changes in technology and service offerings.[8] For example, with respect to government surveillance, the law gives greater protection to email in transit than it does to email that has arrived in a user's in-box at a service provider. In addition, under the law, email that is more than 180 days old is more easily accessible to the government than newer email.[9] Because some ISPs now offer massive or unlimited storage for email, the result is a significantly differing degree of legal protection for email depending on factors that many users no longer view as significant. Other questions arise with respect to newer services such as Voice over Internet Protocol. Documents placed on cloud computing sites may also have fewer protections under current law than email because ECPA only covers electronic communications and the transfer of information to a cloud computing provider may not qualify for protection.[10]

The 1976 decision of the Supreme Court in *U.S. v. Miller*[11] illustrates an important aspect of third party storage of information under the Fourth Amendment. The Supreme Court held that the Fourth Amendment does not recognize an expectation of privacy in an individual's financial records held by a bank. Therefore, the Court allowed the government to obtain the records from the bank without providing the individual notice or an opportunity to contest the demand. The conclusion in *Miller* with its broad implication that an individual has no expectation of privacy in any record held by a third party[12] is an ever-increasing concern to civil libertarians and privacy advocates because most records of an individual's existence—and especially an individual's Internet activities—are held by third parties. ECPA partly curbs the effect of *Miller* by establishing rules and procedures that limit the ability of the government to obtain electronic communications.

2. Other Approaches to *Miller*

Shortly after the decision in *Miller*, Congress passed the Right to Financial Privacy Act.[13] The Act established limited statutory privacy protections for bank records that the Supreme Court declined to recognize under the Fourth Amendment. The Act requires the federal government (but not state governments) to notify a bank customer when it uses a subpoena or summons to obtain a record about that customer

---

[6]Id. at § 2701(c)(1).

[7]See *City of Ontario v. Quon*, 560 U.S. ___ (2010).

[8]The Center for Democracy and Technology (CDT) is leading a broad effort of privacy groups, businesses, and Internet companies to seek amendment and modernization of ECPA. See CDT, *Digital Due Process Coalition (Including Microsoft, Google, and More) Call for Tougher Online Privacy Laws*, http://www.cdt.org/press_hit/digital-due-process-coalition-including-microsoft-google-and-more-call-tougher-online-priv; accessed April 20, 2010.

[9]18 U.S.C. § 2703(a).

[10]*Cloud computing* involves the sharing or storage by users of their own information on remote servers owned or operated by others and accessed through the Internet. The proper characterization for ECPA purposes of cloud documents, which differs greatly in type and terms of service, is far from clear. See Robert Gellman, *Privacy in the Clouds: Risks to Privacy and Confidentiality from Cloud Computing* at 17 (World Privacy Forum, 2009), available at http://www.worldprivacyforum.org/pdf/WPF_Cloud_Privacy_Report.pdf; accessed April 20, 2010.

[11]425 U.S. 435 (1976).

[12]See *Smith v. Maryland*, 442 U.S. 735, 743-44 (1979), ("a person has no legitimate expectation of privacy information he voluntarily turns over to third parties").

[13]12 U.S.C. §§ 3401-3422.

from a bank. The customer then has an opportunity to contest the process in court before the bank hands over the records. The Act's value is questionable since the grounds upon which a customer can challenge the government are limited (must show that the records are not relevant to a legitimate law enforcement investigation), and exceptions to customer notice cover many important agencies and activities.

The federal health privacy rule[14] also contains a provision that requires notice to a patient of a subpoena for the patient's record held by a health care provider or insurer. For patients and for civil litigation, the health privacy rule's provisions are stronger than in the Right to Financial Privacy Act, but the exceptions for law enforcement investigations provide even fewer rights for data subjects than the Right to Financial Privacy Act.[15]

Recent legislation, including updates to the USA PATRIOT Act, Foreign Intelligence Surveillance Act, and ECPA also modify some effects of *Miller* by expanding requirements for judicial involvement in some electronic searches. None of the legislative changes to the *Miller* holding has broad effect with respect to all or most information held by third party record keepers, however.

Because of the tremendous volume and range of personal information held by ISPs and other third party record keepers, privacy advocates want to create a protectable privacy interest that would undermine the broad holding in *Miller*. ECPA provides some protection for electronic communications. However, email only represents a portion of the information now held by third party Internet providers, which include social networks, cloud computing service providers, photograph storage services, financial management websites, and a nearly unlimited number of other services. Indeed, a very large portion of Internet activities create records held by third parties, and the ongoing expansion of cloud computing will shift additional materials from locally owned and controlled computers to third parties. Whether and how Congress (or the courts) revise the principle that there is no privacy interest in records held by third parties will determine both the scope of that privacy interest and the ease with which government investigators can obtain personal and business records held by third parties.

Any expansion of the privacy rights of data subjects with respect to records held by ISPs and other third party record keepers could affect the conduct of cyberattack prevention and investigation activities by creating substantive or procedural barriers to government acquisition of information about Internet activities. These activities may not be affected any more than any other government investigatory activities that center on Internet conduct. It remains to be seen how broadly any future ECPA reforms will affect the basic *Miller* holding that there is no privacy interest in records held by a third party. Any significant change to these privacy protections could produce a major shift in the balance between individual rights and the government's investigatory capabilities. The stakes grow larger as the Internet continues to expand as a central feature of modern life.

At the same time, however, the issue in *Miller* is personal privacy, and not every record created on or off the Internet qualifies as personal information. Government access to non-personal information held by third parties might be unaffected by any change in the privacy interest granted to individuals in third party records. This could include, perhaps, the content of many webpages, commercial transactions, foreign government operations, activities that occur outside the United States and beyond the scope of the Fourth Amendment, and more.

3. Data Retention

In March 2006, the EU enacted a Data Retention Directive calling for the mandatory retention of communications traffic data.[16] A leading argument for the directive is for combating terrorism. The

---

[14]45 C.F.R. Part 164, issued under the authority of the Health Insurance Portability and Accountability Act (HIPAA). Public Law 104–191, title II, § 264, 110 Stat. 2033 (1996), 42 U.S.C. § 1320d-2 note.

[15]Id. at § 164.512(e) & (i).

[16]Directive 2006/24/EC of the European Parliament and of the Council of 15 March 2006 on the retention of data generated or processed in connection with the provision of publicly available electronic communications services or of public communications networks and amending Directive 2002/58/EC, 2006 O.J. (L 105) 54, available at http://eur-lex.europa.eu/LexUriServ/LexUriServ.do?uri=OJ:L:2006:105:0054:0063:EN:PDF; accessed April 20, 2010.

same general argument in support of data retention could be made with respect to cyberattack prevention either because cyberattacks may qualify as terrorism or because data retention would be useful in preventing cyberattacks regardless of motivation. The EU and many of its Member States required data retention to create a new capability in combating criminal and other undesirable activities. The extent to which data retention will work to achieve the stated goals is open to question and beyond the scope of this paper. Nevertheless, data retention is a tool with some potential application to cyberattack prevention.

The EU Data Retention Directive requires Member States to adopt measures to ensure that electronic communications traffic data and location data generated or processed by providers of publicly available electronic communications services be retained for not less than six months and not more than two years from the date of the communication. The Data Retention Directive requires the retention of data necessary:

- to trace and identify the source of a communication
- to trace and identify the destination of a communication
- to identify the date, time and duration of a communication
- to identify the type of communication
- to identify the communication device
- to identify the location of mobile communication equipment.[17]

The retention requirement applies only to data generated or processed as a consequence of a communication or a communication service. It does not apply to the *content* of a telephone call or of electronic mail. The data retained must be made available to competent national authorities in specific cases "for the purpose of the investigation, detection and prosecution of serious crime, as defined by each Member State in its national law."[18] Thus, each Member State can establish its own standards for serious crime as well as its own judicial or other procedures for access.

The data retention directive has been controversial throughout Europe, with Internet activists strongly opposed to its implementation in many EU Member States. Litigation has resulted in some national courts finding laws implementing the directive unconstitutional. The German law suspended by the Federal Constitutional Court in early March 2010.[19] The German Court ordered the deletion of data collected. The decision did not exclude the possibility that a data retention law could pass constitutional muster, but it found that the law's provisions for security of data were inadequate and that the uses of the data were not sufficiently clear. The Romanian Constitutional Court found the Romanian data retention implementation law unconstitutional.[20]

A data retention law has been proposed for the United States, although it has not received much attention from Congress to date.[21] The constitutionality of any data retention proposed will surely be contested on First Amendment and Fourth Amendment grounds. Much will depend on the scope and the details of any enacted law. For example, a data retention requirement for Internet activities could entail the storage of information about electronic mail that could include data about the sender, recipient, header, attachment, content, and more. The retained data could be available to criminal or civil law enforcement, intelligence agencies, or private litigants after a showing of probable cause, reasonable cause, relevance, or another standard. Data subjects could have rights to object before or after retained information is disclosed or could have no rights. The details affect any privacy and civil liberties evalu-

---

[17]Id at Article 5.

[18]Id. at Article 1.

[19]*German High Court Limits Phone and E-Mail Data Storage*, Spiegel Online International (March 2, 2010), available at http://www.spiegel.de/international/germany/0,1518,681251,00.html; accessed April 20, 2010. The decision itself (in German) is at http://www.bundesverfassungsgericht.de/pressemitteilungen/bvg10-011; accessed April 20, 2010.

[20]*Romanian Constitutional Court: Data Retention Law Unconstitutional*, The Sofia Echo (Oct. 9, 2010), available at http://www.sofiaecho.com/2009/10/09/797385_romanian-constitutional-court-data-retention-law-unconstitutional; accessed April 20, 2010.

[21]See S.436, 111th Congress (2009).

ation, and any discussion of the possibilities would exceed the space available here. However, it seems clear that to the extent that a law requires the preservation of content rather than non-content information, the law will be harder to justify because existing precedents provide greater protections for the content of communications.

However, if a data retention law covers traffic, location, or transaction data only, there are some precedents in U.S. law that allow for government access with fewer or no procedural protections for the privacy of the individuals involved. For example, U.S. law allows for the use of pen registers that record dialed numbers without a search warrant.[22] The Stored Communications Act allows the government to order a provider of wire, electronic communication services, or remote computing services, to preserve records and other evidence in its possession pending the issuance of a court order or other process.[23] The Bank Secrecy Act requires banks to keep records of various transactions, including some cash activities and, effectively, all checks.[24] The Supreme Court upheld the law in 1974 as a valid exercise of federal power under the Commerce Clause.[25]

The distinction that the law makes for Fourth Amendment purposes between content and non-content has increasingly been the subject of litigation under ECPA but litigation remains, in the words of a leading Fourth Amendment scholar, "remarkably sparse."[26] The step-by-step analogies that the courts have used to move legal reasoning from postal mail to telephone calls begin to break down when it comes to Internet activities because the content vs. non-content distinction is much harder to sustain over the wide range of Internet functions that extend far beyond basic communications. For email, the substance of a message may not be limited to the actual content of a message but may be visible in part from the header, subject line, title of attachments, or other elements. In a 2010 decision pertaining to electronic communications (albeit not on the content/non-content issue), the Supreme Court was tentative in offering guidance, observing that "[r]apid changes in the dynamics of communication and information transmission are evident not just in the technology itself but in what society accepts as proper behavior."[27] How the law develops in this area could make a significant difference to the ability of the government to prevent or investigate cyberattack activities on the Internet. Any expansion in the ability of the government to see content or content-like elements of Internet activities without a showing of probable cause will be strongly contested using Fourth Amendment arguments. However, at the same time, it will be argued that many Internet activities are voluntary, and a user's expectations of privacy in this context are open to debate. Those expectations may be affected by the expansive monitoring of Internet activities for commercial purposes.[28] The routine and largely unrestricted commercial availability of the entrails of a user's Internet activities could undermine arguments that the user had a reasonable expectation of privacy. Thus, privacy legislation affecting Internet monitoring of individuals by commercial entities could also be relevant to the discussion.

First Amendment challenges to data retention requirements can also be anticipated. The right to associate, to speak, and to receive information would all be affected by data retention, with the specific arguments depending on the precise requirements of a data retention regime and on the standards and procedures under which the government could retrieve information from a service provider. Advocates would argue that the First Amendment requires that a retention law be justified under a strict scrutiny

---

[22]*Smith v. Maryland*, 442 U.S. 735 (1979). 18 U.S.C. §§ 3121-3127.

[23]18 U.S.C. § 2703(f). The Act is part of the Electronic Communications Privacy Act. An order under this provision is generally called *data preservation*. Data retention generally means a blanket requirement for the maintenance of some information on all communications.

[24]31 C.F.R. § 103.34(b)(10).

[25]*California Bankers Association v. Schultz*, 416 U.S. 21 (1974)

[26]Orin S. Kerr, *Applying the Fourth Amendment to the Internet: A General Approach*, 62 Stanford Law Review (forthcoming 2010), available at http://ssrn.com/abstract=1348322; accessed July 1, 2010.

[27]*Ontario v. Quon*, 560 U. S. __ (2010) (slip op. at 11).

[28]For more on the current controversy over behavioral targeting of Internet users for advertising and other purposes, see, e.g., Federal Trade Commission, *Staff Report: Self-Regulatory Principles for Online Behavioral Advertising: Tracking, Targeting, and Technology* (Feb. 2009), available at http://www.ftc.gov/os/2009/02/P085400behavadreport.pdf; accessed April 20, 2010.

standard—the most stringent standard of judicial review that requires that a law address a compelling governmental interest, that a law be narrowly tailored to achieve that interest, and that a law be the least restrictive means for achieving its objective.

In some contexts, however, data retention may be largely unremarkable. Routine business activities, whether online or offline, create records that must be retained for tax, credit, or many other purposes. In private networks, all activities may be monitored and recorded by the network operator, who may be a service provider, employer, or other person acting with or without notice to or the consent of the individual. Backup systems retain copies of an entire network at regular intervals. Broad rights to use, maintain, and disclose an individual's information can be reserved by a service provider through routine privacy policy or terms of service that its clients "consent" to by using the service. A recent report on cloud computing and privacy observed that a cloud provider may acquire rights over materials placed in the cloud "including the right to copy, use, change, publish, display, distribute, and share with affiliates or with the world the user's information."[29] These rights may exceed anything that laws mandating data retention require.

4. Terrorism and Cybersecurity

Congress enacted the USA PATRIOT Act less than two months after the events of September 11, 2001.[30] The Act is long and complex, and Congress amended it on several occasions, and more amendments are under consideration. Challenges to the Act have resulted in courts finding parts of the law unconstitutional. The details of the Act and subsequent litigation are too complex for this space. Generally, the Act expanded the ability of federal agencies to prevent and prosecute terrorism, with one title of the Act setting out enhanced surveillance procedures. For example, provisions make it easier for law enforcement agencies to search telephone and electronic communications and other records.

The Act also amended laws that make terrorism a crime. The basic definition of terrorism in the criminal code provides that terrorism must

(A) Involve violent acts or acts dangerous to human life that are a violation of the criminal laws of the United States or of any State, or that would be a criminal violation if committed within the jurisdiction of the United States or of any State;
(B) appear to be intended—
(i) to intimidate or coerce a civilian population;
(ii) to influence the policy of a government by intimidation or coercion; or
(iii) to affect the conduct of a government by mass destruction, assassination, or kidnapping.[31]

Whether cyberattacks would fall within the definition of *terrorism* is not immediately clear, but it seems a possibility, perhaps depending on the motivation of the attacker. The analysis might well depend on the facts of any given case. The USA PATRIOT Act added the Computer Fraud and Abuse Act[32] to the predicate offense list for wiretapping so at least some of the powers of the Act would be available for cyberattack prevention or investigation.[33] Other authorities provided in the Act may also be available today for some cyberattack prevention activities.

---

[29]Robert Gellman, *Privacy in the Clouds: Risks to Privacy and Confidentiality from Cloud Computing* at 17 (World Privacy Forum, 2009), available at http://www.worldprivacyforum.org/pdf/WPF_Cloud_Privacy_Report.pdf; accessed April 20, 2010.

[30]Public Law No. 107-56, 115 Stat. 272 (2001). The Act's full name is *Uniting and Strengthening America by Providing Appropriate Tools Required to Intercept and Obstruct Terrorism Act of 2001.*

[31]18 U.S.C. § 2331. There is a separate definition for *international terrorism* and for *domestic terrorism*. Both use a similar definition, with the location of the activity being the difference. The part quoted here represents the core of the two definitions.

[32]18 U.S.C. § 1030.

[33]18 U.S.C. § 2516(1)(c).

A broader question is whether Congress or the public would consider cyberattack prevention to be of equal importance to terrorism prevention to justify the granting or use of powers equivalent to those under the USA PATRIOT Act. The Act has remained highly controversial and the subject of continuing congressional actions. Any expansion of the Act or enactment of a similar law for cyberattack prevention would raise the same legal, constitutional, and political controversies that have dogged the Act from its inception.

5. The Fourth Amendment and Special Needs Cases

Ordinarily, the Fourth Amendment requirement that searches and seizures be reasonable means that there must be individualized suspicion of wrongdoing. In some circumstances, the usual rule does not apply. Whether the prevention of cyberattacks could justify an exemption from strict application of the Fourth Amendment is an open question.

In the so-called *special needs* cases, the courts have upheld suspicionless searches in some circumstances. For example, the Supreme Court allowed random drug testing of student athletes; drug tests for some Customs Service employees; and drug and alcohol tests for railway employees involved in train accidents. Searches were allowed for certain administrative purposes without particularized suspicion of misconduct, provided that the searches are appropriately limited. The Supreme Court also upheld brief, suspicionless seizures of motorists at a fixed Border Patrol checkpoint designed to intercept illegal aliens and at a sobriety checkpoint aimed at removing drunk drivers from the road.[34]

Because of the international scope of cyberattacks, any inquiry must consider other law that establishes diminished Fourth Amendment protections in international matters. The Foreign Intelligence Surveillance Act establishes lower standards for conducting surveillance in cases involving agents of a foreign power or a foreign terrorist group. The details of FISA, its amendments, litigation, and history are far beyond the scope of this paper. However, even the diminished FISA standards have been held to give way to the lower standards recognized in special needs cases. Thus, the United States Foreign Intelligence Surveillance Court of Review held in 2008 that a foreign intelligence exception to the Fourth Amendment's warrant requirement exists when surveillance seeks foreign intelligence for national security purposes and is directed against foreign powers or agents of foreign powers reasonably believed to be located outside the United States.[35]

Whether prevention of cyberattacks could qualify as a special needs case is unknown. Any expansion of special needs would be controversial, and a special needs case involving domestic cybersecurity matters would be especially controversial.

III. ISSUES RELATING TO SPEECH AND ASSOCIATION

The Internet raises a host of First Amendment speech and association issues, some of which are relevant to activities seeking to prevent cyberattacks. This is an area where it is especially difficult to be comprehensive and to disentangle issues.

Two preliminary observations are offered. First, the First Amendment does not protect against actions taken by private entities, although there can be some overlap between the public and private spheres at times. The First Amendment is a protection against abridgment of speech by government, state or federal. Second, it has been famously said that on the global Internet, the First Amendment is a local ordinance. To the extent that cyberattack protections involve other nations, First Amendment protections may not be available with respect to Internet activity that originates in or passes through those other nations.

---

[34]*City of Indianapolis v. Edmond*, 531 U.S. 32 (2000). However, the Court refused to allow a general interest in crime control to provide a justification for suspicionless stops. Id.

[35]*In Re Directives Pursuant to Sec. 105B*, 551 F. 3d 1004 (FISA Ct. Rev., 2008).

1. Internet as a Human Right

The Internet has rapidly become a vibrant public forum for speech of all types, including news, political discussions, government communications, commercial speech, and everything else. In some countries, access to the Internet is a fundamental right of its citizens.[36] In Finland, broadband access is a legal right.[37] However, rhetoric about the fundamental importance of the Internet does little to advance the present discussion of preventing cyberattacks. Whatever right may exist is not an unlimited right.

A new law in France illustrates the point. As originally enacted, the law would have allowed a government agency to suspend an individual's user account. The French constitutional court found that the law violated constitutional free speech protections. After an amendment that required a judge to make the decision to suspend, the court allowed the law to stand.[38] During the controversy over the French law, the European Parliament voted to make it illegal for any EU country to sever Internet service unless a court finds a citizen guilty.[39]

Whatever the scope of an individual's right to use the Internet may be, the view in Europe seems to be that the right may be restricted through actions that are not disproportionate and that involve a decision by an independent and impartial judge. The right to use the Internet is, in essence, the right to due process of law before the ability to exercise the right to use the Internet is removed or restricted. The same principles may apply when the reasons for seeking termination of Internet access relate to cyberattack prevention. It may be possible to argue in some cases that immediate threats to critical infrastructure would justify a different or lesser set of due process procedures prior to termination of Internet access rights.[40] Regardless, any rules or procedures with the potential to deny an individual access to the Internet will be controversial and the subject of considerable scrutiny on constitutional or legal grounds.

2. Anonymity

Anonymity on the Internet is a feature prized by many Internet users, often for different reasons. Many Internet activities can be conducted with a significant degree of anonymity using onion routers,[41] free email accounts that do not require any form of identification, public kiosks, blogs that do not ask posters to register, and in other ways. Whistleblowers, political activists, dissidents, and ordinary users value anonymity. The extent to which Internet activities are truly anonymous is uncertain. Even a user who takes concerted action to protect identity may not succeed all the time, especially against a person or government determined to uncover that identity.

Discussing the right to anonymity online is difficult for several reasons. First, the scope of a First Amendment right to anonymity is not clear, and tracking down the borders of anonymity leads far afield from the Internet without necessarily providing clarity. Second, there are many different objectives that a right to (or interest in) online anonymity may satisfy in whole or in part. For example, victims of

[36]Colin Woodward, *Estonia, Where Being Wired Is a Human Right*, Christian Science Monitor (July 1, 2003), available at http://www.csmonitor.com/2003/0701/p07s01-woeu.html. A 2010 poll taken in 26 countries found that almost 79% of those questioned said they either strongly agreed or somewhat agreed with the description of the Internet as a fundamental right. *Internet Access Is a Fundamental Right*, BBC News (March 8, 2010), available at http://news.bbc.co.uk/2/hi/technology/8548190.stm.

[37]Saeed Ahmed, *Fast Internet Access Becomes a Legal Right in Finland*, CNN.com (2009), available at http://www.cnn.com/2009/TECH/10/15/finland.internet.rights/index.html.

[38]Eric Pfanner, France Approves Wide Crackdown on Net Piracy (Oct. 23, 2009), New York Times, available at http://www.nytimes.com/2009/10/23/technology/23net.html.

[39]Kevin J. O'Brien, *French Anti-Piracy Proposal Undermines E.U. Telecommunications Overhaul*, New York Times, (May 7, 2009), available at http://www.nytimes.com/2009/05/07/technology/07iht-telecoms.html.

[40]The discussion below regarding the administrative license suspension for driver's licenses may suggest a precedent.

[41]With onion routing, messages are repeatedly encrypted and sent sequentially through different nodes. Each node removes a layer of encryption to find instructions for sending the message to the next node. Intermediary nodes do not know the origin, destination, or contents of the message.

domestic violence have some unique interests that are not relevant here. Third, it is hard to cover every possible cybersecurity activity that might affect an anonymity interest.

In cases involving political speech, the Supreme Court has consistently overturned laws that prohibited the distribution of anonymous handbills and similar laws that prevented anonymous political speech. Political speech is the most highly favored speech under the First Amendment. However, as one scholar described cases in this area, "the Court failed to embrace the notion of a free-standing right to anonymity and instead employed what would become a characteristic (and maddening) level of ambiguity."[42]

In other areas, a right to anonymity is not clearly established. In 2004, the Supreme Court upheld the conviction of an individual who refused to identify himself to a police officer during an investigative stop involving a reported assault. A state statute required a person detained by an officer under suspicious circumstances to identify himself.[43] The case raised Fourth and Fifth Amendment issues, but it was also seen as raising broader questions about the right to remain anonymous. The case's relevance to cyberspace is limited, but it illustrates that the Court does not universally favor anonymity.

The right to anonymity on the Internet has also been raised in a series of cases that balance the right to speak anonymously against the right of those who claim injury from anonymous defamatory speech. The law here is under development in many different courts and, not surprisingly, with the adoption of different approaches. Courts tend to require a plaintiff to show that a suit is viable before ordering disclosure of the speaker's identity. According to one scholar, the standard that appears to be becoming dominant requires a showing of evidence sufficient to establish a prima facie case of defamation coupled with a balancing of the right to speak anonymously and the right to pursue a libel claim.[44]

Anonymity concerns are likely to be raised by whistleblowers, i.e., individuals who raise concerns about wrongdoing occurring in an organization. Scattered federal and state laws provide some protections for whistleblowers, and the whistleblower community continues to press for stronger protections. Anonymity can be a method for whistleblowers to raise issues while avoiding the consequences of identification. To the extent that activities take place on a private network that does not support anonymity, the availability of the Internet as an alternative way to communicate about possible wrongdoing lessens concerns about the closed nature of a particular network and the lack of any anonymous methods of communications.

Political and other dissidents may also rely on anonymity to protect their identities when complaining about government or other activities. Anonymity can also assist activists who seek to find and communicate with others who hold similar views and to organize their efforts. Anonymity can also allow those with minority views, with unpopular views, or with other needs or fears to speak and organize. Here too, restrictions on a closed network may be of lesser concern if, at the same time, the Internet otherwise allows anonymity for communications and activities. However, if protections against cyberattacks undermine or interfere with the ability to use the Internet anonymously, those protections will be significantly more controversial politically and legally. It does not seem possible in the abstract to draw a line where the federal government can lawfully prevent or punish anonymous speech, although it has broader powers with respect to a network that it operates.

3. Restraining Publication of Security Information

One method that may be relevant to preventing cyberattacks is to limit or prevent the publication of information about vulnerabilities of computer systems, whether the information is held by govern-

---

[42]Jonathan Turley, *Registering Publius: The Supreme Court and the Right to Anonymity*, Cato Supreme Court Review (2001-02), available at http://www.cato.org/pubs/scr/2002/turley.pdf; accessed April 20, 2010.

[43]*Hiibel v. Sixth Judicial District Court of Nevada*, 542 U.S. 177 (2004).

[44]Lyrissa Barnett Lidsky, *Anonymity in Cyberspace: What Can We Learn from John Doe?*, 50 Boston College Law Review 1373, 1378 (2009).

ment or private actors.[45] Restrictions on the availability of information about security vulnerabilities raise First Amendment issues. The practical difficulties of restricting speech on the Internet are real but not necessarily material to the legal or constitutional issues.

Source Code

It is not entirely settled that the publication of source code constitutes speech protected under the First Amendment. In a leading case that arose in the context of export regulations, the Ninth Circuit concluded in the context of that case that encryption software qualified for First Amendment protections.[46] An alternate view expressed in the dissent is that source code is a method of controlling computers and is more function than speech.[47] The case has a complex history and does not offer a broad holding. The proper characterization of source code for First Amendment purposes has many different perspectives.

Copyright

The anti-circumvention provisions of the Digital Millennium Copyright Act[48] (DMCA) principally sought to stop copyright infringers from defeating anti-piracy protections in copyrighted works. The DMCA bans both acts of circumvention and the distribution of tools and technologies used for circumvention. The law exempts some activities, including security testing and encryption research. The DMCA has been used in a variety of ways to stop publication of information about security vulnerabilities, remove content from the Internet, affect research activities, and in other ways.[49] Opponents of the law contend that many of these uses chill free speech activities. The DMCA has some relevance to private sector attempts to prevent cyberattacks, but federal government information is not subject to copyright so the DMCA may not be relevant.[50]

Contractual Methods

Tools, techniques, and policies allow for government controls over publication of some information by some individuals. Contracts that require government employees not to publish any information without pre-publication review by the government offer one approach. In the leading case, the Supreme Court upheld a contract signed by an employee of the Central Intelligence Agency that imposed the restriction as a condition for access to classified information.[51]

Classification

The classification and control of federal government information in the interest of national defense or foreign policy (security classification) is another possible approach to cyberattack prevention. Classification protects security information controlled by the federal government, makes its use and disclo-

---

[45]See 6 U.S.C. § 133 (establishing restrictions on the use and disclosure of information regarding the security of critical infrastructure voluntarily submitted to a Federal agency).

[46]*Bernstein v. U.S. Dept. of Justice*, 176 F.3d 1132 (9th Cir. 1999), *withdrawn*, 192 F.3d 1308 (9th Cir. 1999).

[47]176 F.3d at 1147.

[48]17 U.S.C. § 1201.

[49]See generally, Electronic Frontier Foundation, *Unintended Consequences: Twelve Years under the DMCA*, available at https://www.eff.org/wp/unintended-consequences-under-dmca; accessed April 20, 2010.

[50]17 U.S.C. § 105.

[51]*Snepp v. United States*, 444 U.S. 507 (1980).

sure subject to controls, and subjects its publication to sanction.[52] To the extent that private parties not working for the government hold the information, classifying the information may be difficult as well as expensive.

Even information in private hands is arguably subject to classification. The Atomic Energy Act provides that data about the design and manufacture of atomic weapons is *restricted data* that is *born classified* regardless of who created the information.[53] Doubts about the constitutionality of this provision persist.[54] Enforcement of a *born classified* policy in the current international Internet environment seems challenging at best and impossible at worst.

Generally, however, restricting access to or publication of information in the possession or control of the government is different from restricting information in private hands. When restrictions on information become censorship is a matter of judgment. Some countries expressly restrict the ability of citizens to access websites or to find material they want through search engines.[55] The United States has on several occasions enacted legislation to restrict access by minors to obscene material or harmful material,[56] but the Supreme Court overturned the laws on First Amendment grounds.[57] Whether a law restricting publication of or access to cybersecurity information would be constitutional is unclear, but much could depend on the justification, structure, and application. The Supreme Court upheld the Children's Internet Protection Act,[58] a law that tied certain federal financial assistance to a library to a policy of Internet safety for minors that includes the operation of filtering technology to protect against access to material that is obscene, child pornography, or harmful to minors.[59] There is no specific precedent upholding statutory limitations on publication of cybersecurity information on the same basis as Atomic Energy restricted data or in a manner analogous to allowable controls on obscenity.

Prior Restraint

Prior restraint (government banning expression of ideas prior to publication) is another possible tool that could be used to protect cybersecurity information. However, prior restraint of publication is not favored, and the Supreme Court has stated on several occasions that, "[a]ny system of prior restraints of expression comes to this Court bearing a heavy presumption against its constitutional validity."[60] Whether or when computer security or national security interests could justify a prior restraint is uncertain. Practical considerations suggest that any restraint on publication could be difficult to maintain.

4. Domain Name System

The WHOIS database is an integral part of the registration system for Internet domain names. The database records and identifies the registrant or assignee of Internet resources, such as a web site domain name or an Internet Protocol address. The database includes information on a registrant, including name,

---

[52]Information that is properly classified is exempt from mandatory disclosure under the Freedom of Information Act (FOIA), 5 U.S.C. §552(b)(1). The ability of the government to withhold cybersecurity information from public requesters appears to be broad even if the information is not subject to classification. Nothing prevents the government from enacting additional exemptions to the FOIA. See 5 U.S.C. § 552(b)(3).

[53]42 U.S.C. §§ 2014(y), 2162(a).

[54]An important case is *U.S. v. The Progressive*, 467 F. Supp. 990 (W.D. Wis. 1979), appeal dismissed, 610 F. 2d. 819 (7th Cir. 1979).

[55]See, e.g., Andrew Jacobs, *Follow the Law, China Tells Internet Companies*, New York Times, Jan. 14, 2010, available at http://www.nytimes.com/2010/01/15/world/asia/15beijing.html, accessed August 30, 2010.

[56]See Communications Decency Act of 1996, 47 U.S.C. § 223(a) and (d); Child Online Protection Act, 47 U.S.C. § 231.

[57]*Reno v. ACLU*, 521 U.S. 844 (1997); *Ashcroft v. ACLU*, 535 U.S. 564 (2002), aff'd on remand, 322 F.3d 240 (3d Cir. 2003), aff'd and remanded, 542 U.S. 656 (2004), judgment entered by *ACLU v. Gonzales*, 478 F.Supp.2d 775 (E.D. Pa. 2007), aff'd sub nom. *ACLU v. Mukasey*, 534 F.3d 181 (3rd Cir. 2008), cert. denied, __ U.S. __, 129 S. Ct. 1032 (2009).

[58]20 U.S.C. §§9134(f)(1)(A)(i) and (B)(i); 47 U. S. C. §§254(h)(6)(B)(i) and (C)(i).

[59]*U.S. v. American Library Association*, 539 U.S. 194 (2003).

[60]See, e.g., the Pentagon Papers case, *New York Times v. United States*, 403 U.S. 713 (1971) (per curium).

address, telephone number, and email address. The information in the WHOIS database is often public and available to any inquirer. However, domain name registrars offer to list themselves as the owner of a domain name to shield information about the real owner (i.e., proxy registrations).

A government move to prevent proxy registrations—or to require additional disclosures—in the interest of cyberattack prevention would generate First Amendment and privacy concerns. Registrants who want anonymity to avoid identification and possible harassment and registrants who merely want to shield their personal information from marketers and other secondary users of their information would object. The conflicts over the privacy of the WHOIS database have raged for some time, involve privacy laws in other countries, and will require international coordination. It is impossible to predict how the conflicts might be resolved.

Government actions seeking to cancel domain names issued to those believed to be engaged in activities that threaten cybersecurity would raise due process issues similar to the taking of any other private property by the government. However, because depriving someone of a domain name affects the ability to communicate, First Amendment arguments would likely accompany the due process issues as major points of contention. Cutting off or limiting the ability of a speaker to use the Internet or other recent means of communication will be viewed by many as a direct prohibition on speech and, especially, on political speech. Further, because domain name registration is an international activity, federal efforts could be ineffective or could have to consider international standards.

5. Beyond the First Amendment

The First Amendment does not protect some types of speech, including defamation, incitement, obscenity, and pornography produced with real children.[61] Congress has enacted laws prohibiting child pornography.[62] ISPs are required to report evidence of child pornography offenses.[63] Some state laws require computer technicians to report to police child pornography found while working on computers.[64]

Could similar laws or principles establish limits on or mandate monitoring or reporting of cybersecurity communications, information, or activities? It is possible to characterize those who undermine security protections for computers and computer networks as threatening, among other things, the exercise of free speech rights guaranteed by the First Amendment. Arguably, a case could be made that reducing or eliminating First Amendment protections for speech or actions that present cybersecurity threats actually protect the First Amendment rights of others. Framed this way, the issue might call for a balancing of interests rather than a one-sided evaluation of the rights of a speaker versus the powers of the government. The use of First Amendment values to defend some restrictions on speech is an interesting prospect.[65]

Closely related issues involving tradeoffs between speech and privacy have been a topic of debate in the context of deep packet inspection (DPI). Internet messages are broken into units called packets that are composed of header information (analogous to an envelope) and a data field (analogous to content). Packets move from place to place using the header information alone. DPI involves the opening and

---

[61]*Ashcroft v. Free Speech Coalition*, 535 U.S. 234, 245-6 (2002). See generally Henry Cohen, *Freedom of Speech and Press: Exceptions to the First Amendment* (2009) (Congressional Research Service), http://www.fas.org/sgp/crs/misc/95-815.pdf; accessed April 14, 2010.

[62]See, e.g., Protection of Children From Sexual Predators Act of 1998, Public Law 105-314, 112 Stat. 2974 (1998).

[63]18 U.S.C. § 2258A. There is an exception allowing this type of disclosure in the Electronic Communications Privacy Act, 18 U.S.C. § 2702(b).

[64]See National Conference of State Legislatures, *Child Pornography Reporting Requirements (ISPs and IT Workers)*, http://www.ncsl.org/IssuesResearch/TelecommunicationsInformationTechnology/ChildPornographyReportingRequirementsISPsand/tabid/13460/Default.aspx; accessed March 29, 2010.

[65]Robert Morris's 1988 release of the so-called Internet worm that had the effect of denying service on infected computers resulted in his conviction for violation of the federal Computer Fraud and Abuse Act. The conviction shows that some computer actions are subject to criminal sanction. The line between speech, which is harder to sanction, and non-speech, which may be easier to sanction, is complex.

reading the content of a Web browsing session, email, instant message, or whatever other data the packet contains. ISPs, who assemble packets for users, can and do use DPI to identify network threats including spam, viruses and other malware, and denial-of-service attacks. These actions may well increase cyber-attack protections. DPI could be used to search for personal information, child pornography, copyright infringement, or almost anything else. DPI can also be used to set priorities for Internet activities, an issue in Net Neutrality debates.

The basic idea of using DPI to screen Internet activities for unwanted activities is not simple. Fears about the use of DPI include threats to privacy through the collection or use of more personal information for commercial or other uses;[66] filtering standards that will monitor or block non-objectionable activities or speech; increased government surveillance; interference with Net Neutrality; and other problems. Commercial use of DPI for marketing purposes has given rise to litigation.[67]

Whether government-mandated DPI program for cybersecurity purposes would pass constitutional muster would depend, in significant part, on the factual predicate for the requirement and on the level of scrutiny required by the courts. The availability and effectiveness of other tools and techniques to accomplish the same purpose would also be relevant in any ruling. The specific focus of DPI, whether for malware, spam, copyright infringement, or other purposes, would also make a difference. The waters here are largely uncharted.

Private ISPs already engage in filtering of email for spam and malware. This often happens with some degree of consent from users, although it is unclear whether consumers grant consent knowingly. In general, it is much debated today whether consent is a reasonable way of engaging consumers for privacy and other purposes. Privacy advocates and others express doubts about the value and viability of the notice-and-consent regime used for privacy and other purposes on the Internet today.[68]

IV. ISSUES RELATING TO INFORMATION PRIVACY

The general approach of the United States to the protection of information privacy is often called *sectoral*. Privacy laws often pass in response to specific incidents, and the laws often respond narrowly to the facts, industries, or institutions identified in those incidents. The result is a disparate set of laws that address the collection, maintenance, use, and disclosure of personally identifiable information often in incomplete or inconsistent ways. No privacy statute applies to many types of records and record keepers. In contrast, Europe, Canada, and much of the rest of the developed world operates under omnibus laws that establish uniform, high-level rules for most record keepers. Other nations often expressly base their privacy laws on Fair Information Practices (FIPs), a set of principles for information privacy.[69] U.S. laws often reflect elements of FIPs, and some laws address most or all of the principles to some extent.

The first law anywhere to meet FIPs standards was the Privacy Act of 1974.[70] The Privacy Act of 1974 is a federal statute that applies to records about individuals maintained by federal agencies and

---

[66]"DPI poses unique risks to individual privacy." Statement of Leslie Harris, President and Chief Executive Officer Center for Democracy & Technology, Before the House Committee on Energy and Commerce, Subcommittee on Communications, Technology and the Internet, The Privacy Implications of Deep Packet Inspection at 8 (April 23, 2009), http://www.cdt.org/privacy/20090423_dpi_testimony.pdf; accessed March 29, 2010.

[67]See Jacqui Cheng, *NebuAd, ISPs sued over DPI snooping, ad-targeting program*, ars technica, Nov. 11, 2009, http://arstechnica.com/tech-policy/news/2008/11/nebuad-isps-sued-over-dpi-snooping-ad-targeting-program.ars, accessed August 30, 2010. The lawsuit alleges, among other things, that DPI violates ECPA.

[68]See, e.g., Introductory Remarks, Federal Trade Commission Chairman Jon Leibowitz, FTC Privacy Roundtable (Dec. 7, 2009), http://www.ftc.gov/speeches/leibowitz/091207privacyremarks.pdf; accessed March 29, 2010.

[69]A classic statement of FIPs much more likely to be cited than the original is from the Organisation for Economic Cooperation and Development, *OECD Guidelines on the Protection of Privacy and Transborder Flows of Personal Data*, http://www.oecd.org/document/20/0,3343,en_2649_34255_15589524_1_1_1_1,00.html, accessed March 26, 2010. For a short history of FIPs and some of the many variations of FIPs, see Robert Gellman, *Fair Information Practices: A Basic History*, http://bobgellman.com/rg-docs/rg-FIPshistory.pdf; accessed March 26, 2010.

[70]5 U.S.C. § 552a.

by contractors that maintain systems of records on behalf of agencies. Congress took the substance of the Act largely from the recommendations of the 1972 Department of Health, Education & Welfare Advisory Committee that originally developed and proposed FIPs.[71] In establishing a privacy office at the Department of Homeland Security in 2003, the Congress assigned the office responsibility for "assuring that personal information contained in Privacy Act systems of records is handled in full compliance with fair information practices as set out in the Privacy Act of 1974."[72] This was the first direct U.S. statutory mention of FIPs. DHS now has its own version of FIPs, which it calls Fair Information Practice Principles.[73]

Because the Privacy Act of 1974 applies to federal agencies, it is the privacy law of greatest relevance here and is described here in modest detail. Other privacy laws applicable to the private sector or to state governments are less likely to be important in the context of cyberattack prevention, although there could be circumstances in which other laws could affect access to records needed for investigatory purposes.

1. Privacy Act of 1974

The Privacy Act of 1974 does not apply to all personal information in the possession of federal agencies. It mostly applies to personal information maintained in a *system of records*.[74] This is a group of records from which information is actually retrieved by name, social security number, or other personal identifier. The retrieval standard is a *factual* one. While much personal information in agency hands is covered, some is not because the information is not actually retrieved by personal identifier. This "loophole" exists because of the need to attach many of the Act's requirements to an identified record-keeping structure.[75] It is one of the elements of the Act that has grown outdated with the power of modern computers to readily search and retrieve disorganized information. An agency can collect and use large quantities of personal information, but the Privacy Act is not triggered if the information is not retrieved by individual identifier.[76] Activities designated as *data mining*[77] do not have any separate requirements or distinct status under the Act. The Act generally applies to data mining if personal information in records maintained in a system of records is retrieved by individual identifier and does not apply otherwise.

Despite the evolution of record keeping from paper to mainframe computers to personal computers to databases to networks and to cyberspace since passage of the Act, the basic structure of the Act remains unchanged. Further, the explosion of private sector record keeping and the commercial availability of those private sector records allow federal agencies to examine and use more personal information on a systematic basis without maintaining system of records. Privately maintained records do not become subject to the Privacy Act merely because the federal government uses them. The record keeper

---

[71]Secretary's Advisory Committee on Automated Personal Data Systems, *Records, Computers and the Rights of Citizens* (1972), http://aspe.os.dhhs.gov/datacncl/1973privacy/tocprefacemembers.htm; accessed March 26, 2010.

[72]6 U.S.C. §142. See also 50 U.S.C. § 403-3d(b)(5) (establishing a Civil Liberties Protection Officer within the Office of the Director of National Intelligence).

[73]http://www.dhs.gov/xlibrary/assets/privacy/privacy_policyguide_2008-01.pdf; accessed March 26, 2010.

[74]5 U.S.C. § 552a(a)(5). The Act's protections cover citizens and resident aliens. Id. at § 552a(a)(2) (definition of *individual*). Foreigners are not protected by the Act. Data protection laws in other countries usually cover all individuals regardless of citizenship or residency status. This limitation of the Privacy Act of 1974 has been a point of contention in disputes with the EU over the processing of travel and other information.

[75]Some provisions of the Privacy Act of 1974 have been interpreted as applying generally to agencies maintaining systems of records rather than only to information in systems of records. See Department of Justice, *Overview of the Privacy Act of 1974* (2010) at Definitions, E. Systems of Records, 3. Other Aspects, http://www.justice.gov/opcl/1974definitions.htm#aspects; accessed March 26, 2010.

[76]Whether IP addresses or even email addresses constitute personal information under the Act is not resolved. Many agencies have not established systems of records covering email activities.

[77]For a definition of *data mining*, see the Federal Agency Data Mining Reporting Act of 2007, 42 U.S.C. 2000ee-3.

must maintain the records under a contract with a federal agency, by or on behalf of the agency, and to accomplish an agency function.[78] These limitations often allow an agency to avoid the Act by using private sector records that serve additional purposes other than the agency's purpose. This limitation is a widely recognized shortcoming of the Act.

For example, if an agency reviews a credit report maintained by a credit bureau, the relevance of the Privacy Act of 1974 to the agency's review is limited because of the absence of a system of records. The situation would be different if the agency retrieved the credit report and stored it in a system of records. However, a federal agency's mere use of an Internet search engine or review of a social networking page does not by itself appear to trigger the Act. If ISPs were required by law to retain data about their customers' Internet activities, the records stored by the ISPs would not be covered by the Privacy Act of 1974 because of the absence of a contract with a federal agency, among other reasons. Federal agencies might be able to retrieve those records from ISPs without triggering the Act unless and until the records were made part of a system of records.

The Act's requirements can be generally described using FIPs principles:

- *Openness.* Each agency must publish in the Federal Register a description of personal data record-keeping policies, practices, and systems.[79] No systems or agencies are exempt from the publication requirement.
- *Individual participation.* Each agency must allow an individual to see and have a copy of records about himself or herself. An individual also has the right to seek amendment of any information that is not accurate, timely, relevant, or complete.[80]
- *Data quality.* Each agency must make reasonable efforts to maintain relevant and necessary records that are accurate, relevant, timely, and complete when disclosed to anyone other than another agency.[81] Agencies are prohibited from maintaining information about how individuals exercise rights guaranteed by the First Amendment to the U.S. Constitution unless expressly authorized by statute or unless within the scope of an authorized law enforcement activity.[82] Notably, this First Amendment provision applies to agency records even if not maintained in a system of records.[83]
- *Use limitation.* The Act establishes general rules governing the use and disclosure of personal information.[84] The broad policy that the Act attempts to implement is that information collected for one purpose may not be used for another purpose without notice to or the consent of the subject of the record. However, this policy has so many exceptions, some the result of later enacted laws, that the relevance of the general principle is questionable. The standard for uses within an agency is *need for the record in the performance of duties,*[85] although it is not clear that agencies apply this standard with much rigor.
- *Purpose specification.* The Act grants all agencies authority to make some basic disclosures.[86] However, most disclosures rely on the authority of a *routine use.*[87] Agencies have considerable discretion in defining *routine use* disclosures through a regulatory-like process. When a program changes or a subsequent law directs agencies to use records for a new purpose, the agency defines a new *routine use*

---

[78]5 U.S.C. § 552a(m).

[79]Id. at § 552a(e)(4).

[80]Id. at § 552a(d).

[81]Id. at §§ 552a(e)(1), (e)(5).

[82]Id. at § 552a(e)(7).

[83]*Albright v. United States,* 631 F.2d 915 (D.C. Cir. 1980).

[84]5 U.S.C. § 552a(b).

[85]Id. at § 552a(b)(1).

[86]Id. at § 552a(b)(4) to (b)(12).

[87]Id. at § 552(a)(7), (b)(3).

authorizing a new disclosure. For example, the President's Identity Theft Task Force[88] recommended that all agencies adopt a routine use for all systems of records to allow disclosures to address identity theft problems arising from security breaches. The effectiveness of the routine use provision as a protection against expansive uses of personal information has been questioned for years.

If the Congress or the President established deterrence of cyberattacks as a purpose of the federal government, then agency sharing of personal information would be allowable under the Act pursuant to a routine use.[89] Conceivably, if the charge were broad enough and the identity theft example were used as a model, every system of records in the federal government could include a routine use allowing disclosures for deterrence of cyberattacks. Some in the privacy community would object to the breadth and scope of such an approach, but the Privacy Act may be loose enough to allow it. As a practical matter, however, it seems highly unlikely that all agency systems of records would have information relevant to that purpose.

• *Security.* Agencies must maintain information with appropriate administrative, technical, and physical safeguards to insure the security and confidentiality of the information and to protect against anticipated threats or hazards.[90] The security requirements are general and have been effectively superseded by later, more specific legislation.[91]

• *Collection limitation.* Agencies are required to maintain only information that is relevant and necessary to accomplish an allowable purpose.[92] In addition, agencies are supposed to collect information directly from the data subject *to the extent practicable* if the information may result in an adverse determination.[93]

• *Enforcement.* The Act includes legal remedies that permit an individual to seek enforcement of rights. Civil lawsuits provide the basic enforcement mechanism.[94] In addition, the government may seek relatively minor criminal penalties for Federal employees who fail to comply with the Act's provisions.[95] The Office of Management and Budget has a limited oversight role.[96]

All federal agencies must comply with the Privacy Act of 1974, including law enforcement and national security agencies. The Act does not completely exempt any activity or any agency from the Act. However, the Act includes two different categories of exemption that allow some agencies and some activities to avoid compliance with some provisions of the law. An agency invokes an exemption for a specific system of records through a formal rulemaking process.[97] The exemption becomes part of the agency's Privacy Act of 1974 rules and of the exempted system of records published notice.

---

[88]The Task Force issued a strategic plan in April 2007, http://www.idtheft.gov/reports/StrategicPlan.pdf; accessed March 23, 2010, and a follow-up report in September 2008. http://www.idtheft.gov/reports/IDTReport2008.pdf; accessed March 23, 2010.

[89]See, for example, the information sharing provisions of the Intelligence Reform and Terrorism Prevention Act of 2004, 6 U.S.C. § 485, which direct the establishment of an information sharing environment for terrorism information. The Act also calls for attention to the protection of privacy and civil liberties in the information sharing environment but includes no specifics. From a Privacy Act perspective, this statute would likely authorize agencies operating relevant systems of records to adopt routine uses allowing broad sharing of personal information with appropriate federal agencies for the purposes stated in the Act. Given the statutory direction, the Privacy Act's barriers to information sharing are essentially procedural.

[90]5 U.S.C. § 552a(e)(10).

[91]See Fair Information Principles and Federal Information Security Management Act (FISMA), 44 U.S.C. § 3541 et seq.

[92]5 U.S.C. § 552a(e)(1).

[93]Id. at § 552a(e)(2).

[94]Id. at § 552a(g).

[95]Id. at § 552a(i). Other criminal penalties under other laws may also be used to punish actions that violate the Privacy Act of 1974.

[96]Id. at § 552a(v).

[97]Id. at § 552a(j), (k).

The Act's *general exemptions* are available for (1) all records of the Central Intelligence Agency and (2) records maintained by an agency or component that performs as its principal function any activity pertaining to the enforcement of criminal laws.[98] The general exemptions allow an agency or component to not comply with many provisions of the Act for an exempt system of records. The net effect of the exemptions is to remove many of the protections that the law provides, but a core of privacy provisions remain.

The Act also provides for *specific exemptions* that are narrower than the general exemptions. Systems specifically exempt can be exempted only from access requirements, obligations to limit records to those relevant and necessary, and several other minor provisions. The specific exemptions are available for record systems that contain seven categories of records, of which only three are potentially relevant to cybersecurity. One exemption is for a system of records that has information classified for national defense or foreign policy reasons.[99] Another is for investigatory material compiled for law enforcement purposes (other than material subject to the general criminal law enforcement purposes).[100] This exemption covers civil as well as some criminal law enforcement activities. However, if an agency uses a record to deprive an individual of a right, benefit, or privilege, the agency must disclose the record except if it would reveal the identity of a source who furnished the information under an express promise of confidentiality. The third covers investigatory material compiled for determining eligibility for federal employment, contracts, or access to classified information.[101] The exemption is available only to protect a source expressly promised confidentiality.

Together, the Act's exemptions allow national security and law enforcement activities to comply with some or most of the privacy requirements otherwise applicable to the federal government. One of the principal purposes of the Act was to stop secret government record keeping, and the Act does not exempt any agency from the requirement for openness. However, all exempt systems have some protection from the access and amendment provisions of the Act and can have broad authority to collect information free from relevance requirements.

This type of special treatment that allows national security and law enforcement activities to avoid full compliance with privacy standards is not unusual. The European Union's Data Protection Directive[102] applies broadly to record keepers within Europe. However, under Article 3 of the Directive, the regulatory scheme does not apply to activities that fall outside the scope of community law, processing operations for public security, defense, state security, and criminal law activities. EU Member States may provide privacy protections for these activities.

The Privacy Act of 1974 also restricts computer matching. However, the definition of matching programs both narrow and technologically outmoded.[103] It only covers matching for federal benefit programs, for recouping overpayments for those programs, and of federal personnel records. In addition, the definition expressly excludes matching for some civil or criminal law purposes, for foreign counterintelligence, and for some other purposes. The matching restrictions are not likely to be relevant to computer matching activities supporting cyberattack prevention.

The Privacy Act of 1974 would apply to federal agency cyberattack prevention activities that create systems of records. Technical and policy activities would not likely create any covered records about individuals (except for employment records), but criminal and civil investigatory activities would. There could well be some gray areas. For example, if cyberattack prevention involved offensive and not just defensive actions—e.g., seeking to disrupt the actions of a hacker—it might not be clear whether the

---

[98]Id. at § 552a(j)(1) & (2).

[99]Id. at § 552a(k)(1).

[100]Id. at § 552a(k)(2).

[101]Id. at § 552a(k)(5).

[102]Directive 95/46/EC of the European Parliament and of the Council of 24 October 1995 on the protection of individuals with regard to the processing of personal data and on the free movement of such data, http://ec.europa.eu/justice_home/fsj/privacy/law/index_en.htm; accessed March 26, 2010.

[103]5 U.S.C. § 552a(a)(8).

activity qualifies as a law enforcement activity that could be exempted from some of the Act's provisions. If classified, however, the activity could utilize an exemption regardless of its law enforcement characterization.

In the end, the Privacy Act of 1974 would not create a barrier to cyberattack prevention activities that is any more significant or disruptive than the low barriers it presents to intelligence, defense, or law enforcement functions. In the decades since the Act became effective, there have been few reported problems in these spheres and few amendments. This is not to suggest that the law provides the privacy rigor that advocates or civil libertarians might like or that some agencies would not prefer a broader exemption. Some controversies have not arisen sharply because of the Act's increasing technological obsolescence. For example, not all agencies define electronic mail systems as falling within the Act's scope.

Depending on the scope of cybersecurity activities, however, information privacy controversies could easily arise. The routine collection and maintenance of personal information about the Internet activities of individuals in the absence of a specific law enforcement investigation would raise questions about the scope of the activity and the corresponding obligations regarding the maintenance, use, and disclosure of the information. Obviously, the limitations of the Fourth Amendment and of surveillance statutes would be highly relevant here, establishing procedures and standards for some government actions. The Privacy Act of 1974's standards define additional privacy obligations for personal information collected, compiled, and retrieved by individual identifier. The Act's technological shortcomings create some loopholes that cybersecurity activities might lawfully use.

To the extent that personal information processing can be accomplished using de-identified data or using data minimization policies and practices,[104] privacy issues can be avoided or diminished, and privacy laws may be inapplicable. However, while advocates welcome these approaches, their utility can be limited. Although the Privacy Act's policies may gently push agencies toward using less data, most agencies have no difficulty justifying the collection and maintenance of more personal information except where another statute directs otherwise. The Act's actual barriers are minor, and an agency that wants to can always find a justification for more data. Another reality is that anonymized or de-identified information can often be re-identified, often without much difficulty. There is growing recognition that personal data cannot be successfully anonymized or de-identified.[105] Professor Latanya Sweeney, an authority on anonymity, put it this way: "I can never guarantee that any release of [deidentified] data is anonymous, even though for a particular user it may very well be anonymous."[106] That does not mean that efforts to remove identifiers will never protect a privacy interest, only that the protections that come with de-identification may be overcome.

One possible model for the sharing of de-identified data can be found in the federal health privacy rule issued under the authority of the Health Insurance Portability and Accountability Act (HIPAA). The rule provides that the removal of 18 specific data elements from a health record generally creates anonymized data that is no longer subject to the rule's requirements.[107] A second provision allows for the creation of a *limited data set* containing more data elements and that can potentially be re-identified. A limited data set can be shared for specified purposes and then only under a *data use agreement* that specifies the terms of use and disclosure and that prohibits re-identification.[108]

---

[104]See, e.g., the minimization procedures for electronic surveillance included in the Foreign Intelligence Surveillance Act, 50 U.S.C. § 1801(h).

[105]See, e.g., Paul Ohm, *Broken Promises of Privacy: Responding to the Surprising Failure of Anonymization,* 57 UCLA Law Review 1701 (2010). See also Robert Gellman, *Privacy for Research Data,* Panel on Confidentiality Issues Arising from the Integration of Remotely Sensed and Self-Identifying Data, National Research Council, Putting People on the Map: Protecting Confidentiality with Linked Social-Spatial Data (2007) (Appendix A), http://books.nap.edu/catalog.php?record_id=11865, accessed June 29, 2010.

[106]National Committee on Vital and Health Statistics, Subcommittee on Privacy and Confidentiality, *Proceedings of Roundtable Discussion: Identifiability of Data* (Jan. 28, 1998), available at http://ncvhs.hhs.gov/980128tr.htm.

[107]45 C.F.R. § 164.514(b)(2).

[108]Id. at § 164.514(e).

Neither HIPAA de-identification method is perfectly suited to the cybersecurity arena, but the notion of limited use, written limitations, and prohibitions on re-identification may be adapted as part of information collection or sharing. These or additional controls could be provided by statute, Executive Order, contract, oversight mechanisms, public or other reporting, administrative procedures, or other mechanisms that would impose, enforce, and oversee restrictions on personal data use and sharing. The policy could allow some or all data restrictions to be overridden under a defined standard and procedure that could be as rigorous as desired, even requiring probable cause and judicial approval at the high end. There is much opportunity here for creativity in policy and legislation.

2. Foreign Privacy Laws

Because the Internet is global, cyberattack prevention will not necessarily be domestic in scope and may involve other governments and may focus on events and activities in other countries. To the extent that cybersecurity activities involve the transfer of personal information across national borders, foreign data protection laws may impose some barriers on the export of data to the United States.[109] The best example comes from the European Union, where the EU Data Protection Directive establishes rules for the transfer of personal data to third countries.[110] The general standard allows data exports to third countries that ensure an *adequate level of protection*.[111] The EU has not made any determination whether the United States generally meets this standard, and it is unlikely to do so. Some other countries were found to be adequate, including Canada. In the absence of adequacy, the Directive allows for data exports under specified circumstances.[112] One category of allowable transfers covers those necessary or legally required on important public interest grounds.[113] This would allow personal transfers for some cybersecurity-related activities just as it allows transfers for law enforcement activities.

Outside the EU, other nations have different policies regarding personal data exports. Depending on the nature and purpose of a cyberattack prevention data export restriction, national privacy laws may or may not impose meaningful barriers. Much depends on the details. In general, data protection rules do not prevent law enforcement or national security cooperation. However, as the EU's Article 29 Working Party observed in an opinion about international cooperation on anti-doping activities in sports, "controllers in the EU are responsible for processing personal data in compliance with domestic law and must therefore disregard the World Anti-Doping Code and International Standards insofar as they contradict domestic law."[114] In other words, national data protection laws can matter regardless of international cooperative efforts.

---

[109]U.S. privacy laws rarely address the export of regulated data to other nations. Some data restrictions may continue to apply to exported data or to the exporters of the data, but this may not always be the case. Restrictions on use of data by financial institutions subject to Gramm-Leach-Bliley, 15 U.S.C. § 6802, would apply to international transfers to affiliates. However, health data sent to a foreign health care provider as allowed by the Health Insurance Portability and Accountability Act Privacy Rule, 45 C.F.R. Part 164, would pass outside the scope of the rule and be unregulated by U.S. law. On the other hand, the restrictions imposed by the Children's Online Privacy Protection Act, 15 U.S.C. §§ 6501-6506, apply to any website located "on the Internet" directed at children. Cross border enforcement of privacy laws is often problematic.

[110]The Directive establishes standards that each Member State must comply with through its own national laws. Article 4.

[111]Article 25.1.

[112]Article 26.1.

[113]Article 26.1.c.

[114]ARTICLE 29 Data Protection Working Party, *Second opinion 4/2009 on the World Anti-Doping Agency (WADA) International Standard for the Protection of Privacy and Personal Information, on related provisions of the WADA Code and on other privacy issues in the context of the fight against doping in sport by WADA and (national) anti-doping organizations* (April 6, 2009) (WP 162), http://ec.europa.eu/justice_home/fsj/privacy/docs/wpdocs/2009/wp162_en.pdf; accessed March 29, 2010.

V. ISSUES RELATING TO DUE PROCESS, LICENSING, AND IDENTIFICATION

This section reviews three existing identification/authentication systems in order to provide background for possible consideration of licensing systems for Internet users, for software programs, services, or equipment used to access the Internet. Microsoft's chief research and technology officer recently suggested licensing individuals, machines, and programs using the Internet as a response to the crime, fraud, spying, and other unwelcome Internet activities that have become commonplace.[115] Some type of Internet licensing scheme may have application for cyberattack prevention.

The United States has experience with issuing credentials in a wide variety of contexts. We identify and authenticate people to varying degrees, depending on the purpose of the activity. Each system has its own process rules and privacy rules. The purpose here is not to suggest that any of these systems is a model for identification, authentication, or licensing on the Internet. The goal is to illustrate how we have dealt with privacy, identification, due process, and other facets of identification/authentication systems that affect the ability of people to function.

The first system described here is the security clearance system that regulates who can have access to national security information. The issuance of a security clearance for TOP SECRET information requires an intensive investigation as a precondition. The second system is the driver's license system. Because driver's licenses have become standard identifiers in many contexts, the licenses have a significance far beyond control of driving. With the enactment of the REAL ID Act of 2005, the level of controversy surrounding drivers' licenses has expanded considerably, and changes to the Act remain under consideration by the Congress. The third system is Secure Flight, the airline passenger pre-screening program run by the Transportation Security Administration. Unlike the other two systems highlighted here, Secure Flight operates in more of a real-time, case-by-case mode.[116]

1. The Security Clearance Model

A. Issuance

Only those who have a security clearance can have access to federal government information classified in the interest of national defense or foreign policy.[117] Information pertaining to cybersecurity can qualify under this standard, and those who need access to the information will require a security clearance.

---

[115]See Barbara Kiviat, *Driver's Licenses for the Internet*, The Curious Capitalist Blog (Jan. 30, 2010), at http://curiouscapitalist. blogs.time.com/2010/01/30/drivers-licenses-for-the-internet (discussing comments of Craig Mundie); accessed April 12, 2010.

[116]Another system of potential interest is a recently adopted federal government identification and credentialing system for federal government employees and contractors. The new system began with the issuance of Homeland Security Presidential Directive 12 (HSPD-12) in August 2004, available at https://www.dhs.gov/xabout/laws/gc_1217616624097.shtm#1; accessed March 16, 2010. This directive called for the establishment of a mandatory, interoperable, government-wide standard for secure and reliable forms of identification for federal government employees and contractors who access government-controlled facilities and information systems. The National Institute of Standards and Technology issued the standard in 2005. National Institute of Standards and Technology, *Personal Identity Verification (PIV) of Federal Employees and Contractors* (FIPS 201) (2006), available at http://csrc.nist.gov/publications/fips/fips201-1/FIPS-201-1-chng1.pdf; accessed March 16, 2010. The standard has two parts. The first part sets out uniform requirements for verifying the identity of individuals applying for official agency credentials, issuing credentials, maintaining related information, and protecting the privacy of the applicants. The second part specifies the technical requirements for the smart cards used in the system. The identity proofing requires a background investigation, such as a National Agency Check with Written Inquiries; a FBI National Criminal History Fingerprint Check; requiring applicants to appear in person at least once before the issuance of an ID card; and requiring applicants to provide two original forms of identity source documents.

[117]Differences between clearance standards and procedures among federal agencies are not material here, nor are additional types of higher-level clearances that are prerequisites to access to specific classes of information with greater sensitivity. The description here is of the basic Department of Defense program. See generally Department of Defense, Personal Security Program, DoD 5200.2-R (1996), available at http://www.dod.mil/dodgc/doha/5200.2-R.pdf; accessed March 16, 2010. Legislation on security clearances can be found in 50 U.S.C. Chapter 15 (§§ 435-438).

Prior to issuing a clearance, the federal agency conducts an investigation, with most investigations now done by the Office of Personnel Management. The investigation inquires into an individual's loyalty, character, trustworthiness, and reliability to ensure eligibility for access to national security information. The policy sets out thirteen relevant criteria: allegiance to the United States; foreign influence; foreign preference; sexual behavior; personal conduct; financial considerations; alcohol consumption; drug involvement; emotional, mental, and personality disorders; criminal conduct; security violations; outside activities; and misuse of information technology systems.[118]

The extent of the investigation depends on whether access is required to information classified as CONFIDENTIAL, SECRET, or TOP SECRET. For a CONFIDENTIAL or SECRET clearance, the investigation consists of a National Agency Check (FBI and other federal agency files), a Local Agency Check (local law enforcement files), and a Financial Check (credit record). For a TOP SECRET clearance, the investigation adds field interviews of references, employers, and others; checks of records held by employers, courts, and rental offices; and an interview with the applicant. The TOP SECRET clearance is considerably more costly, intensive, and invasive than the lower-level clearances.

Government employees, military personnel, civilian contractors, and others who require classified information may receive clearances. Only U.S. citizens are eligible for a security clearance. Foreign nationals may be granted a "Limited Access Authorization" (LAA) in "rare circumstances" when a non-U.S. citizen possesses a unique or unusual skill or expertise urgently needed for a specific requirement involving access to specified classified information for which a cleared or clearable U.S. citizen is not available.

Applicants for a clearance complete Standard Form 86 (Questionnaire for National Security Positions),[119] a 21-page document that calls for the disclosure of large amounts of personal information. SF 86 requires the applicant to authorize broadly the disclosure of information from third parties, including employers, schools, landlords, financial institutions, criminal justice agencies, healthcare providers, retail business establishments, and others.

The security clearance process operates subject to the Privacy Act of 1974,[120] a law that provides a reasonably full set of fair information practices. Standard Form 86 includes a Privacy Act notice, an explanation of the process, and a statement that false or inaccurate statements may be a criminal violation of law.

The cost and time to obtain a clearance are not simple numbers to report. A statutory standard calls for completion of at least 80 percent of initial clearances within an average of 120 days.[121] In 2008, the Government Accountability Office (GAO) found that the Office of Personnel Management and DOD made initial decisions on clearances within 87 days.[122] However, GAO also found that 39 percent took more than 120 days. The cost of the basic background investigation for a TOP SECRET clearance begins at $3888, and this does not include other required investigations and administrative costs. Depending on the specifics of any individual clearance, cost can exceed $10,000.[123] CONFIDENTIAL or SECRET clearance do not take as long (estimates of one to three months) and cost less (several hundred dollars to $3,000).

People with security clearances must be routinely reinvestigated at intervals depending on their level of clearance. For a TOP SECRET clearance, periodic reinvestigations should occur every five years.

---

[118]Congress has also intervened from time to time to establish some specific standards for denial of clearances. For a discussion of recent legislation, see Sheldon I. Cohen, *The Smith Amendment, 10 U.S.C. §986 Has Been Repealed and Replaced By 50 U.S.C. 435b § 3002* (2008), available at http://www.sheldoncohen.com/publications/Smith_Amendment2008.pdf; accessed March 16, 2010.

[119]http://www.opm.gov/forms/pdf_fill/sf86.pdf; accessed March 16, 2010.

[120]5 U.S.C. § 552a.

[121]50 U.S.C. § 435b(g). The statutory goal is to reduce the time to 60 days.

[122]*Personnel Security Clearances: Progress Has Been Made to Reduce Delays but Further Actions Are Needed to Enhance Quality and Sustain Reform Efforts* (GAO-09-684T) (2009), available at http://www.gao.gov/new.items/d09684t.pdf; accessed March 16, 2010.

[123]See Office of Personnel Management, *Investigations Reimbursable Billing Rates for FY 2009* (Notice 08-04) (2008), available at http://www.wrc.noaa.gov/wrso/forms/Investigations%20Reimbursable%20Billing%20Rates.pdf; accessed March 16, 2010. The quoted cost is for the Single-Scope Background Investigation.

B. Denial and Revocation

For investigations that do not produce results favorable to the applicant, the due process protections include two levels of review by higher-ranking adjudicative officials. The denial process also provides additional reviews at a higher level and approval of a letter of intent to deny or revoke. The subject of an unfavorable action must receive a written statement of the reasons for the action. The statement must be as comprehensive and detailed as permitted by national security and by the confidentiality provisions of the Privacy Act of 1974 that protect information from sources expressly promised confidentiality. The individual is entitled to request a copy of releasable records of the investigation. The individual has 30 days to reply in writing, and the individual is entitled to a prompt written response to any submission.

The individual also has an opportunity to appeal a letter of denial to the appropriate DOD Component Personnel Security Appeals Board. If requested, an administrative law judge of the Defense Department's Office of Hearings and Appeals holds a hearing. The individual is entitled to a written final decision. Judicial review of a security clearance denial appears precluded under current law, although some argue that there should be limited appeal rights. Judicial deference to the executive branch in national security matters explains the absence of a judicial appeal.

Once granted, an agency can suspend a security clearance if it has information raising serious questions as to the individual's ability or intent to protect classified information or to execute sensitive duties until a final determination. The individual is entitled to written notice and a brief statement of the reason. Resolution of the suspension must occur as expeditiously as circumstances permit

C. Discussion

A security clearance is typically a requirement for employment, so the interest of an applicant for or holder of a clearance is high. The administrative procedures that surround the approval and revocation of a clearance generally reflect both the importance of that interest to the individual and the interest of the government in protecting material that would "cause exceptionally grave damage" to national security if publicly available (the standard for information classified as TOP SECRET). The process for granting a clearance is complex and expensive, can be time consuming, includes significant procedural and other protections, and has established written standards. The system operates under general federal government privacy rules, although it can and does make use of exemptions that exist in those rules. While the granting or denial of a clearance requires considerably judgment ("an overall common sense determination based upon all available facts"), the layers of review and the rights to appeal are designed to address the possibility of bias or unfairness.

While it would be too strong to suggest that there is no concern at all about the due process protections of the security clearance process, it is probably fair to suggest that the existing procedures are not so unbalanced as to raise significant public concerns or to cause ongoing debates. Congress has intervened from time to time to adjust the standards, although that intervention has been controversial, potentially disruptive, and hard to change, all features typical for the political process. Congress has also expressed concern about and legislated to limit delays in the clearance system in the interest of efficiency. Delays in obtaining clearances for employees are costly to the government and to its contractors that hire employees with security clearances.

2. The Driver's License Model

A. Issuance and Identification

The issuance of licenses for drivers is a state function, and the rules and procedures vary across the states and territories. Different types of drivers' licenses (car, truck, motorcycle, taxi, etc.) exist, including permits for learners issued before driving proficiency has been demonstrated. The parts of the licensing process of greatest interest in a civil liberties and privacy context are the identification requirements and the rules for revoking a license. Rules about demonstrating ability to drive are not material here and are not discussed.

The driver's license has become a de factor identifier accepted for many purposes in the United States.[124] As a result, Departments of Motor Vehicles also issue an identification card comparable to a driver's license that identifies individuals but does not authorize driving. An ID card typically resembles a driver's license and has the same security and identification features as a license to drive. Some states also issue enhanced licenses and ID cards that combine a regular driver's license with the specifications of the new US passport card, a wallet-size travel document that can be used to re-enter the United States from Canada, Mexico, the Caribbean, and Bermuda.[125] Driver's licenses may include other information (e.g., organ donor status).

The most important current federal law on the issuance of licenses is the REAL ID Act of 2005.[126] This controversial law establishes federal standards for security, authentication, and issuance of state driver's licenses. While the federal standards are not exactly mandatory, a state license must meet those standards for the federal government to accept the license for official purposes, such as using a driver's license for boarding commercially operated airline flights and for entering federal buildings and nuclear power plants.

The current status of REAL ID is somewhat uncertain, and Congress is considering amendments that would make some significant changes.[127] Nevertheless, the law provides an example of a stricter set of policies for identifying and authenticating recipients. Unlike a security clearance that requires regular renewal following a reinvestigation, a driver's license can usually be retained and renewed without further review of the holder.[128]

REAL ID requirements include:

Document Standards: A license must include: (1) individual's full legal name, (2) date of birth, (3) gender, (4) DL/ID number, (5) digital photograph, (6) address of legal residence, (7) signature, (8) physical security features designed to prevent tampering, counterfeiting or duplication for fraudulent purposes, and (9) a common machine-readable technology. Radio frequency identification (RFID) is not required [for] a card meeting REAL ID standards. Compliance with a bar code standard is required.

Minimum Issuance Standards: (1) A photo identity document; (2) documentation showing date of birth; (3) proof of a SSN or verification that the individual is not eligible for an SSN; and (4) documentation showing name and address of principal residence.

Foreign Documents: A state may not accept any foreign document other than an official passport.

Verification of Documents: A state must (1) verify, with the issuing agency, the issuance, validity and completeness of each document presented; (2) confirm a full SSN with the Social Security Administration; and (3) establish an effective procedure to confirm or verify a renewing applicant's information.

---

[124]Interestingly, federal law at one time required states to put Social Security Numbers on the license. Now it prohibits displaying an SSN on a license.

[125]Department of State, 7 Foreign Affairs Manual 1300, Appendix P (The Passport Card), available at http://www.state.gov/documents/organization/122897.pdf; accessed March 15, 2010.

[126]49 U.S.C. § 30301 note. For a summary of the law from the non-partisan National Conference of State Legislatures, see http://www.ncsl.org/IssuesResearch/Transportation/RealIDActof2005Summary/tabid/13579/Default.aspx; accessed March 15, 2010.

The Driver's Privacy Protection Act (DPPA), 18 U.S.C. § 2721-2725, is a federal law that regulates the disclosure of personal information by state motor vehicle departments. The law allows non-consensual disclosures for specified purposes, including for governmental, judicial, law enforcement, and motor vehicle activities. Disclosure for a marketing use requires affirmative consent. The law largely ended the availability of information about drivers and vehicles for marketing purposes. Some motor vehicle licensing and registration information still ends up in the hands of commercial database companies because they manage automobile recall activities. The information disclosed for authorized purposes is not supposed to be used otherwise. The DPPA pre-dates and bears no express relationship to the REAL ID Act, but the two laws are not incompatible.

[127]See, e.g., PASS ID Act, S.1261, 111th Congress (2009).

[128]Some states require older drivers to demonstrate a continued ability to drive.

Immigration Requirements: A state can only issue a REAL ID license to citizens, lawfully admitted residents, and selected other immigrants and only with verified and valid documentary evidence of status.

Security and Fraud Prevention Standards: A state must (1) ensure security for document materials and locations where they are produced; (2) have security clearance requirements for producers of IDs; and (3) establish fraudulent document recognition training programs for employees engaged in the issuance of licenses.

Data Retention and Storage: A state must (1) capture digital images of identity source documents for storage and transfer; (2) retain paper copies of source documents for at least seven years or images at least ten years; and (3) maintain a state motor vehicle database that contains all data fields printed on a license, and drivers' histories, including violations, suspensions, and points.

Linking of Databases: A state must provide all other states with electronic access to information contained in the motor vehicle database of the state.

Many aspects of REAL ID have drawn objections, including but not limited to the cost of compliance by states and individuals and the unfunded mandate. A study conducted by the National Conference of State Legislatures, National Governors Association, and the American Association of Motor Vehicle Administrators estimated that state costs could be more than $11 billion over five years. The Department of Homeland Security estimate is $3.9 billion.[129] Many states have taken some formal action to object to—or even to prohibit compliance with—REAL ID.[130] State objections are not solely based on cost.

There are also strong objections to REAL ID among public interest and advocacy organizations all along the political spectrum. Some contend that REAL ID will become a national identity system or internal passport used to track and control individuals' movements and activities. Another objection is that it will not be effective against terrorism because ID documents do not reveal anything about evil intent and because fraudulent documents will be available. Bureaucratic concerns are the center of other objections because of the difficulty of verifying documents (e.g., foreign birth certificates and the like), long times for the issuance process, and higher fees.

Other objections to REAL ID center on the creation of a single interlinked database and on the storage of copies of every birth certificate and other documents as a new resource for identity thieves. Some fear exploitation of a machine-readable card by private sector actors scanning a magnetic strip on a driver's license for credit card or age verification purposes and then collecting additional data for marketing or other purposes. Another concern is that the REAL ID database will grow over time and acquire additional identity-based missions. Objections also focus on the effects on immigrants and possible discrimination against foreigners or those who look foreign.[131] The Act's failure to accommodate those who have a religious objection to having their photographs taken is a point of controversy.[132] Constitutional objections include First and Tenth Amendment arguments, as well as arguments about limitations on the right to travel.

---

[129]For a summary of various REAL ID cost estimates, see National Conference of State Legislatures, *REAL ID Cost Estimates*, available at http://www.ncsl.org/Default.aspx?TabId=13578; accessed March 15, 2010.

[130]For a summary of anti-REAL ID activities in the states, including some states that enacted laws prohibiting implementation, see http://www.realnightmare.org/news/105/, accessed August 30, 2010.

[131]For a website of REAL ID opponents, see http://www.realnightmare.org/; accessed March 15, 2010. For a Department of Homeland Security website on REAL ID, see http://www.dhs.gov/files/laws/gc_1172765386179.shtm; accessed March 15, 2010. The rule establishing minimum standards is at http://edocket.access.gpo.gov/2008/08-140.htm; accessed March 15, 2010.

[132]Religious objections can arise with any form of required identification. See Cynthia Brougher, *Legal Analysis of Religious Exemptions for Photo Identification Requirements* (2009) (Congressional Research Service), available at http://www.fas.org/sgp/crs/misc/R40515.pdf; accessed March 15, 2010. See also Council on American-Islamic Relations Research Center, *Religious Accommodation in Driver's License Photographs: A review of codes, policies and practices in the 50 states* (2005), available at http://moritzlaw.osu.edu/electionlaw/litigation/documents/LWVJ.pdf; accessed March 15, 2010. The Religious Freedom Restoration Act, 42 U.S.C. § 2000bb et seq., which statutorily mandates a standard of protection of heightened scrutiny for government actions interfering with a person's free exercise of religion, may have bearing on any resolution of these issues.

Some DHS actions to address privacy and other concerns include: (1) a phased enrollment that allows states to put off compliance on those born before December 1, 1964 an additional three years; (2) technical measures for verifying documents from issuing agencies in other states through a hub-based network and messaging system with end-to-end data encryption; (3) requiring states to collect a minimum of information; (4) and issuing a set of privacy and security best practices that are built on the Fair Information Principles and Federal Information Security Management Act[133] (FISMA) standards to help guide the states in protecting the information collected, stored, and maintained pursuant to the REAL ID; and (5) no preemption of state law that may provide additional protections.

Not every aspect of REAL ID has drawn complaints. There is more support for the standardization of drivers' licenses among the states and for better security in the issuance process. Because a driver's license is a breeder document (i.e., an identification document that can be readily used to obtain other documentation that confers status or privileges), greater control over issuance draws broader support.

B. Revocation

The revocation of a driver's license can arise under a variety of circumstances. In most cases, notice, a right to a hearing, and other elements of procedural due process are routinely available and do not usually raise major fairness concerns. The proceedings address the conflicting interests, and decisions come through a process designed to be fair and balanced.

The cases that raise the sharpest due process issues are those involving administrative license suspension (ALS) laws. ALS involves the automatic suspension of a license when a driver refuses to submit to chemical testing for alcohol or when a driver submits to testing and the results indicate a high level of blood alcohol content. The consequences come immediately and without formal proof of guilt. Case law on the constitutionality of ALS is clear.

It is worth noting as a preliminary matter that the traditional distinction between a right and a privilege does not appear particularly helpful here. Whether a license is viewed as a right protected by constitutional guarantees or a privilege granted by the state that can be revoked, it is not permissible for the state to impose unconstitutional conditions or to act in most instances without appropriate due process. A license holder typically has a clear property interest in the license, and that interest must be respected.

In a leading case on this specific subject, the Supreme Court held that the "suspension of a driver's license for statutorily defined cause implicates a protectable property interest; accordingly, the only question presented by this appeal is what process is due to protect against an erroneous deprivation of that interest."[134] The Court identified three relevant factors:

> First, the private interest that will be affected by the official action; second, the risk of an erroneous deprivation of such interest through the procedures used, and the probable value, if any, of additional or substitute procedural safeguards; and finally, the Government's interest, including the function involved and the fiscal and administrative burdens that the additional or substitute procedural requirement would entail.[135]

While the driver's interest in the license is substantial, ALS provides for a limited period of suspension with an opportunity for a hearing in a reasonable period. The state's substantial interest in keeping drunk drivers off the roads is an important factor in upholding the immediate suspension. The Court observed that it "traditionally accorded the states great leeway in adopting summary procedures to protect public health and safety."[136] Presumably, the Court was well aware of heightened public concern in recent decades about the dangers of drunk driving.

---

[133]44 U.S.C. § 3541 et seq.

[134]*Mackey v. Montrym*, 443 U.S. 1 (1979) (footnote omitted).

[135]Id. at 10.

[136]Id. at 17.

C. Discussion

The system for licensing drivers has some significant differences from the system for granting security clearances. The driver's license process is decentralized among the states, whereas only the federal government grants clearances (albeit different agencies have their own policies and procedures). While drivers must demonstrate skills, knowledge, and physical abilities, no substantive standard requires judgments about an individual's intentions or loyalty. Drivers of the proper age and skill expect to obtain and keep a driver's license for most of their lives without further questioning. However, security clearances must be renewed regularly after an updated investigation, although a clearance is not normally revoked if a required reinvestigation has not occurred.

The driver's license system operated successfully under privacy regimes that varied considerably from state to state until the federal Driver's Privacy Protection Act (DPPA) established a national floor of privacy protection.[137] While controversial in some respects, the DPPA did not undermine the fairness of the licensing system from a driver's perspective.

Revocations are not that dissimilar for clearances and for licenses. Using recognized grounds, both can be revoked or suspended immediately with due process rights for affected individuals that can be pursued after-the-fact rather than before.

It remains unclear at this time how, when, and whether REAL ID will be fully implemented. Therefore, it is impossible to predict how the existing process will change. However, if nothing else, the history of REAL ID demonstrates that identification systems can generate considerable public controversy in the United States. An identification system that affects more people and that has more consequences for them will be the subject of political debate and likely litigation. Millions of people have security clearances, but hundreds of millions of people are likely to need REAL ID identification.

3. The Air Travel Clearance Model

A. Clearance

Following the events of September 11, 2001, and subsequent air travel incidents, the systems for clearing passengers for air travel have changed and evolved. An early program called *Computer Assisted Passenger Prescreening System* (CAPPS II) has been replaced by *Secure Flight* administered by the Transportation Safety Administration (TSA) of the Department of Homeland Security (DHS).[138] Secure Flight offers a different model for clearing individuals for a particular activity, one that is based on weeding out those who have been determined through an independent (and largely secret) process not to be allowed to fly.

Secure Flight makes individualized decisions of who may fly on commercial flights. A major part of Secure Flight is matching names of passengers with the *No Fly* list of individuals not allowed to fly and with the *Selectee* list of individuals who must undergo additional security screening before boarding an aircraft. These two lists are maintained by the Terrorist Screening Center (part of the Federal Bureau of Investigation) and are subsets of the Terrorist Screening Center Database compiled using information from law enforcement and intelligence agencies. At times, TSA may consult lists other than the *No Fly* and *Selectee* lists for clearing passengers, and the process can include random searches and real-time decision making based on interactions between would-be travelers, airline staff, TSA, and intelligence and law enforcement agencies.

The clearance process mostly takes place behind-the-scenes by TSA and the airlines. The process compares information in airline reservation systems, including but not limited to the information pro-

---

[137]18 U.S.C. §§ 2721-2725.

[138]The Secure Flight program is authorized under 49 U.S.C. § 44903. TSA's 2008 Privacy Impact Assessment for the Secure Flight Program is available at http://www.dhs.gov/xlibrary/assets/privacy/privacy_pia_secureflight2008.pdf; accessed March 15, 2010.

vided by a passenger when making an airline reservation, with information on the watch lists. In order to do better matches of records, TSA and the airlines started requiring passengers to provide full name, data of birth, and gender at the time of a reservation. These additional elements are supposed to help prevent misidentification of passengers with similar names. Other information that TSA receives from the airline includes itinerary, passport number (for an international flight or if otherwise available to the airline), and reservation control number. TSA can obtain a full Passenger Name Record (PNR), which reveals other information including food, health, and other preferences.

TSA retains records for individuals not identified as potential matches by the automated matching tool for seven days after completion of travel. TSA keeps records of an individual who is potential or confirmed match for no less than seven years. TSA keeps records of an individual who is a confirmed match for 99 years. Data retained by airlines is not subject to these limits, and TSA may obtain the data from the airlines.

A *registered traveler* program allowed passengers who paid a fee and submitted to a background check to use reserved security lanes with shorter waits at airport checkpoints. The program was voluntary and run by the private sector. An applicant provided additional information, including a biometric, and received a smart card credential. When the company that provided the bulk of the service went out of business, the registered traveler program disappeared. Some criticized the program as providing special treatment for wealthy travelers.

B. Redress

TSA has a program offering redress to travelers who experience denied or delayed airline boarding, who experience denied or delayed entry into and exit from the U.S., or who are continuously referred for additional (secondary) screening. The *Travel Redress Inquiry Program* (DHS TRIP) basically allows an individual to ask for a review in order to minimize or eliminate future watch list name confusion. TSA will not reveal whether an individual is on a watch list, however. An individual seeking redress fills out a form and may be asked to provide additional documentation. A successful traveler will receive a Redress Control Number that airlines collect and that may help to minimize identification or screening problems. An individual who is dissatisfied with the DHS TRIP process may file an appeal with DHS. Effective judicial review of DHS actions may not be available.

The Secure Flight program collects and maintains information on international travelers from airlines, travel agencies, and tour operators in other countries. This brings aspects of the program under the purview of foreign data protection laws. For example, in 2007, the European Union and DHS entered into an agreement about the processing and transfer to DHS of Passenger Name Records (PNR) by airlines operating in Europe.[139] The agreement reflects a determination by the European Commission that U.S. laws, in conjunction with DHS policies regarding the protection of personal data and the U.S.-EU Passenger Name Record Agreement, are adequate to permit transfers of PNR data to the U.S government and that the transfers comply with EU standards under the Data Protection Directive. The agreement is now subject to ratification by the European Parliament,[140] where some members have been critical of the terms of the data transfers.

C. Discussion

The Secure Flight process differs significantly from the process for granting security clearances and drivers' licenses. While Secure Flight is not quite a real-time clearance, it can be close to that. Normally,

---

[139]http://www.dhs.gov/xlibrary/assets/pnr-2007agreement-usversion.pdf; accessed March 15, 2010.

[140]See European Parliament, Legislative Observatory, available at http://www.europarl.europa.eu/oeil/file.jsp?id=5836052; accessed March 15, 2010. On May 5, 2010, the European Parliament showed its displeasure with the agreement by postponed voting on its approval. http://www.europarl.europa.eu/news/expert/infopress_page/019-74146-125-05-19-902-20100505IPR74145-05-05-2010-2010-false/default_en.htm; accessed May 21, 2010.

there is no review of identity documents other than a limited check at an airport security checkpoint or the presentation of passports for international travel. The program mostly matches individuals against lists of people not allowed to fly or who require additional screening. These lists are compiled by TSA and other agencies separately and based on criteria that are not publicly known. TSA will not directly inform an individual if he or she is on one of the lists, although inferences are possible from the way that the individual is treated at the airport. Clearance operations are not conducted in public view, and travelers do not know the details of the review process. Secure Flight clears as many as several million people daily and hundreds of millions of people annually, many more people than seek security clearances or drivers' licenses.

The Secure Flight redress process came as a legislative direction that followed regular news reports of continuing problems with the clearance process. Congress intervened several times during the development and implementation of airport passenger clearance systems to express concern about privacy and about redress. Secure Flight also raises directly issues of international privacy standards that are absent from drivers' licenses and security clearances. It is possible that the international consequences of any standards for cybersecurity activities would require negotiations with other countries similar to the negotiations with the EU about Secure Flight. Finally, Secure Flight has been controversial, with interest groups raising privacy and constitutional objections to the data collection, screening, and secrecy.

4. Other Methods, Other Models

Broader use of identification for general purposes or for cybersecurity purposes will raise harder political, legal, and constitutional issues. The precise terms of any identification use, issuance procedures, due process rules, and information processing policies will shape the arguments about constitutionality and effects on civil liberties and privacy. It is not possible here, to make all the arguments or resolve any of them. However, it is apparent that an identification system has the potential to impinge on anonymity, inhibit speech and association, affect the right to travel, affect other fundamental constitutional or statutory rights, and perhaps exceed the authority of the federal government in other ways (Tenth Amendment). Whether the courts would recognize any of these concerns at the constitutional level is impossible to predict, but it seems certain that these issues will arise.

In 2008, the Supreme Court upheld a state law requiring citizens voting in person to present government-issued photo identification.[141] It may or may not be telling that the identification requirement did not extend to those who did not vote in person. However, the Help America Vote Act of 2002 requires first time registrants voting by mail to include a copy of identification with the ballot.[142] The Court did not require strict scrutiny of the voter ID law, but judicial consideration of a requirement that affects broad First Amendment speech issues is less likely to use the same, weaker standard of judicial review. Regardless, it is difficult to use this decision to assess possible Internet identification requirements because the facts and the particulars could make a major difference. Still, the Court upheld the identification requirement here and reached a similar outcome in the *Hiibel* case discussed above. Clearly, the Court is not strongly averse to identification requirements.

The federal government is already exploring and implementing identity, credentialing, and access management systems to provide a consistent approach for clearing and managing individuals requiring access to federal information systems and facilities.[143] Identification and authorization systems can be unremarkable from a privacy and civil liberties perspective, but they can also raise a host of questions depending on the standards used, due process procedures, scope of application, and data collected and retained. These same issues can arise with any type of identification or licensing system.[144]

---

[141] Crawford v. Marion County Election Bd., 553 U.S. ___, 128 S. Ct. 1610 (2008).

[142] 42 U.S.C. § 15483(b)(3).

[143] See http://www.idmanagement.gov/drilldown.cfm?action=icam; accessed April 15, 2010.

[144] See generally Committee on Authentication Technologies and Their Privacy Implications, National Research Council, *Who Goes There? Authentication Through the Lens of Privacy* (2003).

In particular, an Internet identification or authentication system can be a surveillance mechanism if the system routinely creates a central record of all Internet activities of each user as a result of the clearance process. An Internet identification or authentication system would raise privacy and security concerns that could easily exceed in range and detail the information about the exercise of First Amendment rights collected in a driver's licensing system, by Secure Flight, or even through the security clearance process. A system that fails to properly assess the degree of risk involved or that makes unwarranted demands on users may exacerbate civil liberties and privacy concerns.[145] If the federal government relied on credentials issued by private entities, those concerns could extend beyond government functions and spill over into the rules and procedures of those private entities.

The federal government's use of systems to control access to *government* computers is not the most troublesome part of credentialing or licensing. A broader government requirement for a license for general use of the Internet beyond access to government facilities would be of greater concern. If licensing were the only way to overcome security problems that made the Internet significantly dysfunctional, the argument for licensing might be stronger than if the purpose of the licensing were to require complete identification and accountability for all Internet activities so that criminals could be identified more readily after the fact. The circumstances that result in licensing of users would make a significant difference to the analysis.

The narrower the purpose and application of an ID system/technology, the less likely it will be to raise these concerns. Despite their widespread de facto use as general-purpose identifiers, drivers' licenses were not as controversial until the REAL ID Act sought to alter the process of issuance, mandated collection and maintenance of more personal information, and established requirements and potential for its use that extended beyond established norms. The 1994 Driver's Privacy Protection Act addressed some of the privacy concerns that surrounded the marketing and other secondary uses of drivers' information.

The widespread use of Social Security numbers (SSNs) for identification has, after many years, brought legislative responses at the federal and state level restricting the collection, use, or display of SSNs in some contexts.[146] Many but not all of these responses followed the explosion of identity theft and of complaints from individuals about the consequences of identity theft.

For many individuals, an identification requirement or other prerequisite for using the Internet (as opposed to a prerequisite for using a particular website) would almost certainly be viewed today as similar in importance to a driver's license, if not more important. Access to the Internet, whether or not a fundamental human right, is now for most people in the United States necessary for employment, communication, routine commercial activities, and many other essential, routine, and daily activities.

None of the licensing models described in this section affects an activity as close to the heart of First Amendment values as an Internet licensing scheme would. A governmentally established identification/authorization prerequisite to general Internet access would be, to say the least, controversial. The level of controversy would vary with the scope of the requirement and the amount of information about Internet access and usage that was retained.

However, a governmentally established prerequisite to access a non-public government network would not be controversial or even novel. The federal government operates classified systems with access limited to individuals who have security clearances. A private requirement for access to a private network or website is largely unremarkable as well. It is not that civil liberties and privacy concerns are entirely absent, but that the basic notion of controlling access to some information and facilities is familiar.

---

[145]The Office of Management and Budget calls for a risk assessment for authentication and a matching of risks to an appropriate assurance level. OMB Memorandum to the Heads of all Departments and Agencies, *E-Authentication Guidance for Federal Agencies* (Dec. 16, 2003), http://www.whitehouse.gov/omb/memoranda/fy04/m04-04.pdf; accessed April 15, 2010.

[146]Section 7 of the Privacy Act of 1974, Public Law 93-579, 88 Stat. 1909 (1974), 5 U.S.C. § 552a note, restricts collection of SSNs by federal, state, and local government agencies. This was one of the first legislated restrictions on SSN use. Many more followed in the 1990s and later.

When an identification/authorization requirement is narrow in application, limited in scope, and simple to meet (e.g., user name and password), controversy is less likely to arise. Indeed, simple, limited purpose identification and authorization systems are in widespread use today with few objections. To the extent that private activities (whether voluntary or required by law) collect and maintain additional records about Internet usage by individuals, those records can become available to the government without notice to or participation by the subject of the records. The availability to the government of a list of every website visited by every Internet user would be controversial, to say the least.[147] The earlier discussion about *U.S. v. Miller* and the lack of privacy protections for records held by third party record keepers is relevant here.

If we split the issue of authorization from identification, we face different choices and analyses. Identification might be required for some functions, but there might be a range of allowable activities that call for demonstrating other attributes (e.g., age) rather than identification.[148] An individual might only receive authorization to undertake some activities (e.g., change computer settings or use a private network) after showing competence in security matters.

Drawing lines, however, is not that simple. Even if restricting access to private networks—whether operated by the government or others—is not on its face problematic, much will depend on what activities occur on the private network. We already have private systems with varying identification and authentication prerequisites. Some may raise civil liberties or privacy concerns, but private sector activities will fall outside most constitutional and statutory protections. However, if a citizen must have some form of identification or authorization in order to communicate or conduct ordinary, non-national security business with a government agency, the argument about the propriety of the identification requirement would turn in part on the nature of the communication or the business at issue. The requirement would raise, for example, concerns about impinging on the right to petition the government for a redress of grievances, the right to associate with others, or perhaps the right to practice a religion, all rights protected by the First Amendment.

An Internet identification/authentication requirement could make it impossible or unduly difficult for a citizen without identification to fulfill legal duties (e.g., file tax returns), obtain benefits available by law, or exercise rights. The REAL ID Act is controversial, in part, for this reason. That Act could make it difficult or impossible for a citizen to enter a federal building without an identification document that qualifies under the Act. The analysis would be different if the user of a particular government activity had no alternative to using an identification-restricted Internet than if use of a restricted Internet were one of several options. For example, if meeting particular Internet identification requirements in order to vote or receive Social Security benefits were the only option, the conclusion might be different than if in-person or postal mail alternatives also existed at the same time.

Even an Internet identification/authentication requirement for a private network operated principally for private purposes, it still could raise concerns about how citizens can carry out basic tasks essential to function in society, many of which remain entangled with government activities or regulations. For example, for many people the health care sector is an amalgam of private and government players and actions. A private requirement for an Internet ID that effectively served as a prerequisite to interfacing with the governmental part of the health care system could raise more intensive civil liberties

---

[147]The issuance of a driver's license or an automobile license plate has not in the past resulted in the reporting or collection of information about where an individual or automobile goes. However, with the use of electronic toll collection devices, congestion pricing for highways, and other automated automobile information collection systems, the compilation of additional records about driving habits may become both more commonplace and more controversial. One difference between driving and Internet usage is that driving typically takes place in a public space and much Internet usage does not. The extent of privacy rights in public spaces appears to be undergoing some rethinking at present. *United States v. Maynard*, decided in August 2010 by the D.C. Circuit, is one of several recent cases where the issue of the applicability of the Fourth Amendment to tracking an automobile in public by use of a GPS device arose. http://pacer.cadc.uscourts.gov/docs/common/opinions/201008/08-3030-1259298.pdf.

[148]Identification or authentication requirements could offer additional privacy protections (by limiting identity theft) or assist with other objectives (keeping children away from websites aimed at adults). Whatever other benefits might arise, they do not necessarily relate to the cybersecurity matters under discussion here.

concerns. Additionally, if a government Internet ID were adopted by the private sector and became a practical prerequisite to using the Internet even for private activities, the government process might be questioned for its practical effect on citizens, for any discriminatory effect that the process might have in design or in practice, for its privacy consequences, and otherwise.

Depending on the purpose of identification in the narrower context of preventing cyberattacks, it remains open to debate whether a greater use of identification would be successful in either deterring bad actors or finding them after the fact. The prevalence of identity theft suggests that those interested in using the credentials of others for cyberattack purposes might have little difficulty doing so by stealing the elements needed to impersonate another. Further evidence on this point is the ability of malfeasors to establish and control remotely other computers connected to the Internet. A significant percentage of computers connected to the Internet may be part of a botnet. Botnets could be another channel for cyberattacks unaffected by identification requirements for users because the computers on the network have credentials.

In addition to identifying individuals using the Internet, it is also possible that the government could require Internet users to demonstrate proficiency in some important Internet skills pertaining to security or otherwise. Automobile drivers must pass both written tests and road tests that demonstrate knowledge of laws and rules and the ability to drive. Arguably, the same types of prerequisites could apply to some or all Internet usage. The cost and difficulty of managing a proficiency requirement and keeping it up-to-date aside, any proposal would likely be challenged as a limit on the exercise of First Amendment rights. It would likely be seen as the equivalent of requiring a government license to read a newspaper, use a telephone, or mail a postal letter. It might well prove difficult or impossible to show that a proficiency requirement is compatible with the First Amendment. An employer, including the government, may impose training requirements on its workers, but a general-purpose rule applicable to the population at large would be more challenging to justify.[149]

In all of these cases, whether or not an Internet prerequisite violated a constitutional standard, it is nevertheless the case that civil liberties, due process, and privacy would be affected by the rules and procedures that attach to the prerequisite, by the process for issuing the identification, by the amount of personal information collected and maintained, and by the secondary uses for the information. Even with privately issued identification, some or all of these issues would arise, whether or not a public or private network relied on the identification. Laws prohibiting discrimination would presumably apply to private sector identification schemes, for example. The discussion of security clearances, driver's licenses, and flight clearance shows is that we have found ways to balance the rights and interests involved in licensing schemes. That does not mean, however, that acceptable balances will always be found for the next licensing idea.

Licensing computer technicians, programmers, cybersecurity specialists, or other professionals whose activities directly affect cybersecurity on the Internet is another possibility. We have considerable experience in licensing professionals through state or private sector actions, with due process and privacy concerns similar to the licensing activities discussed above. Licensing of Internet professionals would be less controversial than licensing Internet users. Licensing requirements for computer programs is another possibility, and one that would raise more civil liberties concerns because computer programs are intertwined with speech and are protected by the First Amendment. Whether any of these types of licenses would have any significant effect on preventing unlicensed actors or malware from affecting use of the Internet is far from clear, however. For some users, computer maintenance is accomplished by grandchildren and not by professionals. A system that effectively controls computer programs is difficult to envision. As with any licensing system, a criminal who engages in an illegal activity is not likely to care that his or her actions also violate the obligation to obtain a license.

---

[149]The HIPAA health privacy rule contains a requirement that covered entities train health care workers in privacy. 45 C.F.R. § 164.530(b). This seems unremarkable. However, a training requirement for *patients* would be another matter and considerably more difficult to carry out or justify.

We have not exhausted the identification requirements that might arguably be relevant to preventing cyberattacks. Instead of, or in addition to, licensing individuals to use the Internet, it is possible for government to require identification or licensing of machines that access the Internet. Individual computers or other devices could be required to have and to disclose as a condition of access to the Internet a unique identifier that might be required to be registered in advance or subject to association with particular individuals after the fact. An alternative approach might require that computers accessing the Internet contain specific hardware or software with particular functionality (e.g., virus checking software). Another approach could require regular inspection of Internet devices to determine if they meet specific requirements and are up-to-date.

All of these techniques are used today for automobiles. Each automobile has a Vehicle Identification Number (VIN), a unique serial number used by the automotive industry to identify individual motor vehicles. Automobiles must display unique license plates issued by governments. Most states mandate some form of safety inspection, including an inspection for emissions in some areas.[150] Federal rules require auto manufacturers to install safety equipment, such as airbags. States require proof of insurance before allowing an automobile to be registered.

The federal government likely has the power under the Commerce Clause to regulate computers in similar ways, at least up to the point where the regulations clash with First Amendment interests. Requiring serial numbers for some or most Internet access devices may be possible. For technical reasons, cell phones are identified to the cellular network in order to function so identification seems less of an issue. Internet devices typically use Internet Protocol addresses, which offer a type of identification that may or may not be constant for each device over time. A fixed IP address could serve as an identifier.[151] Registration or identification requirements for other devices would be controversial, of course. In the last 1990s, Intel proposed to produce computer chips with a unique Processor Serial Number (PSN). Objections from the privacy community ("Big Brother Inside") pressured the company into abandoning its plans, and the PSN was dropped.[152] Google released its Chrome browser with a unique identifier with criticism from some privacy advocates, but reports suggest that Google plans to abandon the identifier.[153]

Computers that access the Internet now include many types of devices—including televisions and refrigerators—and requiring some types of inspection seems impractical. The so-called Internet of things (connection of routine objects and devices to the Internet) could result in a vast expansion of items connected to the Internet, including every household item connected to the electrical grid, articles of clothing, body parts, and much else.[154] As a practical matter, it may be unworkable to design and implement a system that mandates and enforces an identification requirement for every Internet device.

One can envision, possibly, a remote inspection of all Internet access devices for security purposes. The government might be able to mandate remote inspection using powers available under the Commerce Clause. A possible precedent is the Communications Assistance for Law Enforcement Act (CALEA), a 1994 law intended to "to make clear a telecommunications carrier's duty to cooperate in the interception of communications for law enforcement purposes, and for other purposes."[155] The law requires telecommunications carriers and manufacturers of telecommunications transmission and switching equipment to ensure that equipment, facilities, and services allow the government to isolate and intercept all wire and electronic communications. Essentially, CALEA forces telecommunications

---

[150]See generally 42 U.S.C. § 7401 et seq.

[151]It is a contested issue today whether an IP address is a personal identifier. The value of an IP address as a personal identifier is cloudy when there are multiple users for a single computer.

[152]See http://bigbrotherinside.org/; accessed March 17, 2010.

[153]Ryan Whitwam, *Google to Drop Unique IDs from their Chrome Browser*, MaximumPC, available at http://www.maximumpc.com/article/news/google_drop_unique_ids_their_chrome_browser; accessed March 17, 2010.

[154]See, e.g., Commission of the European Communities, *Internet of Things—An Action Plan for Europe* (June 18, 2009) (COM(2009) 278 final), http://ec.europa.eu/information_society/policy/rfid/documents/commiot2009.pdf; accessed April 15, 2010.

[155]47 U.S.C. §§ 1001-1010.

carriers to design their networks so as not to impede authorized law enforcement surveillance requests. CALEA does not directly affect consumer devices, but Congress might require consumer devices include the capability of allowing for government access via remote inspection under specified circumstances. Again, the practicalities of implementing and enforcing a remote inspection scheme for all Internet devices seem overwhelming, and the constitutional issues are most difficult.

Enforcement of some or all of these requirements would be additionally challenging because many of these devices enter the country or access the Internet from abroad every day. The government has broad authority to conduct suspicionless border searches of laptops and other electronic storage devices, although it would be hard to do a search of every person and every device.[156] Further, devices in other countries that access networks in the United States present additional compliance and enforcement issues. A uniform international scheme for controlling Internet devices seems a remote possibility at best. The global nature of the Internet and the presence of multiple and potentially overlapping regulatory regimes raise other vexing questions. These include the extent to which any national government could impose or seek to impose requirements on Internet users in other countries or users crossing borders, whether their own citizens or others, that would affect privacy or civil liberties.

It would certainly be argued that any type of regulation that affects the means of speech on the Internet would be akin to regulating speech directly or to licensing printing presses. The regulation would be strongly challenged on First Amendment grounds. The level of judicial scrutiny of an Internet access regulatory scheme would be an important and debatable point. If the government's actions were strictly content neutral, proponents would argue for intermediate scrutiny under which the actions would only have to serve an important or substantial governmental interest unrelated to the suppression of speech and could not burden speech more than is necessary to satisfy that interest. For example, a mandate that personal computers use parts that are readily recyclable would be more likely to be seen as a content neutral regulation.

Yet it is much more likely that a requirement that every computer include a permanent and unerasable keystroke logger would draw very strong objections on First Amendment grounds, with demands for review under the strictest scrutiny standard that would require the government to demonstrate that the regulation furthered an overriding state interest and was drawn with narrow specificity to avoid any unnecessary intrusion on First Amendment rights. A potentially intermediate example might be a requirement that every computer have virus protection software installed and kept up-to-date. Other possible intermediate examples are a requirement that all ISPs examine Internet messages for malware or a mandate that all browsers include specific features.

Regardless of the standard that would apply for constitutional assessment of these requirements, it seem certain that there would be considerable political controversy about any increased role for the federal government in defining prerequisites for access to or use of the Internet. There would likely be strong objections to even the most mild-mannered mandate because it would open the door to stronger and more invasive legislative mandates in the future.

In the absence of a specific identification, licensing, or authentication system, the discussion is quite abstract and unsatisfying. Controls that may have some appeal at a high level of abstraction can face overwhelming practical implementation problems and significant costs in additional to the legal, constitutional, and political objections. The REAL ID law, which is much less sweeping in scope than an Internet licensing scheme would be, started with enough political support to become law, but rapidly became the target of practical, cost, and civil liberties objections. Years after passage, REAL ID languishes with few steps toward implementation actually accomplished.

---

[156]In 2009, the Department of Homeland Security issued directives on border searches of electronic media. U.S. Customs and Border Protection, *Border Search of Electronic Devices Containing Information* (CBP Directive No. 3340-049, (Aug. 20, 2009), available at http://www.dhs.gov/xlibrary/assets/cbp_directive_3340-049.pdf; accessed March 18, 2010; U.S. Immigration and Customs Enforcement, *Border Search of Electronic Devices* (Directive No. 7-6.1) (Aug. 18, 2009), available at http://www.dhs.gov/xlibrary/assets/ice_border_search_electronic_devices.pdf; accessed March 18, 2009. The Department's Privacy Impact Assessment for these policies is available at http://www.dhs.gov/xlibrary/assets/privacy/privacy_pia_cbp_laptop.pdf; accessed March 18, 2009.

It is easy to suggest that licensing of users or similar schemes will have benefits, but it another thing to develop a system that will actually work to meet its objectives in the worldwide Internet with untold number of devices connected to it, hundreds of millions of users connecting and disconnecting every day, and rapid technological changes. A licensing system that controlled 99% of users and devices would still leave plenty of opportunities for evasion by those who are motivated, assisted by insiders within the licensing administration, supported by hostile foreign governments, or others.[157] Identity thieves already operate a robust, underground market where stolen information and illegal services are sold and advertised.[158] An expansion of these activities to include information about Internet identities and licensees can be anticipated.

The goals of any licensing system could matter a great deal. We regulate drivers not with the expectation of removing every improper driver or car from the road. The overall regulatory system results in improvements and not perfection. Despite laws, we still have unregistered cars, unlicensed drivers, stolen license plates, and uninsured motorists on the road every day. A system to prevent cyberattacks could have narrower goals of improving privacy and security on the Internet without necessarily expected to avoid everyone who is highly motivated or well-financed. However, to the extent that a licensing system affects the exercise of First Amendment values, narrower goals may make it harder to justify sweeping restrictions.

On the other hand, proponents of regulating Internet devices would argue that licensing and credentialing have the potential to provide *better* privacy and other protections to individuals. Problems for users that result from spam, malware, identity theft, and the like might diminish with the adoption of broad licensing and credentialing systems. Thus, societal costs from computer viruses might decrease if all computers had adequate anti-virus protection. Still, the benefits of licensing Internet users or activities still might not be enough to overcome the constitutional limitations on governmental powers. The issues involved here are obviously multidimensional and cannot be fairly assessed using a single scale.

Regardless of the applicable standard, however, Internet device regulation that restricts or limits speech in any way might well fail to be upheld because of First Amendment concerns. One hypothetical analysis of the constitutionality of licensing printing presses concluded that it is fairly certain licensing would be unconstitutional.

> The difficulty that a licensing regime would have in satisfying First Amendment standards is reflected in the consensus view: "Although it is virtually impossible to find a case that directly so holds, it is fairly clear that any attempt to license a newspaper or magazine would violate the Constitution."[159]

For Internet regulation, the arguments—and perhaps the result—would surely vary depending on the specific type of regulation, the problem that the government sought to address, and the factual justification for the regulation. However, it seems likely that the burden of defending a regulation would be great.

VI. CLOSE

The principal purpose of this closing section is to identify some issues that, for a variety of reasons including lack of space, have not been discussed in any depth. There are no conclusions because meaningful conclusions are not available given the largely abstract review of issues addressed. Proposals for

---

[157]Any type of activity that creates central information about Internet users has a similar potential to create a resource that could be exploited by identity thieves or others for criminal purposes. The same information could also be used by government for other purposes that may affect privacy or civil liberties interests.

[158]See NextAdvisor, *Inside the Internet's Financial Black Markets—How Identity Thieves Buy and Sell Your Personal Information Online*, http://www.nextadvisor.com/blog/2008/09/16/inside-the-internets-financial-black-markets-%E2%80%93-how-identity-thieves-buy-and-sell-your-personal-information-online/; accessed July 2, 2010.

[159]Stuart Minor Benjamin, *The Logic of Scarcity: Idle Spectrum as a First Amendment Violation*, 52 Duke Law Journal 1, 31 (2002) (footnote omitted), available at http://papers.ssrn.com/sol3/papers.cfm?abstract_id=310121; accessed March 17, 2010.

preventing cyberattacks can only be fully evaluated for their civil liberties and privacy consequences when the details are available because the specific elements will make a significant difference to the evaluation.

Criminal laws that seek to deter unwanted activities and to punish those who engage in them have not been addressed. A leading example is the Computer Fraud and Abuse Act,[160] which generally protects computers belonging to the federal government or a financial institution or to any computer affecting interstate or foreign commerce. Laws about identity theft are also not addressed in detail, although some of these laws have non-criminal law components. Generally, the tools and techniques of criminal law enforcement have some relevance to cybersecurity (e.g., deterrence), but further analysis is not possible in the available space.

Some federal and state[161] legislation also establishes security standards for computer systems. For example, the 2002 Federal Information Security Management Act (FISMA)[162] directs the head of each federal agency to provide "information security protections commensurate with the risk and magnitude of the harm resulting from unauthorized access, use, disclosure, disruption, modification, or destruction of" agency information or information systems.[163] Laws establishing private sector security requirements are not common, but there are some, including:

• Section 404 of Sarbanes-Oxley[164] requires a publicly owned company's management and the external auditor to report on the adequacy of the company's internal control over financial reporting. Because the financial reporting processes of many companies depend on information technology systems, controls over those systems may fall within the scope of a required assessment of financial risks.

• The Gramm-Leach-Bliley Financial Services Modernization Act includes a few privacy and security provisions. It expresses a policy that each financial institution has an affirmative and continuing obligation to protect the security and confidentiality of nonpublic personal information about customers.[165] Financial services regulatory agencies issued regulations with more detailed standards.[166]

• The Health Insurance Portability and Accountability Act[167] (HIPAA) requires the Secretary of Health and Human Services to issue security rules for covered entities (mostly health care providers and insurers). The rules cover electronic health information.[168] The HIPAA security requirements are more detailed than some comparable rules, rely on industry standards, and give covered entities considerable discretion in application.

Legislation is a crude tool for mandating security, and legislators appear to understand its limitations. Security legislation is typically stated in broad, high-level terms with few details, and the civil liberties and privacy implications of current legislation are of lesser significance here. That could change. Some security laws call for the use of encryption, which can have value in deterring cyberattacks. Encryption can be employed or mandated in a multitude of different ways and, depending on the specifics, can have significant consequences for privacy and civil liberties. A Clinton Administration proposal (Clipper Chip) for mandatory encryption of data communications involving the escrow of encryption keys

---

[160]18 U.S.C. § 1030.

[161]See, e.g., the Massachusetts Standards for the Protection of Personal Information of Residents of the Commonwealth, 201 CMR 17.00, available at http://www.mass.gov/Eoca/docs/idtheft/201CMR1700reg.pdf; accessed March 15, 2010, and the implementing regulations at 201 CMR 17.00, available at http://www.mass.gov/Eoca/docs/idtheft/201CMR1700reg.pdf, accessed August 30, 2010.

[162]44 U.S.C § 3541 et seq.

[163]44 U.S.C. § 3544(a)(1)(A).

[164]15 U.S.C. § 7262.

[165]15 U.S.C. § 6801.

[166]See, e.g., 16 C.F.R. Part 314 (Federal Trade Commission).

[167]42 U.S.C. §1320d-2(d).

[168]45 C.F.R. Part 160 and Part 164, Subparts A & C.

with the government was highly controversial among civil liberties advocates, Internet users, industry, and others. The proposal was eventually dropped.[169]

Some other subjects that are largely outside the scope here are better training, consumer education, reporting and collaborative efforts,[170] voluntary activities,[171] security breach notification,[172] and polygraph regulation. Most but not all of these activities are less likely to raise privacy or civil liberties concerns.

Emergency powers may allow the President to seize property; organize and control the means of production; seize commodities; assign military forces abroad; institute martial law; seize and control all transportation and communication; regulate the operation of private enterprise; restrict travel; and, in a variety of ways, control the lives of United States citizens.[173] The scope of these powers with respect to the Internet is not immediately clear, but any exercise would raise civil liberties and privacy concerns that cannot be considered here. Recent circulation of a draft legislative proposal by a Senator that would expand the authority of the emergency powers of the President with respect to operation of the Internet attracted considerable controversy. Direct presidential control over the operation of the Internet or the collection of information about Internet activities data raises a large number of issues for individuals, companies, and organizations. The inherent borderlessness of the Internet does nothing to simplify these issues.

Also unexplored here are uses of incentives for those individuals, companies, or other entities that adopt better cyberattack protections. The range of possible incentives is broad, including civil liability that would make software, hardware, service vendors, or users responsible for their failure to provide adequate security measures or their failure to use adequate security measures; civil liability for ISPs who fail to verify the identity of users; and subsidies or tax incentives for "good" behaviors. It is not apparent in the abstract that any of these would necessarily raise significant civil liberties or privacy concerns, although civil liability can raise constitutional questions about violations of the Due Process Clause by grossly excessive or arbitrary punishments.[174] The use of incentives to induce the private sector to adopt protections that the federal government could not impose directly has the potential be controversial.

---

[169]See, e.g., A. Michael Froomkin, *The Metaphor is the Key: Cryptography, the Clipper Chip, and the Constitution*, 143 U. Pa. L. Rev. 709 (1995).

[170]See, e.g., United States Computer Emergency Readiness Team (US-Cert), http://www.us-cert.gov/; accessed March 17, 2010.

[171]See, e.g., the Critical Infrastructure Information Act, 6 U.S.C. §§ 131-134.

[172]Both the federal government and the states have enacted security breach notification laws, but there is no general federal statute (either preemptive or otherwise) despite much congressional activity over several years.

[173]Harold C. Releya, *National Emergency Powers* (2007) (Congressional Research Service), http://www.fas.org/sgp/crs/natsec/98-505.pdf; accessed April 14, 2010.

[174]See, e.g., *State Farm Mutual Insurance Co. v. Campbell*, 538 U.S. 408 (2003).

Group 7—Contributed Papers

Targeting Third-Party Collaboration

Geoff A. Cohen

Elysium Digital

INTRODUCTION

On its way from an attacker to a target, a cyberattack will pass through the control of many third parties. Packets will flow across wires owned by network operators; hacked machines owned by private individuals will use Internet service providers (ISPs) to transmit additional attacks; and Domain Name System (DNS) servers will resolve domain names by querying independent registrars for the current IP address. Packets will be processed by operating system and application software written by independent software vendors, configured by and installed by system integrators on hardware built by yet different companies.[1]

At the same time, it is difficult—perhaps prohibitively so—to reliably attribute attacks to a specific actor. Even when malicious actors are identified with some confidence, they are most often beyond the reach of law enforcement or other retaliation.[2]

These two factors lead to the conclusion that if we are to reduce the level of cyberattacks against private and government facilities, we need to focus efforts on changing the behavior of third parties, in particular making them less willing to cooperate with cyberattackers. These parties may be cooperating with the attacker, may be operating willfully blindly to the uses of their system, or may in fact be unaware that their network has been suborned (such as in the case of corporate networks infected by a botnet). Levying a sufficiently high price on these third parties for enabling attacks, for example by allowing mislabeled IP datagrams, hosting infected machines, or refusing to perform due diligence on clients of domain registration or hosting service, will dissuade these providers from cooperating. Such a price might include economic sanctions, law enforcement measures, and increased scrutiny from technical elements of the military or intelligence communities; they may also include more aggressive measures such as updating global routing tables to isolate the network.

These measures need not—probably can not—be unilateral on the part of the U.S. Government, but can be carried out in cooperation with network operators, the Internet community, foreign law enforcement, etc. However, it does not require complete global cooperation to achieve some measure of success.

---

[1]Goldsmith, Jack Landman and Tim Wu. *Who Controls the Internet? Illusions of a Borderless World* (Oxford University Press 2006).
[2]Menn, Joseph. *Fatal System Error* (Public Affairs, New York, 2010).

Focusing on third-party enablers has a number of advantages. First, over time it reduces the free-dom with which hostile actors can operate. Second, it reduces the amount of damage done over time to private entities by infected networks. Third, it allows law enforcement or intelligence assets to focus attention on a smaller number of recalcitrant actors. Fourth, by limiting the number of routes through which attacks can be sent, it slows the speed at which attackers learn the precise vulnerabilities of U.S. assets and test various attacks.

COLLABORATION AND ITS DISCONTENTS

In English usage, the word "collaboration" has ambiguous connotations; it can be positive when referring, for example, to colleagues collaborating on a project.[3] In wartime, however, collaboration refers to working with the enemy, and is a crime.[4]

We mean to encompass that ambiguity by using the term "collaboration" here. We don't care whether the security failures are caused maliciously by bad actors, or only through inattention (e.g. by allow-ing malware to infect computers under their control). In legal terms, this distinction might go toward punitive damages rather than compensatory damages. But in either case, damage was caused in part through the actions or inactions of the particular party, and it should be held responsible.

The scope is meant to encompass any way in which a third party (intentionally or not) enables an attacker to launch an attack on a defender. This includes Tier 1 ISPs across whose wires (or even through the sky on a wireless signal) an attack might flow. It also includes more distant but still relevant factors such as software vendors that provided software containing the exploited vulnerability; domain name registrars that host a particular malware-containing site; or operators whose networks contain zombie client machines infected by malware. Other examples include software vendors that introduced vulner-abilities; ISPs that failed to perform adequate ingress filtering; hosting services that turned a blind eye to illicit activity or invalid addresses; sovereign nations that neglect to enforce cybercrime laws or refuse to offer cooperation with foreign investigative services, and so on.

Further, we consider the problem of such attacks as they happen in peacetime; we don't consider the appropriate reaction to attacks during declared armed conflict, or in the escalatory stage immedi-ately before major conflict erupts. Nor do we consider the use of information warfare as an adjunct to traditional kinetic operations. The focus here is on the actions that the U.S. government should employ in the face of attacks or evidence of attack capability (such as malware infection) during "normal" peacetime.

A goal of this paper is to suggest a range of appropriate incentives and disincentives to make third parties less likely to collaborate with attacks.

THE URGENT CASE FOR ACTION

The distinction between "cyberwar" and "cybercrime" is a misleading one, leading one to believe that these are fundamentally different, even if related, activities. But they are far more similar: they are attacks on U.S. national interest, using the same techniques, launched by the same computers and using the same infrastructure to carry out the attack, planned and executed by the same people. The only differences are whether the target is U.S. military/government or private individuals or corporations, and whether the attack is happening in peacetime or during a wider conflict. Important distinctions, to be sure, but surely suggesting that an inability to deter cybercrime is a sign of a wider failure in our system of deterrence. And to the extent that we allow cybercrime to continue essentially unchecked, we are giving our adversaries rich opportunities to shape their attacks and render them increasingly

---

[3]cooperation. Thesaurus.com. *Roget's 21st Century Thesaurus*, Third Edition, Philip Lief Group, 2009, http://www.thesaurus.com/browse/cooperation.

[4]Compare with the usage of "cooperation" (always positive) and "collusion" (always negative). Ibid.

effective, sophisticated, and profitable; these improved attacks (again, most likely launched by the same personnel) are the ones we will face in a time of direct conflict. In the meantime, U.S. and allied interests are suffering significant economic losses from cybercrime, resources transferred to hostile parties and used to further develop attacks. We are, in a real sense, paying our adversaries to build weapons with which to attack us; a curious twist on the prediction on the death of capitalism often attributed to Lenin: "They will sell us the rope with which we will hang them."

Viewed more positively, cybercrime and minor cyberattacks are actually providing an important service to U.S. interests, by testing our defenses and revealing vulnerabilities and complicit third parties. If the United States takes advantage of these opportunities by improving defenses and reforming or shutting down third parties, then perhaps cyberattacks against U.S. interests in an actual high-stakes conflict might be considerably less destructive.

Most cyberattacks are minor, and happen hundreds of times a day across the globe. As such, we all live the day after these attacks, and so we worry more—or ought to, anyway—about how to clean up, whether to disclose the attack publicly, how to repair, and, most important for our purposes here, what we might do to prevent a future attack.

INTRODUCTION TO THIRD-PARTY INTERVENTION

The idea of going after third parties when it is difficult to identify or target actual malefactors is not a new one. Classic examples include "dram shop" laws that attempt to reduce drunk driving by threatening sanctions against proprietors of bars. More recent examples include the Unlawful Internet Gambling Enforcement Act (UIGEA), which intended to clamp down on Internet gambling in the United States by forbidding U.S. financial institutions from transferring assets on behalf of customers from U.S. accounts to overseas gambling institutions. Here, a more traditional target would be the casinos, but they were overseas and thus out of the reach of direct regulation. An alternative target would be the individual users who were gambling, but any attempt to monitor and regulate this behavior would be extremely difficult because of the relatively inobvious nature of it and the extreme degree to which the behavior is distributed. By targeting banks, the government identified a point in the business chain that had a fairly small number of actors (and ones quite accustomed, if not happily, to government regulation).

Such efforts have had limited success in the past. Even in the face of dram shop laws, there is still drunk driving (although some analysts have identified a small reduction in drunk driving in the presence of such laws).[5] Shortly after UIGEA went into effect, there is still online gambling, still accessed by U.S. citizens.[6]

A number of existing U.S. or international laws (or proposed laws) provide potential platforms for third-party intervention for cyberattacks. These include the Council of Europe's Convention on Cybercrime, the currently proposed U.S. Cybersecurity Act, in addition to common law or international norms, such as liability law. This section provides an introduction to some of these.

Communications Decency Act

The Communications Decency Act (CDA) was an attempt by Congress in 1996 to regulate pornography and "indecent material" on the Internet. Section 230 of the Act provides a limited immunity for "providers or users of interactive computer services" if they are not the originator of the allegedly defamatory, indecent, or other actionable material. In other words, a website operator is not liable for defamatory statements made by one of its users, even if that user made the statement on the website.

---

[5]*Drinkers, Drivers, and Bartenders: Balancing Private Rights and Public Accountability*, F. A. Sloan, ed., Chicago: University of Chicago Press, 2000.

[6]"On Poker: UIGEA law now official, but effects remain unclear," Chuck Blount, http://www.mysanantonio.com/sports/On_Poker_UIGEA_law_now_official_but_effects_remain_unclear_95472109.html, accessed July 9, 2010.

This immunity has explicit limits: it does not extend to intellectual property (which is dealt with through the DMCA) or criminal matters.

CALEA

The Communications Assistance for Law Enforcement Act (CALEA) of 1994 requires telecommunications carriers—which later court decisions and executive branch guidance make clear include broadband Internet service providers and Tier 1 carriers—to cooperate in enabling law enforcement access to their networks for monitoring communication, that is, "wiretapping."

This statute is only questionably wide enough to allow investigation into security breaches such as botnet activity or hacking, but provides an important precedent and template for future statutory language requiring networking infrastructure companies to cooperate with law enforcement.

The technological measures that complied with such language, however, might create just as much a problem as it was intended to solve. Government-approved backdoors into Tier 1 providers or hosting services would no doubt become attractive targets for hackers and would make the situation worse. However, if compliance required only that carriers and services allow investigative agencies efficient and standardized access to security audit and logging data, then perhaps tech-savvy investigators could more effectively identify hacked machines and trace the exploit back another level.

DMCA

The Digital Millennium Copyright Act (DMCA) contained a set of amendments to Title 17 (Copyrights) passed by Congress in 1996 and designed, in part, to adjust copyright law to respond to technological innovation such as digital computers and networking. Two sections provide potential analogs to mechanisms to combat malicious activity on the Internet.

First, DMCA provides a coupled takedown notice/safe harbor mechanism. Rights-holders can send a "Section 500" takedown notice to an Internet content provider or ISP that copyrighted material is being made available in an unauthorized manner. If the recipient promptly removes the material, then the recipient is in the "safe harbor;" it cannot then be held liable for infringement.

The recent case of Viacom v. YouTube provides some guidance to interpret the scope of this safe harbor. In the case, Viacom, working with many other rights-holders, sued YouTube, claiming that copyright infringement was common on YouTube. YouTube responded that they had complied promptly with all (proper) takedown requests; they won on summary judgment.

A possible parallel with cybercrime would create a similar dynamic. Third parties that had evidence that they were harmed by cybercrime activity, such as a DDoS attack from a botnet hosted in an ISPs network, could send a takedown request to that ISP. If the ISP promptly responded in some way that remediated the threat, then they would have safe harbor protection from further civil or criminal suits under CFAA or similar laws. The cybercrime safe harbor should possibly be narrower than in DMCA: general knowledge of botnet activity and negligence in performing industry-standard countermeasures should certainly block a party from receiving safe-harbor protection, even if it does comply promptly with cybercrime takedown requests.

The second relevant mechanism created by DMCA is the anti-circumvention restrictions. Under DMCA, it is illegal to create or distribute instruments capable of circumventing technological controls intended to limit access to copyrighted material. With appropriate carve-outs for academic and security research (carve-outs unfortunately missing from DMCA), similar language could apply to the construction and distribution of software intended for illegal use in hacking, even if this code is written overseas (as it very often is); see DeCSS case—websites that even link to the offending code were found liable.

In general, it's worth noting that our society and legal code have tried much, much harder to control and regulate culture through copyright law than it has to control the threat of computer crime or computer war. There are multiple legal recourses for private entities to bring down offending material that violates copyright, but very few options for entities under attack that could actually destroy a business. It is perhaps time to rethink our priorities.

CFAA

The Computer Fraud and Abuse Act (CFAA), strictly speaking 18 USC. Sec. 1030, sets out a number of scenarios of malicious and unauthorized access to the computers that trigger criminal sanctions.

Section 1030 was created by the Comprehensive Crime Control Act of 1984, which criminalized for the first time unauthorized access of computers (as a misdemeanor). It was amended in 1986 by the Computer Fraud and Abuse Act, and amended again eight further times, including by the USA PATRIOT Act in 2001 and by the Identity Theft Enforcement and Restitution Act in 2008. It criminalizes a number of actions covering unauthorized access to certain protected computers, defrauding, causing damage to computer systems (or extortion involving threats to perform damage), trafficking in passwords, etc.

A particular crime is to "knowingly cause the transmission of a program, information, code, or command, and as a result of such conduct, intentionally [cause] damage without authorization, to a protected computer." This would seem to cover many forms of attacks, including denial-of-service attacks, transmission of viruses/worms/etc.

Normally, crimes under CFAA are investigated by the U.S. Secret Service (except for espionage-related investigations, which are handled by the FBI) Under certain circumstances, private parties can bring civil suits under CFAA.[7]

Liability

The current state of U.S. law shields software vendors from product liability claims, as software is usually sold as granting a license to use a product, rather than as the sale of a product. This legal regime could be changed by legislation, creating an enormous economic pressure on software vendors to improve the security of their software. The argument for exposing vendors is that the software marketplace has failed to provide adequate security, due to many factors including the illiquidity of the software market (especially the market for operating systems) and the fact that security failures are an externality the cost of which is borne by neither the vendor nor, in many cases, the purchaser. Even under the current legal framework, software vendors are potentially vulnerable to negligence suits.[8]

National Security Measures

There are a host of U.S. Government powers flowing from national security requirements, including the use of National Security Letters,[9] the war powers ability of the President to shut down wired and wireless networks through Section 606 of the Telecommunications Act, and potentially additional powers granted by the Cybersecurity Act of 2010 or other future legislation.

These mechanisms are undoubtedly powerful tools, and may be appropriate in responding to extremely large and time-sensitive attacks. However, they don't scale well; if the President or Federal judges needed to intercede to combat every computer attack, they would quickly have no time to do anything else. Also, these measures raise concerns about civil liberties, the constitutionality of executive

---

[7]*Prosecuting Computer Crimes*, Chapter 1, U.S. Department of Justice, Computer Crime and Intellectual Property Section, Criminal Division, Scott Eltringham, Editor in Chief, February 2007, downloaded from http://www.justice.gov/criminal/cybercrime/ccmanual/.

[8]Chandler, Jennifer A., Improving Software Security: A Discussion of Liability for Unreasonably Insecure Software. *Securing Privacy in the Internet Age*, Stanford University Press, 2006. Available at http://ssrn.com/abstract=610041.

[9]Doyle, Charles. "National Security Letters in Foreign Intelligence Investigations: A Glimpse of the Legal Background and Recent Amendments," Congressional Research Service, September 2009, downloaded from http://www.fas.org/sgp/crs/intel/RS22406.pdf.

branch interference in protected speech, and the possibility of using such mechanisms to attack political enemies rather than actual adversaries.[10]

LEGAL PRINCIPLES

Government Role in Private Security

In general, the private sector is best equipped and structured to respond to an evolving cyber threat.
—National Strategy to Secure Cyberspace, 2003.

Security is a nearly textbook example of a market failure. The cost of security failure is an enormous externality: it is most often not borne by the organization that failed (for example, if the organization is penetrated and its computers turned into a botnet to send out spam, or if the organization makes a great deal of profit selling insecure software). The knowledge on how to best respond to foreign attacks is rare and dispersed; private corporations are notoriously bad at spending money to combat long-term threats that may not materialize.

Even when solutions are known, coordination costs often prevent deployment of the solution for many years. For example, the use of the Domain Name System as an attack vector to hack machines has been known since the early 1990s,[11] and yet the proposed solution, DNSSEC, was still in the process of being deployed in 2010.[12]

Government can efficiently counter coordination cost (by, for example, setting mandatory standards and timetables for deployment), is a center for expertise, and is the agent of the collective public for acknowledging externalities by levying taxes or fines against the initiator and compensating the damaged. As such, it can serve an important, if not critical role in addressing security failures in the private sector. A more extreme version of this claim is a legal principle that the government has an affirmative responsibility for assuring the security of private infrastructure.

Shared Affirmative Responsibility for Security

A broader principle is that all actors in the software marketplace, including vendors, network infrastructure operators, resellers, and corporate and individual users, have an affirmative responsibility to take reasonable and timely measures to assure the secure and legal operation of their systems and services. This includes the duties to monitor their systems for security, detect vulnerabilities or actual exploits, respond to notice from third parties that a security problem exists; inform relevant users, operators, and authorized clearinghouses; and resolve such vulnerabilities and if relevant distributing such patches.

This legal principle, if adopted, would run directly against the legal framework that affords common carrier rights, and would have to be carefully crafted to not create undue burdens on entities such as Tier 1 ISPs that could not possibly be aware of all activity on their network. See below.

Too often cybercrime investigations have been met with studied airs of ignorance; hosting providers are often shocked to hear that they may have been hosting malware.

---

[10]See, for example, Fellow, Avery, "Experts Caution Against Federal Web Regulations," Courthouse News Service, http://www.courthousenews.com/2010/08/26/29911.htm.

[11]See, for example, RFC 3833, message by Jim Galvin posted to dns-security@tis.com on November 19, 1993, and Bellovin, S., "Using the Domain Name System for System Break-Ins," Proceedings of the Fifth Usenix Unix Security Symposium, June 1995.

[12]See, for example, "Status Update, 2010-07-16," http://www.root-dnssec.org/2010/07/16/status-update-2010-07-16/.

Presumption of Harm

Another proposed legal principle is that malware, exploits, vulnerabilities, etc. create a presumption of harm and are presumed to be counter to the public interest. The legal principle proposed here, somewhat parallel to the Supreme Court's standards for considering injunctions,[13] considers the public interest, the possibility of irreparable harm, and the balance of hardships of discovering the security violation, addressing it after the fact, and the (potential) damage inflicted. In situations where security falls behind exploit technology (as it seems we are in today), the balance of hardships surely indicates that actors are more responsible for cleaning up their own house. In situations where security vulnerabilities are rarer and more isolated, perhaps the balance of hardships would give some more lenience to operators.

The Balance of Incentives

To sum up, the central idea in this approach is that all operators in the network system have a responsibility for securing their system, which includes active monitoring for vulnerabilities and exploitations. This responsibility carries with it the potential for serious legal consequences if actors fail to meet their expected standards of behavior.

Third parties can gain immunity from such consequences—enter a safe harbor, in legal terms—through a variety of ways, which include either remediating the problem or providing proper notice to some other actor up or downstream of the problem. Once notified, those other actors are now on the hook to remediate or otherwise respond.

The idea is to balance these incentives appropriately: the threat of punishment, and positive incentives to fix the problem or shift the burden elsewhere.

A scale of degree of punishment would start with merely failing to meet minimal standards of behavior, progress to "knew or should have known" of vulnerabilities, continue to willful negligence, and end with actual collaboration with malicious actors. At each stage, well-defined (by government or neutral parties such as IETF) standards of behavior define exactly the duties and responsibilities of the actor, as well as the mechanisms to inform others of their own responsibilities.

INSTRUMENTS OF POLICY

Here, we discuss potential actions against third parties—the "retaliation" for allowing cyberattacks to take place. Of course, the presumption is that these entities are not actually malicious actors, or they would be facing criminal investigation instead. As such, the penalties are not designed to be overly punitive. However, at the very least they ought to compensate society for the actual, and some fraction of the potential, damage incurred by their failure to secure their system.

Further, such penalties can't merely be part of the cost of business, as long-haul truckers understand that invariably they will get speeding tickets on the highway. The penalties must be significant enough to drive behavioral changes.

One question is whether actual exploitation must happen in order to trigger the penalty, or is merely having an open vulnerability enough? The first case is easier to sell politically and is linked more closely to existing legal and policy concepts of negligence, contributory infringement, and standards of behavior and responsibility. It would also be easier to specify damages, since in fact some damage must have occurred.

However, this narrower range of response would leave out the much larger range of vulnerabilities that have yet to be exploited. Targeting these actors, while much more politically challenging, and more difficult to fairly assess the potential damage, would have a much broader and more significant policy

---

[13]*eBay Inc. and Half.com, v. MercExchange, L.L.C.*, 126 S. Ct. 1837.

impact. First, it would at least in some cases avoid the actual damage from occurring, since vulnerabilities would be patched and addressed before a malicious actor could take advantage of it. Second, it would create incentives for more widespread changes in behavior, since many more people and organizations would be swept up in the regulation, and the chances of getting hit with a fine would be much larger if you can be fined for simply failing to secure a network.

This approach has more in common with public health campaigns against epidemics than traditional security research. Such an approach emphasizes protection of as-yet unattacked populations through isolation, inoculation of key at-risk groups, and only secondarily the treatment of infected groups. And although the applicability of this approach is most obvious for the biological metaphor attacks of viruses and worms, it can apply more broadly to other malware infection or even more general vulnerabilities.

Market Intervention

As computer security represents a market failure, one solution is for the government to try to address the problem by intervening in the market to achieve a better societal outcome. This could include mandating computer security insurance, with higher rates applied to users of known-insecure systems.

In contrast, systems or services that met higher standards of behavior and have good or excellent track records could be certified by the government as being especially secure, a sort of "Energy Star" program for security. Government agencies could be directed to purchase only those products and services that met this certification; certainly, much of the private sector would do so as well. Targeted tax incentives could also accomplish a similar goal of putting a thumb on the balance in the market.

Collective Action

Many counter-malware activities on the Internet require information to be gathered at many points throughout the network, and information to be distributed. By its very nature, some detection and analysis on the Internet requires the examination of thousands, or millions, of sites. Responding appropriately may also require a distributed response. For example, one technique to fight spam is for many users to pool together the knowledge of originators of spam, and then agree to disallow mail from any of those sources (so-called "blacklisting").

The Internet itself enables this kind of loosely coordinated collective action of interested parties (sometimes also called "crowdsourcing"). Prominent examples include spam-tracking services such as SpamHaus, a non-profit which accepts information from any user regarding spam and then makes it available to system operators.

Another example is the Knujon project to examine the complete DNS records. Previous projects to try to inspect the Domain Name System ran against the sheer scope of the task: nearly 120 million registered domain names in the top five generic top-level domains. By distributing the task to volunteers, Knujon was able to identify hundreds of registrars that were violating their registry accreditation agreement with ICANN.[14]

Of course, information must be the base of action to be useful. In SpamHaus' case, the list of suspected spam-sites is made available for other network operators to (voluntarily) use to mark mail as spam and potentially discard it.

It's clear that collective action will be a key technique in fighting malware and cybercrime and cyberwarfare. Especially as other aspects of this report are adopted, there will be an increasing amount of information collected on the relative degree of proper or rogue behavior on the part of networks, hosts, registrars, etc. This information should be widely disseminated and used with discretion in determining

---

[14]*Knujon Internet Security Report: Audit of the gTLD Internet Structure, Evaluation of Contractual Compliance, and Review of Illicit Activity by Registrar -2010.* http://www.knujon.com/knujon_audit0610.pdf.

whether other entities should trust them. For example, BGP route updates from a rogue ISP that had issued faulty or malicious updates in the past should not be automatically accepted, but require system administrator action. Similarly, SSL certificates signed by a certificate authority in an untrusted nation or from an untrusted ISP should be flagged to users.

Collective action is not without risk. Distributed monitoring and blacklisting could metastasize into mob rule or vigilante justice. Smoothly working procedures could be subverted by bad actors. Principles that could guard against such failures include making the operations and decision making process clearly transparent; providing well-documented appeals and grievances procedures; and some notion of outside accountability or authority, even if tenuous. Non-governmental bodies such as the IETF may be able to serve this role, for example by supporting the drafting and publishing of Best Current Practices documents that describe varieties of collective action.

A second variety of problem with collective action is illustrated by the litigation between e360Insight (a bulk emailer) and SpamHaus. Lawsuits or even the potential threat may be enough to shut down many collective efforts. What's needed is clear statutory guidance that establishes a legal presumption of validity for such activity in the face of negligence or other lawsuits. Such a presumption should only be overcome only by evidence of willfulness or malicious intent.

RESPONSIBILITIES OF THIRD PARTIES

We consider any actor in the network to be a third party that may be a target of this policy. This can include elements of the Domain Name System, registrars, ISPs (Tier 1, smaller, and corporate networks), hosting services, hardware and software vendors, and even sovereign nations. Of course, each of these has different vulnerabilities, presents a different threat model to outsiders, and is responsive to different levers of power. Registrars must comply with rules set by ICANN, while smaller ISPs are dependent on Tier 1 ISPs for connectivity. Sovereign nations may be the hardest case, but even here, diplomatic and economic pressure can be brought to change behavior. For example, Romania was traditionally a haven for cybercrime, but under pressure from the EU and threatened with the withdrawal of technological assistance from richer countries, it became a signatory to the Convention on Cybercrime and is reportedly cooperating more with foreign investigations.[15]

Network Operators

Network operators play a special and challenging role, as they are both in the best position to monitor for security failures and to intervene rapidly and effectively when they occur, but at the same time do not want to be in the business of individually inspecting and approving customers or traffic. To require network operators to monitor the content of traffic would be a significant burden, although it may be that they are doing much of this already for law enforcement purposes.

An important goal of this project is to encourage entities to detect malicious activity and pass the information closer to a location that can take action. For example, local ISPs are well-positioned to identify particular IP addresses (or MAC addresses) as the source of port-scans or spam indicating compromise by malware. They are also best positioned to determine the actual subscriber that was using that particular address at that particular time. The next logical step is for the ISP to communicate its suspicion to the user (presumably with offers of assistance in cleaning up the problem). By providing safe harbor to ISPs that communicate and offer to assist, this policy would encourage ISPs to do that.

Corporate ISPs—that is, companies that provide Internet access to their employees at work, but own and operate their computers—should receive no such safe harbor. They're responsible for their own messes, and any statutory changes in liability should reflect the difference in ISPs.

---

[15]Menn, Joseph, *Fatal System Error*, Public Affairs, New York, 2010.

A basic step is to perform ingress and egress filtering, that is, to check at network boundaries for incoming or outgoing packets that are marked as having impossible origin addresses. IP address spoofing is a key ingredient of the difficulty in attribution: if attacking packets (such as SYN requests used in a DDoS attack) are marked as having come from a false originating machine, then obviously it will be extremely difficult to identify the actual source. Network operators can make such spoofing much more difficult by discarding incoming packets that are marked as having originated at a machine that could not have actually been routed through the peered network. Similarly, outgoing packets should be dropped if they are not marked as having originated within the network or a network with a valid route. A further useful step would be to log and investigate such events. This is not a panacea, of course; it merely restricts the freedom of malevolent actors to spoof. However, it will at least provide some degree of clues to investigators trying to determine the source of attack.

Such filtering is not a new technique—RFC 2827 described it in May 2000.[16] It is considered a "Best Current Practice," but is not required. If a network attack occurs which uses spoofed IP addresses, then any network that transmitted such networks and failed to apply ingress or egress filtering, then it is potentially a target of a retaliatory action by the government.

Such security requirements are, for example, required by the Payment Card Industry Data Security Standard.[17] (More broadly, this is a useful example/model for how private industry could develop stronger security practice requirements, and create a supporting audit/certification regime). Inter-ISP terms of service ought to make sending on unfiltered packets a violation that allows termination.

A similar attack is to publish invalid routes. For example, in March and April of 2010, a small Chinese ISP published invalid routes to more than 30,000 networks using the Border Gateway Protocol (BGP), the Internet's protocol for communicating routes between networks. Many ISPs accepted these routes, thus in effect isolating those networks.[18] Whether a result of a sloppy system administration or an intentional experiment, this clearly demonstrates a critical, current vulnerability in the architecture of the Internet; it's one that can be addressed best by ISPs.

Team Cymru has identified a number of measures by which ISPs can filter BGP messages, including throwing out routing information apparently coming from invalid or valid but unallocated IP blocks.[19]

To reiterate, these technological and administrative defenses are not new; the question is whether the U.S. government can require organizations to follow them, or conversely if a failure to follow them creates enough liability that the organizations could face punitive measures if they fail to follow them and as a result an attack occurs.

Registrars and Hosting Providers

Currently, much of the domain name registration information (that is, the names and contact information associated with a particular registration) is invalid. And yet registrars face no repercussions for allowing false information, nor do they perform any checking. Often, payment is accepted using stolen credit cards. The situation is little different with hosting providers. When investigators tracing an attack come to a hosting provider or seek to determine who registered a domain name, they often hit a dead end.

While it would be overly burdensome and intrusive to require these sorts of companies to police the content being hosted, they certainly should be able to verify the identity—or existence—of the users submitting the form. Those who negligently allow invalid data should face consequences when such a

---

[16]http://tools.ietf.org/html/rfc2827. It was updated in May 2004 by RFC 3704 (see http://tools.ietf.org/html/rfc3704).
[17]https://www.pcisecuritystandards.org/security_standards/pci_dss.shtml.
[18]http://www.computerworld.com/s/article/9175081/A_Chinese_ISP_momentarily_hijacks_the_Internet_again_.
[19]http://www.team-cymru.org/Services/Bogons/.

site is used in an attack. This approach is analogous to the "Know Your Customer" regulations applied to financial institutions after 9/11 by the Bank Secrecy Act and the USA PATRIOT Act.[20]

Individuals

Ultimately, the vast majority of the unsecured aspect of computing is the individuals who operate or own personal computers. Any other efforts by security vendors, operating system authors, ISPs, or even police, intelligence agencies, or the military to secure the computing infrastructure—or even merely erect minimal defenses against attack—will be an uphill struggle if the endpoints remain compromised. For all the malevolence of malware authors or criminal website operators, in most situations there's no damage until someone's machine becomes infected. (Even in snooping or man-in-the-middle attack, it's often because the intermediate node has itself become infected first.)

Without yet raising the question of legal responsibility, it's straight-forward and well-documented that the security burden on individuals comprises ensuring that they're running the most recent patched version of system software and applications; running an updated virus scanner and security suite; and avoiding risky behavior such as installing software from untrusted sources or visiting shady websites.

This is all too well known and has been for years; clearly it is insufficient to merely announce these burdens. It is no more effective than fighting the obesity epidemic by publishing another diet book or exhorting people to eat less and exercise more. Clearly, if endpoints are to be secured, then some more proactive and regulatory action on behalf of the government is necessary.

Can individuals be punished if their infected computers are found to have been used in an attack? Even determining such data could raise significant privacy and civil liberties concerns. Instituting mechanisms to detect and legal infrastructure to, for example, punish citizens for visiting certain cites is, even if well-intentioned, a mechanism for oppression. Counterintuitively, a broader and stronger mandate that applied to all users would be a more effective while encroaching less on liberty.

No doubt an individual mandate requiring individuals who used networked computers to buy, install, and maintain security software would be as controversial as the mandate to purchase health insurance—indeed, the issues are quite similar both in legal analysis and in the way an individual's choices affect global outcomes. Unflattering parallels will undoubtedly be drawn with China's mandate for computer manufacturers to install Green Dam, its Internet filter that would prevent access to sites containing content on, for example, pornography and democracy. (The parallels may be deeper: some security researchers hypothesized that due to security flaws in Green Dam, it would become compromised by malicious actors, and the population of all connected PCs in China could become an enormous botnet.)

And yet this is no different than requiring drivers to have bought insurance from the market. A requirement for security software is even less burdensome than one for auto insurance, since effective free options are available.

It's certainly true that the aggregate cost of maximally securing every end-point is enormous and probably prohibitive; and yet it is not necessary to reach that goal to be effective. As long as the number of vulnerable nodes decreases to such an extent that certain types of hacking become unprofitable (relative to other activities), then this approach will have some value. This is not to mention the reduced pain and damage accruing to those individuals that will not be harmed given this higher—even if not maximal—level of security.

WILL THIS STRATEGY BE EFFECTIVE?

As described above, efforts to prevent bad behavior by controlling third parties has had mixed results, from gambling and drunk driving to counterfeit goods. More immediately, successful efforts

---

[20]See http://en.wikipedia.org/wiki/Know_your_customer.

to shut down known malicious ISPs have resulted in dramatic drops in spam rates in the short run (estimated up to 70% reductions in world-wide spam[21]); however, spammers quickly develop new techniques and find (or establish) new ISPs willing to convey spam.[22]

For these reasons, it is perhaps overly optimistic to consider that such a technique could work. However, much of the problem in computer security is that there is little learning; each round is played as if it is the entire game. Repeated instances of the same security hole don't seem to result in changed behavior by other actors. For example, consider the Chinese ISP that was responsible twice in two months for hijacking global routing tables. As the saying goes, fool me once, shame on you; fool me twice, shame on me. And yet knowledge of bad actors isn't encoded into the system in any way; there is, for example, no easy way for end-users to know that they have visited a site which is known to host malware, that is registered through a registrar that is known to work with spammers, that is using a certificate generated by a certifying authority in a country known for protecting hackers, and so on.

A legal/technical framework that consistently applied standards of liability for negligence and safe harbors for responsible actions could conceivably raise the level of secure behavior across the system, rather than simply playing whack-a-mole against particularly extreme bad actors such as McColo or Waledac.

Future analysis might be able to more precisely predict effects of improved security measures. For example, game theoretic or complex adaptive system simulation models of threats and responses, tied with white-hat/black-hat exercises, could suggest ranges of effectiveness, or more narrowly describe the regimes in which particular approaches might be effective. Such models might also suggest the adversary's countermoves.

Distant Third Parties

It is easy enough to imagine a broad range of regulatory regimes to apply to companies acting within the U.S., and most likely such an approach could also be introduced into close allies in the industrialized West. But how to address software vendors, hosting providers, or other services in other nations? This is the problem of the Russian Business Network (RBN), a so-called "bulletproof" network of services that has been implicated in major hacking schemes and cyberattacks. And yet due to its complicated, interlocking structure with shifting identifies (mostly forged), it is extremely difficult for agents in the West to identify a particular malefactor with any confidence. And given the lack of cooperation provided by Russian law enforcement, the RBN operates with impunity.[23] Can the overflight approach advocated here help with this situation?

It can in three ways, although of course no domestic peace-time regulatory regime will be able to fully shut down offensive capability or even action in an uncooperative nation. First, it reduces the ability of a malicious actor's ability to launch attacks from within the defensive perimeter of the United States. Most recent offensive information operations, such as the Korean attack, involved U.S.-located assets in at least some stage, whether zombie-compromised PCs on U.S. ISPs, U.S. registrars or hosting providers, botnet control communication servers (e.g. IRC servers), or even compromised machines used as botnet controllers. Increased regulatory retaliation for security failures against U.S. agencies will drive these activities overseas, making attacks easier to defend against because they will come through a much smaller number of nodes.

Second, from the other point of view, we would be denying the advantages of the use of U.S. infrastructure to malevolent actors. There's a reason that world businesses—legitimate and otherwise—want to use hosting services in the U.S.: high-quality, comparatively cheap, universally available, 24/7 electric

[21]"Web Provider Busted, Spam Drops," Stefanie Hoffman, CRN, Nov. 13, 2008, http://www.crn.com/security/212002482.

[22]"Analyzing the Aftermath of the McColo Shutdown," Steve DiBenedetto, Dan Massey, Christos Papadopoulos, Patrick Walsh, Workshop on Trust and Security in the Future Internet, (FIST'09), Seattle, WA, July 2009, downloaded from http://www.cs.colostate.edu/~christos/papers/DiBenedetto09a.pdf.

[23]*Inside Cyber Warfare: Mapping the Cyber Underworld*, Jeffrey Carr, O'Reilly Media, December 2009.

power; convenient access to electronic replacement parts (including highly available parcel delivery); and in general an uncorrupted polity in which business expenses are reasonable and predictable, and relatively safe from gang warfare. In general, the U.S. is a friendly location for Internet-based business. Denying these advantages to attackers forces them to rely on inferior infrastructure in non-cooperating nations. This is no mere coincidence: nearly by definition, those nations that refuse to prosecute cyber-crimes (because in fact cybercrime gangs are an extension of state power) are the ones where criminal elements define the rules, an inherently dangerous place for business.

Improved security will also have spill-over benefits to other nations. If large operating system vendors, for example, improve the security of their product for U.S. consumption, then the security of endpoints around the world will improve. If Tier 1 ISPs accelerate adoption of improved protocols, such as IPv6, then that will further develop the international marketplace in products and software that support those protocols, as well as validating standards of behavior that will encourage worldwide adoption. Individually these measures may not result in large improvements in security. IPv6, in par-ticular, is no guarantee of security. However, increasing U.S. spending (public and private) and activity in the realm of securing computing systems should have an aggregate benefit in reducing the cost and increasing the availability of secure software, as well as increasing the number of skilled professionals world-wide. Perhaps most importantly, it will help establish and strengthen norms of behavior among software and networking professionals and researchers that securing their products and services is a necessary element to allowing the Internet to continue to grow and thrive.

Thinking Through Active Defense in Cyberspace

Jay P. Kesan and Carol M. Hayes
University of Illinois at Urbana-Champaign

I. INTRODUCTION

To the collective eyes of the information technology (IT) industry, cyber attacks appear to occur with disturbing frequency. One source indicates that during the six months between September 2007 and March 2008, 1,300 distributed denial of service attacks (DDoS attacks) occurred each day on average.[1] The Pentagon reported being electronically attacked 6 million times during one day in 2008, and a New York executive of a financial house indicated that his company was attacked 1 million times over the course of another day.[2] The danger of cyber crime that defies jurisdictional boundaries is an example of an area where the legal approach requires updating. The current legal system is very effective at addressing attacks using conventional weapons intended to inflict bodily harm, like guns, knives, and bombs. This same legal system, however, is ill-equipped to adequately address issues surrounding attacks where the weapons and targets are computers. This paper is meant to be forward-looking, addressing the use of self defense in response to cyber attacks, which is currently a controversial topic with a questionable legal status, but this topic is also one which many members of the IT industry find attractive.

Cyber attacks, though they generally do not involve bodily harm, are nonetheless very dangerous. Massive economic damage is possible if an important server goes down due to an attack. The damage may be localized, including lost sales due to website down time and substantial costs to replace damaged hardware, but the damage can also be far-reaching due to the extent to which the modern economy relies on Internet activities.[3] Beyond economic harm, if the targeted system is part of the critical infrastructure (such as dams or power plants), damage to the system's network could have dangerous physical consequences. Cyber attacks are also very unpredictable by nature. Because malicious hackers only need a computer and an Internet connection to cause harm throughout the world, the number of possible

---

[1]Chenfeng Vincent Zhou, Christopher Leckie, Shanika Karunasekera, A survey of coordinated attacks and collaborative intrusion detection, 29 *Computers & Security* 124 (2010).

[2]Patrick W. Franzese, *Sovereignty in Cyberspace: Can It Exist?*, 64 A.F. L. Rev. 1, 2 (2009).

[3]An estimated $3.5 billion in damage was caused by the Sasser worm in 2004, which exploited a vulnerability in the Windows Operating System. Amitai Aviram, Network Responses to Network Threats: The Evolution into Private Cybersecurity Associations, in *The Law and Economics of Cybersecurity* 143, 144 (Mark F. Grady & Francesco Parisi, eds., 2006).

origins of attack is nearly limitless.[4] This inability to accurately predict the location of attackers on an on-going basis currently renders it difficult for governments to protect attack victims.

Cyber attacks, however, are just one possible avenue of cyber harm. Another category of harm may be referred to as "cyber exploitation," where the goal of the hacker is to obtain data from the target system. This is different from the idea of "cyber attacks," which are executed with the goal of causing direct harm to the target. However, there is some overlap, since an act that is considered cyber *exploitation* may be aimed at obtaining information necessary for executing a future cyber *attack*. The ideas of this paper generally apply to cyber attacks, but there are some implications for cyber exploitation as well. When an issue only implicates cyber exploitations, that term will be used. When both types of harm are implicated, the term "cyber intrusion" will be used. Otherwise, the term "cyber attack" will be used.

What sort of recourse might the organization have in the case of a malicious cyber intrusion? Currently, there are three primary options: civil liability, criminal liability, and purely defensive response. However, it would be difficult to sue the hackers because in almost all cases, hackers route their malicious signals through many different computer systems, finding vulnerable networks that the hacker can use toward his ultimate ends. Even if fast and accurate software could locate the attacking computer, it would be almost impossible to establish who was using the computer to conduct the attack. Criminal liability is also difficult because of criminal jurisdiction issues, since it could be difficult to subject the hackers to criminal liability in another country even if the attacking computer could be found using effective technology to trace the signal back to its original source *and* the human operator of the attacking computer could be identified with sufficient certainty for purposes of prosecution. A purely defensive approach is sometimes effective, but it may be inadequate for mitigating the harm to the system or deterring attacks, and therefore that approach may be insufficient as well.

A fourth more controversial option is that the actors could employ active defense by returning fire at the hackers in order to prevent further disruption of the target system. Active defense can be accomplished by using a combination of intrusion detection systems (IDS) and traceback technology, and then sending data back at the attacker to disrupt the attack. Counterstrikes of this nature have already been occurring on the Internet over the last decade, by both government[5] and private actors,[6] and full software packages designed to enable counterstriking have also been made commercially available,[7] even though such counterstrikes are of questionable legality under the current regime. It is thus apparent that cyber counterstriking is already a practice within the IT industry, and the question then arises as to whether this active defense practice of cyber counterstriking should be regulated and standardized. This paper promotes the idea that currently, technology may not be sufficient to ensure safely executed counterstrikes, and thus continued prohibition may be appropriate. Such prohibition, however, should be explicit and should be in the context of encouraging technological developments so that the sorts of behaviors that are currently being undertaken in secret may eventually be permitted within the optimal framework.

This paper will first discuss a model that evaluates factors to determine whether and when active defense is the socially optimal solution to address cyber attacks. The focus will then shift to a discussion of the policy considerations implicated by this model. What are the capabilities of the current

---

[4]Even developing countries regularly have internet kiosks available in urban areas.

[5]In late 1998, when the activist group Electronic Disturbance Theater attacked the Pentagon's website with a flood of requests, the Pentagon redirected the requests and sent graphics and messages back to the group's system to cause it to crash. Winn Schwartau, *Striking Back*, Network World (Jan. 11, 1999), http://www.networkworld.com/news/0111vigilante.html.

[6]In 2002, secure software developer Mullen developed a technology for identifying and loading a code on the attacking system in order to "neutralize" the attacking process and stop the propagation of the Code Red and Nimda worms. *See* Thomas C. Greene, *Attacking Nimda-infected Attackers*, The Register (Aug. 8, 2002), http://www.theregister.co.uk/2002/08/08/attacking_nimda infected_attackers/.

[7]In 2004, Symbiot Security announced a new product, iSIMS, that would permit firms to counterstrike when their network came under fire from malicious hackers. Press Release, Symbiot Security Announces World's First Solution to Strike Back Against Network-Based Attackers, http://www.symbiot.com/pdf/pr.030404.pdf (Mar. 4, 2004) ("Symbiot provides the equivalent of an active missile defense system.").

technology, and how might those capabilities shape policy? What sort of attacks (type and strength) could justify counterstrike? Who should be permitted to counterstrike: private companies, the government, or an agency representing the interests of both? If the government is permitted to counterstrike on the behalf of private companies, what might be some possible advantages and controversies arising from such an arrangement? If the government is involved with conducting counterstrikes, what sort of process should be utilized? Lastly, this paper will examine how to address potential harm caused to third parties by active defense.

II. GAME THEORETIC MODEL—WHEN IS ACTIVE DEFENSE THE SOCIALLY OPTIMAL SOLUTION?

In an earlier paper, we proposed using game theory to model the interaction between several measures: technology (IDS and traceback), legal remedies (criminal law and tort-based litigation), and the economic incentives to engage in active defense.[8] One observation was that sufficiently strong criminal enforcement would effectively deter cyber intrusions such that there would be no need for active defense. As noted above, however, there are significant issues with criminal enforcement of laws against cyber crime because of jurisdiction issues and the ease with which hackers can currently render themselves almost impossible to find.

One potential solution to the problem of insufficient criminal enforcement could be to coordinate an international cyber crime treaty to permit enforcement under international law. The Council of Europe's Convention on Cybercrime could potentially provide a regime for international enforcement, but the relatively low participation in the convention makes it difficult to enforce on a wide scale at this time. In an environment where there was accurate technology to identify the origin of cyber intrusions and a capability to hold the hacker criminally liable across national borders, there would be sufficient incentives against cyber crime to avoid needing active defense as an option. Proposing a specific international criminal law treaty on cyber crime is beyond the scope of this paper, but it is an action that we would support and strongly urge the international community to undertake.[9]

As discussed above, criminal enforcement is just one possible way to address cyber crime. Two other alternatives are civil litigation and a purely defensive approach. Active defense is anticipated by the model to be more appealing than civil litigation in situations where litigating would be impractical.[10] The model also concludes that active defense may be appropriate when purely defensive strategies, such as simply dropping incoming packets, would not effectively mitigate harm.

These three primary methods for addressing cyber intrusions (criminal sanctions, litigation, and purely defensive remedies), thus must all be found to be unavailable, impractical, or ineffective in order for active defense to be the socially optimal solution. The model further emphasizes the importance of the technology utilized: reasonable effort must be exerted to employ good IDS technology to assist the firm in detecting intrusions, and advanced traceback technology must also be employed to ensure that the victim firm is accurately targeting the hacker.[11]

The model also anticipates holding counterstrikers liable for damage to innocent third parties, with the expectation that potential tort liability will give firms incentive to not use unnecessary force when engaging in active defense. Potential tort liability to third parties also provides incentive for counterstrikers to use the most accurate technology. The model further posits that third-party damages are an

---

[8]Ruperto P. Majuca & Jay P. Kesan, Hacking Back: Optimal Use of Self-Defense in Cyberspace (Mar. 2009 Working Paper, Illinois Public Law Research Paper No. 08-20), available at http://papers.ssrn.com/sol3/papers.cfm?abstract_id=1363932. References to "the model" in this paper refer to the findings of this working paper.

[9]*See* Monika Ermert, *ITU Calls for Global Cybersecurity Measures, The H Security* (May 24, 2009), http://www.h-online.com/security/news/item/ITU-calls-for-global-cybersecurity-measures-741711.html (discussing proposals by the International Telecommunication Union for the establishment of a "Cybersecurity Toolkit").

[10]Majuca & Kesan, supra note 8.

[11]Id.

important factor in attaining the socially optimal solution.[12] However, some injured third parties may not have the knowledge or resources to litigate harm caused by a counterstrike, so one possibility is that active defense could be subject to government regulation to protect those third parties. The model also emphasizes that counterstrikers must be permitted to only use necessary and proportionate force and refrain from wantonly damaging hackers' systems out of retaliation.[13] The model does not, however, address who should be permitted to engage in active defense.

At its core, proportionate cyber-counterstriking is self-defense. The right to self-defense springs from the natural instinct for self-preservation, and self-defense is viewed as the use of reasonable force for self-protection. The model focuses on applying this idea of self-defense to the issue of cyber intrusions. The model promotes a view that the socially optimal solution to the threat of cyber intrusions, in the absence of effective remedies being available through criminal law enforcement, civil litigation, or effective passive defense strategies, is to permit (but not require) parties to act in self-defense when reliable technology can be utilized, subject to potential liability for harm caused to the systems of innocent third parties, whose interests are further protected by making counterstrikes subject to government regulation. This liability rule ensures that firms have sufficient incentive to utilize the most effective IDS and traceback technologies to ensure that any counterstrike will have a genuine prospect of hitting the attacker. In sum, this model provides helpful guidance concerning the optimal use of self-defense in cyberspace.

III. THE HOW, WHEN, AND WHO OF ACTIVE DEFENSE IN CYBERSPACE

Having examined the results of our model establishing the socially optimal framework for active defense, the next important questions address the technology involved in active defense, the situations where active defense would be appropriate, and who should be permitted to engage in active defense in a context where such counterstrikes are subject to government regulation. As to the latter question, the two primary possibilities are that the firms themselves could be permitted to counterstrike, or that the government could be the entity entrusted with engaging in counterstriking on behalf of the victim of the cyber intrusion.

A. The Technology Involved in Active Defense

Even in situations where permitting active defense would be socially optimal, allowing cyber counterstriking may still be irresponsible if the technology is inadequate to ensure the accuracy of counterstrikes. In-depth analysis of the full state of the art is outside of the scope of this paper, but it is important to note that the technology involved in active defense is not in its infant stages, and that it is currently the subject of a significant amount of research aimed at improving accuracy and efficiency.

Cyber attacks occur very rapidly, so responses must be prompt in order to best mitigate harm to the targeted system. Detecting a cyber intrusion may require an attack to continue for some time so that a pattern may be detected.[14] Once an attack is detected, however, tracing it to its origin can take a matter of seconds, with error potentially being measured in milliseconds.[15]

When engaging in active defense, the first essential technology is IDS, which has been developing significantly over the past decade. IDS works partly by detecting patterns of attack by a particular attacker, so there is a challenge in detecting intrusions when the intrusion is being executed remotely

[12]Id.

[13]Id.

[14]*See* Zhou, Leckie, & Karunasekera, supra note 1, at 131.

[15]*See* Ethan Katz-Bassett, et. al, Reverse Traceroute 2, 12, USENIX Symposium on Networked Systems Design & Implementation (NSDI) (2010), available at http://www.cs.washington.edu/research/networking/astronomy/reverse-traceroute.html (Awarded Best Paper). Traceroute and traceback are not interchangeable terms, but the underlying technology is similar enough that measurement of errors in traceroute may be used as a description of potential error level in traceback.

by one person attacking through thousands of compromised computers in a botnet. One possible way of addressing collaborative attacks of this nature is to develop collaborative intrusion detection systems (CIDS), and a number of researchers have been examining various methods of doing so.[16] The three primary categories for an approach to CIDS are (1) centralized; (2) hierarchical; and (3) fully distributed.[17] The Zhou et. al article provides a helpful survey of the research concerning CIDS, and also sets out the areas that should be the focus for further research in the topic, including expressiveness, scalability, and accuracy.[18]

Once an attack has been detected, the next step in active defense is to identify the source of the attack. This identification is achieved through some form of traceroute, which is the most widely used diagnostic tool on the Internet.[19] Traceroute is commonly used to evaluate Internet traffic to ensure that data is transmitted effectively, but similar technology can also be utilized to identify an attack's source, and traceroute technology used to achieve that end may be referred to as traceback. Guan's overview of network forensics provides a helpful look into the state of the art of traceback, giving summaries of the four primary IP traceback schemes: (1) active probing; (2) ICMP traceback; (3) packet marking; and (4) log-based traceback.[20] A recent study into reverse traceroute is a helpful illustration of the improvements to the technology.[21] The researchers' reverse traceroute technique was found to offer improvements over both the accuracy and coverage of traditional direct traceroute techniques.[22] The reverse traceroute study found that the median accuracy of reverse traceroute was 87%, compared to 75% median accuracy for direct traceroute.[23]

One additional concern about the technology used in active defense is that the attacker might be spoofing his IP address in order to evade detection. Issues caused by IP spoofing (including harm to third parties) would be most acute in a situation where only traceback technology was used to determine an attack's origin. However, IDS provides additional information to the victim that can indicate if the apparent origin identified by traceback may be inaccurate due to IP spoofing, and this knowledge can prevent the victim from counterstriking against an incorrect IP address, and also potentially help locate the actual source of the attack.[24]

The amount of research into IDS and traceback technology and the results of research into these topics provide strong evidence that the state of the art relevant to active defense is steadily improving. Because the state of the art indicates that the technology will eventually have the capability of addressing some current attribution problems, this paper contains a forward-looking analysis of the potential directions that might be taken by policymakers concerning active defense once the technology is sufficiently advanced. This paper focuses on an idea of active defense that utilizes IDS and traceback technology combined with counterstrikes, in a detect-trace-counterstrike pattern, where the attack is detected via IDS, traced with traceback technology, and then an active response occurs.

Further research is needed to determine what level of confidence in a traceback should be necessary to permit cyber-counterstrikes; for example, is an accuracy rating of 85% sufficient, or should counterstrikes remain illegal until traceback technology's standard error is 5% or less? While additional technological improvements would be beneficial, it is clear that the current state of the technology is adequately advanced to permit the discussion about active defense to move forward into an evaluation of how an

[16] Zhou, Leckie, & Karunasekera, supra note 1.
[17] Id.
[18] Id. at 136 (2010).
[19] Katz-Bassett, supra note 15, at 2, 12.
[20] Yong Guan, *Network Forensics* (Chapter 20), *Computer and Information Security Handbook* (2009).
[21] Katz-Bassett, supra note 15, at 2, 12.
[22] Id. at 9, 11.
[23] Id. at 9.
[24] *See* Tom Chmielarski, Intrusion Detection FAQ: Reconnaissance Techniques Using Spoofed IP Addresses, SANS (Apr. 4, 2001), http://www.sans.org/security-resources/idfaq/spoofed_ip.php. ("One way to help determine which hosts did not send the packets (and therein which host did) is to search firewall and router logs for incoming error messages from the ten hosts that were spoofed, as those hosts react to the packets sent by the target in response to the stimulus from the attacker.")

active defense scheme should be implemented, even if implementation is delayed until the technology is sufficiently accurate. Because one of the key determinants of whether active defense is socially optimal is the availability of accurate technology, this paper does not condone the current vigilante behavior of those currently using less reliable active defense techniques, and instead supports the continued prohibition of cyber-counterstriking until such time as the technology is sufficiently advanced to enable victims to obtain reliable attribution data. The goal of this paper, then, is to provide a framework that can be looked to when the circumstances are ripe for new policy concerning active defense.

B. When Would Active Defense Be Appropriate?

Having established that accurate active defense may be feasible, the discussion now turns to when active defense might be appropriate. This question has two parts: What types of intrusions may justifiably result in counterstrike, and how severe must these intrusions be?

1. What Types of Intrusions Can Be Addressed by Active Defense?

One important consideration is the type of intrusions that could be appropriately addressed using active defense. For our purposes, the key point in the process is the detection stage. Because of the nature of IDS as requiring multiple attempts at accessing the target, active defense would likely not be applicable in circumstances where the intrusion is a single event. There are two types of intrusion that this paper anticipates as being appropriate to address by active defense: DDoS attacks and spiders.

DDoS attacks would be categorized as cyber attacks. One way that a DDoS attack can be undertaken is for the attacker to compromise a large number of computers to create a hoard of zombie systems in order to flood a target with data to knock it off line. When an attacker undertakes a DDoS attack of this type, he first must identify a vulnerability to target and disseminate malicious code to take advantage of that vulnerability (like a virus or a worm) in a large number of systems (perhaps hundreds of thousands). Once the hacker has control of this zombie hoard, he has at his disposal an army of computers that can be ordered to attack repeatedly until the target is taken out. The repetitive nature of a DDoS attack makes it well-suited for the detect-trace-counterstrike pattern of active defense.

The use of spiders to mine data would be categorized as cyber exploitation, rather than cyber attack, because the goal is to obtain data, not to cause immediate harm. Because the hacker accesses the target system repeatedly, there would likely be sufficient activity for a firm's IDS to detect a pattern, making the use of spiders another kind of intrusion that can be appropriately handled using active defense. Whether active defense *should* be used to respond to the threat of spiders, however, is a question related to the severity of the attack.

2. How Severe Should an Attack Be to Justify Active Defense?

The model discussed in Section II sets out a number of factors to consider when determining if active defense is the socially optimal solution. It may be advisable, however, to establish a concrete definition to determine when counterstriking is appropriate. Walker supports a consequences-based approach, where an information-based attack (such as DDoS) would be considered an "act of violence" under international humanitarian law if said information-based attack is aimed at causing the sort of harm (including the damage or destruction of property) that international humanitarian law is intended to prevent.[25] Such an approach provides an important standard that could be applied in the context of active defense, whereby counterstriking would not be deemed an appropriate recourse except in

---

[25]Paul Walker, Rethinking Computer Network "Attack": Implications for Law and U.S. Doctrine at 23 (Journal of National Security Law and Policy, Forthcoming, 2010), available at http://papers.ssrn.com/sol3/papers.cfm?abstract_id=1586504.

relatively narrow situations where the initial intrusion was severe enough to rise to the level of being an "act of violence."

Since responsive counterstriking is most easily justified as self-defense, and the U.N. Charter permits self-defense in response to an armed attack, another standard is to look at whether the initial attack is an "armed attack" under Article 51 of the U.N. Charter. An armed attack is more than a "use of force," as discussed below, and therefore mere intrusions would not provide sufficient justification for the use of active defense. A threat to critical infrastructure, such as to an electrical grid, would probably rise to the level of being an armed attack, but it is not clear what other type of intrusion would be considered an armed attack such that self-defense would be permissible. It is also unclear whether a cyber exploitation could ever be considered an "armed attack," or if that designation would be restricted to cyber attacks.

C. Should Firms Participate Directly in Active Defense?

In the socially optimal situation where accurate technology is used and no other means of recourse would be practicable, there are potential advantages to permitting the attacked firms to counterstrike directly, such as the increased speed with which counterstrikes could be undertaken, but there are many concerns about permitting this as well. Technology often outpaces legal developments, so private sectors would likely have access to technology that potentially has significant negative effects on third parties, but that essentially exists outside the law. This could lead to hundreds of companies competing to provide IDS, traceback, and counterstrike technologies to thousands of private firms in the absence of any kind of oversight to ensure quality and protect third parties. The lack of technological uniformity could also raise issues. If there is a significant amount of variation and competition among software providers, developers may have incentive to cut costs in order to compete, leading to some software being cheaper but lower quality than others.

Beyond the issues of consistency of implementation and product quality, there is a more significant downside of entrusting active defense to private firms. Our model addressing the optimal use of active defense emphasizes that there are threshold points where permitting counterstrikes would be the socially optimal solution. However, it does not define these thresholds, and determining these thresholds requires some sort of standardization. It would be unwise to allow individual companies to make these decisions on a case by case basis. Some companies would be more risk averse, while some may be more inclined to behave like cyber vigilantes. It is thus important to not place this significant discretion in the hands of private firms, because that would result in a wide array of differing results. In order to ensure that only socially optimal usage of active defense occurs, there needs to be some form of standardization for how an active defense program is implemented. One possible way to achieve this sort of standardization is to utilize a central government entity for the purpose of deciding when counterstriking would be appropriate.

If private firms were permitted to directly engage in active defense, one possible restriction that the government could place would be a requirement that a counterstriking firm have a certain percentage of its capital invested in IT infrastructure. This could potentially help ensure that counterstriking was only engaged in by firms that had the most to lose from an attack that cripples its IT system. If this sort of restriction is adopted, it should probably not apply to firms that control essential services such as hospitals and power grids. However, given the significant downsides of permitting private firms to counterstrike directly, an alternative implementation may be advisable.

D. Should the Government Be Responsible for Conducting Active Defense?

As an alternative to entrusting active defense to the private firms who are injured by the initial cyber intrusions, the government (or a government contractor) may also be placed in charge of any counterstrike deemed necessary. This proposal has several advantages, though there are also some potential pitfalls that must be carefully monitored.

1. Advantages and Disadvantages to Requiring Government Control of Active Defense

If the government were placed in charge of any necessary counterstrike, this would simplify matters by ensuring technological uniformity in the software utilized for detection, traceback, and counterstriking. IDS and traceback technologies are developing rapidly, and having one actor responsible for acquiring the technology will ensure that the best technology is put into place for the benefit of society. Another advantage of placing the responsibility for counterstriking with government entities is that there will be uniformity of personnel, and the uniformity can help ensure that all employees responsible for counterstriking will be adequately informed of the processes and dangers.

Our previous paper concluded that a liability rule is important to preserve the optimality of active defense. Targeted firms, under such a liability rule, would be responsible for harm a counterstrike causes to innocent third parties. We also suggest retaining this liability rule if government is responsible for coordinating active defense. If the original liability rule is preserved and firms are still held responsible for harm caused to innocent third parties, on the theory that the government was acting as an agent of the counterstriking firm, that would ensure that firms will not capriciously submit a request to the relevant government agency for counterstrike assistance. A potential liability rule is discussed in more detail below in Section IV.

Another advantage of placing active defense under government control is that such a system would help to control for the dangers of rapid escalation. The future battlefields of cyber wars will likely be found in the private sector. As discussed above, some members of the private sector are already resorting to self-help to defend themselves against cyber attacks. This could lead to a dangerous pattern of attack-counterstrike-countercounterstrike that will escalate rapidly and cause significant damage. Placing control of active defense implementation with the government could help to control this and prevent potentially dangerous rapid escalation of cyber attacks.

On the other hand, there are some potential downsides of permitting the government to control all aspects of active defense. Any advantage that the government has in putting the best technology in place, for instance, is almost exclusively an advantage on the front end only, as once that technology is in place, there may be insufficient incentive to ensure that the technology is consistently kept up to date. Additionally, the nature of government action requires that all actions are undertaken slowly and carefully. While this serves to protect third parties from the hasty responses of others, it may cause issues for those who are the actual victims of attacks due to the increase in response time.

Government involvement could also lead to international political conflicts in the event that a government action has negative effects on another nation's government or population. If individual actors in one country took cyber action against aggressors in another country and inadvertently harmed innocent individuals, the government would likely not be held responsible if it did not somehow encourage the harmful acts. The same government, however, would be the party held responsible if government-sanctioned active defense caused harm to innocents in the other country. This sort of accountability could also be an advantage of government involvement, but it would likely only be optimal if governments uniformly accepted responsibility for active defense within their borders to ensure that the behavior was addressed consistently between all potentially affected countries.

2. Potential Legal Issues with Active Defense

There are many possible issues that might arise from counterstrikes. Some of these potential issues would arise in the context of counterstrikes being conducted by state actors, while other potential issues would exist regardless of the party engaging in the counterstrike.

Legal Implications Resulting from Active Defense by State Actors   Because of the nature of counterstriking, the act of mitigating harm to the victim's computer could potentially be viewed as inflicting punishment to the attacker in a manner inconsistent with Procedural Due Process under the 5th

Amendment. Under the United States Constitution, the 5th amendment's Due Process clause guarantees that procedures will be adequate to ensure against improper deprivation of life, liberty, or property.[26] However, that is why the model emphasizes the importance of only using as much force as is necessary to mitigate harm to the counterstriker.[27] Our view is that when properly executed, active defense is proportionate response, not punishment, and that it is grounded solely on self-defense and mitigation. Accepting this characterization of active defense, if there is ever an incident where the force inflicted during counterstriking is disproportionate to the amount of force inflicted during the initial intrusion, there may be a Due Process violation. However, if the model is followed appropriately, standard use of active defense should not raise due process concerns.

In addition to constitutional concerns, it is also important to consider the implications of international law. The DOD General Counsel issued an opinion in 1999 stating that the law of war should apply to cyber attacks, and therefore any attacks must be based on the necessity of war in order to avoid potential war crimes charges.[28] The law of war includes requirements such as that the attacker must be able to make effective distinction between combatants and noncombatants, that attacks be founded on military necessity, that steps are made to ensure that any collateral damage is proportionate to the military advantage attained from the attack, and that only weapons that can be targeted with precision at combatants may be used.[29] There would also be a danger of retaliation or retorsion by governments whose citizens are harmed by cyber counterstrikes executed by the U.S. government, which is another reason why it is essential for any government involvement in counterstriking to be very careful and precise. The potential danger of war crimes charges is why our previous paper on the optimality of active defense urges decisions about counterstriking to be made consistent with the idea of a just war.[30]

Other Legal Implications of Active Defense   Two other significant areas of law are implicated by active defense, regardless of the party conducting the counterstriking: international humanitarian law, and the Computer Fraud and Abuse Act (CFAA).

War crimes charges would likely only be implicated when the counterstrike is executed by the government, but some international law implications could apply even if the actor was not a state actor. Cyber counterstrikes implicate several elements of international humanitarian law. The initial attack may violate the U.N. Charter if the attack rises to the level of "use of force."[31] However, the U.N. Charter would prohibit the target of an attack from responding in self-defense unless the initial attack was severe enough to be considered an "armed attack."[32] This dichotomy indicates that it is possible for an attack to violate the U.N. Charter without the attack being severe enough to justify the use of self-defense.

On its face, the U.N. Charter applies to states, but because of the nature of cyberspace, it has become apparent to many that private entities will play a key role in future cyberwars. When many government websites operated in the country of Georgia were shut down by DDoS attacks (which evidence linked to computers in Russia), the Georgian government sought "cyber refuge" by moving many of its important websites to private servers in the United States.[33] This action was without the consent of the U.S. govern-

---

[26]US Const. amend. V. Another potentially relevant clause in the 5th amendment is the Takings Clause, which prohibits the government from taking private property for public use. If state actions cause damage to someone's computer due to cyber counterstriking, this could potentially be a taking under the 5th amendment. It is unclear, however, how Supreme Court takings jurisprudence would apply in this cyber context. Beyond the threshold question of whether a taking occurred, a takings argument would likely fail unless it is shown that the interference with computer property was related to a "public use."

[27]Majuca & Kesan, supra note 8.

[28]Office of General Counsel, Department of Defense, An Assessment of International Legal Issues in Information Operations (May 1999), available at http://www.au.af.mil/au/awc/awcgate/dod-io-legal/dod-io-legal.pdf.

[29]Id. at 10-11.

[30]Majuca & Kesan, supra note 8.

[31]U.N. Charter art. 2 para. 4.

[32]U.N. Charter art. 51.

[33]Joshua E. Kastenberg, *Non-Intervention and Neutrality in Cyberspace: An Emerging Principle in the National Practice of International Law*, 64 A.F.L. Rev. 43, 46-47 (2009).

ment, and at least one commentator views this as illustrating that international law issues like neutrality may potentially be implicated by the actions of private actors. The language of Article 51 refers to "the inherent right of individual or collective self-defense" in the event that an armed attack occurs against a U.N. Member,[34] which may suggest that individual actions may be included in the language just like state actions. Since the language seems to permit it and the reality of cyber warfare may even require it, considerations relating to articles of the U.N. Charter should be interpreted as potentially applying to private actors in the context of cyberspace where national boundaries are at best amorphous.

Another domestic legal issue is the implications for active defense from the CFAA. The CFAA's broad language prohibits knowingly transmitting data to intentionally cause damage to a protected computer, and also prohibits the intentional unauthorized accessing of a protected computer where damage is caused recklessly.[35] Some commentators have persuasively observed that even the act of tracing an attack through intermediaries might violate the CFAA if harm is caused to the intermediaries.[36] The phrase "protected computers" is defined as computers that are at least sometimes used by or for financial institutions or the U.S. government where the conduct of the offense affects that protected use, *or* computers that are used in or affect interstate or foreign commerce.[37] The latter category could potentially make all computers connected to the Internet into "protected computers" under the CFAA.

It is an issue of statutory interpretation as to whether a statute enacted in 1986 was passed with the intent that it should apply to the Internet age reality of 2010. The CFAA clearly distinguished between sections that apply to all computers and sections that apply only to "protected computers."[38] The provisions at issue here, the ones prohibiting actions that cause damage, use the phrase "protected computer," whereas provisions that just use the term "computer" cover activities like hacking into systems to obtain information relevant to national security. A broad interpretation of the phrase "protected computers" would be inconsistent with the canons of statutory interpretation, since it would mean that the phrase "protected computer" is redundant of the same concepts communicated by the larger label "computer."[39] If the CFAA was intended to potentially cover every computer in the United States as a "protected computer," there would not have been some sections that referred to "computers" while others specified "protected computers." Therefore, to preserve the vitality of the CFAA, the phrase "protected computer" must be reunderstood in the statute to bring this decades-old statute in line with the reality of the Internet age in 2010.

Preserving the vitality of the CFAA as it was intended can be accomplished in a couple of ways. First, courts can adopt a more narrow interpretation of the second half of the definition of "protected computers," interpreting it to apply only to computers containing sensitive, commerce-related information that would affect a large number of people. This could leave open the possibility of CFAA-based liability for harm caused to health institutions by active defense, without imposing liability under the CFAA for most incidental intrusions into the computers of private individuals whose computers only participate in interstate commerce by virtue of being connected to the Internet. A second way to preserve the integrity of the CFAA for these purposes would be to amend the statute to either eliminate the second half of the definition of "protected computers" or to amend the language in such a way as to narrow the scope of the definition.

International humanitarian law and the CFAA are thus two areas that must be considered when forming a policy concerning active defense. The CFAA is potentially more prohibitive of the sorts of

---

[34] U.N. Charter art. 51.

[35] 18 USC. § 1030 (2008).

[36] *See* Bruce P. Smith, *Hacking, Poaching, and Counterattacking: Digital Counterstrikes and the Contours of Self-Help*, 1 J.L. Econ. & Pol'y 171, 182 (2005).

[37] 18 USC. § 1030(e)(2) (2008).

[38] *E.g.*, 18 USC. § 1030(a)(2) (2008) ("... intentionally accesses a computer without authorization ..."); 18 USC. § 1030(a)(4) (2008) ("... knowingly and with intent to defraud, accesses a protected computer without authorization ...").

[39] 18 USC. § 1030(e)(1) (2008) ("[T]he term "computer" means an electronic, magnetic, optical, electrochemical, or other high speed data processing device performing logical, arithmetic, or storage functions ...").

behaviors that would be involved with active defense, but it is our position that a broad reading of the CFAA would be inconsistent with the canons of statutory interpretation, and thus the CFAA would likely not prove to be a substantial obstacle to implementation of a system to permit active defense.

3. *Public-Private Partnerships as an Alternative to Pure Government Control*

Even though there are several advantages to permitting the government to have control over active defense, it is important to acknowledge the weaknesses of a pure, state-run regime. As noted in subsection (1), while there is a benefit to having uniformity in software due to a single state entity having control, that benefit exists primarily on the front end, and the benefit would degrade over time if the contractor who supplies the software is not given incentive to continue to improve its product. A purely private regime, on the other hand, would be undesirable, because the lack of uniformity in software and procedure for active defense indicates that a privately run active defense regime would be unpredictable at best.

The importance of the private sector to the future of handling cyber conflicts cannot be under emphasized, however, since the private sector arguably has an interest in addressing vulnerabilities that is at least equal to that of the government. The private sector also may have access to more advanced technologies and more experts than are readily available to the government, since considerable development is undertaken as part of for-profit ventures. One core competency of the private sector, then, is its potentially superior technological expertise and access to cutting edge technology. The corresponding core competencies of the public sector include access to highly relevant, non-public information, the ability to develop uniform procedures, and its access to enforcement mechanisms. One potential way to address these disparities in strengths is to establish a public-private partnership to address active defense issues. A situation where the private sector and government routinely coordinate on matters of active defense would provide the uniformity and legal benefits of government-coordinated active defense, while taking advantage of the private sector's access to top technologies and experts.

Looking to a public-private partnership as a model could be very helpful in forming and shaping a new organization designed to bring private and public actors together to address security and active defense issues. One possible model for such a public-private partnership in this context is the Information Sharing and Analysis Centers (ISACs), which have the goal of advancing and protecting "the physical and cyber security of the critical infrastructures of North America."[40] There are several different ISACs to cover major sectors relating to critical infrastructure, including the Communications ISAC and the Information Technology ISAC.[41] The IT ISAC only lists 20 current members on its website,[42] which does not sound like a significant proportion since some sources indicate that over 70,000 IT companies exist in the United States.[43] However, the member list of the IT ISAC includes Microsoft, IBM, McAfee and Symantec, representing a significant proportion of several areas of the IT market.

The website of the IT ISAC contains several sections, most of which are viewable by members only. The public area of the website includes a Daily News section, a collection of Best Practices documents from a variety of sources, alerts and advisories issued by the United States Computer Emergency Readiness Team (US-CERT), alerts issued by X-Force (a service of IBM Internet Security Systems[44]), a form for members of the public to submit suspicious files to the organization's attention, and a collection of legal documents.[45] The sort of information that is publicly available on the IT ISAC website demonstrates the sort of coordination between private enterprise and government that characterizes public-private

---

[40]ISAC Council Home Page, http://www.isaccouncil.org/about/ (last visited July 6, 2010).

[41]Id.

[42]IT-ISAC, https://www.it-isac.org/memberlist.php (last visited July 6, 2010).

[43]Information Technology in the United States, manta.com, http://www.manta.com/mb_33_G4_000/information_technology (last visited July 6, 2010).

[44]Internet Security Systems—Research, http://xforce.iss.net/ (last visited July 8, 2010).

[45]IT-ISAC, https://www.it-isac.org/ (last visited July 6, 2010).

partnerships. An analogous arrangement in the context of active defense could consist of frequent updates concerning IDS and traceroute/traceback research, reports concerning potential cyber intrusion trends, and alerts about newly discovered vulnerabilities.

However, public-private partnerships can be difficult to implement. The private sector and government are dominated by two very different cultures, and getting the two groups to work together can be problematic. For instance, there may be a lack of trust between the two groups, with resistance on both sides to share fully with the other, leading to informational asymmetry where one party knows more than the other with respect to some matters. To mitigate these informational asymmetries, the public and private parties need to be encouraged to trust each other and share their expertise so that they can work together in a coordinated fashion in order to attain the expected synergies that drive the collaboration. If a public-private partnership is to succeed, building trust between the parties will be extremely important.

ISACs are generally not viewed as being hugely successful, in part due to the relatively low private sector participation. This low participation is perhaps due to the inherent difficulties of fostering trust between the private and public sectors, and perhaps also because of the resistance some members of the private sector might have to engaging in full cooperation and information sharing with their competitors. A full case study of the ISAC regime is outside the scope of this paper, but would likely be helpful in understanding the advantages and pitfalls of public-private partnerships in the cyber context.

E. Potential Process for Active Defense

Having evaluated the possible advantages and pitfalls of active defense, the next important consideration is the process that should be followed in the event that government-involved active defense is concluded to be the optimal approach. Because of the necessity for quick action when engaging in counterstrike, the first important point is that the process should contain elements conducive to expedited review.

One possible approach might be to establish a process that in some ways resembles the manner in which wiretapping approvals are obtained. Currently, wiretaps are available through the Foreign Intelligence Surveillance Act (FISA), which provides a process for requesting surveillance of a foreign power or an agent of a foreign power through the FISA court.[46] An analogous process could be developed whereby decisions concerning potential counterstrikes are made by an independent body staffed by persons skilled in Internet-related legal issues and who are also specialists in matters concerning complicated computer network and cyber intrusion issues. Such a body could be responsible for evaluating whether counterstrike was appropriate, and could also serve to verify the precision of the technology used.

The agency responsible for active defense must also establish criteria to clearly set forth the threshold requirements necessary to justify active defense intervention. When experiencing a cyber intrusion, the entity requiring assistance should be permitted to petition the agency for such assistance, providing specific information about the intrusion and any harm currently inflicted or anticipated to be inflicted if the harm is not mitigated. The agency in charge of active defense might decide that it would be appropriate to have higher threshold requirements in situations where the victim organization is a private entity versus when the victim organization is a government entity. Such disparate treatment may be justified given the national security importance of prompt termination of cyber intrusions on sensitive government systems. Also, the agency in charge of the active defense process could potentially contract the counterstriking activity out to a private organization with employees that fulfill government or military functions.

IV. EFFECT OF ACTIVE DEFENSE ON THIRD PARTIES

Hackers who engage in cyber intrusions generally seek to avoid getting caught, and one method that they use to evade detection is to route their message through other computers on the Internet in order

---

[46]50 USC. § 1805 (2008).

to obscure the origin of their original signal. In addition to using other computers to evade detection, a hacker who compromises a large number of systems could use those computers against the ultimate victim. One possibility is that a hacker might use a virus to gain access to the computers of unsuspecting third parties, turning the computers into "zombies." A hacker with a large army of zombie computers can now initiate DDoS attacks against a firm, flooding the firm's network with data until it crashes.[47] A firm that is monitoring for such attacks could then initiate the process necessary to counterstrike, but what if the ultimate counterstrike causes harm to the zombie computers, whose owners were not involved with or aware of the hacker's malicious intentions?

One very important concern is that these third parties, who we will refer to as "oblivious intermediaries," should be protected from damage caused by counterstrike—but if ignorance of the law is no excuse, why should ignorance of the technology (or at least the basic protections provided by easily available support software) be acceptable? In addition, in some circumstances, the oblivious intermediaries may be unaware not only of the intrusions by the initial hacker, but also of harm caused by counterstrikes. If those oblivious intermediary firms are unaware that their system has been harmed, has their system truly been harmed? And if the oblivious intermediary firms unwittingly became tools of the hacker because of their negligence in maintaining their own systems, why should they be afforded extra protection? One possible solution, then, is to afford no protection for injured third parties, because additional protection creates a moral hazard by permitting firms to avoid the consequence of their own negligence. Policymakers could point to the risk of damage due to counterstrikes as another incentive for computer operators to be more diligent in installing security updates for their operating systems and programs, as well as providing incentive for operators to be more consistent in their usage of firewalls and anti-virus/anti-malware products.

As a policy matter, however, such a harsh approach may be inappropriate. A company with a thousand responsible computer-using corporate employees should not necessarily be punished (via the denial of a remedy) for the careless actions of a single employee on the network. It is standard practice to hold a firm responsible for the negligence of its employees, but ineligibility for remedy would likely be too harsh, since it would be a per se rule that does not easily lend itself to flexibility when considering the circumstances of the situation. Therefore, the firm that finds itself as an oblivious intermediary should be afforded remedy by being permitted to sue the original target of the attack if the oblivious intermediary's system suffered harm as a result of a negligent or reckless counterstrike.

However, we are still left with the problem of avoiding the moral hazard posed by rewarding computer users who willingly remain ill-equipped to handle the threats of modern cyber attacks. The first step that should be taken is education. In order to minimize potential zombie armies, educational materials should be disseminated to underscore the importance of timely security updates and use of software packages that prevent infiltration and that detect if the system has been compromised. Using education to reduce the number of potential third parties that can be harmed could potentially ease the implementation of a liability rule as part of a regime designed to permit defensive actions under the appropriate circumstances.

Failure to protect their systems appropriately should not render parties ineligible for causes of action, but allowing the neglect of the oblivious intermediaries to decrease the damages owed may be an appropriate compromise to ensure that all firms are provided with the incentive to exercise due care in managing their IT infrastructure. Because of variations in tort law between the states, federal statutory intervention may be necessary, potentially in the form of some type of federal cybercrime tort statute. Such a statute should include provisions stating that contributory negligence is not a defense available to a counterstriker in a lawsuit brought by the oblivious intermediary. The statute should, however, make available a comparative negligence option for reducing damages owed. For example, a firm with one careless employee who inadvertently renders the firm's entire network vulnerable would

---

[47]How Zombie Computers Work, http://computer.howstuffworks.com/zombie-computer3.htm (last visited July 8, 2010).

likely be entitled to a larger damage award than a firm that lacks any systematic controls of network content and quality.

If the government is placed in control of conducting counterstrikes, one possibility to extend civil liability may be to permit suits by foreign citizens against the United States under the Federal Tort Claims Act (FTCA).[48] The government could then resolve the dispute, and then begin a new process to recover the damages from the party that required government assistance. The most significant problem with using the FTCA in this manner, however, is that the FTCA contains an exception for claims that arise in a foreign country.[49] The nature of the Internet age leads to many complications when the question becomes where a cyber harm "arises." One possible solution could be to treat the harm as arising in the state where the counterstrike began, given the almost instantaneous effect that the counterstrike would have on the third party, to be governed by the tort law for negligence of that state.

V. CONCLUSION

In certain circumstances, counterstrikes in response to cyber attacks can be the socially optimal solution. The optimal approach to active defense is to permit (but not require) counterstriking in certain circumstances, while making the exercise of counterstrikes subject to potential liability for damages that the counterstrike causes to the systems of the oblivious intermediaries whose computers have been compromised by the original hacker. Current technology is supported by a large body of research indicating a steady improvement in accuracy in active defense technologies, thus the current state of the art does not necessarily detract from the social optimality of permitting active defense, though further technological developments may be necessary if higher degrees of accuracy are found to be needed.

If active defense is deemed necessary, its existence should be carefully regulated by the government in order to prevent harm to third parties and to prevent escalation by private entities that could potentially lead to crises of international relations. It may also be advisable for a government entity to control the application of active defense in order to ensure consistency and accuracy in counterstriking. Centralizing the exercise of active defense may be preferable to permitting private firms to counterstrike directly due to the need for standardization and consistency when making determinations about whether to counterstrike. A related option could be to create a public-private partnership to address active defense issues, where government and private enterprise would work together on designing and implementing an active defense program.

There are some potential concerns with permitting the government to coordinate active defense efforts. A possible constitutional objection to state involvement in counterstrikes is the danger of a Due Process violation. This paper, however, is based in part on a model emphasizing that the force used during counterstrike should be proportionate and should be no more than that necessary to mitigate the effects of an attack. If this model is followed appropriately, there will be no Due Process violation in standard execution of active defense, because any response will be proportionate and responsive, not punitive. There are, however, other legal provisions, including the self-defense provision of the U.N. Charter, that suggest that the use of active defense would be inappropriate in most cyber intrusion situations.

If the use of active defense is limited to narrow situations and is found to not be inconsistent with current law (including the CFAA), the implications of counterstriking on third parties must also be considered. This paper stresses that the third parties whose computers are used by hackers in furthering attacks against a target must be given incentive to exercise due care in the maintenance of their systems and networks. Offering a pure liability rule that will permit these oblivious intermediaries to recover significant amounts in damages regardless of their own actions would create a moral hazard.

---

[48]See 28 USC. 1346(b) (2008).

[49]Henry Cohen and Vanessa K. Burrows, CRS Report for Congress, Federal Tort Claims Act 5 (Dec. 11, 2007), available at http://www.fas.org/sgp/crs/misc/95-717.pdf.

Avoiding this problem consists of two parts. First, people must be provided with educational material to underscore the importance of maintaining their systems adequately, including installation of all security updates and the usage of functional firewalls and anti-virus/anti-malware software packages. Second, the cause of action brought by the oblivious intermediary against the target of the hacker's attack could be governed by a new federal cybercrime tort statute, which would provide for a comparative negligence scheme, or potentially by an extension of the Federal Tort Claims Act.

In the absence of effective deterrents under international criminal law, a self-help method like active defense offers sufficient deterrence to malicious hacker activity, with the added advantage of possibly mitigating damage to the target of the intrusion. Since there are some situations where the socially optimal solution would be to permit counterstrikes, active defense should not be perpetually prohibited as a matter of policy, but it should be regulated carefully to ensure that counterstrikes are used only in the socially optimal way. Further research in this area is required to ensure the optimal implementation of a potential active defense legal regime.

Appendixes

Appendix A

Reprinted Letter Report from the Committee on Deterring Cyberattacks

March 25, 2010

Mr. Brian Overington
Assistant Deputy Director of National Intelligence
Office of the Director of National Intelligence
Washington, DC 20511

Dear Mr. Overington:

This letter report from the National Research Council's (NRC's) Committee on Deterring Cyberattacks is the first deliverable for Contract Number HHM-402-05-D-0011, DO#12. This committee (biographies of committee members are provided in Attachment 1) was created to help inform strategies for deterring cyberattacks and to develop options for U.S. policy in this area. The project statement of task is provided below:

> An ad hoc committee will oversee an activity to foster a broad, multidisciplinary examination of deterrence strategies and their possible utility to the U.S. government in its policies toward preventing cyberattacks. In the first phase, the committee will prepare a letter report identifying the key issues and questions that merit examination. In the next phase, the committee will engage experts to prepare papers that address key issues and questions, including those posed in the letter report. The papers will be compiled in a National Research Council publication and/or published by appropriate journals. This phase will include a committee meeting and a workshop to discuss draft papers, with authors finalizing the papers following the workshop.

This letter report satisfies the deliverable requirement of the first phase of the project by providing basic information needed to understand the nature of the problem and to articulate important questions that can drive research regarding ways of more effectively preventing, discouraging, and inhibiting hostile activity against important U.S. information systems and networks. (Attachment 2 acknowledges the reviewers of this letter report.) The second phase of this project will entail selection of appropriate experts to write papers on questions raised in this report. Much of the analytical framework of this letter

---

NOTE: National Research Council, "Letter Report from the Committee on Deterring Cyberattacks: Informing Strategies and Developing Options for U.S. Policy," The National Academies Press, Washington, D.C., March 25, 2010, available at http://www.nap.edu/catalog/12886.html.

report draws heavily on reports previously issued by the NRC.[1] In particular, it builds in large part on the work of a previous NRC panel (the NRC Committee on Offensive Information Warfare), which issued a report entitled *Technology, Policy, Law, and Ethics Regarding Acquisition and Use of U.S. Cyberattack Capabilities* in April 2009, and extracts without specific attribution sections from Chapters 2, 9, and 10 of that report. In addition and as requested by the Office of the Director of National Intelligence (ODNI), the committee reviewed the ODNI-provided compendiums on three summer workshops conducted by the ODNI,[2] and incorporated insights and issues from them into this report as appropriate.

This report consists of three main sections. Section 1 describes a broad context for cybersecurity, establishing its importance and characterizing the threat. Section 2 sketches a range of possible approaches for how the nation might respond to cybersecurity threats, emphasizing how little is known about how such approaches might be effective in an operational role. Section 3 describes a research agenda intended to develop more knowledge and insight into these various approaches.

As for the second phase of this project, a workshop will be held in June 2010 to discuss a number of papers that have been commissioned by the committee and possibly additional papers received through the NRC's call for papers. This call for papers is at the heart of a competition sponsored by the NRC to solicit excellent papers on the subject of cyberdeterrence. The call for papers can be found at http://sites.nationalacademies.org/CSTB/CSTB_056215.

1. THE BROAD CONTEXT FOR CYBERSECURITY[3]

Today, it is broadly accepted that the U.S. military and economic power is ever more dependent on information and information technology. Accordingly, maintaining the security of important information and information technology systems against hostile action (a topic generally referred to as "cybersecurity") is a problem of increasing importance to policy makers.

Accordingly, an important policy goal of the United States is to prevent, discourage, and inhibit hostile activity against these systems and networks. This project was established to address cyberattacks, which refer to the deliberate use of cyber operations—perhaps over an extended period of time—to alter, disrupt, deceive, degrade, usurp, or destroy adversary computer systems or networks or the information and/or programs resident in or transiting these systems or networks.[4] Cyberattack is not the same as cyber exploitation, which is an intelligence-gathering activity rather than a destructive activity and refers to the use of cyber operations—perhaps over an extended period of time—to support the goals and missions of the party conducting the exploitation, usually for the purpose of obtaining information resident on or transiting through an adversary's computer systems or networks.

Cyberattack and cyber exploitation are technically very similar, in that both require a vulnerability, access to that vulnerability, and a payload to be executed. They are technically different only in the nature of the payload to be executed. These technical similarities often mean that a targeted party may not be able to distinguish easily between a cyber exploitation and a cyberattack.

---

[1]National Research Council (NRC), *Technology, Policy, Law, and Ethics Regarding U.S. Acquisition and Use of Cyberattack Capabilities* (William Owens, Kenneth Dam, Herbert Lin, editors), The National Academies Press, Washington, D.C., 2009; NRC, *Toward a Safer and More Secure Cyberspace* (Seymour Goodman and Herbert Lin, editors), The National Academies Press, Washington, D.C., 2007.

[2]These workshops addressed the role of the private sector, deterrence, and attribution.

[3]The discussion in this section is based on Chapter 1, NRC, *Technology, Policy, Law, and Ethics Regarding U.S. Acquisition and Use of Cyberattack Capabilities*, 2009; and Chapter 2, NRC, *Toward a Safer and More Secure Cyberspace*, 2007.

[4]This report does not consider the use of electromagnetic pulse (EMP) attacks. EMP attacks typically refer to nonselective attacks using nuclear weapons to generate an intense electromagnetic pulse that can destroy all unprotected electronics and electrical components within a large area, although a tactical EMP weapon intended to selectively target such components on a small scale is possible to imagine. For a comprehensive description of the threat from EMP attacks, see *Report of the Commission to Assess the Threat to the United States from Electromagnetic Pulse (EMP) Attack*, available at http://www.globalsecurity.org/wmd/library/congress/2004_r/04-07-22emp.pdf.

Because of the ambiguity of cyberattack and cyber exploitation from the standpoint of the targeted party, it is helpful to have a word to refer to a hostile cyber activity where the nature of the activity is not known (that is, an activity that could be either a cyberattack or a cyber exploitation)—in this report, the term cyberintrusion is used to denote such activity.

The range of possibilities for cyberintrusion is quite broad.[5] A cyberattack might result in the destruction of relatively unimportant data or the loss of availability of a secondary computer system for a short period of time—or it might alter top-secret military plans or degrade the operation of a system critical to the nation, such as an air traffic control system, a power grid, or a military command and control system. Cyber exploitations might target the personal information of individual consumers or critical trade secrets of a business, military war plans, or design specifications for new weapons. Although all such intrusions are worrisome, some of these are of greater significance to the national well-being than others.

Intrusions are conducted by a range of parties, including disgruntled or curious individuals intent on vandalizing computer systems, criminals (sometimes criminal organizations) intent on stealing money, terrorist groups intent on sowing fear or seeking attention to their causes, and nation-states for a variety of national purposes. Moreover, it must be recognized that nation-states can tolerate, sponsor, or support terrorist groups, criminals, or even individuals as they conduct their intrusions. A state might tolerate individual hackers who wish to vandalize an adversary's computer systems, perhaps for the purpose of sowing chaos. Or it might sponsor or hire criminal organizations with special cyber expertise to carry out missions that it did not have the expertise to undertake. Or it might provide support to terrorist groups by looking the other way as those groups use the infrastructure of the state to conduct Internet-based operations. In times of crisis or conflict, a state might harbor (or fail to discourage, or encourage, or control) "patriotic hackers" or "cyber patriots" who conduct hostile cyberintrusions against a putative adversary. Note that many such actions would also be plausibly deniable by the government of the host state.

The threats that adversaries pose can be characterized along two dimensions—the sophistication of the intrusion and the damage it causes. Though these two are often related, they are not the same. Sophistication is needed to penetrate good cyberdefenses, and the damage an intrusion can cause depends on what the adversary does after it has penetrated those defenses. As a general rule, a greater availability of resources to the adversary (e.g., more money, time, talent) will tend to increase the sophistication of the intrusion that can be launched against any given target and thus the likelihood that the adversary will be able to penetrate the target's defenses.

Two important consequences follow from this discussion. First, because nation-state adversaries can bring to bear enormous resources to conduct an intrusion, the nation-state threat (perhaps conducted through intermediaries) is the most difficult to defend against. Second, stronger defenses reduce the likelihood but cannot eliminate the possibility that even less sophisticated adversaries can cause significant damage.

2. A RANGE OF POSSIBILITIES

The discussion below focuses primarily on cyberattacks as the primary policy concern of the United States, and addresses cyber exploitation as necessary.

2.1 The Limitations of Passive Defense and Some Additional Options

The central policy question is how to achieve a reduction in the frequency, intensity, and severity of cyberattacks on U.S. computer systems and networks currently being experienced and how to prevent the far more serious attacks that are in principle possible. To promote and enhance the cybersecurity of

---

[5]Chapter 1, NRC, *Technology, Policy, Law, and Ethics Regarding U.S. Acquisition and Use of Cyberattack Capabilities*, 2009.

important U.S. computer systems and networks (and the information contained in or passing through these systems and networks), much attention has been devoted to passive defense—measures taken unilaterally to increase the resistance of an information technology system or network to attack. These measures include hardening systems against attack, facilitating recovery in the event of a successful attack, making security more usable and ubiquitous, and educating users to behave properly in a threat environment.[6]

Passive defenses for cybersecurity are deployed to increase the difficulty of conducting the attack and reduce the likelihood that a successful attack will have significant negative consequences. But experience and recent history have shown that they do not by themselves provide an adequate degree of cybersecurity for important information systems and networks.

A number of factors explain the limitations of passive defense. As noted in previous NRC reports,[7] today's decision-making calculus regarding cybersecurity excessively focuses vendor and end-user attention on the short-term costs of improving their individual cybersecurity postures to the detriment of the national cybersecurity posture as a whole. As a result, much of the critical infrastructure on which the nation depends is inadequately protected against cyberintrusion.

A second important factor is that passive defensive measures must succeed every time an adversary conducts a hostile action, whereas the adversary's action need succeed only once. Put differently, attacks can be infinitely varied, whereas defenses are only as strong as their weakest link. This fact places a heavy and asymmetric burden on a defensive posture that employs only passive defense.

Because passive defenses do not eliminate the possibility that an attack might succeed, it is natural for policy makers to seek other mechanisms to deal with threats that passive defenses fail to address adequately. Policy makers understandably aspire to a goal of preventing cyberattacks (and cyber exploitations as well), but most importantly to a goal of preventing **serious** cyberattacks—cyberattacks that have a disabling or a crippling effect on critical societal functions on a national scale (e.g., military mission readiness, air traffic control, financial services, provision of electric power). In this context, "deterrence" refers to a tool or a method used to help achieve this goal. The term "deterrence" itself has a variety of connotations, but broadly speaking, deterrence is a tool for dissuading an adversary from taking hostile actions.

Adversaries that might conduct cyberintrusions against the United States span a broad range and may well have different objectives. Possible adversaries include nation-states that would use cyberattacks to collect intelligence, steal technology, or "prepare the battlefield" for use of cyberattacks either by themselves or as part of a broader effort (perhaps involving the use or threat of use of conventional force) to coerce the United States; sophisticated elements within a state that might not be under the full control of the central government (e.g., Iranian Revolutionary Guards); criminal organizations seeking illicit monies; terrorist groups operating without state knowledge; and so on.

In principle, policy makers have a number of approaches at their disposal to further the broad goal of preventing serious cyberattacks on the United States. In contrast to passive defense, all of these approaches depend on the ability to attribute hostile actions to specific responsible parties (although the precise definition of "responsible party" depends to a certain extent on context).

The first approach, and one of the most common, is the use of law enforcement authorities to investigate cyberattacks, and then identify and prosecute the human perpetrators who carry out these attacks. Traditionally, law enforcement actions serve two purposes. First, when successful, they remove such perpetrators from conducting further hostile action, at least for a period of time. Second, the punishment imposed on perpetrators is intended to dissuade other possible perpetrators from conducting similar actions. However, neither of these purposes can be served if the cyberattacks in question cannot be attributed to specific perpetrators.

---

[6]As an example, see NRC, *Toward a Safer and More Secure Cyberspace*, 2007.

[7]National Research Council, *Cybersecurity Today and Tomorrow: Pay Now or Pay Later*, The National Academies Press, Washington, D.C., 2002; NRC, *Toward a Safer and More Secure Cyberspace*, 2007.

In a cyber context, law enforcement investigations and prosecutions have had some success, but the time scale on which such activities yield results is typically on the order of months, during which time cyberattacks often continue to plague the victim. As a result, most victims have no way to stop an attack that is causing ongoing damage or loss of information. In addition, the likelihood that any given attack will be successfully investigated and prosecuted is low, thus reducing any potential deterrent effect. Notwithstanding the potential importance of law enforcement activities for the efficacy of possible deterrence strategies, law enforcement activities are beyond the scope of this report and will not be addressed further herein. A second approach relies on deterrence as it is classically understood. The classical model of deterrence (discussed further in Section 0) seeks to prevent hostile actions through the threat of retaliation or responsive action that imposes unacceptable costs on a potential adversary or denies an adversary the benefits that may result from taking those hostile actions. Deterrence thus includes active defense, in which actions can be taken to neutralize an incoming cyberattack. A third approach takes note of the fact that the material threat of retaliation underlying deterrence is not the only method of inhibiting undesirable behavior.

Behavioral restraint (discussed further in Section 1.2) is more often the result of formal law and informal social norms, and the burden of enforcement depends a great deal on the robustness of such rules and the pressures to conform to those rules that can be brought to bear through the social environment that the various actors inhabit.

These approaches—and indeed an approach based on passive defense—are by no means mutually exclusive. For example, some combination of strengthened passive defenses, deterrence, law enforcement, and negotiated behavioral restraint may be able to reduce the likelihood that highly destructive cyberattacks would be attempted and to minimize the consequences if cyberattacks do occur. But how well any of these approaches can or will work to prevent cyberattacks (or cyberintrusions more broadly) is open to question, and indeed is one primary subject of the papers to be commissioned for this project.

2.2 Classical Deterrence[8]

Many analysts have been drawn to the notion of deterring hostile activity against important IT systems and networks, rather than just defending against such activity. Deterrence seems like an inevitable choice in an offense-dominant world—that is, a world in which offensive technologies and tactics are generally capable of thwarting defensive efforts. As noted in Section 1.1, a major difficulty of defending against hostile actions in cyberspace arises from the asymmetry of offense versus defense.

Deterrence was and is a central construct in contemplating the use of nuclear weapons and in nuclear strategy. Because effective defenses against nuclear weapons are difficult to construct, using the threat of retaliation to persuade an adversary to refrain from using nuclear weapons is regarded by many as the most plausible and effective alternative to ineffective or useless defenses. Indeed, deterrence of nuclear threats in the Cold War establishes the paradigm in which the conditions for successful deterrence are largely met.

Although the threat of retaliation is not the only possible mechanism for practicing deterrence, such a threat is in practice the principal and most problematic method implied by use of the term.[9] Extending traditional deterrence principles to cyberattack (that is, cyberdeterrence) would suggest an approach that seeks to persuade adversaries to refrain from launching cyberattacks against U.S. interests, recognizing that cyberdeterrence would be only one of a suite of elements of U.S. national security policy.

---

[8]The discussion in Section 2.2 is based on Chapter 9, NRC, *Technology, Policy, Law, and Ethics Regarding U.S. Acquisition and Use of Cyberattack Capabilities*, 2009.

[9]Analysts also invoke the concept of deterrence by denial, which is based on the prospect of deterring an adversary through the prospect of failure to achieve its goals—facing failure, the adversary chooses to refrain from acting. But denial is—by definition—difficult to practice in an offense-dominant world.

But it is an entirely open question whether cyberdeterrence is a viable strategy. Although nuclear weapons and cyber weapons share one key characteristic (the superiority of offense over defense), they differ in many other key characteristics, and the section below discusses cyberdeterrence and when appropriate contrasts cyberdeterrence to Cold War nuclear deterrence. What the discussion below will suggest is that nuclear deterrence and cyberdeterrence do raise many of the same questions, but indeed that the answers to these questions are quite different in the cyber context than in the nuclear context.

The U.S. Strategic Command formulates deterrence as follows:[10]

> Deterrence [seeks to] **convince adversaries** not to take **actions that threaten U.S. vital interests** by means of decisive influence over their decision-making. Decisive influence is achieved by **credibly threatening** to **deny benefits** and/or **impose costs**, while **encouraging restraint** by convincing the actor that restraint will result in an **acceptable outcome**.

For purposes of this report, the above formulation will be used to organize the remainder of this section, by discussing at greater length the words in bold above. Nevertheless, the committee does recognize that there are other plausible formulations of the concept of deterrence, and that these formulations might differ in tone and nuance from that provided above.

2.2.1 *"Convince"*

At its root, convincing an adversary is a psychological process. Classical deterrence theory assumes that actors make rational assessments of costs and benefits and refrain from taking actions where costs outweigh benefits. But it assumes unitary actors (i.e., a unitary decision maker whose cost-benefit calculus is determinative for all of the forces under his control), and also that the costs and benefits of each actor are clear, well-defined, and indeed known to all other actors involved, and further that these costs and benefits are sufficiently stable over time to formulate and implement a deterrence strategy. Classical deterrence theory bears many similarities to neoclassical economics, especially in its assumptions about the availability of near-perfect information (perfect in the economic sense) about all actors.

Perhaps more importantly, real decisions often take place during periods of crisis, in the midst of uncertainty, doubt, and fear that often lead to unduly pessimistic assessments. Even a cyberattack conducted in peacetime is more likely to be carried out under circumstances of high uncertainty about the effectiveness of technology on both sides, the motivations of an adversary, and the effects of an attack.

In addition, cyber conflict is relatively new, and there is not much known about how cyber conflict would or could evolve in any given situation. History shows that when human beings with little hard information are placed into unfamiliar situations in a general environment of tension, they often substitute supposition for knowledge. In the words of a former senior administration official responsible for protecting U.S. critical infrastructure, "I have seen too many situations where government officials claimed a high degree of confidence as to the source, intent, and scope of a [cyber]attack, and it turned out they were wrong on every aspect of it. That is, they were often wrong, but never in doubt."[11]

As an example, cyber operations that would be regarded as unfriendly during normal times may be regarded as overtly hostile during periods of crisis or heightened tension. Cyber operations X, Y, and Z undertaken by party A (with a history of neutrality) may be regarded entirely differently if undertaken by party B (with a history of acting against U.S. interests). Put differently, reputations and past behavior matter—how we regard or attribute certain actions that happen today will depend on what has happened in the past.

This point has particular relevance as U.S. interest in obtaining offensive capabilities in cyberspace becomes more apparent. The United States is widely regarded as the world leader in information technology, and such leadership can easily be seen by the outside world as enabling the United States to

---

[10]U.S. Department of Defense, *Deterrence Operations: Joint Operating Concept*, Version 2.0, December 2006, available at http://www.dtic.mil/futurejointwarfare/concepts/do_joc_v20.doc.

[11]See NRC, *Technology, Policy, Law, and Ethics Regarding Acquisition and Use of U.S. Cyberattack Capabilities*, 2009, page 142.

conceal the origin of any offensive cyber operation that it might have conducted. That is, many nations will find it plausible that the United States is involved in any such operation against it, and even if no U.S.-specific "fingerprints" can be found, such a fact can easily be attributed to putative U.S. technological superiority in conducting such operations.

Lastly, a potential adversary will not be convinced to refrain from hostile action if it is not aware of measures the United States may take to retaliate. Thus, some minimum of information about deterrence policy must be known and openly declared. This point is further addressed in Section 1.1.3.

2.2.2 "Adversaries"

In the Cold War paradigm of nuclear deterrence, the world is state-centric and bipolar. It was reasonable to presume that only nation-states could afford to assemble the substantial infrastructure needed to produce the required fissile material and develop nuclear weapons and their delivery vehicles. That infrastructure was sufficiently visible that an intelligence effort directed at potential adversaries could keep track of the nuclear threat that possible adversaries posed to the United States. Today's concerns about terrorist use of nuclear weapons arise less from a fear that terrorists will develop and build their own nuclear weapons and more from a fear that they will be able to obtain nuclear weapons from a state that already has them.

These characteristics do not apply to the development of weapons for cyberattack. Many kinds of cyberattack can be launched with infrastructure, technology, and background knowledge easily and widely available to nonstate parties and small nations. Although national capabilities may be required for certain kinds of cyberattack (such as those that involve extensive hardware modification or highly detailed intelligence regarding truly closed and isolated system and networks), substantial damage can be inflicted by cyberattacks based on ubiquitous technology.

A similar analysis holds for identifying the actor responsible for an attack. In the nuclear case, an attack on the United States would have been presumed to be Soviet in origin because the world was bipolar. In addition, surveillance of potential launch areas provided high-confidence information regarding the fact of a launch, and also its geographical origin—a missile launch from the land mass of any given nation could be safely attributed to a decision by that nation's government to order that launch.

Sea-based or submarine-based launches are potentially problematic in this regard, although in a bipolar world, the Soviet Union would have been deemed responsible. In a world with three potential nuclear adversaries (the United States, Soviet Union, and China), intensive intelligence efforts have been able to maintain to a considerable extent the capability for attributing a nuclear attack to a national power, through measures such as tracking adversary ballistic missile submarines at sea. Identification of the distinctive radiological signatures of potential adversaries' nuclear weapons is also believed to have taken place.

The nuclear deterrence paradigm also presumes unitary actors, nominally governments of nation-states—that is, it presumes that the nuclear forces of a nation are under the control of the relevant government, and that they would be used only in accordance with the decisions of national leaders.

These considerations do not hold for cyberattack, and for many kinds of cyberattack the United States would almost certainly not be able to ascertain the source of such an attack, even if it were a national act, let alone hold a specific nation responsible. For example, the United States is constantly under cyberattack today, and it is widely believed (though without conclusive proof) that most of these cyberattacks are not the result of national decisions by an adversary state, though press reports have claimed that some are.

In general, prompt technical attribution of an attack or exploitation—that is, identification of the responsible party (individual? subnational group? nation-state?) based only on technical indicators associated with the event in question—is quite problematic, and any party accused of launching a given cyberintrusion could deny it with considerable plausibility. Forensic investigation might yield the identity of the responsible party, but the time scale for such investigation is often on the order of weeks or months. (Although it is often quite straightforward to trace an intrusion to the proximate node, in general, this will not be the origination point of the intrusion. Tracing an intrusion to its actual origination point past intermediate nodes is what is most difficult.)

Three factors mitigate to some (unknowable) degree this bleak picture regarding attribution. First, for reasons of its own, a cyberattacker may choose to reveal to its target its responsibility for a cyberattack. For example, it may conduct a cyberattack of limited scope to demonstrate its capability for doing so, acknowledge its responsibility, and then threaten to conduct a much larger one if certain demands are not met.[12]

Second, over time a series of cyberintrusions might be observed to share important technical features that constitute a "signature" of sorts. Thus, the target of a cyberattack may be able to say that it was victimized by a cyberattack of type X on 16 successive occasions over the last 3 months. An inference that the same party was responsible for that series of attack might under some circumstances have some plausibility.

Third, the target of a cyberattack may have nontechnical information that points to a perpetrator, such as information from a well-placed spy in an adversary's command structure or high-quality signals intelligence. If such a party reports that the adversary's forces have just launched a cyberattack against the United States, or if a generally reliable communications intercept points to such responsibility, such information might be used to make a plausible inference about the state responsible for that attack. Political leaders in particular will not rely only on technical indicators to determine the state responsible for an attack—rather, they will use all sources of information available to make the best possible determination.

Nevertheless, it is fair to say that absent unusually good intelligence information, high confidence in the attribution of a cyberattack to a nation-state is almost certain to be unattainable during and immediately after that attack, and may not be achievable for a long time afterward. Thus, any retaliatory response to a cyberattack using either cyber or kinetic weaponry may carry a significant risk of being directed improperly, perhaps with grave unintended consequences.

2.2.3 "Actions That Threaten U.S. Vital Interests"

What actions is the United States trying to deter, and would the United States know that an action has occurred that threatens its vital interests?

A nuclear explosion on U.S. territory is an unambiguously large and significant event, and there is little difficulty in identifying the fact of such an explosion. The United States maintains a global network of satellites that are capable of detecting and locating nuclear explosions in the air and on the ground, and a network of seismic sensors that provide additional information to localize nuclear explosions. Most importantly, a nuclear explosion would occur against the very quiet background of zero nuclear explosions happening over time.

But U.S. computer and communications systems and networks are under constant cyberintrusion from many different parties, and against this background noise, the United States would have to notice that critical systems and networks were being attacked and damaged. A cyberattack on the United States launched by an adversary might target multiple sites—but correlating information on attacks at different sites against a very noisy background to determine a common cause is today technically challenging. Target sets may be amorphous and complex, especially when massively complex and globally scaled supply chains are involved. And the nature of a questionable event (an intrusion) is often in doubt—is it an attack or an exploitation? If an attack, does a destructive cyberattack take place when the responsible

---

[12]Of course, a forensic investigation might *still* be necessary to rule out the possibility that the putative attacker was only claiming responsibility for the attack when in fact it had no real ability to conduct the attack on its own. To mitigate the possibility that it might not be believed, the party claiming responsibility could leave a "calling card" in the wake of an attack whose contents only it could know.

software agent is *implanted* in a critical U.S. system, or when it is *activated*? Even knowing the effect or impact of an attack or exploitation is difficult, as the consequences of some intrusions will play out only over an extended period of time. (For example, an attack may be designed to have no immediate impact and only later to show destructive consequences.)

Another profound difference between the nuclear and cyber domains is that nuclear weapons are not thought to target individual private sector entities—it would be highly unusual for a major corporation, for example, to be the specific target of a nuclear weapon. By contrast, major corporations are subject to cyberattacks and cyber exploitations on a daily basis. This difference raises the question of whether deterrence of such intrusions on individual private sector entities (especially those that are regarded as a part of U.S. critical infrastructure) is an appropriate goal of U.S. policy—as suggested by recent allegations of Chinese cyberintrusions against human rights activists using Google's gmail.com service and against multiple private sector companies in the United States seeking important intellectual property of these companies.[13] The question is important, because targeted private entities might seek to defend themselves by retaliating against attackers or cyber spies, notwithstanding criminal prohibitions, with consequences damaging to U.S. national interests.

The question is important for a number of reasons. First, U.S. military forces have not been used in recent years to support the interests of specific private sector entities, at least not as a matter of declared public policy. Thus, an explicit threat to respond with force, whether cyber or otherwise, to a cyberattack on an individual private sector entity would constitute a major change in U.S. policy. Second, targeted private entities might seek to defend themselves by retaliating against attackers or cyber spies, even though such actions are currently illegal under U.S. law, and such retaliation by these entities might well have consequences damaging to U.S. national interests.

2.2.4 *"Credible Threat"*

A credible threat is one that an adversary believes can and will be executed with a sufficiently high probability to dissuade the adversary from taking action. (The definition of "sufficiently high" is subject to much debate and almost certainly depends on the specific case or issue in question. In some cases, even a low absolute probability of executing the deterrent threat is sufficient to dissuade.) In the nuclear domain, the United States developed strategic forces with the avowed goal of making them survivable regardless of what an adversary might do. Survivability means that these forces will be able to execute the retaliatory threat for which they are responsible under any possible set of circumstances. In addition, the United States conducts many highly visible military training exercises involving both its conventional and nuclear forces, at least in part to demonstrate its capabilities to potential adversaries.

On the other hand, U.S. capabilities for offensive cyber operations are highly classified, at least in part because discussing these capabilities in the open may point the way for adversaries to counter them. That is, at least some capabilities for conducting offensive cyber operations depend on a vulnerability that an adversary would be able to fix, if only he knew about it. To the extent that U.S. capabilities for cyber operations are intended to be part of its overall deterrent posture, how should the United States demonstrate those capabilities? Or is such demonstration even necessary given widespread belief in U.S. capabilities?

A credible deterrent threat need not be limited to a response in kind—the United States has a wide variety of options for responding to any given cyberattack, depending on its scope and character; these options include a mix of changes in defense postures, law enforcement actions, diplomacy, economic actions, cyberattacks, and kinetic attacks.[14]

---

[13]See, for example, Ariana Eunjung Cha and Ellen Nakashima, "Google China Cyberattack Part of Vast Espionage Campaign, Experts Say," *Washington Post*, January 14, 2010.

[14]Chapter 1, NRC, *Technology, Policy, Law, and Ethics Regarding Acquisition and Use of U.S. Cyberattack Capabilities*, 2009. As illustrations, a change in defensive posture might include dropping low-priority services, installing security patches known to cause inconvenient but manageable operational problems, restricting access more tightly, and so on. Law enforcement actions might call

Another dimension of making a threat credible is to communicate the threat to potential adversaries. A nation's declaratory policy underpins such communication and addresses, in very general terms, why a nation acquires certain kinds of weapons and how those weapons might be used. For example, the declaratory policy of the United States regarding nuclear weapons is stated in the National Military Strategy, last published in 2004:[15]

> Nuclear capabilities [of the United States] continue to play an important role in deterrence by providing military options to deter a range of threats, including the use of WMD/E and large-scale conventional forces. Additionally, the extension of a credible nuclear deterrent to allies has been an important nonproliferation tool that has removed incentives for allies to develop and deploy nuclear forces.

For the use of cyber weapons, the United States has no declaratory policy, although the DOD Information Operations Roadmap of 2003 stated that "the USG should have a declaratory policy on the use of cyberspace for offensive cyber operations."[16]

Lastly, a "credible threat" may be based on the phenomenon of blowback, which refers to a bad consequence affecting the instigator of a particular action. In the cyberattack context, blowback may entail direct damage caused to one's own computers and networks as the result of a cyberattack that one has launched. For example, if Nation X launched a cyberattack against an adversary using a rapidly multiplying but uncustomized and indiscriminately targeted worm over the Internet, the worm might return to adversely affect Nation X's computers and networks. Blowback might also refer to indirect damage—a large-scale cyberattack by Nation X against one of its major trading partners (call it Nation Y) that affected Nation Y's economic infrastructure might have effects that could harm Nation X's economy as well. If concerns over such effects are sufficiently great, Nation X may be deterred (more precisely, self-deterred) from conducting such attacks against Nation Y (or any other major trading partner). Blowback may sometimes refer to counterproductive political consequences of an attack—for example, a cyberattack launched by a given government or political group may generate a populist backlash against that government or group if attribution of the attack can be made to the party responsible.

For blowback to be the basis of a credible threat, the dependencies that give rise to blowback should be apparent (or at least plausible) to a potential attacker. (As a possible example, it may be that given massive Chinese investment in U.S. securities, the Chinese have a large stake in the stability of U.S. financial markets, and thus might choose to refrain from an attack that might do significant harm to those markets.)

2.2.5 "Denying Benefits"

The ability to deny an adversary the benefits of an attack has two salutary results. First, an attack, if it occurs, will be futile and not confer on the adversary any particular advantage. Second, if the adversary believes (in advance) that he will not gain the hoped-for benefits, he will be much less likely to conduct the attack in the first place.

In the nuclear domain, ballistic missile defenses are believed to increase the uncertainty of an attack's success. For this reason, they need not be perfect—only good enough to significantly complicate an adversary's planning to the point at which it becomes impossible to carry out an attack with a high probability of success.

In the cyber domain, a number of approaches can be used to deny an adversary the benefits of an attack. Passive defenses can be strengthened in a number of ways, such as reducing the number of vulnerabilities present in vital systems, reducing the number of ways to access these systems, configuring

---

for investigation and prosecution of perpetrators. Diplomacy might call for demarches delivered to a perpetrator's government or severing diplomatic relations. Economic actions might involve sanctions.

[15]Joint Chiefs of Staff, "The National Military Strategy of the United States of America," 2004, available at http://www.strategic studiesinstitute.army.mil/pdffiles/nms2004.pdf.

[16]Available at http://www.gwu.edu/~nsarchiv/NSAEBB/NSAEBB177/info_ops_roadmap.pdf.

these systems to minimize their exposed security vulnerabilities, dropping traffic selectively, and so on. Properties such as rapid recoverability or reconstitution from a successful attack can be emphasized.

Active defense may also be an option. Active defense against an incoming cyberattack calls for an operation, usually a cyber operation, that can be used to neutralize that incoming attack. A responsive operation (often described within the U.S. military as a "computer network defense response action") must be conducted while the adversary's cyberattack is in progress, so that there is an access path back to the facilities being used to mount the attack. In practice, active defense is possible only for certain kinds of cyberattack (e.g., denial-of-service attacks) and even then only when the necessary intelligence information on the appropriate targets to hit is available to support a responsive operation.

On the other hand, whether improvements in denying benefits are sufficient to deter a cyber adversary is open to question. Experience to date suggests that strengthening a system's passive defense posture may discourage the casual attacker, but will only suffice to delay a determined one. That is, the only costs to the attacker result from the loss of time and thus an increased uncertainty about its ability to conduct a successful attack on a precise timetable. Such uncertainty arguably contributes to deterrence if (and only if) the action being deterred is a necessary prelude to some other kind of attack that must also be planned and executed along a particular timetable.

2.2.6 "Imposing Costs"

Costs that may be imposed on an adversary typically involve the loss of assets or functionality valued by the adversary.

In the nuclear case, the ability to attribute an attack to a national actor, coupled with a knowledge of which specific states are nuclear-capable, enables the United States to identify target sets within each potential nuclear adversary, the destruction of which the United States believes would be particularly costly to those adversaries.

In the context of cyberattack, an attacker determined to avoid U.S. retaliation may well leave a false trail for U.S. forensic investigators to follow; such a trail would either peter out inconclusively or even worse, point to another nation that might well see any U.S. action taken against it as an act of war. (Catalytic conflict, in which a third party instigates mutual hostilities between two nations, is probably much easier in cyberspace than in any other domain of potential conflict.)

That said, the ability to attribute political responsibility for a given cyberattack is the central threshold question.

If responsibility cannot be attributed, the only hope of imposing any costs at all lies in identifying an access path to the platforms involved in launching the cyberattack on U.S. interests. For example, if it is possible to identify an access path to the attacking platforms in the midst of an ongoing cyberattack, knowledge of the national (or subnational) actor's identity may not be necessary from a technical perspective to neutralize those platforms. (An analogy would be an unidentified airplane dropping bombs on a U.S. base—such an airplane could be shot down without knowing anything about the airplane or its pilot other than the fact that it was dropping bombs on a U.S. base.) Under these circumstances, a strike-back has some chance of neutralizing an incoming cyberattack even if the identity of the adversary is not known. By developing capabilities to deny the adversary a successful cyberattack through neutralization, the United States might be able to deter adversaries from launching at least certain kinds of cyberattack against the United States. Yet neutralization is likely to be difficult—destroying or degrading the source of a cyberattack while the attack is in progress may simply lead the adversary to launch the attack from a different source. It is also extremely likely that the attacking platforms will belong to innocent parties.

The attacking platforms may also be quite inexpensive—personal computers can be acquired for a few hundred dollars, and any software used to conduct an attack is virtually free to reproduce. Thus, the attacking platforms may not be assets that are particularly valuable to the attacker. Intermediate nodes that participate in an attack, such as the subverted computers of innocent parties used in a botnet, cost nothing from a capital standpoint, although they do represent some non-zero cost to the attacker of electronically capturing and subverting them.

The location(s) of the attacking platforms may be valuable to the attacker—more precisely, keeping such locations secret may be important to the attacker. But an adversary that chooses to conduct a cyberattack using platforms located in a particular location has also probably made the choice that he is willing to lose that secret location.

If responsibility can be attributed to a known actor, the range of possibilities for response becomes much larger. For example, if a nation-state can be identified as being responsible, anything of value to that state can be attacked, using any available means.[17] Indeed, options for responding to cyberattacks span a broad range and include a mix of changes in defensive postures, law enforcement actions, diplomacy, economic actions, and kinetic attacks, as well as cyberattacks.[18] Further, if individual/personal responsibility can be ascertained (or narrowed to a sufficiently small group of individuals), severe penalties could also be imposed, ranging from law enforcement prosecutions to permissible kinetic responses.

A variety of considerations might apply to choosing the appropriate retaliatory mode. For example, a "tit-for-tat" retaliatory response against an adversary might call for a cyberattack of comparable scale against a comparable target. However, a threat to do so might not be credible if the United States has a great deal to lose from such an action, thus throwing doubt on the viability of an "in-kind" deterrence strategy. On the other hand, a near-peer competitor might well be deterred from launching a large-scale cyberattack by the knowledge that it too would have much to lose if the United States launched an in-kind counterattack.

It may even be the case that when the responsible party is known, a responsive cyberattack is among the least useful tools for responding. Because a cyber adversary knows the time of his cyberattack, he can take action to mitigate the costs that the United States will attempt to impose following his attack. For example, the adversary can take steps in advance to invalidate the intelligence information on cyber targets that the defender has already collected on him, thus strengthening its defensive posture. Such an action could force the United States into either a nonselective retaliation or a retaliation delayed until new intelligence information can be collected. In the first case, the United States may not be willing to risk the large-scale escalation that might accompany a non-selective retaliatory cyberattack, and in the second case, the adversary may have already achieved its objectives by the time a new retaliatory strike can be planned.

Whether the **prompt** imposition of costs is necessary for deterrence is another unknown. U.S. nuclear forces and their command and control are structured to support prompt responses (in part because of a "use-it-or-lose-it" concern not necessarily present in a cyber context), and such a structure is believed to be an important element of deterring nuclear attack against the United States.

By contrast, the relationship between the pace at which responses are made and the deterrent effect of such responses in a cyber context is not well understood. Although a prompt response to an incoming cyberattack may have a number of possible benefits (e.g., a demonstration of resolve, an earlier termination of the damage resulting from an attack), such a response also raises the risk that a response may be

---

[17]One particular option deserves mention along these lines. As noted earlier, the U.S. Joint Chiefs of Staff write that "Nuclear capabilities . . . [provide] military options to deter a range of threats, including the use of WMD/E and large-scale conventional forces. The same document defines WMD/E as follows: "The term WMD/E relates to a broad range of adversary capabilities that pose potentially devastating impacts. WMD/E includes chemical, biological, radiological, nuclear, and enhanced high explosive weapons as well as other, more asymmetrical 'weapons.' They may rely more on disruptive impact than destructive kinetic effects. For example, cyberattacks on U.S. commercial information systems or attacks against transportation networks may have a greater economic or psychological effect than a relatively small release of a lethal agent." Although the use of nuclear weapons against a known adversary could indeed impose very substantial costs, the threat to use nuclear weapons in response to any kind of cyberattack on the United States would not be credible to all adversaries.

[18]Some of these potential responses are less escalatory (e.g., changes in defensive postures); others, more so (e.g., retaliatory cyberattacks or kinetic attacks). Implementing less escalatory responses would seem to require lower levels of authority than would more escalatory responses, and thus would be more easily undertaken.

misdirected or even undertaken mistakenly. There may be more to gain by seeking more information and being more confident about the necessary attributions.

2.2.7 "Encouraging Restraint"

Under the Cold War paradigm of nuclear deterrence, the technical prerequisite to encourage restraint on an adversary's part was the ability to execute a devastating response no matter what the adversary did first. In particular, the existence of a powerful ballistic missile submarine force was regarded as the element of force structure that precluded a successful counterforce first strike by an adversary. More abstractly, it was the existence of a secure second-strike capability that was the foundation of encouraging restraint on the adversary's part.

In the cyber environment, there appears to be no realistic possibility of a targeted counterforce attack that will eliminate a nation's ability to execute offensive operations in cyberspace. Cyberattack forces are too easily dispersed (indeed, can operate covertly in other nations) and can launch attacks from myriad venues. (A broad and indiscriminate attack on the Internet infrastructure—analogous to a countervalue strike—might make it hard to mount a response in kind, at least until Internet services were restored.)

But it is still an open question if a secure second-strike cyberattack capability is an enabling condition for encouraging restraint on an adversary's part. That is, does the existence of a secure U.S. cyberattack capability contribute materially to encouraging an adversary to refrain from conducting offensive operations against the United States in cyberspace? Or could other U.S. capabilities for responding compensate for any shortfall in U.S. cyberattack capabilities? A related question is whether U.S. cyberattack capabilities contribute to deterring hostile adversary actions outside cyberspace. In this context, pre-emption to eliminate an adversary's cyberattack capabilities does not seem likely or plausible, although U.S. cyberattack capabilities could be used to disrupt an adversary's impending kinetic attack.

Restraint is also a concept that is relevant to escalation after conflict has begun. That is, after conflict has broken out (whether in cyberspace or kinetically), policy makers will seek to deter an adversary from escalating the conflict to greater levels of violence. In general, deterring escalation requires that the adversary believe that escalation will result in a worse outcome than maintaining the status quo, which implicitly requires that the United States have reserve capabilities (whether cyber or kinetic) that can produce such an outcome.

2.2.8 "Acceptable Outcome"

Whatever else it may be, an acceptable outcome surely involves a cessation of hostilities. A cessation of hostilities necessarily involves the transmission of orders from the cognizant political authority to its "shooters" to refrain from undertaking further offensive actions. A reciprocal or mutual cessation of hostilities involves both sides taking such action, and one party's cessation is generally conditional on the other side's cessation. Each party must therefore be convinced that the other side has ceased or will cease hostilities.

When conventional or nuclear conflict is involved, a cessation of hostilities is reasonably easy to recognize—no more missiles fly, no more nuclear weapons explode, and so on. But when cyber conflict is involved, recognizing a cessation of hostilities is quite problematic.

For example, given that there exists a background level of ongoing cyberattacks affecting the United States, how would the United States recognize that an adversary had ceased its cyberattacks? What evidence would be acceptable as proof positive that an adversary was complying with a cyber cease-fire?

Cessation of hostilities may also call for the removal of destructive elements emplaced in an adversary's information technology infrastructure. For example, if the United States had implanted Trojan horse software agents useful for cyberattack in an adversary's infrastructure, it might be obliged to remove them or render them harmless under the terms of a cease-fire. This could entail either some direct communications between the United States and these agents (which could be monitored and thus could reveal sensitive operational secrets of the United States) or keeping track of where such agents were implanted. Autonomous attack agents that require no further command direction after deployment and replicate themselves as they spread through adversary networks are particularly problematic in this regard.

Finally, both sides may have actors under their nominal jurisdiction that do not necessarily respond to national decisions to cease and desist. For example, in the aftermath of the August 2001 incident in which a Chinese fighter airplane was destroyed and a U.S. reconnaissance airplane forced to land on Chinese territory, private individuals on each side (so-called "patriotic hackers") began to conduct cyberattacks against various web sites of the other. In ordinary kinetic hostilities, private individuals do not generally have the physical wherewithal to participate directly in combat operations. But where cyberattack is concerned, they often do, and "combat operations" takes on an expanded meaning of "operations that damage or destroy adversary information technology or information."

2.2.9 Observations about Cyberdeterrence

An analysis of cyberdeterrence as traditionally conceived requires a knowledge of the specific adversary being deterred, the undesirable action to be deterred, the specific threat that constitutes the basis for deterrence, and the target(s) against which the threat is to be exercised.[19] These factors are not independent—for example, the nature of the relevant specific threat and target set for effective deterrence of a nation-state may well be different than that for a terrorist group, because what is both valuable and vulnerable to the former adversary (e.g., targets of economic significance) may not be to the latter (which does not have targets of economic significance and may not care if such targets are destroyed in its host nation). In short, a generalized cyberdeterrence strategy that does not account for individual adversaries and hostile actions is less likely to succeed than one that is appropriately tailored. Of course, the price for tailored deterrence is high—a great deal of knowledge and intelligence about specific adversaries is necessary to execute such a strategy.

Where cyberattacks launched by nation-states are at issue, cyberdeterrence should not be conceptualized as being necessarily separate from other spheres of potential conflict. Although it is possible that conflict between nations might occur entirely within cyberspace, there is no reason to presume that a sufficiently serious cyberattack would not have consequences in physical space. One reason, of course, is that computer systems and the physical world often do interact—computer systems control physical artifacts and accept data from the physical world. Adversary cyberattacks may also be accompanied by other hostile behavior, such as kinetic attacks or adverse economic actions.

The threats that are at the center of deterrence need not be limited to in-kind responses. Options for responding to cyberattacks on the United States span a broad range and include a mix of changes in defensive postures, law enforcement actions, diplomacy, cyberattacks, and kinetic attacks, and there is no reason that a retaliatory cyberattack would necessarily be favored over a retaliatory kinetic attack.

There is also a broad range of conflict scenarios to which cyberdeterrence may be applicable. For example, analysts often refer to strategic or tactical conflict between adversaries. A large-scale use of cyberattack against the critical infrastructure of a nation (e.g., against its electric grid, against its financial systems) might well be regarded as strategic in nature, whereas a cyberattack against an air defense radar system would almost certainly be regarded as tactical. Such different scenarios, or scenarios located at any point along this continuum of potentially deterrable cyberattacks, may well pose different challenges for how and to what extent deterrence is relevant to them. (For example, there may well be differences in the nature of the relevant deterrent threat or the likelihood that the deterrent threat would be carried out.)

---

[19]See Box 9.1, NRC, *Technology, Policy, Law, and Ethics Regarding U.S. Acquisition and Use of Cyberattack Capabilities*, 2009.

The feasibility of cyberdeterrence and of international regimes to constrain cyberattacks on the United States is profoundly affected by the fact that the technology for cyberattacks is broadly and inexpensively available to everyone, nation-states and subnational entities down to the level of single individuals. Such broad availability means that the assumption of unitary actors is not necessarily valid.

Furthermore and as mentioned in Section 1.1.3, an environment in which certain critical infrastructures are highly interconnected across national boundaries leaves open a possibility (of unknown magnitude) that a cyberattack conducted in one nation may have global effects, including effects on the instigating nation. Perhaps the most prominent example is the existence of myriad cross-border links between financial institutions, and the consequent possibility that the U.S. financial sector (for example) might be harmed from an attack against another country's financial system.

Lastly, the private sector has a direct stake in U.S. cyberattack policy—uniquely more so than for policy regarding most other kinds of military action because of the extent of private sector ownership and operation of many of the national critical infrastructure systems that must be protected. In addition, to the extent that policy needs require certain cyberattacks to be carried out, private sector cooperation may well be required. (At the very least, accidental or inadvertent interference with a U.S. government cyberattack will have to be avoided.) And as noted in Section 1.1.2, questions arise about whether deterrence of cyberattacks against individual private sector entities is properly a component of U.S. policy. An answer in the affirmative will raise the question of whether granting private sector entities the right to engage in active defense as a response to cyberattacks directed at them would enhance or detract from cyberdeterrence.

2.3 International Regimes That Limit or Require Certain Behaviors

The preceding discussion suggests that at the very least, classical deterrence theory (as construed for deterring nuclear attacks on the United States) is quite problematic when applied to cyberattacks on the United States because many of the conditions necessary for nuclear deterrence are absent from the cyber domain.

Whether a deterrence framework can be developed for the cyber domain is open to question, and indeed is one primary subject of the papers to be commissioned for this project. But whatever the useful scope for deterrence, there may also be a complementary and helpful role for international legal regimes and codes of behavior designed to reduce the likelihood of highly destructive cyberattacks and to minimize the realized consequences if cyberattacks do occur. That is, participation in international agreements may be an important aspect of U.S. policy.

In the past, nations have pursued a variety of agreements intended to reduce the likelihood of conflict and to minimize the realized consequences if conflict does occur (and also to reduce the financial costs associated with arms competitions) under the broad rubric of arms control. To achieve these objectives, arms control regimes often seek to limit capabilities of the signatories or to constrain the use of such capabilities. Thus, in the nuclear domain, agreements have (for example) been reached to limit the number and type of nuclear weapons and nuclear weapons platforms of the signatories—a limitation on capability that putatively reduces the destructiveness of conflict by limiting the capabilities on each side.

Agreements have also been reached for purposes of constraining the use of such capabilities—for example, the United States and Russia are parties to an agreement to provide advance notice to each other of a ballistic missile launch. Other proposed restrictions on use have been more controversial—for example, nations have sometimes sought agreement on "no first use of nuclear weapons." Agreements constraining the use of such capabilities are intended to reduce the possibility of misunderstandings that might lead to conflict and thus reduce the likelihood of conflict.

Lastly, international legal regimes and codes of behavior can make certain kinds of weapons unacceptable from a normative standpoint. For example, most nations today would eschew the overt use of biological weapons, and thus the likelihood of such use by any of these nations is lower than it would be in the absence of such a behavioral norm.

In the present case (that is, in thinking about ways to prevent cyberattacks of various kinds), one of the most powerful rationales for considering international agreements in the cyber domain is that all aspects of U.S. society, both civilian and military, are increasingly dependent on information technology, and to the extent that such dependencies are greater for the United States than for other nations, restrictions on cyberattack asymmetrically benefit the United States. Proponents of such agreements also argue that aggressive pursuit of cyberattack capabilities will legitimize cyberattack as a military weapon and encourage other nations to develop such capabilities for use against the United States and its interests, much to its detriment.

Objections to such regimes usually focus on the difficulty (near-impossibility) of verifying and enforcing such an agreement. But the United States is a party to a number of difficult-to-enforce and hard-to-verify regimes that regulate conflict and prescribe rules of behavior—notably the Biological Weapons Convention (BWC). In recent years, the BWC has been criticized for lacking adequate verification provisions, and yet few policy makers suggest that the convention does not further U.S. interests.

In the cyber domain, meaningful agreements to limit acquisition of cyberattack capability are unlikely to be possible. Perhaps the most important impediment to such agreements is the verification issue—technology development for cyberattack and the testing of such technology would have few signatures that could be observed, even with the most intrusive inspection regimes imaginable.

Agreements to constrain cyberattack capabilities are also problematic, in the sense that little can be done to verify that a party to such an agreement will in fact restrict its use when it decides it needs to conduct a cyberattack. On the other hand, such agreements have a number of benefits.

- They help to create international norms regarding the acceptability of such behavior (and major nation-states tend to avoid engaging in broadly stigmatized behavior).
- They help to inhibit training that calls for such use (though secrecy will shield clandestine training).
- The violation of such agreements may be detectable. Specifically, cyberattacks that produce small-scale effects may be difficult to detect, but massively destructive attacks would be evident from their consequences, especially with appropriate rules to assist forensic assessment. If a violation is detected, the violator is subject to the consequences that follow from such detection.

Lastly, even though the development of regimes constraining use would address only cyberattacks associated with nation-states, they could have significant benefit, as nation-states do have advantages in pursuing cyberattack that most nonstate-supported actors do not have. Although such regimes would not obviate the need for passive defenses, they could be useful in tamping down risks of escalation and might help to reduce international tensions in some circumstances.

As illustrations of regimes constraining use, nations might agree to Confidence-building measures that committed them to providing mutual transparency regarding their activities in cyberspace, to cooperate on matters related to securing cyberspace (e.g., in investigating the source of an attack), to notify each other regarding certain activities that might be viewed as hostile or escalatory, or to communicate directly with each other during times of tension or crisis. Agreements to eschew certain kinds of cyberattack under certain circumstances could have value in reducing the likelihood of kinetic conflict in those cases in which such cyberattacks are a necessary prelude to a kinetic attack.

Limitations on cyber targeting (e.g., no cyberattacks on civilian targets; requirements that military computers be explicitly identified; no first use of cyberattack on a large scale; or no attacks on certain classes of targets, such as national power grids, financial markets or institutions, or air traffic control systems) could prevent or reduce the destructiveness of an attack, assuming that collateral and/or cascading damage could be limited. Agreements (or unilateral declarations) to abide by such agreements might be helpful in establishing appropriate rules of conduct (norms of behavior) and a social structure to enforce those rules.

On the other hand, U.S. policy makers and analysts have not seriously explored the utility and feasibility of international regimes that deny the legitimacy of cyberattacks on critical infrastructure assets, such as power grids, financial markets, and air traffic control systems.[20] How useful would such a regime be, especially applied in concert with a significantly improved cyberdefensive posture for these assets? How would difficulties of verification and enforcement affect relative national military postures and the credibility of the regime? What meaningful capabilities would the United States be giving up if it were to agree to such a regime? These and other related questions find few answers in the literature. The feasibility of these or other regimes to limit use of cyberattack is unclear, especially in light of the difficulties of working out the details of how the regime would actually operate. It is for this reason that research is needed to explore their feasibility.

Agreements in a cyber context might also usefully address important collateral issues, such as criminal sanctions or compensation for damages sustained under various circumstances. They might also require signatories to pass national laws that criminalize certain kinds of cyber behavior undertaken by individuals and to cooperate with other nations in prosecuting such behavior, much as the Convention on Cyber Crime has done.[21]

There are a number of major complications associated with arms control regimes for cyberattack. These include:

- The functional similarity between cyber exploitation and cyberattack. That is, from the target's perspective, it may be difficult or impossible to distinguish between a cyber operation intended for attack and one intended for exploitation. Restrictions on cyberattack will almost certainly restrict cyber exploitation to a large degree, and nations—including the United States—may well be loath to surrender even in principle any such capability for gaining intelligence.
- The lack of state monopoly over cyber weapons. For kinetic weaponry, the destructiveness and potency of any given weapon has some significant correlation with the extent to which it is only available to nation-states—almost everyone has access to rifles, whereas jet fighters and submarines are mostly restricted to nations. For cyber weapons, this correlation is far less strong, and private parties can and do wield some cyber weapons that can be as destructive and powerful as some of those wielded by nation-states. Although as a rule nation-states do have major operational advantages in conducting cyberattacks (e.g., intelligence agencies that can support cyberattack), nonstate actors are certainly capable of acquiring cyber weaponry that can cause enormous damage.
- "Positive inspection" arrangements to increase the confidence that each side is abiding by an agreement not to engage in proscribed activities could be easily thwarted or circumvented. One primary reason is that the footprint of personnel and equipment needed to conduct cyber operations is small, and thus could be located virtually anywhere in a nation (or even in another nation).
- In contrast to nuclear weapons, the private sector has essentially unlimited access to most of the technology that underlies cyberattack weapons, and the scope for destructive use varies over a much wider range. Thus, an extraordinary degree of intrusiveness would be required to impose controls on the private acquisition and use of cyber weapons. It would be impractical and unacceptable, not to mention futile, to subject every personal computer and all forms of electronic communication to inspection to ensure that cyber weapons are not present on computers or concealed within e-mails. On the other

---

[20]Indeed, the United States has until recently avoided discussions on military uses of cyberspace. In December 2009, it was publicly reported that the United States had begun to engage with Russian officials and with UN officials (see John Markoff and Andrew E. Kramer, "U.S. and Russia Open Arms Talks on Web Security," *New York Times*, December 13, 2009, available at http://www.nytimes.com/2009/12/13/science/13cyber.html), although the emphasis of the United States in these talks was apparently directed toward combating Internet crime and as a collateral effect strengthening defenses against any militarily-oriented cyberattacks.

[21]See http://conventions.coe.int/Treaty/EN/Treaties/html/185.htm.

hand, special rules might help to regulate access to the operations of critical social infrastructure in order to improve the attribution of parties that come into contact with them.

• The inherent anonymity of cyberattacks, mentioned above, greatly complicates the attribution of responsibility for an attack, and thus it is difficult to hold violators of any agreement accountable. Any alleged violation could simply be met with a strongly worded denial, and unambiguous evidence supporting the allegation would be hard to provide. Moreover, behavioral norms are generally much harder to instill and enforce in an environment in which actors can act anonymously.

Suggestions are often made to create a parallel Internet (call it an SAI, for strongly authenticated Internet) that would provide much stronger authentication of users than is required on today's Internet and would in other ways provide a much more secure environment.[22] If important facilities, such as power grids and financial institutions, migrated to an SAI, accountability for misbehavior would be much greater (because of the lack of anonymity) and the greater security of the environment would mean that only very sophisticated parties could mount attacks on it or within it.

Although the availability of an SAI would certainly improve the security environment over that of today, it is not a panacea. Perhaps most importantly, SAI users would immediately become high-priority targets to be compromised by nontechnical cyberattacks. A compromised SAI user would then become an ideal platform from which to launch IT-based cyberattacks within the SAI—and in particular, would become an ideal jumping-off point for slowly and quietly assembling an array of computing resources that can be used for attack—all of which would be on the SAI. In addition, experience with large networks indicates that maintaining an actual air-gap isolation between an SAI and the standard Internet or dial-up or wireless connections would be all but impossible—not for technical reasons but because of a human tendency to make such connections for the sake of convenience.

• Subnational groups can take action independently of governments. Subnational groups may be particularly difficult to identify, and are likely to have few if any assets that can be targeted. Some groups (such as organized hacker groups) regard counterattacks as a challenge to be welcomed rather than a threat to be feared. Finally, a subnational group composed of terrorists or insurgents might seek to provoke retaliation in order to galvanize public support for it or to provoke anti-American sentiments in its supporting public.

This last point is particularly relevant to any international agreements or regime that the United States might deem helpful in reducing cyberattacks against it—any legal agreement or regime must be respected by all parties, including the United States. If the United States wishes other nations to eschew certain actions or to abide by certain behavioral requirements or to grant it certain rights under certain circumstances, it too must be willing to do the same with respect to other nations.

As an example, some analysts have suggested that it is an appropriate strategy for the United States to seek the right to retaliate against a nation for offensive acts emanating from within its borders, even if that nation's government denies responsibility for those attacks and asserts that those responsible are nonstate actors. Doing so, they argue, would give states an incentive to crack down on harmful private offensive actors in its borders. On the other hand, it is not clear that it is in the U.S. interest for the United States to be subject to such a regime, given that parties within the United States are themselves responsible for conducting many cyberattacks against the rest of the world. Any solution proposed for other nations must (most probably) be tolerable to the United States as well, but accepting such consequences may be politically, or economically, or legally infeasible.

---

[22]For example, the White House Cyberspace Policy Review of May 2009 called for the nation to "implement, for high-value activities (e.g., the Smart Grid), an opt-in array of interoperable identity management systems to build trust for online transactions." White House, *Cyberspace Policy Review*, 2009, available at http://www.whitehouse.gov/assets/documents/Cyberspace_Policy_Review_final.pdf. More recently, a trade press article reported on the intent of the Defense Information Systems Agency of the U.S. Department of Defense to establish an enclave for its unclassified networks that is isolated from public Internet access (Amber Corrin, "DISA to Establish Safe Haven Outside the Internet," *DefenseSystems.com*, February 12, 2010, available at http://defensesystems.com/articles/2010/02/12/disa-dmz.aspx?s=ds_170210).

It should also be noted that the traditional arms control agreements are not the only form of agreement that might be helpful.[23] For example, nations have sometimes agreed on the need to protect some area of international activity such as airline transport, telecommunications, maritime activities, and so on, and have also agreed on standards for such protection. They may declare certain purposes collectively with regard to a given area of activity on which they agree, often in the form of a multilateral treaty, and then establish consensus-based multilateral institutions (generally referred to as "specialized agencies" composed of experts rather than politicians) to which to delegate (subject to continuous review) the task of implementing those agreed purposes.

It has sometimes been easier to obtain agreement among the nations involved on standards and methods concerning the civilian (commercial) aspects of a given activity than to obtain agreement on the military (governmental) aspects of the same activity.[24] For example, civil aviation is regulated internationally through agencies that have promulgated numerous agreements and regulations, all by consensus. Over the years, some precedents, and some forms of regulation, have been established, again largely by consensus, that have enhanced the protection of civilian aviation and reduced the uncertainties regarding governmental (military) aviation. A similar pattern of international regulation has resulted in increased maritime safety.

In both areas, states have agreed to criminalize terrorist attacks, and to prosecute or extradite violators. These commitments have not uniformly been kept, but security has been enhanced in these areas of international commerce because of the virtually universal support given to protecting these activities from identified threats. It is an open question whether such an approach might enhance cybersecurity internationally, whether or not it excludes any direct application or restriction on the national security activities of signatories.

2.4 Domestic Regimes to Promote Cybersecurity

Law enforcement regimes to prosecute cyber criminals are not the only ones possible to help promote cybersecurity. As noted in *Toward a Safer and More Secure Cyberspace*, the nation's cybersecurity posture would be significantly enhanced if all owners and operators of computer systems and networks took actions that are already known to improve cybersecurity. That is, the nation needs to do things that the nation already knows how to do.

What that report identified as a critical problem in cybersecurity was a failure of action. That report attributed the lack of adequate action to two factors—the fact that decision makers discount future possibilities of disaster so much that they do not see the need for present-day action (that is, they weigh the immediate costs of putting into place adequate cybersecurity measures, both technical and procedural, against the potential future benefits (actually, avoided costs) of preventing cyber disaster in the future—and systematically discount the latter as uncertain and vague) and the additional fact that the costs of inaction are not borne by the relevant decision makers (that is, the nation as a whole bears the cost of inaction, whereas the cost of action is borne by the owners and operators of critical infrastructure, which are largely private-sector companies).

Accordingly, that report called for changes in the decision-making calculus that at present excessively focuses vendor and end-user attention on the short-term costs of improving their cybersecurity postures. The report did not specify the nature of the necessary changes, but rather noted the need for more research in this area to assess the pros and cons of any given change.

The present report reiterates the importance of changing the decision-making calculus described above, but suggests that developing the necessary domestic regime (including possibly law, regulation, education, culture, and norms) to support a new calculus will demand considerable research.

---

[23]Chapter 10, NRC, *Technology, Policy, Law, and Ethics Regarding U.S. Acquisition and Use of Cyberattack Capabilities*, 2009.

[24]Abraham D. Sofaer and Seymour E. Goodman, *A Proposal for an International Convention on Cyber Crime and Terrorism*, Center for International Security and Cooperation, Stanford University, August 2000.

3. A POSSIBLE RESEARCH AGENDA

Although the preceding section seeks to describe some of the essential elements of cyberdeterrence, it is sobering to realize the enormity of intellectually unexplored territory associated with such a basic concept. Thus, the committee believes that considerable work needs to be done to explore the relevance and applicability of deterrence and prevention/inhibition to cyber conflict. At the highest level of abstraction, the central issue of interest is to identify what combinations of posture, policies, and agreements might help to prevent various actors (including state actors, nonstate actors, and organized criminals) from conducting cyberattacks that have a disabling or a crippling effect on critical societal functions on a national scale (e.g., military mission readiness, air traffic control, financial services, provision of electric power).

The broad themes described below (lettered A-H) are intended to constitute a broad forward-looking research agenda on cyberdeterrence. Within each theme are a number of elaborating questions that are illustrative of those that the committee believes would benefit from greater exploration and analysis. Thoughtful research and analysis in these areas would contribute significantly to understanding the nature of cyberdeterrence.

A. Theoretical Models for Cyberdeterrence

1. Is there a model that might appropriately describe the strategies of state actors acting in an adversarial manner in cyberspace? Is there an equilibrium state that does not result in cyber conflict?

2. How will any such deterrence strategy be affected by mercenary cyber armies for hire and/or patriotic hackers?

3. How does massive reciprocal uncertainty about the offensive cyberattack capabilities of the different actors affect the prospect of effective deterrence?

4. How might adversaries react technologically and doctrinally to actual and anticipated U.S. policy decisions intended to strengthen cyberdeterrence?

5. What are the strengths and limitations of applying traditional deterrence theory to cyber conflict?

6. What lessons and strategic concepts from nuclear deterrence are applicable and relevant to cyberdeterrence?

7. How could mechanisms such as mutual dependencies (e.g., attacks that cause actual harm to the attacker as well as to the attacked) and counterproductivity (e.g., attacks that have negative political consequences against the attacker) be used to strengthen deterrence? How might a comprehensive deterrence strategy balance the use of these mechanisms with the use of traditional mechanisms such as retaliation and passive defense?

B. Cyberdeterrence and Declaratory Policy

8. What should be the content of a declaratory policy regarding cyberintrusions (that is, cyberattacks and cyberintrusions) conducted against the United States? Regarding cyberintrusions conducted by the United States? What are the advantages and disadvantages of having an explicit declaratory policy? What purposes would a declaratory policy serve?

9. What longer-term ramifications accompany the status quo of strategic ambiguity and lack of declaratory policy?

10. What is the appropriate balance between publicizing U.S. efforts to develop cyber capabilities in order to discourage/deter attackers and keeping them secret in order to make it harder for others to foil them?

11. What is the minimum amount and type of knowledge that must be made publicly available regarding U.S. government cyberattack capabilities for any deterrence policy to be effective?

12. To the extent that a declaratory policy states what the United States will not do, what offensive operational capabilities should the United States be willing to give up in order to secure international cooperation? How and to what extent, if at all, does the answer vary by potential target (e.g., large nation-state, small nation-state, subnational group, and so on)?

13. What declaratory policy might help manage perceptions and effectively deter cyberattack?

C. Operational Considerations in Cyberdeterrence

14. On what basis can a government determine whether a given unfriendly cyber action is an attack or an exploitation? What is the significance of mistaking an attack for an exploitation or vice versa?

15. How can uncertainty and limited information about an attacker's identity (i.e., attribution), and about the scope and nature of the attack, be managed to permit policy makers to act appropriately in the event of a national crisis? How can overconfidence or excessive needs for certainty be avoided during a cyber crisis?

16. How and to what extent, if at all, should clear declaratory thresholds be established to delineate the seriousness of a cyberattack? What are the advantages and disadvantages of such clear thresholds?

17. What are the tradeoffs in the efficacy of deterrence if the victim of an attack takes significant time to measure the damage, consult, review options, and most importantly to increase the confidence that attribution of the responsible party is performed correctly?

18. How might international interdependencies affect the willingness of nations to conduct certain kinds of cyberattack on other nations? How can blowback be exploited as an explicit and deliberate component of a cyberdeterrence strategy? How can the relevant feedback loops be made obvious to a potential attacker?

19. What considerations determine the appropriate mode(s) of response (cyber, political, economic, traditional military) to any given cyberattack that calls for a response?

20. How should an ostensibly neutral nation be treated if cyberattacks emanate from its territory and that nation is unable or unwilling to stop those attacks?

21. Numerous cyberattacks on the United States and its allies have already occurred, most at a relatively low level of significance. To what extent has the lack of a public offensive response undermined the credibility of any future U.S. deterrence policy regarding cyberattack? How might credibility be enhanced?

22. How and to what extent, if at all, must the United States be willing to make public its evidence regarding the identity of a cyberattacker if it chooses to respond aggressively?

23. What is the appropriate level of government to make decisions regarding the execution of any particular declaratory or operational policy regarding cyberdeterrence? How, if at all, should this level change depending on the nature of the decision involved?

24. How might cyber operations and capabilities contribute to national military operations at the strategic and tactical levels, particularly in conjunction with other capabilities (e.g., cyberattacks aimed at disabling an opponent's defensive systems might be part of a larger operation), and how might offensive cyber capabilities contribute to the deterrence of conflict more generally?

25. How should operational policy regarding cyberattack be structured to ensure compliance with the laws of armed conflict?

26. How might possible international interdependencies be highlighted and made apparent to potential nation-state attackers?

27. What can be learned from case studies of the operational history of previous cyberintrusions? What are the lessons learned for future conflicts and crises?

28. Technical limitations on attribution are often thought to be the central impediment in holding hostile cyber actors accountable for their actions. How and to what extent would a technology infrastructure designed to support high-confidence attribution contribute to the deterrence of cyberattack and cyber exploitation, make the success of such operations less likely, lower the severity of the impact

of an attack or exploitation, and ease reconstitution and recover after an attack? What are the technical and nontechnical barriers to attributing cyberintrusions? How might these barriers be overcome or addressed in the future?

D. Regimes of Reciprocal/Consensual Limitations

29. What regimes of mutual self-restraint might help to establish cyberdeterrence (where regimes are understood to include bilateral or multilateral hard-law treaties, soft-law mechanisms [agreements short of treaty status that do not require ratification], and international organizations such as the International Telecommunication Union, the United Nations, the Internet Engineering Task Force, the Internet Corporation for Assigned Names and Numbers, and so on)? Given the difficulty of ascertaining the intent of a given cyber action (e.g., attack or exploitation) and the scope and extent of any given actor's cyber capabilities, what is the role of verification in any such regime? What sort of verification measures are possible where agreements regarding cyberattack are concerned?

30. What sort of international norms of behavior might be established among like-minded nations collectively that can help establish cyberdeterrence? What sort of self-restraint might the United States have to commit to in order to elicit self-restraint from others? What might be the impact of such self-restraint on U.S. strategies for cyber conflict? How can a "cyberattack taboo" be developed (perhaps analogous to taboos against the use of biological or nuclear weapons)?

31. How and to what extent, if any, can the potency of passive defense be meaningfully enhanced by establishing supportive agreements and operating norms?

32. How might confidence-building and stability measures (analogous to hotline communications in possible nuclear conflict) contribute to lowering the probability of crises leading to actual conflict?

33. How might agreements regarding nonmilitary dimensions of cyberintrusion support national security goals?

34. How and to what extent, if at all, should the United States be willing to declare some aspects of cyberintrusion off limits to itself? What are the tradeoffs involved in foreswearing offensive operations, either unilaterally or as part of a multilateral (or bilateral) regime?

35. What is an act of war in cyberspace? Under what circumstances can or should a cyberattack be regarded as an act of war.[25] How and to what extent do unique aspects of the cyber realm, such as reversibility of damage done during an attack and the difficulty of attribution, affect this understanding?

36. How and to what extent, if any, does the Convention on Cyber Crime (http://conventions.coe.int/Treaty/EN/Treaties/html/185.htm) provide a model or a foundation for reaching further international agreements that would help to establish cyberdeterrence?

37. How might international and national law best address the issue of patriotic hackers or cyber patriots (or even private sector entities that would like to respond to cyberattacks with cyber exploitations and/or cyberattacks of their own), recognizing that the actions of such parties may greatly complicate the efforts of governments to manage cyber conflict?

E. Cyberdeterrence in a Larger Context

38. How and to what extent, if at all, is an effective international legal regime for dealing with cyber crime a necessary component of a cyberdeterrence strategy?

39. How and to what extent, if at all, is deterrence applicable to cyberattacks on private companies (especially those that manage U.S. critical infrastructure)?

---

[25]The term "act of war" is a colloquial term that does not have a precise international legal definition. The relevant terms from the UN Charter are "use of force," "threat of force," and "armed attack," although it must be recognized that there are no internationally agreed-upon formal definitions for these terms either.

40. How should a U.S. cyberdeterrence strategy relate to broader U.S. national security interests and strategy?

F. The Dynamics of Action/Reaction

41. What is the likely impact of U.S. actions and policy regarding the acquisition and use of its own cyberattack capabilities on the courses of action of potential adversaries?

42. How and to what extent, if at all, do efforts to mobilize the United States to adopt a stronger cyberdefensive posture prompt potential adversaries to believe that cyberattack against the United States is a viable and effective means of causing damage?

G. Escalation Dynamics

43. How might conflict in cyberspace escalate from an initial attack? Once cyber conflict has broken out, how can further escalation be deterred?

44. What is the relationship between the onset of cyber conflict and the onset of kinetic conflict? How and under what circumstances might cyberdeterrence contribute, if at all, to the deterrence of kinetic conflict?

45. What safeguards can be constructed against catalytic cyberattack? Can the United States help others with such safeguards?

H. Collateral Issues

46. How and to what extent do economics and law (and regulation) affect efforts to enhance cyber-security in the private sector? What are the pros and cons of possible solution elements that may involve (among other things) regulation, liability, and standards-setting that could help to change the existing calculus regarding investment strategies and approaches to improve cybersecurity? Analogies from other "protection of the commons" problem domains (e.g., environmental protection) may be helpful.

47. What are the civil liberties implications (e.g., for privacy and free expression) of policy and technical changes aimed at preventing cyberattacks, such as systems of stronger identity management for critical infrastructure? What are the tradeoffs from a U.S. perspective? How would other countries see these tradeoffs?

48. How can the development and execution of a cyberdeterrence policy be coordinated across every element of the executive branch and with Congress? How should the U.S. government be organized to respond to cyber threats? What organizational or procedural changes should be considered, if any? What roles should the new DOD Cyber Command play? How will the DOD and the intelligence community work together in accordance with existing authorities? What new authorities would be needed for effective cooperation?

49. How and to what extent, if any, do private entities (e.g., organized crime, terrorist groups) with significant cyberintrusion capabilities affect any government policy regarding cyberdeterrence? Private entities acting outside government control and private entities acting with at least tacit government approval or support should both be considered.

50. How and to what extent are current legal authorities to conduct cyber operations (attack and exploitation) confused and uncertain? What standards should govern whether or not a given cyber operation takes place? How does today's uncertainty about authority affect the nation's ability to execute any given policy on cyberdeterrence?

51. Cyberattack can be used as a tool for offensive and defensive purposes. How should cyberattacks intended for defensive purposes (e.g., conducted as part of an active defense to neutralize an incoming attack) differ from those intended for offensive purposes (e.g., a strategic cyberattack against the critical infrastructure of an adversary)? What guidelines should structure the former as opposed to the latter?

Research contributions in these areas will have greater value if they can provide concrete analyses of the offensive actors (states, criminal organizations, patriotic hackers, terrorists, and so on), motivations (national security, financial, terrorism), actor capacities and resources, and which targets require protection beyond that afforded by passive defenses and law enforcement (e.g., military and intelligence assets, critical infrastructure, and so on).

4. CONCLUSION

The research agenda described in the questions above is intellectually challenging and fundamentally interdisciplinary. The committee hopes that a variety of scholarly communities, including those in political science, psychology, and computer science and information technology, are able to find ways of working together to address the very important question of deterring cyberattacks against the societal interests of the United States.

Moving forward and in accordance with the requirements of the relevant contract, the committee has commissioned a number of papers that address some of the questions articulated above. Drafts of these papers will be discussed in a workshop to be held in June 2010. Although resource limitations will constrain the number of papers commissioned, the committee is of the belief that all of these questions are important and deserve further significant attention.

Respectfully,

John D. Steinbruner, *Chair*
Committee on Deterring Cyberattacks
Computer Science and Telecommunications Board
Division on Engineering and Physical Sciences
Division on Policy and Global Affairs

ATTACHMENT 1
BIOGRAPHIES OF COMMITTEE MEMBERS AND STAFF

Committee Members

John D. Steinbruner, *Chair*, is a professor of public policy at the School of Public Policy at the University of Maryland and director of the Center for International and Security Studies at Maryland (CISSM). His work has focused on issues of international security and related problems of international policy. Steinbruner was director of the Foreign Policy Studies Program at the Brookings Institution from 1978 to 1996. Prior to joining Brookings, he was an associate professor in the School of Organization and Management and in the Department of Political Science at Yale University from 1976 to 1978. From 1973 to 1976, he served as an associate professor of public policy at the John F. Kennedy School of Government at Harvard University, where he also was assistant director of the Program for Science and International Affairs. He was assistant professor of government at Harvard from 1969 to 1973 and assistant professor of political science at the Massachusetts Institute of Technology from 1968 to 1969. Steinbruner has authored and edited a number of books and monographs, including: *The Cybernetic Theory of Decision: New Dimensions of Political Analysis* (Princeton University Press, originally published 1974, second paperback edition with new preface, 2002); *Principles of Global Security* (Brookings Institution Press, 2000); "A New Concept of Cooperative Security," co-authored with Ashton B. Carter and William J. Perry (*Brookings Occasional Papers*, 1992). His articles have appeared in *Arms Control Today*, *The Brookings Review*, *Dædalus*, *Foreign Affairs*, *Foreign Policy*, *International Security*, *Scientific American*, *Washington Quarterly* and other journals. Steinbruner is currently co-chair of the Committee on International Security Studies of the American Academy of Arts and Sciences, chairman of the board of the Arms Control Association, and board member of the Financial Services Volunteer Corps. He is a fellow of the American Academy of Arts and Sciences and a member of the Council on Foreign Relations. From 1981 to 2004 he was a member of the Committee on International Security and Arms Control of the National Academy of Sciences, serving as vice chair from 1996 to 2004. He was a member of the Defense Policy Board of the Department of Defense from 1993 to 1997. Born in 1941 in Denver, Colorado, Steinbruner received his A.B. from Stanford University in 1963 and his Ph.D. in political science from the Massachusetts Institute of Technology in 1968.

Steven M. Bellovin is a professor of computer science at Columbia University, where he does research on networks, security, and especially why the two don't get along. He joined the faculty in 2005 after many years at Bell Labs and AT&T Labs Research, where he was an AT&T Fellow. He received a B.A. degree from Columbia University, and an M.S. and a Ph.D. in computer science from the University of North Carolina at Chapel Hill. While a graduate student, he helped create Netnews; for this, he and the other perpetrators were given the 1995 Usenix Lifetime Achievement Award (The Flame). He is a member of the National Academy of Engineering and is serving on the Department of Homeland Security's Science and Technology Advisory Committee; he has also received the 2007 NIST/NSA National Computer Systems Security Award. Bellovin is the co-author of *Firewalls and Internet Security: Repelling the Wily Hacker*, and he holds a number patents on cryptographic and network protocols. He has served on many National Research Council study committees, including those on information systems trustworthiness, the privacy implications of authentication technologies, and cybersecurity research needs; he was also a member of the information technology subcommittee of an NRC study group on science versus terrorism. He was a member of the Internet Architecture Board from 1996 to 2002; he was co-director of the Security Area of the Internet Engineering Task Force (IETF) from 2002 through 2004.

Stephen Dycus, a professor at Vermont Law School, teaches and writes about national security and the law, water rights, and wills and trusts. The courses he has taught at Vermont Law School include International Public Law, National Security Law, Estates, Property, and Water Law. He was founding chair of the National Security Law Section, Association of American Law Schools. Dycus is the lead author of *National Security Law* (the field's leading casebook), and was a founding co-editor in chief of the *Journal of National Security Law & Policy*. Dycus earned his B.A. degree in 1963 and his LLB degree in 1965 from Southern Methodist University. He earned his LLM degree in 1976 from Harvard University. He has been a faculty member at Vermont Law School since 1976. Dycus was a visiting scholar at the University of California at Berkeley's Boalt Hall School of Law in 1983 and at the Natural Resources Defense Council in Washington, D.C., in 1991. He was a visiting professor at the United States Military Academy in West Point, New York, from 1991 to 1992 and at Petrozavodsk State University in Karelia, Russia, in 1997. Dycus is a member of the American Law Institute. Dycus also served as a reviewer of the recent NRC report *Technology, Policy, Law, and Ethics Regarding U.S. Acquisition and Use of Cyberattack Capabilities*.

Sue E. Eckert is senior fellow at the Thomas J. Watson Jr. Institute for International Studies at Brown University, after having served as assistant secretary of commerce in the Clinton administration. Her current research focuses on issues at the intersection of economic and international security—terrorist financing, targeted sanctions, and critical infrastructure. At the Watson Institute, she co-directs the projects on terrorist financing and targeted sanctions. Recent publications include: *Countering the Financing of Terrorism* (2008) and "Addressing Challenges to Targeted Sanctions: An Update of the 'Watson Report'" (2009). She works extensively with United Nations bodies to enhance the instrument of targeted sanctions. From 1993 to 1997, she was appointed by President Clinton and confirmed by the Senate as assistant secretary for export administration, responsible for U.S. dual-use export control and economic sanctions policy. Previously, she served on the professional staff of the U.S. House of Representative's Committee on Foreign Affairs, where she oversaw security/nonproliferation issues, technology transfer policies, and economic sanctions.

Jack L. Goldsmith III has been a professor of law at Harvard Law School since 2004. From 2003 to 2004 he was the assistant attorney general in the U.S. Department of Justice's Office of Legal Counsel. He was a professor of law at the University of Virginia Law School from 2003 to 2004. He served on the faculty of the University of Chicago Law School as an associate professor from 1994 to 1997 and as special counsel to the General Counsel in the Department of Defense. Goldsmith received his B.A. in philosophy summa cum laude from Washington and Lee University in 1984, a B.A. in philosophy, politics, and economics with first class honors from Oxford University in 1986, a J.D. from Yale Law School in 1989, and a diploma in private international law from The Hague Academy of International Law in 1992. After law school he clerked for Judge J. Harvie Wilkinson of the United States Court of Appeals for the Fourth Circuit, Justice Anthony M. Kennedy of the Supreme Court of the United States, and Judge George A. Aldrich of the Iran-US Claims Tribunal. He also previously has served as an associate at Covington & Burling. Goldsmith's scholarly interests include international law, foreign relations law, national security law, conflict of laws, and civil procedure. Goldsmith served on the NRC Committee on Offensive Information Warfare.

Robert Jervis is the Adlai E. Stevenson Professor of International Affairs at Columbia University. He specializes in international politics in general and security policy, decision making, and theories of conflict and cooperation in particular. His most recent book is *American Foreign Policy in a New Era* (Routledge, 2005), and he is completing a book on intelligence and intelligence failures. Among his previous books are *System Effects: Complexity in Political and Social Life* (Princeton, 1997); *The Meaning of the Nuclear Revolution* (Cornell, 1989); *Perception and Misperception in International Politics* (Princeton, 1976); and *The Logic of Images in International Relations* (Columbia, 1989). Jervis also is a coeditor of the Security Studies Series published by Cornell University Press. He serves on the board of nine scholarly journals and has authored more than 100 publications. He is a fellow of the American Association for the Advancement of Science and of the American Academy of Arts and Sciences. He has also served as president of the American Political Science Association. In 1990 he received the Grawemeyer Award for his book *The Meaning of the Nuclear Revolution*. Professor Jervis earned his B.A. from Oberlin College in 1962. He received his Ph.D. from the University of California, Berkeley in 1968. From 1968 to 1974 he was appointed an assistant (1968-1972) and associate (1972-1974) professor of government at Harvard University. From 1974 to 1980 he was a professor of political science at the University of California, Los Angeles. His research interests include international political, foreign policy, and decision making.

Jan M. Lodal was president of the Atlantic Council of the United States from October 2005 until the end of 2006. Currently, Lodal is chairman of Lodal and Company. Previously, he served as principal deputy under secretary of defense for policy and as a senior staff member of the National Security Council. He was founder, chair, and CEO of Intelus, Inc., and co-founder of American Management Systems, Inc. During the Nixon and Ford administrations, Lodal served on the White House staff as deputy for program analysis to Henry A. Kissinger, and during the Johnson administration as director of the NATO and General Purpose Force Analysis Division in the Office of the Secretary of Defense. Lodal is a member of the Board of Overseers of the Curtis Institute of Music, a Trustee of the American Boychoir, and a member of the Council on Foreign Relations and the International Institute of Strategic Studies. He was previously executive director of the Aspen Strategy Group and president of the Group Health Association. He is the author of numerous articles on public policy, arms control, and defense policy, and of *The Price of Dominance: The New Weapons of Mass Destruction and Their Challenge to American Leadership*. Lodal is the recipient of Rice University's Distinguished Alumnus Award for Public Service and Achievement in Business and was twice awarded the Department of Defense Medal for Distinguished Public Service, the Department's highest civilian honor. Lodal remains an active member of the Atlantic Council's Board and its treasurer.

Phil Venables has graduate and postgraduate qualifications in computer science and cryptography from York University and The Queen's College, Oxford, and is a chartered engineer. He has worked for more than 20 years in information technology in a number of sectors including petrochemical, defense, and finance. He has held numerous positions in information security and technology risk management at various financial institutions. He is currently managing director and chief information risk officer at Goldman Sachs. Additionally, he is on the board of directors for the Center for Internet Security and is a committee member of the U.S. Financial Sector Security Coordinating Council.

Staff

Herbert S. Lin, study director, is chief scientist for the National Research Council's Computer Science and Telecommunications Board, where he has been a study director for major projects on public policy and information technology. These studies include a 1996 study on national cryptography policy (*Cryptography's Role in Securing the Information Society*), a 1999 study of Defense Department systems for command, control, communications, computing, and intelligence (*Realizing the Potential of C4I: Fundamental Challenges*), a 2000 study on workforce issues in high-technology (*Building a Workforce for the Information Economy*), a 2004 study on aspects of the FBI's information technology modernization program (*A Review of the FBI's Trilogy IT Modernization Program*), a 2005 study on electronic voting (*Asking the Right Questions About Electronic Voting*), a 2005 study on computational biology (*Catalyzing Inquiry at the Interface of Computing and Biology*), a 2007 study on privacy and information technology (*Engaging Privacy and Information Technology in a Digital Age*), a 2007 study on cybersecurity research (*Toward a Safer and More Secure Cyberspace*), a 2009 study on health care information technology (*Computational Technology for Effective Health Care*), and a 2009 study on U.S. cyberattack policy (*Technology, Policy, Law, and Ethics Regarding Acquisition and Use of U.S. Cyberattack Capabilities*). Before his NRC service, he was a professional staff member and staff scientist for the House Armed Services Committee (1986-1990), where his portfolio included defense policy and arms control issues. He received his doctorate in physics from MIT.

Tom Arrison is a senior staff officer in the Policy and Global Affairs Division of the National Academies. He joined the National Academies in 1990 and has directed a range of studies and other projects in areas such as international science and technology relations, innovation, information technology, higher education, and strengthening the U.S. research enterprise. He holds M.A. degrees in public policy and Asian studies from the University of Michigan.

Gin Bacon Talati is a program associate for the Computer Science and Telecommunications Board of the National Academies. She formerly served as a program associate with the Frontiers of Engineering program at the National Academy of Engineering. Prior to her work at the Academies, she served as a senior project assistant in education technology at the National School Boards Association. She has a B.S. in science, technology, and culture from the Georgia Institute of Technology and an M.P.P. from George Mason University with a focus in science and technology policy.

ATTACHMENT 2
ACKNOWLEDGMENT OF REVIEWERS

This report has been reviewed in draft form by individuals chosen for their diverse perspectives and technical expertise, in accordance with procedures approved by the National Research Council's Report Review Committee. The purpose of this independent review is to provide candid and critical comments that will assist the institution in making its published report as sound as possible and to ensure that the report meets institutional standards for objectivity, evidence, and responsiveness to the study charge. The review comments and draft manuscript remain confidential to protect the integrity of the deliberative process. We wish to thank the following individuals for their review of this report:

Thomas A. Berson, Anagram Laboratories
Catherine Kelleher, Brown University
Dan Schutzer, Financial Services Technology Consortium
Jeffrey Smith, Arnold and Porter, Inc.
William A. Studeman, U.S. Navy (retired)

Although the reviewers listed above have provided many constructive comments and suggestions, they were not asked to endorse the conclusions or recommendations, nor did they see the final draft of the report before its release. The review of this report was overseen by David Clark, of the Massachusetts Institute of Technology. Appointed by the National Research Council, he responsible for making certain that an independent examination of this report was carried out in accordance with institutional procedures and that all review comments were carefully considered. Responsibility for the final content of this report rests entirely with the authoring committee and the institution.

Appendix B

Workshop Agenda

8:15   Chairman's Opening Remarks
John Steinbruner, University of Maryland

8:30   *Law and Economics of Cybersecurity*—Tyler Moore, Harvard University
Discussion Leader: Jack Goldsmith, Harvard Law School

9:15   *Paper on the Council of Europe's Convention on Cybercrime*—Michael Vatis,
Steptoe & Johnson
Discussion Leader: Sue Eckert, Brown University

10:00   Break

10:30   *Survey Paper on Challenges in Attribution*—W. Earl Boebert
Discussion Leader: Steven Bellovin, Columbia University

11:15   *Decision Making Under Uncertainty*—Rose McDermott, Brown University
Discussion Leader: Jan Lodal, Lodal and Company

Noon   Break for Lunch

12:30 PM   *The Role of Declaratory Policy in Deterring the Use of Cyber Force*—Stephen Lukasik,
Georgia Institute of Technology
Discussion Leader: Robert Jervis, Columbia University

1:15   *Civil Liberties and Privacy Implications of Policies to Prevent Cyberattacks*—Robert Gellman
Discussion Leader: Stephen Dycus, Vermont Law School

2:00   *The Role of Offensive Cyber Capability in National Military Strategy and Tactics*—Greg Rattray and Jason Healey
Discussion Leader: Committee/Staff

2:45 *Issues of Organization and Process*—Paul Rosenzweig
Discussion Leader: Jack Goldsmith

3:30 Break

4:00 *Launching "Wars" in Cyberspace: The Legal Regime*—Michael Schmitt, Durham University
Discussion Leader: Stephen Dycus

4:45 *Applicability of Traditional Deterrence Concepts and Theory to the Cyber Realm*—Patrick Morgan, University of California at Irvine
Discussion Leader: Robert Jervis

5:30 Adjourn to Reception and Working Dinner / Small Group Discussions
Keck Center—3rd Floor Atrium | 500 Fifth Street, NW

FRIDAY JULY 11, 2010

8:15 *Limitations on Offensive Operations*—Martin C. Libicki, RAND
Discussion Leader: Steven Bellovin

9:00 *Untangling Attribution*—David Clark and Susan Landau
Discussion Leader: Jan Lodal

9:45 *Possible Forms of International Cooperation for Enhancing Cyber Security*—Abraham Sofaer
Discussion Leader: Sue Eckert

10:30 Break

11:00 *Deterrence Theory and Cyber Conflict: Historical Insights and Contemporary Challenges*—Richard Weitz
Discussion Leader: John Steinbruner

11:45 *Implementing Hackback: A Policy Analysis*—Jay Kesan
Discussion Leader: Jack Goldsmith

12:30 PM Break for Lunch

1:00 *Deterring Third-party Collaboration*—Geoff Cohen
Discussion Leader: Jan Lodal

1:45 *Strategic Policies for Cyberdeterrence: A Game-Theoretic Framework*—M. Gupte, A.D. Jaggard, R. McLean, S.R. Rajagopalan, R.N. Wright
Discussion Leader: Committee/Staff

2:30 *Use of Multi-Modeling to Inform Cyber Deterrence Policy and Strategies*—Robert Elder, Alexander Levis
Discussion Leader: Steven Bellovin

Appendix C

Biosketches of Authors

W. Earl Boebert is an expert on information security, with experience in national security and intelligence as well as commercial applications. He recently retired as senior scientist at Sandia National Laboratories and currently consults for Sandia's Office of Intelligence and Counterintelligence. He has 30 years' experience in communications and computer security and is the holder or co-holder of 13 patents. Prior to joining Sandia, he was the technical founder and chief scientist of Secure Computing Corporation, where he developed the Sidewinder security server, a system that currently protects several thousand sites. Before that he worked 22 years at Honeywell, rising to the position of senior research fellow. At Honeywell Mr. Boebert worked on secure systems, cryptographic devices, flight software, and a variety of real-time simulation and control systems, and he won Honeywell's highest award for technical achievement for his part in developing a very large scale radar landmass simulator. He also developed and presented a course on systems engineering and project management that was eventually given to more than 3,000 students in 13 countries. Prior to joining Honeywell he served as an EDP Officer in the U.S. Air Force where he was awarded the Air Force Commendation Medal. He graduated from Stanford University in 1962. He has served on the National Research Council committees that produced *Computers at Risk: Computing in the Information Age; For the Record: Protecting Electronic Health Information; Information Technology for Counterterrorism: Immediate Actions and Future Possibilities;* and *Risk-Based Approaches for Securing the DOE Nuclear Weapons Complex*. He was a special advisor to the Committee on Information Systems Trustworthiness.

David Clark is a senior research scientist for the Computer Science and Artificial Intelligence Laboratory at the Massachusetts Institute of Technology. Since the mid 1970s, Dr. Clark has been leading the development of the Internet; from 1981 to 1989 he acted as chief protocol architect in this development, and he chaired the Internet Activities Board. Recent activities include extensions to the Internet to support real-time traffic, explicit allocation of service, pricing and related economic issues, and policy issues surrounding local loop employment. New activities focus on the architecture of the Internet in the post-PC era. He is a former chair of the Computer Science and Telecommunications Board of the National Research Council.

Geoff A. Cohen is a computer scientist at Elysium Digital, a technology litigation consulting company. He specializes in computer intellectual property, networking, mobile phone technology, computational biology, and security. His previous experience includes the M.I.T. Communications Futures Program, where he led the Internet Security & Privacy working group; the National Academies, where he consulted on research at the intersection of computer science and biology; the Ernst & Young Center for Business Innovation; IBM; and Data General. He also worked as an analyst in the National Security Division of the Congressional Budget Office. He holds a Ph.D. in computer science from Duke University and an A.B. from the Woodrow Wilson School of Public and International Affairs at Princeton University.

Whitfield Diffie is vice president for Information Security and Cryptography at the Internet Corporation for Assigned Names and Numbers and Visiting Scholar at the Center for International Security and Cooperation at Stanford University. He is a U.S. cryptographer and one of the pioneers of public-key cryptography. In 1991 he joined Sun Microsystems as a Distinguished Engineer, working primarily on public policy aspects of cryptography. Promoted to vice president and fellow, Diffie remained with Sun, serving as its chief security officer, until 2009. He received a bachelor of science degree in mathematics from the Massachusetts Institute of Technology in 1965. In 1992 he was awarded a doctorate in technical sciences (Honoris Causa) by the ETH Zurich and, in July 2008, a degree of doctor of science (Honoris Causa) by Royal Holloway College, University of London. He is also a fellow of the Marconi Foundation and a Franklin Institute Laureate. He has received recognition from numerous organizations, most recently the Hamming Award of the Institute for Electrical and Electronic Engineers. Diffie and Martin Hellman's 1976 paper "New Directions in Cryptography" introduced public-key cryptography, a radically new class of cryptographic system whose asymmetry made it possible to manage cryptographic keys on an unprecedented scale. The article set off an explosion of cryptographic research by academic and industrial researchers and led to the rise of an open cryptographic community. Diffie and Susan Landau's book *Privacy on the Line* about the politics of wiretapping and encryption was published in 1998; an updated and expanded edition appeared in 2007.

Robert Gellman is an information and privacy consultant. Since 1995, he has assisted large and small companies, organizations, U.S. government agencies, and foreign governments to develop, implement, and maintain policies for personal privacy and fair information practices. Specialty areas include privacy policy for health (including HIPAA), the Internet and Internet websites, the homeless (HMIS), freedom of information policy, and other information policy areas. He previously served as chief counsel for the Subcommittee on Information, Justice, Transportation, and Agriculture, part of the House Committee on Government Operations.

Carol M. Hayes completed her JD at the University of Illinois College of Law in 2010. During law school, she worked as a research assistant to Professor Jay Kesan and was the Recent Developments Editor of the *Journal of Law, Technology and Policy* (JLTP). Her student note, which was published in the Fall 2009 issue of JLTP, examined regulatory questions surrounding network neutrality. Prior to law school, Hayes received a B.A. in psychology from the University of Arkansas at Fayetteville. She is a member of the Fall 2010 class of the Christine Mirzayan Science and Technology Policy Graduate Fellowship at the National Academies, working with the Committee on Law and Justice.

Jason Healey has worked cyber security policy and operations since 1996—from the White House to Wall Street. In addition to being a world-class cyber defense strategist, he has experience in crisis management, business continuity, and intelligence collection and analysis. He is currently teaching the cyber conflict curriculum for Delta Risk to bring together national security expertise with the technical problems of conflict in cyberspace. Mr. Healey is also executive director and a founding board member of the Cyber Conflict Studies Association, which seeks to create a multidisciplinary discussion of issues related to warfare in cyberspace. Most recently, he worked for Goldman Sachs in Hong Kong—first as the Asia head of business continuity, and then as crisis manager, overseeing preparation and response for all hazards in Asia including the Sichuan earthquake, terrorist attacks in India, and the 2006 Asia-wide network outages. Earlier in his career, working from New York, Mr. Healy was Goldman's first computer emergency response coordinator and was also the vice chair of the Financial Services Information Sharing and Analysis Center. During his time at the White House as director of critical infrastructure protection, he assisted the President in prioritizing and overseeing the government's efforts in cyber security, resilient telecommunications, and infrastructure protection. He is a certified information systems security professional (CISSP) has a bachelor's degree in political science from the U.S. Air Force Academy and master's degrees in liberal arts (Johns Hopkins University) and information security (James Madison University).

Jay P. Kesan's academic interests are in the areas of technology, law, and business. Specifically, his work focuses on patent law, intellectual property, entrepreneurship, Internet law/regulation, digital government (e-gov), agricultural biotechnology law, and biofuels regulation (recent publications are on SSRN). At the University of Illinois, Professor Kesan is appointed in the College of Law, the Institute of Genomic Biology, the Information Trust Institute, the Coordinated Science Laboratory, the Department of Electrical & Computer Engineering, the Department of Agricultural & Consumer Economics, and the College of Business. Professor Kesan continues to be professionally active in the areas of patent litigation and technology entrepreneurship. He was appointed by federal judges to serve as a special master in patent litigations, and he has served as a technical and legal expert and counsel in patent matters. He also serves on the boards of directors/advisors of start-up technology companies. He serves as faculty editor-in-chief of the University of Illinois's *Journal of Law, Technology & Policy*, which published its inaugural issue in spring 2001. He has also developed an online course, "Legal Issues in Technology Entrepreneurship," supported by a grant from the Coleman Foundation. Professor Kesan received his J.D. summa cum laude from Georgetown University, where he received several awards, including the Order of the Coif, and served as associate editor of the *Georgetown Law Journal*. After graduation, he clerked for Judge Patrick E. Higginbotham of the U.S. Court of Appeals for the 5th Circuit. Prior to attending law school, Professor Kesan—who also holds a Ph.D. in electrical and computer engineering—worked as a research scientist at the IBM T.J. Watson Research Center in New York. He is a registered patent attorney and practiced at the former firm of Pennie & Edmonds LLP in the areas of patent litigation and patent prosecution. In addition, he has published numerous scientific papers and obtained several patents in the United States and abroad.

Susan Landau is a fellow at the Radcliffe Institute for Advanced Study during the academic year 2010-2011. From 1999 to 2010 Landau was a Distinguished Engineer at Sun Microsystems Laboratories, where she worked on security, cryptography, and policy, including surveillance and digital-rights management issues. Landau had previously been a faculty member at the University of Massachusetts and Wesleyan University, where her research was in algebraic algorithms. Landau's book *Surveillance or Security? The Risks of New Wiretapping Technologies* will be published by MIT Press in the spring of 2011. She is the coauthor, with Whitfeld Diffie, of *Privacy on the Line: The Politics of Wiretapping and Encryption* (MIT Press, original edition: 1998; updated and expanded edition: 2007), a participant in a 2006 ITAA study on the security risks of applying the Communications Assistance for Law Enforcement Act to VoIP, lead author on the 1994 ACM study *Codes, Keys, and Conflicts: Issues in U.S. Crypto Policy*, and author of numerous computer science and public policy papers. She has also written several op-ed pieces on computer science policy issues and has appeared on National Public Radio a number of times. Landau is a member of the National Research Council's Computer Science and Telecommunications Board, serves on the advisory committee for the National Science Foundation's Directorate for Computer and Information Science and Engineering, and serves on the Commission on Cyber Security for the 44th Presidency, established by the Center for Strategic and International Studies. She is also an associate editor for *IEEE Security and Privacy* and a section board member of *Communications of the ACM*. Landau serves on the executive council for the Association for Computing Machinery Committee on Women in Computing, and she served for many years on the Computing Research Association Committee on the

Status of Women in Computing Research. She was a member of the National Institute of Standards and Technology's Information Security and Privacy Advisory Board for 6 years. Landau is the recipient of the 2008 Women of Vision Social Impact Award, a AAAS Fellow, and an ACM Distinguished Engineer. She received her B.A. from Princeton University, her M.S. from Cornell University, and her Ph.D. from MIT.

Martin Libicki has been a senior management scientist at RAND since 1998, focusing on the impacts of information technology on domestic and national security. This work is documented in commercially published books (*Conquest in Cyberspace: National Security and Information Warfare [2007] and Information Technology Standards: Quest for the Common Byte* [1994]) as well as in numerous monographs, notably *How Insurgencies End (with Alfred Connable), How Terrorist Groups End* (with Seth Jones), *Exploring Terrorist Target Preferences* (with Peter Chalk), *Cyber-Deterrence and Cyber-War,* and *Who Runs What in the Global Information Grid.* He was also the editor of the RAND textbook *New Challenges New Tools for Defense Decisionmaking.* His most recent assignments were on the subjects of cyber/IT acquisition, multi-factor authentication, organizing the Air Force for cyber-war, exploiting cell phones in counterinsurgency, developing a post-9/11 information technology strategy for the U.S. Department of Justice, using biometrics for identity management, assessing the Defense Advanced Research Projects Agency's (DARPA's) Terrorist Information Awareness program, conducting information security analysis for the FBI, and evaluating In-Q-Tel. Prior employment includes 12 years at the National Defense University, 3 years on the Navy Staff as program sponsor for industrial preparedness, and 3 years as a policy analyst for the Government Accountability Office's (GAO's) Energy and Minerals Division. He has received a master's degree (1974) and a Ph.D. (1978) in city and regional planning, both from the University of California, Berkeley.

Steve J. Lukasik received a B.S. in physics from Rensselaer Polytechnic Institute and a Ph.D. in physics from the Massachusetts Institute of Technology. His early research at Stevens Institute of Technology was on the physics of fluids and plasmas. While a member of the Defense Advanced Research Projects Agency (DARPA), he was responsible for research in support of nuclear test ban negotiations and subsequently served from 1967 to 1974 as deputy director and director of the agency. Later government service was as chief scientist of the Federal Communications Commission (1979-1982), where he was responsible for advising the commission on technical issues in communication regulation and for the management of nongovernment use of the electromagnetic spectrum. He is a member of the International Institute for Strategic Studies, the American Physical Society, and the American Association for the Advancement of Science. Dr Lukasik was awarded the Department of Defense Distinguished Service Medal in 1973 and 1974 and a D. Eng. (Hon.) from Stevens Institute of Technology. He is a founder of *The Information Society: An International Journal,* and he has served on the boards of trustees of Harvey Mudd College and Stevens Institute of Technology. He currently holds an appointment as distinguished senior research fellow at the Center for International Strategy, Technology, and Policy, at Georgia Institute of Technology.

Rose McDermott is a fellow at the Radcliffe Institute for Advanced Study during the 2010-2011 academic year. Previously, she was a professor in the Brown University Department of Political Science. Professor McDermott's main area of research concerns political psychology in international relations. She is the author of *Risk Taking in International Relations: Prospect Theory in American Foreign Policy* (University of Michigan Press, 1998), *Political Psychology in International Relations* (University of Michigan Press, 2004), and *Presidential Illness, Leadership and Decision Making* (Cambridge University Press, 2007). She is co-editor of *Measuring Identity: A Guide for Social Science Research,* with R. Abdelal, Y. Herrera, and A. I. Johnson (Cambridge University Press, 2009). She has written numerous articles and book chapters on experimentation, evolutionary and neuroscientific models of political science, political behavior genetics, and the impact of emotion on decision making. Professor McDermott has held fellowships at the

John M. Olin Institute for Strategic Studies and the Women and Public Policy Program, both at Harvard University. Prior to joining Brown University, she was a fellow at the Stanford Center for Advanced Study in the Behavioral Sciences.

Tyler Moore is a postdoctoral fellow at Harvard University's Center for Research on Computation and Society. His research interests include the economics of information security, the study of electronic crime, and the development of policy for strengthening security. Moore completed his Ph.D. in computer science at the University of Cambridge, supervised by Professor Ross Anderson. His Ph.D. thesis investigated cooperative attack and defense in the design of decentralized wireless networks and through empirical analysis of phishing attacks on the Internet. Dr. Moore has also co-authored a report for the European Union detailing policy recommendations for overcoming failures in the provision of information security. As an undergraduate, he studied at the University of Tulsa, identifying several vulnerabilities in the public telephone network's underlying signaling protocols. He is a 2004 Marshall Scholar.

Patrick M. Morgan is the Tierney Chair of Peace & Conflict in the Political Science Department at University of California, Irvine's School of Social Sciences. Professor Morgan has concentrated his research primarily on national and international security matters—deterrence theory, strategic surprise attack, arms control, and related subjects. He has also had a longstanding interest in theoretical approaches to the study of international politics. Currently he is involved in projects on the theory and practice of deterrence in the post-Cold War era, security strategies for global security management, and security in Northeast Asia.

Gregory Rattray is an internationally recognized cyber defense and policy expert with more than 20 years of experience in cyber security, operations, and intelligence. He served as the director of cyber security on the White House National Security Council Staff under Richard Clarke and Dr. Condoleezza Rice. He is currently the chief Internet security advisor for ICANN—the Internet Corporation for Assigned Names and Numbers—and he continues to advise the White House, Department of Defense, intelligence community, academic education, and research programs on global risk and enterprise policy. Additionally, Mr. Rattray is a partner at Delta Risk, where he provides consulting services for the development of cyber security initiatives across both the government and private sectors. From 2003 to 2005, while serving as the director for cyber security on the National Security Council (NSC), he led national policy development and NSC oversight for cyber security to include the Executive Order on Information Sharing, Homeland Security Policy Directives on Critical Infrastructure and Incident Response, the establishment of cyber security roles for the Department of Homeland Security, and interagency responsibilities in the National Response Plan. Prior to working on the NSC, he was an Air Force fellow serving the President's Critical Infrastructure Protection Board. During his tenure he was a key contributor to the President's National Strategy to Secure Cyberspace and served on the White House team for legislation and policy on establishment of the Department of Homeland Security.

Paul Rosenzweig is the founder of Red Branch Consulting PLLC, which provides comprehensive advice to companies, individuals, and governments seeking homeland security and privacy solutions for the challenges they face. Mr. Rosenzweig formerly served as deputy assistant secretary for policy in the Department of Homeland Security and twice as acting assistant secretary for international affairs. He also serves as an adjunct professor at the National Defense University, College of International Security Affairs, a professorial lecturer in law at George Washington University, a senior editor of the *Journal of National Security Law & Policy*, and as a visiting fellow at the Heritage Foundation. Mr. Rosenzweig is a cum laude graduate of the University of Chicago Law School. He has an M.S. in chemical oceanography from the Scripps Institution of Oceanography, University of California at San Diego and a B.A from Haverford College. Following graduation from law school he served as a law clerk to the Honorable

R. Lanier Anderson III of the U.S. Court of Appeals for the Eleventh Circuit. He is the coauthor (with James Jay Carafano) of the book *Winning the Long War: Lessons from the Cold War for Defeating Terrorism and Preserving Freedom.*

Michael N. Schmitt is the chair of public international law at Durham Law School in the United Kingdom. He was previously dean of the George C. Marshall European Center for Security Studies in Garmisch-Partenkirchen, Germany, where he had served as professor of international law since 1999. From 2007 through 2008, he occupied the Charles H. Stockton Visiting Chair of International Law at the U.S. Naval War College. He was the 2006 Sir Ninian Stephen Visiting Scholar at Melbourne University and has been a visiting scholar at Yale Law School and the Australian National University. Before joining the Marshall Center, Professor Schmitt served 20 years in the U.S. Air Force, specializing in operational and international law. Professor Schmitt's works on law and military affairs have been published in Belgium, Chile, Germany, Israel, Italy, Norway, Peru, Sweden, Switzerland, the Netherlands, the United Kingdom, and the United States. He is the general editor of the *Yearbook of International Humanitarian Law* and serves on the editorial boards of the *International Review of the Red Cross*, *International Peacekeeping*, the *Journal of Military Ethics*, *Connections*, *Journal of International Humanitarian Legal Studies*, and the *International Humanitarian Law Series* (Brill). Professor Schmitt sits on numerous international advisory boards and has been active in multiple expert working groups, including those on the Manual on the International Law of Air and Missile Warfare (Harvard Program on Conflict Research) and Direct Participation by Civilians in Hostilities (ICRC). A frequent speaker on international humanitarian law, Professor Schmitt delivered the 2003 Waldemar A. Solf Lecture at the U.S. Army's Judge Advocate General's School and the 2008 Hilaire McCoubrey Lecture at the University of Hull Law School.

Abraham D. Sofaer, who served as legal adviser to the U.S. Department of State from 1985 to 1990, was appointed the first George P. Shultz Distinguished Scholar and Senior Fellow at the Hoover Institution in 1994. Mr. Sofaer's work has focused on separation of powers issues in the American system of government, including the power over war, and on issues related to international law, terrorism, diplomacy, national security, the Middle East conflict, and water resources. He has taught a course on transnational law at the Stanford Law School. During his distinguished career, Mr. Sofaer has been a prosecutor, legal educator, federal judge, government official, and attorney in private practice. His most recent book is *Best Defense? Legitimacy and Preventive Force* (Hoover Institution Press, 2010). Mr. Sofaer has extensive experience in international negotiations. During his 5 years as legal adviser to the U.S. Department of State, he was the principal negotiator in various interstate matters that were successfully resolved, including the dispute between Egypt and Israel over Taba, the claim against Iraq for its attack on the USS Stark, and the claims against Chile for the assassination of diplomat Orlando Letelier. He received the Distinguished Service Award in 1989, the highest State Department award given to a non-civil servant. In 2000, Mr. Sofaer, along with Seymour Goodman, published a proposed multilateral treaty aimed at enhancing cyber security, along with a commentary on the issues then being considered.

Michael A. Vatis is a partner in the New York office of Steptoe & Johnson LLP. His practice focuses on Internet, e-commerce, and technology matters, providing legal advice and strategic counsel on matters involving privacy, security, encryption, intelligence, law enforcement, Internet gambling, and international regulation of Internet content. He also is an experienced appellate litigator, representing clients before the U.S. Supreme Court and federal courts of appeals.

Mr. Vatis has spent most of his career addressing cutting-edge issues at the intersection of law, policy, and technology. He was the founding director of the National Infrastructure Protection Center at the FBI, the first government organization responsible for detecting, warning of, and responding to cyber attacks, including computer crimes, cyber terrorism, cyber espionage, and information warfare. Before that, Mr. Vatis served as associate deputy attorney general and deputy director of the Executive Office for National Security in the Department of Justice, where he advised the attorney general and deputy attorney general and coordinated the department's activities involving counterterrorism, intelligence, encryption, and cyber crime. In that capacity, he also helped lead the development of the nation's first policies regarding critical infrastructure protection. Mr. Vatis served as special counsel at the Department of Defense, where he handled sensitive legal and policy issues for the secretary and deputy secretary of defense and the general counsel, receiving the Secretary of Defense Award for Excellence.

After leaving the government in 2001, Mr. Vatis served as the first director of the Institute for Security Technology Studies at Dartmouth, a federally funded counterterrorism and cyber security research institute. He was simultaneously the founding chairman of the Institute for Information Infrastructure Protection (I3P). I3P, a consortium of leading cyber security research organizations, worked with industry, government, and academia to develop a comprehensive research and development agenda to improve the security of the nation's computer and communications networks. Mr. Vatis also served as the executive director of the Markle Task Force on National Security in the Information Age, a highly influential group of technology company executives, former government officials, and civil libertarians that recommended ways the government could more effectively use information and technology to combat terrorism while preserving civil liberties. Mr. Vatis was the principal author of the group's second report, whose recommendations were adopted by the 9/11 Commission and included in the 2004 Intelligence Reform Act.

Mr. Vatis has been a senior fellow at New York University Law School's Center on Law and Security and a member of numerous expert working groups on counterterrorism, intelligence, and technology issues. He recently served as a member of both the National Research Council Committee on Offensive Information Warfare and the Commission on Cyber Security for the 44th presidency. Mr. Vatis has also regularly testified before congressional committees on counterterrorism, intelligence, and cyber security issues. He is also interviewed frequently on television, radio, and in print media and has been a guest lecturer at many prestigious law schools and universities and a speaker at industry conferences worldwide.

Appendix D

Biosketches of Committee and Staff

COMMITTEE MEMBERS

John D. Steinbruner is a professor of public policy at the School of Public Policy at the University of Maryland and director of the Center for International and Security Studies at Maryland (CISSM). His work has focused on issues of international security and related problems of international policy. Dr. Steinbruner was director of the Foreign Policy Studies Program at the Brookings Institution from 1978 to 1996. Prior to joining Brookings, he was an associate professor in the School of Organization and Management and in the Department of Political Science at Yale University from 1976 to 1978. From 1973 to 1976, he served as associate professor of public policy at the John F. Kennedy School of Government at Harvard University, where he also was assistant director of the Program for Science and International Affairs. He was an assistant professor of government at Harvard from 1969 to 1973 and an assistant professor of political science at the Massachusetts Institute of Technology from 1968 to 1969. Dr. Steinbruner has authored and edited a number of books and monographs, including *The Cybernetic Theory of Decision: New Dimensions of Political Analysis* (Princeton University Press, originally published 1974, second paperback edition with new preface, 2002); *Principles of Global Security* (Brookings Institution Press, 2000); and *A New Concept of Cooperative Security*, with Ashton B. Carter and William J. Perry (Brookings Occasional Papers, 1992). His articles have appeared in *Arms Control Today*, *The Brookings Review*, *Dædalus*, *Foreign Affairs*, *Foreign Policy*, *International Security*, *Scientific American*, *Washington Quarterly*, and other journals. Dr. Steinbruner is currently co-chair of the Committee on International Security Studies of the American Academy of Arts and Sciences, chairman of the board of the Arms Control Association, and board member of the Financial Services Volunteer Corps. He is a fellow of the American Academy of Arts and Sciences and a member of the Council on Foreign Relations. From 1981 to 2004 he was a member of the Committee on International Security and Arms Control of the National Academy of Sciences, serving as vice chair from 1996 to 2004. He was a member of the Defense Policy Board of the Department of Defense from 1993 to 1997. Dr. Steinbruner received his A.B. from Stanford University in 1963 and his Ph.D. in political science from the Massachusetts Institute of Technology in 1968.

Steven M. Bellovin is a professor of computer science at Columbia University, where he does research on networks, security, and especially why the two don't get along. He joined the faculty in 2005 after many years at Bell Labs and AT&T Labs Research, where he was an AT&T fellow. He received a B.A.

from Columbia University and an M.S. and a Ph.D. in computer science from the University of North Carolina at Chapel Hill. While a graduate student, he helped create Netnews; for this, he and the other perpetrators were given the 1995 Usenix Lifetime Achievement Award (The Flame). He is a member of the National Academy of Engineering and is serving on the Computer Science and Telecommunications Board of the National Academies, the Department of Homeland Security's Science and Technology Advisory Committee, and the Technical Guidelines Development Committee of the Election Assistance Commission. He has also received the 2007 NIST/NSA National Computer Systems Security Award. Dr. Bellovin is the co-author of *Firewalls and Internet Security: Repelling the Wily Hacker*, and he holds a number patents on cryptographic and network protocols. He has served on many National Research Council (NRC) study committees, including those on information systems trustworthiness, the privacy implications of authentication technologies, and cyber security research needs. He was also a member of the information technology subcommittee of an NRC study group on science versus terrorism. He was a member of the Internet Architecture Board from 1996 to 2002, and he was co-director of the Security Area of the IETF from 2002 through 2004.

Stephen Dycus has been a member of the faculty at Vermont Law School since 1976. He teaches national security law, public international law, estates, property, and water law. Professor Dycus is the lead author of two casebooks, *National Security Law* (4th ed., 2007) and *Counterterrorism Law* (2007) and the author of *National Defense and the Environment* (1996). He was a founding co-editor in chief of the *Journal of National Security Law & Policy*. He was also founding chair of the National Security Law Section, Association of American Law Schools. Professor Dycus earned B.A. and LLB degrees from Southern Methodist University and an LLM degree from Harvard University. He was a visiting scholar at the University of California, Berkeley's Boalt Hall School of Law in 1983-1984 and the Natural Resources Defense Council in Washington, D.C., in 1991. He was a visiting professor at the U.S. Military Academy at West Point in 1991-1992 and at Petrozavodsk State University in Karelia, Russia, in 1997. Professor Dycus is a member of the American Law Institute.

Sue Eckert has spent her career in the policy arena focusing on issues at the intersection of international security and political economy. As a senior fellow at the Watson Institute for International Studies at Brown University, her research concentrates on making UN sanctions more effective through targeting and combating the financing of terrorism and strengthening private-sector cooperation in critical infrastructure protection. At the Institute of International Economics in Washington, D.C., she coauthored a policy primer on global electronic commerce. From 1993 to 1997, Ms. Eckert was appointed by the President and confirmed by the Senate as assistant secretary of commerce for export administration, responsible for U.S. dual-use export control policy and defense industrial base programs. Previously, she served on the professional staff of the U.S. House of Representatives' Committee on Foreign Affairs, where she oversaw technology transfer, international trade, and national security/nonproliferation issues. In addition, she has worked extensively with UN entities, as well as business groups, and she has served on numerous working groups and committees addressing security and technology issues, including the Resource Group advising the UN's High-Level Panel on Threats, Challenges, and Change, established by then-Secretary-General Kofi Annan, the Club of Madrid's International Summit on Democracy, Terrorism, and Security, and the NRC Committee on the Science, Technology, and Health Aspects of the Foreign Policy Agenda of the United States.

Jack L. Goldsmith III has been a professor of law at Harvard Law School since 2004. From 2003 to 2004 he was the assistant attorney general of the U.S. Department of Justice's Office of Legal Counsel. He was a professor of law at the University of Virginia Law School from 2003 to 2004. He previously served on the faculty of the University of Chicago Law School as an associate professor from 1994 to 1997 and was special counsel to the general counsel in the Department of Defense. Mr. Goldsmith received his B.A. in philosophy summa cum laude from Washington and Lee University in 1984, a B.A. in philosophy,

APPENDIX D

387

politics, and economics with first class honors from Oxford University in 1986, a J.D. from Yale Law School in 1989, and a diploma in private international law from The Hague Academy of International Law in 1992. After law school he clerked for Judge J. Harvie Wilkinson of the U.S. Court of Appeals for the Fourth Circuit, Justice Anthony M. Kennedy of the Supreme Court of the United States, and Judge George A. Aldrich of the Iran-U.S. Claims Tribunal. He also previously has served as an associate at Covington & Burling. Mr. Goldsmith's scholarly interests include international law, foreign relations law, national security law, conflict of laws, and civil procedure. Mr. Goldsmith served on the NRC Committee on Offensive Information Warfare.

Robert Jervis is the Adlai E. Stevenson Professor of International Politics at Columbia University. His most recent book is *Why Intelligence Fails: Lessons from the Iranian Revolution and the Iraq War* (Cornell University Press, 2010). His book *System Effects: Complexity in Political Life* (Princeton University Press, 1997) was a co-winner of the APSA's Psychology Section Best Book Award, and *The Meaning of the Nuclear Revolution* (Cornell University Press, 1989) won the Grawemeyer Award for Ideas Improving World Order. He is also the author of *Perception and Misperception in International Politics* (Princeton University Press, 1976), *The Logic of Images in International Relations* (Princeton University Press, 1970; 2d ed., Columbia University Press, 1989), *The Illogic of American Nuclear Strategy* (Cornell University Press, 1984), and *American Foreign Policy in a New Era* (Routledge, 2005). He was president of the APSA in 2000-2001 and has received career achievement awards from the International Society of Political Psychology and ISA's Security Studies Section. In 2006 he received the National Academy of Sciences' tri-annual award for behavioral sciences contributions to avoiding nuclear war. He was a Guggenheim Fellow in 1978-1979 and is a fellow of the American Association for the Advancement of Science and the American Academy of Arts and Sciences. He chairs the Historical Review Panel for the Central Intelligence Agency (CIA) and is a National Intelligence Council associate. His current research problems include the nature of beliefs, IR theory and the Cold War, and the links between signaling and perception.

Jan M. Lodal is the immediate past president of the Atlantic Council of the United States and chair of Lodal and Company. Previously, he served as principal deputy under secretary of defense for policy, where he had significant responsibilities for cyber security, and as a senior staff member of the National Security Council. He was founder, chair, and CEO of Intelus Inc. and co-founder of American Management Systems, Inc. During the Nixon and Ford administrations, Mr. Lodal served on the White House staff as deputy for program analysis to Henry A. Kissinger, and during the Johnson administration as director of the NATO and General Purpose Force Analysis Division in the Office of the Secretary of Defense. Mr. Lodal is a member of the board of overseers of the Curtis Institute of Music, a trustee of the American Boychoir, and a member of the Council on Foreign Relations and the International Institute of Strategic Studies. He was previously executive director of the Aspen Strategy Group and president of Group Health Association. He is the author of numerous articles on public policy, arms control, and defense policy, and of *The Price of Dominance: the New Weapons of Mass Destruction and Their Challenge to American Leadership*. Mr. Lodal is the recipient of Rice University's Distinguished Alumnus Award for Public Service and Achievement in Business and was twice awarded the Department of Defense Medal for Distinguished Public Service, the Department's highest civilian honor.

Philip Venables is a managing director and chief information risk officer for Goldman Sachs. He leads the Information Security, Technology Risk and Business Continuity Programs. He is part of the Technology Infrastructure Management Team, co-chairs the Business Resilience Committee, and is a member of the Operational Risk Committee. Prior to joining the firm, Mr. Venables was chief information security officer at Deutsche Bank. He also functioned as the global head of technology risk management for Standard Chartered Bank, and he served in various technology and network management positions at Barclays Bank. He is a member of the BITS/FISAP Advisory Council and serves on the Committee of the U.S. Financial Sector Security Coordinating Council. Mr. Venables is on the board of referees of the journal *Computers and Security*, the board of directors for the Center for Internet Security, and the advisory board of the London School of Economics Information Systems Integrity Group. Mr. Venables earned a B.Sc. (Hons.) in computer science from York University in the United Kingdom in 1989 and an M.Sc. in computation and cryptography from the Queen's College at Oxford University in 1990. Additionally, Mr. Venables was awarded the designation of chartered engineer in 1995 and chartered scientist in 2002. In 2005, he was elected a fellow of the British Computer Society.

STAFF

Herbert S. Lin, study director, is chief scientist for the National Research Council's Computer Science and Telecommunications Board, where he has been a study director for major projects on public policy and information technology. These studies include a 1996 study on national cryptography policy (*Cryptography's Role in Securing the Information Society*), a 1999 study of Defense Department systems for command, control, communications, computing, and intelligence (*Realizing the Potential of C4I: Fundamental Challenges*), a 2000 study on workforce issues in high-technology (*Building a Workforce for the Information Economy*), a 2004 study on aspects of the FBI's information technology modernization program (*A Review of the FBI's Trilogy IT Modernization Program*), a 2005 study on electronic voting (*Asking the Right Questions About Electronic Voting*), a 2005 study on computational biology (*Catalyzing Inquiry at the Interface of Computing and Biology*), a 2007 study on privacy and information technology (*Engaging Privacy and Information Technology in a Digital Age*), a 2007 study on cyber security research (*Toward a Safer and More Secure Cyberspace*), a 2009 study on health care information technology (*Computational Technology for Effective Health Care*), and a 2009 study on U.S. cyber attack policy (*Technology, Policy, Law, and Ethics Regarding Acquisition and Use of U.S. Cyberattack Capabilities*). Before his NRC service, he was a professional staff member and staff scientist for the House Armed Services Committee (1986-1990), where his portfolio included defense policy and arms control issues. He received his doctorate in physics from the Massachusetts Institute of Technology.

Tom Arrison is a senior staff officer in the Policy and Global Affairs Division of the National Academies. He joined the National Academies in 1990 and has directed a range of studies and other projects in areas such as international science and technology relations, innovation, information technology, higher education, and strengthening the U.S. research enterprise. He holds M.A. degrees in public policy and Asian studies from the University of Michigan.

Gin Bacon Talati is an associate program officer for the Computer Science and Telecommunications Board of the National Research Council. She formerly served as a program associate with the Frontiers of Engineering program at the National Academy of Engineering. Prior to her work at the Academies, she served as a senior project assistant in education technology at the National School Boards Association. She has a B.S. in science, technology, and culture from the Georgia Institute of Technology and an M.P.P. from George Mason University with a focus in science and technology policy.